CRUELTY

AN ANALYSIS OF ARTICLE 3

AUSTRALIA
Law Book Co.
Sydney

CANADA and USA
Carswell
Toronto

NEW ZEALAND
Brookers
Wellington

SINGAPORE and MALAYSIA
Sweet & Maxwell Asia
Singapore and Kuala Lumpur

CRUELTY

AN ANALYSIS OF ARTICLE 3

JOHN COOPER LL.B. (Hons)
Middle Temple.
Barrister of the English and Australian Bar

London
Sweet & Maxwell
2003

Published in 2003 by
Sweet & Maxwell Ltd., of
100 Avenue Road
London NW3 3PF
(http://www.sweetandmaxwell.co.uk)
Typeset by Interactive Sciences Ltd, Gloucester
Printed and bound in Great Britain
by TJ International Ltd, Cornwall

No natural forests were destroyed to make this product;
only farmed timber was used and replanted.

A CIP catalogue for this book is
available from the British Library

ISBN 0421 836 806

FOREWORD

It would not be right to say that Article 3 is the most important of all the articles in the European Convention for the Protection of Human Rights and Fundamental Freedoms. Article 2, which protects the right to life, almost certainly has the claim to that distinction. But Article 3 is without doubt one of the most challenging and most controversial. Its scope depends so much on the meaning of words.

> "When *I* use a word," Humpty Dumpty said in rather a scornful tone, "it means just what I choose it to mean—neither more nor less."

> "The question is," said Alice, "whether you can make words mean so many different things."

> "The question is," said Humpty Dumpty, "which is to be master—that's all."

> [*Through the Looking Glass*, Chapter VI]

It is possible to find some guidance in decisions of the European Court of Human Rights as to the scope of the article. We all think that we know what is meant by "torture". As for "ill-treatment", we are told that the conduct which is complained of must attain a minimum level of severity if it is to fall within the scope of the article. We are told that the absolute prohibition which it contains is not capable of modification. We are also told that where a positive obligation is to be implied issues of proportionality can arise. But at the root of the whole matter is the question what the words really mean. They are the masters of what is acceptable and what is not. Extreme cases will be easy to identify. Much more difficult are cases where relatively slight injuries or trivial ill-treatment is inflicted on those who are disadvantaged or who are vulnerable. It is hard to avoid the impression that at the end of the day the question of whether the article has been breached will depend on all the circumstances of the case.

If that is so, the area which Article 3 covers appears to be rather uncertain and rather grey. Nevertheless the consequences of a finding that the article has been breached by thoughtless or ill-considered conduct are likely to be far reaching, and they may indeed be profound. Its effect must not be underestimated by anyone who is in a position of authority in any public service or any institution which deals with people who are vulnerable to any extent to acts which in the slightest degree may be considered to be acts of cruelty. Preconceptions as to the meaning of the words used in the article will be an uncertain guide as to what is and what is not likely to be acceptable. A thorough understanding of its scope and of the remedies available is the best way to overcome one of the most dangerous of all attitudes, which is complacency. It will pay many dividends.

It is into this uncertain but vitally important field that Mr Cooper has chose to venture. He has done us all a valuable service by devoting his attention in this carefully researched book exclusively to this very important and demanding article.

October 2002   *Lord Hope of Craighead*

To Laura and Frank

ACKNOWLEDGEMENTS

As far as I am aware, this is the first book to be devoted to an analysis of Article 3 of the European Convention on Human Rights and other associated provisions. The Article provides that "no one shall be subjected to torture or to inhuman or degrading treatment or punishment". It was my decision to use one generic word to encompass the three prohibited ills as well as breaches of physical integrity covered by Article 8. I decided on the word cruelty, conscious that it is not a precise legal definition of prohibited treatment or punishment under the Convention, but nevertheless encapsulating what it is that European jurisprudence endeavours to eliminate from civilised society.

Article 3 is the most wide-ranging of provisions within the European Convention on Human Rights. A perusal of the chapter titles in this book proves its range from police interrogation, prison detention and immigration to medical treatment, death row and corporal punishment. It is arguably the most influential of all Convention Articles. It demands a book of its own.

The last year has seen the relentless application of Article 3 through the domestic and European courts and I am enormously grateful to Clair Brissenden (Context) who has painstakingly provided me with over 600 case references and whose invaluable help in assimilation of material has meant that this book met its deadline.

Further thanks are due to Jacqui Mowbrey at Sweet & Maxwell who has continued to support this project, for which I am eternally grateful.

Many thanks to Liberty who provided me with their up to date case reports and to Nicola Makanjuola who was a pupil in my chambers at 25 Bedford Row, formerly 3 Gray's Inn Square, for providing me with useful source material.

Finally, thanks and gratitude to Alli Wakefield whose skill, patience and good humour when laying out the text of the original draft was priceless.

The case citations in this book are current up to the end of October 2002 and any omissions and errors are all mine.

It should be noted that in the process of publishing this book, there were case developments involving Article 3. On November 12, 2002, a legal challenge was launched in the High Court relating to the imprisonment of children. The Howard League for Penal Reform, which is bringing the case, is arguing that the Children Act 1989 and the protection it affords to children should apply to children in prison.

Statistics show that between April 2000 and February 2002, 296 children sustained injury after the application of restraints and control in prison. There is concern that Article 37 of the UN Convention, which protects children from inhuman and degrading treatment is not being respected in prisons and that the UK may be in breach of Article 3, due in part to safety, health and number and suitability of staff, as well as supervision.[1]

---

[1] See article in Howard League for Penal Reform publication, H.L.M., December 2002.

[ix]

As this book went to press, *R. v. Lichniak* and *R. v. Pyrah*, concerning mandatory life sentences, were decided by the House of Lords. In essence, the Court held that most mandatory life sentences do not breach Article 3.[2]

October 2002   *John Cooper*

---

[2] *The Times*, November 26, 2002.

CONTENTS

CONTENTS

CONTENTS

TABLE OF CASES

TABLE OF STATUTES

TABLE OF STATUTORY INSTRUMENTS

TABLE OF INTERNATIONAL TREATIES AND CONVENTIONS

CRUELTY

The inhuman treatment caused by the interrogators in the *Ireland v. United Kingdom* "five techniques" case was referred by the perpetrators as "interrogation in depth".

Some commentators have even tried to excuse the use of torture or at least to downgrade its abhorrence. An interviewee on CNN television in the United States of America when commenting upon the treatment of so-called enemy combatants arrested as a result of the clampdown in that country following on from the attacks of September 11, observed:

> "Torture is bad. Some things are worse and under certain circumstances it may be the lesser of two evils".

Another fallacy is that allegations of torture, inhuman and degrading treatment whilst highly relevant to other countries is not relevant to the United Kingdom. This was brought to book at a very early stage in the life of the European Convention on Human Rights.

Whilst the United States of America were distracted by the Cold War with Soviet Russia, western European nations created the European Convention on Human Rights. Britain was the first nation to ratify it and the words of Ernest Bevin, "if you open that Pandora's Box you never know what Trojan horses will jump out" soon came to pass. When Britain extended the Convention to the majority of its colonies, the Greeks complained to Europe that British colonial administration in Cyprus was breaching the European Convention by use of its collective punishments, the whipping of adolescents and ill-treatment of prisoners. In 1956 the European Commission on Human Rights agreed to investigate matters. This was the first time that it had ever taken up an interstate complaint. Britain was in the dock.

In her book *"The Rise and Rise of Human Rights"*,[1] Kirsten Sellars quotes an English barrister, Peter Benenson who visited Cyprus and commented upon the colonial regime:

> "When I first arrived in Cyprus, in October 1956, the entire Greek Cypriot Bar was inundated with complaints against the authorities. I have seen a queue of anxious parents at the chambers of the present Ministry of Justice so long that it stretched outside the front door. The authorities insisted that the Greek lawyers were mischievously inventing allegations of violence. To prevent them talking to their arrested clients, they were refused information as to their whereabouts. Independent Greek doctors were denied access to prisons or prison hospitals. Regulations were passed permitting the Government to hold arrested persons administratively in close confinement for 16 days without charge . . . in these circumstances the Government could have scarcely expected anything else except that the rumour of torture should grow, until it is swept like a cloud across to mainland Greece".

---

[1] Sutton Publishing, 2002.

I refer to the Greek Cases later on in this book[2] but the groundbreaking cases which included a revealing attitude of the British to corporal punishment, made it abundantly clear at a very early stage of European jurisprudence that there was and still is no room for complacency in the United Kingdom. Some of the most fundamental cases concerning Article 3 have arisen as a result of violations by U.K. prisons, medical establishments, schools and security forces. Torture, inhuman and degrading treatment affects every Contracting State, there are no exceptions, one must not be seen in any way as superior to the other.

The question is therefore whether there is a single foundation for human rights that spans so many cultures and societies which justifies intervention across national boundaries? The Convention for the Protection of Human Rights and Fundamental Freedoms articulates various rights, which include the right to liberty and security,[3] the right to a fair trial,[4] the right to no punishment without law,[5] the right to freedom of thought, conscience and religion,[6] the right to freedom of expression,[7] the right to freedom of assembly and association,[8] the right to marry[9] and the prohibition of slavery and forced labour[10] are some of the principle human rights and fundamental freedoms enshrined by the Convention.

Some of these rights such as freedom of expression, freedom of thought, conscience and religion and even the Article 6 right to a fair trial are open to interpretation depending upon the culture of the society in which you live. But the Article 3 prohibition on torture, inhuman and degrading treatment or punishment must, along with the right to life, be the most inviolate protections provided by the Convention.

But even this seems open to some debate. Most recently the courts have observed that the minimum severity thresholds incumbent upon a finding of Article 3 should not be made so low as to make findings of torture, inhuman or degrading treatment "commonplace". There still seems to be a tolerance level.

Today, any State which recognises the rule of law has reason to fear a condemnation under Article 3, which has so far been synonymous with a major lapse, attracting international opprobrium, because it is only applied exceptionally and in particularly serious situations.[11] Article 3 is one of the Convention's basic provisions. The European Court of Human Rights has referred to "its hard core of rules".[12] It enshrines one of the human rights which cannot be limited, even in time of war or public emergency threatening the life of the nation.

The injuries received by the applicant in *Tomasi v. France*[13] were described as "relatively slight" but these injuries inflicted upon the applicant by police officers nevertheless, according to the European Court, constituted:

---

[2] See Chapter 1: Torture, Inhuman and Degrading Treatment, para. 1–08.
[3] Article 5.
[4] Article 6.
[5] Article 7.
[6] Article 9.
[7] Article 10.
[8] Article 11.
[9] Article 12.
[10] Article 4.
[11] See *Tomasi v. France* (1992) 15 E.H.R.R. 1.
[12] See *Tomasi v. France* (1992) 15 E.H.R.R. 1.
[13] (1992) 15 E.H.R.R. 1.

"outward signs of the use of physical force on an individual deprived of his liberty and thus vulnerable and in a state of inferiority. Such treatment cannot be justified and in the circumstances of the case, may be considered both inhuman and degrading".

In other words, however slight the injuries, the degree of gravity arises from the fact that the victim is deprived of liberty, vulnerable and in a state of inferiority. As such, the consequence of the victim's position of inferiority, may make extremely slight injuries consistent with inhuman and degrading treatment. The courts have retreated from taking the view that this will constitute a breach of Article 3 and fear a great increase in the number of complaints and findings of inhuman and degrading treatment as a result of applicants detained in police stations, hospitals and other places where they are made vulnerable and deprived of their liberty.

The courts fear that inhuman and degrading treatment will be devalued as a concept greatly reducing its preventative effect. The European Court of Human Rights has also noted that whilst there is growing recognition of the overriding importance of the prohibition of torture, it does not find it established that there is yet acceptance in international law of the proposition that States were not entitled to immunity in respect of civil claims for damages for alleged torture committed outside the forum State.[14]

So, can such a devalued Article 3 really continue to act as an obstacle, for instance, to those extraditions and expulsions which it seeks to prevent?

In 1969, the European Commission for Human Rights, after careful consideration of the Greek cases, made the first attempt to lay down the parameters of Article 3. It went on to describe the concept of inhuman treatment and degrading treatment in the following way:

"The notion of inhuman treatment covers at least such treatment as deliberately causes suffering, mental or physical, which, in the particular situation, is unjustifiable.

The word 'torture' is often used to describe inhuman treatment, which has a purpose, such as the obtaining of information or confessions or the infliction of punishment, and it is generally an aggravated form of inhuman treatment.

Treatment or punishment of an individual may be said to be degrading if it grossly humiliates him before others or drives him to act against his will or conscience".

But the Commission in the Greek Cases was criticised for contemplating the possibility of "the justification" of inhuman treatment. It took the opportunity in putting this right in the Northern Ireland cases, concluding:

"That the prohibition under Article 3 of the Convention is an absolute one and that there can never be, under the Convention or under international law, a justification for acts in breach of that provision".

Again, the Northern Ireland cases which developed the so-called "five techniques" was also a case which involved the United Kingdom when they were criticised for their behaviour at interrogation centres for IRA detainees. When the European Court of Human Rights downgraded the finding of the Commission from torture to inhuman or degrading treatment, a degree of consternation was caused within the Commission since it heard all the witnesses which numbered nearly 150 and the court had not. Further surprise was caused because the United

---

[14] See *Al-Adsani v. United Kingdom* (2002) 34 E.H.R.R. 11.

[3]

Kingdom Government had accepted the unanimous finding by the Commission.

The fact that the European Court did not explain its assertion that the techniques failed to cause suffering sufficiently intense to be labelled torture, has also added to the unease that one feels when reading the text of the case.

In the introduction to Michael Ignatieff's book "*Human Rights as Politics and Idolatry*",[15] Amy Gutmann observes:

> "What counts as a minimal set of human rights is by no means either obvious or agreed upon by even good willed people. Even the means of protecting people against 'cruel, inhuman, or degrading . . . punishment' is open to reasonable disagreement. When the Taliban stoned women to death for adultery, this is about as clear a violation of a human right against cruel, inhuman, and degrading treatment as any. But does the United States violate a human right that belongs in the minimal set when its judicial system sentences people to death. Does capital punishment as practised today in the United States constitute a human rights violation under Article 7?
>
> To answer in the affirmative, one need not think that capital punishment is equivalent to the worst atrocities committed by the Taliban. To answer in the negative, one need not approve of capital punishment or even be anything less than an ardent opponent of the practice.
>
> This example illustrates the problem of determining how to characterise even a minimal set of human rights . . . the example of capital punishment reveals that the sovereignty of a constitutional democratic regime is no guarantee against tyranny of the majority or minority".

The influences of the Convention go far beyond Europe. The advance to independent statehood of many former colonies under entrenched Constitutions expressed to be the supreme law of the State has embraced the principles of the European Convention on Human Rights. They have adopted and set out within the constitutions a series of fundamental rights and freedoms which will be protected under their constitution. It is well established that in drafting these chapters containing the statements of protection, heavy reliance was placed upon the European Convention. In some instances, they adopt the language used in Article 10 of the Bill of Rights 1689,[16] the Eighth Amendment to the Constitution of the United States 1791 and Section 12 of the Canadian Charter of Rights and Freedoms 1982; the Prohibition on Inhumane Treatment has referred to "cruel and unusual treatment or punishment".

For instance, the European Convention applies to Belize as a dependent territory of the Crown from October 25, 1953 when it came into force until September 21, 1981 when Belize became independent. On September 25, 1981, Belize adhered to the Universal Declaration, in January 1991 to the American Declaration and in June 1996 to the International Covenant (although it has not adopted the optional protocol to the International Covenant nor has it become a party to the American Convention). The Privy Council has no licence to read in to such Constitutions its own predilections and moral values but it is required to consider the substance of the fundamental right to issue and ensure contemporary protection of that right in the light of evolving standards of decency that mark the

---

[15] Princeton University Press, 2001.
[16] 1 Will. and Mary. Sess. 2 c.2.

progress of a maturing society.[17] In carrying out its task of constitutional inter-pretation the court is not concerned to evaluate and give effect to public opinion, for reasons given by Chaskalson P. in *S v. Makwanyane*[18]:

"Public opinion may have some relevance to the enquiry, but, in itself, it is not substitute for the duty vested in the courts to interpret the Constitution and to uphold its provisions without fear or favour. If public opinion were to be decisive, there would be no need for Constitutional adjudication. The protection of rights could then be left to Parliament, which has a mandate from the public, and is answerable to the public for the way its mandate is exercised, but this would be a return to Parliamentary Sover-eignty, and a retreat from the new legal order established by the 1993 Constitution. By the same token, the issue of the constitutionality of capital punishment cannot be referred to a referendum, in which a majority view would prevail over the wishes of any minority. The very reason for establishing the new legal order, and for vesting the power of judicial review of all legislation in the courts, whilst to protect the rights of minorities and others who cannot protect their rights adequately through the democratic process. Those who are entitled to claim this protection include the social outcasts and margin-alised people of our society".

Steven Kay Q.C., the experienced international law barrister, who is presently *Amicus Curriae* in the Milosovic Trial, has recently observed that:

"No State should call itself civilised unless it is willing to expose and take steps to prevent inhuman and degrading treatment to its citizens.

The mark of a civilised society is its willingness to prevent and expose acts of inhuman and degrading treatment perpetrated upon its citizens.

An act of inhuman and degrading treatment by a person upon a fellow human being arises from the lack of respect the one human is prepared to give the other. Once such decency is missing between people the rights to peace and security that should be enjoyed by all, are violated.

Civilised societies should not be measured by their artistic achievements, but by their treatment of people who live in their streets. Art may conceal the truth of life".

It is usually apparent that it is the vulnerable who seek protection of Article 3 and its associated rights. Of their nature, those who seek the protection of this Article are "marginalised". Article 3 will be their fundamental protection.

What is apparent from a study of Article 3 and indeed Article 8, is that although there are minimum standards which should be upheld as to the treat-ment of human beings fundamentally at the hands of the State, these protections, by no means rule out every incident of maltreatment.

It is one of the purposes of this book to lay down for the first time in a structured way each and every category in which human beings are subject to maltreatment and to attempt to discern whether that aspect of maltreatment qualifies as torture, inhuman or degrading treatment and/or punishment or a breach of physical integrity.

The use of the rack was discredited many years ago but it would be a mistake born perhaps of arrogance and complacency to suggest that in fields such as immigration, medical treatment, children, prisons and maltreatment in custody that the 21st century cannot breed its own hybrid.

---

[17] See *Trop v. Dulles* 356 U.S. 86 at 101.
[18] 1995 (3) SA 391 at 431, para. 88.

The European Convention on Human Rights and Fundamental Freedoms is regularly referred to by the courts as a "living instrument". This emphasises its ability to grow and adapt to the times and circumstances in which it is being applied. So too, torture, inhuman and degrading treatment. The words are still with us, it is just that they have different connotations.

What remains the same is the potential brutality that they can inflict upon human beings.

Chapter 1

TORTURE, INHUMAN AND DEGRADING TREATMENT

1. Article 3

The guarantee. Article 3 of the European Convention for the Protection of **1–01** Human Rights and Fundamental Freedoms[1] became part of the law of England, Wales and Northern Ireland on October 2, 2000. It prohibits in absolute terms torture or inhuman or degrading treatment or punishment.[2] It is one of the most categoric of Convention guarantees, providing a minimum standard by which a State must comply.

Lord Cooke of Thorndon in his eloquent dissenting judgement in *Higgs v. Minister of National Security*[3] articulated the critical status of Article 3:

> "Self evidently every human being has a natural right not to be subjected to inhuman treatment. A right inherent in the concept of civilisation, it is recognised rather than created by international human rights instruments such as the Universal Declaration of Human Rights 1948, the International Covenant on Civil and Political Rights[4] and the European Convention for the Protection of Human Rights and Fundamental Freedoms[5] . . .
>
> A duty of governments and courts in every civilised State must be to exercise vigilance to guard against violation of this fundamental right. Whenever violation is in issue a court will not fulfil its function without a careful examination of the facts of each individual case and a global assessment of the treatment in question. Commonly, decisions in this field are findings of fact and degree, not expositions of law. If more than the assessment is open, the choice made is not one of law or legal principle but one of evaluation. Although it may properly have some influence on a latter court faced with somewhat similar facts and anxious to achieve consistency of results, it cannot be a binding precedent. To subscribe to a contrary doctrine of precedent would be to insist on 'the austerity of tabulated legalism'. If I venture to state these dogmatically, it is only because they seem dictated by the very idea of civilisation".

Breaches cannot be justified by lack of resources.[6]

Inter-linked terms. The terms "torture", "inhuman" and "degrading treat- **1–02** ment" or "punishment" are often considered to be placed in a hierarchy. Firstly, torture as the most severe; followed by inhuman treatment or punishment; and then degrading treatment or punishment with the protection of physical integrity offered under Article 8 performing some sort of "mopping up" exercise.

---

[1] (1953) (Cmd. 8689).
[2] See *Ireland v. United Kingdom* (1978) 2 E.H.R.R. 25, 79, para. 163; *Selcuk and Asker v. Turkey* (1998) 26 E.H.R.R. 477, 515–515, para. 75.
[3] See [2000] 2 A.C. 288 at pp. 260–261.
[4] (1977) (Cmnd. 6702).
[5] (1953) (Cmd. 8969).
[6] See Lester and Pannick, *Human Rights Law and Practice* (1999), para. 4.3. 1–4. 3.8; Jacobs and White, *The European Convention on Human Rights*, Second Edition (1996) p. 49.

The European Committee for the Prevention of Torture takes a somewhat different view and are unwilling to produce a clear and comprehensive inter-pretation of these terms. Their approach is that the expressions torture, inhuman and degrading treatment or punishment reflect not so much a hierarchy of severity of ill-treatment as different types of ill-treatment, more or less closely linked.[7] European jurisprudence seems to make it clear that the European Court of Human Rights is more willing to find inhuman treatment than torture. The intensity of the suffering required to constitute inhuman treatment is less, although the threshold is still high. The suffering does not have to be deliberately caused.

Domestic courts have commented that it will not serve the cause of human rights to set such demanding standards that breaches were commonplace.[8] Whilst one can appreciate that if the standard is set too low there may be a risk that the protections offered by Article 3 and its associated Articles may be devalued, one should not interpret this dicta as indicating that the court will shirk from imposing the strictures of Article 3 if applicants have been ill-treated, regardless of how many there are.

This has not avoided controversy over the findings of the European Court of Human Rights as to what constitutes torture, inhuman or degrading treatment. An early example of this has been seen in *Ireland v. United Kingdom*[9] wherein the five interrogation techniques instituted by the security forces were categorised as torture by the Commission but somewhat downgraded by the court.

Again, in the more recent case of *Z v. United Kingdom*[10] in which children were exposed to appalling living conditions which included gross neglect and emotional abuse, the European Court, somewhat surprisingly, declined to come to a finding of torture. The facts of *Z* displayed some appalling examples of ill-treatment to children who were left in unsanitary conditions and subjected to them, amongst other things, chronic food shortages. The European Court of Human Rights held that the neglect and abuse suffered by the four child applicants reached the threshold of inhuman and degrading treatment. This treatment was brought to the local authority's attention and that local authority, the court held, was under a statutory duty to protect the children. The children were over a period of $4\frac{1}{2}$ years, subject to what a child consultant psychiatrist referred to "as horrific experiences". Although the court acknowledged the difficult and sensitive decisions facing social services they were in no doubt that the failure of the system to protect the children from suffering serious long term neglect and abuse, violated Article 3.

1–03   **Article 3.** This Article provides that:

"No one shall be subjected to torture or to inhuman or degrading treatment or punishment".

The Convention prohibits in absolute terms torture and inhuman or degrading treatment or punishment, irrespective of the victim's conduct.

---

[7] See Evans and Morgan, *Preventing Torture* (June 27, 2000) at 253–256.
[8] See *Thomas v. Baptiste* [2000] 2 A.C. 1 at 27.
[9] (1978) 2 E.H.R.R. 25.
[10] [2002] 34 E.H.R.R. 3.

No derogation. Unlike most of the substantive clauses of the Convention and   **1–04** of Protocols 1 and 4, Article 3 makes no provision for exceptions and derogation, express or implied, is not possible in peacetime conditions even in the event of a public emergency threatening the life of the nation.[11] Prohibition is equally applicable during time of war. Article 15 reads:

> "(1) In time of war or other public emergency threatening the life of the nation, any High-Contracting Party may take measures derogating from its obligations under this Convention to the extent strictly required by the extringencies of the situation, provided that such measures are not inconsistent with its other obligations under international law.
> (2) No derogation from Article 2, except in respect of deaths resulting from lawful acts of war, or from Articles 3, 4(1) and 7 shall be made under this provision".

The courts readily accept that counter-terrorist activities are important measures to protect society. But violations of Article 3 will not even be condoned when the excuse given is the suppression of terrorism or to counter violent crime.[12] This stance is of a particular interest when one considers the approach of the United States Administration post-September 11 and the *laissez faire* attitude in that country to the treatment of so-called "enemy combatants".

Court to take into account the entire circumstances of the case. It is for the   **1–05** court to pronounce if the facts before it amount to torture, inhuman or degrading treatment, having regard to the entire circumstances of the case under investigation.[13]

Three categories. As can be seen from the text of Article 3, three separate   **1–06** categories of prohibited treatment or punishment are encompassed, that of, torture; inhuman treatment or punishment; and degrading treatment or punishment.

2. TORTURE

Definition. Torture is defined in the Convention Against Torture And Other   **1–07** Cruel, Inhuman Or Degrading Treatment Or Punishment 1984[14] as:

> "any act by which severe pain or suffering, whether physical or mental, is intentionally inflicted on a person for such purposes as obtaining from him or a third person information or a confession, punishing him for an act he or a third party has committed or is suspected of having committed, or intimidating or coercing him or a third person, or for any reason based on discrimination of any kind, when such pain or suffering is inflicted by or at the instigation of or with the consent of acquiescence of a public official or other person acting in an official capacity. It does not include pain or suffering arising only from, inherent in or incidental to lawful sanctions".[15]

---

[11] See *Ireland v. U.K.* (1978) 2 E.H.R.R. 25 and Article 15(2).
[12] See *Tomasi v. France* (1992) 15 E.H.R.R. 1, 33, para. 15.
[13] See *Ireland v. U.K.* (1978) 2 E.H.R.R. 25, p. 116.
[14] See Appendix 5.
[15] See also the International Covenant on Civil and Political Rights 1996, Article 7 and Chapter 8: Children and Young People.

In the Greek case,[16] the Commission considered allegations of ill-treatment and torture in Greek prisons which seemed, in many instances, to be carried out as a matter of routine. They defined the word torture as an aggravated form of inhuman treatment which as a purpose such as the obtaining of information or confession, or the infliction of punishment.

1–08   **The Greek Cases.** There is a large body of materials on the 49 cases in the Public Record Office. Most of the allegations are of crude violence, mostly by interrogators or police officers, some being Special Branch officers and some military as well as civilian police. Referring to the cases by their number, the level of ill-treatment can be graphically illustrated.

Case 10 concerned a person who was tried but acquitted of murder, his confession being ruled inadmissible, where he alleged he was beaten by an interrogator.

Case 15 involved a woman who alleged that pencils were placed between her fingers and her hand crushed against them by an interrogator, who then also beat her unconscious.

Case 18 detailed allegations that a victim was stripped naked and beaten with a belt.

Case 25 detailed allegations of a beating by a police officer, both with his fist and with a cane.

Case 32 involved allegations of water torture by Special Branch officers which probably included the practice of pouring large quantities into the victim's mouth, to produce the fear of drowning.

Case 37 alleged the application of electricity.

Case 44 details a floodlight being turned on to the victim whilst being interrogated.

Case 21 involves sexual assault, indecent and degrading treatment of a woman.

1–09   **Intensity of suffering.** In *Ireland v. United Kingdom*,[16–17] the court observed that the distinction between torture, inhuman or degrading treatment derived principally from a difference in the intensity of the suffering inflicted.[18] They went on to observe that "special stigma" should be attached to "deliberate inhuman treatment causing very serious and cruel suffering".[19]

1–10   **Aggravated and deliberate.** The court emphasised European jurisprudence and stressed that "torture constitutes an aggravated and deliberate form of cruel, inhuman or degrading treatment or punishment".[20]

In his dissenting opinion Judge Zekia prays in aid paragraph 1 of Article 1 of Resolution 3452 of the General Assembly of December 9, 1975 which reads:

[16–17] (1978) 2 E.H.R.R. 25.
[18] See p. 80.
[19] See para. 168.
[20] See Article 1 of Resolution 3452 adopted by the General Assembly of the United Nations on December 9, 1975, para. 2 of Article 1.

"For the purpose of this declaration, torture means any act by which severe pain or suffering, whether physical or mental, is intentionally inflicted by or at the instigation of a public official ... for ... obtaining ... information or confession ... ".

He is of the view that this paragraph, dealing with the meaning to be attached to the word torture, is more relevant for the purpose of interpretation of Article 3 of the Convention. He goes on to say:

"I do not share the view that extreme intensity of physical or mental suffering is a requisite for a case of ill-treatment to amount to torture within the purport and object of Article 3 of the Convention. The nature of torture admits gradation in its intensity, in its severity and methods adopted. It is, therefore, primarily the duty and responsibility of the authority conducting the enquiries from close quarters, after taking into account all the surrounding circumstances, evidence and material available, to say whether in a particular case inhuman ill-treatment reached the degree of torture. In other words, this is a finding of fact for the competent authority dealing with the case in the first instance and, for reasons we give hereunder, we should not interfere with".

The Commission's decision in *Ireland v. United Kingdom*. In his important   **1–11** dissenting judgement, Judge Zekia reminds the court that the Commission was unanimously of the opinion that the effect of the combined application of the five techniques detailed in the *Ireland v. United Kingdom* case, amounted to torture. These techniques were:

(a) Forcing suspects to stand against a wall, spread-eagled, with their fingers put high above their head against the wall, their legs spread apart and their feet back, causing them to stand on their toes with the weight of the body mainly on the fingers;

(b) Placing a hood on the suspects consisting of a black or navy coloured bag and keeping it there for a significant period of time;

(c) Subjecting the suspects to noise which consisted of holding the suspects in a room pending interrogation where there was a continuous loud and hissing noise;

(d) Depriving the suspects of sleep;

(e) Depriving the suspects of food and drink in that the detainees were subjected to a reduced diet during their detention at the interrogation centre and pending their interrogations.

Nevertheless, the majority view of the European Court of Human Rights was that the "five techniques" could not be categorised as torture but amounted to inhuman and degrading treatment. This indicates the high threshold which has to be reached to establish the most serious strand of Article 3, that of torture.

Special stigma. *Aydin v. Turkey*[21] was a case where the European Court did   **1–12** find that the treatment qualified as torture. The facts of that case bear analysis.

---

[21] (1998) 25 E.H.R.R. 251.

The applicant, a Turkish citizen of Kurdish origin, alleged that she had been arrested by the Turkish Security Forces and that during a period of detention lasting three days she was beaten, tortured and raped. At the request of the Public Prosecutor she was examined by three doctors during July and August, each of whom confirmed that she had recently lost her virginity. She complained to the European Court that she had been violated in breach of Article 3.[22] Upholding her complaint, the court held that Article 3 prohibited in absolute terms torture and inhuman or degrading treatment. They emphasised again that there were no exceptions and no derogations, even having regard to the imperatives of a public emergency threatening the life of the nation.[23] The court also emphasised that the special stigma of torture attached only to deliberate inhuman degrading treatment causing very serious and cruel suffering.[24] In the instant case, the accumulation of acts of physical and mental violence inflicted upon the applicant, and especially the act of rape, amounted, in the court's view, to torture sufficient to violate Article 3.

Here, the court seemed to be emphasising that an *accumulation* of ill-treatment may cause their infliction to amount to torture.

In *Aksoy v. Turkey*,[25] the court held that a practice known as "Palestinian hanging"[26] which caused paralysis amounted to torture in contravention of Article 3. This treatment was inflicted upon the applicant in an attempt by the Turkish authorities to obtain admissions or information from him.

Rape has also been recognised by the European Court of Human Rights as constituting torture.[27] Rape of a detainee by a State official "must be considered to be an especially grave and abhorrent form of ill-treatment, given the ease with which the offender can exploit the vulnerability and weakened resistance of the victim" (see para. 83).

Reference should also be made to the case of *Furundzija*,[28] which was a matter from the International War Crimes Tribunal for the Former Yugoslavia which in 1995 issued indictments charging rape as a crime against humanity "like torture, rape is used for such purposes as intimidation, degradation, humiliation, discrimination, punishment, control or destruction of a person. Like torture, rape is a violation of personal dignity, and rape in fact constitutes torture when inflicted by or at the instigation of or with the consent or acquiescence of a public official or other person acting in an official capacity" (para. 65).

In times of armed conflict, rape is a violation of international law, and punishable as a crime against humanity under the Geneva Conventions of 1949 and their 1977 Protocols.[29]

---

[22] She also claimed breach of Article 3 on the basis that no effective investigation of her allegations by the Public Prosecutor had exacerbated her condition.

[23] See *Aksoy v. Turkey* (1997) 23 E.H.R.R. 553.

[24] Applying *Ireland v. U.K.* (1978) 2 E.H.R.R. 25.

[25] (1997) 23 E.H.R.R. 553.

[26] This process includes the victim being stripped naked, his arms tied behind his back and being suspended by the arms.

[27] see *Aydin v. Turkey* [1997] 3 B.H.R.C. 300.

[28] IT-95-17/1-T, December 10, 1998.

[29] See the Geneva Convention relative to the Protection of Civilian Persons in Time of War of 1949 and the Additional Protocols of 1977 which provide that women shall especially be protected against any attack on their honour, in particular against humiliating and degrading treatment, rape, enforced prostitution or any form of indecent assault. It was the Vienna Declaration and Programme of Action, adopted by the World Conference on Human Rights, which stated that "violations of the human rights of women in situations of armed conflict are violations of the fundamental principles of international human rights and humanitarian law".

European jurisprudence seems to make it clear that the European Court of Human Rights is more willing to find inhuman treatment than torture. The intensity of the suffering required to constitute inhuman treatment is less, although the threshold is still high. The suffering does not have to be deliberately caused. The most important element of degrading treatment is humiliation. It must reach a sufficient level of severity to be degrading.

Cross-examination by a defendant accused of rape. Cross-examination by   1–13
a defendant accused of rape of an alleged rape complainant during the course of a trial may, in some circumstances, amount to inhuman or degrading treatment, depending upon the length and manner of the cross-examination[30] where the complainant was cross-examined by the defendant for six days.

Mental suffering. One of the essential features of torture is the effect on the   1–14
state of mind of the individual as well has his physical well-being.[31]
As Judge O'Donoghue stated in *Ireland v. United Kingdom*[32]:

"One is not bound to regard torture as only present in a medieval dungeon where the appliances of rack and thumb screw or similar devices were employed.
Indeed, in the present day world there can be little doubt that torture may be inflicted in the mental sphere".[33]

Flexible interpretation. There is a considerable dynamic between the defini-   1–15
tions of torture, inhuman or degrading treatment and the courts reflect that changing standards within society mean that, for example, what was not considered torture 20 years ago will be considered so now. The Convention is regarded as a living instrument, one which serves the society in which it operates.

As the protection of human rights has come to achieve greater prominence, acts that were formerly seen as "inhuman and degrading" are becoming classifiable as torture, particularly when inflicted on those in custody.[34] Furthermore, the changing attitudes of society towards basic respect of individual integrity has had the effect of widening the categories of each example of ill-treatment in Article 3 and by association in Article 8.

The European Court of Human Rights in this case referred to the Convention as "a living instrument", they went on to say:

"The court has previously examined cases in which it concluded that there had been treatment which could only be described as torture . . . however, having regard to the

---

[30] See *J M v. United Kingdom*, September 28, 2000.
[31] See *R. v. Secretary of State for the Home Department ex p. Singh (Sarbjit)* [1999] Imm. A.R. 445.
[32] (1978) 2 E.H.R.R. 25, p. 116.
[33] This judge again dissented and concluded that the combination of the "five techniques" constituted a practice of inhuman treatment and torture in breach of Article 3. He is rather scathing of the proceedings before the Commission and states "Although the charges under Article 3 were vigorously contested by the respondent government in the proceedings before the Commission, the finding against that government by the Commission in its Report has not been contested by the respondent government before the court. It must be stated again that, while the evidence of the applicant government was quite properly subjected to rigorous cross-examination, the same attitude was not displayed to all the witnesses for the respondent government. Here was a lamentable lack in the manner adopted in carrying out a search in an even handed investigation".
[34] See *Selmouni v. France* (2000) 29 E.H.R.R. 403.

fact that the Convention is a 'living instrument', which must be interpreted in the light of present day conditions . . . the court considers that certain acts which were classified in the past as 'inhuman and degrading treatment' as opposed to 'torture' could be classified differently in the future. It takes the view that the increasingly high standard being required in the area of the protection of human rights and fundamental liberties correspondingly and inevitably requires greater firmness in assessing breaches of the fundamental values of democratic societies."[35]

The dynamic nature of this aspect of Article 3 can be seen in an analysis of two cases.

1–16   *Cakici v. Turkey*.[36] This case concerned the treatment following the applicant's detention during an operation against Kurdish Separatists. During a period of about 3 months, he was beaten, with a rib being broken and his head being split open and had received electric shock treatment in the course of his interrogation.

The court did not actually evaluate this violence either as regards the pain and suffering which was inflicted on the victim or the purpose for which it was used but it is self-evident that its use was extreme. This is consistent with the approach taken by the Commission in the Greek case[37] which in that case found that the use of electric shocks to be within a range of treatment constituting "torture and ill-treatment".[38] The treatment of the applicant was intended to obtain information or to punish.

The court had no hesitation in finding that the applicant had been tortured during his detention.[39]

1–17   *Selmouni v. France*.[40] The treatment that was inflicted upon the applicant's brother in *Cakici*[41] did indeed come within the established view of what constituted torture but it is arguable that the violations which were held to have occurred in *Selmouni* would in older cases have been classed as inhuman and the court were conscious that they were in effect reclassifying the treatment as torture, bearing firmly in mind modern principles and attitudes.

---

[35] See para. 101.

[36] July 8, 1999.

[37] (2001) 31 E.H.R.R. 5.

[38] See (1969) 12 Y.B. 1 501.

[39] In *Cakici*, the court had to consider whether the relative of a disappeared person had suffered sufficient anguish and distress so as to establish a breach of Article 3. The factors considered important for this purpose were the strength of the bond between the relatives, presence at the abduction, involvement in attempts to get information about the disappeared person and most important of all, the reaction and attitudes of the authorities to such attempts. These factors were seen as being required to distinguish the situation from the distress which the court regarded as inevitably caused to relatives by such a serious violation as disappearance but, although there is undoubtedly a need to require some degree of proximity, it is considered worrying that a State that is responsible for the disappearance of an individual to be allowed to evade liability for the inevitable consequences of this wrongdoing by then stipulating that their first has to be an additional aggravating fact on the State's part. See also *Kurt v. Turkey*, May 25, 1998 where the applicant was the brother and not the mother of the disappeared person, he was not present at the abduction, he did not bear the brunt of the enquiries and, despite the finding of a violation of Article 13, there was no aggravating feature in the authorities' response to them and thus the claim failed (see dissenting opinions). In a consideration of proximity, one should also refer to the nervous shock cases such as *White v. Chief Constable of South Yorkshire Police* [1999] 1 All ER 1.

[40] (2000) E.H.R.R. 403.

[41] July 8, 1999.

The facts of *Selmouni* concern the treatment of a Moroccan national after his arrest for drug trafficking. One of the allegations concerned the insertion of a small truncheon into his anus[42] but the court did not regard either this or blows resulting in damage to his sight as having been proved. The applicant alleged that he was made to kneel down while one officer pulled him by the hair, a second hit him repeatedly with something like a baseball bat and others kicked him and, standing on his feet, crushed them.

He was subjected to a second session of ill-treatment in which the rape was said to have occurred. Furthermore, one officer showed his penis, asking him to suck it, and then urinated over him. The applicant was threatened with a blow lamp and a syringe. The national French Courts accepted that Selmouni had been assaulted but, although viewing this as a very serious wrong, saw it as "particularly degrading treatment" and not torture.[43] The European Court of Human Rights maintained that torture still required very serious and cruel suffering, and concluded the pain and suffering was sufficiently severe to constitute torture. It accepted that the suffering inflicted upon the applicant was inflicted intentionally for the purpose of making Selmouni confess. In concluding that the treatment constituted torture, the court relied upon three factors:

(a) The presumption that the intensity of blows would cause substantial pain;

(b) The repetition of the treatment over a number of days;

(c) The need for greater firmness in assessing breaches of the fundamental values of democratic societies because of the increasingly high standard being required in the area of the protection of human rights.

It was (3) above that caused the court to recognise that the Convention was a living instrument, and to confirm that certain acts not previously classified as torture could now be so viewed.

The European Committee for the Prevention of Torture[44] were of the view that:

"This approach appears to be recognising the need for a tougher line to be taken in the face of abuse of authority but, although welcome in principle, it also manages to give the impression of a lowering of standards which could actually undermine respect for them . . . the ruling may, of course, be a recognition that in the past suspects were expected to tolerate too much physical pain but this points to the test perhaps not previously being applied with sufficient rigour rather than a dilution of the test itself. Moreover, although the repetition and duration of particular treatment will undoubtedly reinforce its unacceptable character, it is improbable that the suffering of Salmouni at any one interrogation session could have been regarded as insufficient to support a finding of torture".

State motive or purpose. Recent cases have started to stress the importance **1–18** of consideration of a state motive or purpose in assessing the level of violation, this suggests that the court is beginning to develop an alternative or at least a

---

[42] The courts have previously regarded rape alone as sufficient to constitute torture (see *Aydin v. Turkey* (1998) 25 E.H.R.R. 553).

[43] This is inconsistent with the court's view of similar beatings as inhuman and degrading in *Tomasi v. France* (1993) 15 E.H.R.R. 1 and *Ribitsch v. Austria* (1996) 21 E.H.R.R. 573.

[44] (2000) 25 E.L.Rev. Human Rights Survey.

parallel approach which adopts the stricter test of the United Nations Convention Against Torture.

The United Nations Convention against Torture and Other Cruel, Inhuman or Degrading Treatment or Punishment 1984 at Article 1(1),[45] imposes a four-part test, to establish torture:

(a) The intentional infliction;

(b) of severe pain or suffering whether physical or mental;

(c) for any purpose including, for example, to obtain information, inflict punishment or intimidate him or a third person, or for any reason based on discrimination of any kind;

(d) with the consent or acquiescence of a public official or person acting in an official capacity.

It does not include pain or suffering arising only from inherent in or incidental to lawful sanctions.

1–19   **Extracting confessions.** In *Aksoy v. Turkey*,[46] a case which produced the first finding of torture by the court, the applicant had been stripped naked by police officers and then suspended by his arms which had been tied behind his back.

The treatment had involved severe pain and subsequent temporary paralysis of both arms; its deliberate infliction had also required "a certain amount of preparation and exertion" by State officials; and its purpose appeared to be to extract information or a confession from the applicant. The conclusion was a finding of torture within the meaning of Article 3.

In *Aydin v. Turkey*,[47] the court again highlighted the motive of the State when considering the treatment of a 17 year old Kurdish girl who was stripped, beaten, sprayed with cold water and subsequently raped by soldiers. The court accepted[48] that the detention had been with a view to interrogation, and thus the suffering inflicted should be seen as having been calculated to *serve the same purpose*.

This is a significant development from the approach taken in *Ireland v. United Kingdom*,[49] where the court acknowledged[50] that the object of the ill-treatment was "the extraction of confessions, the naming of others and/or information", but seemed from a reading of their judgement to discount the importance of this motive.

The court observed "although the five techniques, as applied in combination, undoubtedly amounted to inhuman and degrading treatment, although their object was extraction of confession, the naming of others and/or information and although they were used systematically, they did not occasion suffering of the particular intensity and cruelty implied by the word torture as so understood".

1–20   **Severity of pain and suffering inflicted.** Although the court has not abandoned its long-standing view that the severity of the pain and suffering inflicted

---

[45] Misc. 12 (1985), Cmnd. 9593. The Convention entered into force in 1987.
[46] (2002) 34 E.H.R.R. 57.
[47] (1998) E.H.R.R. 553.
[48] See para. 5.
[49] (1978) 2 E.H.R.R. 25.
[50] See para. 167.

is an important distinction between torture and inhuman treatment, an analysis of case law indicates a willingness to review the way in which it categorises particular treatment.[51]

The importance of precision in definition. The prohibition articulated within **1–21** Article 3 can often be applied without too much concern as to which particular element, torture, inhuman or degrading treatment, is involved. Nevertheless, precision in definition is important to ascertain the gravity of the response which the treatment concerned may require, for instance, criminal sanctions should be applied to torture but may not always be an appropriate step for treatment found to be inhuman or degrading. Furthermore, precision is necessary so that clarity can be obtained about the boundary between what is acceptable and what is unacceptable.

Thus, Article 3 provides considerations as to torture which is seen as an aggravated form of inhuman treatment which is deliberately inflicted and has a purpose, such as obtaining a confession; degrading treatment which entails gross humiliation or has the effect of driving a person to act against his will or conscious, and inhuman treatment which additionally requires severe mental or physical suffering to have been caused without any justification.

Proving violation. The standard of proof required for a finding that an **1–22** applicant had been subjected to torture, is the criminal standard of beyond reasonable doubt, or satisfying the tribunal so that they are sure.

Although no criminal responsibility is imposed by the courts finding, the Convention Against Torture and Other Cruel, Inhuman or Degrading Treatment or Punishment 1984[52] at Article 4 states:

(1) Each State Party shall ensure that all acts of torture are offences under its criminal law. The same shall apply to an attempt to commit torture and to an act by any person which constitutes complicity or participation in torture.
(2) Each State Party shall make these offences punishable by appropriate penalties which take into account their grave nature.

Article 5

(1) Each State Party shall take such measures as may be necessary to establish its jurisdiction over the offences referred to in Article 4 in the following cases:

(a) when the offences are committed in any territory under its jurisdiction or on board a ship or aircraft registered in that State;
(b) when the alleged offender is a national of that State;
(c) when the victim is a national of that State if that State considers it appropriate.

(2) Each State Party shall likewise take such measures as may be necessary to establish its jurisdiction over such offences in cases where the alleged offender is present in any territory under its jurisdiction and it does not extradite him pursuant to Article 8 to any of the States mentioned in paragraph 1 of this Article.
(3) This Convention does not exclude any criminal jurisdiction exercised in accordance with internal law.

---

[51] There is a similar tendency within the court not to distinguish significantly between inhuman and degrading treatment and/or punishment.
[52] See Appendix 5.

Article 6

(1) Upon being satisfied, after an examination of information available to it, that the circumstances so warrant, any State Party in whose territory a person alleged to have committed any offence referred to in Article 4 is present shall take him into custody or take other legal measures to ensure his presence. The custody and other legal measures shall be provided in the law of that State but may be continued only for such time as is necessary to enable any criminal or extradition proceedings to be instituted.

The State will only be held liable where it can safely be concluded that torture has been committed.

1–23   **Problems of proof.** The usual problems of proof arise, other than the alleged victim there may be an absence of direct witnesses to the ill-treatment. *Ireland v. United Kingdom*,[53] attempted to deal with this problem by observing that such proof can "follow from the coexistence of a sufficiently strong, clear and concordant inferences or of similar unrebutted presumptions of fact . . . the conduct of the Parties when evidence is being obtained has to be taken into account".[54] It should be emphasised that the object of the proceedings in the European Court of Human Rights is not to secure a conviction despite the fact that criminal conduct may be the basis for a State's responsibility.

Where an applicant is in good health at the time of the alleged ill-treatment and then clearly suffers from injuries when released, the State will be expected to provide a plausible explanation for those injuries and any suggestion that they were self-inflicted or in some way legitimately inflicted will have to be overcome by medical evidence to the contrary.[55] In *Selmouni*,[56] the court recognised several medical certificates which were "precise and concordant" as to the injuries suffered and the absence of any plausible explanation as to their cause were together considered sufficient for the court to conclude that the majority of the applicant's allegations were proved to the required standard of proof, beyond reasonable doubt. The courts have recognised that trauma as a result of ill-treatment may inhibit the making of an early complaint.[57]

In *Cakici*,[58] evidence given as to what witnesses saw, in effect the applicant in a bad condition with dried blood on his clothing, was considered admissible. Furthermore, what the applicant had told witnesses, namely what he had told them about the beatings, the breaking of his rib, the splitting open of his head and the use of electric shock treatment on two occasions, was also admissible and considered by the Commission to be reliable and credible. The Commission also took into account the brief and contradictory statements previously made by the witnesses to the police and a prosecutor, as well as a statement about Mr Cakici's detention and ill-treatment made by another detainee to a non-Governmental organisation.

---

[53] (1978) 2 E.H.R.R. 25.
[54] See para. 161.
[55] See *Tomasi v. France* (1992) 15 E.H.R.R. 1 and *Ribitsch v. Austria* (1996) 21 E.H.R.R. 573: also see *Klaas v. Germany* (1994) 2 E.H.R.R. 305, a case where no violation of Article 3 was found on the basis that the medical evidence could not rule out an alternative explanation of ill-treatment.
[56] (2000) 29 E.H.R.R. 403.
[57] See *Stubbings v. United Kingdom* (1997) 23 E.H.R.R. 213.
[58] (2001) 31 E.H.R.R. 5.

The evidence which the courts will rely upon in considering torture may never sustain a conviction but the focus of the court's attitude will be to hold States responsible to ensure that it has the determination to either prevent ill-treatment occurring or to respond effectively in the event of such violations.

Racial discrimination. This area may engage Article 3 as it may constitute **1–24** degrading treatment. In the *East African Asian cases* the Commission stated:

"Deferential treatment of a group of persons on the basis of race, might therefore be capable of constituting degrading treatment where deferential treatment on some other ground would raise no such question . . . While recognising the unique worth of each person, the Constitution does not presuppose that a holder of rights is an isolated, lonely and abstract figure possessing a disembodied and socially disconnected self. It acknowledges that people live in their bodies, their communities, their cultures, their places and their times. The expression of sexuality requires a partner, real or imagined . . . if this is a right enjoyed by heterosexual people under Article 8, then it must also be accorded to homosexuals. Discrimination is prohibited by Article 14 of the Convention".[59]

Article 14 states:

"The enjoyment of the rights and freedoms set forth in this Convention shall be secured without discrimination on any ground such as sex, race, colour, language religion, political or other opinion, national or social origin, association with a national minority, property or other status".

Article 14 is not a free-standing right. It is defined in terms of, and thus compliments the enjoyment of the other rights contained in the Convention. However, this does not mean that a breach of another Article is required.

In November 2000 the Council of Europe agreed a new Protocol 12 to the Convention. Article 1 provides for a free-standing right to equal treatment, but the United Kingdom has so far refused to ratify it.

The leading case is probably *Belgian Linguistics*[60] where the court stated that:

"While it is true that this guarantee has no independent existence in the sense that under the terms of Article 14, it relates solely to 'the rights and freedoms set forth in the Convention', a measure which in itself is in conformity with the requirements of the Article enshrining the right or freedom in question may however infringe this Article when read in conjunction with Article 14 for the reason that it is of a discriminatory nature".

The State therefore has no obligation to avoid discrimination in relation to rights that are not protected by the Convention.

However, the court went on to say that:

"Article 6 of the Convention does not compel States to institute a system of appeal courts. A State which does set up such courts consequently goes beyond its obligations under Article 6. However, it would violate that Article, read in conjunction with Article

---

[59] However, the court was not permitted to apply s.3(1) of the 1998 Act so as to constitute the 1975 Act in a way different from that which is binding upon the lower tribunals at the time, and the appeal was dismissed.
[60] (1968) 1 E.H.R.R. 252.

14, were it to debar certain persons from these remedies without legitimate reason while making them available to others in respect of the same type of actions".

Thus, where a State chooses to do more than the Convention requires it to do, or in cases where there is no actual breach of a substantive right, Article 14 still has application so long as the matter remains within the ambit of the Convention. The test is as follows:

> "The principle of equality of treatment is violated if the distinction has no objective and reasonable justification. The existence of such a justification must be assessed in relation to the aim and effects of the measure under consideration, regard being had to the principles which normally prevail in democratic societies.
>
> A difference in treatment in the exercise of a right laid down in the Convention must not only pursue a legitimate aim; Article 14 is likewise violated when it is clearly established that there is no reasonable relationship of proportionality between the means employed and the aim sought to be realised".[61]

1–25   **Discrimination based upon sexual orientation.** Ill-treatment of individuals as a result of their sexual orientation is not considered by the courts to reach the minimum level of severity required for violation of Article 3 in any of its categories.[62] In *Smith and Grady v. United Kingdom*,[63] the court considered the operation of a policy precluding homosexuals from serving in the armed forces.

Both of the applicants had been in the forces for a considerable number of years but were discharged following investigations into allegations that they were homosexual. The investigations entailed detailed questioning of the applicants about their past and present sex lives, the risk of HIV, the seizure of many personal items and, in the case of one applicant, the possibility of a sexual relationship with her foster-daughter. The applicants were discharged and both the manner of the investigations and the consequent discharge were held to be in violation of the applicants' right to respect for their private life. But although their treatment was accepted by the court as having intruded into the most intimate part of private life, the court did not consider that the undoubted distress and humiliation for both applicants reached the minimum level of severity required. Nevertheless, the court acknowledged the possibility that the treatment concerned was "grounded upon a predisposed bias on the part of a heterosexual majority against a homosexual minority" which could, in principle, fall within Article 3.[64] The court seems to be concentrating on the intensity of suffering which they consider more appropriate for inhuman treatment.

3. INHUMAN TREATMENT AND/OR PUNISHMENT

1–26   **Definition.** Inhuman treatment and/or punishment will be so classified if the ill-treatment causes "intense physical and mental suffering".[65]

---

[61] See also *Abdulaziz Cabales and Balkandali v. United Kingdom* (1985) 7 E.H.R.R. 471; *R. v. Manchester City Council* [2001] EWHC Admin 707.
[62] But see Article 8: Chapter 9.
[63] (2001) 31 E.H.R.R. 24.
[64] See the East African Asians case (1973) 3 E.H.R.R. 76.
[65] See *Ireland v. United Kingdom* (1978) 2 E.H.R.R. 25, para. 159.

The treatment can fall short of actual bodily injury and include "acute psychiatric disturbances".[66]

In *X & Y v. Netherlands*,[67] the Commission were of the view that "mental suffering leading to acute psychiatric disturbances falls into the category of treatment prohibited by Article 3 of the Convention".[68]

The threat of prohibited conduct. Provided it is sufficiently real and immediate, a threat of conduct prohibited by Article 3 may itself be in conflict with that Article. Therefore, to threaten an individual with torture may in some circumstances constitute at least inhuman treatment.[69]   **1–27**

The degree of suffering. The distinction between torture and inhuman treatment and/or punishment centres around the degree of suffering caused by the alleged ill-treatment. The minimum severity threshold[70] applies in matters of inhuman treatment and/or punishment as with any other aspect of Article 3's application. Nevertheless, the threshold for inhuman treatment to breach Article 3 is lower when an applicant is held in custody. As was stated in *Tomasi v. France*[71]:   **1–28**

> "Although the injuries observed might appear to be relatively slight, they nevertheless constituted outward signs of the use of physical force on an individual deprived of his liberty and therefore in a state of inferiority. The treatment had therefore been both inhuman and degrading".

The court emphasised the "cowardly" nature of the attack by those in authority upon the applicant.

Intention. As with degrading treatment and/or punishment, the absence of an intention to humiliate or debase will not conclusively rule out a finding of a violation.[72]   **1–29**

Ill-treatment at the point of arrest. Authorities suggest that ill-treatment at the point of arrest or deprivation of liberty may be considered by the court as a less serious violation of Article 3. In *Egmez v. Cyprus*,[73] the State accepted that the applicant had been intentionally subjected by police officers to violence at the time of his arrest and its immediate aftermath. But the court determined that the facts disclosed a finding of inhuman treatment rather than torture since the injuries had been inflicted over a short period of heightened tension at the time of arrest, no convincing evidence had been adduced to show that the ill-treatment had resulted in any long term consequences, and it had not been shown that the officers' aim had been to extract a confession. It was the absence of the intent to extract information that was particularly important in the court's finding that despite violence at the hands of the police, it should not be characterised as torture.   **1–30**

---

[66] See *Ireland v. United Kingdom* (1978) 2 E.H.R.R. 25 at para. 159.
[67] (1986) 8 E.H.R.R. 235.
[68] See Commission Report at p. 22.
[69] See *Campbell and Cosans v. U.K.* (1982) 4 E.H.R.R. 293 at para. 26.
[70] See Chapter 2: Proving Violations of Article 3.
[71] (1992) 15 E.H.R.R. 1 at para. 113.
[72] See *T v. U.K.* and *V v. U.K.* (1999) 30 E.H.R.R. 121.
[73] (2002) 34 E.H.R.R. 29.

In the case of *Chrysostomos and Papachrysostomou v. Turkey*,[74] it was held by the court that the use of rough treatment by police officers did not meet the minimum threshold test for Article 3 in view of the public disorder at the time the applicants were taken into custody.[75] It seems that the court will find that the circumstances pertaining at the time of the ill-treatment can mitigate the effect of police behaviour, thus reducing culpability under Article 3.

4. DEGRADING TREATMENT AND/OR PUNISHMENT

1–31   **Definition.** Treatment will be deemed to fall within this category of Article 3 violation if it is adjudged as to arouse in a victim the feeling of fear, anguish and inferiority capable of humiliating and debasing them and possibly breaking their physical and moral resistance.[76]

1–32   **The distinction.** Again, the distinction embodied in Article 3 between degrading treatment and/or punishment and that of inhuman treatment and/or punishment or torture, derives principally from a difference in the intensity of the suffering inflicted.[77]

1–33   **Humiliation.** Ill-treatment itself will not be degrading unless the person concerned has undergone, in the eyes of others or in his own eyes, humiliation or debasement attaining a minimum level of severity.[78] That level has to be assessed with regard to the circumstances of the case.[79] The level of humiliation or debasement must be over and above that inherent in legitimate punishment. In *Costello-Roberts v. United Kingdom*,[80] the European Court held that a "slippering" administered to a 7 year old boy at a private school did not reach the minimum level of severity to amount to degrading treatment.

1–34   **Persons deprived of their liberty.** In respect of a person deprived of their liberty, any recourse to physical force which has not been made strictly necessary by his own conduct of its nature diminishes human dignity and is in principle an

---

[74] (1993) D.R. 86.

[75] The European Committee for the Prevention of Torture in its Report to the United Kingdom, CPT/Inf. (94) 17, para. 30: stated "The CPT fully recognises that the arrest of a criminal suspect is often a hazardous task in particular, if the person concerned resists arrest and/or is someone who the security forces have good reason to believe may be armed and dangerous. The circumstances of an arrest may be such that injuries are sustained by the person concerned (and by members of the security forces) without this being the result of an intention to inflict ill-treatment. However, no more force than is reasonably necessary should be used when effecting an arrest. Furthermore, once arrested persons have been brought under control, there can be no justification for them being struck by members of the security forces. In the light of the information gathered by its delegation, the CPT recommends that members of the security forces be reminded of these precepts".

[76] See *Ireland v. U.K.* (1978) 2 E.H.R.R. 25 at para. 167.

[77] See *Ireland v. U.K.* (1978) 2 E.H.R.R. 25 at para. 167: we remind ourselves that the European Court in this case concluded that the five techniques of ill-treatment amounted to a practice of inhuman and degrading treatment (but see the view of the Commission).

[78] See *Tyrer v. United Kingdom* (1979–80) 2 E.H.R.R. 1 at pp. 15–16.

[79] See *Ireland v. United Kingdom* (1978) 2 E.H.R.R. 25 at paras 162, 167 and 179–181.

[80] (1995) 19 E.H.R.R. 112.

infringement of Article 3 and classified as degrading treatment and/or punishment.[81] Suffering or humiliation must go beyond that inevitable element associated with legitimate treatment or punishment. In order for a punishment or treatment associated with it to be degrading the suffering or humiliation involved must in any event go beyond that inevitable element of suffering or humiliation connected with a given form of legitimate treatment or punishment.[82]

For example, in the context of the treatment of prisoners, the treatment must go beyond the usual element of humiliation associated with imprisonment after a criminal conviction.[83] The public nature of the treatment is relevant as is its adverse effect,[84] but the absence of publicity will not necessarily prevent a given punishment from being degrading, for it may be sufficient that the victim is humiliated in his own eyes, even if not in the eyes of others. This aspect has been developed further when the courts have considered matters concerning the infliction of corporal punishment.

Effects of treatment. The punishment or treatment need not cause any severe **1–35**
or long-lasting physical effects.[85]

Behaviour of victim. The fact that the person concerned brought the treatment **1–36**
on himself may be relevant,[86] but that fact alone cannot absolve the State from
its obligations under Article 3.[87]

Deterrent effect. A degrading punishment does not lose its degrading charac- **1–37**
ter just because it is believed to be, or actually is, an effective deterrent or aid to
maintain discipline.[88]

No need for intention to cause degrading treatment.[89] Of course, if the **1–38**
purpose of the treatment was to humiliate or debase a victim, then that is a factor
that has to be taken into account. But the absence of any such purpose will not
conclusively rule out a finding of a violation under Article 3.[90] Article 3 is an
absolute right from which there is no derogation under any circumstances,[91] and
Article 8 is a qualified right where the right is disclosed and then interference
with it is permitted in certain circumstances.

Relationship between Article 3 and Article 8. Article 3 and Article 8 often **1–39**
run in tandem. This can be seen in the recent case of *Wilkinson v. RMO
Broadmoor Hospital*[92] in the Court of Appeal. W had been sectioned under the
Mental Health Act and obtained permission to apply both for judicial review of
the treatment decisions taken by the first and second respondents and for an

---

[81] See *Ribitsch v. Austria* (1996) 21 E.H.R.R. 573 at para. 38.
[82] See *T v. United Kingdom* and *V v. United Kingdom* (1999) 30 E.H.R.R. 121 at para. 71.
[83] See *Tyrer v. United Kingdom* (1979–80) 2 E.H.R.R. 1 at pp. 9–10.
[84] See *Raninen v. Finland* [1997] 26 E.H.R.R. 563.
[85] See *Tyrer v. United Kingdom* (1979–80) 2 E.H.R.R. 1 at pp. 10–11.
[86] See *McFeeley v. United Kingdom* [1980] 3 E.H.R.R. 161 at p. 198.
[87] See *X v. United Kingdom* [1982] 28 D.R. 5 at p. 32.
[88] See *Tyrer v. United Kingdom* (1980) 2 E.H.R.R. 1 at p. 10, para. 31; and Chapter 4; Prisoners.
[89] But see *Abduaziz, Cabales and Balkandali v. U.K.* (1985) 7 E.H.R.R. 471 which held that degrading treatment must be intentional to violate Article 3.
[90] See *T v. U.K.* and *V v. U.K.* (1999) 30 E.H.R.R. 121 at para. 71.
[91] See Article 15.
[92] October 22, 2001, unreported.

injunction prohibiting any further such treatment until the hearing of the substantive challenge. The respondents sought to treat him without consent. Issues were taken as to Article 3 because the forcible injection of an unwilling patient must constitute, it was argued, at the very least degrading treatment and, if he is properly to be regarded as capacitated, it clearly violated his fundamental right to autonomy and bodily inviolability.

But even if Article 3 were not breached, Article 8 was considered, there being no sufficient justification under Article 8(2) was breached as there was such a fundamental invasion of his autonomy and inviolability that his basic rights to privacy were breached.

1–40   **The court's role in reviewing decisions.** The decision maker retains the ultimate decision and bears the burden of proving that he had not violated human rights.[93]

In *R. v. Secretary of State for the Home Department ex p. Isiko*,[94] the court emphasised that it will not substitute its own views for that of the executive. It will simply apply the law. It went on to state:

> "When a court reviews a decision which is required to comply with the Convention by the Human Rights Act 1998, it does not substitute its own decision for that of the executive. It reviews the decision of the executive to see if it was permitted by law—in this instance the Human Rights Act. In performing this exercise the court has to bear in mind that, just as individual States enjoy a margin of appreciation which permits them to respond within the law in a manner which is not uniform, so there will often be an area of discretion permitted to the executive of a country which needs to be exceeded before an action must be categorised as unlawful. In this difficult area choices may have to be made by the executive or the legislature between the rights of the individual and the needs of society".

1–41   **The effect of the Human Rights Act 1998 on decisions before incorporation of that Act.** In *R. v. Secretary of State for the Home Department ex p. Mahmood (Amjad)*,[95] the applicant was a Pakistani national who had entered the country illegally in 1994. At the date of the Secretary of State's decision to remove him he had been married for less than two years to a woman settled in the United Kingdom and had two children by that marriage. He sought to challenge the decision to remove him by way of judicial review. An argument was made by the applicant that the court should treat the Convention as being incorporated vis a vis the decision even though the decision being impugned was dated prior to incorporation. The applicant's argument, which was supported by the Secretary of State was that although the judicial review challenge was in relation to past decisions of the Secretary of State, in truth the court is or should be considering the legality of the action which will or would be taken in the future by the Secretary of State to put that decision into effect. This argument though was rejected by the court and Laws L.J. said:

> " . . . it is to be born in mind that the court's primary role is historic: that is, to review the legality of decisions already arrived at.
>
> But I recognise that in the present context this conclusion may produce an artificial state of affairs.

---

[93] *R. v. Secretary of State for the Home Department ex p. Mahmood.*
[94] [2001] H.R.L.R. 15.
[95] December 8, 2000.

We cannot in reality tolerate a position in which the court says one thing about the legality of a decision taken before October 2, 2000, while (notionally at least) reserving a potentially different riposte in relation to the decision's implementation after October 2. The answer, as so often with the common law, is a pragmatic one. By definition the case will involve fundamental rights or freedoms, recognised as such here and in Strasbourg. The law intrusive mode of supervision—the second approach which I have earlier described—which is apt by our domestic law to the review of decisions affecting fundamental freedoms will, in my judgement, in broad terms and in most instances suffice also at least as the beginning of a proper touchstone for review when the Convention is directly in play. It will of course fall to be tailored and adapted as the courts confront disparate situations in which, by force of Section 2 of the Act of 1998, they are obliged to take account of the Strasbourg jurisprudence".

The court would only intervene when the decision fell outside the range of responses open to a reasonable decision maker. The court decided in this case that there were reasonable grounds for the Secretary of State's decision that the applicant's deportation was necessary in the interests of an orderly and fair control of immigration and that his right to respect for his family life was not violated.

Section 3 of the Human Rights Act 1998 obligation on the court. Section **1–42** 3 of the Human Rights Act imposes an interpretative obligation on the courts, it reserves the amendment of legislation to Parliament thereby preserving Parliamentary Sovereignty. In *S re: W*,[96] the House of Lords observed that to interpret the proposed starring system initiated by the Court of Appeal in Children Act 1989 cases, went further than Sections 7 and 8 of the Human Rights Act allows interpretatively—it would impose obligations on local authorities when there has been no finding of unlawfulness and before identification of a breach of a Convention right.

The question arises as to whether the Children Act 1989 is generally incompatible with Article 8 (and Article 6). In respect of Article 8, the manner in which a local authority discharges its responsibility may evoke the Article. It may cease to be Article 8(2) justifiable as not pursuing a legitimate aim or disproportionate to the original care order aim.[97]

The effect on common law. The courts are obliged to correct common law **1–43** cases to bring them in line with the Convention. As has been stated "the Human Rights Act empowers, nay commands, the courts to amend common law rules so as to ensure compatibility with the Convention".[98]

The approach to European and other jurisprudence. It has been suggested **1–44** that "a court should take account of any Strasbourg decision, but there seems no reason why it should not develop those decisions and fill in gaps where they exist, taking a principled rather than a predictive approach".[99]

---

[96] [2002] U.K.H.L. 10 [March 14, 2002].
[97] The absence of a remedy in the Children Act 1989 for the local authority failings does not in itself make the legislation incompatible—there are other means available to the parent and child.
[98] See Andrew Ashworth, Crim.L.R. [2000] 564 at 566.
[99] See Andrew Ashworth, Crim.L.R. [2000] 564: "The Human Rights Act and the Substantive Criminal Law: A Non-Minimalist View".

To do so, the court will take into account other jurisprudence. For instance, in *Lee Kwong-Kut v. R.*,[1] Lord Woolf drew upon Commonwealth and United States Constitutional decisions to deal with an issue little developed in Europe. Furthermore, in *T and V v. U.K.*,[2] the European Court of Human Rights considered various sources, including United Nations material. In *McKerry v. Teesdale and Wear Valley Justices*,[3] Lord Bingham cited the European Convention on the Rights of the Child, the United Nations Standard Minimum Rules for the Administration for Juvenile Justice and Recommendation No. R(87) 20 of the Committee of Ministers of the Council of Europe in Social Reactions to Juvenile Delinquency.

It is not necessarily the court's role to predict how a particular point would be decided in Strasbourg according to the arguments of Sir Richard Buxton in his article in Law Quarterly Review.[4]

---

[1] [1993] A.C. 951: Privy Council.
[2] (1999) 30 E.H.R.R. 1.
[3] Times Law Reports, February 29, 2000.
[4] Sir Richard Buxton "The Human Rights Act and Private Law", (2000) 116 L.Q.R. 48.

Chapter 2

PROVING VIOLATIONS OF ARTICLE 3

1. Severity

The minimum level of severity. The guarantee under Article 3 is a universal **2–01**
minimum standard, the breach of which is protected by the Convention. The only
qualification laid down by Convention case law and jurisprudence is that in order
for the conduct to be prohibited, the ill-treatment must attain a minimum level of
severity if it is to fall within the scope of Article 3. The assessment of what
constitutes a minimum level of severity is relative and will depend upon all the
circumstances of the case but includes such matters as the duration of the ill
treatment, its physical or mental effects and, in some cases, the sex, age and state
of health of the victim. The effect of this stricture has resulted in the courts
developing a boundary, across which every applicant must cross into the protection afforded by Article 3. It has produced a wealth of case law.

Ireland v. United Kingdom.[1] Because the Convention contains no prohibition **2–02**
covering intermediate forms of maltreatment that clearly fall short of, that degree
of severity which would justify a classification as in human or degrading or as
amounting to torture, the Courts have been required to develop their own code as
to what is acceptable and what has reached that minimum level of severity which
contravenes Article 3.

One of the earliest cases to develop guidelines was *Ireland v. U.K.* which
concerned the British Government's response to terrorism in Northern Ireland in
the late 1970s. The United Kingdom approved "five techniques" of interrogation
of terrorist suspects which included wall standing, hooding, subjection to noise,
deprivation of sleep and deprivation of food and drink. On each of these activities
the European Court of Human Rights was asked to adjudicate as to whether they
breached Article 3. All activities were said to do so, but were not necessarily
categorised as torture bringing it into conflict with the Commission.

The Commission unanimously found that the five techniques did constitute a
practice of torture. When one analyses the techniques, this may not be surprising.
Wall standing consisted of forcing the detainees to remain for periods of some
hours in a "stress position" described by those who underwent it as being
"spread-eagled against the wall with their fingers put high above the head against
the wall, the legs spread apart and the feet back, causing them to stand on their
toes with the weight of the body mainly on the fingers".

Hooding consisted of putting a black or a navy coloured bag over the detainees' heads and, at least initially, keeping it there all the time except during
interrogation.

---

[1] (1978) 2 E.H.R.R. 25.

Subjection to noise consisted of holding the detainees in a room pending their interrogation where there was a continuous loud and hissing noise.

Deprivation of sleep meant that the detainees were deprived of their sleep pending interrogation.

Deprivation of food and drink subjected the detainees to a reduced diet during their detention at the interrogation centre and pending their interrogations.

In the judgement of the European Court of Human Rights at paragraph 167, the court's condemnation is clear, "the five techniques were applied in combination, with premeditation and for hours at a stretch; they caused, if not actual bodily harm, at least intense physical and mental suffering to the persons subjected thereto and also led to acute psychiatric disturbances during interrogation. They accordingly fell into the category of inhuman treatment within the meaning of Article 3. The techniques were also degrading since they were such as to arouse in their victims feelings of fear, anguish and inferiority capable of humiliating and debasing them and possibly breaking their physical or moral resistance".

Their conclusion that the techniques fell short of torture, sits somewhat awkwardly with modern attitudes and standards and demonstrates how positions taken as recently as 1979 can seem somewhat out of step.

2–03   **Relativity.** In *Toomey v. United Kingdom*,[2] the applicant was recommended for assessment under the Sex Offenders Treatment Programme and transferred to prison where he underwent a Penile Polygraph Assessment (PPG). The first test lasted for one hour and 20 minutes wherein the applicant was put in a small room without windows and with bolts both inside and outside the door. A video recorder was adjusted to the level of his face. Monitoring was possible via a camera and a microphone.

The applicant then had to attach a sensor clip to his penis and to leave his underpants and trousers removed throughout the test. The applicant was shown sets of slides which included nude images of young children, scenes of consensual sex, rape and non-sexual violence. The slides were left on for about 20 seconds and each were shown approximately 6 times.

The test then continued with a *"key score"* pad on which the applicant had to mark his sexual attraction to the slides with a score from 0–9. A second PPG test similar to the first one was conducted. Both tests disclosed no strong indication of a deviant PPG profile. The conclusion of a forensic psychologist was that the applicant presented a low risk of re-offending. The applicant was therefore not considered a suitable candidate for the Sex Offenders Treatment Programme. He complained to the European Commission of a violation of Article 3 arguing that the PPG tests amounted to torture, inhuman or degrading treatment. The court declared the application inadmissible (by majority).

They emphasised that the minimum level of severity was relative depending upon the above cited circumstances and although they accepted that the applicant's participation in the tests was humiliating for him, the question that had to be decided was whether, given all the relevant circumstances of the case, the PPG assessments amounted to degrading treatment within the meaning of Article 3. The court did not believe that the treatment could be so categorised.

---

[2] Application. No. 37231/97.

2. THE ABSOLUTE NATURE OF ARTICLE 3

No exceptions. A feature of Article 3 interpretation and correct application is   **2–04**
the absolute nature of the provision. Unlike some other provisions of the Convention,[3] Article 3 provides no exceptions, no special cases and no derogations on emergency grounds. In *Venables and Thompson v. Newsgroup Newspapers and Associated Newspapers Limited*,[4] Dame Elizabeth Butler-Sloss stated:

> "It is important to have regard to the fact that the rights under Articles 2 and 3 are not capable of derogation, and the consequences to the claimants if those rights were to be breached. It is clear that, on the basis that there is a real possibility that the claimants may be objects of revenge attacks, the potential breaches of Articles 2, 3 and 8 have to be evaluated with great care".

In that case, the court was concerned with the treatment of two children charged with the murder of a child. It could not provide a better example of how Article 3 will bite, regardless of public clamour and consequence.

Severity rule counterbalances absolute nature of Article 3. Despite the fact   **2–05**
that it was argued that the "five techniques" employed by the State in *Ireland v. United Kingdom* produced some very important results in terms of counter-terrorism, this was considered to be irrelevant.

This must be correct, any relaxation as to the strictures of Article 3 would give rise to very grave possibilities of abuse. The motivation of the alleged treatment, such as obtaining information for public protection is rendered irrelevant by the unconditional wording of Article 3. This rigid approach is clearly counter-balanced by the minimum level of severity rule. Therefore, the applicant must prove that he has suffered the treatment complained of and that it is above the minimum level of severity so as to cross the threshold required by Article 3. The applicant must also establish in practice that this engages the responsibility of the State.

Victim's conduct irrelevant. The absolute prohibition of Article 3 violation   **2–06**
has been reasserted in subsequent case law and prohibition persists irrespective of the victim's conduct. In *Ahmed v. Austria*,[5] a Somalian national sought refugee status in Austria on the basis that his father and brother had been executed in that country as part of a political oppression.

The deportation order against Ahmed was upheld on the ground that he had revealed a tendency towards aggressive behaviour and constituted a danger to Austrian society. Ahmed appealed on the basis that his expulsion to Somalia would violate Article 3 in that it would expose him to a real risk of torture or degrading treatment in that country. The court upheld that submission and ruled that Article 3 implied the obligation not to expel a person to a country where substantial grounds had been shown that if the person were expelled he would face a real risk of being subjected to torture or degrading treatment. The court emphasised that there was no provision for exceptions and no derogation was

---

[3] See Article 8: Qualified Rights.
[4] [2001] 2 W.L.R. 1038.
[5] (1997) 24 E.H.R.R. 278.

permissible and that the activities of an individual applicant, however undesirable or dangerous, could not be a material consideration.[6]

It follows that there will be no relaxation of the absolute nature of Article 3 even when it is suggested that serious crime requires special dispensation.

This was argued in *Selmouni v. France*[7] where the applicant was held in custody for 4 days in connection with a police investigation into a drug ring. The applicant complained that he had also been physically abused, beaten, urinated upon and dragged by the hair. Again, it was reiterated that there are no exceptions to the absolute application of Article 3.

3. HUMILIATION

2–07   **Whether the object is to humiliate and debase.** In considering whether a treatment is degrading within the meaning of Article 3, the court will have regard to whether its object is to humiliate and debase the person concerned. In *Peers v. Greece*,[8] the court held that whilst there was no evidence that there was a positive intention of humiliating or debasing the applicant, a remand prisoner who was held in a psychiatric unit, the question whether the purpose of the treatment was to humiliate or debase is a factor which can be taken into account. Even if there is an absence of purpose on behalf of the authorities to humiliate or debase a victim, a finding of violation of Article 3 will not be conclusively ruled out.[9] Humiliation or debasement attaining the minimum level of severity can be in either the eyes of others or the applicant's own eyes.[10] That level has to be assessed with regard to the circumstances of the case.[11] For instance, racial discrimination has been held to engage Article 3 as it may constitute degrading treatment. In the *East African Asian cases*,[12] the Commission stated:

> "Deferential treatment of a group of persons on the basis of race, might therefore be capable of constituting degrading treatment where deferential treatment on some other ground would raise no such question".

2–08   **Humiliation in applicant's own eyes.** In *Campbell and Cosans v. United Kingdom*,[13] a case concerning the threat of corporal punishment but not its infliction,[14] the European Court of Human Rights considered whether the juveniles were humiliated or debased in their own eyes. The court observed, firstly, that a threat directed to an exceptionally insensitive person may have no significant effect on them but nevertheless, incontrovertibly degrading; and conversely, an exceptionally sensitive person might be deeply affected by a threat that could be described as degrading only by a distortion of the ordinary and usual meaning of the word.

---

[6] *Tomasi v. France* (1993) 15 E.H.R.R. 1; *Chahal v. United Kingdom* (1997) 23 E.H.R.R. 413; *Aydin v. Turkey* (1998) 25 E.H.R.R. 251.

[7] (2000) 29 E.H.R.R. 403.

[8] 33 E.H.R.R. 51.

[9] *V v. United Kingdom* 71 E.C.H.R. IX.

[10] See *Tyrer v. U.K.* (1980) 2 E.H.R.R. 1 at p. 16, para. 32.

[11] See *Ireland v. U.K.* (1978) 2 E.H.R.R. 25 at p. 65, para. 162, p. 66, para. 167 and pp. 69–70, paras 179–181.

[12] (1981) 3 E.H.R.R. 76.

[13] (1991) 31 E.H.R.R. 441.

[14] See Chapter 8: Children and Young People.

The test propounded by *Campbell and Cosans*[15] when considering whether the applicant has been humiliated in their own eyes seems to be subjective and in noting that it has not been shown by means of medical certificates or otherwise that the juveniles had suffered any adverse psychological or other effects, the court were clearly indicating that expertise will be required in many cases to establish a proper level of humiliation or debasement.

Adverse effect on personality. Whether a treatment is degrading to a degree **2–09** which violates Article 3 may also be effected with reference to the consequences of the errant behaviour, as to whether it adversely affects the personality of the victim in a manner incompatible with Article 3. In *Peers v. Greece*, the court accepted that there was no evidence that there was a positive intention of humiliating or debasing the applicant.

But the facts of that case established that the authorities took no steps to improve the objectively held unacceptable conditions of the applicant's detention. On the facts of that case, the court took particular account that for at least two months the applicant had to spend a considerable part of each 24 hour period confined to his bed in the cell with no ventilation and no window which would at times become unbearably hot. The applicant also had to use the toilet in the presence of another inmate and be present while the toilet was being used by his cell mate. The court rejected the Government's argument that the conditions had not affected the applicant in a manner incompatible with Article 3. The court were of the opinion that the prison conditions complained of diminished the applicant's human dignity and arose in him feelings of anguish and inferiority capable of humiliating and debasing him and possibly breaking his physical or moral resistance.

They held that the conditions in which the applicant was detained in a segregation unit amounted to degrading treatment within the meaning of Article 3 of the Convention.[16]

The mere threat of torture, inhuman or degrading treatment. Provided the **2–10** threat is sufficiently real and immediate, and relates to conduct prohibited by Article 3, this in itself may be in conflict with that provision. Therefore, to threaten an individual with torture might in some circumstances constitute at least inhuman treatment.[17]

The standard of proof. The standard of proof required for Article 3 is the **2–11** criminal standard of "beyond reasonable doubt". In *Ireland v. United Kingdom*, the court added that such proof may follow from the coexistence of sufficiently strong, clear and "concordant inferences or of similar unrebutted presumptions of fact".

The conduct of parties when evidence is being obtained is a matter which will be taken into account when assessing evidence.[18]

The burden of proof. The European Court does not place a burden of proof **2–12** on either party. In cases referred to it the court will examine all materials put

---

[15] (1991) 31 E.H.R.R. 441.
[16] *Raninen v. Finland* (reports of judgments and decisions) (1998) 26 E.H.R.R. 563.
[17] See *Campbell and Cosans v. U.K.* (1982) 4 E.H.R.R. 293 at para. 26.
[18] See *Ireland v. U.K.* (1978) 2 E.H.R.R. 25 at para. 161.

before it, whether they originate from the Commission, the parties or other sources and if necessary the court will obtain material of its own motion.[19] The court are encouraged to take an investigative role.[20]

4. INVESTIGATIONS

2–13   **The duty of the court to offer protection.** The Human Rights Act 1998 Section 6 lays down obligations upon the courts to proactively protect human rights by preventing breaches and it is likely that positive obligations will be placed upon the courts and other public authorities under the Human Rights Act to facilitate this protection.[21]

The pertinent part of Section 6 reads:

"(1) It is unlawful for a public authority to act in a way which is incompatible with a Convention right. . . .

(3) In this section 'public authority' includes—

    (a) a court or tribunal, and

    (b) any person certain of whose functions are functions of a public nature, but does not include either Houses of Parliament or a person exercising functions in connection with proceedings in Parliament;

(4) In sub-section (3) 'Parliament' does not include the House of Lords in its judicial capacity;

(6) 'An act' includes a failure to act but does not include a failure to—

    (a) introduce in, or lay before, Parliament a proposal for legislation; or

    (b) make any primary legislation or remedial order".

As a result of this the courts can require an investigation as to the adequacy of the level of protection for Convention rights which is in place in any given policy or administrative area. The court will not just be required to examine the conduct of any particular authority which is named as respondent, it will also be expected to assess the adequacy of the standard of protection provided by the relevant legal framework as a whole in combination with the practice of the array of responsible public authorities.

Examples of instances where the European Court have held that the State's duty to protect rights under the Convention has not been properly fulfilled include investigations into the circumstances of deaths in custody.[22] The European Court have held that the State's duty to safeguard rights under Articles 2 and 3 will extend beyond measures to determine criminal liability and include a duty to take steps to prevent future violations.[23]

In *R. (on the application of Wright and Bennett) v. Home Office*,[24] the court referred to the Human Rights Act 1998, Section 6, Section 7 (Proceedings) and Section 8 (Judicial Remedies) in finding breaches of Articles 2 and 3, and that in

---

[19] See *Ireland v. U.K.* at para. 160.

[20] *Ireland v. U.K.* (1978) 2 E.H.R.R. 25 at para. 160.

[21] See *W and B (Children: W (Children))* [2001] EWCA Civ 757 and the forthcoming House of Lords decision.

[22] See Chapter 4: Prisoners and *R. (on the applicant of Wright and Bennett) v. Home Office* [2001] EWHC Admin 520.

[23] See *R. (Amin) v. Secretary of State for the Home Department* [2001] EWHC Admin 719.

[24] See above.

that case civil proceedings under the Fatal Accidents Act 1976 had been settled before any court hearing took place.[25]

The court's duty under Section 6 extends beyond a mere procedural role and go beyond ensuring the right to a fair trial under Article 6.[26]

The independence of the court. The Court of Appeal have held that where **2–14** fundamental rights are in issue, the court must reach an "independent" view of the merits of a case. Sometimes this will mean departing from normal court practices. In *R. v. Responsible Medical Officer Broadmoor Hospital and Mental Health Act Commission Second Opinion Doctor, ex p. Wilkinson and Secretary of State for Health (Interested Party)*,[27] a detained mental health patient sought by way of judicial review to challenge the administration of medical treatment without his consent. The Court of Appeal emphasised that in taking the independent approach to the merits of the medical decision to treat this should include the disputed issues of fact. They directed that the court should depart from the usual practices inherent within judicial review by ordering the attendance of the medical personnel concerned with the administration of the proposed medical treatment so that they could be cross-examined. If this was done, then the court would have discharged its duty.[28]

The State's obligations. The State is required to take measures designed to **2–15** ensure that individuals within the jurisdiction are not subjected to torture or inhuman or degrading treatment or punishment, this includes vigilance as to how an applicant will be treated if he is sent back to a country where he fears persecution and whether ill-treatment will be administered by private individuals, for instance, in the area of corporal punishment. There is a positive obligation on States to "take those steps that could reasonably be expected of them to avoid a real and immediate risk of ill-treatment contrary to Article 3 of which they knew or ought to have had knowledge".[29-30] Although treatment contrary to Article 3 must be prohibited by the criminal law, which must be implemented in a manner so as to ensure that the prohibition is effective,[31] the obligation of the State under Article 3 extends beyond this in cases where private individuals have behaved contrary to Article 3.[32]

State's obligation to take preventative measures. In stating that the criminal **2–16** law was not enough to protect children, the court observed in *Z v. U.K.*:

" . . . that the protection of children who by reason of their age and vulnerability are not capable of protecting themselves requires not merely that criminal law provides protection against Article 3 treatment but that, additionally, this provision will in appropriate circumstances imply a positive obligation on the authorities to take preventative measures to protect a child who is at risk from another individual. The Commission

---

[25] The proceedings were found to be flawed, in particular during the inquest the families of the deceased were inadequately represented.
[26] See also *R. (on the application of Holding and Barnes) v. Secretary of State for the Environment, Transport and the Regions* [2001] 2 W.L.R. 1389, in a planning context.
[27] *The Times*, November 2, 2001.
[28] See Appendix 2 The Human Rights Act.
[29-30] See *Z v. United Kingdom* (2002) 34 E.H.R.R. 3.
[31] See *A v. United Kingdom* (1998) 27 E.H.R.R. 611.
[32] See *Z v. United Kingdom* otherwise entitled *X v. Bedfordshire County Council* [1995] 3 All E.R. 353 for proceedings in the domestic arena.

notes in this regard the international recognition accorded to this principle in Article 19 of the United Nations Convention on the Rights of the Child which enjoins States to take all appropriate measures 'to protect the child from all forms of physical and mental violence, injury or abuse' ".

The Commission observed that the State had:

"failed in its positive obligation under Article 3 of the Convention to provide the applicants with adequate protection against inhuman and degrading treatment".

The Commission were clearly concerned that no steps had been taken to place children who are being abused by their parents on the "at risk" register until after 4 years of ill-treatment.

The Commission in *Z v. United Kingdom*[33] stated:

"The court emphasised that Article 3 enshrined one of the most fundamental values of a democratic society, prohibiting in absolute terms torture or inhuman or degrading treatment or punishment. States that had ratified the Convention were bound to ensure that individuals within their jurisdiction were not subjected to inhuman or degrading treatment, including such ill-treatment administered by private individuals. Those measures had to provide effective protection, in particular, of children and other vulnerable people and included reasonable steps to prevent ill-treatment of which the authorities had or ought to have had knowledge. The court said that there was no dispute that the neglect and abuse suffered by the four child applicants reached the threshold of inhuman and degrading treatment".

2–17   **State investigations.**[34] The court in *Z v. United Kingdom* derived the following general principles of good practice regarding an investigation into death which can be added to guidelines laid down by subsequent case law. The investigation must be:

1. *Effective*

"The essential purpose of such investigation is to secure the effective implementation of the domestic laws which protect the right to life and, in those cases involving State agents or bodies, to ensure their accountability for deaths occurring under their responsibility . . . the authorities must act of their own motion, once the matter has come to their attention. They cannot leave it to the initiative of the next of kin either to lodge a formal complaint or to take responsibility for the conduct of any investigative procedures" (para. 105).

The investigation must also be "capable of leading to a determination of whether the force used was or was not justified in the circumstances and to the identification and punishment of those responsible" (para. 106).

The investigation should also be plausible. In the case of *Tanli v. Turkey*,[35] the applicant's son was taken away by Gendarme Commanders following a search in

---

[33] (2002) 34 E.H.R.R. 3.
[34] Although the cases of *Jordan v. United Kingdom* (Application No. 24746/94): see *The Times*, May 18, 2001; *McKerr v. United Kingdom* (2002) 34 E.H.R.R. 20; *Kelly v. United Kingdom* (Application No. 30054/96) and *Shanaghan v. United Kingdom* (Application No. 37715/97) . . . were cases involving the so-called "shoot to kill" cases as a result of individuals who had been shot and killed by the RUC, they do lay down useful guidance as to the court's expectations of a proper investigation.
[35] Application No. 26129/95, April 10, 2001.

his village. Two days later the applicant was informed at the police station that his son had died of a heart attack whilst in custody. The applicant maintained that his son's death was caused by torture. An investigation, which was undertaken by the Public Prosecutor, failed to establish the cause of death and three defendants were acquitted.

The court observed that the Government had not provided a plausible explanation for the death of the applicant's son in custody after he entered in apparently good health. While the applicant and other witnesses referred to seeing bruising on the body, there was no medical substantiation that this was attributable to traumatic injury rather than post-mortem changes in the body. In the circumstances, the court found that it had not been established that there had been a violation of Article 3. (Reassuringly, they did find a violation of Article 2 in that the authorities had failed to provide any plausible or satisfactory explanation for the death of the applicant's son and that their responsibility for his death was therefore engaged.)[36]

2. Independent

"For an investigation . . . to be effective, it may generally be regarded as necessary of the persons responsible for and carrying out the investigation to be independent from those implicated in the events" (para. 106)

3. Prompt and expeditious

"A requirement of promptness and reasonable expedition is explicit in this context . . . a prompt response by the authorities in investigating a use of lethal force may generally be regarded as essential in maintaining public confidence in their adherence to the rule of law and in preventing any appearance of collusion or intolerance of unlawful acts" (para. 108).

4. Public

"There must be a sufficient element of public scrutiny of the investigation and its results to secure accountability in practice as well as in theory".[37]

5. Participation of family

"In all cases, . . . the next of kin of the victim must be involved in the procedure to the extent necessary to safeguard his or her legitimate interests".[38]

The Lawrence Enquiry recommendations[39] were also pertinent where they stated[40] that:

"This development must be regarded as a positive contribution to the openness and fairness of the inquest procedures . . . the court considers that the right of the family of

---

[36] The case of *Adali v. Turkey* is presently before the court (January 21, 2002) which concerns the applicant's complaints (under Articles 3, 6, 8, 10, 11, 12, and 14 of the Convention) about, amongst other things, the failure to investigate the killing of her husband, a writer who had published articles critical of the Turkish Government and the Turkish Republic of Northern Cyprus. Her claim also deals with harassment of herself by TRNC officials, including the monitoring of her telephone and correspondence.

[37] (para. 109).

[38] (para. 109).

[39] McPherson report.

[40] At para. 134.

the deceased whose death is under investigation to participate in the proceedings requires that the procedures adopted ensure the requisite protection of their interests, which may be in direct conflict with those of the police or security forces".

2–18   **Payment of damages not enough.** The court reiterated that the obligation on the State to investigate (in that case under Article 2) could not be satisfied by the payment of damages. A similar principle must apply to investigations regarding Article 3. Compensation must be accompanied by measures to prevent further violations of Article 3.

In *Donnelly v. United Kingdom*,[41] the court observed:

"[C]ompensation could not . . . be deemed to have rectified a violation in a situation where the state had not taken responsible measures to comply with its obligations under Article 3.

The obligation to provide a remedy does not constitute a substitute for or alternative to those obligations, but rather an obligation to provide redress within the domestic system for violations which may, inevitably occur despite measures taken to ensure compliance with the substantive provisions of Article 3 . . . [I]f the higher authorities of the State pursued a policy or administrative practice whereby they authorised or tolerated conduct in violation of Article 3, compensation would not of itself constitute an adequate remedy . . .

[C]ompensation can only be seen as an adequate remedy in a situation where the higher authorities have taken reasonable steps to comply with their obligations under Article 3 by preventing, as far as possible, the occurrence of repetition of the acts in question".

2–19   **Inquests fall short of satisfying requirements.** On *inquests*, the court stated:

"Notwithstanding the useful fact finding function that an inquest may provide in some cases, the court considers that in this case it could play on effective role in the identification or prosecution of any criminal offences which may have occurred and, in that respect, falls short of the requirements of Article 2" (see para. 130).

2–20   **The "horizontal" effect of Section 6.**[42] The traditional concept of human rights limits them to the relationship between the individual and their Government. The European Court of Human Rights does not itself hear actions against individuals, it is limited to hearing complaints of violations by Signatory States. Nevertheless, it has considered whether "horizontal" violations, that is actions between private parties, can occur. The indications are that it thinks that they can.[43]

In a string of cases, the court has found the State guilty of a violation because it failed to provide protection for one individual from another. In other words, it failed to fulfil the State's positive obligations. In *Plattform "Arzte fur das Leben"*[44] the Austrian Government was held to have failed to protect a doctor's freedom of speech when a private group intimidated pro life doctors in Austria to the point where they could not speak freely. Some have concluded that the

---

[41] 4 D.R. 4 at 78–79.

[42] See Appendix 2.

[43] See *Young, James and Webster*, August 13, 1981, No. 44; *X & Y v. Netherlands* (1985) 8 E.H.R.R. 235, March 25, 1985 No. 91; and *Plattform "Arzte fur das Leben"* (1991) 13 E.H.R.R. 204, June 21, 1988, No. 139.

[44] (1991) 13 E.H.R.R. 204, June 21, 1988, No. 139.

European Court has thus accepted the conceptual possibility that the actions of private parties may comprise a violation of human rights and that this has opened the way to horizontal use of Article 6.[45]

In *Young, James and Webster v. United Kingdom*,[46] a case concerning corporal punishment in private schools, the European Court held that although the defendant before the court was a State, the primary harm was caused by the actions of non-State persons or bodies. The court found the State guilty of a violation because it failed to protect one individual from another.

Considering the growing controversy of media invasions of privacy or cases of genocide and war crimes across international boundaries, there is a strong argument that a mature human rights code must be activated by the nature of violations and the consequent suffering of the victims rather than whether the perpetrator was a State of "public authority".[47] For instance, much case law has been developed in the sphere of asylum claims as to whether it is the State or rebel forces which are for potential persecution if a refugee is returned to the receiving country. The effect upon the refugee will be the same regardless of whether the State flies the flag of its country when it inflicts the torture, or if the abusive behaviour perpetrates from a rebel standard.

5. CIVIL JURISDICTION

Court findings in breach of Convention rights. According to the Human **2–21** Rights Act 1998 Section 6(3), courts of law are considered to be part of the State. Without doubt, a criminal court which convicts a defendant in breach of a Convention right does so unlawfully and therefore itself commits a violation. But it is unclear whether civil courts are similarly constrained. For instance, will a civil court act unlawfully if it decides a case between private parties in a fashion which is irreconcilable with the Convention?

It has been argued[48] that since a major element of the court's role as "public authorities" is to settle disputes between individuals, the Human Rights Act horizontality arises as a matter of necessary implication.[49] There is little case law on the point although observations have been made in the area of privacy. In *Douglas v. Hello! Limited*,[50] Sedley L.J. was of the opinion that the point had been reached where "it can be said with confidence that the law recognises and will appropriately protect personal privacy".[51]

---

[45] See the "Horizontal" Effect of the Human Rights Act by Gareth Davies, New Law Journal, June 2, 2000 839.

[46] (1981) 4 E.H.R.R. 38.

[47] See Appendix 1.

[48] See Wade H.R.W. (2000) "Horizons of Horizontality" L.Q.R. 217–2224: Hunt M., "The Horizontal Effect of the Human Act Rights", (1998) P.L. 423–443.

[49] The American case of *Shelley v. Kramer* (1948) 343 U.S. 1 resolves an issue of horizontal application by capitalising all common law rules, irrespective of the identities of the parties contesting them, as part of the apparatus of Government. Although *Shelley v. Kramer* only operates as a negative restraint on a court action by forcing it to withhold previously available remedies and not as a positive requirement to create new remedies, it does present a useful indication as to how the dilemma of the civil courts in the "horizontal" debate can be resolved.

[50] [2001] 2 W.L.R. 992 at 1021, para. 110.

[51] See also *Venables v. Newsgroup Newspapers* [2001] 2 W.L.R. 1038 where Article 8 was used to develop a right to privacy.

2–22   **A judge may violate Article 3.** This issue was obliquely raised in *Price v. United Kingdom*[52] where a four-limb deficient Thalidomide victim was detained in a police cell and a prison and kept in degrading conditions. It was observed that the judge in committing the applicant to prison without ascertaining whether there were adequate facilities for her was following "English law and practice" at the time, although this is no longer in accordance with the law, as Section 6 of the Human Rights Act 1998 requires the court, as well as other public authorities, to act compatibly with Convention rights.

Now, a judge will violate Article 3 by committing an applicant to prison without first ascertaining that there were adequate facilities to look after the proper needs of that detainee.

Judge Greve stated in his Separate Opinion that:

"The applicant's disabilities are not hidden or easily overlooked".

Sir Nicholas Bratza, the British judge, and Judge Costa, the presiding judge, also issued a separate statement which laid responsibility firmly upon the judge, in that in their view, there was:

"No justification for the decision to commit the applicant to an immediate term of imprisonment without at the very least ensuring in advance that there existed both adequate facilities for detaining her and conditions of detention in which her special needs could be met".

2–23   **Relationship with Article 14.** Article 14 is often inextricably linked with Article 3 and Article 8. In the case of *Pearce v. Governing Body of Mayfield School*,[53] although a case concerning the acts of a public authority which occurred prior to the coming into force of the Act, nevertheless contains a forceful judgement from Lady Justice Hale concerning sexual harassment and homophobia.

The appellant was a science teacher of many years standing. She was also a lesbian. From the early 1990s she was subjected to repeated abuse from the pupils, both in words and behaviour. The response of the school was, in her view, seriously inadequate.

Eventually her health suffered and she took early retirement in 1996 and brought proceedings under the Sex Discrimination Act 1975.

Lady Justice Hale considered the rights under Article 8 and observed:

"Autonomy must mean far more than the right to occupy an envelope of space in which a socially detached individual can act free from interference by the State. What is crucial is the nature of the activity, not its site. While recognising the unique worth of each person, the Constitution does not presuppose that a holder of rights is an isolated, lonely and abstract figure possessing a disembodied and socially disconnected self. It acknowledges that people live in their bodies, their communities, their cultures, their places and their times. The expression of sexuality requires a partner, real or imagined . . . if this is a right enjoyed by heterosexual people under Article 8, then it must also be accorded to homosexuals. Discrimination is prohibited by Article 14 of the Convention".

---

[52] (2002) 34 E.H.R.R. 53.
[53] Unreported, CA July 31, 2001.

Racial discrimination may also engage Article 3 as constituting degrading treatment. The European Commission distinguished "deferential treatment of persons on the basis of race" attracting Article 3 from such other treatment on some other ground which does not so activate that Article.[54]

Court's willingness to participate in policy. The courts have shown an   **2–24** increasing willingness to engage in policy debates. It is apparent from a reading of *S.R. v. Nottingham Magistrates' Court*[55] that considerable deference is paid to the stated policy intent behind the legislative measures. Nevertheless, it appears that the courts are becoming more willing to engage in policy type debates albeit in a cautious and restricted manner, in which the validity of that policy is examined.[56]

The status of Statements of Compatibility. Lord Hope has held in the case   **2–25** of *"A"*,[57] that a Statement of Compatibility attached to a Bill is no more than an "expression of opinion by the Minister", which is not even of persuasive authority in court.

---

[54] *East African Asian* cases (1981) 3 E.H.R.R. 76.

[55] [2001] EWHC Admin 802.

[56] See *Reynolds v. Secretary of State for Works and Pensions*, unreported, March 7, 2002 Administrative Court, dealing with the justification for deferential payment of Jobseekers Allowance (payable at a lower rate for those under 25). *Hooper v. Secretary of State for Works and Pensions*, unreported, February 14, 2002, Administrative Court, dealing with the non-availability of a widow's payment, the widow's mother's allowance and widow's pension for men and *Wilkinson v. Inland Revenue Commissioners*, unreported, February 14, 2002 in the Administrative Court concerning non-availability of widow's bereavement allowance for men.

[57] [2001] 2 W.L.R. 1546 at para. 69.

CHAPTER 3

THE POLICE

Bullet points. To establish violation of Article 3 during police interview or   **3–01**
interrogation, the following should be ascertained:

- Ascertain the good health of the applicant before going into custody;

- Obtain medical evidence after release from custody—see *Akkoc v. Turkey*;

- Ascertain whether there has been an independent investigation of complaints—see *Dikme v. Turkey*, Application No. 20869/92;

- Is the applicant vulnerable?—see *Tomasi v. France*;

- Was the purpose of the ill-treatment to obtain a confession?—see *Aksoy v. Turkey* and *Ireland v. United Kingdom*;

- Can the treatment be described as "oppressive"?—see *R. v. Fulling*;

- What is the cumulative effect of the alleged violations?—see *Tomasi v. France*;

- Physical assault unnecessary—see *Ireland v. United Kingdom*.

1. The Starting Point

Burden on the State. When an individual is taken into police custody in good   **3–02**
health but is found to be injured at the time of release, it is incumbent upon the
State to provide a plausible explanation of how those injuries were caused,
failing which a clear issue will arise under Article 3 of the Convention. In
Selmouni v. France,[1] the applicant complained that he had been physically
abused during his detention. The judge ordered a forensic medical examination
of the applicant which revealed that there was evidence to support his allegation
of physical assault. The court held that there was an onus upon the court to
investigate the matter properly and identify and deal with those who may be
responsible.

In *Dikme v. Turkey*,[2] the burden upon the State to provide plausible explanation
for injuries caused in police custody was reiterated.

Requirements of an investigation cannot justify violation. In respect of a   **3–03**
person deprived of their liberty, recourse to physical force which has not been
made strictly necessary by the applicant's own conduct diminishes human dignity and is in principle an infringement of the Article 3 right. *Dikme v. Turkey*

---

[1] (2000) 29 E.H.R.R. 403.
[2] Application No. 20869/92.

[41]

emphasised that in this connection, the requirements of an investigation and the undeniable difficulties inherent in the fight against terrorist crime cannot justify placing limits on the protection to be afforded in respect of the physical integrity of individuals.

3–04   **Outcome of trial is irrelevant.** As was stated in *Ribitsch v. Austria*,[3] the Austrian Government were obliged to provide a plausible explanation of how the applicant's injuries were caused. Merely referring to the outcome of criminal proceedings before the national courts where the high standard of proof necessary to secure a criminal conviction was not satisfied, was not enough.

3–05   **Totality of allegations need not be proved.** At times the totality of the applicant's allegations may not be proved. In *Tomasi v. France*,[4] the applicant alleged that whilst in police custody he was beaten and ill-treated. In short, he alleged that he was slapped, kicked and punched by police officers. The medical evidence did not fully support these allegations but nevertheless confirmed that blows of considerable force were inflicted upon the applicant. The court were of the view that such treatment was sufficiently serious to be categorised as inhuman and degrading as defined by Article 3.

2. ARREST

3–06   **Effecting an arrest.** In principle, the way an arrest is effected can amount to inhuman or degrading treatment contrary to Article 3 although it will be extremely difficult to establish even if the arrest was unlawful or beyond what is reasonably necessary in the circumstances. There are few cases on this point although *Klaas v. Germany*[5] establishes that in principle Article 3 covers this area. Klaas was arrested for driving with excess alcohol and during an altercation with the police she suffered personal injuries. Her civil action for damages failed but she claimed that the way she was arrested amounted to inhuman and degrading treatment.

The European Court of Human Rights held that there had been no violation of Article 3 and that the evidence before the German court was consistent with both the applicant's version of events and the version given by police officers, effectively cancelling each other out.

The Domestic Court found that on the balance of the evidence the case fell against Klaas and the European Court were of the view that no cogent elements had been provided which could lead the court to differ from the German court. Although this case failed on the evidence it is highly unlikely that an Article 3 violation will be upheld unless physical or mental injury can be established or that the police intended to humiliate the individual who they were arresting.

3. QUESTIONING

3–07   **Police interrogation.** In *Ireland v. United Kingdom*, the "five techniques" which were applied in combination, with premeditation and for hours at a stretch

---

[3] (1996) 21 E.H.R.R. 573.
[4] (1993) 15 E.H.R.R. 1.
[5] (1994) 18 E.H.R.R. 305.

caused, in the view of the court, if not actual bodily injury at least intense physical and mental suffering to the person subjected thereto and also led to acute psychiatric disturbances during the interrogation. The court were in no doubt that they fell into the category of inhuman treatment within the meaning of Article 3.

They were also of the view that the techniques were degrading since there was such as to arouse in their victims feelings of fear, anguish and inferiority capable of humiliating and debasing them and possibly breaking their physical or moral resistance.[6]

It is of course a matter of degree whether behaviour is categorised as torture, inhuman or degrading treatment or indeed whether it be considered not in violation of the Article.

4. INVESTIGATIONS

Failure to hold official investigation. Where there has been a failure to   **3–08** conduct a thorough and effective investigation into an applicant's arguable allegation that he has been ill-treated whilst in police custody the courts will hold that of itself that is a violation of Article 3.[7]

In *Dikme v. Turkey* the rationale for this principle was stated to be that such investigation should be capable of leading to the identification and punishment of those responsible for an alleged breach of Article 3.

Otherwise, the general legal prohibition of torture and inhuman and degrading treatment and punishment would, despite its fundamental importance, be ineffective in practice and it would be possible in some cases for the agents of errant states to abuse the rights of those within their control with virtual impunity.[8]

The facts of *Dikme v. Turkey* show an extreme example of state in action in that more than 8 years after the incident in issue the investigation did not appear to have produced any tangible results and at the date the judgement was given in *Dikme v. Turkey* members of the branch not were responsible for Dikme during his time in police custody and consequently of the ill-treatment confirmed by medical certificates whose contents were known to the authorities had still not been identified. In those circumstances, the European Court concluded that there had been no thorough and effective investigation into the applicant's allegations and thus of itself there had been a breach of Article 3.[9]

---

[6] In *D'Haeses Le Compte v. Belgium* (1984) 6 E.H.R.R. 114, the courts considered that extreme and continuous police surveillance was capable of being degrading treatment.

[7] The case of *Adali v. Turkey* is presently before the court (January 21, 2002) which concerns the applicant's complaints under Articles 3, 6, 8, 10, 11, 12 and 14 of the Convention about, amongst other things, the failure to investigate the killing of her husband, a writer who had published articles critical of the Turkish Government and the Turkish Republic of Northern Cyprus. Her claim also deals with harassment of herself by TRNC officials, including the monitoring of her telephone and correspondence.

[8] *Labita v. Italy* (GC) ECHR 2000—IV.

[9] Article 13 of the European Convention on Human Rights provides that "everyone whose rights and freedoms as set forth in this Convention are violated shall have an effective remedy before a national authority notwithstanding that the violation has been committed by persons acting in an official capacity". This is otherwise known as the right to an effective remedy and applies with particular relevance to Article 3 in that an applicant must be provided with redress and necessary procedural safeguards against abuses by State officers. In *Dikme v. Turkey* the applicant did not rely on Article 13 although this was certainly open to him. See also Chapter 10: Effective Remedy.

3–09   **Inquests.** The courts consider that the primary purpose of the inquest is to pinpoint the faults, if any, within the system rather than identify specific individuals involved. The Coroners Rules 1984,[10] Rule 42, provides that no verdict must be framed in such a way as to appear to determine any question of criminal liability on the part of a named person or any civil liability.

3–10   **Medical reports.** Usually an applicant will be isolated and have no evidence to substantiate potential violations of Article 3. The likelihood of official denial or excuse may indeed add to the difficulties of proof.

The European Court have stressed that where an individual alleges that he has been ill-treated while in custody, the State is under an obligation to provide a complete and sufficient explanation as to how any injuries were caused. In *Akkoc v. Turkey*,[11] the court stressed the importance that independent and thorough examinations of persons on release from detention. Proper medical examinations are an essential safeguard against ill-treatment of persons in custody. Such examinations must be carried out by a properly qualified doctor, without any police officer being present and the report of the examination must include not only the detail of any injuries found but the explanations given by the patient as to how they occurred and the opinion of the doctor as to whether the injuries are consistent with those explanations. This approach has been endorsed by the European Committee of the Prevention of Torture.[12]

The problem of proving mistreatment sufficient to violate Article 3, is a real problem and continues to be a barrier to providing adequate protection for detainees. This is graphically illustrated in *Labita v. Italy*[13] where the applicant had been allegedly subjected to physical and mental ill-treatment whilst in prison.

The applicant did not produce any conclusive evidence or supply a detailed account of the abuse to which he had allegedly been subjected, and he had never suggested that he had ever been refused permission to see a doctor. A further difficulty for the applicant was that he had inexplicably taken more than a year to complain about his treatment, notwithstanding the fact that he had made several applications through his lawyers to the judicial authorities shortly after the alleged ill-treatment had diminished or ceased. As such, the European Court concluded that there was insufficient evidence to support a conclusion that the applicant had been subjected to physical and mental ill-treatment. Nevertheless, at paragraph 125 of the judgment "the court recognises that it may prove difficult for prisoners to obtain evidence of ill-treatment by their prison warders" and a powerful dissenting opinion places considerable weight upon the practical difficulties facing a prisoner who seeks to allege ill-treatment. Effectively, it is recognised that the prisoner is placed in a situation in which he is vulnerable and hamstrung in his ability to gather and bring evidence before the court. Although this particular case relates to those in prison, the view expressed by the court, though in a dissenting judgement, continues to recognise the difficulties faced by

---

[10] SI 1984/552.

[11] (2002) 34 E.H.R.R. 51.

[12] Now in the second decade of its work, the mandate of the European Committee for the Prevention of Torture is "to examine the treatment of persons deprived of their liberty with a view to strengthening, if necessary, the protection of such persons from torture and from inhuman or degrading treatment or punishment". Article 1 of the European Convention for the Prevention of Torture or Inhuman or Degrading Treatment or Punishment.

[13] April 6, 2000.

those who are detained and it is incumbent upon the legal advisers to ensure that as compelling a case as possible be placed before the court.

5. PURPOSE

The purpose of ill-treatment. Once the hurdle of proving ill-treatment in **3–11** police custody has been overcome, and the issue has been proven, the precise purpose as to why the ill-treatment was inflicted upon an applicant will become important.

In *Aksoy v. Turkey*,[14] the court held that the ill-treatment inflicted upon Aksoy was so severe as to be categorised as torture because, amongst other things, it was administered during the course of interrogation with the aim of extracting admissions or confessions from the applicant. This approach is consistent with the earlier case of *Ireland v. United Kingdom* where the court concluded that five particular interrogation practices had the stated objective of obtaining information concerning terrorist activities. It was nevertheless held to be in violation of Article 3.

6. CHARACTERISTICS OF APPLICANT

Vulnerability of applicant. Another factor which may influence a positive **3–12** violation of Article 3 concerns the nature of the applicant and in particular whether the individual is vulnerable.[15]

A useful classification of vulnerability has been provided by the Department of Psychology at Leicester University in their paper "New Guidelines for the Interviewing of Vulnerable and Intimidated Witnesses". It has been adopted by the Bar Council as a new memorandum of good practice and provides a useful list of individuals who may be classified as vulnerable, as well as children and juveniles, it lists witnesses with learning disabilities, witnesses with communication difficulties, witnesses with "mental disorders", and witnesses with physical disabilities.

Domestic law regarding juveniles in police custody. The attitude taken by **3–13** the domestic criminal courts in England and Wales as to when a person is to be classified as a juvenile is somewhat contradictory. This dichotomy was highlighted in *R. v. Stratford Youth Court on the application of the Director of Public Prosecutions*.[16] In that case, the prosecution were appealing a decision made by the District Judge which they asserted was wrong in law, the District Judge having ruled that, in the circumstances of that case, interviewing a 17 year old suspect without an appropriate adult was in breach of Code C of the Police and Criminal Evidence Act 1984.[17]

Code C.1.5 states "If anyone appears to be under the age of 17 then he shall be treated as a juvenile for the purpose of this Code in the absence of clear evidence to show that he is older".

---

[14] (1997) 23 E.H.R.R. 53.
[15] In *Tomasi v. France*, at paragraphs 113 and 115, this issue was addressed.
[16] Decision of July 26, 2001, unreported.
[17] See Appendix 8.

At paragraphs 11 and 12 of Lord Justice Sedley's decision in *Stratford Youth Court*, his Lordship states "What I would however say before coming to the question of disposal is this: it is clearly relevant if the point is taken as it needs to be taken under section 76 [Police and Criminal Evidence Act 1984] though not under section 78, but a young man of 17 although not a juvenile for Code C purposes, is a juvenile for other legal purposes, being interviewed both at his own election without representation and without an appropriate adult because Code C does not apply to him. In at least two of these cases we know that the youth in question had not been in a police station before. Nobody should underestimate any more than they should overestimate the kind of pressure to get things over and done with that such a youngster may experience. This is part of the picture".

The Commission have held that evidence obtained by ill treatment contrary to Article 3 cannot be admitted in a criminal trial consistently with Article 6.[18] This principle is fully reflected in the Police and Criminal Evidence Act 1984, Section 76.

Lord Justice Sedley highlights the peculiarity of domestic criminal law which categorises a 17 year old individual as an adult for criminal purposes but a juvenile for other legal purposes.

Code C.11(b) contained in the Police and Criminal Evidence Act 1984 states "It is important to bear in mind that although juveniles or people who are mentally disordered or mentally handicapped are often capable of providing reliable evidence, they may without knowing or wishing to do so, be particularly prone in certain circumstances to provide information which is unreliable, misleading or self-incriminating. Special care should therefore always be exercised in questioning such a person and the appropriate adult should be involved if there is any doubt about a person's age, mental state or capacity. Because of the risk of unreliable evidence, it is also important to obtain a corroboration of any facts admitted whenever possible".

It is certainly arguable that a consideration of vulnerability for an individual even when they have attained 17 is appropriate. Furthermore, the absence of an appropriate adult at a police interview for any witness classified or potentially classified as vulnerable will also be an issue to consider as to the conduct of the interrogation.

3–14   **The Police and Criminal Evidence Act 1984.** The Police and Criminal Evidence Act addresses itself to oppression applied during police interviews which result in confessions.

Section 76 lays down that a confession made by an accused person may be given in evidence against him but "if, in any proceedings where the prosecution proposes to give in evidence a confession made by an accused person, it is represented to the court that the confession was or may have been obtained—(a) by oppression of the person who made it . . . the court shall not allow the confession to be given in evidence against him except insofar as the prosecution proves to the court beyond reasonable doubt that the confession (notwithstanding that it may be true) was not obtained as aforesaid".

Section 76(8) of the Act defines oppression " 'Oppression' includes torture, inhuman or degrading treatment, or the use or threat of violence (whether or not amounting to torture)".

---

[18] See *Austria v. Italy* (1963) 6 Yearbook 740.

Oppression in earlier cases has been defined in accordance with its ordinary dictionary meaning. *R. v. Fulling*[19] cited the Oxford English Dictionary which defined oppression as the "exercise of authority or power in a burdensome, harsh, or wrongful manner; unjust or cruel treatment of subjects, inferiors, etc. or the imposition of unreasonable or unjust burdens".[20]

Interestingly, the wording of section 76(8) reflects the wording of Article 3.

Application of the Police and Criminal Evidence Act 1984,[21] section 76 does not require a minimum level of severity threshold. Each case will be considered on its merits. But a finding of section 76 violation and in particular a finding of oppression as defined by section 76(8), will be of assistance in building up the overall required level of severity to establish violation of Article 3 particularly as the wording of section 76(8) is virtually identical to that of Article 3.

Physical force unnecessary. *Ireland v. United Kingdom* and cases subsequent   **3–15**
to it have established that physical force is not necessary to establish violation of Article 3. The five interrogation techniques criticised by the court in *Ireland v. United Kingdom* involved excessive standing in uncomfortable positions, the wearing of hood, deprivation of sleep, noise abuse and deprivation of food and drink. The court considered each issue separately and held them to be inhuman and degrading treatment, but surprisingly not torture.

7. HANDCUFFING

Difficult to establish violation. *Raninen v. Finland*[22] demonstrates how diffi-   **3–16**
cult it is to establish a violation of Article 3 based upon the police handcuffing of an applicant. In that case, handcuffing had not been made necessary by Raninen's conduct and had been imposed upon him in the context of an unlawful arrest and detention.

Furthermore, the applicant had been visible to the public upon entering a military police vehicle outside the prison gate and had felt humiliated by appearing handcuffed in front of members of his support group. The court held that although these considerations were relevant to a determination of whether his treatment was degrading within the meaning of Article 3, they were by no means conclusive. What seems to be vital for any claim to succeed under this head is that the handcuffing adversely affected the applicant's mental state or some physical injury which could be associated of the application of handcuffs. Alternatively, the applicant will need to make out that the handcuffing was aimed at debasing or humiliating him.

Proof.   **3–17**

- To establish an Article 3 violation based partly or solely on the use of handcuffs, it must be established that:

---

[19] [1987] Q.B. 426.
[20] *Per* Lord Lane C.J. at pp. 432, 142.
[21] The obtaining of evidence by violation of a Convention right (usually Article 8, the right to respect of family life), does not render a trial unfair under Article 6 and that in all cases it is a question for the judge's discretion under Section 78 of the Police and Criminal Evidence Act 1984: see also *R. v. P* [2001] W.L.R. 463 (HL): *Loveridge* Times Law Reports, May 3, 2001; *Wright v. McGregor* June 14, 2001 and *Sultan Khan* [1997] A.C. 558 interpreting *Khan v. U.K.* [2000] Crim.L.R. 684.
[22] (1998) 26 E.H.R.R. 563.

- The handcuffs were used in connection with an unlawful arrest or unlawful detention;

- That the use of the handcuffs went beyond what could reasonably be considered to be necessary in the circumstances;

- That the application of handcuffs caused some mental injury to the applicant; or

- Some physical injury to the applicant;

- A clear indication that the authority's purpose in using handcuffs was to humiliate the applicant.[23]

8. Challenging Treatment

3–18   **Cross-examination of police officers.** The court have identified three basic principles to assist the cross-examination of police officers who face an allegations of misconduct which must encompass suggestions that they have been in breach of Article 3.

In *R. v. Twitchell (Keith)*,[24] the appellant appealed against a conviction of manslaughter and robbery on a reference by the Criminal Cases Review Commission on the basis that he had been the victim of torture instigated by police officers in charge of his case, some of whom had later been found to have conducted themselves inappropriately during investigations in *R. v. Treadaway*.[25]

A powerfully constituted Court of Appeal which included Lord Justice Rose endorsed the three principles of cross-examination which were:

1. That the test was mainly one of relevance;

2. That whereas cross-examination on criminal or disciplinary convictions was allowed, it was not permitted about complaints that had not resulted in conviction or where it concerned misconduct by other officers; and

3. Cross-examination was allowed on matters surrounding an earlier acquittal where they were such that the jury could not have believe the same officers.

   It was emphasised that the role of the Court of Appeal, Criminal Division, was not to make findings of fact.[26] The court should assess new evidence that had become available since the trial and make a decision as to the safety of the earlier conviction.

3–19   **Death.** Where an individual has died as a result of police action, the State are obliged to carry out an effective, independent enquiry into the incident.

In *R. (on the application of Green) v. Prosecution Service Court of Appeal*,[27] the applicant was severely injured when hit by an unmarked police car driven by

---

[23] See *Albert v. Belgium* (1983) 5 E.H.R.R. 533.
[24] [2000] 1 Cr.App.R. 373.
[25] Unreported, November 18, 1986.
[26] *R. v. C (Trevor Anthony)* unreported, October 14, 1999.
[27] (2002) EWCA Civ 389.

a detective sergeant. The applicant complained to the Police Complaints Authority that the officer had been attempting to kill him.

The Police Complaints Authority refused to disclose documents to the applicant so he undertook judicial review proceedings which ordered that the documents, including eye witness accounts and experts' accounts regarding the scene were in principle discloseable.

Mr Justice Moses reasoned that Article 2 and Article 3 imposes an obligation to secure an effective independent enquiry into an incident such as this. Furthermore, the applicant was himself an eye witness. The court went on to conclude that there was no particularly sensitive aspect to the documents. As such, the applicant had a right to comment on other people's accounts as there was no other way of recognising his special status or safeguarding his rights.

The Police Complaints Authority have appealed this decision.[28]

Death in police custody. The same rules which applies to deaths in prison **3–20** custody, equally apply to any form of State custody. The courts have held that there is a procedural obligation to investigate such deaths.[28a]

The extent and scope of that duty is for the domestic courts to determine according to each individual case. The case of *R. (on the application of Amin) v. Secretary of State for the Home Department,*[29] concerned a murder in State custody and was one which demanded a thorough and rigid investigation, although family participation was not considered to be a compulsory requirement which needed to be fulfilled in every case. All measures taken by the public authorities so far to investigate the deceased's death had to be taken into account when determining whether the procedural duty had been fulfilled.[30]

Compare the decision in *Edwards v. United Kingdom*[31] where the deceased was placed in a cell with another prisoner who had a history of violent outbursts and assaults, including an assault on a cell-mate in prison. A prison officer heard continuous banging on a cell door and, on investigating, it was found that the deceased had been stamped and kicked to death and that the other prisoner was making continual references to being possessed by evil spirits. He was diagnosed as a paranoid schizophrenic. The European Court of Human Rights held that amongst other oversights, the failure of the authorities to pass on information available which would have identified the prisoner as a danger breached the deceased's Article 2 rights. Furthermore, the applicant could not be regarded as having been involved in the procedure, investigating his death to the extent necessary to safeguard their interests as the enquiry set in private and they were unable to question witnesses. It was a failure to hold an effective investigation.

Procedure relating to the Police Complaints Authority investigations. A **3–21** case such as *Green* had to be referred to the Police Complaints Authority as it

---

[28] See para. 3–20: "The complainant's rights".
[28a] See also *United Kingdom Deaths in Custody: lack of police accountability* published by Amnesty International, May 2000 EUR 45/42/00.
[29] [2002] EWCA Civ. 390.
[30] See *R. (on the application of Middleton) v. Coroner for West Somerset* [2002] EWCA Civ. 390: *R. v. North Humberside and Scunthorpe Coroner ex p. Jameson* [1994] 3 All E.R. 972 CA; *Jordan v. U.K.* (2001) 11 B.H.R.C. 11 ECtHR; *Edwards v. United Kingdom* (2002) Times Law Reports, April 1, 2002.
[31] (2002) Times Law Reports, April 1, 2002.

concerned serious injury. The investigation must be conducted by another force to that of the force implicated.

Sections 73–76 of the 1996 Act deal with the procedure at the end of an investigation:

- The investigating officer submits a report to the Police Complaints Authority and sends a copy to the relevant police force;

- The Authority considers the report and then submits the statement to the relevant police force enquiring as to whether they are satisfied with the investigation and, if not, why not;

- If the relevant force believes that an offence has been committed, they must send it to the DPP;

- The relevant police force then sends a memorandum to the PCA regarding any disciplinary action considered or declined;

- The PCA may recommend and direct relevant forces to bring disciplinary proceedings if they are unwilling to do so.

3–22   **The complainant's rights.** In *Green*, the appeal was allowed and an order for disclosure set aside when the court held that the legitimate interests of the complainant had been protected by the proper acknowledgement of:

- His right to a thorough and independent investigation;

- The right to contribute evidence where he can;

- The right to be kept informed of the progress of the investigation (the PCA encourages forces to provide limited documentary evidence and oral summaries of witness statements);

- His right to be given reasoned conclusions.

3–23   **Family members of a victim.** Whether a family member of a victim may claim that their own Article 3 rights have been violated will depend upon special circumstances. In *Akdeniz v. Turkey*,[32] the applicants alleged that their relatives had disappeared after they were detained by soldiers during an operation in South East Turkey. As the factual situation was disputed, the Commission conducted a fact finding mission. It found that a large number of people, including the applicants' relatives were detained by the security forces.

Among other things, it was found that during their detention, the majority of the applicants' relatives were tied up, were kept outside during the day and at night, were questioned by soldiers, and were in a state of some distress and apprehension. All those who had been detained except for the applicants' relatives were released. The families attempted through a variety of means to discover what had happened to their relatives. Following their application to the European Court of Human Rights, all bar one of the applicants were questioned (and some detained) regarding their applications.

The court held that the treatment of the applicants' relatives attained the minimum level of severity to fall within Article 3 human and degrading treatment. The evidence showed that the applicants' relatives had suffered not only from cold, but also from fear and anguish about what might happen to them.

---

[32] Application No. 23954/94, May 31, 2001.

As for the applicants themselves, the court considered whether or not they had suffered an Article 3 violation. It noted that in *Kurt v. Turkey*[33] it did not establish the general principle that a family member of a "disappeared person" is thereby a victim of treatment contrary to Article 3. The court stated:

"Whether a family member is such a victim will depend on the existence of special factors which gives the suffering of the applicant a dimension and character distinct from the emotional distress which may be regarded as inevitably caused to relatives of a victim of a serious human rights violation.

Relevant elements will include the proximity of the family tie—in that context, a certain weight will attach to the parent-child bond, the particular circumstances of the relationship, the extent to which the family member witnessed the events in question, the involvement of the family member in the attempts to obtain information about the disappeared person and the way in which the authorities responded to those enquiries. The court have emphasised that the essence of such a violation does not so much lie in the fact of the 'disappearance' of the family member, but rather concerns the authorities' reactions and attitudes to the situation when it is brought to their attention. It is especially in relation to the latter that a relative can claim to be a victim of the authorities' conduct" (see *Cakici v. Turkey*[34]).

Although the applicants in this case had clearly suffered, the court was not satisfied that he case disclosed the special circumstances required.

---

[33] May 25, 1998.
[34] Application No. 23657/94.

CHAPTER 4

PRISONERS

Bullet points. The following general criteria will constitute ill-treatment in **4–01** respect of prisoners in the variety of situations to which they may be exposed:

- The treatment must go beyond the usual element of humiliation associated with imprisonment after a criminal conviction (*Tyrer v. United Kingdom*);

- The public nature of the treatment is relevant as is its adverse effect (*Raninen v. Finland*);

- The absence of publicity will not necessarily prevent a given punishment from being degrading for it may be sufficient that the victim is humiliated in his own eyes even if not in the eyes of others—see *Costello-Roberts v. United Kingdom* (1993) 19 E.H.R.R. 112;

- The punishment or treatment need not cause any severe or long lasting physical effects (*Tyrer v. United Kingdom* at pp. 10–11);

- The fact that the person concerned has brought the treatment on himself may be relevant (*McFeeley* at 198);

- This fact cannot absolve the State of its obligations under Article 3 (*X v. U.K.* [1982] 28 D.R. 5 at 32);

- A degrading punishment does not lose its degrading character just because it is believed to be, or actually is, an effective deterrent or aid to maintain discipline (see *Tyrer v. United Kingdom* at p. 10, para. 31).

1. THE STATUS OF A PRISONER

Civil rights are not taken away. A convicted prisoner retains all his civil **4–02** rights which are not taken away expressly or by necessary implication.[1] Since a sentence of imprisonment is intended to restrict the rights and freedom of a prisoner, the prisoner's liberty, personal autonomy and freedom of movement and association are necessarily limited, but the starting point is to assume that a civil right is preserved unless it has been expressly removed or its loss is an inevitable consequence of lawful detention in custody.[2]

The principle of legality means that, in the absence of express words or unnecessary implications to the contrary, even the most general words of an Act of Parliament and subordinate legislation, must be presumed to be intended to be subject to the basic rights of the individual and accordingly, prison regulations

---

[1] *Raymond v. Honey* [1983] A.C. 1 at 10G.
[2] See *R. v. Home Secretary ex p. Simms* [1999] 3 W.L.R. 328 at 331 *per* Lord Steyn.

expressed in general language are presumed to be subject to fundamental human rights, a presumption which enables them to be valid.[3]

Where the question arises as to the extent to which a power is impliedly conferred by statute to interfere with those fundamental rights, there must be established a self-evident and pressing need for that power and the interference must be the minimum necessary to fulfil that need.[4]

4–03 **Changing attitudes.** Case law has been developing with considerable speed in this area of application of Article 3. The court's decisions reflect the changing attitudes within society to the treatment of those detained in prisons. What was acceptable 20 years ago is not acceptable now and a consideration of the older cases will not assist in appreciating the drastic steps that the courts have taken in developing the law in this area.

In *R. v. Board of Visitors of Hull Prison ex p. St Germain*,[5] Lord Justice Shaw observed:

"Despite the deprivation of his general liberty, a prisoner remains invested with residuary rights appertaining to the nature and conduct of his incarceration.

Now the rights of a citizen, however circumscribed by a penal sentence or otherwise, must always be the concern of the courts unless their jurisdiction is clearly excluded by some statutory provision.

The courts are in general the ultimate custodians of the rights and liberties of the subject whatever his status and however attenuated those rights and liberties may be as the result of some punitive or other process . . . Once it is acknowledged that such rights exist, the courts have function and jurisdiction.

It is irrelevant that the Secretary of State may afford redress where the Rules have been infringed or their application has been irregular or unduly harsh. An essential characteristic of the right of a subject is that it carries with it a right of recourse to the courts unless some statute decrees otherwise. What should be the nature and measure of the relief accorded must be a matter for the courts. Public policy or expediency as well as merits may be factors to consider and they may influence the answer to any application for relief, but to deny jurisdiction on the ground of expediency seems to me . . . to be tantamount to abdicating a primary function of the judiciary".

4–04 **Minimum level of severity.** As with any consideration of Article 3 for the complainant to establish a breach it is again necessary to show that the treatment complained of had reached a minimum level of severity which was relative and dependent on all the circumstances of the case.

But in considering whether a treatment is degrading within the meaning of Article 3, the court will have regard to whether its object is to humiliate and debase the person concerned and whether as far as the consequences are concerned, it adversely affected his or her personality in a manner incompatible with Article 3.[6]

4–05 **Absence of intention to humiliate does not preclude violation.** Nevertheless, the absence of such an intention to humiliate does not necessarily preclude a complainant from establishing a violation. In *Price v. United Kingdom*,[7] the applicant was a disabled person who was four-limb deficient and

---

[3] See *R. v. Home Secretary ex p. Simms* 2000 WL 1084379 at pp. 341–342 *per* Lord Hoffmann.
[4] See *R. v. Home Secretary ex p. Leech* [1994] Q.B. 198.
[5] [1979] Q.B. 425.
[6] *Raninen v. Finland* (1998) 26 E.H.R.R. 563.
[7] [2001] Crim.L.R. 916.

suffered from kidney problems. The cell in which Price stayed for her first night of detention contained a wooden bed and mattress which were not adapted to the needs of a disabled person, so that she had to sleep in her wheelchair. The toilet was also inaccessible to her and she persistently complained of the cold which she felt more acutely as a disabled person. To add to her indignity, male officers had to lift her onto a toilet. The European Court of Human Rights confirmed that her treatment was in breach of Article 3 and could be properly classified as degrading.

The Court concluded that she had failed to show an intention to humiliate or debase her, but observed that her detention in circumstances where she was likely to suffer cold, develop sores, and was unable to use the toilet or keep clean, constituted degrading treatment in contravention of Article 3.

This view was repeated in *Peers v. Greece*[8] where the applicant was detained in a cell with no ventilation which resulted in it being exceedingly hot. Furthermore, the toilet facilities were inadequate and were not separated from the rest of the cell by a screen. The applicant was not the cell's only inhabitant. Again, the court held a violation of Article 3, degrading treatment, despite the fact that there was no evidence that there was a positive intention of humiliating or debasing the applicant.[9]

Ill-treatment need not be deliberate. The prison may not intend to ill-treat a   **4–06** prisoner but the very conditions which are prevalent in the place of detention may very well activate the detainee's Convention rights. In the Second General Report of the CPT,[10] it was stated:

> "44. Ill-treatment can take numerous forms, many of which may not be deliberate but rather the result of organisational failings or inadequate resources. The overall quality of life in an establishment is therefore of considerable importance to the CPT".

Must go beyond mere fact of imprisonment. Of course, the very fact that an   **4–07** individual is confined in prison is of itself humiliation. Any ill-treatment complained of must go beyond this.[11]

In *Valasinas v. Lithuania*,[12] the court stressed that the suffering and humiliation involved must in any event go beyond that inevitable element of suffering or humiliation connected with a given form of treatment or punishment. The court reiterated its earlier jurisprudence that measures depriving a person of his liberty may involve such an element. The State must ensure that a person is detained in conditions which are compatible with the respect for his human dignity, but the manner and method of the execution of the measure do not subject him to distress or hardship of an intensity exceeding the unavoidable level of suffering inherent in detention and that, given the practical demands of imprisonment, his health and well being are adequately secured.[13]

---

[8] 33 E.H.R.R. 51.
[9] See also *V v. United Kingdom* 71 ECHR—IX and Chapter 8: Children and Young People.
[10] CPT/Inf. (92) 3.
[11] *Tyrer v. United Kingdom* (1979–80) 2 E.H.R.R. 1 and Chapter 8: Children and Young People.
[12] Application No. 44559/98.
[13] *Kudla v. Poland*, Application No. 30210/96.

It is arguable that the courts will not treat convicted prisoners and remand prisoners differently, except in the basic principle that a remand prisoner is yet to be convicted.[14]

2. CONDITIONS OF THE CELL

4–08   **Bullet points.** The courts have laid down basic conditions in which a prisoner should be detained: see *Dougaz v. Greece* (2000) 29 E.H.R.R. CD 147; *Napier v. The Scottish Ministers* (2001) GWD 23-876; *Peers v. Greece*:

- A cell should not be overcrowded;

- Sleeping facilities should be adequate;

- Temperatures should be tolerable, neither too hot or too cold;

- Ventilation should be appropriate;

- Appropriate lighting should be provided;

- Sanitary arrangements should reach the proper standards;

- The amount of time a prisoner is confined to his cell should not be excessive;

- There should be proper periods of exercise and recreation outside the cell;

- There should be proper steps by the authority to remedy the position;

- The overall period of time a prisoner serves in such conditions his highly relevant.

4–09   **Overcrowding.** The recent cases have developed a checklist of general minimum standards required for the accommodation of prisoners. As recently as the 1970s, it was deemed acceptable that a prisoner could be held overnight in a cell containing the stale smell of urine and faeces of an earlier occupant.

Furthermore, the courts were also willing to accept that it was acceptable for a prisoner to spend 3 weeks in a cockroach-infested cell.[15]

Fortunately, times have now changed. In *Dougoz v. Greece*,[16] the applicant was confined in a cell with inadequate sanitation, insufficient sleeping accommodation, deprived of fresh air, daylight, hot water and exercise.

The European Court stated that the conditions of the applicant's detention, in particular the serious overcrowding and lack of sleeping facilities, together with the amount of time he was detained in those conditions, amounted to degrading treatment and a violation of Article 3.

---

[14] *Napier v. Scottish Ministers* 2001 GWD 23–876, *The Times*, November 15, 2001.
[15] *Reed v. United Kingdom* (1983) 5 E.H.R.R. 114.
[16] (2000) 29 E.H.R.R. CD 147.

The CPT, in its Second General Report,[17] stated at para. 45 that:

"The level of overcrowding in a prison, or in a particular part of it, might be such as to be in itself inhuman or degrading from a physical standpoint".

This is a powerful persuasive argument when considering overcrowding in prisons.

During several visits of the CPT they encountered prison overcrowding.[18] Overcrowding is often particularly acute in prisoners used to accommodate remand prisoners. The CPT pointed out in its 2nd General Report that prison overcrowding is an issue of direct relevance to the Committee's mandate.[19] Hand-in-hand with prison overcrowding comes cramped, unhygienic accommodation, a constant lack of privacy, reduced out of cell activities, an overburdened health care facility, increased tension and more violence between prisoners and prison staff. The CPT has concluded that the adverse effects of overcrowding have resulted in inhuman and degrading conditions of detention.

The CPT seems far from convinced that providing additional prison accommodation alone with offer a lasting solution.

The use of physical control. The 2nd General Report[20] also emphasises at **4–10** para. 53 that prison staff will on occasions have to use force to control violent prisoners and exceptionally may need to resort to "instruments of physical restraint". In such circumstances the CPT advises:

"a prisoner against whom any means of force has been used should have the right to be immediately examined and, if necessary, treated by a medical doctor.

This examination should be conducted out of the hearing and preferably out of the sight of non-medical staff, and the results of the examination (including any relevant statements by the prisoner and the doctor's conclusions) should be formally recorded and made available to the prisoner".[21]

As to effective grievance procedures, para. 54 of the CPT's Report states that effective grievance and inspection procedures are "fundamental safeguards against ill-treatment in prisons".

The CPT goes on to say that it "attaches particular importance to regular visits to each prison establishment by an independent body (e.g. a board of visitors or supervisory judge) possessing powers to hear (and if necessary take action upon), complaints from prisoners and to inspect the establishment's premises".[22]

Time spent in conditions is vital. Significantly, in *Dougoz v. Greece*, the **4–11** applicant was detained in these conditions for about 17 months and the court observed that the amount of time that the applicant was imprisoned for in such

---

[17] CPT/Inf (92) 3.
[18] 7th General Report (CPT Inf (1997)) 10.
[19] CPT/Inf (92) 3, para. 46.
[20] CPT/Inf (92) 3.
[21] See para. 53.
[22] See para. 54.

degrading conditions was vital. It seems to follow that the longer the conditions of ill-treatment, the more likely a finding of violation.

The court took account that "for at least two months, the applicant had to spend a considerable part of each 24 hour period practically confined to his bed in a cell with no ventilation and no window which would at times become unbearably hot".

The CPT observed in its Second General Report[23] at paragraph 47 that:

" . . . prisoners cannot simply be left to languish for weeks, possibly months, locked up in their cells, and this, regardless of how good material conditions might be within the cells.

The CPT considers that one should aim at ensuring that prisoners in remand establishments are able to spend a reasonable part of the day (8 hours or more) outside their cells, engaged in purposeful activity of a varied nature. Of course, regimes in establishments for sentenced prisoners should be even more favourable.

Specific mention should be made of outdoor exercise. The requirement that prisoners be allowed at least one hour of exercise in the open air every day is widely accepted as a basic safeguard (preferably it should form part of a broader programme of activities). The CPT wishes to emphasise that all prisoners without exception (including those undergoing cellular confinement as punishment) should be offered the possibility to take outdoor exercise daily. It is also axiomatic that outdoor exercise facilities should be reasonably spacious and whenever possible offer shelter from inclement weather".

In *Napier v. The Scottish Ministers*,[24] the Court of Session held that a remand prisoner's human rights were prima facie infringed when he was required to spend most of each day in a shared cell without integral toilet facilities.

The court ordered the Government to secure his transfer to conditions of detention compliant with Article 3. The facts of this case indicate that the appellant was 21 years of age and had been detained in Barlinnie Prison in Scotland in a cell which provided grossly inadequate living space, lighting and ventilation, particularly since the appellant was required the share the cell with another prisoner.

He further alleged that the sanitary arrangements, which involved a process known as "slopping out", that is urination and defecation in vessels which were kept in the cell and emptied two or three times a day were grossly inadequate.

Complaint was made about the excessive extent to which he was confined in his cell and that the periods of exercise and recreation outside the cell were inadequate.

The particular condition of this petitioner was also preyed in aid in that he suffered from eczema. As a result of his incarceration he displayed an acute exacerbation of this condition affecting his face which required treatment.

The court held that the conditions in which the petitioner had been detained might well have played a causative role in the exacerbation of his medical condition. The Court of Session were of the view that in all the circumstances the petitioner had made out a prima facie case of infringement of his rights.

The court were particularly assisted by a report compiled by the European Committee for the Prevention of Torture and Inhuman or Degrading Treatment or

---

[23] CPT/Inf (92) 3.
[24] 2001 GWD 23–876, *The Times*, November 15, 2001.

Punishment which corroborated the applicant's allegations[25] and provides an invaluable yardstick to judge European standards that are required of the Prison Service.

Again, the observations of the CPT are helpful:

> "48. Ready access to proper toilet facilities and the maintenance of good standards of hygiene are essential components of a humane environment (no "slopping out"). Further, prisoners should have adequate access to shower or bathing facilities. It is also desirable for running water to be available within cellular accommodation.
> 50. The CPT would add that it is particularly concerned when it finds a combination of overcrowding, poor regime activities and inadequate access to toilet-washing facilities in the same establishment. The cumulative effect of such conditions can prove extremely detrimental to prisoners".

State not absolved from responsibility. The applicant in *Peers v. Greece* had   **4–12** been treated for heroin addiction in the United Kingdom but was arrested at Athens airport for drug offences. In due course, he was placed in a segregation unit in a Greek prison. He complained that whilst in the segregation unit he was confined to his bed for a considerable part of the day in a cell with no ventilation and no window. He further alleged that the prison did not provide inmates with sheets, pillows, toilet paper or toiletries. The court observed that the fact that the applicant could have obtained toiletries and toilet paper from his co-detainees did not absolve the Government from responsibility under the Convention.

State inactivity exacerbates allegations. Again, the applicant complained   **4–13** that he had to use the toilet in the presence of other inmates and be present whilst the toilet was being used by a fellow cell mate. As a result of all this, Peers complained that he felt humiliated and distressed and that the conditions of his detention had had an adverse physical and mental affect upon him. In finding that the treatment was degrading the court observed that the competent authorities

---

[25] See Murdock 26 E.L.Rev. Human Rights Survey 398 which emphasises that there are 43 countries bound by the Convention increasing the number of individuals deprived of their liberty and who are direct subjects of the Committee's mandate. The Committee's figures suggest that the total European prison population is approaching 1.9 million and once other places of detention are included (such as immigration centre, police stations, mental health institutions and military detention centres), the uncomfortable conclusion is that the number of Europeans deprived of their liberty exceeds 200 per 100,000 of the population. The Committee periodically visits contracting countries and in 1990 found that conditions prevailing in Wandsworth, Brixton and Leeds prisons amounted to inhuman and degrading treatment. After a visit to the North Caucasian region, the Committee concluded that "no circumstances whatsoever can justify the infliction of torture or inhuman or degrading treatment or punishment upon persons who are in the custody of State authorities" (Press Release, April 2, 2000). While visits of the Committee provide the opportunity for inspection and face to face discussion, a continuous and effective dialogue relies upon written communication. States are expected to provide an interim report within 6 months of receipt of the report on the visit containing details of action already taken and how it is intended to implement any remaining recommendations, and to provide a follow-up report within 12 months which provides a full account of action taken. The Committee expect the States to publish the reports. However, the United Kingdom has not entirely embraced the principle of openness. After the Committee's visit to that country in 1997 the Committee examined the efficacy of legal remedies for police misconduct. The delegation considered four particular cases of named individuals who had sought damages against the Metropolitan Police. In each instance, the part of the report which outlined the advice given by police solicitors to the Force's Complaints and Investigations Branch was deleted, the report carrying the explanation that "at the request of the United Kingdom Government, the European Committee for the Prevention of Torture has decided to omit from the published version of this report certain passages of professional legal advice ... to which its delegation had access, for reasons of legal professional privilege".

had taken no steps to improve the objectively unacceptable conditions of the applicant's detention. The court went on to say that "this omission denotes lack of respect for the applicant".

The degrading treatment was clearly brought to the authorities' attention and they chose to do nothing about it. This extra element will exacerbate the conditions in which applicants find themselves and be an extra ingredient to assist in a finding of violation.

In short, the court were of the view that the prison conditions complained of "diminished the applicant's human dignity and arose in him feelings of anguish and inferiority capable of humiliating and debasing him and possibly breaking his physical or moral resistance". The conditions as outlined in *Peers v. Greece* were categorised as degrading within the meaning of Article 3 of the Convention.

4–14   **Prison discipline.** A period of 7 days solitary confinement with a minimum diet and hard bed although not corresponding with the minimum standards that are laid down within statutory guidelines were nevertheless not adjudged to be conditions which could be described as inhuman and degrading treatment. The critical aspect of this finding was the fact that only 7 days were spent in these conditions and that that short period was for disciplinary reasons rather than as a result of a criminal conviction.[26]

4–15   **Prolonged solitary confinement.** The European Court has turned its face against prolonged solitary confinement unless there are exceptional reasons.

On this point, the Commission admissibility decision in *X v. FRG*[27] is instructive:

> "Opportunities for communication are denied to the applicant. They are nevertheless essential to enable a prisoner to stand a long period of compulsory social isolation without lasting mental effects, since a minimum of social contacts is one of the elementary needs of every human being. That enforced an almost complete social isolation leads ultimately to serious mental damage has long been recognised by specialists . . .
>
> The Commission first wishes to state its opinion that prolonged solitary confinement is undesirable, particularly where the prisoner concerned is in detention on remand. In the latter case, if exceptional reasons have justified such continuous detention, it can obviously best be shortened by expediting the trial proceedings".

3. Medical Care

4–16   **Bullet points.** It can be argued that prison authorities have the following duties:

- To safeguard the health and well-being of prisoners—see *McFeeley v. United Kingdom* (1981) 3 E.H.R.R. 611;

---

[26] See *X v. FRG* 10 D.R. 221.
[27] 10 D.R. 221.

- Where there is reasonable cause to fear for the health of a prisoner, to take reasonable steps to monitor his medical condition and/or to offer him access to medical care—see *Keenan v. United Kingdom* (2001) 33 E.H.R.R. 38;

- A prisoner must be treated in the most appropriate way to reflect his medical or psychiatric needs—see *Aerts v. Belgium* (2000) 29 E.H.R.R. 56;

- To obtain medical reports and act upon them—see *Chartier v. Italy* (1983) 33 D.R. 41;

- To maintain adequate records of a prisoner's progress whilst under medical supervision—see *Keenan v. United Kingdom* (2001) 33 E.H.R.R. 38;

- Not to impose a further sentence and/or punishment which may threaten the prisoner's physical and/or moral resistance and/or adversely affect his personality—see *Keenan v. United Kingdom* (2001) 33 E.H.R.R. 38.

Lack of care. The lack of proper medical treatment has been held to amount **4–17** to a violation of Article 3, in a prison context. Indeed, whilst the fact that a detainee is elderly will not cause his incarceration to be in breach of Article 3, nevertheless, if it can be established that he will not receive appropriate medical treatment in custody then a violation may be established.[28]

General duties upon the State. Where there is reasonable cause to fear for a **4–18** health of a detainee, reasonable steps should be taken to monitor his or her medical condition and to offer him or her access to medical care as required. Each case will be decided upon its own particular facts but the State is under no obligation to force a prisoner to take medical care.[29]

There is a general duty on the State to safeguard and well-being of prisoners when they are being detained in a place of custody.[30] Indeed, the prisons are under an obligation to protect the health of people who have been deprived of their liberty[31] and at the very least a sick patient deprived of the care that he requires may well have suffered inhuman and degrading treatment.

Insufficient medical treatment in prison.[32] According to case law of the **4–19** Convention, the following are essential considerations for any Article 3 issue:

- Ill-treatment must attain a minimum level of severity if it is to fall within the scope of Article 3;

- The lack of medical treatment in prison may raise an issue under Article 3;

- The court will consider the seriousness of the applicant's condition;

- The quality of the medical care he receives in prison;

---

[28] See *Papon v. France* (2001) Crim.L.R. 918 and *Sawoniuk v. United Kingdom* (2001) Crim.L.R. 917.

[29] *R. v. Monney* [1999] 1 S.C.R. 652.

[30] *McFeeley v. United Kingdom* (1981) 3 E.H.R.R. 161.

[31] *Hurtado v. Switzerland* July 8, 1993 (1994) Series A, No. 28-A; *D v. United Kingdom* [1997] 24 E.H.R.R. 423.

[32] See the Commission's observations in *Andrzej Jastrzebski v. Poland* (Report of the Commission, Application No. 25669/94).

- Whether the applicant's state of health is compatible with detention;

- The State has no obligation under Article 3 to release a detainee or to transfer him to the civil hospital, even when he has a disease which is particularly difficult to treat (see *Chartier v. Italy*[33]);

- The State has an obligation to maintain a continuous review of the detention arrangements employed with a view to ensuring the health and well-being of all prisoners, having due regard to the ordinary and reasonable requirements of imprisonment.[34]

4–20   **Suicidal prisoners.** If the State is aware of the depressive nature of a prisoner then the fact that they are being held in detention and suffer from a serious depressive state imposes a duty of particular diligence upon the prison. In *Kudla v. Poland*,[35] a Polish national suffering from chronic depression and with a diagnosed personality disorder, spent more than two years in detention on remand. Whilst in detention he had twice attempted suicide and had undergone numerous psychiatric examinations.

In rejecting the applicant's complaint that he had not received adequate psychiatric treatment whilst detained and that this amounted to inhuman and degrading treatment, the court observed that ill-treatment had to reach a minimum level of severity to constitute a breach of Article 3 and that detention on remand was not of itself inhuman or degrading treatment but the State had to ensure that the conditions of detention showed respect for human dignity.

In Kudla's case he had regularly sought and obtained medical assistance and the court were of the view that there was insufficient evidence to indicate that the applicant's suicide attempts were in any way due to failures on the part of the authorities. As such they found no violation of Article 3. Had the applicant's suicide attempts been attributable to a failure on behalf of the State, then it seems that the court are paving a way for a violation to be substantiated.

4–21   **Proof of effect upon the person may not be determinative.** In *R. v. Keenan*,[36] the court stated:

> "It is not possible to distinguish with any great certainty to what extent his symptoms during this time, or indeed his death, resulted from the conditions of his detention imposed by the authorities.
>
> The court considers however that this difficulty is not determinative of the issue as to whether the authorities fulfilled their obligation under Article 3 to protect Mark Keenan from treatment or punishment contrary to this provision. While it is true that the severity of suffering, physical or mental, attributable to a particular measure has been a significant consideration in many of the cases decided by the court under Article 3, there are circumstances where proof of the actual effect on the person may not be a major factor . . .
>
> treatment of a mentally ill person may be incompatible with the standards imposed by Article 3 in the protection of fundamental human dignity, even though that person may not be able, or capable of, pointing to any specific ill effects".

---

[33] (1983) 33 D.R. 41.
[34] See *Bonnechaux v. Switzerland*, Comm. Report 5.12.79, D.R. 18, p. 100, see also *Lukallv v. Bulgaria*, Eur. Comm. HR, No. 21915/93, December 1, 1995, D.R. 80-A, p. 128–130.
[35] (1998) E.H.R.L.R. 630.
[36] [1990] 2 Q.B. 54.

The court pointed to the lack of medical notes and noted that this showed an adequate concern to maintain full and detailed records of his mental state.

Internal disciplinary sentences. Prison authorities must also take into 4–22
account the vulnerability of prisoners when deciding whether any internal disciplinary sentences are appropriate. In *Keenan v. United Kingdom*,[37] a prisoner who had been receiving anti-psychotic medication was imprisoned for four months. During his transfer from the prison health care centre to the main prison, he badly assaulted two hospital officers and despite the prison health staff being aware of his problems, he was further remanded for a period of 28 days, along with a 7 day segregation period as punishment. Within 24 hours of that decision, he hanged himself. The court observed that while the prison authorities had made a reasonable response to the deceased's conduct by placing him in hospital care and subject to daily medical supervision, they had shown inadequate concern to maintain records of his progress and had failed to refer him to a psychiatrist for advice regarding his medication and future care.

The deceased had been found by the prison doctors to be fit for segregation and there had been no breach of the right to life under the Human Rights Act 1998 Schedule 1, Part 1, Article 2. However, the court were of the view that the deceased's vulnerability should have been taken into account by the authorities and the prison had an obligation to protect his health. The European Court of Human Rights observed that the imposition of the further sentence and punishment might have threatened the deceased's physical and moral resistance and adversely affected his personality to the extent that it was degrading and inhuman treatment and therefore in breach of Article 3.[38]

The special duty of care. The prison authorities are under a particular duty to 4–23
care for suicide risk detainees and not expose them to harm as a result of inappropriate disciplinary regimes.

The court went on to observe in *Keenan*'s case:

"The lack of effective monitoring of Mark Keenan's condition and the lack of informed psychiatric input into his assessment and treatment disclosed significant defects in the medical care provided to a mentally ill person known to be a suicide risk.
This belated imposition on him in those circumstances of a serious disciplinary punishment—7 days segregation in the punishment block and an additional 28 days to his sentence imposed 2 weeks after the event and only 9 days before his expected date of release—which may well have threatened his physical and moral resistance, is not compatible with the standard of treatment required in respect of a mentally ill person. It must be regarded as constituting inhuman and degrading treatment and punishment within the meaning of Article 3 of the Convention".[39]

Psychiatric treatment. There is increasing concern that detainees who require 4–24
the assistance of psychiatric attention are being detained in prisons instead. Concern is increased when prisoners are detained in psychiatric wings of a prison because they are adjudged too mentally ill to be criminally responsible and there

---

[37] (2001) 33 E.H.R.R. 38.
[38] The Court awarded the family of the deceased £10,000 in compensation.
[39] Para. 115. This case was subsequently applied in *Orange v. Chief Constable of West Yorkshire Police*, *The Times*, June 5, 2001, CA and *The Queen (on the application of Wright and Bennett) v. The Home Office* (see above).

is no other place to put them. The State have an obligation to take reasonable and necessary measures to treat a prisoner in the most appropriate way. In *Aerts v. Belgium*,[40] the applicant complained of his detention in the psychiatric wing of a prison himself having been adjudged to be too mentally ill to be criminally responsible. In essence he complained that his detention was unlawful and that the treatment he received in the psychiatric wing was inhuman and degrading. The court held that in principle, the detention of a person as a Mental Health patient would only be lawful for the purposes of the Convention rights if it was effected in a hospital, clinic or other appropriate institution.[41]

In *Aerts'* case, the psychiatric wing of the prison could not be regarded as an appropriate institution since it was not a therapeutic environment and there was no regular medical attention.

The proper relationship between the aim of the detention and the conditions in which it took place was deficient and was in breach of Article 5(1)(e), dealing with the detention of persons of "unsound mind".

In ruling that the minimum level of severity had not been breached and therefore Article 3 not violated, the court concluded that while the general conditions in the psychiatric wing of the prison were unsatisfactory and not conducive to the effective treatment of inmates, there was no proof of deterioration of the applicant's mental health and it had not been established that he suffered treatment that was inhuman or degrading.

4–25 **Duty to respect human dignity.** The State do have a duty to ensure that the conditions of detention show respect for human dignity. In *Kudla v. Poland*,[42] the applicant was a chronic depressive with a diagnosed personality disorder who spent more than two years in detention on remand. While in detention he twice attempted suicide and underwent numerous psychiatric examinations and the repeated applications and appeals for release. Kudla alleged that he had not received adequate psychiatric treatment while detained on remand and that this amounted to inhuman and degrading treatment.

Although in the circumstances of this particular case the detention on remand was not found of itself to be inhuman or degrading, the European Court of Human Rights affirmed that the State had to ensure that the conditions of detention showed respect for human dignity.

4–26 **Provision of medical assistance.** Critical in avoiding liability the State were able to prove that the applicant had regularly sought and obtained medical assistance and that there was insufficient evidence to indicate that his suicide attempts were in any way due to the failures on the part of the authorities. Thus, where the authorities can show that they have taken reasonable and necessary steps to treat a detainee by, for example, seeking and obtaining medical assistance and are able to show that harm to the prisoner was not in any way due to the failures of the State, it is unlikely that a breach of Article 3 will be found. The State has an obligation to maintain a continuous review of the detention arrangements employed with a view to ensuring the health and well-being of all

---

[40] (2000) 29 E.H.R.R. 50.
[41] *Ashingdane v. United Kingdom* 7 E.H.R.R. 528.
[42] [1998] E.H.R.L.R. 630.

prisoners, having due regard to the ordinary and reasonable requirements of imprisonment.[43]

No obligation to release. The State has no obligation under Article 3 to **4–27** release a detainee or to transfer him to the civil hospital, even when he has a disease which is particularly difficult to treat[44]

4. JUVENILES[45]

Definition. In its ninth report, the European Committee for the Prevention of **4–28** Torture considered that juveniles were to be classified as persons under the age of 18.[46]

Imprisonment must be a last resort. The detention of minors is increasing, **4–29** particularly as youth crime is receiving considerable political attention. The European Committee for the Prevention of Torture (CPT) have highlighted the growing concern about abuse of children by adults entrusted with their care or inappropriate use of incarceration in the face of lack of alternatives to custody.[47]

It is a recognised principle of international law that "juveniles should only be deprived of their liberty as a last resort and for the shortest possible period of time".[48]

Distinguish from adults. The effective safeguards provided for juveniles will **4–30** be the same as those applied to adult detainees but the State will, in addition, have to take account of the immaturity and vulnerability of young people and they have to accept that additional measures must be put in place. The CPT recommends that juveniles be accommodated separately from adults.[49]

Physical punishment. Although there is a paucity of case law concerning the **4–31** treatment of juveniles in custody, the CPT's recommendations give an important insight into what the courts may in future find indicative of violation of Article 3.

The CPT have indicated that they would wish to see all forms of physical chastisement prohibited and emphasise that the carrying of batons by custodial staff who have direct contact with juveniles should be discouraged. If the staff

---

[43] See *Bonnechaux v. Switzerland*, Comm. Report 5.12.79, D.R. 18, p. 100.
[44] See *Chartier v. Italy* (1983) D.R. 41.
[45] See also Chapter 8: Children and Young People.
[46] It is interesting to compare this with the attitude of the courts in England and Wales to the classification of juveniles in criminal cases. See *Stratford Youth Justices v. Attorney General, DPP* [2001] EWHC Admin 615; (2001) 165 J.P. 761.
[47] The European Convention for the Prevention of Torture and Inhuman or Degrading Treatment or Punishment: Activities in 1999 (2000) 25 E.L.Rev. Human Rights Survey (Jim Murdock).
[48] Convention on the Rights of the Child, Article 37(b) and Rules 13 and 19 of the Beijing Rules.
[49] The CPT recognises that there may be exceptional situations, for instance, children and parents being held as immigration detainees in which it is plainly in the best interests of juveniles not to be separated from particular adults (para. 25 above).

consider it indispensable to carry such weapons, they should be hidden from view, according to the ninth general report of the CPT at paragraph 27.[50]

4-32   **Searching.** As should be encouraged with adult detainees, prisoners should only be searched by staff of the same gender with any search involving undressing being conducted out of the sight of the opposite gender.

4-33   **Accommodation and regime.** In short, the Committee recommend that juveniles should be held in detention centres specifically designed for persons of their age and which can offer a multi disciplinary regime offered by a range of professionals including teachers and psychologists and tailored to meet the individual needs of juveniles "within a secure educative and socio-therapeutic environment", employing "special efforts to reduce the risks of long-term social maladjustment". Staff should be carefully selected on the basis of personal maturity and an ability to work with, guiding and motivating, and safeguarding the welfare of young people. The training aspect of those assigned to care for young detainees is emphasised in that specific training and appropriate support and supervision are considered to be crucial. The Committee emphasise that the management of juvenile detention centres requires "advanced leadership skills" and the ability to respond to the competing demands of detainees and staff.

In the absence of compelling considerations of security, detainees should be permitted to retain personal items. For female detainees, the Committee are of the view that failure to provide sanitary and washing facilities and hygiene items (such as sanitary towels) can indeed amount to degrading treatment.[51] This of course again could apply to adult as well as juvenile prisoners.

Regime activities should involve "a full programme of education, sport, vocational training, recreation and other purposeful activities", including in particular physical education with female detainees enjoying equal access to such rather than being provided with stereotypical activities such as sewing or handicrafts.[52] The Committee advise that contact with the outside world should never be restricted or denied as a disciplinary measure. Any resort to the placement of a juvenile in conditions resembling solitary confinement could only be justified if for the shortest possible period of time and accompanied by appropriate human contact, access to reading material and at least one hour of outdoor exercise every day.

4-34   **Discipline.** As to general disciplinary measures, the right to be heard and appeal to a higher authority is emphasised along with the proper recording of any

---

[50] The CPT also observe that juveniles run a higher risk in Europe of ill-treatment in police establishments than in other places of detention (paras 22–23 above). The period immediately following deprivation of liberty carries the greatest risk, according to the CPT, of torture and ill-treatment, and thus requires to be safeguarded through the provision of the usual range of rights, such as reasonable cell accommodation, the right to notify a relative or other third party of detention, access to a lawyer and access to a doctor from the very outset of detention. The CPT welcomes but apparently does not prescribe the practice of placing police officers under a formal duty to ensure that the appropriate person is notified even if the juvenile has not requested that this be done and only to interview any juvenile in the presence of any appropriate person with or without a lawyer being present. See again, the domestic case of *Stratford Youth Justices v. Attorney General, DPP* [2001] EWHC Admin 615; (2001) 165 J.P. 761.

[51] Paras 29–30 of the ninth general report.

[52] The Beijing Rules, Rule 26.4 provides that female juveniles deprived of their liberty "by no means receive less care, protection, assistance, treatment and training than young male offenders". This is cited with approval by the CPT.

sanction imposed which is considered by the Committee to be central to the prevention of ill-treatment. This, coupled with effective complaints and inspection procedures, including the right of lodging a complaint both within and outside the detention centre's administrative system, is important and confidential access to an appropriate authority is vital.

Medical provision. Along with the provision of proper medical services **4–35** within the detention centre, the CPT advise that the monitoring of food is particularly important for juveniles since, they say, "the consequences of inadequate nutrition may become evident more rapidly (and be more serious) than for prisoners who have reached full physical maturity".

Whilst all of the above observations form the basis of recommendations only, some or all of these benchmarks will be used if absent from the regime provided to detain the juvenile, to mount an argument that Article 3 has been violated.

It can be argued with some force that many of the recommendations and observations will also apply to the care and custody of adults.

Sentence of detention during Her Majesty's Pleasure. In the case of *R. v.* **4–36** *Secretary of State for the Home Department, ex p. Venables,*[53] the Court of Appeal considered whether the character of the sentence of detention during Her Majesty's Pleasure under Section 53(1) of the Children and Young Persons Act 1933,[54] which replaced Section 103 of the Children Act 1908 and whether it was a form of life sentence or a sentence for discretionary custody of such duration as should thereafter be decided.

The view which prevailed was that it was not a life sentence but was a wholly discretionary sentence. Lord Browne-Wilkinson stated[55]:

> "Detention during Her Majesty's Pleasure is wholly indeterminate in duration: it lasts so long as Her Majesty (i.e. the Secretary of State) considers appropriate [it is not] a sentence of the same kind as the mandatory life sentence imposed on an adult murderer, the duration of which is determined by the sentence of the court and is for life. In the cases of detention during Her Majesty's Pleasure the duty of the Secretary of State is to decide how long that detention is to last, not to determine whether or not to release prematurely a person on whom the sentence of the court is life imprisonment".[56]

The policy which underlies such an approach is to maintain flexibility and to enable the duration of the defendant's detention to take into account his welfare, the desirability of reintegrating him into society and his developing maturity through his formative years.[57] It is also accepted that punishment is part of the purpose of the sentence and therefore that the Secretary of State in exercising his statutory discretion regarding the duration of the detention, should have regard to the need to punish the defendant.[58]

Lord Steyn said[59]:

---

[53] [1998] A.C. 407.
[54] As substituted by section 1(5) of the Murder (Abolition of Death Penalty) Act 1965.
[55] At page 498.
[56] Lord Steyn and Lord Hope expressed similar views at pp. 521 and 531–532.
[57] *per* Lord Brown-Wilkinson at pp. 499–500.
[58] See *per* Lord Steyn at pp. 519–520.
[59] At pp. 522–523.

"Parliament differentiated between the two sentences. An order of detention during Her Majesty's Pleasure involves merely an authority to detain indefinitely. That means that the Home Secretary must decide from time to time, taking into account the punitive element, whether detention is still justified. Life imprisonment involves an order for custody for life".[60]

5. HEALTHY PRISONERS WHO BECOME ILL

4–37   **Illness during incarceration.** A perfectly healthy prisoner may nonetheless become ill during his incarceration. If it can be established that imprisonment of itself causes ill-health, the court may find this to be inhuman treatment. For instance, in *B v. FRG*,[61] the applicant claimed that depression experienced during his detention on remand resulted in his conditions of detention causing him to re-experience his imprisonment in a Nazi concentration camp.

The Commission will pay particular attention both to whether the prisoner has shown a willingness to make use of the medical services available and will examine the medical treatment that was at the prisoner's disposal should he choose to take it.[62]

6. DEATH IN CUSTODY

4–38   **Death of prisoner.** The State has a positive obligation to protect life in accordance with Article 2 and failure to take the appropriate preventative steps when the prison authority is aware that the life of a detainee may be under threat be it for external reasons or that the prisoner is in a depressive or suicidal state will also constitute a breach of Article 2. A full consideration of these issues is beyond the scope of this work.[63]

4–39   **Treatment leading to death.** It is sometimes the case that ill-treatment of a prisoner can lead to death and in these circumstances it is usual to see a joint submission under Article 2 and Article 3, Article 3 dealing with the pre-death treatment of the detainee. In *R. (on the application of Wright) v. The Secretary of State for the Home Department*,[64] the mother of a prisoner who died after suffering a severe asthma attack whilst in a prison cell, sought judicial review of the Secretary of State's continued failure to hold an independent investigation into her son's death. She had previously brought an action under the Fatal Accidents Act 1976 over the treatment her son had received for his asthma whilst in prison, and liability and damages had been agreed.

It was held to be arguable that Article 3 had been breached given the fact that there was evidence that the deceased's asthma condition worsened because of

---

[60] See also *Browne v. The Queen* [2000] A.C. 45.
[61] Application. No. 55 D.R. 271.
[62] See *Lockwood v. United Kingdom* 15 E.H.R.R. CD 48 where the Commission declined to find a violation of Article 3 where a medical officer delayed for four months in seeking a second opinion which ultimately resulted in a diagnosis of a malignant tumour.
[63] But see *Osman v. United Kingdom* (1998) 29 E.H.R.R. 245 and *Keenan v. United Kingdom* (Application no. 27229/95, June 22, 1998), ECmHR.
[64] [2001] EWHC Admin. 520.

inadequate medical attention and that fact that the conditions in his cell were such that he did not have access to prompt medical attention.

The facts. The facts of *R. (on the application of Wright) v. The Secretary of* **4–40** *State for the Home Department* bear analysis and demonstrate a growing willingness of the courts to invoke Article 3 in death in custody cases.

An inquest was heard into the death of Paul Wright and in the absence of the medical officer responsible for Mr Wright's care, Mr Wright's family representatives and the cell mate of the deceased, a jury returned a verdict of death by natural causes. During the inquest there was no independent consideration of the medical treatment that the deceased had received nor was there any suggestion that it was or could have been inadequate. As such, the jury's verdict in the inquest cannot be criticised on the evidence that it had before it. The family of the deceased later discovered that the medical officer who had been responsible for the deceased's care had been suspended from the Prison Service in 1999 and had been found guilty of serious professional misconduct by the General Medical Council (GMC) in 1994. Mr Wright died from his asthma attack on November 7, 1996 having suffered from serious asthma all his life. In April 2000, the defendant, the Home Office, admitted liability and then settled the proceedings for a substantial sum of money.

Despite this, the Home Secretary refused to initiate an independent investigation as to how it was that a prisoner should die in these circumstances.

It was this catalyst that encouraged the family to issue proceedings under the Human Rights Act 1998 seeking disclosure of the expert report which led to the Home Office admitting liability in the Fatal Accidents Act 1979 proceedings, a mandatory order requiring the Home Office to initiate an investigation into Mr Wright's death, a declaration that the Home Office's treatment of the family following Mr Wright's death was in breach of the family rights under Article 8 of the European Convention on Human Rights (right to private and family life) and finally, damages.

When the medical report was finally disclosed, serious flaws were seen in the medical treatment and it concluded that "Compliance with these characteristics of good medical practice would properly have averted his death".

It was upon this basis that the family of the deceased as well as arguing breach of Article 2 argued breach of Article 3.[65]

Proper investigation. There is a right for the families of the deceased to **4–41** obtain a competent and official investigation of any death in custody. This right has often properly been prescribed to the provisions of Article 2, the absence of which will in itself be a breach.[66]

But there also seems to be a concurrent duty under Article 3. In *Timurtas v. Turkey*,[67] the applicant's father was aware that his son had been taken into custody but was never able to get satisfactory information from the authorities and no explanation was given as to why his son had not been seen since. His family brought an action claiming that the disappearance of his son by the Turkish authorities and the anguish this had caused him violated his rights under

---

[65] See also *Jordan v. United Kingdom, The Times,* May 18, 2001, and New Law Journal pp. 677 at 808–809.

[66] *McCann v. United Kingdom* (1995) 21 E.H.R.R. 97; *Kaya v. Turkey* (1998) 28 E.H.R.R. 1; *Assenov v. Bulgaria* (1998) 28 E.H.R.R. 652; *Salman v. Turkey,* June 27, 2000, ECtHR.

[67] (2001) 33 E.H.R.R. 6.

Articles 2, 3 and 5. The court assumed that his son had died in custody and the lack of an explanation by the authorities meant that Turkey would be held responsible for his death in violation of Article 2. The court were also of the view that the lack of an effective investigation into the prisoner's death further violated Article 2. When one reads the judgment in *R. (on the application of Wright) v. The Secretary of State for the Home Department*,[68] it is arguable that the lack of an effective investigation into the ill-treatment of the deceased is also in breach of Article 3.

Mr Justice Jackson in *Wright* articulated five propositions from the case law considered in argument:

1. That Article 2 and Article 3 enshrine fundamental rights, and where it is arguable that a breach of either provision has occurred, the State must procure an effective official investigation;

2. Such investigations are required to maximise future compliance with the Convention;

3. There is a prescribed form that an investigation must take. Whether or not it is sufficient to discharge the obligations under the Convention will depend on the facts of the case and the procedures of the investigation;

4. Where there is an arguable breach of Article 2 or Article 3 the investigation must comply with the conditions set down in *Jordan*, in short, the next of kin must be involved in the procedure and the investigation must be independent, public, effective, prompt and reasonably expeditious;

5. The holding of an inquest may or may not (depending on the facts of the case) satisfy the obligations inherent in Article 2 and Article 3.

Clearly, the investigations into the death of Wright were not adequate. The court rejected the Home Secretary's argument that the duty to investigate had been discharged by the inquest and the Fatal Accidents Act proceedings. Mr Justice Jackson emphasised that the inquest did not comply with the requirements set out in *Jordan v. United Kingdom* and it could never have been an effective hearing because of the lack of disclosure of the medical officer's history, the failure to call the cell mate, the failure to call an independent medical expert and because of the absence of legal representation of family members the family had no effective chance of participating in the investigation.

As to the Fatal Accidents Act proceedings, the court in *Wright* considered that these proceedings were irrelevant to the duties of the Prison Service under Articles 2 and 3. As such, the Home Secretary was ordered to initiate an independent investigation. At the time of writing, the Home Office are appealing this decision.

In *McShane v. United Kingdom*,[69] the court again recognised that the obligation to protect human life (and by implication to protect against ill-treatment), read in conjunction with the State's general duty under Article 1 to secure to everyone within its jurisdiction the rights and freedoms defined in the Convention, also required by implication that there should be some form of effective official investigation. One of the reasons for this was to secure the effective

---

[68] [2001] EWHC Admin 520.
[69] *The Times*, June 3, 2002.

implementation of domestic laws and in those cases involving State agents or bodies, to ensure their accountability. In finding that there had been a number of shortcomings in an investigation into the applicant's death, which had been caused during his attempted apprehension, the European Court of Human Rights isolated six failings. They were:

- The police officers investigating the incident were not independent of the officers implicated in the incident;

- The police investigation lacked expedition;

- The soldier who drove the vehicle which fatally injured the applicant could not be required to attend the inquest as a witness;

- The inquest procedure did not allow any verdict or findings which could have played an effective role in securing a prosecution should a criminal offence have been disclosed;

- The non-disclosure of witness statements and other relevant documents contributed to long adjournments in the proceedings;

- The inquest proceedings were not started promptly.

No universal set of rules. There is no universal set of rules for the form of an **4–42** effective official investigation. What is required is a flexible approach responsive to the dictates of the facts of the case. The court should look at the matter pragmatically, taking into account all investigative initiatives that have been undertaken. For instance, publicity and family participation in any investigation while they may be desirable in some cases are not compulsory requirements which must be distinctly and separately fulfilled in every case where the procedural duty to investigate is engaged. In *The Queen (on the application of Amin) v. Secretary of State for the Home Department and HM Coroner for West London*,[70] the Court of Appeal observed that the overall question for the court is whether the State had fulfilled its procedural obligation to investigate.

Positive acts and omissions. The facts of *Wright* distinguish it from *Keenan* **4–43** *v. United Kingdom*[71] in that the negligent medical care of Wright involved positive acts and omissions and that the treatment involved greater culpability over a longer period. Furthermore, Mr Justice Jackson observed that in a moment leading up to his death, Wright would have endured considerable pain and suffering which might be categorised as a breach of Article 3 and that if a breach was found in *Keenan* then there was arguably a breach in *Wright*.

Decisions not to prosecute. There is no absolute obligation imposed on **4–44** the Director of Public Prosecutions to give reasons for a decision not to prosecute.

But the courts have observed[72] that since the death of a person in the State's custody which results from violence inflicted by its agents necessarily arouses concern, the Director of Public Prosecutions will be expected, in the absence of compelling grounds to the contrary, to give reasons for such a decision where it

---

[70] Court of Appeal, March 27, 2002.
[71] (2001) 33 E.H.R.R. 38.
[72] See *R. v. Director of Public Prosecutions ex p. Manning* [2001] Q.B. 330.

relates to a death in custody in respect of which an inquest jury has returned a lawful verdict of unlawful killing implicating an identifiable person against whom there was prima facie evidence, in order to meet the expectation that, if a prosecution did not follow, a plausible explanation would be provided, and to vindicate the decision by showing the existence of solid grounds to support it.

Skill and care will be required to draft such reasons in order to protect the public and third party interests, but the Queen's Bench Division in *Ex p. Manning* held that a citizen should not be obliged to challenge the lawfulness of the decision in order to seek, in judicial review proceedings, the response which "*good administrative practice ordinarily requires*".[73]

Ex parte Manning was concerned with the highly publicised death in Blakenhurst prison of a defendant awaiting trial. He was restrained by two prison officers during a violent altercation and during a prolonged struggle was suffocated.

The Report to the United Kingdom Government of the European Committee for the Prevention of Torture,[74] stated:

"Reference should also be made to the high degree of public interest in Crown Prosecution Service decisions regarding the prosecution of police officers (especially in cases involving allegations of serious misconduct).

Confidence about the manner in which such decisions are reached would certainly be strengthened were the Crown Prosecution Service to be obliged to give detailed reasons in cases where it was decided that no criminal proceedings should be brought. The CPT recommends that such requirement be introduced".

Reference should also be made to the Victims Charter published by the Home Office which states:

"The Crown Prosecution Service, on request, will meet the family of someone killed as a result of a crime, to explain their decision on prosecution".

4–45   **Realistic prospect of conviction.** General responsibility for the institution and conduct of prosecutions in England and Wales is entrusted to the Director of Public Prosecutions, subject to the involvement of the Attorney General and the responsible staff of the Crown Prosecution Service, although the power to institute a private prosecution is preserved.

Section 10 of the Prosecution of Offences Act 1985 requires the Director to issue a Code for Crown Prosecutors giving guidance on general principles to be applied by them in determining, in any case, whether proceedings for an offence should be instituted. The Code, in essence, provides:

"Crown prosecutors must be satisfied that there is enough evidence to provide a 'realistic prospect of conviction' against each defendant on each charge. They must consider what the defence case may be and how that is likely to affect the prosecution case . . . a realistic prospect of conviction is an objective test. It means that a jury or bench of magistrates, properly directed in accordance with the law, is more likely than not to convict the defendant of the charge alleged . . . when deciding whether there is enough evidence to prosecute, Crown prosecutors must consider whether the evidence can be used and is reliable".[75]

---

[73] See pp. 344E–G and 347B–348A.
[74] Published in January 2000 at p. 20.
[75] See the Code for Crown Prosecutors at 5.1; 5.2; and 5.3.

The evidential test of a "realistic prospect of conviction" has to be satisfied. If it is not satisfied, there will be no prosecution, no matter how great the public interest might seem in having the matter ventilated in court. It is not the role of the Crown Prosecution Service simply to give cases a public hearing, regardless of the strength of the evidence. It is clear that there must be an objective assessment of that evidence. The Crown Prosecution Service will not look for the same standard of proof that a jury or bench of magistrates would need to find before it could convict, this will set too high a standard and tend to usurp the role of the court. The test as laid out in the Code is based on "more likely than not".

Judicial review. The decision by the Director of Public Prosecutions not to **4–46** prosecute is susceptible to judicial review.[76]

The power of review is one which will be exercised sparingly because the primary decision to prosecute or not to prosecute is entrusted by Parliament to the Director of Public Prosecutions as head of an independent, professional prosecution service, answerable to the Attorney General in his role of guardian of the public interest. It is considered that it will make no difference that in practice the decision will ordinarily be taken by a senior member of the Crown Prosecution Service and not by the Director personally.

Of course, there may be borderline cases where the decision may be one of acute difficulty, since while a defendant whom a jury would be likely to convict should properly be brought to justice and tried, a defendant whom a jury would be likely to acquit should not be subjected to the trauma inherent in a criminal trial.[77]

7. ELDERLY PERSONS

Imprisonment. It is unlikely whether the imprisonment of elderly persons per **4–47** se can amount to inhuman or degrading treatment although this has been argued in the recent cases of *Sawoniuk v. United Kingdom*[78] and *Papon v. France*.[79] These cases challenge the imprisonment of elderly persons who were convicted of war crimes.

If detention will cause extreme suffering, then it is arguable that a violation of Article 3 has been committed. In the case of *B v. Germany*,[80] the applicant had spent 5 years in a Nazi concentration camp and claimed that any period of incarceration would force him to relive his experiences during World War II. The European Commission observed that:

> "The detention today of a person such as the applicant . . . might well raise serious issues under Article 3 of the Convention, if, as a direct consequence of his detention, he is allegedly force to relive and suffer again the terrible experiences of the years 1940–45".

---

[76] See *R. v. Director of Public Prosecutions ex p. C* [1995] 1 Cr.App.R. 136.
[77] See *R. v. Director of Prosecutions ex p. Manning* [1995] 1 Cr.App.R. 136.
[78] (2001) Crim.L.R. 918, ECHR.
[79] (2001) Crim.L.R. 917, ECHR.
[80] 55 D.R. 271.

No Member States of the Council of Europe has an upper age limit for detention. In certain circumstances, the imprisonment of an elderly person over a lengthy period might activate Article 3.

Regard must be had to the particular circumstances of the case. In *Papon v. France*,[81] the court held that in view of the applicant's general state of health and his conditions of detention, his treatment had not reached the level of severity required to bring it within the scope of Article 3 of the Convention.

In *Sawoniuk v. United Kingdom*,[82] another admissibility decision of the European Court of Human Rights[83] concerned the murder trial of a former commander in World War II of a German controlled police force responsible for implementing genocide against the Polish-Jewish population. The European Court repeated that there is no prohibition in the Convention on the detention of the elderly, although failure to provide adequate health care to a prisoner might give rise to an issue under Article 3.[84]

8. WOMEN

4–48 **Imprisonment.** Recently, the Court of Appeal have issued guidelines as to circumstances when a mother who is responsible for the care of her young children and is of previous good character, should not serve a term of imprisonment, where an alternative is available.

In *R. v. Mills*,[85] the Lord Chief Justice laid down certain guidelines which a court should consider before imprisoning such women. He stated:

"1. Although one reason for a custodial sentence was "the clang of prison doors" factor, namely that it gave an offender the opportunity to know what a prison sentence involved, the ability of the prison service to achieve anything of benefit in a short period of time was limited;
2. Where an offender was the sole supporter of young children, the court had to bear in mind the consequences to the children of their mother being sent to prison;
3. Since 1993 there had been a remarkable and undesirable increase in the female prison population. Short sentences were always difficult for the prison service to accommodate, as was imprisoning mothers close to their homes".

His Lordship went on to state that this did not mean that if it was necessary for an offender to be sent to prison, she should not be, but in borderline cases such as cases which did not involve violence or which had financial consequences

---

[81] Admissibility decision of the Court of Human Rights, Third Section, June 7, 2001 (2001) Crim.L.R.
[82] (2001) Crim.L.R. 918.
[83] Admissibility Applications usually go forward for determination by the court, but the decision that an application is inadmissible can give some indication and therefore be of value in predicting the court's approach, especially where an issue has not yet been subject to a court judgment.
[84] See also the Sentencing Appeals of *John Francis C* (1993) 14 Cr.App.R. (S) 562: *Harold Nicholas S* (1998) 1 Cr.App.R. (S) 261 which were cases involving elderly defendants where the approach of the Domestic Court has been to calculate the sentence by reference to the age and infirmities of the offender and then to rely on extra-judicial, executive discretion to enable release if there is a significant deterioration of the defendant's condition: see also *Togher v. U.K.* [1998] E.H.R.L.R. 636 where the defendant was a woman with a young child.
[85] *The Times*, January 30, 2002.

only for a commercial concern, the court would have to consider the above mentioned factors.

Further aspects which should be taken into account concerned the personality of the offender, the positive good character, the offences being out of character with normal behaviour and the indications that there would be no reoffending.

9. THE PROVISION OF FOOD

The general duty. The Prison Rules 1999 Section 24(1) provides as follows: **4–49** "Subject to any directions of the Secretary of State, no prisoner shall be allowed, except as authorised by the medical officer . . . to have any food other than that ordinarily provided". Section 24(2) provides "the food provided shall be wholesome, nutritious, well prepared and served, reasonably varied and sufficient in quantity".

No punishment can be imposed which takes the form or has the effect of withholding or limiting the right of a prisoner to receive such food. As the Prison Rules 1999, Rule 21 (the predecessor of Rule 24) stipulates "no . . . prisoner shall be given less food than is ordinarily provided except . . . upon the written recommendation of the medical officer". The rights of a prisoner to the provision of adequate food cannot be withdrawn or limited as a punishment or sanction or as a method of coercion.[86]

Although this provision is not to be found in Rule 24, its prohibition is implicit in a reading of Rule 24(2). Furthermore, it must be implicit in the Rules that the Governor is under an overriding and continuing obligation to prisoners in his care to take reasonable care to prevent prisoners suffering any serious harm.

The Governor has an overriding duty to care for those in his custody who have no means to obtain food (or clothing) save from him. The Governor must make immediately available for consumption food to prisoners who want it.[87] The Governor has no right or duty to force-feed prisoners on hunger strike and that a prisoner's autonomy in this regard must be respected as was held in *Secretary of State for the Home Department v. Robb.*[88]

Governor's Discretion. In *R. v. Governor of HMP Frankland ex p. Russell*   **4–50** *and Wharrie*,[89] the court considered the extent to which the prison authorities were obliged to provide nutrition to inmates in the context of Article 3. Mr Justice Lightman reasserted that Rule 24 of the Prison Rules 1999 must be fully respected but that adequate food does not necessarily mean three meals a day. The judge went on to observe: "What, however, is self evident is that the Governor should provide three meals a day unless and until he is satisfied that less than three meals is adequate to meet the prisoners' nutritional needs. Such a decision cannot be made lightly".

---

[86] See *R. and the Governor of HMP Frankland ex p. Russell and Wharrie* (2000) 1 W.L.R. 2027.
[87] Food includes drink, see Prison Rules 1999, Rule 24(4).
[88] [1995] Fam. 127.
[89] (2000) 1 W.L.R. 2027.

The Court in *HMP Frankland*[90] emphasised that no disciplinary sanction should involve the reduction of food to inmates.[91]

4–51   **Freely available.** The obligation of the Governor is to provide adequate food and is an obligation to make food immediately available to prisoners who want to eat it. Food is made immediately available if the prisoners are allowed free access to the place where it is to be collected or eaten.

If the Governor lays down conditions for obtaining such access, for example the wearing of prison clothes, so long as the prisoners are content to comply with those conditions, the Governor is to be seen as providing free access to them; but if the prisoners refuse to comply with those conditions, and for that reason are excluded from access, their free access to the food is withdrawn and a potential violation of Article 3 may be a consequence.

4–52   **Governor can decide time and place.** Subject to his overriding obligation to provide prisoners with adequate food, the Governor, in his exercise of his powers of management, is free to decide the times and places where food is to be made available and, for example, whether the cutlery shall be metal or otherwise.

4–53   **Governor can lay down reasonable conditions.** The Governor can lay down conditions which regulate access to the place where food is to be made available, for instance, requiring the wearing of clothes or particular clothes; and he may order prisoners to comply with such conditions, for instance, to get appropriately dressed; and he may treat disobedience to such an order as a disciplinary offence. But neither the imposition of such conditions nor the failure of a prisoner to comply with them (or with an order requiring compliance) can excuse the Governor from performance of the obligation to provide food to that prisoner or can detract from the fundamental right of the prisoner to adequate food. That does not mean that the Governor must accede to the prisoner's demands and, for example, allow the prisoner to wear other clothes or to go to the servery naked; but that, since the Governor cannot comply with his obligation to provide food in the ordinary way (*i.e.* in the servery), *he must adopt some alternative way.* Simply doing nothing is not an option.

4–54   **Provision of food to cell.** The obvious alternative is to provide food to the prisoner in his cell. This does not mean that he had to provide the same number of meals or the same food or provide food at the same time as to other prisoners. All that Rule 24 and the fundamental rights of the prisoner requires is that the prisoner is provided with adequate food which meets the requirements of Rule 24 and adequacy is not to be measured by the criterion of whether it is sufficient to ensure that the prisoner will survive or be unlikely to suffer any medical problems, rather it must meet the nutritional requirements of the prisoner and the

---

[90] (2001) 1 W.L.R. 2027.

[91] The days of bread and water are now consigned to the history books. In *McFeeley v. United Kingdom* [1980] 3 E.H.R.R. 161, prisoners were placed on a restricted diet as a disciplinary measure. The Commission in that case observed (at page 204), "That a restricted diet such as the above, coupled with an award of cellular confinement is a stringent and wholly undesirable form of punishment. However, in the present case it notes that it was employed for short periods in respect of both complainants and is thus of the opinion, though harsh, it does not amount to a sufficiently rigorous punishment where the level of physical or mental suffering or the degree of humiliation amounts to inhuman or degrading punishment in breach of Article 3".

food provided in the servery for prisoners is to be taken as meeting such requirement.

If a prisoner is to be provided with less food than, or different food from, that provided to other prisoners in the servery, care must be taken, and professional advice obtained, to ensure that the provision made is adequate to meet the requirements of the individual prisoner in question. *If the quality of the food must inevitably suffer because of the need to transport it to the cell, that is not a matter of which the prisoner can complain.*

Food and prison clothing.[92] The Governor may lay down policies for the   **4–55** treatment and feeding of prisoners unwilling to wear prison clothes, but the policy must be flexible and calculated to ensure in the case of each individual prisoner that he receives adequate nourishment and, if any question can arise whether he will receive adequate nourishment, must provide safeguards to protect the prisoner's health.

In *HMP Frankland*, the Governor laid down policies for the treatment and feeding of prisoners unwilling to wear prison clothes, limiting provision of one meal a day whilst they remained in segregation. This operated on an arbitrary basis irrespective of the impact on the individual prisoner. The court were firmly of the view, particularly in the absence of any facility to monitor this regime that the policy was unlawful and could not be authorised by the Prison Rules and in view of the possible indefinite duration of the segregation of a prisoner in the unit may well have breached the fundamental rights protected by Article 3.

In coming to the conclusion that this was a potential violation of Article 3, the High court emphasised that the regime arbitrarily cut down for an indeterminate period to one third the provision of food to the prisoners effected without any or any proper or sufficient regard to the entitlement of prisoners under Rule 24 to adequate food. The regime was inflexible and it failed to provide the elementary health safeguards which such a reduction in provision, if otherwise lawful, would require.[93]

10. ASSAULTS BY PRISON OFFICERS

The general rule. Any gratuitous assault by prison officers will be in breach   **4–56** of Article 3. The principles were enunciated in *Tomasi v. France*[94] where although the assault had taken place whilst in police custody, the principles were clear, that Article 3 had been violated and that such treatment was sufficiently serious to be inhuman and degrading.[95]

Breach of trust. A prison officer who assaults a prisoner commits a breach of   **4–57** trust not only against the officer but against society itself. In the joined cases of

---

[92] See *Hurtado v. Switzerland*, unreported, A/280-A(1994) where the authority's refusal to allow a suspect to change their clothing which had been soiled by the suspect's own defecation was held to be capable of being degrading and contrary to Article 3.

[93] This is just one example of how conditions in segregation units and Place Supervision Centres may be challenged under Article 3. In March 2000 the Chief Inspector of Prisons criticised the "*extreme levels of sensory deprivation at Woodhill Close Supervision Centre in Milton Keynes*".

[94] (1993) 15 E.H.R.R. 1.

[95] The applicant received compensation of 700,000 French francs plus costs.

R. v. Fryer, Nicol and Lawrie,[96] in the Court of Appeal, Mr Justice Newman emphasised that prisoners were entitled to the protection of the law from assault on them by prison officers. The onerous responsibilities of prison officers had to be discharged in a way which was not a perversion of the system. In this case a remand prisoner at Wormwood Scrubs prison was subjected to a series of sustained attacks by the appellant prison officers.

11. SEGREGATION AND SOLITARY CONFINEMENT

4–58   **Segregation Units.** There is nothing degrading or inhuman about the locating of prisoners in a segregation unit.[97] Isolation of detainees is often justified by the prison authorities on the grounds of discipline, security of particularly high risk prisoners, to maintain order within the prison and consequently the prevention of crime within that prison structure. Case law in this area endorses that within a prison regime such forms of discipline are acceptable although what will be tolerated by the Convention will be a matter of degree.

    In the case of *Ensslin, Baader and Raspe v. The Federal Republic of Germany*,[98] the simultaneous use of sensory isolation and complete social isolation of the applicant's was deemed unjustifiable. The court in considering the facts of this case which hinged upon terrorist offences were of the view that the two methods of treatment employed could ultimately destroy the personality and as such would not be tolerated. The facts of *Ensslin, Baader and Raspe* were extreme and were a reaction to the terrorist activities of the Red Army Faction in the late 1970s.[99]

    It is therefore clear that solitary confinement and segregation of high security prisoners will not automatically breach Article 3. This includes prisoners who are put upon Rule 43. In *X v. United Kingdom*,[1] the detainee served 760 days on Rule 43. His cell was illuminated 24 hours a day. The Commission took note of the fact that he was able at times to mix with other category A inmates and thus held no breach of Article 3.[2] It is, as is often the case, in a consideration of Article 3 a matter of degree as to whether the treatment of a detainee in segregation is to be considered as a violation.

Reference should be made to the CPT's observations:

> "51. It is also very important for prisoners to maintain reasonably good contact with the outside world. Above all, a prisoner must be given the means of safeguarding his relationships with his family and close friends.
>
>   The guiding principle should be the promotion of contact with the outside world; any limitations upon such contact should be based exclusively on security concerns of an appreciable nature or resource considerations.
>
> 56. The CPT pays particular attention to prisoners held for whatever reason (for disciplinary purposes; as a result of their 'dangerousness' or their 'troublesome'

---

[96] *The Times*, April 10, 2002.
[97] *McFeeley v. United Kingdom* [1980] 3 E.H.R.R. 161.
[98] 14 D.R. 64.
[99] See also *Krocher & Moller v. Switzerland*, 34 D.R. 24.
[1] 21 D.R. 95.
[2] Category A prisoners are divided into three sub-categories: standard risk, high risk and extreme risk.

behaviour; in the interests of a criminal investigation; at their own request) under conditions akin to solitary confinement.

The principle of proportionality requires that a balance be struck between the requirements of the case and the application of a solitary confinement-type regime, which is a step that can have very harmful consequences for the person concerned. Solitary confinement can, in certain circumstances, amount to inhuman and degrading treatment; in any event all forms of solitary confinement should be as short as possible.

In the event of such a regime being imposed or applied on request, an essential safeguard is that whenever the prisoner concerned, or a prison officer on the prisoner's behalf, requests a medical doctor, such a doctor should be called without delay with a view to carrying out a medical examination of the prisoner. The results of this examination, including an account of the prisoner's physical and mental condition as well as, if need be, the foreseeable consequences of continued isolation, should be set out in a written statement to be forwarded to the competent authorities."

It should be emphasised that exclusion of a prisoner from the main prison community is not without further factors a violation of Article 3.

Denial of access to lawyers and to close family. It is an important principle **4–59** that a prisoner's unimpeded right of access to a solicitor for the purpose of receiving advice and assistance in connection with the possible institution of civil proceedings in the courts form an inseparable part of the right of access to the courts themselves.[3]

In June 1995, the Home Secretary announced the immediate introduction of a closed visits regime for Exceptional Risk category A prisoners. It is a category into which detainees regarded as IRA terrorists would ordinarily fall. The lawfulness of this regime was challenged in *Patrick Hugh Sean Martin*.[4]

Lord Justice Rose, dismissing the application in the Divisional Court, observed that:

"This judgment is not to be understood as recognising a power in the Home Secretary to impose a general closed visits regime on other categories of prisoners . . . nor do I mean that closed visits can necessarily lawfully continue indefinitely in relation to these applicants.

This case relates to the order made in the circumstances prevailing in June 1995; changed circumstances may require a changed regime".

The facts of this case centred around the applicant's solicitor who was very properly pressing for greater and easier facilities to interview and take instructions from the applicant. He received a response from the prison which conceded extremely little. At a plea and directions hearing before the trial judge at the Central Criminal Court on November 28, 1996, the judge expressed the view that every effort should be made for the defence to have adequate access to their clients. But again, little headway was achieved with the prison.

When this case came before the Lord Chief Justice in the Court of Appeal, it was observed that: "criticisms of the closed visits regime has been expressed

---

[3] See *Golder v. U.K.* 1 E.H.R.R.: *R. v. Secretary of State for the Home Department ex p. Anderson* [1984] Q.B. 778 at 794.
[4] [1998] EWCA Crim 2336, July 14, 1998.

both on medical grounds and by Amnesty International,[5] and in a report of the United Nations Special Rapporteur. The culmination of this criticism appeared to come earlier this year when it was announced that the mandatory closed visits regime had been abolished. This, however, was too late to avail the applicant and the other defendants, who, from their arrest in July 1996, had been subjected to it, only relieved by the decision following the application for judicial review".[6]

It was argued by counsel for the applicant that the facilities finally provided for legal advisors to see their clients prevented the proper relationship between lawyer and client being established, seriously impeding the proper preparation of the applicant's case and putting him under severe emotional pressure as to lead him to wish for the case to be concluded so that he could have freer access to his wife. It was contended by the applicant that he was induced to give instructions to his counsel that an adjournment should not be sought and to do nothing to explore the possibilities of obtaining further relief by way of judicial review.

The Lord Chief Justice confirmed that it was essential that a defendant facing trial on a very serious charge should have adequate opportunities to take legal advice and prepare his defence. Nevertheless, the Lord Chief Justice observed the applicant did not seek any adjournment "for whatever reasons".

It was submitted in the perfected grounds of appeal that "the conditions in which the applicant was held in Belmarsh Special Secure Unit were in violation of international Conventions and amounted to inhuman and degrading treatment contrary to law. In particular, the denial of proper access to defence lawyers was a gross interference with the administration of justice and rendered the subsequent trial unfair to the applicant. Denial of the possibility of any physical contact with his family for a prolonged period imposed an unacceptable pressure upon the applicant. As a result of this pressure he began his trial without adequate preparation and made decisions . . . including the decision whether or not to give evidence . . . within that context".

Insofar as the applicant argued inhuman and degrading treatment and preyed in aid denial of proper access to defence lawyers, the court were of the view that the nature of the defence disclosed imposed "a much less stringent duty on those advising the applicant to comb through the fine detail of what the various witnesses said that they saw". It seems therefore that in a complex case of identity, for instance, where a client's input may be vital in the preparation stage of a case, a finding of violation may be more likely. As such, in the circumstances of this particular case, lack of legal access was not considered to have reached the threshold of inhuman or degrading treatment.

4–60   **Correspondence.** Authorised intrusion of a prisoner's correspondence must be the minimum necessary to ensure that the correspondence is in true bona fides

---

[5] Influential pressure groups such as Amnesty International have campaigned for an end to closed (non-contact) visits, on the ground that in their view they seriously impede remand prisoners' rights to a fair trial, undermine the defendant's capacity to prepare his defence, restrict the facilities for the preparation of the prisoner's defence through "closed" legal visits and jeopardise the maintenance of relationships between prisoners and their families. See Amnesty International Press Release, 8 August 1997.

[6] See para. 20 of the Report.

legal correspondence. In *Solosky v. The Queen*,[7] the court explained this principle in concrete terms. It stated:

"In my view the 'minimum extent necessary to establish whether it is properly the subject of solicitor-client privilege' should be interpreted in such manner that:

(1) the contents of an envelope may be inspected for contraband;

(2) in limited circumstances, the communication may be read to ensure that it, in fact, contains a confidential communication between a solicitor and client written for the purpose of seeking or giving legal advice;

(3) the letter should only be read if there are reasonable and probable grounds for believing the contrary, and then only to the extent necessary to determine the bona fides of the communication;

(4) the authorised penitentiary official who examines the envelope, upon ascertaining the envelope contains nothing in breach of security, is under a duty at law to maintain the confidentiality of the communication".

Again, the court in *Leech* supported this statement of principle. Further assistance can be obtained from the Prison Rules.

Rule 37A[8] reads:

"(1) A prisoner who is a party to any legal proceedings may correspond with his legal advisor in connection with the proceedings and unless the Governor has reason to suppose that any such correspondence contains a matter not relating to the proceedings it shall not be read or stopped under Rule 33(3) of these Rules.

(2) A prisoner shall on request be provided with any writing materials necessary for the purposes of paragraph (1) of this Rule.

(3) Subject to any directions given in the particular case by the Secretary of State, a registered medical practitioner selected by or on behalf of such a prisoner as aforesaid shall be afforded reasonable facilities for examining him in connection with the proceedings, and may do so out of hearing but in sight of an officer.

(4) Subject to any directions of the Secretary of State, a prisoner may correspond with a solicitor for the purpose of obtaining legal advice concerning any course of action in relation to which the prisoner may become a party to civil proceedings or for the purpose of instructing the solicitor to issue such proceedings".

Rule 37A was added to the Prison Rules as a result of the decision in the European Court of Human Rights in *Golder v. United Kingdom*.[9] Rule 37 refers to a prisoner who is a party to legal proceedings. The Rules refer to legal proceedings which are already duly constituted.

Contact with family. It was also argued by the applicant that the detainee had **4–61** been deprived of any physical contact with his family for a prolonged period. This too was not considered to be sufficient as to violate Article 3. This seems to be consistent with earlier authorities which established that Article 3 will not

---

[7] (1979) 105 D.L.R. (3d) 745. At page 760 Dickson J. described the impact of a right to read a prisoner's correspondence as follows: "Nothing is more likely to have a 'chilling' effect upon the frank and free exchange and disclosure of confidences, which should characterise the relationship between inmate and counsel, than knowledge that what has been written will be read by some third person, and perhaps used against the inmate at a later date". The court in *R. v. Home Secretary ex p. Leech* (1994) Q.B. 198 agreed with this statement of principle.

[8] As inserted by the Prison (Amendment) Rules 1972 (S.I. 1972 No. 1860) and 1976 (S.I. 1976 No. 503).

[9] (1975) 1 E.H.R.R. 524.

have been violated if the prison authorities refused to transfer a prisoner from one prison to another in order to facilitate visits by a relative.

The CPT at paragraph 57 of its Report[10] deals with this aspect:

> "The transfer of troublesome prisoners is another practice of interest to the CPT. Certain prisoners are extremely difficult to handle, and the transfer of such a prisoner to another establishment can sometimes prove necessary.
>
> However, the continuous moving of a prisoner from one establishment to another can have very harmful effects on his psychological and physical well being. Moreover, a prisoner in such a position will have difficulty in maintaining appropriate contacts with his family and lawyer. The overall effect on the prisoner of successive transfers could under certain circumstances amount to inhuman and degrading treatment."

In *Wakefield v. United Kingdom*,[11] a prisoner applicant requested transfer from a prison in England to a prison in Scotland so he could have visits from his fiancee. The prison refused and the European Court did not consider that this refusal was in breach of Article 3.[12]

4–62   **Every citizen has a right of unimpeded access to a court.** This right applies to prisoners as much as any other citizen. The right was described by Lord Wilberforce in *Raymond v. Honey*[13] as a "basic right". The Court of Appeal in the case of *R. v. Home Secretary ex p. Leech*[14] observed that:

> "Even in our unwritten Constitution it must rank as a constitutional right".[15]

4–63   **There is no right to be transferred to a prison of choice.** It is well established that a prisoner has no right as such under the Convention to choose the place of his confinement and that the separation of a detained prisoner from his family and the hardship resulting from it are the inevitable consequences of detention.[16]

In *William Ballantyne v. United Kingdom*,[17] the Commission noted that the applicant's location in a secure prison further north was a result of his history of violence and further offences. The Commission also noted that the authorities had made arrangements for transfers for accumulated visits and escorted home visits.

In the light of those circumstances, the Commission found that insofar as the detention of the applicant hundreds of miles from his family may be construed as an interference with his right to respect for his family life, it was justified as being in accordance with the law unnecessary in a democratic society for the prevention of disorder and crime within the meaning of Article 8(2).

4–64   **Culmination and duration.** Recent authorities indicate that two matters are vital, the cumulation of deprivations inflicted upon the detainee, such as sensory

---

[10] CPT/Inf. (92)3.

[11] 66 D.R. 251.

[12] The situation is a little more complex when one considers whether a mother and baby should be separated, see *Togher v. U.K.* [1998] E.H.R.L.R. 637.

[13] [1983] 1 A.C. 1 at 13.

[14] [1994] Q.B. 198.

[15] At p. 210.

[16] See Case No. 5229/71, Dec. 5.10.72, collection 42p 14, No. 5712/72, Decision of July 15, 1974, collection 46p 112 and No. 9054/80, Dec. 8.10.82, Br. 30p 113.

[17] Application No. 14462/88) (Commission Admissibility Decision of April 12, 1991.

and social isolation, rather than say, sensory or social isolation, and the amount of time that the detainee has to suffer these deprivations. Furthermore, the Commission will take into account the purpose or object of the deprivation. As is common in cases involving the segregation of prisoners, the individuals involved are either convicted or suspected of terrorist offences, and that the object of their segregated confinement was that of security. This is considered to be acceptable.

Destruction of personality and breaking of resistance. The line will be **4–65** crossed if it can be found that the conditions inflicted upon the detainees had deliberately subjected them to a range of physical and mental suffering designed to punish them, to destroy their personality or break down their resistance. If medical evidence is provided to the Commission which can substantiate that the conditions destroyed the personality or caused severe mental and physical suffering, or would have done so, then a breach of Article 3 can be substantiated.

In *Krocher and Moller v. Switzerland*,[18] the total isolation of the detainees lasted for the first month after which they had contact with their lawyers and their family again. The Commission in that case were at pains to point out that the conditions were then gradually relaxed. The reasons for this restrictive detention was that of security and the effects could not have been considered, according to the Commission, to have destroyed the personality or caused severe mental and physical suffering. As such, the Article 3 argument failed.

12. Self Imposed Deprivations

Generally. The fact that the person concerned has brought the treatment upon **4–66** himself may be a relevant consideration.[19] Nevertheless, this fact will not automatically absolve the State of its obligations under Article 3.[20]

In *McFeeley*, the applicants were prisoners in Northern Ireland who in pursuit of the goal of achieving the status of political prisoners protested against the requirement to wear prison uniform and to work, and as part of this protest engaged in a strategy involving "a self-inflicted debasement and humiliation to an almost sub-human degree".[21] Because of the prisoner's protest over clothing, the prison authorities imposed conditions as to their access of washing and toilet facilities with which the prisoners refused to comply which resulted in them stopping washing and remaining in their cells to urinate and defecate. This became what is known as "a dirty protest".

The applicants complained that their treatment by the prison authorities constituted a breach of various articles of the Convention, including Article 3. The Commission were of the view that the undoubted harsh conditions of detention which developed from the applicant's decision not to wear prison uniform and use the toilet and washing facilities provided and other self-imposed deprivations associated with their protest, cannot engage the responsibility of the respondent Government.

---

[18] 34 D.R. 24.
[19] See *McFeeley v. United Kingdom* (1981) 3 E.H.R.R. 161 at 198.
[20] See *X v. United Kingdom* [1982] 28 D.R. 5 at 32.
[21] At p. 196.

The Commission went on to reason that it must also consider whether the Convention imposed upon the Government an obligation to accept the demands of the applicants not to wear prison uniform or work in the face of a dispute which continues to deteriorate in such a drastic way to the detriment of everyone concerned. They did not consider that such an obligation existed in *McFeeley.*[22]

4–67 **Hunger strikes.** An adult of sound mind and capacity has a specific right of self-determination which entitles him to refuse nutrition and hydration. Thus, when an adult prisoner refuses all nutrition and medical experts agree that he is of sound mind and fully understands the consequences of his decision to refuse food and that death will result, there maintains a prima facie right of the prisoner to continue his actions, it is not diminished when he becomes a prisoner.[23] This must be balanced against potentially countervailing State interests in preserving life, preventing suicide and protecting innocent third parties.[24]

4–68 **State's refusal to comply with Convention.** Matters may be significantly different if a detainee is protesting about a deprivation caused as a result of a contracting Government's refusal to honour an obligation under the Convention. One presumes that because the Commission were at pains to point out that in *McFeeley* the Government had no obligation to accept the demands of the applicants not to wear prison uniform or work, then no violation would be considered. Had the applicants been deprived of food, for instance, and as a result of such deprivation protested, then it is arguable that the State would be held responsible for any self-inflicted inhuman or degrading conditions.

4–69 **Article 3 can be violated even if prisoners' actions are unlawful.** Whether or not the prisoners are engaged in what is regarded as an unlawful challenge to the authority of the prison administration, Article 3 could still bite.

Although short of an obligation to accept the applicant's demands, the Convention requires that the prison authorities with due regard to the ordinary and reasonable requirements of imprisonment, exercise the custodial authority to safeguard the health and well-being of all prisoners, including those engaged in protest insofar as may be possible in the circumstances. Such a requirement makes it necessary for the prison authorities to keep under constant review their reaction to recalcitrant prisoners engaged in a developing and protracted protest.

4–70 **Prison authorities should resolve deadlock rather than punish.** The attitude of the prison authority to the behaviour of prisoners is also important. In *McFeeley* the Commission went on to express concern at the adoption by the authorities of an inflexible approach more concerned to punish offenders against prison discipline than to explore ways of resolving such a serious deadlock, but

---

[22] At p. 196.
[23] See *Secretary of State for the Home Department v. Robb* (1995) Fam. 127.
[24] See also *Thor v. Supreme Court* (1993) 855 P 2d 375 where the prison authorities failed in their application for an order authorising force feeding of a quadriplegic prison inmate who had determined to refuse food and medical treatment necessary to maintain his life. The conclusion of the court was that the right of self-determination prevailed subject to certain State interests. This balancing exercise was further articulated in the United States case *Re Caulk* (1984) 480 A 2d 93. This case observed the need to preserve internal order, discipline and security within the confines of the gaol.

in view of the magnitude of the institutional problems posed by the protest and the precautions taken, it was held that the failure by the authorities did not amount to a breach of Article 3.[25]

Non-deliberate behaviour. Sometimes the mental or physical health of a   **4–71**
detainee deteriorates through no fault of his own. In *Hilton v. United Kingdom*,[26] the detainee's mental state of health deteriorated so markedly that he was reduced to an animal-like state whereby he would roll around in his own excrement. The facts of this case indicate a detainee who would have been far better served by hospital treatment than in a prison.[27] A mark of the prison's inability to cope with such troubled detainees, their response was an unnecessarily rigorous regime of discipline. Because the Commission were of the view that the prison authority had taken some positive measures to assist him, no violation of Article 3 was found. Perhaps a more modern approach can be found in the four dissenting opinions of the Commissioners.

13. HANDCUFFING

Should not debase or humiliate. The case of *Raninen v. Finland*[28] clearly   **4–72**
lays down that there will be no violation of Article 3 if a detainee is handcuffed in such a way as is unnecessarily and unlawful. Simply transporting a prisoner in handcuffs back to a prison was not considered to have breached the minimum level of severity.[29]

The courts findings may be different if an individual is taken in handcuffs whilst in the custody of prison authorities to a hospital for treatment. Furthermore, if a detainee is handcuffed whilst receiving treatment or indeed handcuffed to a hospital bed, then it is highly arguable that Article 3 will have been breached when one considers the guidelines in *Raninen v. Finland*. In establishing that the handcuffing is unnecessary and unlawful, a causal link could be made between that treatment and any psychological problem which could have been caused to the detainee as a result of this form of restraint in hospital. Furthermore, it may be far easier to prove that the use of handcuffs was aimed at

---

[25] See also *T v. U.K.* (1983) 49 D and R 5, which concerned an analogous situation, namely the continued right under Article 10(1) of a prisoner who refused to wear prison clothes to "receive information" notwithstanding that his conduct led to an exceptional degree of segregation from human contact. The Commission held that the authorities could properly prevent him obtaining access to the library when undressed, but that this did not justify the restriction on his access to newspapers and periodicals in his cell. The Commission held (at para. 49) that authorities had to adopt a flexible approach to disciplinary problems where it becomes clear that an individual or group shows an intransigent resolve against the disciplinary system; and it went on to say: "While it is true that (a degree of) segregation was necessary, in the interest of good order and discipline (Rule 43 of the Prison Rules [1964]), this alone does not mean that the restrictions on the applicant's access to information, can equally be considered as necessary until Article 10, para. 2, since his access to information itself was not relevant to the good order of the prison even though it might not have been possible for the applicant to collect books or other publications in person". The Commission went on to conclude that Article 10 required the prison authorities during the period of the applicant's segregation (including punishment periods) to consider alternative means which were administratively practical to ensure continued access by the applicant to newspapers and periodicals.
[26] (1981) 3 E.H.R.R. 104.
[27] See *Aerts v. Belgium* (2000) 29 E.H.R.R. 50.
[28] [1998] E.H.R.L.R. 344.
[29] See *Raninen v. Finland* (1998) 26 E.H.R.R. 563.

debasing or humiliating a detainee when they are handcuffed during medical treatment or to a hospital bed than simply when they are being handcuffed in transfer from one place to another place of detention.

4–73 **Mental health institutions.** The same principles apply to mental health institutions as to prisons. In *Sylvain Dhoest v. Belgium*,[30] the principal issue was whether the applicant's conditions of detention and treatment in the custodial mental health institution amounted to a breach of Article 3. He complained that he spent most of his time in isolation. The Commission repeated the criteria relating to solitary confinement in prisons and added that:

> "The same reasoning applies mutatis mutandis to persons who have been committed to a mental hospital in the framework of criminal proceedings".

4–74 **Responsibility of judicial authorities.** Judicial authorities are primarily responsible for the care of detainees. In *Price v. United Kingdom*,[31] the court unanimously found that there had been a violation of Article 3. The primary responsibility for the treatment of Adele Price was that of the judicial authorities who committed her to an immediate term of imprisonment for contempt of court without at the very least ensuring in advance that her special needs could be met by adequate facilities whilst in prison. Treating Price like others, particularly in light of her sleeping requirements, also constituted discrimination, as Price's disabilities are not easily overlooked. The treatment to which Price was subjected violated the entire spirit of the Standard Minimum Rules for the Treatment for Prisoners.

14. CLOSE BODY SEARCHES

4–75 **Depends on the facts of each case.** At times the authorities consider it appropriate to strip-search or intimately examine a detainee. This behaviour was considered in *McFeeley v. United Kingdom*.[32] In that case it was argued by the prison authority that detainees had previously been found with razor blades, flints, matches and cigarette lighters in the recta and that they had used these objects to disrupt prison discipline.

Once again, it as held that close body searches, which on the facts of *McFeeley* involved the prisoner squatting naked while a mirror was put up close to his anus did not breach the minimum level of severity. In coming to this finding, the Commission emphasised that the prison authorities had attempted to reduce the degree of humiliation and had actively attempted to provide safeguards against abuse. The Commission were also persuaded by the fact that the prisoners must have been aware by reason of their various campaigns of disruption that a substantial security threat had been posed. These two factors taken together allowed the Commission to reject an Article 3 violation.[33]

---

[30] Application No. 10448/83, Report of the Commission.
[31] (2002) 34 E.H.R.R. 53.
[32] (1981) 3 E.H.R.R. 161.
[33] See *AB v. Switzerland* 80-B.D.R. 66 which lays down that when a prisoner is forced to provide a urine sample for drug testing there is no breach of Article 3. One can imply from this that the result would be equally the same if any other bodily substance or fluid was taken from a prisoner for that purpose.

In *Valasinas v. Lithuania*,[34] the applicant was a Lithuanian prisoner placed in the Separate Segregation Unit of a prison. He complained about his conditions of detention, alleging that they were overcrowded and unsanitary. He also complained in particular about one body search which took place in front of a female officer, after he had a personal visit. He was ordered to strip, his body including his testicles and sexual organs were searched by male officers who did not wear gloves. The officers then searched the applicant's food without washing their hands. The applicant was also ordered to do sit-ups to establish whether he had concealed anything in his anus. He alleged that this was done to embarrass him in front of a female officer.

The court stated that the absence of any record of an enquiry by the prison doctor into the applicant's complaints at the material time about this search shows a reluctance on the part of the prison authorities to investigate the incident properly. It concluded that the circumstances of the search showed a clear lack of respect for the applicant and diminished in effect his human dignity. It stated:

> "It must have left him with feelings of anguish and inferiority capable of humiliating and debasing him".

This amounted to a violation of Article 3.

Where a detainee is strip-searched for no apparently compelling reason, the courts will not be slow to find a violation of Article 3. In *Rawanczuk v. Poland*,[35] the court considered that given the applicant's personality, his peaceful behaviour during detention, and the fact that he was not charged with a violent crime and had no previous convictions, it had not been shown that there were grounds on which to fear that he would behave violently. It had not consequently been shown that the body search had been justified.

The court observed:

> "Against the above background, the court observes that the applicant was ordered to strip naked in front of a group of prison guards. No compelling reasons have been adduced to find that this order was, in the light of the applicant's personality and all the other circumstances of the case, necessary and justified by security reason.
>
> In addition, whilst strip searches may be necessary on occasions to ensure prison security or prevent disorder in prisons, they must be conducted in an appropriate manner. In the present case, the prison's guards verbally abused and derided the applicant. Their behaviour was intended to cause in the applicant feelings of humiliation and inferiority. This, in the court's view, showed a lack of respect for the applicant's human dignity.
>
> Given that such treatment was afforded to a person who, as stated above, wished to exercise his right to vote within the framework of arrangements specifically provided for in Wroclaw Prison for persons detained on remand, and in view of the absence of persuasive justification therefore, the court is of the view that in the present case such behaviour which humiliated and debased the applicant, amounted to degrading treatment contrary to Article 3" (paras 58 and 59).

Review of the applicant's complaints. Again, in *Valasinas v. Lithuania*,[36] the **4–76** applicant was subjected to disciplinary penalties including cleaning duties, temporary restrictions on his socio-economic rights, restrictions on his freedom of

---

[34] Application No. 44559/98.
[35] Application No. 25196/94: Judgment of November 15, 2001.
[36] Application No. 44591/98.

movement, or recorded disciplinary warnings. The court concluded that these did not attain the minimum level of severity as the applicant had not produced medical evidence to show that he had suffered any pain or distress. The review of the applicant's complaints at the executive level and by the Ombudsman satisfied the requirements of Article 3. It seems that as long as the complaint is properly reviewed at executive level, then an Article 3 violation will not be maintained. Although it is right to point out that review of the Ombudsman is not always considered to be adequate, depending upon the powers available to him.

4–77   **Remand prisoners.** The European Court of Human Rights have recognised that for remand prisoners there is a presumption of innocence and that this should be respected in custody as well as in court. The case of *Rawanczuk v. Poland*[37] concerned an applicant who complained under Article 3 about his treatment whilst on remand. He complained that when he requested to vote in the Parliamentary Elections as there were voting facilities for detainees in the prison, he was taken by a prison guard to the guards' room. There, he was told by a group of four guards that in order to be allowed to vote,[38] he must get undressed and undergo a body search. The applicant removed all his clothing except his underwear. The guards ridiculed him, exchanged humiliating remarks about his body and abused him verbally. He was ordered to strip naked. He refused to do so and repeatedly requested permission to vote without a body search. This was refused. The applicant was taken back to his cell without being allowed to vote. This also happened to another group of prisoners in the prison when they too requested to vote.

The court stressed that the applicant had not been convicted and therefore enjoyed a presumption of innocence. This did not just apply to his procedural rights in the criminal proceedings, but also to the legal regime governing the rights of detained persons, including the manner in which a person should be treated by prison guards.

4–78   **Discrimination against prisoners.** The Commission has found that the position of prisoners and persons outside prison cannot be considered as analogous for the purposes of Article 14 of the Convention. Prisoners, who are detained, inevitably suffer a lack of choice or freedom as to the medical advice to which they have access. The applicant's situation in the case of *Lockwood v. United Kingdom*[39] therefore was not considered comparable to that of a person who is not detained.

---

[37] Application No. 25196/94: judgment of November 15, 2001.
[38] The court considered that it was doubtful whether the exercise of the basic right to vote by people detained on remand should be subject to any special conditions other than those dictated by normal requirements of prison security. The court did not find that it was justified that such conditions include an order to strip naked in front of a group of prison guards. The court noted that the Government had pointed simply to the lawfulness of the measures complained of, but had not addressed the question of how the relevant provisions of domestic law were applied in practice at the material time in the context of voting in Parliamentary Elections organised in prisons and detention centres. The Government had not argued or shown that the measure was applied uniformly to all detainees in the detention centre on that day.
[39] Application No. 18824/91.

CHAPTER 5

IMMIGRATION

Bullet points. To establish an Article 3 violation, there are nine considera- **5–01**
tions:

- Substantial grounds must be shown for believing that the person to be extradited, if extradited, faces a real risk of being subjected to torture or to inhuman or to degrading treatment or punishment in the Requesting Country—see *Jabari v. Turkey* (2000) 29 E.H.R.R. CD 178; *Ahmed v. Austria* (1997) 24 E.H.R.R. 278;

- The personal record or antecedents of an applicant is irrelevant—see *Ahmed v. Austria* (1997) 24 E.H.R.R. 278;

- The court can take account of the conditions in the Requesting State—see *Chahal v. United Kingdom* (1997) 23 E.H.R.R. 413;

- Past persecution of the applicant is relevant—see *R. v. Secretary of State for the Home Department ex p. Dahmas, Independent*, January 24, 2000;

- Isolated incidents of ill-treatment may not be enough—see *R. v. Immigration Appeal Tribunal ex p. Cosgun*, unreported, 1999;

- The need for medical treatment is not conclusive—see *Bensaid v. United Kingdom* (2001) 33 E.H.R.R. 10;

- The possibility of internal flight can mitigate violation of Article 3—see *Hilal v. United Kingdom* (2001) 33 E.H.R.R. 2;

- No applicant will be deported to face a possibility of capital punishment—see *Jabari v. Turkey* (2000) 29 E.H.R.R. CD 178;

- It may be sufficient to belong to a particular social group—see *R. v. Immigration Appeal Tribunal ex p. Shah and Islam* (1999) 2 A.C. 629.

1. AN ABSOLUTE RIGHT

State cannot derogate responsibility. The prohibition against torture, inhu- **5–02**
man and degrading treatment under Article 3 is of such fundamental importance
that no State can derogate its responsibility under that Article. In short, there is
no passing of responsibility from one State to another.

In *IT v. United Kingdom*,[1] the European Court of Human Rights held that the
Secretary of State could not derogate his responsibility under the Dublin Convention 1990. *T*, a Sri Lankan Tamil, was refused asylum in Germany and claimed
asylum in the United Kingdom. The Secretary of State rejected the claim and

---

[1] [2000] 1 N.L.R. 211.

certified the case under the Asylum and Immigration Act 1996 Section 2 ordering his removal to Germany which acknowledged responsibility for his claim under the Dublin Convention 1990. The court held that the United Kingdom could not derogate its responsibility to investigate by relying upon those provisions.[2]

5–03   **The State's right to control entry.** Every contracting State has a right to control entry, residence and expulsion of aliens although the court's main consideration must always be whether there has been or potentially will be ill-treatment of the applicant if deported rather than the imperatives of the State.

In *Chahal v. United Kingdom*,[2a] the court held that the European Convention on Human Rights absolutely prohibited torture or inhuman or degrading treatment, regardless of the circumstances of the case, and although the court understood the problems faced by States in the fight against terrorism, the main consideration in the decision was not national security but the possibility of ill-treatment of an applicant if deported. Although States have a right to control who cross and live within their borders, there are significant restrictions to how this can be exercised.

2. ASYLUM SEEKERS

5–04   **The United Nations Convention Relating To The Status Of Refugees.** Asylum will be granted where the applicant fulfils the criteria in the 1951 Convention[3] unless the applicant may reasonably be expected to seek asylum in a third country.[4] The 1951 Convention sets out the criteria which must be fulfilled if an individual is to be granted Convention refugee status[5]:

"Article 1A(2)   Definition of the term 'refugee'

A For the purposes of the present Convention, the term 'refugee' shall apply to any person who: . . . (2) as a result of events occurring before January 1 1951 and owing to well founded fear of being persecuted for reasons of race, religion, nationality, membership of a particular social group or political opinion, is outside the country of his nationality and is unable or, owing to such fear, is unwilling to avail himself of the protection of that country; or who, not having a nationality and being outside the country of his former habitual residence as a result of such events, is unable or, owing to such fear, is unwilling to return to it".

---

[2] Nevertheless the court held that the U.K. was not in breach of Article 3 on the basis that asylum seekers including Tamils, faced with non-state persecution had been given protection by Germany under the Aliens Act 1990 Section 53(6) and that, although Germany set rigorous standards for asylum seekers, the threshold was not unreasonably high so that T's asylum application would be given due consideration by Germany.

[2a] (1997) 23 E.H.R.R. 413.

[3] See also the 1967 Protocol.

[4] Or the Dublin Convention applies.

[5] See also *El Ali v. Secretary of State for the Home Department*, Times Law Reports, August 12, 2002, a case in the Court of Appeal which held that children of Palestinian Arabs who came within the definition of those to be treated automatically as refugees when seeking asylum did not have the same status and had to establish a well-founded fear of persecution. Lord Justice Laws analysed the United Nations Convention, Article 1D, and rejected the wide interpretation of it in relation to children and stated that the Immigration Appeal Tribunal's more restrictive interpretation was correct.

There is no universally accepted definition of 1951 Convention "*persecution*", however, it seems that persecution is to be distinguished from punishment,[6] but it is clear that a threat to life or freedom on account of an action is always persecution. Furthermore, there may be occasions when excessive punishment may constitute persecution (see the United Nations Handbook on Procedures and Criteria for Determining Refugee Status, a practical guide based on the knowledge accumulated by the High Commissioners Office, which although it does not enjoy the force of law is frequently referred to by domestic authorities and the Council of the European Union has acknowledged it as being "a valuable aid to member States in determining refugee status".[7]

When considering whether the applicant has a well founded fear of persecution in accordance with the 1951 Convention, the presence of fear is tested on a subjective basis and will require an evaluation of the applicant's statements. However, a subjective fear alone is not sufficient and that fear must be measured alongside the factual situation as it presently exists. The United Nations Handbook[8] observes that an evaluation of this subjective element is inseparable from an assessment of the personality of the applicant.[9]

There is also an objective element when the State should refer to the prevailing political and legal situation within the applicant's country of origin.

Comparisons with Article 3. Article 3 is considerably broader in its protec-   **5–05** tion than the Refugee Convention.

This is so in various ways:

- There are no exclusions from Article 3's protection, on national security grounds or on grounds of commission of particularly serious crimes;

- There is no need to show that the harm feared is causally linked to the applicant's race, religion, nationality, membership of a particular social group or political opinion, to establish Article 3 violation;

- Article 3 has no requirement of "persecution". So a real risk of exposure to "wide spread clan and sub-clan killing and torture" in a civil war context[10] has not been held constitute persecution unless there was "differential impact" and so not to give rise to a good refugee claim, would, conversely, engage Article 3.

- For the same reason, an Article 3 route is available where Convention refugee status might be excluded on the basis that the harm feared was "prosecution for a common law offence" or attributable to "peace-keeping functions" or without the requisite degree of repetition or continuity to constitute persecution,[11] or where there might be harsh punishment (for

---

[6] See the UNHCR Handbook on Procedures and Criteria for Determining Refugee Status, which observed that the refugee is a victim, or potential victim, of injustice and not a fugitive from justice.
[7] See *R. v. Secretary of State ex p. Mehari* [1994] Q.B. 474 and *IT v. Secretary of State for the Home Department* (2001) 1 N.L.R. 211.
[8] See above.
[9] At para. 40.
[10] See *Secretary of State for the Home Department v. Adan* [1998] I.N.L.R. 325, HL.
[11] See *Faraj* [1999] I.N.L.R. 451; but see also *Demirkaya* [1999] 1 I.N.L.R. 441.

example that imposed by Islamic law for adultery within the Refugee Convention[12]);

- The concept of Article 3 "inhuman treatment" has been applied with much more regard to the characteristics of the individual than it has the concept of refugee Convention "persecution".

Article 3 will significantly be relied upon where the applicant is excluded by virtue of Article 1F of the Refugee Convention or where there is no Convention ground, or where the harm feared has nothing to do with persecution at all (for instance, destitution). It should of course be observed that Refugee Convention protection is much more secure, providing a proper legal status with civil, social, economical and political rights set out in the Convention and in domestic law. The Refugee Convention has as its basis an adherence to the fundamental human rights in a non-discriminatory regime. The same was recognised by the House of Lords in *R. v. Secretary of State for the Home Department, ex p. Shah: Islam v. IAT.*[13]

5–06   **Asylum Seeker.** An asylum seeker is anyone arriving in the U.K. who demonstrates a well founded fear of persecution because of race, religion, nationality or membership of a particular social group or political opinion.

5–07   **Persecution.** In refugee case law there is no universally accepted definition of the word "persecution". However, we may infer that a threat to life or freedom on account of an action is always persecution. Persecution should be distinguished from punishment

5–08   **Failure to satisfy the United Nations Convention 1951.** If the applicant does not qualify for asylum in accordance with the strictures laid down in the 1951 Convention, the court will consider whether the applicant should be granted exceptional leave to remain in their country and it is here that the European Convention on Human Rights comes into play.[14]

5–09   **Generally.** The largest growth area of Article 3 applications is presently within the category of asylum seekers. The court is faced with the unenviable task of having to decide which applicant has a legally, legitimate and Conventionally enforceable right to remain within the borders of the Contracting State and which applicant will fail to meet that standard. To do so, the courts have developed guidelines which seek to establish whether the asylum seeker has a legitimate claim.

The vast amount of time spent in court on this issue centres around an interpretation of whether the enforced return of the applicant to his former country will be in breach of Article 3 and the courts have developed criteria upon which adjudication can be based. As with any consideration of Article 3, whether there has been a violation is a matter of degree including the frequency and period of time over which the ill-treatment took place. Nevertheless, some decisions are somewhat controversial. In *R. v. Special Adjudicator ex p.*

---

[12] See *Danaei v. Secretary of State for the Home Department* [1998] Imm. A.R. 84.
[13] [1999] I.N.L.R. 144.
[14] The Asylum Directorate also instruct their case workers to take into account "compelling compassionate reasons" at p. 3.; June 1999.

Okonkwo[15] the applicant claimed asylum in the United Kingdom but the Secretary of State refused her application having concluded that there was no reasonable likelihood that she had been tortured in the past. The applicant appealed, arguing that she had been raped by a number of soldiers in Nigeria. The Adjudicator upheld the Secretary of State's certificate and the applicant applied for judicial review on the basis that the Adjudicator erred in not considering rape to be a form of torture.

Somewhat surprisingly, in dismissing the application, the Queen's Bench Division held that the issue of whether rape constituted torture required a consideration of the motive. On the facts, the rape, perpetrated by a number of men who sought sexual gratification, could not amount to torture but constituted a very serious assault. The court reasoned that because violence alone would not constitute torture, unless it followed a persistent course, rape, viewed as one incident of violence, could not itself be regarded as torture.

This was despite the facts of the case which alleged not by one soldier but by a number of soldiers and should be treated with caution. *Ex parte Okonkwo* illustrates a fundamental trend in the case law which is consistent with an interpretation of Article 3, ill-treatment is not enough it must breach the minimum threshold. That threshold in asylum cases is often high.[16]

Article 3 further prohibits, in absolute terms, torture or inhuman or degrading treatment or punishment, irrespective of the victim's conduct. It makes no provisions for exceptions and no derogation is permissible from it even in the event of a public emergency threatening the life of the nation.[17] The principle is equally valid in expulsion cases and the activities of the individual, however undesirable or dangerous, cannot be a material consideration.[18]

Real risk of torture or inhuman or degrading treatment. If an individual is   **5–10**
subjected to a real risk of torture or inhuman or degrading treatment contrary to Article 3, then the State must not expel or extradite that individual, regardless of the particular circumstances. Although Contracting States have a right to control entry and expel aliens, they are under an obligation not to order an expulsion if there is a real risk of inhuman or degrading treatment in terms of Article 3.

Jabari v. Turkey[19] was a death penalty case in that the Iranian national applicant faced the possibility of death by stoning or flogging if deported back to Iran, having been accused of committing adultery.

The risk of exposure to this particular form of death sentence violated Article 3.

In *Soering v. United Kingdom*,[20] the court was prepared to accept that Article 3 had been violated despite the fact that the applicant might be acquitted and that some form of assurance had been given that even upon conviction the death penalty would not be implemented.[21]

---

[15] [1998] Imm. A.R. 502.
[16] [1998] Imm. I.R. 502.
[17] *Ireland v. United Kingdom* 2 E.H.R.R. 25; *Tomasi v. France* 15 E.H.R.R. 1; *Chahal v. United Kingdom* (1997) 23 E.H.R.R. 413.
[18] See *Ahmed v. Austria* (1997) 24 E.H.R.R. 278.
[19] (2000) 29 E.H.R.R. CD 178.
[20] (1989) E.H.R.R. 439.
[21] See also *A. v. Switzerland* (1986) 46 D.R. 257 and *Altun v. Germany* (1983) 36 D.R. 209, both of which establish that prosecution for politically orientated offences which attract substantial sentences can violate Article 3. The courts in these instances were no doubt concerned about political oppression.

If of course the death penalty is mandatory within a certain State, then this will increase the probability of a violation of Article 3 being made out.[22]

In *Ahmed v. Austria*,[23] the risk emanated from non-State agents holding substantial power. Ahmed, a Somalian national sought refugee status in Austria. His application was based on the fact that his father and brother had been executed and that his family had been assaulted on suspicion of belonging to an opposing organisation. The applicant was later convicted of a criminal offence and served a prison sentence and the State sought to forfeit his refugee status on the basis that he had committed a "particularly serious crime", one punishable by up to 10 years' imprisonment.

The Austrian authorities concluded that by referring to the applicant's previous behaviour and convictions he constituted a danger to Austrian society and reaffirmed that his refugee status should be forfeited. The applicant challenged this decision and his subsequent deportation proceedings on the basis that if he returned to Somalia his life would be at risk. Despite the State relying upon the applicant's aggressive and criminal behaviour, the court reaffirmed that if he faced real risk of being subjected to torture or inhuman or degrading treatment or punishment, in the country who requested his deportation, then Article 3 would be breached regardless of his conduct in the host nation.

In *Ahmed v. Austria*,[24] the European Court were of the view that there had been no observable improvement in the conditions in Somalia and that the applicant's deportation to Somalia in those circumstances would breach Article 3 for as long as he faced a serious risk of being subjected to torture or inhuman or degrading treatment.

5–11 **Conditions of former country.** The court also took into account the conditions in the applicant's former country of residence in *Chahal v. United Kingdom*[25] when the European Court took account of the substantial evidence of serious human rights abuses by the Indian authorities in case heard in 1996. Despite India's promise that Chahal would be safe if deported, the court held that was not wholly convincing and that therefore deportation would violate Article 3.

5–12 **Past persecution relevant.** The court can reasonably conclude that if evidence is presented of past persecution of an applicant by the regime to which he would be returned that can properly find a well-founded fear of further persecution if he returned and as such, that enforced repatriation would be in breach of Article 3. In *R. v. Secretary of State for the Home Department ex p. Dahmas*,[26] an Algerian applied for asylum on entry to the United Kingdom. Originally, his application had been turned down by Denmark, the Convention country in which he originally sought asylum. The applicant applied for judicial review of the Secretary of State's decision, contending that the Danish decision not to grant him asylum had been perverse. The Danish Refugee Board had accepted the applicant's history, save for a past conviction and sentence, and on this basis the applicant had contended that his previous history of torture and incarceration had been too readily set aside.

---

[22] See *Woodson v. North Carolina* (1976) 428 U.S. 280; *Furman v. Georgia* (1972) 408 U.S. 238.
[23] (1997) 24 E.H.R.R. 278.
[24] (1997) 24 E.H.R.R. 278.
[25] *The Independent*, January 24, 2000.
[26] *The Independent*, January 24, 2000 (CS).

As a member of the Islamic Salvation Front who had suffered from previous persecution and imprisonment, the applicant contended that a return to Denmark would inevitably result in his deportation to Algeria where he had a legitimate fear of further persecution. The application for judicial review was granted and the decision of the Danish Refugee Board held as perverse. An influential Court of Appeal consisting of Kennedy L.J., Mantell L.J. and Mummery L.J., were of the view that the Danish Refugee Board had unjustifiably discounted an important element of the applicant's evidence concerning his past persecution. The applicant was being sought by the same regime which had imprisoned him.

Compare this to *Dereva v. Secretary of State for the Home Department*[27] where a Kenyan asylum seeker had her appeal dismissed. She claimed that she had been tortured because of her membership of a militant opposition group, but was no longer at risk of persecution. The Court of Appeal were therefore of the view that the Immigration Appeal Tribunal were right to refuse her application for asylum.

But, in *R. v. Secretary of State for the Home Department ex p. P*,[28] the court held that the Secretary of State of the Home Department had misdirected himself by failing to take into account the past persecution and by failing to relate the past events to the authority's current interest.

In *R. (on the application of Sugeetharan) v. Immigration Appeal Tribunal*,[29] in the Queen's Bench Division Administrative Court, Mr Justice Maurice Kay held that the Special Adjudicator's finding that the applicant was not at risk of future persecution was unsustainable given that he had accepted the applicant's account of his treatment by the army and for circumstances surrounding his subsequent release from detention. Once again, the Special Adjudicator should have considered past persecution when assessing the future risk of persecution.

General history of persecution. It is not only the past persecution of the   **5–13** individual applicant that should be taken into account by the court, but also the general history of persecution in the country to which the applicant will be sent if he fails in his quest for refugee status. In the Queen's Bench Division Administrative Court in the case of *R. (on the application of Vatheeswaran) v. Immigration Appeal Tribunal*,[30] the court considered the application of a Sri Lankan for judicial review of a decision of the Immigration Appeal Tribunal refusing him permission to appeal against the Special Adjudicator's dismissal of his appeal against the refusal of his asylum claim. It was contended that the Special Adjudicator, in finding that the applicant lacked a subjective fear of persecution, had made erroneous factual findings regarding the history of torture he had allegedly suffered and had failed to give consideration to the background of persecution existing in Sri Lanka.

Although the court refused this application, it emphasised that the Special Adjudicator had properly considered the background situation in Sri Lanka. It seems to follow that if a country has a particularly bad record of general persecution, then that is a matter which the courts can properly take into account when considering whether there is a potential breach of Article 3.

---

[27] [2001] EWCA Civ 1520.
[28] [1992] COD 295.
[29] Unreported, 2000.
[30] [2001] EWHC Admin 169.

5–14　　**Persecution must be for a Convention reason.** The fact that an applicant fears that money may be extracted from him if he is returned to the country from which he has fled will not found a successful claim for asylum. In *Montoya v. Secretary of State for the Home Department*,[31] a member of a wealthy Colombian family claimed refugee status on the basis that his life had been threatened by Marxist groups if he did not pay them a sum of money per month. The Court of Appeal refused his application for refugee status and concluded that even if he was a member of a particular social group and that he had a well-founded fear of persecution upon his return to Colombia, the Tribunal were nevertheless entitled to conclude that if he returned to Colombia he was likely to be persecuted because the persecutors wanted his money, rather than by reason of membership of a group or for his political beliefs. Accordingly, the court were of the view that he would not be persecuted for a Convention reason.

The Convention and Protocol Relating to the Status of Refugees[32] is clear in its terms. Article 1A provides:

> " ... the term "refugee" shall apply to any person who ... (2) ... owing to a well-founded fear of persecution for reasons of ... membership of a particular social group or political opinion, is outside the country of his nationality and ... is unable or, owing to such fear, is unwilling to avail himself of the protection of that country".

This definition does not include a persecutor's demand for money and indicates that the courts will be very restrictive in interpretation as to what Convention friendly persecution actually means.

5–15　　**Specific application to the individual.** The existence of a consistent pattern of gross, flagrant or mass violations of human rights in a country is not in itself a sufficient ground for determining whether a person would be in danger of being subjected to torture, inhuman or degrading treatment upon their return to that place. There must be in addition to that, specific grounds indicating that the individual concerned would personally be at risk.[33]

5–16　　**Group persecution.** Of course, if the applicant can neither establish that the country has a history of persecution or that the individual applicant has not been persecuted himself, then his application will be hopeless. It will not assist the

---

[31] [2002] EWCA Civ 620.
[32] (1951) (Cmd 9197) and (1967) (Cmnd 3906).
[33] See *Alan v. Switzerland* [1997] I.N.L.R. 29; 1 B.H.R.C. 598, in this case a Turkish citizen of Kurdish background had been arrested by the Turkish police who he claimed tortured him and he sought asylum in Switzerland. One of his grounds of argument was that deportation to Turkey would violate Switzerland's obligation under the Convention against Torture and Other Cruel, Inhuman or Degrading Treatment or punishment 1984, Article 3, not to expel or return a person to another State where there was substantial grounds for believing that he would be in danger of being subjected to torture. He produced evidence that although Turkey had ratified the Convention, torture was systematically practised there, and that his background and record of involvement with an outlawed Kurdish communist organisation, the KAWA, indicated he belonged to several target groups of Turkish repression and stood at risk of being arrested and tortured. The court found that the mere fact that a country was a party to the Convention and recognised the UN Committee against Torture's competence did not constitute sufficient guarantee for a person's security. The combination of the applicant's ethnic background, political affiliation and history of detention and internal exile, *combined* with the Turkish Security Force's activities and the fact that torture was still systematic in Turkey, constituted substantial grounds for believing that he would be in danger of torture if he returned there and the deportation of the applicant would therefore violate Switzerland's obligations under the Convention.

applicant to say that he was simply part of a group that had been detained and ill-treated. It must be proved that the individual suffered the necessary level of degradation. This was a hurdle which the applicant in *Bekele v. Secretary of State for the Home Department*[34] in the Court of Appeal could not overcome. The Court approved the Special Adjudicator's approach had been correct in refusing the application on the basis that Bekele had failed to establish that he was part of a group that had been detained and tortured in Ethiopia during a student demonstration.

But compare *Faraj v. Secretary of State for the Home Department*[35] which held that whereas a single case of torture suffered by an individual asylum seeker would not constitute persecution on its own, persecution could exist where the single asylum seeker was part of a group whose members had suffered similar incidents.

Some assistance may be given by the House of Lords interpretation of the phrase "particular social group" for the purpose of the 1951 Convention. In *R. v. Immigration Appeal Tribunal ex p. Shah and Islam*,[36] the House of Lords found that members of a social group had to have in common an immutable character-istic, that is a characteristic which is either beyond the power of an individual to change, or is so fundamental to his identity or conscience that it ought not to be required to be changed. The court went on to hold that whilst the social group must exist independently of persecution, discrimination against the group could be *taken into account* in identifying it as a social group, in other words discrim-ination against a group can be a factor contributing to the identity of a social group. In the facts of Shah and Islam, the House of Lords held that in the context of Pakistani society women are a social group and that the applicants, two Pakistani women, were persecuted by reason of their membership of that group.

In that case the persecution comprised violence from their husbands, which the State was unable or unwilling to prevent. It seems therefore that in societies in which women are subject to serious discrimination which reaches the degree of severity found by the House of Lords in *Shah and Islam*, women will be considered a social group and that those who fear or receive violence at the hands of their husbands will be able to show persecution if they can show that the State is unable or unwilling to protect them. The Asylum Directorate, in the light of *Shah and Islam*, have conceded that "we can no longer argue that homosexuals (or other persons defined by sexual orientation) are not capable of being a social group.[37] Discrimination against homosexuals in a society may be such as to single them out as a single group, depending on the factual circumstances in the

---

[34] 2000 WL 774973.

[35] [1999] I.N.L.R. 451.

[36] [1999] 2 A.C. 629.

[37] In *Karner v. Austria* (Application No. 40016/98), the applicant, a homosexual, lived with his partner in a flat. The landlord of the flat brought eviction proceedings which were upheld by the domestic courts. The Austrian Supreme Court observed that it found that " 'life companion' . . . was to be interpreted at the time it was enacted and that it had not been the intention of the legislature in 1974 to include a person of the same sex. The applicant complained that the domestic court's ruling amounted to discrimination on the grounds of sexual orientation in violation of Article 14 in conjunction with Article 8(1) of the Convention". On September 11, 2001, the application was declared unanimously admissible. The court will have an opportunity to consider whether homo-sexuals as a group deserve general protection as a group under Article 14 "the enjoyment of the rights and freedoms set forth in this Convention shall be secured without discrimination on any ground such as sex, race, colour, language, religion, political or other opinion, national or social origin, association with a national minority, property, birth or other status".

country concerned". The Directorate go on to advise that each case will be considered on its merits and that to qualify for asylum, a member of a social group will have to show that they have a well founded fear of persecution and that the authorities were unable or unwilling to offer protection and that the persecution was *because of* their social group.

5–17   **Isolated incidents not enough.** Where previous detention and ill-treatment, even if it breaches the threshold has been of an isolated nature and on the facts the applicant has continued to live or work within the complained of country without hindrance, or had delayed departing that country following alleged persecution, a violation of Article 3 will be difficult to maintain.

5–18   **Applicant's actions after persecution.** The court will look very carefully at the actions of the applicant immediately following the allegations of persecution and will not apply Article 3 unless that applicant leaves the country relatively promptly or has remained in the perpetrating State and been subject to continuing persecution.

In *R. v. Immigration Appeal Tribunal ex p. Cosgun*,[38] in the Queen's Bench Division, the applicant, a Turkish Kurd, accepted that he had been detained only on a single occasion some years previously but nevertheless during the detention he suffered torture. On the facts of that case, the Special Adjudicator concluded that the applicant's delay in leaving Turkey and the fact that he had worked unhindered in several areas of Turkey undermined his assertions of persecution.

5–19   **Fact and degree.** The question as to whether particular conduct amounts to persecution is a question of fact and degree. Unless a single beating is of particular severity or there is a real risk of repetition, it is open for a court to hold that a single beating does not amount to persecution, and as such is a bar to a finding under Article 3.[39]

In *Demirkaya v. Secretary of State for the Home Department*, the Court of Appeal held that a finding of persecution did not necessarily follow from the Tribunal's decision that the applicant would probably be beaten upon his return, but the Tribunal ought to have considered the history of the applicant's treatment before he left Turkey as relevant to his likely treatment on returning. In the absence of any evidence of a change in the treatment of members of the PKK by the Turkish authorities, the Court of Appeal held that the Tribunal had been wrong to conclude that the applicant would not be subject to persecution on returning to Turkey.[40]

5–20   **Isolated criminal acts.** It seems that an isolated incident amounting to a criminal act will not indicate any policy of persecution towards an applicant. In *R. v. Secretary of State for the Home Department ex p. Roomy*,[41] the applicant, a

---

[38] Unreported, 1999.
[39] See *Demirkaya v. Secretary of State for the Home Department* [1999] I.N.L.R. 441; [1999] Imm. A.R. 498.
[40] See *Vilvarajah v. United Kingdom* (1992) 14 E.H.R.R. 248; the European Court will consider all relevant material including the general situation in the receiving country and the individual's personal circumstances and political developments in a country between the decision to expel or otherwise and expulsion will be taken into account. *Cruz Varas v. Sweden* (1991) 14 E.H.R.R. 1.
[41] [1999] Imm. A.R. 483.

citizen of Sri Lanka, applied for asylum claiming that he had been raped and forced to commit an act of gross indecency with one of his captors, a member of the Sri Lankan army.

The Adjudicator, while prepared to accept that the incident had taken place, stated that the assault was a criminal act and therefore could not be accepted as proof of torture. The Queen's Bench Division in refusing the application confirmed that the Adjudicator had not erred in reasoning that the ill-treatment had been a criminal act and had not received any evidence to suggest that it had amounted to persecution or that it was a product of a persecutory attitude towards the applicant. Although the court concluded that the conduct of the soldier was deplorable, it was nevertheless an isolated incident amounting to a criminal act and did not necessarily indicate any policy of persecution.[42]

A slightly different approach was taken in *R. v. Secretary of State for the Home Department ex p. Kameswaran* where the applicant contended that he had been hit or beaten on one occasion whilst being detained and that he had therefore established a real likelihood that he had been a victim of torture and that it had therefore been incumbent on the Special Adjudicator to give reasons for a finding that such conduct did not amount to torture.[43] Mr Justice Blofeld in the Queen's Bench Division refused judicial review against the Adjudicator's decision and held that he had been entitled to reach the conclusion that he had in relation to the single incident referred to, given the applicant's lack of credibility when his evidence was assessed as a whole. This seems to indicate that a single incident of mistreatment may, if it reaches the required threshold, be sufficient to establish torture, inhuman or degrading treatment and that success depends more on credibility than on quantum, creating a degree of uncertainty as to exactly how the courts will approach single incident issues in the future.

As a matter of logic it must be right that a single incident can, depending upon its degree of severity and upon the credibility of the evidence before the court, amount to a violation of Article 3. Each case will depend upon its own merits.

Asylum Directorate Guidelines to Case Workers. The Asylum Directorate **5–21** have laid down in their guidance documents what they consider amounts to Human Rights violations which can be categorised as persecution. They state at paragraph 8.2:

"The following will amount to persecution:

— unjustifiable attack on life and limb;
— slavery, torture, cruel, inhuman or degrading punishment or treatment.

Acts in this category would include:

— unjustifiable killing, or maiming, or

---

[42] The issue of whether rape constitutes torture requires a consideration of the motive. The disturbing facts of *R. v. Special Adjudicator ex p. Okonkwo* reveal that a citizen of Nigeria had been raped by a number of soldiers in that country and that on her application for asylum the Adjudicator considered rape not to be a form of torture. The Queen's Bench Division dismissed her appeal stating that on the facts, the rape, perpetrated by a number of men who sought sexual gratification could not amount to torture, but constituted a very serious assault. Given that violence alone would not constitute torture, unless it followed a persistent course, rape, viewed as one incident of violence, could not itself be regarded as torture.
[43] See Asylum and Immigration Appeals Act 1993, paragraph 5(5) as further defined in *Ireland v. U.K.* (1979) 2 E.H.R.R. 25.

— physical or psychological torture, rape and other serious sexual violence.

8.3 Acts of discrimination or ill-treatment which might amount to persecution. Acts in this category include violations of the right to:

— freedom of thought, conscience and religion;
— be free from arbitrary arrest and detention;
— freedom of expression, assembly and association;
— privacy;
— access to public employment without discrimination;
— access to normally available services such as:

  — food
  — clothing
  — housing
  — medical care
  — social security
  — education
  — right to work

— or a combination of such measures assessed cumulatively.

The official authorities of a country may need to take measures which restrict the exercise of certain freedoms. Such restrictions may not in themselves constitute persecution. However, if the restrictions are being applied in a discriminatory manner and have sufficiently serious consequences . . . they may amount to persecution.

Measures may be directed against certain sections of the population which includes the applicant. Such measures can be relied on by the applicant in advancing his claim; he need not have personally suffered the persecution to have a well founded fear of it.

However, to amount to persecution measures must amount to persistent and serious ill-treatment without just cause.

They must be of a substantially prejudicial nature and must strike at a fundamental part of the individual's or group's existence so as to result in making the individual's life intolerable if he were to return to the country in which he is likely to be persecuted. All claims of persecution must be viewed in the round, assessing both the cumulative effect and any mitigating factors".

5–22   **The requirement that ill-treatment be specified.** The mere possibility of ill-treatment is not enough to activate Article 3. Furthermore, ill-treatment in itself is not sufficient to establish a breach. In *Vilvarajah v. United Kingdom*,[44] a group of Tamil asylum seekers alleged that their removal from the United Kingdom to Sri Lanka would amount to a violation of Article 3.[45] The European Court of Human Rights held that the Home Secretary's decision, that the applicant's position was no worse than the majority of other members of the Sri Lankan Tamil community, was reasonable and that some form of specific violation above and beyond ill-treatment must be made out. Once again, the minimum level of severity threshold comes into play.

5–23   **The need for medical treatment.** The absence of medical treatment in the State to which the applicant would be returned upon a failure to prove Article 3 can be a factor to establish violation. But where the application is based upon the proposition that the source of the treatment is beyond the State, the applicant

---

[44] (1992) 14 E.H.R.R. 248.
[45] As it then was under the European Convention on Human Rights 1950, Article 3.

must pass a high threshold where that State is not directly responsible for the harm.

In *Bensaid v. United Kingdom*,[46] an Algerian national came to the United Kingdom as a visitor in 1989 and married a United Kingdom citizen in 1993. Between 1994 and 1995, he began receiving treatment for schizophrenia on the National Health Service. The Secretary of State for the Home Department decided to remove the applicant on the grounds that his marriage was one of convenience. The applicant claimed that his removal would violate his rights under the European Convention on Human Rights, Article 3,[47] as the difficulties in obtaining the necessary treatment in Algeria would amount to his suffering inhuman and degrading treatment. It is apparent from the evidence in that case that the applicant could have obtained treatment for his condition at a hospital 75 km from his home village. The European Court of Human Rights were of the view that the fact that it would be harder to obtain such treatment in Algeria than in the United Kingdom was not conclusive for the purposes of Article 3. Evidence that difficulties in obtaining treatment in Algeria could exacerbate his condition did not bring the matter within Article 3 as he was also at risk of relapse if he stayed in the United Kingdom, given the long-term nature of his condition.

To succeed in an application under Article 3 on the basis that medical treatment is required and cannot be obtained in the State to which the applicant would be returned, will not be easy and the court will be required to make an analysis of what treatment is available to the applicant should he be returned and just because it is more difficult in that country to obtain required medical treatment will not be a guarantee of success. It is clear that the court will take into account the nature of the condition suffered by the applicant.

Withdrawal of care. If withdrawal of care, support or treatment that the **5-24** applicant is currently receiving in his present location would have a serious consequence for him then the court may hold that there will be a violation of Article 3 if he is deported. Nevertheless, such an approach should be considered as exceptional and involve compelling humanitarian factors. In *D. v. United Kingdom*,[48] the applicant, who was a serving prisoner following convictions relating to controlled drugs, was suffering in the advanced stages of AIDS. By the time he was released, he was provided with accommodation and care by a United Kingdom charity as well as receiving medical treatment for his condition. The immigration authorities ordered his removal to St Kitts and the applicant claimed violation of Article 3 as he would not receive adequate medical treatment and had no family in St Kitts who could care for him.

The European Court of Human Rights upheld this application emphasising that withdrawal of the care, support and treatment of the applicant would have serious consequence for him and that whilst the conditions in St Kitts did not themselves breach the standards demanded by Article 3, the applicant's removal there would expose him to a real risk that he would die in distressing circumstances, which the European Court concluded would amount to inhuman treatment, contrary to Article 3. The court went on to emphasise that released alien prisoners did not

---

[46] (2001) 33 E.H.R.R. 10.
[47] He also claimed violation of Article 8.
[48] (1997) 24 E.H.R.R. 423.

normally have the right to remain so as to continue to receive medical or welfare services and classified the applicant's case in *D. v. United Kingdom* as exceptional.[49]

The case of *R. v. Secretary of State for the Home Department ex p. Cardoso*,[50] presents an interesting comparison. In that case, the applicant, a Brazilian national, had been resident in the United Kingdom since 1981 during which time he had twice entered the United Kingdom illegally, falsely claiming benefits and having a marriage of convenience. In 1995, he was diagnosed as HIV Positive and contracted AIDS-related symptoms. Cardoso made an application for leave to enter the United Kingdom which was refused by the Secretary of State, and upon appeal to the Queen's Bench Division, the court agreed confirming that in that case the requirement for medical treatment was not determinative. Mr Justice Sullivan concluded that the applicant would receive adequate treatment in Brazil.[51]

5-25   **Possibility of internal flight.** If an applicant establishes that he may be ill-treated in such a way as to violate Article 3, he must also satisfy the court that the risk of a further violation cannot be avoided by going to another part of that country or State where he will not be so affected. In *Hilal v. United Kingdom*,[52] the European Court upheld a violation of Article 3 based upon the evidence that the applicant who fled from the island of Zanzibar following detention and torture because of his connections to the opposition political party in Tanzania would also be at risk on the mainland of Tanzania. The court emphasised that internal flight was not a viable option as the situation in mainland Tanzania was no less dangerous and extradition to Zanzibar was a possibility. It is clear that the court will take into account the possibility of extradition from one State to another as to whether the applicant needs protection from that possible eventuality.

5-26   **Countries who practice the death penalty.** The European Court are particularly vigilant to prevent applicants being returned to a country who may subsequently sentence them to death. The leading case is *Soering v. United Kingdom*[53] where the applicant faced extradition to the United States of America and in particular Virginia, a State notorious for its enthusiasm for the death penalty. But it was not only the actual execution which concerned the court, it

---

[49] The court were at pains to point out that Contracting States do have the right to control the entry and residence of aliens and to impose severe sanctions, including expulsion, for the commission of Drug Trafficking offences, but the Prohibition Against Torture or Inhuman or Degrading Treatment or punishment in Article 3 was an absolute one which applied regardless of the conduct of the individual concerned and had to be respected when a State was considering an expulsion.

[50] [2000] Imm. A.R. 1.

[51] A further strand of Cardoso's Article 3 argument included the ground that the refusal of his initial application by the Secretary of State and the requirement for him to appeal from abroad of itself constituted inhuman or degrading treatment in view of his medical condition. This was also dismissed by the court which emphasised that it was a well established principle that an appeal from a decision to refuse leave to enter had to be made from abroad, save in exceptional circumstances, which were not applicable in Cardoso's case. See *R. v. Secretary of State for the Home Department ex p. Swati* [1986] 1 W.L.R. 477.

[52] (2001) 33 E.H.R.R. 2.

[53] [1990] C.O.D. 162.

was the conditions in which the condemned man would be held whilst awaiting execution. Many condemned prisoners wait decades on "Death Row".[54]

The European Court concluded that three consequences of "Death Row phenomenon" would mean an automatic violation of Article 3. Those three circumstances were:

1. the length of detention pending execution (an average of 6–8 years);

2. the strict and harsh conditions on death row; and

3. the applicant's age and mental state.[55]

Different States practice different sorts of death penalty and the method used of execution will be a relevant consideration when considering a possible violation of Article 3.[56]

Visible injury. Whether or not an applicant has a visible injury in the absence of medical reports can be considered by the court. In *R. (on the application of Atputharajah) v. Immigration Appeal Tribunal*,[57] the court refused an application for judicial review of the refusal to grant asylum on the basis that the fact that visible, non-facial scarring did not suggest torture or military combat or training, did not make out the applicant's case and was a proper reason for a refusal of asylum. **5–27**

Medical reports. The Special Adjudicator must give appropriate weight to medical reports and reports of independent agencies when considering the evidence of torture, inhuman or degrading treatment.[58] Indeed, when it is held that a Special Adjudicator has not properly considered a medical report, the court will hold that that admission could have materially affected the outcome of the Adjudicator's decision.[59] It will be important to consider in detail how thorough the Special Adjudicator's consideration of the medical evidence has been and simply making a claim that the Adjudicator has not been diligent in this respect will not be enough without specific examples. In *R. (on the application of Njike) v. Immigration Appeal Tribunal*,[60] the court held that the Adjudicator had accurately underlined the limits to the medical evidence and considered it in the correct context. **5–28**

---

[54] Sometimes the condemned prisoners are in solitary confinement which will add to the ill-treatment inflicted. In his book "Prisoners of Isolation: Solitary Confinement in Canada" (University of Toronto Press: Toronto 1992), Professor Michael Jackson quotes Charles Dickens who wrote in 1842: "I believe that very few men are capable of estimating the immense amount of torture and agony which this dreadful punishment, prolonged for years, inflicts upon the sufferers and in guessing at it myself, and from reasoning from what I have seen written upon their faces, from what to my certain knowledge they feel within, I am only the more convinced that there is a depth of terrible endurance in it which none but the sufferers themselves can fathom in which no man has a right to inflict upon his fellow creatures."
[55] See Chapter 7: Death Row and Long Term Prisoners.
[56] See *Ng v. Canada* (1993) 1 I.H.R.R. 161.
[57] See also *R. (on the application of Atputharajah) v. Secretary of State for the Home Department.*
[58] [2001] EWHC Admin 156. See *R. v. Secretary of State for the Home Department ex p. Celi-Loaiza*, 2000 WL 33348547, Judgment date, May 23, 2000.
[59] See *R. (on the application of Judes) v. Immigration Appeal Tribunal* [2001] EWCA Civ 825.
[60] 2000 WL 1675170, Judgment date October 12, 2000.

5-29   **The quality of the medical evidence required.** There must be more than a
presumption from the medical evidence that an applicant has been tortured,
exposed to inhuman or degrading treatment or otherwise persecuted.[61]

5-30   **Applicants subject to the Mental Health Act 1983, Section 48.** Operation of
the Immigration Act 1971 relating to illegal entrants and the Mental Health Act
1983 Section 48 detaining an individual in hospital for medical treatment should
run in tandem.[62] Accordingly, an applicant's detention in hospital under the
provisions of the 1983 Act does not prevent the Secretary of State from directing
his removal pursuant to the 1971 Act. Removal therefore does not amount to
inhuman or degrading treatment in breach of Article 3 even if the applicant
claims that such removal would create an increased risk of suicide or self-
harm.[63]

3. SOURCE OF THE RISK

5-31   **The danger may emanate from persons or groups of persons who are not
public officials.** Article 3 may be applied to a case where the danger emanates
from persons who are not public officials. In the case of *HLR v. France*,[64] the
European Court of Human Rights accepted the contention that drug traffickers in
Colombia could in certain circumstances be the source of a threat to an applicant.
In *HLR v. France*, the applicant, a Colombian national, was arrested in Italy in
possession of cocaine. During questioning, he provided information which led to
the conviction of a Colombian drug dealer. The applicant was understandably
concerned that if he was deported to Colombia he would be running a serious risk
of reprisals at the hands of drug traffickers as a result of his informing behaviour
and be subject to torture, inhuman or degrading treatment, contrary to
Article 3.

The court concluded that it did not rule out the possibility that Article 3 of the
Convention may also apply "where the danger emanates from persons or groups
of persons who are not public officials. However, it must be shown that the risk
is real and that the authorities in the receiving State are not able to obviate the
risk by providing appropriate protection".[65]

In *R. (on the application of Roszkowski) v. Special Adjudicator*,[66] the applicant
argued that the Special Adjudicator had erred in her interpretation of the definition of torture by placing reliance on definitions found within the Convention

---

[61] See *R. v. Secretary of State for the Home Department ex p. Panther* (1996) 8 Admin.L.R. 155.
[62] See *R. (on the application of X) v. Secretary of State for the Home Department* [2001] 1 W.L.R.
740.
[63] See *R. v. (on the application of X) v. Secretary of State for the Home Department* [2001] 1 W.L.R.
740.
[64] (1997) 26 E.H.R.R. 29.
[65] The court also held that the general situation of violence in Colombia did not entail, *in itself*, a
violation of Article 3 in the event of the applicant's deportation. While evidence had been adduced
to show that drug traffickers sometimes took revenge on informers, there was no relevant evidence
to show in the applicant's case that the risk was real. There were no documents to support the claim
that the applicant's situation would be worse than that of other Colombians. Furthermore, the
applicant had not shown that the Colombian authorities were incapable of affording him the
appropriate protection. In the light of these considerations, the European Court held that no substantial grounds had been established in this case for believing that the applicant, if deported, would
be exposed to a real risk of treatment contrary to Article 3.
[66] [2001] EWCA Civ 650.

against Torture and Other Cruel, Inhuman or Degrading Treatment or Punishment 1984 (United Nations) Article 1(1) and the Criminal Justice Act 1988, Section 134(1), both of which refer to acts by an official or acquiescence by an official. The applicant maintained that those definitions differed from that found within Schedule 2, paragraph 5(5) of the 1993 Act which made no mention of official acts and sub-paragraph 2 under Schedule 2, paragraph 5(5), torture did not have to be linked to the facts of the asylum application but could be "free-standing" of the applicant itself.

In dismissing the appeal, the Court of Appeal confirmed the view of the Queen's Bench Division Administrative Court in that with regard to an asylum seeker's claim to have suffered from torture under Schedule 2, paragraph 5(5) of the Asylum and Immigration Appeals Act 1993, such torture had to be either by Agents of the State, or were carried out by persons who were not agents of the State of a kind which that State was not able to disinclined to provide adequate protection against.[67]

The source of the feared ill-treatment. In *Ahmed v. Austria*[68] the risk   5–32
emanated from non-State agents holding substantial power, the court held that these individuals were properly considered in an application under Article 3 as it was unlikely that any public authority could afford protection from it. In *Ould Barar v. Sweden*,[69] the fear was of a slave master, from whom the applicant feared punishment for seeking to escape, in the absence of adequate protection from the authorities.

Acts or omissions of a non-receiving State. In the exceptional case of *D v.*   5–33
United Kingdom,[70] the court held that Article 3 could apply to a situation which did not directly or indirectly concern the responsibilities of the public authorities and emphasised again that Article 3 should not only be applied to the acts or admissions of public authorities in the Receiving State. *D* was in the advanced stage of AIDS and being treated in the United Kingdom. He contended that if he were deported to St Kitts, he would not receive adequate medical treatment and care. The court concluded that the withdrawal of the care, support and treatment that he was currently receiving within the United Kingdom would have serious consequences for him. Whilst emphasising that the conditions in St Kitts did not in themselves breach the standards demanded by Article 3, the applicant's removal there would expose him to a real risk that he would die in distressing circumstances, which would, the European Court concluded, would amount to inhuman treatment, contrary to Article 3.

---

[67] It seems that the Special Adjudicator in this case may have erred in law but the Court of Appeal reasserted the principle that if there was an error it would not have vitiated the underlying decision on the merits; see *R. v. Secretary of State for the Home Department ex p. Singh*, unreported March 3, 2000. The Court of Appeal went on to state that the sole reason likely for the Special Adjudicator's decision was that the evidence did not establish a reasonable likelihood that the events which had caused the applicant to leave Poland amounted to severe pain or suffering and was therefore torture for the purposes of the Convention against Torture and Other Cruel and Inhuman and Degrading Treatment and Punishment 1984, Article 1(1). It was observed in this case that torture had to be related to the underlying application. See *R. v. Immigration Appeal Tribunal ex p. Brylewicz*, unreported March 26, 2000.
[68] (1996) 24 E.H.R.R. 278.
[69] Application No. 42367/98, January 19, 1999.
[70] See previously (1997) 24 E.H.R.R. 423.

At the time this was a ground-breaking case and at paragraph 49 the court developed the principle upon which applicants would not be expelled. Having observed that in the past the risk of ill-treatment sufficient to violate Article 3 must emanate from "intentionally inflicted acts of the public authorities in the Receiving Country or from those of non-State bodies in that country when the authorities there are unable to afford him protection".

The court went on to say that:

"Aside from these situations and given the fundamental importance of Article 3 in the Convention system, the court must reserve to itself sufficient flexibility to address the application of that Article in other contexts which might arise. It is therefore not prevented from scrutinising an applicant's claim under Article 3 where the source of the risk of prescribed treatment in the Receiving Country stems from factors which cannot engage either directly or indirectly the responsibility of the public authorities in that country, or which, taken alone, do not in themselves infringe the standards of that Article. To limit the application of Article 3 in this manner would undermine the absolute character of its protection".

5–34   **The prohibition of sending an applicant back to a country which may itself return that applicant to a persecuting country.** The Secretary of State must not send back an applicant if the Secretary of State considers that the other State's interpretation of immigration law as perceived by the Convention would lead to an individual being sent back by that State to a State where he has established a fear of persecution which the Secretary of State finds to be covered by the Convention. In other words, the question is not whether the Secretary of State thinks that any alternative approach is reasonable or permissible or legitimate or arguable but whether the Secretary of State is satisfied that the application of the other State's interpretation of the Convention would mean that the individual will still not be sent back otherwise than in accordance with the Convention.[71]

5–35   **Dual nationality.** It is likely that a person who has more than one nationality and who has a well founded fear of persecution in one of his countries of nationality will not be considered a refugee if he is able to avail himself of the protection of another country of nationality. This seems logical in that the applicant will not be required to return to a country in which he faces a danger of persecution.

Even where there are differences between tests applied in two countries as to who qualifies for asylum, one being more stringent than the other, *R. (on the application of Yogathas) v. Secretary of State for the Home Department; R. (on the application of Thangarasa) v. Secretary of State for the Home Department*,[71a] this was not considered sufficient to prevent removal of the applicants, given that such differences were not so great as to render the application permissible.

5–36   **Stateless applicants.** If an applicant has not nationality it is probable that he must be outside the country of his former habitual residence before he can be

---

[71] See *R. v. Secretary of State for the Home Department ex p. Adan* [2001] 2 A.C. 477 at 509.
[71a] [2002] U.K.H.L. 36; [2002] 3 W.L.R. 1276.

recognised as a refugee and his fears must be in that country, not in the country of which he was once a national.[72]

4. The Duties of the Special Adjudicator

Credibility of applicants. As with all contested litigation, the credibility of   **5–37** the witnesses and in particular the applicant, is of vital importance and in Article 3 cases will be the overall deciding feature upon which the Special Adjudicator will make their decision. Even if the medical reports consider that torture, inhuman or degrading treatment has been inflicted upon an applicant the Special Adjudicators often ignore those findings if they feel overall the applicant lacks credibility.

In *R. (on the application of Arulseelan) v. Special Adjudicator*[73] in the Queen's Bench Division (Administrative Court), it was held that notwithstanding the existence of a bad record of maltreatment of supporters allied to a Tamil political organisation, the Special Adjudicator had properly considered the risk of persecution in the applicant's case and had been entitled to find that he lacked credibility.[74]

In *Bekele v. Secretary of State for the Home Department*,[75] the Court of Appeal upheld the Adjudicator's approach when he considered that the applicant lacked credibility even in the face of evidence from the Human Watch Organisation which corroborated his claims of persecution and torture. In that case, the evidence objectively verified the applicant's account of the demonstrations but he had nevertheless failed to establish that he was part of the group that had been detained and tortured.

In *Singh (Amrik) v. Secretary of State for the Home Department*,[76] a psychiatrist found that the shortcomings in details provided by the applicant of past events were in fact consistent with a person who had suffered torture. Nevertheless, the Court of Appeal confirmed the approach of the Immigration Appeal Tribunal when they found that notwithstanding the psychiatrist's findings, there were no grounds to conclude differently than the Special Adjudicator, there was no error in law. The Tribunal had not ignored the evidence of the psychiatrist but rather, as they had been entitled to do, concluded that her findings did not alter the position in relation to the applicant's credibility. They added that the Tribunal had not made findings as to credibility in isolation from the underlying picture.[77]

Totality of evidence. The Adjudicator must examine the totality of the evi-   **5–38** dence without having to separate the parts from each other. In *R. v. Secretary of State for the Home Department ex p. Thirugnanasampanther*, a Sri Lankan Tamil alleged that she had been tortured and raped by security forces. An expert

---

[72] The Asylum Directorate instruct its case workers to consider "the practicality of removal or deportation of a Stateless person as Stateless persons may not always be re-admitted to countries where they were previously permitted to live". Case workers are directed to seek advice from the Immigration Service and other Government bodies before proposing outright refusal.
[73] Judgment of November 20, 2000.
[74] See *Horvath v. Secretary of State for the Home Department* [1999] Imm. A.R. 121.
[75] Judgment date, May 16, 2000 in the Court of Appeal.
[76] [2000] Imm. A.R. 340.
[77] *R. v. Immigration Appeal Tribunal, ex p. Ahmed* [1999] I.N.L.R. 473 distinguished.

instructed by the Medical Foundation for the Care of Victims of Torture supported her account.[78]

Despite the fact that the Medical Foundation supported her account and that
two legal practitioners from Sri Lanka wrote letters verifying the facts, the
Special Adjudicator did not accept the applicant's account of the manner in
which she had been tortured. He found that, although she had been brutally
treated, that was not as a result of persecution as defined by the Convention
relating to the Status of Refugees 1951. This case once again highlights the
classic situation in matters particularly before Special Adjudicators and the
frustration that many practitioners experience in establishing cogent evidence of
torture, inhuman or degrading treatment but having that separate though vital
issue nullified by the "totality of the evidence".

5–39   **The Standard of Proof.**[79] The correct test as laid out in *R. (on the application
of Shohan) v. Special Adjudicator*,[80] in the Queen's Bench Administrative Court
is whether there is a reasonable likelihood that the applicant had been
tortured.[81]

5–40   **Burden of Proof.** The burden of proof to show risk of persecution, which
includes the risk of torture, inhuman or degrading treatment is on the applicant.
This was reiterated in the case of *R. (on the application of Hussein-Deen) v.
Immigration Appeal Tribunal*[82] in the Queen's Bench Division Administrative
Court. If it is contended that due to changed circumstances in an individual's
home country that individual is safe to leave international protection and return

---

[78] The Medical Foundation for the Care of Victims of Torture is a highly reputable organisation which
has an unrivalled expertise in treating and assessing victims of torture. Their reports are often held
in high esteem by courts although the waiting list for such reports to be compiled often means that
applicants are unable to avail themselves of their services.

[79] Where a prospective breach of Article 3 of the Convention is alleged under section 65 of the
Immigration and Asylum Act 199, the standard of proof is the same as in an asylum case (see *Kacai*,
July 19, 2001). This is the lower standard of proof. The question of course is has the claimant
established that there is a real risk of their rights under Article 3 being breached? Section 65 reads:
"(1) A person who alleges that an authority has, in taking any decision under the Immigration Acts
relating to that person's entitlement to enter or remain in the United Kingdom, acted in breach of his
human rights may appeal to an adjudicator against that decision unless he has grounds for bringing
an appeal against the decision under the Special Immigration Appeals Commission Act 1997. (2) For
the purposes of this Part, an authority acts in breach of a person's human rights if he acts, or fails to
act, in relation to that other person in a way which is made harmful by section 6(1) of the Human
Rights Act 1998. (3) Subsections (4) and (5) apply if, in proceedings before an adjudicator or the
Immigration Appeal Tribunal on an appeal, a question arises as to whether an authority has, in taking
any decision under the Immigration Acts relating to the appellant's entitlement to enter or remain in
the United Kingdom, acted in breach of the appellant's human rights. (4) The adjudicator, or the
Tribunal, has jurisdiction to consider the question. (5) If the adjudicator, or the Tribunal, decides that
the authority concerned acted in breach of the appellant's human rights, the appeal may be allowed
on that ground. (6) No appeal may be brought under this section by any person in respect of a decision
if (a) that decision is already the subject of an appeal brought by him under the Special Immigration
Appeals Commission Act 1997; and (b) the appeal under that Act has not been determined. (7)
'Authority' means—(a) the Secretary of State; (b) an immigration officer; (c) a person responsible for
the grant or refusal of entry clearance".

[80] *Independent*, November 27, 2000 (CS). See also *R. v. Special Adjudicator ex p. Shohan*.

[81] The court also held that in relying upon an authority not brought to the party's attention, the Special
Adjudicator had wrongly failed to give the parties the opportunity to deal with the authority that she
had relied upon. This, of itself, was not considered a fatal error but in combination with other errors,
the case was remitted back for consideration by another Adjudicator. See also *R. (on the application
of Dhothar) v. Special Adjudicator* [2001] Imm. A.R. 210.

[82] Judgment of October 27, 2000.

the burden of proof is on the host country and it is for the Secretary of State to discharge that burden.[83]

Special Adjudicator's power to cross-examine. The Special Adjudicator is   **5–41** entitled to conduct a searching examination of an applicant in the absence of any representation from the Home Office. In *R. (on the application of Malibet) v. Immigration Appeal Tribunal*,[84] the Queen's Bench Divisional Court held that the Special Adjudicator had acted unfairly on a number of grounds, including the fact that he acted unfairly in treating the applicant's pregnancy to her husband shortly after she had allegedly been raped and tortured by police officers as casting doubt on her credibility without giving her the opportunity to comment upon that issue.[85]

Rulings must be clear and precise. The Adjudicator must make clear findings   **5–42** as to what evidence he accepts and what evidence he rejects.[86] Findings on the evidence must be clear and precise and Adjudicators are under an obligation to demonstrate to the parties involved that no error of law has been made when reaching a decision, which includes stating, with the requisite degree of clarity, their findings on the evidence.[87] Again, in *R. (on the application of Malibet) v. Immigration Appeal Tribunal*[88] the Queen's Bench Division held that the reasons provided by the Special Adjudicator for his decision did not satisfy the requirement that the applicant be able to understand why her credibility had in that case been doubted.

In *R. v. Immigration Appeal Tribunal ex p. Pal*,[89] the Queen's Bench Division granted an application for judicial review of the Immigration Appeal Tribunal's decision to refuse the applicant permission to appeal against the dismissal of his asylum application. The court accepted that the Tribunal was only required to give brief reasons for their decision, in that particular case they failed to give the requisite minimum reasons to illustrate how their decision had been reached and they had not dealt with the fresh evidence adduced by the applicant at all. The Court of Appeal added that notwithstanding the fact that the medical and psychological reports were unsatisfactory, they were not worthy of total disregard and the application was therefore remitted to the Immigration Appeal Tribunal for fresh consideration.[90]

Judge's duty to give reasons. It is the duty of the judge to produce a judg-   **5–43** ment that gives a clear explanation for his or her order. In *English v. Emery Reimbold and Strick Limited*,[91] the Court of Appeal considered the duties of a judge in the domestic courts and gave certain guidance as to the form of a

---

[83] See *Arif v. Secretary of State for the Home Department* [1999] Imm. A.R. 271 where the Secretary of State argued before the Immigration Appeals Tribunal that the political complexion of Azad Kashmir had changed since the applicant's flight and it would now be safe for him to return.
[84] Judgment of October 30, 2000.
[85] See *R. v. Special Adjudicator ex p. Demeter* [2000] Imm. A.R. 424 considered.
[86] See *R. v. Immigration Appeal Tribunal ex p. Amin (Mohd)* [1992] Imm. A.R. 367.
[87] See *R. v. Immigration Appeal Tribunal ex p. Moniz*, Judgement date July 31, 2000.
[88] 2000 WL 1720381.
[89] Judgment of June 16, 2000; 2000 WL 1720381.
[90] See *Singh (Ramel) v. Secretary of State for the Home Department* 2000 GWD 26–999 confirming that the Special Adjudicator does not have to resolve every particular question of fact.
[91] [2002] EWCA Civ 605: see also *Flannery v. Halifax Estate Agencies Limited* [2000] 1 W.L.R. 377.

judgment which affects the substantive rights of the parties. The Master of the Rolls, Lord Phillips of Worth, commented:

"Strasbourg law required that the decision should be reasoned".

The European Commission of Human Rights has recognised that there are circumstances where the reasoning would be implicit from the decision itself so that it did not need to be expressly set out by the judge. For instance, the practice of giving decisions on costs in summary form without reasons following oral arguments after judgement complies with Article 6 rights to a fair trial only if the reason for the costs decision was clearly implicit from the circumstances In which the award was made.

In *English*, the court stated that:

"Where it was not obvious, the judge should, usually briefly, explain why he has made the order . . . at common law, justice would not be done if it was not apparent to the parties why one party had won and one had lost".

It seems that the adequacy of reasons given depends on the nature of the case. A judge is not obliged to deal with every argument, but for the appellate process to work satisfactorily the judgement has to enable the appellate court to understand why the judge reached his decision. Not every factor which weighs with the judge has to be identified and explained, but the issues the resolution of which were vital to the judge's conclusion should be identified and the manner in which he resolved them explained. In cases of conflict of expert evidence the judge should explain why he has accepted the evidence of one expert and rejected that of another.

5–44   **The courts are only concerned with procedure.** The decision whether or not a person is entitled to political asylum and for the purpose of this book, whether they have been subjected to torture, inhuman or degrading treatment, is the responsibility of the Secretary of State for the Home Department. The courts are only concerned with the question whether the procedures have been properly observed.[92]

In *Nunongo (Mbangala) v. Secretary of State for the Home Department*,[93] although medical reports presented by the applicant were consistent with torture, the same applicant went on to give inconsistent accounts in evidence and as a result of these discrepancies the Secretary of State refused the application for asylum stating the usual reasons of lack of credibility. The Court of Appeal were of the view that given all the facts and circumstances of the case, it was not Wednesbury unreasonable for the Secretary of State for the Home Department to have concluded that the applicant's case lacked credibility and was to be refused.

5–45   **The correct time to make a decision.** If the Special Adjudicator has any doubt about his final conclusions on the issue of torture, inhuman or degrading treatment, he ought to refrain from making a decision as to whether to discharge the Secretary of State's certificate under the Asylum and Immigration Appeals

---

[92] See *Bugdaycay v. Secretary of State for the Home Department* [1987] C.L.Y. 1989 applied.
[93] [1991] Imm. A.R. 616.

Act 1993, Schedule 2, paragraph 5(5) until such time as he has reached a final decision on the merits of the case.[94]

In *Nanthakumar v. Secretary of State for the Home Department*,[95] the applicant gave evidence before the Special Adjudicator of having suffered torture in Sri Lanka. The Special Adjudicator discharged the Schedule 2, paragraph 5(5) certificate, pending his consideration of the substantive case. By the time of his written decision, delivered several months later, he had reached a different conclusion, namely that there was a reasonable likelihood that the applicant had been tortured, or that he would be persecuted, if returned to Sri Lanka.

The applicant contended in the Court of Appeal that those two determinations were directly in conflict and could not stand. Lord Woolf, the Master of the Rolls, concluded that it had been inappropriate of the Special Adjudicator to discharge the certificate because that step gave the appearance of accepting that the evidence relied established a reasonable likelihood of torture. The appeal was allowed for this and other reasons.

Reconsidering findings of fact by the Adjudicator. The Immigration Appeal **5–46** Tribunal will only overturn the Adjudicator's findings of fact if it is clearly wrong. This seems to correlate with the observations in *DF v. United Kingdom*[96] where the European Court of Human Rights observed that it will not interfere with the findings of domestic courts on issues of fact unless that court has come to a decision which is grossly unfair or arbitrary on the facts before it.

In *McPherson v. Secretary of State for the Home Department*,[97] a female Jamaican national entered the United Kingdom as a visitor. Following her conviction for drug offences, she was recommended for deportation. She appealed under section 65 of the Immigration and Asylum Act 1999 that deportation would violate her rights under Article 3 and Article 8 of the Convention. The adjudicator held that Jamaican society was such that she would be at risk if she returned. The Immigration Appeal Tribunal allowed the appeal but did not consider the Article 8 claim as it was of the view that it should not reconsider findings of fact made by an adjudicator unless persuaded that they were clearly wrong, in other words, that there was insufficient evidence to support such a finding.

The adjudicator had determined as a matter of fact the applicant would be at risk. The crucial question was could the State protect her? The Immigration Appeal Tribunal set out its reasons for overturning the adjudicator on these matters as it was perfectly entitled to do. The important issue was were they entitled to overturn the adjudicator's decision without remitting the matter? The appeal was allowed and the Articles 3 and 8 issue was remitted back.

5. NEW CLAIMS OF ILL-TREATMENT

Later elaboration will not suffice. Normally where ill-treatment was initially **5–47** alleged, later further elaboration of much worse ill-treatment will not amount to

---

[94] The Asylum and Immigration Appeals Act 1993, Schedule 2, paragraph 5(5) must be applied to all of the material before the Special Adjudicator, not merely to that relating to the alleged torture, inhuman or degrading treatment.

[95] [2000] I.N.L.R. 480.

[96] Application No. 12016/86. See Chapter 6: Medical Treatment.

[97] (2001) All E.R. (D) 294, judgment of December 19, 2001.

a new claim. In *R. v. Secretary of State for the Home Department ex p. Ejon*,[98] the applicant initially alleged that she had been beaten and questioned by soldiers in Uganda. The Secretary of State refused the application. The applicant appealed and claimed that she had been the victim of multiple rapes by Ugandan soldiers and that she had been regularly raped by a soldier who provided her with protection against further rapes by other soldiers. Her new claims of rape and trauma were supported by reports from Women Against Rape and the Medical Foundation for the Care of Victims of Torture. It was submitted by the Secretary of State that there had not been a fresh application for asylum, because the new claim repeated the previous application and that the applicant had had ample opportunity to present all available evidence to the Secretary of State.

The applicant then obtained and submitted a psychiatric report which concluded that she was suffering from Post Traumatic Stress Disorder and her efforts to avoid the experiences had prevented her from mentioning the relevant incidents earlier. Again, the Secretary of State refused to accept that a fresh application for asylum had been made.

In the Queen's Bench Division hearing, the Secretary of State accepted that the new evidence was "apparently credible" but contended that it did not satisfy the "unavailability" limb of the test in *Ladd v. Marshall*.[99]

5–48   **The test in *Ladd v. Marshall*.** In normal circumstances where ill-treatment is initially alleged, further elaboration of much worse ill-treatment will not amount to a new claim as the *Ladd v. Marshall* hurdles of "availability", "significance" and "credibility" would have to be overcome.

Denning L.J. (as he then was) put it this way:

> "The principles to be applied are the same as those always applied when fresh evidence is sought to be introduced.
>
> In order to justify the reception of fresh evidence or a new trial, three conditions must be fulfilled: first, it must be shown that the evidence could not have been obtained with reasonable diligence for use at the trial; second, the evidence must be such that, if given, it would probably have an important influence on the result of the case, although it need not be decisive; third, the evidence must be such as is presumably to be believed, or in other words, it must be apparently credible, although it need not be incontrovertible".

These principles apply whether it is alleged that a witness in a previous hearing has told a lie or indeed simply omitted to tell an accurate version of what happened for perfectly honest reasons, although to admit fresh evidence of a dishonest witness may not satisfy the third condition of credibility. In that case, to justify the reception of the fresh evidence, some good reason must be shown why a lie was told in the first incident, and good ground given for thinking the witness will tell the truth on the second occasion.

Denning L.J. went on to say:

> "If it were proved that the witness had been bribed or coerced into telling a lie at the trial, and was now anxious to tell the truth, that would, I think, be a ground for a new trial, and it would not be necessary to resort to an action to set aside the judgement on the ground of fraud.

---

[98] [1998] I.N.L.R. 195.
[99] [1954] 3 All E.R. 745.

Again, if it were proved that the witness made a mistake on a most important matter and wished to correct it, and the circumstances were so well explained that his fresh evidence was presumably to be believed, then again there would be ground for a new trial".[1]

It is important that applicants present the full panoply of their ill-treatment to the court at the first available opportunity otherwise the obstacle course provided by *Ladd v. Marshall* will have to be overcome which will not be easy.[2]

6. INABILITY OF RECEIVING STATE TO OFFER PROTECTION

Evidence to show inability. It is for the applicant to produce evidence to show 5–49 that a Receiving State will be unable to offer him protection. If there is no such evidence produced, the Secretary of State does not have to take the matter into consideration. But the standard of protection offered by the Receiving State must be such as to remove the real risk of ill-treatment.[3]

In *R. (on the application of Kiramburi) v. Secretary of State for the Home Department*,[4] the applicant contended that the Kenyan authorities were unable to protect him and it would be wrong to send him to France which applied the so-called accountability theory, denying refugee status if a State were willing, though unable, to provide protection.[5] It follows that had the applicant been able to produce evidence to substantiate his allegation that Kenya would be unable to offer him protection, it was a matter which the Secretary of State would be directed to take into account when considering any applications.

7. PARTICULAR DUTIES OF THE SECRETARY OF STATE

No requirement to carry out particular investigations. The Secretary of 5–50 State is not required to carry out any particular investigations in relation to

---

[1] See also *Richardson v. Fisher* (1823) 1 Bing 145.

[2] Somewhat reassuringly, the applicant in *R. v. Secretary of State for the Home Department ex p. Ejon* succeeded in her appeal in that once her evidence had been accepted as "apparently credible", it was perverse for the Secretary of State to have then categorised a person suffering from the degree of suffering and trauma described in the reports as "unwilling to give evidence" as opposed to "unable to give evidence". The evidence of repeated and sustained rapes was, the Queen's Bench Division considered, in a different league altogether from the isolated incidents of ill-treatment described earlier by the applicant, and the new evidence, accepted as "apparently credible" and containing an explanation as to why it had not been produced earlier presented a wholly different view of what the applicant might have to fear if she returned to Uganda. Considering the gravity of the sexual violence alleged, the court considered that the Secretary of State had been unreasonable to conclude that there had been no new claim for asylum.

[3] See also *R. v. Secretary of State for the Home Department ex p. Kebbeh*, where an amputee with serious medical and psychological problems would receive no financial or medical support in Gambia and therefore his deportation was quashed (April 30, 1998, Hidden J: see also *R. v. Secretary of State for the Home Department ex p. M* 23 July 1999: and *R. (on the application of Njai) v. Secretary of State for the Home Department*, December 1, 2000). See also *R. v. SS SS ex p. JCWI* where the court held that the imposition of conditions of destitution breached fundamental human rights [1997] 1 W.L.R. 275.

[4] Judgment of October 13, 2000.

[5] An approach which had led the court to refuse to permit the removal of an asylum seeker in *R. v. Secretary of State for the Home Department ex p. Adan (Lul Omar)* [1999] 3 W.L.R. 1274.

individual allegations of potential ill-treatment in Receiving States. The Secretary of State is entitled to rely upon information that he obtains through the Foreign and Commonwealth Office.

In *Akdag (Sabri) v. Secretary of State for the Home Department,*[6] a Turkish Kurd applied for political asylum. This was refused but on receipt of the news the applicant became mentally disordered and showed suicidal tendencies. The Secretary of State was asked to reconsider his decision but maintained his position. The Court of Appeal upheld the Secretary of State's decision not to carry out investigations in Turkey to verify the truth or falsehood of the applicant's claims as proper discharge of his duties.[7]

5-51   **State should not conduct balancing exercise.** The European Court overturned the observations of the Queen's Bench Division,[8] that the Secretary of State for the Home Department, in considering the applicant's claim for refugee status and deciding whether to deport him was required to balance the applicant's interests as identified by the Convention against those of national security.

The Queen's Bench Division were of the view that the Secretary of State for the Home Department had acted reasonably on the material available to him in weighing the risk of torture against the risk to national security and reaching the conclusion he did. This view was rejected by the European Court in *Chahal v. United Kingdom*[9] which stressed that though "well aware of the immense difficulties faced by States in modern times in protecting their communities from terrorist violence ... even in these circumstances, the Convention prohibits in absolute terms torture or inhuman or degrading treatment or punishment, irrespective of the victim's conduct ... ". There is no balancing exercise to be conducted when weighing the risk of torture, inhuman or degrading treatment against the risk to national security.[10]

---

[6] [1993] Imm. A.R. 172.

[7] It was further held that deportation of an applicant for asylum who has had his application lawfully refused cannot amount to inhuman or degrading treatment where the applicant has suffered mental or physical disorder as a result of the dismissal of his application for asylum.

[8] See *R. v. Secretary of State for the Home Department ex p. Chahal (No. 2)* [1995] 1 W.L.R. 526.

[9] (1997) 23 E.H.R.R. 413.

[10] Assessing whether an applicant is indeed a "terrorist" is often difficult as the term is often subjectively applied. In *Sivakumar v. Secretary of State for the Home Department; R (on the application of Sivakumar) v. Secretary of State for the Home Department* [2001] EWCA Civ 1196, a Sri Lankan Tamil appealed against the refusal of his application for judicial review ([2001] EWHC Admin 109) of a decision to refuse his asylum claim. The Special Adjudicator had concluded that whilst the applicant's evidence concerning the torture he had been subjected to by the authorities was credible, such torture had not been the result of any political opinion that S might have been believed to have held but instead resulted from a suspicion that he was involved in violent terrorism. The applicant contended that the Special Adjudicator had erred and that he should have been found to have a well founded fear of persecution on three Convention grounds, namely, imputed political opinion, race and membership of a particular social group. He further maintained that imputed political opinion and suspicion of involvement in violent terrorism were not mutually exclusive concepts and that an individual suspected of involvement in violent terrorism could equally have a political opinion imputed to him. The Court of Appeal upheld this view and confirmed that where an individual had been persecuted for his alleged involvement in violent terrorism, it did not necessarily follow that he had been persecuted for his political opinion. Each case had to be assessed on its merits and the particular reason for persecution determined. It was not necessarily the case that excessive and arbitrary punishment for political offences would amount to persecution for Convention purposes but such treatment, the court held, raised a strong inference that that was in fact the case; see also *Paramanathan v. Minister for Immigration and Multicultural Affairs* (1998) 160 A.L.R. 24.

The court's power to review legality of subordinate legislation. The court   **5–52**
is entitled to review on the grounds of illegality, procedural impropriety or
unreasonableness, the legality of subordinate legislation made by a minister and
approved by affirmative resolution of both Houses of Parliament.[11] The starting
point for the domestic court's approach to Parliamentary legislation goes as far
back as Article 9 of the Bill of Rights 1689[12] which provides:

> "That the freedome of speech and debates or proceedings in Parlyament ought not to
> be impeached or questioned in any court or place out of Parlyament".

But the courts have asserted their right to review the legality of subordinate
legislation:

> "The fact that, in the course of debate, the Secretary of State or others make statements
> of fact that support the legitimacy of the subordinate legislation and that the House
> thereafter approves the subordinate legislation, cannot render it unconstitutional for the
> court to review the material facts and form its own judgement, even if the result is
> discordant with statements made in Parliamentary debate".[13]

In the above case, the Secretary of State for the Home Department, in purported
exercise of the powers conferred upon him under the Asylum and Immigration
Appeals Act 1993[14] as substituted by the Asylum and Immigration Act 1996,
Section 2(3), laid before Parliament an order designating Pakistan as a country in
respect of which there was "in general no risk of persecution". The applicant
disagreed.

Particular reference to Article 3. The Secretary of State's decisions will be   **5–53**
particularly examined in issues relating to Article 3.[15]
In *R. v. Secretary of State for the Home Department ex p. Turgut*,[16] a case
concerning Article 3, Simon Browne L.J. observed[17]:

> "I therefore conclude that the domestic court's obligation on an irrationality challenge
> in an Article 3 case is to subject the Secretary of State's decision to rigorous examina-
> tion, and this it does by considering the underlying factual material for itself to see
> whether or not it compels a different conclusion to that arrived at by the Secretary of
> State. Only if it does will the challenge succeed . . . all that said, however, this is not an
> area in which the court will pay any especial deference to the Secretary of State's
> conclusion on the facts. In the first place, the human right involved here—the right not
> to be exposed to a real risk of Article 3 ill-treatment—is both absolute and fundamental:
> it is not a qualified right requiring a balance to be struck with some competing social
> need. Secondly, the court here is hardly less well placed than the Secretary of State
> himself to evaluate the risk once the relevant material is placed before it.
>   Thirdly, whilst I would reject the applicant's contention that the Secretary of State
> has knowingly misrepresented the evidence or shut his eyes to the true position, we
> must, I think, recognise at least the possibility that he has (even if unconsciously)
> tended to depreciate the evidence of risk and, throughout the protracted decision

---

[11] See *R. (Asif Javed) v. Secretary of State for the Home Department* [2002] Q.B. 129.
[12] 1 Will. and Mary, sess 2, c.2.
[13] See *R. (Asif Javed) v. Secretary of State for the Home Department* [2002] Q.B. 129 at p. 147,
para. 37.
[14] Para. 5(2) of Schedule 2.
[15] See *R. v. Ministry of Defence ex p. Smith* [1996] Q.B. 517.
[16] [2001] 1 All E.R. 719.
[17] At p. 729.

making process, may have tended also to rationalise the further material adduced so as to maintain his pre-existing stance rather than reassess the position with an open mind.

In circumstances such as these, what has been called the 'discretionary area of judgment'—the area of judgment within which the court should defer to the Secretary of State as the person primarily entrusted with the decision on the applicant's removal[18] is a decidedly narrow one."

It seems in the above circumstances the courts will not hesitate to question the decision making process of the Secretary of State.

8. THE NEED TO EXHAUST DOMESTIC REMEDIES

5–54   **Formal requirements and time limits to be complied with.** While the prohibition of torture contained in Article 3 of the Convention is absolute in expulsion cases as in other cases, applicants invoking Article 3 are not for that reason excused as a matter of course from exhausting domestic remedies that are available and effective. It seems to follow that even in cases of expulsion to a country where there is an alleged risk of ill-treatment contrary to Article 3, the formal requirements and time limits laid down in domestic law should normally be complied with.

Whether there are special circumstances which absolve an applicant from the obligation to comply with such rules will depend on the facts of each case. Furthermore, any procedural means which may prevent a breach of the Convention should be used.[19]

In *Bahaddar v. Netherlands*,[20] the European Court held that the applicant had failed to exhaust his domestic remedies despite the fact that his lawyer had failed to submit grounds of appeal when required, failed to request any extension of time and failed to explain the delay when the grounds were finally submitted, three months late.[21]

5–55   **Court of Appeal is reluctant to permit second appeals.** In *Koller v. Secretary of State for the Home Department*,[22] the court laid down that it is reluctant to permit a second appeal if the Immigration Appeal Tribunal sets out the relevant principles of law correctly and the facts clearly before applying the law to the facts. An appeal from the Immigration Appeal Tribunal does not fall into the category of Tribunal Appeals identified by the court in *Cooke v. Secretary of State for Social Security*[23] to which a stricter approach should be applied to the granting of permission to make second appeals.[23a]

---

[18] See Lord Hope of Craighead's Speech in *R. v. Director of Public Prosecutions, ex p. Kebilene* [2000] 2 A.C. 326, at 380–381.

[19] See *Akdivar v. Turkey* (1997) 23 E.H.R.R. 143.

[20] (1998) 26 E.H.R.R. 278.

[21] The Court also held that it would be open to the applicant to lodge a further application for refugee status and if necessary to apply for an interim injunction restraining his expulsion.

[22] [2002] EWCA Civ 1267.

[23] [2001] EWCA Civ 734.

[23a] See *Gardi v. Secretary of State for the Home Department (No. 2)* [2002] EWCA Civ 1560, *The Times*, October 25, 2002 which held that the Court of Appeal has no jurisdiction to entertain an appeal from the Immigration Appeal Tribunal where the detention has been made by an adjudicator in Scotland. Such an appeal lies with the Court of Session.

9. COMPARATIVE INTERNATIONAL APPROACHES TO ASYLUM

Different approaches. Countries throughout the world have different attitudes   **5–56**
towards refugees and asylum seekers and it is important to appreciate attitudes of
countries from which or to which applicants have travelled.

United States. American law offers asylum to anyone with a "credible fear"   **5–57**
of persecution because of race, religion, nationality, membership of a particular
social group, or political opinion. In 2001, the United States received 60,853
asylum applications. Most came from Mexico with 12,675, followed by China
with 9,142. In total, only 7,839 people were granted asylum. As to the accommodation of applicants, at any time about 20,000 asylum applicants are being
held in custody, many of them in local prisons. About 40 per cent of those
awaiting asylum will abscond and disappear into America as illegal immigrants.

Australia. Australia defines an asylum seeker as someone who is unwilling or   **5–58**
unable to return to their homeland due to a well founded fear of being persecuted
for race, religion, nationality or political opinions. In 2000–2001, 13,733 applicants for refugee or asylum seeker status were accepted. About 4,000 of these
were boat people and about 1,500 who claimed to be refugees arrived by air.
Those who applied for asylum once they arrive in Australia can often face a long
and bureaucratic delay.

Denmark. Early in May, Denmark's Parliament passed new legislation tight-   **5–59**
ening controls on immigration. The Bill abolishes the concept of de facto
refugees, allowing only individual asylum seekers and refugees entitled to
protection under international law to live in Denmark. The State-run Danish
Immigration Service records that a total of 12,512 asylum seekers came to
Denmark in 2001, mainly from Iraq, Afghanistan, Bosnia and Yugoslavia. 53 per
cent were granted asylum, the process taking on average 240 days.

Germany. Asylum is given to refugees who flee their countries for political   **5–60**
reasons, according to the Geneva Convention. A second group is tolerated
because they would face political persecution if they returned to their home
countries. A third group is tolerated on humanitarian grounds. Refugees who are
given asylum for political reasons can stay for life. This could change with the
new immigration law that has not yet been passed by the German Parliament. In
2001, German authorities received 88,287 applications (12.4 per cent more than
the previous year). 5,716 applications were accepted for political reasons, 17,003
for political persecution, and 3,383 on humanitarian grounds. According to
Germany's official figures, 55,402 asylum seekers were refused asylum. In 2001,
5,566 asylum seekers came from Iraq (19.6 per cent) followed by Turkey (12.3
per cent) and the Federal Republic of Yugoslavia (8.9 per cent).

France. The French received 47,291 asylum requests in 2001, accepting 18   **5–61**
per cent of them on the basis that they fulfilled the terms of the Geneva
Convention on Human Rights. The biggest group of asylum seekers were from
Turkey, mostly from Turkish Kurdistan, with 5,347 claims, followed by the
Democratic Republic of Congo (3,781), China (2,948), Mali (2,940), Algeria
(2,933), Hiaiti (2,730), Mauritania (2,332) and Sri Lanka (2,000). Claims in

France will take between 4 months and 4 years to process. During that period, claimants have no right to work and receive welfare benefit of about £200 a month for a maximum of 12 months.

5–62   **Canada.** Canadian statistics reveal that there were 44,000 refugee claimants in 2001. Canada accepted 13,500 refugees in 2000. The remainder were either sent back, are in the process of being sent back, or their cases are under appeal. While waiting for a hearing, claimants have the right to work in Canada, collect public welfare, receive free education, free hospital treatment, and free language classes. There is a two year of back log of applicants in Canada.

5–63   **Italy.** The Interior Ministry of the Italian authorities states that in 2002 there were 10,000 requests for asylum, of which 1,000 had been accepted, 2,000 rejected and the others are still under consideration.

5–64   **Spain.** Interestingly, in Spain the term asylum is rarely used. There are about 1,000,0000 legal immigrants, about half from the European Union and the rest from Morocco, Latin America and Eastern Europe, and an estimated 150,000 illegal immigrant.

Many Africans escaping sub-Saharan war or famine are also held in Spain's African enclaves of Ceuta and Melilla. In 2001, 13,000 illegal immigrants were deported while, in one of the Spanish Government's occasional amnesties, 120,000 had their status regularised.

10. EXPULSION

5–65   **Generally.** Repeated expulsion of an applicant to a State where the applicant's safety is not guaranteed can give rise to a breach of Article 3.[24] When someone is expelled it is sometimes difficult to be sure of the applicant's fate and there is an onerous duty on the expelling State to attempt to ascertain the safety of the receiving country.[25]

11. REFUSAL OF ENTRY

5–66   **Qualification for Protection.** The physical presence of the applicant within the jurisdiction of the State qualifies that applicant to the absolute protection provided by Article 3.[26]

5–67   **Discrimination.**[27] This is the most prevalent basis of claim under Article 3 in relation to admission cases. In *East African Asian v. United Kingdom*,[28] it was

---

[24] See *Giana v. Belgium* (1980) 21 D.R. 73.
[25] See *Ahmed v. Austria* (1996) 24 E.H.R.R. 278 at paras. 39 and 47.
[26] See *SM and MT v. Austria* (1993) 74 DR 179 and *Amuur v. France* (1996) 22 E.H.R.R. 533.
[27] Racial harassment has been found to be capable of being degrading treatment. See *Hilton v. United Kingdom* (1976) 4 D.R. 177, as has institutionalised racism: see *East African Asians v. United Kingdom* (1973) 3 E.H.R.R. which concerned British passport holders who had been expelled from Uganda, Tanzania and Kenya being refused residence in the United Kingdom. The use of grossly racist remarks was also held in that case to be capable of degrading treatment.
[28] (1981) 3 E.H.R.R. 76.

held by the Commission that discrimination[29] based on race can in prescribed circumstances violate Article 3 as degrading treatment. In a key passage it was observed "A special importance should be attached to discrimination based on race; that publicly to single out a group of persons for differential treatment on the basis of race might, in certain circumstances, constitute a special form of affront to human dignity; and that differential treatment of a group of persons on the basis of race might therefore be capable of constituting degrading treatment when differential treatment on some other ground would raise no such question".

Discrimination of itself will not suffice to violate Article 3 and there must be special or aggravating circumstances to force the issue over the minimum severity threshold. In *Abdulaziz, Cabales and Balkandali v. United Kingdom*,[30] the applicant wives lawfully and permanently settled in the United Kingdom complained that their husbands were refused to permission to join them. The court held no breach of Article 3,[31] and held that "the difference in treatment . . . did not denote any contempt or lack of respect for the personality of the applicants" and "it was not designed to, and did not, humiliate or debase" them. This of course refers back to *Ireland v. United Kingdom*[32] where the European Court on human Rights held that the five techniques were, amongst other reasons, degrading because they were such as to arouse in their victims feelings of fear, anguish and inferiority capable of humiliating them and debasing them and possibly breaking their physical or moral resistance.[33]

The separation of spouses or parents. Often expulsion will cause spouses to   **5–68** be separated or parents to be separated from their children. The increasing phenomena of people being expelled from their spouse or child's country of origin has rarely been considered by the court. This factor was acknowledged in *Boultif v. Switzerland*[34] which was an application under Article 8,[35] where it was held that sending the applicant to Algeria would be a serious impediment to establishing a family life. It was held that the interference was not proportionate to the aim pursued and was therefore in breach of Article 8.

In *Sen v. Netherlands*[36] the European Court found unanimously a violation of Article 8 concerning the refusal of a residents permit to allow the applicant child, living in Turkey, to join her applicant parents who were living in the Netherlands.

---

[29] But see *Hector v. United Kingdom* (*The Guardian*, April 20, 1990 in the European Court on Human Rights) which held that race discrimination *per se* may not amount to an Article 3 violation. In this case the applicant who was black together with several white men went to a private club and asked to enter in order to collect money for charity. The applicant was refused entry to the club. The club's doormen said "If the manager says it's alright for you to collect the rest of you can, but the black lad can't". The applicant complained to the Commission of the European Communities on Human Rights that his treatment had violated the European Convention on Human Rights, Article 3, Article 11, Article 11 and Article 13. The European Court held the application was inadmissible. They observed that the applicant's treatment did not attain such a level of severity as to make it treatment prohibited by Article 3.

[30] (1985) 7 E.H.R.R. 471.

[31] Although they did find breaches of Article 8 and Article 14 on the basis of sex discrimination.

[32] (1978) 2 E.H.R.R. 25.

[33] At page 80, para. 167 and Chapter 3: Interrogation.

[34] (2001) 33 E.H.R.R. 50.

[35] See Chapter 9: Physical Integrity.

[36] Heard on December 21, 2001.

If the applicant's family is capable of resettling with him in his original home, then any request to remain will be refused and there will be no Convention reason to overturn it.[37]

The European Court laid down certain guidelines as to what issues a tribunal should take into account when considering whether an applicant should be expelled. They were:

(a) the nature and seriousness of the offence;

(b) the length of the applicant's stay in the expelling country;

(c) the time elapsed since the offence was committed;

(d) the applicant's conduct during the intervening period;

(e) the nationalities of the persons concerned;

(f) the applicant's family situation, such as the length of marriage and other factors expressing the effectiveness of a couple's family life;

(g) whether the spouse had knowledge of the offence when they entered into the relationship;

(h) whether there are children of the marriage, and their ages;

(i) the seriousness of the difficulties which the spouse is likely to encounter in the country of origin.

On the facts of *Boultif*'s case, the court observed that the applicant was rehabilitated since his offences and that for his Swiss wife to live in Algeria she would suffer "obvious and considerable difficulties".

5–69   **Effect on spouse of deportation.** The Court of Appeal have considered that the detrimental effect on the applicant's spouse of deportation could be a factor to be taken into account when considering whether an overstayer could remain. The case of *Carpenter v. Secretary of State for the Home Department*[38] concerned the Article 49 right to provide services.

Article 49 EC reads that:

"Within the framework of the provisions set out below, restrictions on freedom to provide services within the Community shall be prohibited in respect of nationals of

---

[37] See *R. v. Secretary of State for the Home Department ex p. Mehmet Sezek*, Queen's Bench Division (Administrative Court) December 21, 2000. The claimant S applied for judicial review of the Secretary of State's refusal to revoke a deportation order. S entered the U.K. in 1976 and was granted indefinite leave to remain, together with his wife and daughter in 1983. In March 1994, S was convicted of importing heroin and sentenced to 16 years' imprisonment. In January 1995, S was informed of the decision to deport him. S's appeal to the Immigration Appeal Tribunal was rejected and leave to appeal to the Court of Appeal declined. S claimed that the deportation order should be revoked on compassionate grounds and also because of his good prison record, personal referees and Article 8. The request was refused, on the ground that his family was capable of re-settling in Turkey with him.

[38] *The Times*, July 20, 2002.

Member States who are established in a state of the Community other than that of the person for whom the services are intended . . . ".

The applicant appealed, maintaining that she had a right to remain in the United Kingdom, as her husband's business required him to travel around in other Member States providing and receiving services, and that her presence would make it easier for him to do so as she was looking after his children, so that her deportation would restrict her husband's right to provide and receive services under Article 49 EC.[39]

The court were of the view that a Member State could invoke reasons of public interest to justify a national measure which was likely to obstruct the exercise of the freedom to provide services only if that measure was compatible with the fundamental rights whose observance the court ensured, which included the right to respect for family life within the meaning of Article 8. In short, it was held that the decision to deport the applicant constituted an interference with her husband's exercise of that right.

12. STATE IMMUNITY

Protection for Sovereign States should be in harmony with Convention   **5–70**
rights. The State Immunity Act 1978 grants immunity to Sovereign States for acts committed outside their jurisdiction, without an implied exception for acts of torture. The Act does not apply to criminal proceedings.

This principle of Sovereign Immunity is a concept of international law, by virtue of which one State is not subject to the jurisdiction of another. In *Al-Adsani v. United Kingdom*[40] the European Court considered that granting Sovereign Immunity to a State in civil proceedings pursued the legitimate aim of complying with international law to promote comity and good relations between States through the respect of another State's sovereignty.

The court further observed that the European Convention on Human Rights, should, so far as possible, be interpreted in harmony with other rules of international law of which it formed part, including those relating to State Immunity. It follows from this reasoning that measures which reflect the generally recognised rules of public international law on State Immunity cannot in principle be regarded as imposing a disproportionate restriction on the right of access to court as embodied in Article 6(1).

In *Al Adsani v. United Kingdom*,[41] the European Court recalled that Article 1 required States to "secure" the listed rights and freedoms to persons within its own "jurisdiction" (see *Soering*). Articles 1 and 3 taken together place a number of positive obligations on the States, designed to prevent and provide redress for torture and other forms of ill-treatment. However, the State's obligation only applies in relation to ill-treatment, allegedly committed within its jurisdiction.

---

[39] Previously Article 59 EC.
[40] (2002) 34 E.H.R.R. 11.
[41] (2002) E.H.R.R. 11.

In *Soering* the court recognised that Article 3 has some limited extra-territorial effect, to the extent that the decision by a State to expel an individual might engage the responsibility of that State under the Convention, where substantial grounds had been shown for believing that the person concerned, if expelled, faces a real risk of being subjected to torture or to inhuman and degrading treatment or punishment in the receiving country. However, liability under the Convention might only be incurred if by reason of the State having taken action the individual was exposed as a direct result to prescribed ill-treatment.

"The applicant does not contend that the alleged torture took place within the jurisdiction of the United Kingdom or that the United Kingdom authorities had any causal connection with its occurrence. In these circumstances, it cannot be said that the High Contracting Party was under a duty to provide a civil remedy to the applicant in respect of torture allegedly carried out by the Kuwaiti authorities. It follows that there has been no violation of Article 3 in respect to the present case" (see paras. 40 and 41).

Furthermore, in *Al-Adsani*, while noting the growing recognition of the over-riding importance of the prohibition of torture, the European Court did not find it established that there was yet acceptance in international law of the proposition that States were not entitled to immunity in respect of civil claims for damages for alleged torture committed outside the forum State.

Somewhat surprisingly, the court were of the view that the State Immunity Act 1978 which granted immunity to States in respect of personal injury claims unless the damage was caused within the United Kingdom, was not inconsistent with those limitations generally accepted by the Community of Nations as part of the doctrine of State Immunity. It was therefore considered that the application by the English courts of the provisions of the 1978 Act to uphold Kuwait's claim to immunity, could not, therefore be said to have amounted to an unjustified restriction on the applicant's access to court. Again, it followed that there had been no violation of Article 6(1).[42] The failure to establish an exception for acts of torture, inhuman or degrading treatment from the strictures of the State Immunity Act is both perplexing and of concern.

5–71   **Limitation of State Immunity.** There is a trend in international and comparative law towards limiting State Immunity in respect of personal injury caused by an act or omission within the forum State, although the practice is by no means universal at the moment. The trend primarily refers to insurable personal injury, that is incidents arising out of ordinary road traffic accidents, rather than matters relating to the core area of State Sovereignty, such as the acts of soldiers on foreign territory which, of their very nature, might involve sensitive issues affecting diplomatic relations between States and national security.

In *Fogarty v. United Kingdom*,[43] the European Court observed that there appeared to be a trend in international and comparative law towards limiting State immunity in respect of employment related disputes. However, where the proceedings relate to employment in a foreign mission or embassy, international practice is divided on the question whether State Immunity continues to apply

---

[42] But see the dissenting judgments.
[43] (2002) 34 E.H.R.R. 12.

and, if it did, whether it covers disputes relating to the contracts of all staff or only more senior members of the mission. Questions relating to the recruitment of staff to missions and embassies might by their very nature involve sensitive and confidential issues, relating to the diplomatic and organisational policy of a foreign State.

It is somewhat incongruous that the absolute right not to be tortured or treated in any inhuman or degrading fashion is summarily negated by the State Immunity Act, particularly when in other areas such as road traffic accidents State Immunity is limited.

Duty to provide a civil remedy. If a breach of Article 3 has occurred within **5–72** the territory of a State, then that State has a duty to provide a civil remedy, failure to do so can result in a violation of Article 3. But if the alleged torture took place outside the jurisdiction of the State or that the authority had no causal connection with its occurrence, then no liability can be established.

In *Al-Adsani v. United Kingdom*,[44] the applicant alleged that high ranking officials of the Kuwaiti Government tortured him, and in particular that his head was repeatedly held underwater in a swimming pool containing corpses and was severely beaten for several days as well as receiving 25 per cent burns to his body. He instituted civil proceedings in England for compensation against the Kuwaiti Government and the Sheikh allegedly involved and obtained a default judgement against the Sheikh. Later, the High Court ordered that the action be struck out against the Kuwaiti Government finding that State immunity applied under the State Immunity Act. As such the United Kingdom was not held by the European Court of Human Rights to be under any duty to provide a civil remedy and their failure to do so in that case was not in breach of Article 3.

13. THE FUTURE

The Bill. The Nationality, Immigration and Asylum Bill proposes significant **5–73** changes to procedure in relation to asylum cases:

1. Either a High Court Judge or an Adjudicator of the Immigration Appellate Authority will be "explicitly required" to impose financial penalties on lawyers bringing appeals and applications of "no merit".

   The Legal Services Commission will then have to consider if the lawyers should receive any payment or only partial payment for work done on behalf of the applicant.

2. In further amendments to the Bill, the Government seeks to stop judicial review asylum hearings on points of law by setting up a new review process. Under this process a failed asylum applicant who seeks to challenge a decision on a point of law will, if the Bill passes into legislation, have to apply in two weeks rather than in three months.

---

[44] (2002) 34 E.H.R.R. 11.

> Instead of an oral argument a single High Court Judge will deal with the matter after studying written argument.[45]

These proposed changes are clearly designed to speed up the appeals system but in hearings which have to resolve Article 3 issues, it is often the subjective view of the Tribunal that will assess upon all the criteria before them whether there is a reasonable risk of violation.

It is to be hoped that this subjective view, if it tends to be against the legal advice that the applicant has been given, will not result in a rash of costs awards against lawyers who have properly attempted to interpret a very fluid area of law.

---

[45] The proposals are clearly intended to cut the annual 129 million asylum and immigration legal aid budget and reduce the tens of thousands of applicants who automatically appeal when their case is rejected. A total of 118,000 cases were given initial decisions in 2001. About 10 per cent are given asylum, 25 per cent exceptional leave to remain in the United Kingdom and of the 65 per cent rejected, most appeal against the decision. In 2001, the Immigration Appellate Authority dealt with 19,395 appeals, of which 3,340 or 17 per cent were allowed. 15,580 or 80 per cent were dismissed and 475 or 2 per cent were withdrawn. There are approximately 55,00 appeals still outstanding. The main countries from which applicants have come in, in 2001, are Afghanistan—91,901; Iraq—6,805; Somalia—6,500; Sri Lanka—5,545; Turkey—3,740. The main countries to which failed asylum applicants removed in a third quarter of 2001 were Federal Republic of Yugoslavia—435; Czech Republic—190; Poland—145; Pakistan—140; Albania—1351; India—115; Romania—105. An applicant needing accommodation will be put in temporary accommodation before being disbursed to other premises around the country. If the applicant needs financial support, he or she gets £29.89 a week if aged 18–24 and £37.77 aged 25-. All applicants are eligible for free medical treatment and children are eligible for free education. Applicants are barred for working for six months. It takes, on average, 13 months for an asylum seeker to reach the end of the process, i.e. appeal is determined. It is plain that it is taking two months to deal with an initial application and $3\frac{1}{2}$ months for an appeal to be heard. The gap between the two figures is the time the appeal waits in the Home Office (about 7 months) before being sent to the Immigration Appellate Authority for the appeal. As for accommodation, Oakington Reception Centre in Cambridgeshire is for asylum claimers which, upon initial screening, seems straightforward and suitable for processing within 7–10 days. It has a capacity for 400. There are also detention centres at Harmondsworth, near Heathrow with a capacity for 550; Tinsley House, near Gatwick Airport to accommodate 137; Yarlswood in Bedfordshire which is presently closed because of riot and fire but could accommodate 900 at its peak; Dungavel, in Lanarkshire, Scotland, to accommodate 150; Campsfield House, Oxfordshire accommodating 184; and Dover accommodating 100 which will rise to 316. There are also two prisons which hold immigration detainees, including asylum seekers, whom the authorities fear will abscond—they are Haslar in Hampshire with a capacity of 160 and Lindholme in South Yorkshire accommodating 112. The Government plans in the future to build three accommodation centres each holding 750.

CHAPTER 6

MEDICAL TREATMENT

Bullet points. The following principles can be extracted: **6–01**

- Minimum level of severity rules apply—see *T and V v. United Kingdom* (1999) 7 B.H.R.C. 659;

- Prima facie negligence can activate Article 3—see *Association X v. United Kingdom* (1978) 14 D.R. 31;

- Withdrawal of care with resultant serious consequences for patient may violate Article 3—see *D v. United Kingdom* (1997) 24 E.H.R.R. 423;

- Applicant must be aware of violation (excludes persistent vegetative state)—see *NHS Trust A v. M* [2001] Fam. 348;

- A presumption that mentally competent patients are able to decide whether to receive treatment—see *S v. McC and M* [1972] A.C. 24;

- Disputes to be resolved in High Court if necessary—see *Re MB* [1997] 2 F.C.R. 541;

- Competent adult can refuse medical treatment even though refusal could result in death—see *Re B, The Times*, March 26, 2002;

- A disabled person cannot instruct another to take their life—see *Dianne Pretty v. United Kingdom* (2002) 35 E.H.R.R. 1;

- There is a distinction between causing death and alleviating pain—see *Dianne Pretty v. United Kingdom*; *Airedale National Health Service Trust v. Bland* [1993] A.C. 789;

1. GENERALLY

Duties. It is established law that degrading and inhuman treatment includes the   **6–02** situation of a sick patient deprived of the care that he requires.[1] The State is required to take appropriate measures to preserve life. This principle is laid down within Article 2 of the European Convention on Human Rights which deals with the right of life and is beyond the scope of this book. Nevertheless, it should be observed that in laying down that "everyone's right to life shall be protected by law", any attempt to violate that provision will evoke Article 3 so as to make that safeguard "practical and effective".[2]

---

[1] See *Hurtado v. Switzerland* (1994) Series A, No. 28-A: and *D v. United Kingdom* [1997] 24 E.H.R.R. 423.
[2] See *McCann v. United Kingdom* (1996) 21 E.H.R.R. 97 at para. 146.

In *Tanko v. Finland*,[3] the Commission observed "A lack of proper medical care in a case where someone is suffering from a serious illness could in certain circumstances amount to treatment contrary to Article 3".

6–03   **The minimum level of severity.** As with all aspects of Article 3, ill-treatment must attain a minimum level of severity if it is to fall within the scope of Article 3. The assessment of this minimum is, relative, and will depend upon all the circumstances of the case, such as the nature and context of the treatment, the manner with which it is applied, its duration, its physical or mental effects and in some instances, the sex, age and state of health of the victim.[4]

In order for the treatment to be inhuman or degrading, the suffering or humiliation involved must in any event go beyond that inevitable element of suffering or humiliation connected with a given form of legitimate treatment (or punishment). The question whether the purpose of the treatment debases the victim in the context of medical treatment is a further factor to be taken into account, but the absence of any such purpose will not conclusively rule out a finding of violation of Article 3. As a general rule, a measure which is a therapeutic necessity cannot be regarded as inhuman or degrading.[5] The court must nevertheless satisfy itself that the medical necessity has been convincingly shown to exist.[6]

6–04   **Article 3 is a negative obligation on the State.** Generally, the Article 3 right is described as a negative obligation on the State to refrain from inflicting serious harm on persons within their jurisdiction. If it were to be otherwise, a positive obligation would require that the State sanctions actions *intended* to terminate life, which cannot be derived from Article 3.[7]

6–05   **Negligent medical treatment.** If it can be established that the medical authority has acted negligently in their treatment of a patient, then a *prima facie* Article 3 issue will arise.[8] Establishing negligence sufficient to violate Article 3 will be an altogether more difficult prospect.

Given the minimum severity thresholds, the breach of duty in a Convention case will need to be that much more severe than in the standard tort application of that principle. In order to satisfy that duty, the standard of care and skill to be

---

[3] Application No. 23634/94, unreported, (1994).
[4] See *T and V v. United Kingdom* (1999) 7 B.H.R.C. 659 at 682–683.
[5] See *Herczegfalvy v. Austria* (1992) 15 E.H.R.R. 437 at 484, paragraph 82.
[6] See *X v. Federal Republic of Germany* (1984) 7 E.H.R.R. 152 which related to the forcible feeding of a prisoner on hunger strike which was not found to be in violation of Article 3.
[7] Regarding Article 8, although no court has established that a right of self-determination is contained within that Article, the European Court of Human Rights considers that the notion of personal autonomy is an important principle underlying the interpretation of its guarantees. The ability to conduct one's life in a manner of one's own choosing may also include the opportunity to pursue activities perceived to be physically or morally harmful, or dangerous for the individual concerned. Any imposition of compulsory or criminal sanctions impinging on private life in this respect would require justification in terms of Article 8(2). Similarly, the prevention of exercising choice can interfere with the right to respect for private life. As to Article 8(2) the issue is proportionality as an alleged blanket ban can be at great personal cost to the applicant, as was seen in the case of Dianne Pretty. In that case, the purpose of the Suicide Act 1961 was to protect the weak and vulnerable, it is the vulnerability of the class, including the terminally ill that provides the rationale for this rule and in the Pretty case the court considered that the operation of the law was not disproportionate (see para. 6–20 below).
[8] See *Association X v. U.K.* (1978) 14 D.R. 31

attained is that of the ordinary competent medical practitioner, who is exercising the ordinary degree of professional skill.

It is not required in standard tort litigation that in the discharge of his duty of care he must use the highest degrees of skill, since these may never be acquired by him. Furthermore, it is not incumbent upon the practitioner to use the very latest equipment and techniques. So, where a surgeon had made an incorrect diagnosis, as a result of his failure to use an instrument, which at the time was very rarely to be found in England, negligence was not established against him.[9]

Although the standard is a high one "a defendant charged with negligence can clear himself if he shows that he acted in accord with general and approved practice".[10] A practitioner is not guilty of negligence if he has acted in accordance with practice accepted as proper by a responsible body of medical people skilled in that particular art. Merely because there was a body of opinion who would take the contrary view is not considered to be sufficient to establish negligence.[11] The standard is articulated most clearly by Lord Denning M.R. when he emphasised that "a doctor was not to be held negligent simply because something went wrong".

> "He was not liable for mischance or misadventure; or for an error of judgement . . . He was only liable when he fell below the standard of a reasonably competent practitioner in his field so much so that his conduct might be deserving of censure or inexcusable".[12]

Good faith administration of medical treatment is therefore unlikely to constitute a violation of Article 3.[13]

Medical practitioners' duty to warn patient. The general principles are laid   **6–06** down in *Bolam v. Friern Hospital Management Committee*[14] which concerned the duty of a doctor to warn his patient of inherent risks of medical treatment. The standard of care in these circumstances was held to be that of the ordinary skilled man exercising and professing to have that special skill and that a doctor was not negligent if he acted in accordance with the practice accepted at the time as proper by a responsible body of medical opinion, notwithstanding that other doctors adopted different practices. In matters of diagnosis and the carrying out of treatment, the court has never been tempted to put itself in the surgeon's position.

When it comes to warning about risks, and the volunteering of unsought information about those risks of the proposed treatment failing to achieve the results required or indeed making the patient's physical or mental condition worse rather than better, is considered to be an exercise of professional skill and judgement as in any other part of a doctor's comprehensive duty of care to the individual patient and it will be a matter of expert evidence from the medical profession as to whether this standard of care has been maintained.

---

[9] See *Whiteford v. Hunter* [1950] W.N. 553.
[10] See *Marshall v. Lindsey CC* [1935] 1 K.B. 516 at 540.
[11] See *Bolam v. Friern Hospital Management Committee* [1957] 1 W.L.R. 582 at 587.
[12] See *Hucks v. Cole, The Times*, May 9, 1968.
[13] See *D v. United Kingdom* (1997) 24 E.H.R.R. 423; *T and V v. United Kingdom* (1999) B.H.R.C. 659; *Herczegfalvy v. Austria* (1993) 15 E.H.R.R. 437; *X v. Federal Republic of Germany* (1984) 7 E.H.R.R. 152.
[14] [1957] 1 W.L.R. 582.

6–07 **Termination or withdrawal of existing treatment.** Although there may be no general right to medical treatment, withdrawal of care, support or treatment which an applicant was currently receiving and that would have serious consequences for him if so withdrawn may amount to a violation of Article 3.[15]

In *D v. United Kingdom*,[16] the applicant was in the advanced stages of AIDS and had been provided with accommodation and care by a United Kingdom charity as well as receiving medical treatment for his condition. The immigration authorities ordered his removal to St Kitts and ultimately the applicant applied to the European Court contending that his removal would be in breach of Article 3 as he would not receive adequate medical treatment and had no family in St Kitts who could care for him.

The European Court of Human Rights reaffirmed the absolute nature of Article 3 and observed that withdrawal of the care, support and treatment that the applicant was currently receiving in the United Kingdom would have serious consequences for him and expose him to a real risk that he would die in distressing circumstances, which would amount to inhuman treatment contrary to Article 3. Although *D v. United Kingdom* was a deportation case, the principles concerning medical treatment and the withdrawal of that treatment are, it is arguable, relevant to non-deportation cases.

The European Court were clearly laying down principles concerning the continuation of medical treatment and if the withdrawal of such treatment would or may cause severe consequences to a patient, then Article 3 will be violated, although if the withdrawal of that treatment is not held to have so severe a consequence, then violation may not follow so easily.[17]

In *Bensaid v. United Kingdom*,[18] the European Court held that the risk to health of that particular applicant was largely theoretical and the fact that it would be harder for the applicant to obtain medical treatment in the Receiving State of Algeria than in the United Kingdom was not conclusive for the purposes of Article 3. Evidence that difficulties in obtaining treatment in Algeria could exacerbate the applicant's condition again did not bring the matter within Article 3, particularly as he was also at risk of relapse if he stayed in the United Kingdom, given the long term nature of his schizophrenic condition.

D v. United Kingdom was further distinguished in the Court of Appeal by *K v. Secretary of State for the Home Department*,[19] where a citizen of Uganda who was suffering from AIDS sought permission to apply for judicial review of the Secretary of State's refusal to grant him asylum. The Secretary of State refused to grant exceptional permission to remain. The applicant submitted that he should have followed the case of *D v. United Kingdom* and that to return him to Uganda would be in breach of Article 3. The Court of Appeal distinguished *D v. United*

---

[15] It may also violate Article 2.

[16] (1997) 24 E.H.R.R. 423.

[17] See Chapter 4 on Prisoners and the Provision of Medical and Psychiatric Treatment to Detainees. See also *Keenan v. United Kingdom* (2001) 33 E.H.R.R. 38 who committed suicide whilst in custody and was not given proper hospital care and psychiatric supervision. In that case, although there had been no breach of the right to life under Article 2, the European Court of Human Rights took into account the applicant's vulnerability and the authority's particular obligation to protect his health, and in placing him in segregation, given his need for medical treatment, they threatened his physical and moral resistance and adversely affected his personality to the extent that it was degrading and inhuman treatment, therefore breaching Article 3. Clearly, particular care needs to be taken of detainees, especially those who are vulnerable.

[18] (2001) 33 E.H.R.R. 10.

[19] [2001] Imm. A.R. 11.

Kingdom in that there, no medical facilities had been available in the applicant's country. In the instant case, it had been accepted that treatment was available in Uganda, even if the applicant could not afford such treatment.

The court held that it was not right to suggest that it would constitute inhuman or degrading treatment to send the applicant back to Uganda on the ground that he might, or might not, be able to afford all the treatment he might require. To accept that submission, the court held, would be to adopt a rule that any country without a health service which was available free of charge to all people within its boundaries would be a place to which it would be inhuman and degrading to send someone.

It is clear that the courts will not enter into a comparative study of health facilities within various States when assessing whether there will be a violation of Article 3. If there is medical treatment available, then a breach of Article 3 will not be found. This seems to imply that failure to provide treatment on the National Health Service can never be considered to be in violation of Article 3 if such treatment can be provided privately, regardless of whether the citizen can afford it.

Victim must be aware of the torture, inhuman or degrading treatment. To   **6–08** take advantage of Article 3, the applicant must be aware of the potential violation. In *NHS Trust A v. M*,[20] a hospital trust sought a declaration that it was entitled to discontinue the administration of artificial hydration and nutrition to M, a patient in a persistent vegetative state.[21]

M had been diagnosed as being in a permanent vegetative state in 1997 after having suffered anoxic brain damage and the trust submitted that it would not be in her best interests to continue the treatment. The Family Division held, granting the declaration, that where the continuation of treatment was no longer in the best interests of a patient, action to discontinue that treatment would not constitute an intentional deprivation of life pursuant to Article 2. It followed that in the instant case there was no obligation on the State to prolong M's life.[22] Furthermore, the withdrawal of treatment would not breach the requirement contained in Article 2 to take adequate and appropriate steps to safeguard life as the positive obligation upon a State to protect life was not an absolute obligation to treat a patient if that treatment would be futile.[23]

Dame Elizabeth Butler-Sloss went on to hold that in the instant case discontinuance of the life support machine and treatment was not in breach of Article 3. M was incapable of being aware of the inhuman and degrading treatment as the patient was insensate who had been in a persistent vegetative state for in excess of three years. Article 3 will therefore not be applicable where a patient is unaware of the treatment and will be unaware of its withdrawal.[24]

---

[20] [2001] Fam. 348.

[21] See Practice Note (Persistent Vegetative State: Withdrawal of Treatment) [1996] 4 All E.R. 766: see also definition of "vegetative state" in "The Permanent Vegetative State" (1996) 30 Journal of the Royal College of Physicians 119 which concludes that a diagnosis of permanent vegetative state can reasonable be made when a patient has been in a continuing vegetative state following head injuries for more than 12 months or following other causes of brain damage for more than six months, although Dam Elizabeth Butler-Sloss concluded that the periods suggested might properly be shorter after which artificial nutrition and hydration might properly be discontinued.

[22] See *Airedale NHS Trust v. Bland* [1993] A.C. 789.

[23] See *Osman v. United Kingdom* [1999] 1 F.L.R. 193.

[24] Futile treatment may involve a violation of Article 3, see *Herczegfalvy v. Austria* (1992) 15 E.H.R.R. 437.

In *Airedale NHS Trust v. Bland*,[25] the House of Lords held that the duty of a doctor is to treat the patient as long as it is in his best interests to have the treatment. If, however, it is no longer in the patient's best interests to have that treatment, it is not the duty of the medical team to continue it. Lord Goff of Chieveley said in *Bland*'s case[26] "If the justification for treating a patient who lacks the capacity to consent lies in the fact that the treatment is provided in his best interests, it must follow that the treatment may, and indeed ultimately should, be discontinued where it is no longer in his best interests to provide it".

Lord Browne-Wilkinson went further. He stated[27] "Unless the doctor has reached the affirmative conclusion that it is in the patient's best interest to continue the invasive care, such care must cease . . . only if the doctors responsible for (the applicant's) care held the view that, although he is aware of nothing, there is some benefit to him in staying alive, would there be anything to indicate that it is for his benefit to continue the invasive medical care". The court added that given the discontinuance of life support would be in accordance with proposals contained in the discussion paper on Treatment of Patients in Persistent Vegetative State, issued in September 1992 by the Medical Ethics Committee of the British Medical Association, they were not entitled nor under a duty to continue medical care and therefore would be not guilty of murder if they did discontinue such care.

The continuation of futile treatment or the withdrawal of such treatment cannot be described either as torture or as punishment. The issue is whether either is "degrading treatment".[28] In the context of interrogation practices in Northern Ireland, degrading treatment means ill-treatment designed to "arouse in their victims feelings of fear, anguish and inferiority capable of humiliating and debasing them and possibly breaking their physical or moral resistance".[29]

2. MENTALLY COMPETENT PATIENTS

6–09   **The presumption.** There is a presumption that a patient has the mental capacity to make decisions whether to consent or whether to refuse medical or surgical treatment that is offered. No court has power to authorise any invasive medical procedure on an adult without their consent.[30] An adult is entitled to decline medical advice or treatment for rational or irrational reasons or for no reason at all.[31] No one can be detained or compelled to undergo treatment except by clear statutory authority.[32]

A patient's right to decline medical advice and treatment extends to an emergency situation.[33] It also extends to a situation where the consequences of

---

[25] [1999] A.C. 789.
[26] At p. 867.
[27] At pp. 884–885.
[28] See *NHS Trust A v. M* paragraph 43.
[29] See *Ireland v. United Kingdom* (1978) 2 E.H.R.R. 25, p. 80 at paragraph 167.
[30] See *S v. McC and M (David Samuel Intervener)* [1972] A.C. 24.
[31] See *Sidaway v. Board of Governors of the Bethlem Royal Hospital and the Maudesley Hospital* [1985] A.C. 871; *Re F (Mental Patient Sterilisation)* [1990] 2 A.C. 1; *Re T (Adult Refusal of Medical Treatment)* [1993]. Fam 95; *Airedale NHS Trust v. Bland* [1993] A.C. 789; *Malone v. Metropolitan Police Commissioner* [1979] Ch. 344.
[32] See *R. v. Hallstrom ex p. W* [1986] Q.B. 1090.
[33] See *Re F (Mental Patient Sterilisation)* [1990] 2 A.C. 1.

refusal might be life threatening.[34] If mental capacity is not an issue and the patient, having been given the relevant information and offered the available options, chooses to refuse that treatment, that decision must be respected by the doctors; considerations that the best interests of the patient would involve consent are irrelevant.[35]

Concerns or doubts about mental capacity. Any concerns or doubts about   **6–10** the patient's mental capacity should be resolved as soon as possible by the doctors within the hospital or other normal medical procedures. The Mental Health Act 1983 cannot be deployed to achieve treatment upon an individual against their will merely because their thinking process is unusual, even apparently bizarre and irrational and contrary to the views of the overwhelming majority of the community at large. In *R. v. Hallstrom ex p. W,*[36] Mr Justice McCullough said:

"There is . . . no canon of construction which presumes that Parliament intended that people should, against their will, be subjected to treatment which others, however professionally competent, perceive, however sincerely and however correctly, to be in their best interests . . .

Parliament is presumed not to enact legislation which interferes with the liberty of the subject without making it clear that this was its intention. It goes without saying that, unless clear statutory authority to the contrary exists, no one is to be detained in hospital or to undergo medical treatment or even to submit himself to a medical examination without his consent. That is as true of a mentally disordered person as with anyone else".

The patient must be consulted as to what in the judgment of the doctors is their best interests. It is most important that those considering the issue should not confuse the question of mental capacity with the nature of the decision made by the patient however grave the consequences. Since the view of the patient might reflect a difference in values rather than an absence of competence, the assessment of capacity should be approached with that in mind and doctors should not allow an emotional reaction to, or strong disagreement with, the patient's decision to cloud their judgment in answering the primary question of capacity.[37]

Where disagreement still exists about competence, it is of the utmost importance that the patient be fully informed, involved and engaged in the process, which could involve obtaining independent outside help, of resolving the disagreement since the patient's involvement could be crucial to a good outcome. If

---

[34] See *Airedale NHS Trust v. Bland* [1993] A.C. 789.

[35] An exception to these provisions can be seen with reference to the Mental Health Act 1983 Section 63 which provides for dispensing with consent to medical treatment for a mental disorder. See *B v. Croydon Health Authority* [1995] Fam 133; *Tameside and Glossop Acute Services Trust v. CH* [1996] 1 F.L.R. 762.

[36] See [1986] Q.B. 1090 at 1104. Part IV of the Act provides a carefully structured scheme setting out the circumstances in which the patient's consent to treatment may be dispensed with. Section 63 of the Act may apply to the treatment of any condition which is integral to the mental disorder provided the treatment is given by or under the direction of the responsible medical officer. Detention under the 1983 Act must not undermine or restrict the patient's right to self-determination unless the patient is deprived "either by long term mental capacity or retarded development or by temporary factors such as unconsciousness or confusion or the effects of fatigue, shock, pain or drugs" of their capacity to decide for themselves: see *Re: JT (Adult: Refusal of Medical Treatment)* [1998] 1 F.L.R. 48. In principle a patient may remain competent notwithstanding detention under the Mental Health Act 1983: see *St George's Healthcare NHS Trust v. S* [1999] Fam 26 at 63.

[37] See *Re B (Consent to Treatment: Capacity)* [2002] EWCA Civ 1385.

the hospital is faced with a dilemma which doctors do not know how to resolve, that must be recognised and further steps taken as a matter of priority. Those in charge must not allow a situation of deadlock or rift to occur.[38]

If there is no disagreement about competence but the doctors are for any reason unable to carry out the patient's wishes, it is their duty to find other doctors who will do so.[39]

The treating clinicians and the hospital should always have in mind that a seriously physically disabled patient who was mentally competent had the same right through personal autonomy and to make decisions as any other person with mental capacity.[40]

In many cases the patient's general practitioner or other responsible doctor may be sufficiently qualified to make the necessary assessment, but in serious or complex cases involving difficult issues about the future health and well-being or even the life of the patient, the issue of capacity should be examined by an independent psychiatrist, ideally one approved under the Mental Health Act 1983 Section 12(2). If following this assessment there remains a serious doubt about the patient's competence, and the seriousness or complexity of the issues in the particular case may require the involvement of the court, the psychiatrist should further consider whether the patient is incapable by reason of mental disorder of managing their property or affairs. If so, the patient may be unable to instruct a solicitor and will require a guardian *ad litem* in any court proceedings.

The authority should seek legal advice as quickly as possible. If a declaration is to be sought, the patient's solicitors should be informed immediately and if practicable they should have a proper opportunity to take instructions and apply for Legal Aid where necessary.[41]

6–11   **Procedures for medical practitioners upon a competent refusal.** If the patient is competent and refuses consent to the treatment, an application to the High Court for a declaration will be pointless. In this situation the advice given to the patient should be recorded.

For their own protection, hospital authorities should seek unequivocal assurances from the patient (to be recorded in writing) that the refusal represents an informed decision, that is, that the patient understands the nature of and reasons for the proposed treatment, and the risks and likely prognosis involved in the decision to refuse or accept it. If the patient is unwilling to sign a written indication of this refusal, this too should be noted in writing. Such a written indication is merely a record for evidential purposes. It should not be confused with, or regarded as, a disclaimer.[42]

Where the patients' health and future are at stake, the patient must make the final decision. The patient is free to decide whether or not to submit to treatment recommended by the doctor and therefore the doctor impliedly contracts to provide information which is adequate to enable the patient to reach a balanced

---

[38] See *Re: B (Consent to Treatment: Capacity)* [2002] EWCA Civ 1385.
[39] See *Re: B (Consent to Treatment: Capacity)* [2002] EWCA Civ 1385.
[40] See *Re: B (Consent to Treatment: Capacity)* [2002] EWCA Civ 1385.
[41] Potential witnesses for the authority should be made aware of the criteria laid down in *Re: MB (an Adult: Medical Treatment)* [1997] 2 F.C.R. 541 together with any guidance issues by the Department of Health and the British Medical Association.
[42] See *St George's Healthcare NHS Trust v. S* [1999] Fam. 26 at 64.

judgment, subject always to the doctor's own obligation to say and do nothing which the doctor is satisfied will be harmful to the patient.[43]

Failure to obtain doctors to carry out the patient's wishes. If all appropriate **6–12** steps to seek independent assistance from medical experts outside the hospital have failed, the hospital should not hesitate to make an application to the High Court or seek the advice of the Official Solicitor.[44]

The duties of the medical practitioner if a patient is incapable of giving or 6–13 refusing consent. If a patient is incapable of giving or refusing consent, either in the long term or temporarily (*eg.* due to unconsciousness), the patient must be cared for according to the authority's judgement of the patient's best interests.

Where the patient has given an advance directive, before becoming incapable, treatment and care should normally be subject to the advance directive. However, if there is reason to doubt the reliability of the advance directive (for example, it may sensible be thought not to apply to the circumstances which have arisen), then an application for a declaration may be made.

If the patient is unable to instruct solicitors, or is believed to be incapable of doing so, the authority or its legal advisors must notify the Official Solicitor and invite him to act as guardian *ad litem*. If the Official Solicitor agrees he will no doubt wish, if possible, to arrange for the patient to be interviewed to ascertain their wishes and to explore the reasons for any refusal of treatment.[45]

The hearing. The hearing before the judge should be *inter partes*. As an order **6–14** made in the absence of a patient will not be binding on the patient unless that patient is represented either by a guardian *ad litem* (if incapable of giving instructions) or (if capable) by counsel or solicitor, a declaration granted *ex parte* is of no assistance to the authority.

Although the Official Solicitor will not act for a patient if the patient is capable of instructing a solicitor, the court may in any event call on the Official Solicitor (who has considerable expertise in these matters) to assist as *amicus curaiae*.

The judge must be provided with accurate and all relevant information. This should include the reasons for the proposed treatment, the risks involved in the proposed treatment and, in not proceeding with it, whether any alternative treatment exists, and the reason, if ascertainable, why the patient is refusing the proposed treatment. The judge will need sufficient information to reach an informed conclusion about the patient's capacity and, where it arises, the issue of best interest. The precise terms of any order should be recorded and approved by the judge before its terms are transmitted to the authority. The patient must be accurately informed of the precise terms. Applicants for emergency orders from the High Court made without first issuing and serving the relevant applications and evidence in support have a duty to comply with the procedural requirements (and pay the court fees) as soon as possible after the urgency hearing.

As the court in *St George's Healthcare NHS Trust v. S*[46] which laid down these guidelines accepted that there may be occasions when, assuming a serious question arises about the competence of the patient, the situation facing the

---

[43] See *Sidaway* [1985] A.C. 871 at p. 904.
[44] See *Re B (Consent to Treatment: Capacity)* [2002] EWCA Civ 1385.
[45] The Official Solicitor can be contacted through the Urgent Court Business Officer hours on 0271 936 6000.
[46] (1999) Fam. 26.

authority may be so urgent and the consequences so desperate that it is impracticable to attempt to comply with these guidelines. The court went on to say:

> "The guidelines should be approached for what they are, that is, guidelines. Where delay may itself cause serious damage to the patient's health or put her life at risk then formulaic compliance with these guidelines would be inappropriate".

It must follow that any patient who is mentally competent and who refuses medical treatment has a right to do so and any attempt to inflict medical treatment will be a violation of Article 3 and certainly constitute both a tort and a crime of battery if medical treatment is administered to an adult who is conscious and of sound mind without his consent.[47]

6–15   **Pregnancy.** A child *en ventre sa mere* does not have a distinct human personality in law and its extinguishment does not give rise to any penalties or liabilities at common law.[48] Lord Mustil in the *Attorney General's Reference (No. 3 of 1994)*,[49] stated "the defendant intended to commit and did commit an immediate crime of violence to the mother. He committed no relevant violence to the foetus, which was not a person, either at the time or in the future".

Pregnancy does not diminish the woman's entitlement to decide whether or not to undergo medical treatment. Although human, and protected by the law in the number of different ways set out in the judgment in *Re: MB (an Adult: Medical Treatment)*,[50] an unborn child is not a separate person from its mother. Its need for medical assistance does not prevail over her rights. She is entitled not to be forced to submit to an invasion of her body against her will and in possible violation of Article 3, whether her own life or that of her unborn child depends on it. Her right is not reduced or diminished merely because her decision to exercise it may appear morally repugnant.[51]

3. BRINGING LIFE PREMATURELY TO AN END

6–16   **Fundamental duty upon the State.** The State has a fundamental duty to preserve life and the courts have recognised that a balance must be struck between this and the right of self-determination. There is also a State interest in preventing suicide.[52]

---

[47] See *Re: F (Mental Patient: Sterilisation)* [1990] 2 A.C. 1, Lord Browne-Wilkinson at page 882 observed that any treatment given by a doctor to a patient which is invasive (ie. it involves any interference with the physical integrity of the patient) is unlawful unless done with the consent of the patient it constitutes the crime of battery and the tort of trespass to the person. Thus, in the case of an adult who is mentally competent, the court were of the view that artificial feeding and the necessary steps required to evacuate the bowels and bladder would be unlawful unless the patient consented to it. Furthermore, a mentally competent patient can at any time put an end to life support systems by refusing their consent to their continuation.
[48] See *Re: MB (an Adult: Medical Treatment)* [1997] 2 F.C.R. 541: *Attorney General's Reference (No. 3 of 1994)* [1998] A.C. 245.
[49] [1998] A.C. 245.
[50] [1997] 2 F.C.R. 541.
[51] See *St George's Healthcare NHS Trust v. S* [1998] 3 W.L.R. 936.
[52] See *Secretary of State for the Home Department v. Robb* (above) at 132.

Suicide. The Suicide Act 1961 Section 1, abrogated the rule of law whereby   **6–17**
it is a crime for a person to commit suicide. It had been considered a felony at
common law for a sane person of the age of responsibility to kill themselves
either intentionally or in the course of trying to kill another. As a matter of legal
history, such a suicide was regarded as self-murder. Though the offender was, in
the nature of things, personally beyond the reach of the law, their guilt was not
without importance consequences at common law, since it resulted in the for-
feiture of the deceased's property. The results were more important, however,
where the attempt failed, for then since the individual had attempted to commit
a felony he was guilty, under ordinary common law principles, of the misde-
meanour of attempted suicide. If the unfortunate defendant in the course of trying
to kill himself, killed another, he was guilty of murder under the doctrine of
transferred malice. Though suicide was regarded as "not a very serious crime",[53]
an intention to commit it was thus the *mens rea of* murder.

Following the Suicide Act 1961 Section 1 which removed suicide from the
criminal calendar, it followed that attempted suicide also ceased to be criminal
and that there was no place for the doctrine of transferred malice where the
defendant kills another in the course of trying to kill himself, for there is no
malice to transfer.[54] This old jurisprudence continues to influence the way the law
treats assisted suicide.

Assisted Suicide. In *R: B (Consent to Treatment: Capacity)*,[55] a competent   **6–18**
adult sought a declaration from the court that she was entitled to refuse medical
treatment even though that refusal would result in her death. She had a right to
do so. The position in which Ms B found herself in was one of demanding her
right to take her own life.

When a disabled person is unable to take their own life an entirely different set
of principles will apply. That person cannot ask another to take their life or take
steps which would result in the extinguishment of their life without exposing that
other person to the risk of criminal sanctions.

The Suicide Act 1961 Section 2 laid down that:

"Section 2(1)

A person who aids, abets, counsels or procures the suicide of another, or an attempt
by another to commit suicide, shall be liable on conviction on indictment to imprisonment for a term not exceeding 14 years.

Section 2(2)

If on the trial of an indictment for murder or manslaughter it is proved that the
accused aided, abetted, counselled or procured the suicide of the person in question,
the jury may find him guilty of that offence . . .

---

[53] See *French* (1955) 39 Cr.App.R. 192, *per* Lord Goddard C.J.
[54] For further background on this issue, see Williams *The Sanctity of Life*, Chapter 7; St. John Stevas,
Life, Death and The Law, Chapter 6; and the Second Report of the Criminal Law Revision
Committee, Cmnd. 1187 (1960).
[55] [2002] EWHC 429.

Section 2(4)

> ... no proceedings shall be instituted for an offence under this section except by or with the consent of the Director of Public Prosecutions".[56]

An individual can be criminally liable even if the person encouraged does not in fact commit or attempt to commit suicide. This offence is best categorised as incitement to commit suicide.[57] The presence is unnecessary for aiding, abetting or counselling, particularly where the tools or materials for the suicide are supplied.[58] So far as mens rea is concerned, the important requirement is not presence so much, as encouragement.[59] Knowledge of an intention to commit the crime combined with something down to help in the commission of it has been held to be sufficient.[60] But knowledge of the precise details of the commission of the offence is not necessary.[61]

In the Dianne Pretty case,[62] the European Court ruled that the Suicide Act 1961 Section 2(1) was not disproportionate. In coming to this conclusion it accepted the arguments of the United Kingdom Government that flexibility was provided for in individual cases by the fact that consent it needed from the Director of Public Prosecutions to bring a prosecution. Furthermore, the fact that a maximum sentence is provided, allowing lesser penalties to be imposed in the circumstances of the case led the court to conclude that the legislation was proportionate.

6–19   **The requirements of the offence.** The law surrounding assisted suicide was clarified in *Attorney General v. Able*,[63] in which the defendants who were members of the Executive Committee of the Voluntary Euthanasia Society, published a booklet entitled "A Guide to Self-Deliverance" for distribution to members of the Society, subject to certain qualifications, the expressed aim of which was to overcome the fear of the process of dying. While the booklet could deter a would-be suicide, it could also assist persons to commit suicide who might not otherwise do so. Indeed, it set out five separate methods of suicide.[64]

---

[56] As to sentencing, in *R. v. Sweeney* (1986) 8 Cr.App.R. (S) 419 CA, Watkins L.J. said that it was the policy of the law that even desperate people must be deterred from taking life. In *Hough* (1984) 6 Cr.App.R. (S) 406, Lord Lane C.J. observed that the crime could vary "from the borders of cold-blooded murder down to the shadowy area of mercy killing or common humanity". In that case a 9 month prison term was upheld on a 60 year old woman of unblemished character who had been a regular visitor to an 84 year old woman who as partly blind, partly deaf and suffered from arthritis. The elderly lady had persisted in various statements to the effect that she intended to take her own life, and the offender eventually supplied her with the necessary tablets. When she became unconscious, the offender placed a plastic bag over her head. In *Wallis* (1983) 5 Cr.App.R. (S) 342, a sentence of 12 months' imprisonment was described by the Court of Appeal as "at the extreme of leniency" in a case where the offender pleaded guilty to aiding the suicide of a 17 year old flatmate by buying her tablets and alcohol, sitting with her while she took the tablets, and not calling the ambulance until she was dead.

[57] See *McShane* (1977) 66 Cr.App.R. 97.

[58] See *National Coal Board v. Gamble* [1959] 1 Q.B. 11 at 24 per Devlin J.

[59] See *R. v. Coney* (1882) 8 Q.B.D. 534; *R. v. Allan* [1965] 1 Q.B. 130; *R. v. Clarkson* [1971] 1 W.L.R. 1402.

[60] See *R. v. Bainbridge* [1960] 1 Q.B. 129.

[61] See *Thambiah v. The Queen* [1966] AC 37: *Tuck v. Robson* [1970] 1 W.L.R. 741.

[62] (2002) 35 E.H.R.R. 1.

[63] See [1984] 1 Q.B. 795.

[64] The booklet proved very popular. In less than 18 months after its publication, 8,300 copies had allegedly been sold.

The introduction in the booklet articulates the views of some members of society as to their rights to control the manner and timing of their death. The introduction commences:

"The reasons for writing this pamphlet are quite simple. Those who join Exit do so because they believe that they have a right to a say in the manner and timing of their death, particularly if it seems likely that the process of dying will be a long one and distressing either to them or to their friends and families. For some the main fear will be of continuing pain, while for others the main fear is of paralysis of body or mind or simply weariness with a life that has deteriorated beyond repair".

In *Attorney General v. Able*,[65] Woolf J. (as he then was) laid down three requirements that were necessary as a bear minimum before the crime of assisted suicide can be made out.[66] They are that the conduct of an alleged accessory to suicide should indicate:

(a) that the accused knew that the suicide was contemplated;

(b) that the accused approved of or assented to it; and

(c) that the accused's attitude in respect of the potential suicide in fact encouraged the principal offender to perform (or attempt to perform) the suicide.

---

[65] [1984] Q.B. 795.

[66] In 1976, the Criminal Law Revision Committee made a proposal in a Working Paper that consideration should be given to the creation of a new offence of mercy killing. It was proposed that a person who unlawfully killed another should not be guilty of murder or of manslaughter, but guilty of an offence punishable with two years' imprisonment if he, from compassion, killed another person who was, or was with reasonable cause believed to be (1) subject to great bodily pain or suffering; or (2) permanently helpless from bodily or mental incapacity; or (3) subject to rapid and incurable bodily or mental degeneration. This proposal received a hostile reception and the Criminal Law Revision Committee were persuaded that the public was not prepared to countenance what was seen as a threat to the sanctity of life and, when they published their Report (14th Report, p. 53), the proposal was abandoned. The Law Commission submitted a different proposal to the Select Committee on Murder and Life Imprisonment where it agreed that there should be no separate offence of mercy killing, but that some cases might be covered by a new special defence reducing murder to manslaughter. The Law Commission suggested in 1988 that "the limits of the defence might be: (a) that the killing was done in order to relieve a person who was permanently subject to great bodily pain or suffering, or permanently helpless from bodily or mental incapacity or subject to rapid and incurable mental or bodily degeneration; and (b) at a time when the accused was affected by severe emotional distress". The latter aspect was new. Professor Leonard Leigh argued at the time in favour of a defence of "overwhelming emotional stress". The Law Commission pointed out that such a defence would not excuse a doctor or nurse from liability to conviction of murder and that it would be wrong for the law to appear to be sanctioning such killings by "professionals". This, in effect, would amount to an extension of the defence of diminished responsibility, explicitly bringing with the defence some cases which at present are accommodated only by a straining of the concepts beyond their proper limits and others where the defendant is not so fortunate and is convicted of murder. The British Medical Association's Working Party on Euthanasia (May 5, 1988) concluded that "An active intervention by anybody to terminate another person's life should remain illegal. Neither doctors nor any other occupational group should be placed in a category which lessens their responsibility for their actions" and "the law should not be changed and the deliberate taking of a human life should remain a crime. This rejection of a change in the law to permit doctors to intervene to end a person's life is not just a subordination of individual well being to social policy. It is, instead, an affirmation of the supreme value of the individual, no matter how worthless and hopeless that individual may feel". The Select Committee took all these opinions into account and concluded (at para. 100) that "the introduction of a discretionary sentence for murder will enable the judge to take the full circumstances of the crime into account in passing sentence. The Committee make no recommendation for a change in law on this point".

6–20   **Dianne Pretty.** The litigation surrounding the arguments of Dianne Pretty, a
Motor Neurone Disease sufferer who sought a review of the Directory of Public
Prosecutions' decision to refuse to undertake the path of not prosecuting her
husband if he assisted her to commit suicide has brought into sharp focus issues
of assisted suicide and the application of the European Convention on Human
Rights.[67]

Mrs Pretty was mentally alert and wished to control the time and manner of her
dying so as to avoid the suffering and indignity she would otherwise have to
endure. Because of her chronic incapacities, she could not commit suicide
unaided and wished her husband to help her. He was prepared to do so provided
that the Director of Public Prosecutions gave the undertaking required under the
Suicide Act 1961, Section 2(4) that he would not prosecute her husband. The
Director of Public Prosecutions refused to do so. Of course, if Pretty had been
physically capable of taking her own life unassisted, she would as a matter of law
been able to do so but this freedom has been denied to her by her disability and
the blanket ban under English law which prevents her husband from helping her
unless the Director of Public Prosecutions makes a section 2(4) undertaking.

The Queen's Bench Divisional Court,[68] the House of Lords,[69] and the European Court of Human Rights[70] considered the arguments presented on behalf of
Dianne Pretty. Central to those arguments were consideration of whether Article
3 had been violated. In the Queen's Bench Divisional Court, Lord Justice Tuckey
stated that Articles 2 and 3 of the Convention protected life and preserved the
dignity of life. But he went on to say that they did not protect the right to procure
one's own death or confer a right to die. The right to the dignity of life was not
a right to die with dignity but the right to live with as much dignity as could
possibly be afforded until that life reached its natural end.[71]

In the House of Lords, Lord Bingham confirmed that Article 3 "which was
complimentary to Article 2" enshrined one of the fundamental values of democratic societies. He confirmed again that its prohibition of prescribed treatment
was absolute, not to be derogated from even in times of war and national
emergency. As Article 2 requires States to respect and safeguard the lives of
individuals within their jurisdiction, so, His Lordship observed, Article 3 obliged
them to respect the physical and human integrity of such individuals. But the
House of Lords went on to say that there was nothing in Article 3 which bore on
an individual's right to live or to choose not to live. That was not, the House of
Lords, considered its fear of application.[72]

The absolute and unqualified prohibition on a member State inflicting the
prescribed treatment required "treatment" not to be given an unrestricted or

---

[67] In his arguments before the European Court, Mrs Pretty's counsel Philip Havers Q.C. observed
"This is a case about life, about imminent death and about incurable illness ... it is also, most of
all, a case about an individual, a courageous and determined and dying woman and the extent to
which her individual rights are protected under the Convention".
[68] [2001] EWHC Admin 788.
[69] [2001] UKHL 61.
[70] (2002) 35 E.H.R.R. 1.
[71] That might mean not taking futile and undignified steps to prolong life beyond its natural end. See
Re J (A Minor) (Child in Care: Medical Treatment) [1993] Fam 15.
[72] The House of Lords also observed that a State might, on occasion, be justified in inflicting
treatment which would otherwise be in breach of Article 3 in order to serve the ends of Article 2. We
can assume from this that certain treatment which may be categorised in normal circumstances as in
violation of Article 3 and breach the minimum severity threshold if it preserves life may avoid being
sufficient for a violation of Article 3.

extravagant meaning. The House of Lords went on to provide the boundaries of the definition of "treatment" to be applied in medical cases. In doing so, the court held that it could not be plausibly suggested that the Director of Public Prosecutions or any other agent of the United Kingdom was inflicting the prescribed treatment on Mrs Pretty, whose suffering derived from her cruel disease. The report goes on to state:

> "By no legitimate process of interpretation could the Director of Public Prosecutions' refusal of troleptic immunity from prosecution to Mr Pretty, if he committed a crime, be held to fall within the negative prohibition of Article 3.
>
> If, on the contrary, Article 3 might be applied and there was no arguable breach of the negative prohibition in the article, the state's positive observation was not absolute and unqualified".

In other words, the "negative prohibition" upon States absolutely forbidding the infliction of the prescribed treatment on individuals within their jurisdiction, is absolutely forbidden, but the steps appropriate or necessary to discharge the States' "positive obligation", arguably to ensure that a competent, terminally ill person should be entitled to seek assistance to end their life, would be more judgmental, more prone to variation from State to State, more dependent upon the opinions and beliefs of the people and less susceptible to any universal injunction.

Taking into account all these national traits which the House of Lords considered relevant considerations for a consideration of the "positive obligation", Lord Bingham concluded that the United Kingdom was not under such a positive obligation to ensure that a competent, terminally ill person who wished but was unable to take his or her own life should be entitled to seek the assistance of another without that other being exposed to the risk of prosecution.[73]

The European View. The European Court rejected the contention that Mrs **6–21** Pretty was vulnerable. A person who is contemplating suicide and who is severely disabled should not as a matter of course be regarded as vulnerable.

The judgment of the European Court of Human Rights,[74] in essence reproduces all of Lord Bingham's observations from the House of Lords, but the European Court adds:

> "The very essence of the Convention is respect for human dignity and human freedom. Without in any way negating the principle of sanctity of life protected under the Convention, the court considers that it is under Article 8 that notions of quality of life take on significance. In an area of growing medical sophistication, combined with longer life expectancies, many people are concerned that they should not be forced to linger on in old age or in states of advanced physical or mental decrepitude which conflict with strongly held ideas of self and personal identity".

In ruling that the assisted suicide of Dianne Pretty met with the requirements of Article 8(2), on the basis that States should be entitled to regulate through the operation of the general criminal law activities which are detrimental to life and safety of other individuals, the European Court differed with the opinion of the House of Lords (by majority) which excluded the possibility that a complete ban

---

[73] Mrs Pretty's right to self-determination under Article 3 was significantly engaged in this case.
[74] (2002) 35 E.H.R.R. 1.

on assisted suicide might constitute an interference with the applicant's right to respect of private life.

6–22   **The difference of opinion between the House of Lords and Europe.** Whilst the House of Lords have excluded the possibility that a blanket ban on assisted suicides might constitute an interference with an applicant's right to private life, the European Court were of the view that the interference was in harmony with the requirements of Article 8(2) because States should be entitled through their domestic criminal law regime to control activities which are detrimental to life and safety of other individuals. In short, whilst the House of Lords refused to accept (by majority) that Dianne Pretty's Article 8 rights were capable of violation in the sphere of assisted suicide, the European Court by invoking Article 8(2) disagreed.

What is interesting is that Dianne Pretty's complaint was fully adjudicated upon in the House of Lords and in reconsidering the case, the European Court of Human Rights has for the first time considered a complaint that has already been adjudicated upon in the domestic courts under the Human Rights Act.[75] It is unclear how the domestic courts should deal with a future case based upon the facts of Dianne Pretty, under Article 8.

The Human Rights Act 1998, Section 2 substantably reads:

"2(1) A court or tribunal determining a question which has arisen in connection with a Convention right must take into account any—

(a) judgement, decision, declaration or advisory opinion of the European Court of Human Rights . . .
      whenever made or given, so far as, in the opinion of the court or tribunal, it is relevant to the proceedings in which that question has arisen".[76]

6–23   **The attitude of Parliament.** Precisely which court will prevail in future argument is open to conjecture although it is reasonable to speculate that a future domestic court will take into account European decisions that were not available to domestic courts when they came to their own judgments. This seems to be enforced when one considers the attitude of Parliament during the progress of the Human Rights Bill through both Houses. The Lord Chancellor, Lord Irvine of Lairg, observed during the third reading of the Bill[77] that the Human Rights Act 1998 "does not create new human rights or take any existing human rights away. It provides better and easier access to rights which already exist".

In the Government's document "Bringing Rights Home", the Prime Minister, Tony Blair, in its preface observed that the Human Rights Act is intended to "give people in the United Kingdom opportunities to enforce their rights under the European Convention in British Courts rather than having to incur the cost and delay of taking a case to the European Human Rights . . . Court in Strasbourg".[78] This of itself seems to indicate that the Strasbourg approach in the Dianne Pretty case will be preferred.

---

[75] See Autonomy and the Human Rights Convention by Rosalind English, New Law Journal, May 31, 2002, in which the author predicts *"Fertile ground for future litigation under this Article"*, as a result of the difference of opinion between the two courts.
[76] Compare the European Communities Act 1972, Section 3 which makes European Court of Justice decisions binding on all U.K. domestic tribunals.
[77] See 585 HL Official Report (5th Series) col 755 (February 5, 1998).
[78] See "Rights Brought Home" (Cm 3782, 1997), p. 1.

Further strength is given to this argument by reading part of the text of a speech by the Lord Chancellor on the second reading of the Bill in the House of Lords[79] where he stated:

> "The Bill will bring human rights home. People will be able to argue for their rights and claim their remedies under the Convention in any court or tribunal in the United Kingdom.
>
> Our courts will develop human rights throughout society. A culture of awareness of human rights will develop . . . the protection of human rights at home gives credibility to our foreign policy to advance the course of human rights around the world . . . we are not ceding new powers to Europe. The United Kingdom already accepts that Strasbourg rulings bind".

Lord Bingham of Cornhill, observed in the same debate[80]:

> "It makes no sense, and, I suggest, does not make for justice that those seeking to enforce their rights have to exhaust all their domestic remedies here before embarking on the long and costly trail to Strasbourg . . . British judges have a significant contribution to make in the development of the law of human rights.
>
> It is a contribution which so far we have not been permitted to make . . . at present disappointed litigants leave our courts believing that their exists elsewhere a superior form of justice which our courts are not allowed to administer".[81]

During the second reading of the Bill in the House of Lords,[82] the Lord Chancellor went on to observe that Section 2:

> "requires courts in the United Kingdom to take account of the decisions of the Convention institutions in Strasbourg in their consideration of Convention points which come before them. It is entirely appropriate that our courts should draw on the wealth of existing jurisprudence on the Convention".[83]

Nevertheless, courts and tribunals in the United Kingdom though required to take judgments, decisions, declarations and opinions whether or not delivered in cases concerning the United Kingdom[84] into account because they are potentially relevant to a proper interpretation of Convention rights, domestic courts and tribunals are not bound to follow Strasbourg judgements and other decisions.

The Lord Chancellor observed[85] that Section 2(1) of the 1998 Act does not make the Strasbourg judgments binding. He stated that the United Kingdom courts may "depart from existing to Strasbourg decisions and upon occasion it might well be appropriate to do so, and it is possible they might give a successful lead to Strasbourg". However, "where it is relevant, he would of course expect our courts to apply Convention jurisprudence and its principles to the cases before them".

Judgments of the European Court of Human Rights carry greater weight than decisions of the Commission, especially admissibility decisions. During the

---

[79] 582 HL, Official Report (5th Series), col 1228 (November 3, 1997).
[80] See columns 1245–1246.
[81] Lord Wilberforce observed " 'bringing home the rights' is a lovely phrase. It makes us think of the 'Ashes', or perhaps the bacon", see column 1279.
[82] 582 HL Official Report (5th Series) col. 1230 (3 November 1997).
[83] Commonwealth constitutional case law is also likely to provide considerable assistance.
[84] See 584 HL Official Report (5th Series) col. 1271 (19 January 1998).
[85] At the Committee Stage of the Bill in the House of Lords at 583 HL Official Report (5th Series) cols. 514–515 (November 18, 1997).

House of Commons Committee Stage, the Parliamentary Secretary to the Lord Chancellor's Department, Mr Geoffrey Hoon, explained that the phrase "must take into account" did not mean that the domestic courts were obliged to follow Strasbourg jurisprudence. He resisted an amendment which would have substituted "may take into account".[86] Lord Browne-Wilkinson stated in *Re H (Minors) (Abduction: Acquiescence)*[87]:

> "An international Convention (there the Hague Convention on the Civil Aspects of International Child Abduction), expressed in different languages and intended to apply to a wide range of differing legal systems, cannot be construed differently in different jurisdictions.
>
> The Convention must have the same meaning and effect under the laws of all Contracting States".[88]

If there is a conflict between interpreting a statute in two ways, one compatible with the Convention and one not, it seems that the courts will be encouraged to choose the interpretation which is compatible.[89]

Nevertheless, the 1998 Act does not allow the court to set aside or ignore Acts of Parliament and Section 3 of the Act preserves the effect of primary legislation which is incompatible with the Convention. It does the same for secondary legislation where it is inevitably incompatible because of the terms of the parent statute.

6–24   **Future Convention jurisprudence.** Section 2(1) concludes by stating that a court or tribunal determining a question which has arisen in connection with a Convention right must take into account any judgement decision or opinion of the court or Commission whenever made or given. This phrase is intended to make "clear that the domestic courts are to take into account not only existing jurisprudence of the Convention institutions, but their future jurisprudence".[90]

6–25   **Distinction between intention to cause death and to relieve pain.** Clearly in the light of the ruling in Dianne Pretty, it is important to draw a distinction between an intention to cause death or simply to relieve pain in the application of medical treatment or substances. A court will not order a medical practitioner to treat a patient in a manner contrary to that medical practitioner's clinical judgement and professional duty.

In the recent trial of Dr David Moor, the issue of intent became central to the jury's deliberation. In that case, the patient was receiving oral morphine for pain relief. Dr Moor was administering diamorphine in an increased dose of the substance being administered which caused the patient to fall into a deep and

---

[86] See 313 HC Official Report (6th Series) cols. 388, 402 and 413 (June 3, 1998).

[87] [1998] A.C. 72 at 87.

[88] In *Iyadurai v. Secretary of State for the Home Department* [1998] Imm. A.R. 470, the Court of Appeal stated that the observations in *Re: H* did not apply to the Geneva Convention on Refugees. Lord Woolf M.R. concluded at p. 481 that the Secretary of State may return an asylum seeker to a third country even though it does not adopt the same interpretation of the Convention as the United Kingdom, so long as the third country's interpretation is not "outside the range of responses of a Contracting State acting in good faith to implement its obligations under the Convention".

[89] See "Rights Brought Home" (Cm 3782, 1997), para. 2.4 and the speech of the Lord Chancellor on the second reading of the Bill in the House of Lords, 582 HL Official Report (5th Series) cols. 1230–1231 (November 3, 1997).

[90] As stated by Geoffrey Hoon during the House of Commons Committee Stage: see 313 HC Official Report (6th Series) col. 405 (3 June 1998).

peaceful sleep. Later, Dr Moor was seen to inject the unconscious patient with further quantities of diamorphine. Critical to the jury's deliberations was the intention of the doctor in administering such a large dose. The doctor's position at trial was that the patient was suffering such intense pain which could not be relieved by surgery that he attempted to relieve that pain. To do so he administered the drug in such a dosage that he knew would virtually certainly cause death. The prosecution of Dr Moor proceeded on the basis of Mr Justice Ognall's direction in the case of *Cox*[91] by emphasising the primary intention and distinguishing the secondary effect.

The test was articulated by Ognall J. in the following terms:

"We all appreciate that some medical treatment, whether of a positive, therapeutic character or solely of an analgesic kind—by which I mean designed solely to alleviate pain and suffering—some treatment carries with it a serious risk to the health or even life, the life of the patient. Doctors are frequently confronted with, no doubt, distressing dilemmas. They have to make up their minds as to whether the risk even to the life of their patient, attendant upon their contemplated form of treatment, is such that the risk is, or is not, medically justified. If a doctor genuinely believes that a certain course is beneficial to his patient, either therapeutically or analgesically, then even though he recognises that that course carries with it a risk to life, he is fully entitled, nonetheless, to pursue it. If in those circumstances the patient dies, nobody could possibly suggest that in that situation the doctor was guilty of murder or attempted murder . . . the problem is obviously particularly acute in the case of those who are terminally ill and in considerable pain, if not agony. . . . It was plainly Dr Cox's duty to do all that was medically possible to alleviate . . . pain and suffering, even if the course adopted carried with it an obvious risk that, as a side effect of that treatment, her death would be rendered likely or even certain. . . . There can be no doubt that the use of drugs to reduce pain and suffering will often be fully justified notwithstanding that it will, in fact, hasten the moment of death. What can never be lawful is the use of drugs with the primary purpose of hastening the moment of death".

In short, this approach provides a special defence to those in the medical profession. The defence would not have been available to the husband of Dianne Pretty, for instance.

In Anthony Arlidge's paper,[92] the case of *Adams* is referred to.[93] In that case, which is unreported and heard at the Central Criminal Court in 1957, Devlin J. summed-up in the following terms:

"Murder is an act or series of acts done by the prisoner which were intended to kill and did in fact kill the dead woman. It does not matter for this purpose that her death was inevitable and her days were numbered. If her life was cut short by weeks or months; it is just as much murder as if it were cut short by years".

Devlin J. went on to consider whether there was a special defence in 1957 for doctors. He concluded at that stage that there was not. This was confirmed in *R. v. Arthur*[94] where Farquharson J. observed in his directions to the jury:

"There is no special law in this country that places doctors in a separate category and gives them extra protection over the rest of us".

---

[91] See [2000] Crim. L.R. 37.
[92] See Criminal Law Review, the Trial of David Moor by Anthony Arlidge Q.C.: [2000], Criminal Law Review 31.
[93] p. 33 of Anthony Arlidge's paper.
[94] 12 B.L.N.R. 1.

In *Airedale National Health Service Trust v. Bland*,[95] the House of Lords agreed that it was proper to remove life support from a patient who was in a persistent vegetative state and had been so for three years. In order to maintain this condition, the patient was fed and hydrated mechanically. When this system was removed, death would be inevitable. The House of Lords characterised the removal of the equipment, not as a positive act, but as an omission to sustain life. They observed that whilst it was not lawful for a doctor to kill by a positive act, they could decide not to treat a patient who would die as a result. In short, the House of Lords were making a distinction between omission and commission.

The most recent case in *Moor* allows the special defence in very limited circumstances when a doctor is dealing with a patient who is in pain and in the latter stages of life and so when a doctor who is trying to relieve suffering knows that his actions are virtually certain to cause death in a short time span, may rely on this special defence.[96]

It has latterly been suggested[97] that the following direction is most appropriate by a judge to a jury:

"The Prosecution must make you sure that D intended to cause P's death. In considering his intention, you are entitled to infer he intended to cause death if you feel sure death was a virtually certain result of his actions (barring some unforeseen intervention) and that he appreciated that fact *and* that his primary intention in so acting was not purely to relieve pain and suffering but to cause death".

The above guidelines and case law development provides some succour to the medical profession so that they may not fall foul of any allegations of murder and by implication any suggestion of a violation of Article 3. They provide no assistance at all to non-medical practitioners.

In *Re: J (A Minor) (Wardship: Medical Treatment)*,[98] the court in considering an application relating to a child, stated certain principles, one of which will equally apply to adults:

"There is no question of approving, even in a case of the most horrendous disability, a course aimed at terminating life or accelerating death. The court is concerned only with the circumstances in which steps should not be taken to prolong life".

The court recognised that with a child aged 19 months who had suffered irreversible brain damage, the right to die with dignity, as included in Article 3, was protected by a declaration in that case that there be leave to treat the patient without artificial ventilation unless such a course seemed inappropriate to the doctor in charge given the prevailing conditions at any re-entry of that patient into hospital.

6–26   **Treatment of Children.** In *Re: J. (A Minor) (Wardship: Medical Treatment)*,[99] Lord Donaldson said[1]:

---

[95] [1993] A.C. 789.
[96] See "The Trial of Dr. David Moor" by Anthony Arlidge Q.C. Criminal Law Review, citation above, and "A Postscript to the Trial of Dr David Moor", by James Goss Q.C., Crim.L.R. [2000], 568.
[97] See "A Postscript to the Trial of Dr David Moor", above.
[98] [1991] 1 F.L.R. 366 at 381.
[99] [1991] 1 F.L.R. 366.
[1] At p. 375.

"In *Re: B (A Minor) Wardship: Medical Treatment*[2] it seems to me to come very near to being a binding authority for the proposition that there is a balancing exercise to be performed in assessing the course to be adopted in the best interests of the child. Even if it is not, I have no doubt that this should be and is the law".

The court went on to conclude that there was a strong presumption in favour of a course of action which will prolong life, "but, even excepting the 'cabbage' case to be which special considerations may well apply, it is not irrebuttable . . . account has to be taken of the pain and suffering and the quality of life which the child will experience if life is prolonged. Account has also to be taken of the pain and suffering involved in the proposed treatment itself . . . in the end, there will be cases in which the answer must be that it is not in the interests of the child to subject it to treatment which will cause increased suffering and produce no commensurate benefit, giving the fullest possible weight to the child's, and mankind's, desire to survive".

Medical treatment without consent can be permissible. There are some   **6–27** circumstances in which the application of treatment or care without the consent of a mentally competent patient can amount to a violation of Article 3. Whilst the application of medical treatment without consent certainly activates Article 8 in that it may violate the privacy or physical integrity of a patient, Article 3 may also be activated if the treatment passes the necessary threshold tests. Furthermore, if a patient is force-fed, be it by medical staff or those in a position of authority, then Article 3 may be violated. The court will take into account the circumstances under which the force-feeding occurred and if it is carried out pursuant to the State's obligation to protect life, then it will not amount to inhuman or degrading treatment.[3]

Whether patient is capable of consenting. If there is an issue of whether the   **6–28** patient is capable of consenting to treatment, a full hearing, with evidence, should be conducted to enable the court to reach its own views.

The Court of Appeal observed in *The Queen (on the application of Wilkinson) v. Broadmoor Hospital*[4] that following the coming into force of the Human Rights Act 1998 and given that the prospective Convention breaches were either fundamental or such as obviously raising issues of necessity and proportionality, there was a need for courts to investigate an resolve issues relating to the application of medical treatment. The court in determining the substantive judicial review will have to reach its own view on whether the patient is capable of consenting to treatment and whether such treatment would breach his Convention rights.

Wilkinson's case was an interlocutory appeal from the decision of the court to refuse to order that all three doctors involved in the case should attend the substantive judicial review hearing for cross-examination upon their witness statements. The claimant, a 69 year old mental patient,[5] complained that he had been administered with anti-psychotic medication without his consent. In short,

---

[2] (1982) 3 F.L.R. 117.
[3] See *X v. Germany* (1985) 7 E.H.R.R. 152.
[4] October 22, 2001.
[5] Subject to hospital and restriction orders made under the Mental Health Act 1983, ss.37 and 41.

he complained that the treatment violated his rights under Article 3 and Article 8, in that the forcible injection without consent constituted degrading treatment and violate his rights to autonomy and bodily inviolability.

Lord Justice Simon Brown was of the view that the court must resolve medical issues and decide between competing views in order to reach a proper judgement on the issues such as whether the treatment of Wilkinson was necessary and proportionate having regard to its profoundly invasive effect upon the appellant's right to respect for his private life and dignity. It was said that Article 6 required the court to reach its own conclusions on the disputed issues of fact.

The Court of Appeal held that where a decision to administer medical treatment to a mental patient without his consent under the Mental Health Act 1983, s.58(3)(b),[6] was challenged by way of judicial review, the court was entitled to reach its own view on the merits of the medical decision and whether it infringed the patient's human rights. In such a case, the patient was entitled to require the attendance of medical witnesses for cross-examination.

Lord Justice Simon Brown stated:

"It seems to me that the court must inevitably now reach its own view both as to whether this appellant is indeed incapable of consenting (or refusing consent) to the treatment programme planned for him by the first respondent as his RMO . . .

The super-Wednesbury test (itself an Article 8 case) was, as is well known, subsequently held to be inadequate by the European Court of Human Rights in *Smith & Grady v. United Kingdom*.[7] I can see no basis on which an approach disapproved in the context of homosexuality in the armed forces could be supported in the present context of forcibly treating mental patients. Quite the contrary, given that this case raises also a real question under Article 3 . . . if I am correct in having concluded that the appellant on this challenge is entitled to have the legality of his future treatment plan determined by the court according to its own assessment of the relevant facts, then plainly the requirements of Article 6 are satisfied: the Administrative Court will conduct a merits review on the evidence".

The court stated that it would be prepared to order the attendance of all the medical specialists for cross-examination at the review hearing if there were to be a fresh decision to subject W to forceful treatment. The recent case of *M, Petitioner*,[7a] confirmed that detention and treatment without consent of a patient under the Mental Health (Scotland) Act 1984 did not automatically amount to an infringement of the petitioner's Convention rights. The treatment in issue concerned the administration of an anti-psychotic medicine to which administration the petitioner had to give consent. Article 8 was referred to in a consideration of

---

[6] Section 58(3) reads: "(3) Subject to section 62 below, a patient shall not be given any form of treatment to which this section applies unless—(a) he has consented to that treatment and either the responsible medical officer or a registered medical practitioner appointed for the purposes of this Part of this Act by the Secretary of State has certified in writing that the patient is incapable of understanding its nature, purpose and likely effects and has consented to it; or (b) a registered medical practitioner appointed as aforesaid (not being the responsible medical officer) has certified in writing that the patient is not capable of understanding the nature, purpose and likely effects of that treatment or has not consented to it but that, having regard to the likelihood of its alleviating or preventing a deterioration of his condition, the treatment should be given".

[7] (1999) 29 E.H.R.R. 493.

[7a] *The Times*, August 26, 2001.

whether interference with the petitioner's rights was "necessary in a free and democratic society". It was, of course, a matter of proportionality.[7b]

Children. The main statement of principle regarding the medical treatment of   **6–29**
children appears in the case of *Re J.*[8] where the court observed:

> "No one can dictate the treatment to be given to the child—neither court, parents, nor doctors. There are checks and balances. The doctors can recommend treatment A in preference to treatment B.
>   They can also refuse to adopt treatment C on the grounds that it is medically contra indicated or for some other reason is a treatment which they could not conscientiously administer. The court or parents for their part can refuse to consent to treatment A or B or both, but cannot insist upon treatment C. The inevitable and desirable result is that choice of treatment is in some measure a joint decision of the doctors and the court or parents. This co-operation is reinforced by another consideration. Doctors nowadays recognise that their function is not a limited technical one of preparing or servicing a body. They are treating people in a real life context. This at once enhances the contribution which the court or parents can make towards reaching the best possible decision in all the circumstances".

Further enunciation of these principles appear in *Re R*[9] where the court observed:

> "It is trite law that in general a doctor is not entitled to treat a patient without the consent of someone who is authorised to give that consent . . . however, consent by itself creates no obligation to treat. It is merely a key which unlocks a door".

The court continued[10]:

> "No doctor can be required to treat a child, whether by the court in the exercise of its wardship jurisdiction, by the parents, by the child or anyone else. The decision whether to treat is dependent upon an exercise of his own professional judgement, subject only to the threshold requirement that, save in exceptional cases usually on emergency, he has the consent of someone who has authority to give that consent".

The court of Appeal in *Re J (a Minor)*,[11] emphasised that it is the duty of medical practitioners to make choices and that the court when considering what course to adopt in relation to a particular child has no knowledge of competing claims to a health authority's resources and is in no position to express any view as to how it should elect to deploy them. It seems that the domestic courts have recognised the competing demands on health authorities with limited resources.

Prior hearings in the domestic court. The European Court of Human Rights   **6–30**
will defer to the findings of domestic courts on issues of fact unless the court has come to "grossly unfair or arbitrary conclusions" on the facts before it. In *DF v. United Kingdom*,[12] the applicant complained that the medical treatment which he

---

[7b] Lord Eassie added that there is a current debate as to the definition of those areas in which involuntary treatment was appropriate. It might be added that as a result of that debate, the legislature may change their position.
[8] [1991] Fam. 33 at 41.
[9] [1992] Fam. 11 at 22.
[10] At page 26.
[11] [2000] 2 F.C.R. 133.
[12] Application No. 12016/86.

received was administered without his consent, with physical force and in an inhuman and degrading fashion. He also complained that he did not receive the necessary antidotes to counteract the side effects and was a victim of sadistic and intolerable treatment, which subjected him to a form of mental torture.

The matter was argued before the domestic courts in a claim for assault, battery and trespass to the person against the prison authorities on the grounds that he had not consented to the injections. After considering the evidence presented by the applicant, and the Home Office, the High Court Judge at first instance concluded that the applicant had in fact consented to the administration of drugs and that they had not been administered by force:

> "The issue of fact, namely, whether the applicant did consent to the drug treatment was fully aired before a domestic court. Such a matter necessarily falls within the appreciation of an independent and impartial court and therefore cannot be reviewed by the Commission unless there is an indication that the judge has drawn grossly unfair or arbitrary conclusions from the facts before him. No such indication has been given in the present case. The Commission therefore finds in the circumstances of the present application that the complaint as submitted by the applicant fails to disclose any appearance of violation of Article 3 of the Convention".

CHAPTER 7

THE TREATMENT OF DEATH ROW AND LONG TERM PRISONERS

Bullet points. The act of putting an individual to death does not breach Article   **7–01**
3[1]:

- Length of detention pending execution critical—Death Row Pheno-mena—see *Soering v. United Kingdom* (1989) 11 E.H.R.R. 439;

- Execution should take place as soon as reasonably practicable after sentence—see *Bell v. DPP of Jamaica* [1985] C.L.Y. 181;

- Domestic appeals process should be completed within approximately 2 years—see *Pratt v. Attorney General for Jamaica* [1994] 2 A.C. 1;

- Mandatory term of life imprisonment for murder incompatible with Article 3—see *Reyes v. The Queen* [2002] UKPC 11;

- Imposition of mandatory sentence of life imprisonment for murder committed by young adults not prohibited by Article 3—see *Bromfield v. United Kingdom*, Application No. 32003/96, July 1, 1998;

- Clear distinction between discretionary life sentence which has a protective purpose and mandatory sentence which is punitive—see *Wynne v. United Kingdom* (1994) 19 E.H.R.R. 333;

- Fixing tariff is equivalent to Judge's sentencing power—see *T and V v. United Kingdom* (2000) 30 E.H.R.R. 121;

1. THE DEATH PENALTY

Legal status of death penalty. Although the death penalty is not prohibited   **7–02**
under Article 2, the guiding principle can be found in Optional Protocol 6.[1a] The
Protocol states:

"1. The death penalty shall be abolished. No-one shall be condemned to such penalty or executed.

2. A State may make provision in its law for the death penalty in respect of acts committed in time of war or imminent war; such penalty shall be applied only in the instances laid down in the law and in accordance with its provisions. The State shall communicate to the Secretary General of the Council of Europe, the relevant provisions of the law.

---

[1] Furthermore, of itself, a mandatory sentence of death, which was abolished nearly 40 years ago, will not influence the Criminal Cases Review Commission's decision whether to refer the conviction as to whether to a conviction is unsafe—see *R. v. Knighter (deceased), The Times*, October 28, 2002.
[1a] Ratified by the United Kingdom on January 27, 1999 and given effect to in the Human Rights Act 1998.

3. No derogation from the provisions of this Protocol shall be made under Article 15 of the Convention.

4. No reservation may be made under (Article 57) of the Convention in respect of the provisions of this Protocol".

Some States continue to practice application of a death penalty.

In *Soering v. United Kingdom*,[2] the court observed[3]:

"103 . . . Article 3 cannot be interpreted as generally prohibiting the death penalty.

104 That does not mean however that circumstances relating to a death sentence can never give rise to an issue under Article 3. The manner in which it is imposed or executed, the personal circumstances of the condemned person and the disproportionality to the gravity of the crime committed, as well as the conditions of detention awaiting execution, are examples of factors capable of bringing the treatment or punishment received by the condemned person within the proscription under Article 3. Present day attitudes in the Contracting States to capital punishment are relevant for the assessment whether the acceptable threshold of suffering or degradation has been exceeded".[4]

7–03   **The Death Row Phenomenon.** Whilst the act of putting an individual to death will not breach Article 3, other matters, such as the length of detention pending execution (in America an average of 6–8 years[5]), the strict and harsh conditions on Death Row and the applicant's age and mental state can violate Article 3. Such conditions are known as the Death Row Phenomenon.[6] In *Soering v. United Kingdom*,[7] the United States and German authorities sought extradition of the applicant from the United Kingdom to stand trial for alleged murders which had occurred in the United States. The American prosecutor had called for the imposition of the death penalty if the applicant was convicted. The crux of his

---

[2] (1989) 11 E.H.R.R. 439.

[3] at p. 474.

[4] See *Reyes v. The Queen* [2002] 2 W.L.R. 1034.

[5] On June 20, 2002, the U.S. Supreme Court ruled that executing mentally retarded criminals was unconstitutional because it amounted to "cruel and unusual punishment". This vote was seen to be one of the Supreme Court's most important death penalty decisions in 30 years. There are no reliable figures on how many of the 3,700 inmates currently on Death Row in America are mentally retarded but 35 of the 775 convicted murderers executed since 1976 showed signs of mental retardation, which is different from mental illness. Justice John Paul Stevens wrote in his majority opinion "We are not persuaded that the execution of mentally retarded criminals will measurably advance the deterrent or retributive purpose of the death penalty". The standard barometer of mental retardation is an IQ of 70 or lower; an average IQ is 100.

[6] See also *Jabari v. Turkey* [2001] I.N.L.R. 136 on expulsion and the real risk of inhuman or degrading treatment relating to the death penalty in Iran. See also a case presently before the European Court of *Malmatkulov v. Turkey* (October 23, 2001) which deals with the complaints of an Uzbeks applicant under Articles 3 and 2 that they face torture and the death penalty if extradited to Uzbekistan on suspicion of involvement in the attempted assassination of the president of Uzbekistan. In this case, while the court had applied Rule 39 requesting Turkey not to extradite the two applicants pending the proceedings in the European Court, Turkey had handed both men over to the Uzbek authorities and they had since been convicted and sentenced to terms of imprisonment. The question will therefore arise in due course as to whether the term of imprisonment is sufficient to breach Article 3. Decision awaited.

[7] (1989) 11 E.H.R.R. 439. Bodily injury is not essential and mental anguish alone may constitute torture.

argument was that this would lead to 6–8 years on Death Row amongst other hardships, and contravened Article 3.[8]

The European Court of Human Rights held that if the United Kingdom extradited the applicant to the United States then that would be in contravention of Article 3. The death penalty itself is allowed under certain conditions under Article 2, however, it is the Death Row Phenomenon which the court held as inhuman and degrading. They went on to state that for any prisoner, any delay between sentence and execution would result in "severe stress". As is apparent from the facts of *Soering v. United Kingdom* a consideration of the Death Row Phenomenon usually arises in cases of immigration, asylum, extradition and deportation.[9] It is also argued in death row cases before the Privy Council in the United Kingdom.

The length of time a condemned will spend confined to death row will not *in itself* amount to cruel and degrading treatment or punishment sufficient to violate Article 3, in the absence of other compelling circumstances. In *Johnson v. Jamaica*,[10] a Jamaican citizen was convicted of murder and sentenced to death. Having exhausted his domestic remedies, he made an initial submission to the United Nations Human Rights Committee. During this process, the offence of which he had been convicted was classified as non-capital murder and his death sentence was commuted to life imprisonment.

It was argued before the Human Rights Committee that the applicant's detention on death row for 10 years amounted to cruel and degrading treatment and/or punishment in violation of the International Covenant on Civil and Political Rights 1966, Article 7, or to inhuman treatment in violation of the International Covenant, Article 10(1). The Committee in reaching their decision emphasised that to make the length of detention on death row determinative of such a violation would have been to expedite executions, and inconsistent with the International Covenant's object of reducing the use of the death penalty.

Comparative approaches. Considerable support for the abolition of the death penalty has been generated by the views taken on the death row phenomenon. In *People v. Anderson*, Wright C.J. observed[11]:

> "The cruelty of capital punishment lies not only in the execution itself and the pain incident thereto, but also in the dehumanising effects of the lengthy imprisonment prior to execution during which the judicial and administrative procedures essential to the due process of law are carried out. Penologists and medical experts agree that the process of carrying out a verdict of death is often so degrading and brutalising to the human spirit as to constitute psychological torture . . . [the death penalty] degrades and dehumanises all who participate in its processes. It is unnecessary to any legitimate goal of the State and is incompatible with the dignity of man and the judicial process".

Similar sentiments were expressed in *Catholic Commission for Justice and Peace in Zimbabwe v. Attorney General of Zimbabwe*[12] by Gubbay C.J.[13]:

7–04

---

[8] See also *Ng v. Canada* (1993) I.H.R.R. 161: *Woodson v. North Caroline* (1976) 428; US 2809: *Furman v. Georgia* (1972) 408 U.S. 238. Reference will also be made as to whether Article 3 has been violated to the form the death penalty takes and whether it is mandatory in nature.
[9] See Chapter 5.
[10] 1 B.H.R.C. 37.
[11] 493P.2d 880 Supreme Court of California, at pp. 894, 899.
[12] (1993) (4) SA 239 Zimbabwe Supreme Court.
[13] At 268.

"From the moment he enters the condemned cell, the prisoner is enmeshed in a dehumanising environment of near hopelessness. He is in a place where the sole object is to preserve his life so that he may be executed. The condemned prisoner is the living dead . . . the hope of a reprieve is all that is left. Throughout all this time the condemned prisoner constantly broods over his fate. The horrifying spectre of being hanged by the neck and the apprehension of being made to suffer a painful death is never far from the mind".

Judgments in the Canadian Supreme Court have recognised that capital punishment constitutes a serious impairment of human dignity. Cory J. hearing the case of *Kindler v. Canada*,[14] described the death penalty as:

"The supreme indignity to the individual, the ultimate corporal punishment, the final and complete lobotomy and the absolute and irrevocable castration. [It is] the ultimate desecration of the individual as a human being. It is the annihilation of human dignity".

The Hungarian Constitution Court has declared capital punishment to be unconstitutional on the basis of the guarantees for the right to life and human dignity and the prohibitions on torture, cruel, inhuman or degrading treatment in the Hungarian Constitution.

The Constitutional Courts of Ukraine (December 30, 1999), Albania (December 10, 1999), Lithuania (December 9, 1999) and the Republic of Srpsza have all held that the death penalty is unconstitutional either as violating a right to life or as amounting to inhuman and degrading treatment.

The United Nations Human Rights Committee has held that "every execution of a sentence of death may be considered to constitute cruel and inhuman treatment".[15]

The Californian Supreme Court and Massachusetts Supreme Judicial Court have both held that capital punishment was "impermissibly cruel" and a violation of State constitutions.

Sydney Kentridge Q.C., in advancing the applicant's arguments, in *Ocalan* also relied upon the words of M. Pierre Henri Imbert, the Council of Europe's Director of Human Rights "revenge is kindred with our nature and our instincts but not with the law. The law cannot obey the same rules as human nature. Murder may come naturally to mankind, but the law is not made to imitate or reproduce nature. The law is crafted to correct nature".

7–05   **Period from death sentence to execution.** Nevertheless, the courts have attempted to lay down some form of guidance as to what the law will tolerate in terms of delay. An extreme example, although by no means the longest delay, was recorded in *Pratt v. Attorney General for Jamaica*[16] where the Privy Council held that a prolonged delay of 14 years between sentence of death and proposed execution constituted inhuman punishment and was unconstitutional.[17]

---

[14] [1992] 6 C.C.R. (2d) 193.
[15] See also *Ng v. Canada* (1993) I.H.R.R. 161.
[16] [1994] 2 A.C. 1.
[17] It should be pointed out that *Pratt v. Attorney General for Jamaica* decides that it is normally inhuman or degrading treatment to execute a prisoner more than 5 years after he has been sentenced. It does not decide that he may not be lawfully executed before 5 years have elapsed: see *Guerra v. Baptiste* at pp. 414 to 415. The complaint in cases where the *Pratt* principle has been applied is that the prisoner has been kept too long on death row, not that he has not been kept long enough.

Quite properly, the defendant, following conviction for murder in 1979 and sentenced to death, pursued every avenue open to him to appeal and to petition human rights groups. Finally, a warrant for the defendant's execution was issued in 1991.

Allowing the appeal that Section 17(2) of the Constitution authorised various punishments, it did not prevent the court investigating the circumstances in which the executive intended to carry out the sentence.[18] The Privy Council held that execution should take place as soon as reasonably practicable after the sentence. To carry out executions after a delay of 14 years would, they held, constitute inhuman punishment contrary to Section 17(1) of the Constitution.[19]

Section 17 of the Constitution provides:

"(1) No person shall be subjected to torture or to inhuman or degrading punishment or other treatment;

(2) Nothing contained in or done under the authority of any law shall be held to be inconsistent with or in contravention of this section to the extent that the law in question authorises the infliction of any description of punishment which was lawful in Jamaica immediately before the appointed day".

Pratt v. Attorney General for Jamaica[20] laid down certain guidance as to what will constitute delay sufficient to violate Article 3. They observed that capital appeals must be expedited and legal aid allocated to an appellant at an early stage. The aim should be to hear a capital appeal within 12 months of convictions.

The court were of the view that the entire domestic appeals process should be completed within "approximately 2 years". The Privy Council did not purport to set down any rigid timetable but indicated what appeared to them to be realistic targets which, if achieved, would entail very much shorter delays than have occurred in recent cases and could not be considered to involve inhuman or degrading punishment or other treatment.

The court also concerned itself with applications by prisoners to the IACHR and the UNHRC. In observing that it was reasonable to allow some period of delay for decisions of these bodies in individual cases, it should not be very prolonged.

The UNHRC does not accept the complaint unless the author "has exhausted all available domestic remedies", but the UNHRC in *Pratt v. Attorney General for Jamaica*[21] and in the case of *Carlton-Reid v. Jamaica*,[22] that a constitutional motion to the Supreme Court of Jamaica is not a remedy to which the complainant need resort before making an application to the Committee under the Optional Protocol.

A complainant will therefore be able to lodge a complaint immediately after his case has been disposed of by the Judicial Committee of the Privy Council. If Jamaica is able to revise its domestic procedures so that they are carried out with

---

[18] See also *Henfield v. Attorney General of the Bahamas* [1997] A.C. 413 which reaffirmed that the time limits were not rigid and the court can take account of the circumstances of each case.
[19] See also *Bell v. DPP of Jamaica* [1985] C.L.Y. 181: Dictum in *Riley v. Attorney General of Jamaica* [1982] C.L.Y. 543 not followed.
[20] [1994] 2 A.C. 1.
[21] [1994] 2 A.C. 1.
[22] See 250/1987, Annual Report of the Human Rights Committee 1990, Volume II, GAOR, 45th Session, Supplement No. 40, p. 85.

reasonable expedition, no grounds will exist to make a complaint based upon delay.[23] The Privy Council consider that complaints to the UNHRC should be infrequent but when they do occur it should be possible for the Committee to dispose of them with reasonable dispatch and at most within 18 months.[24]

Putting all these considerations together, Their Lordships were of the view that in any case in which execution is to take place more than 5 years after sentence, there will be *strong grounds* for believing that the delay is such as to constitute inhuman or degrading punishment or other treatment.

In India, where the death penalty is not mandatory, the appellate court takes into account delay when deciding whether the death sentence should be imposed. In *Vatheeswaran v. State of Tamil Nadu*,[25] the court recognised the "dehumanising effect of prolonged delay after the sentence of death" and held that delay exceeding two years in the execution of a sentence of death should be sufficient to entitle a person under such sentence to demand the quashing of that sentence on the ground that it offended Article 21 of the Indian Constitution.[26]

In *Pratt v. Attorney General for Jamaica*,[27] the defendants had been incarcerated in a special section of the prison reserved for condemned men, where they were subjected to the Death Row Phenomenon, an experience amounting to torture when protracted. In addition, three warrants for their execution had been issued, resulting in their transfer to a condemned cell and last minute reprieves, producing severe trauma and disorientation. The Human Rights provisions in the Jamaican Constitution are based upon the European model.[28]

The observations of the Privy Council were foreshadowed by Lord Diplock in *Abbott v. Attorney General of Trinidad & Tobago*,[29] when he said of the Judge's power to stay a long delay execution:

"In such a case, which is without precedent and, in Their Lordships' view, would involve delay measured in years, rather than in months, it might be argued that the taking of the condemned man's life was not by due process of law".

7–06   **Time taken by international bodies to consider appeals.** What is reasonable in relation to time taken to appeal may differ when one considers international time limits as opposed to the time limits of domestic tribunals.

The observations of in *Fisher v. Ministry of Public Safety (No. 2)*[30] are instructive. Lord Lloyd of Berwick states:

"Where, . . . the domestic appeal process has been completed well within the period which was regarded in Pratt's case as a reasonable target period, any delay in dealing with the petition to the IACHR beyond the 18 month target period for this stage ought to be capable of being accommodated within the overall 5 year period. Furthermore, as

---

[23] It is to be remembered that the UNHRC does not consider its role to be that of a further appellate court.

[24] See *Pratt v. Attorney General for Jamaica*, p. 35.

[25] (1983) 2 S.C.R. 348.

[26] Which provides "no person shall be deprived of his life or personal liberty except according to procedure established by law".

[27] [1994] 2 A.C. 1.

[28] See *Minister of Home Affairs v. Fisher* [1980] A.C. 319; De Smith, the New Commonwealth and its Constitutions (1964) at pp. 193–194; *Director of Public Prosecutions v. Nasralla* [1976] 2 A.C. 328; *Thornhill v. Attorney General of Trinidad & Tobago* [1981] A.C. 61.

[29] [1979] 1 W.L.R. 1342 at 1348.

[30] [2000] 1 A.C. 434, p. 453.

the decision in *Guerra v. Baptiste*[31] illustrates, the 5 year period has in practice been treated not as a limit but as a norm, from which, as Lord Goff said in *Henfield's* case,[32] the courts may depart if it is appropriate to do so in the circumstances of the case. The decision in *Reckley v. Minister of Public Safety and Immigration (No. 2)*,[33] in which the petition for special leave to the judicial committee was dismissed more than 5 years after the passing of the death sentence, shows that there is room for some latitude either way in the application of the 5 year period, depending on the circumstances".

In deciding what is reasonable, the courts have decided that it is not right to compare the time taken for domestic proceedings with that taken by international bodies.[34] The court accept that proceedings even in the European Commission and the Court of Human Rights can take 5 years, or occasionally even more.

The IACHR only normally meets twice a year and its members act on a part time basis. Nevertheless, the court have declared that death sentence cases are to be treated as urgent cases which call for the shortening of relevant time tables.

Frivolous delay. The court in *Sher Singh v. State of Punjab*[35] raised the   **7–07** concern of prisoners defeating the ends of justice by pursuing a series of frivolous and untenable proceedings.

Domestic authority takes a different view. Where a State wishes to retain capital punishment it must accept the responsibility of ensuring that execution follows as swiftly as practicable after sentence, allowing a reasonable time for appeal and consideration of reprieve. It is part of the human condition that a condemned person will take every opportunity to save their life through the use of the appellate procedure.

If the appellate procedure enables the prisoner to prolong the appellate hearings over a period of years, the fault is considered to be attributed to the appellate system that permits such delay and not to the prisoner who takes advantage of it.[36] The Privy Council have emphasised that the Death Row Phenomenon "must not become established as part of our jurisprudence".[37]

The correct approach to fault based delay. Although delay which is caused   **7–08** by a fault attributable to the applicant should be disregarded, the court should not conduct a minute examination of the periods of delay in order to apportion it but should have regard to the total period of time which has elapsed since sentence.[38] The right approach is to take the total period of time which has elapsed and then to ask whether the "delay is due entirely to the fault of the accused such as an escape from custody or frivolous and time wasting resort to legal procedures which amount to an abuse of process"[39] or whether there is some other reason for the delay.

Repeated reading of warrant for execution. The repeated reading of a   **7–09** warrant for execution to the applicant was considered by the Court of Appeal to

---

[31] [1996] A.C. 397.
[32] See *Henfield v. Attorney General of the Commonwealth of the Bahamas* [1997] A.C. 413.
[33] [1996] A.C. 527.
[34] See *Fisher v. Ministry of Public Safety (No. 2)* at p. 453.
[35] [1983] 2 S.C.R. 582.
[36] See *Pratt v. Attorney General for Jamaica* at p. 33.
[37] See *Pratt v. Attorney General for Jamaica* at p. 33.
[38] See *Bradshaw v. Attorney General of Barbados* [1995] 1 W.L.R. 936.
[39] See *Pratt v. Attorney General for Jamaica* [1994] 2 A.C. 1 at 29–30.

be a matter to be taken into account by the Advisory Committee on the Power of Pardon in a Trinidad and Tobago death penalty case and did not constitute cruel and unusual treatment of itself.[40]

7–10   **The reprieve process.** The consideration of a reprieve is not a legal process and is not subject to the constitutional requirement of due process.[41] Therefore, a strict interpretation directs that any constitutional committee considering the implementation of the death penalty is not bound to consider the views of any other body such as an Advisory Committee in the jurisdiction of Trinidad and Tobago, as to whether a reprieve should take place.

Nevertheless, good practice dictates that all views should be taken into account, and the failure to take pertinent opinions into the decision making process may well be an element to add to the overall argument of breach of Convention rights.[42]

7–11   **Distinction between inhuman or degrading treatment and inhuman or degrading punishment.** The condemned applicant's detention is not considered to be a punishment because their punishment is to suffer death.[43] This was another capital case from Jamaica establishing that section 17(2) of the Constitution does not legitimise inhuman treatment merely because it is a prelude to execution of lawful punishment, or because lawful punishment by hanging happens to be part of the course of treatment.[44]

7–12   **Absconding.** Delay caused by a prisoner escaping will not be taken into consideration.[45]

7–13   **Pre-trial delay.** The principles laid out in *Pratt v. Attorney General for Jamaica*,[46] have not been extended to address the different problem of pre-trial delay.

In *Fisher v. Minister of Public Safety and Immigration (No. 1)*,[47] the Privy Council were of the view that since the state of mind of a person during the pre-trial period was quite different from that of a person sentenced to execution and the norms chosen to establish whether the delay amounted to inhuman punishment took into account the appeals process, it was inappropriate to extend the principle in *Pratt v. Attorney General for Jamaica*,[48] which was formulated to tackle the problem of individuals sentenced to death being held on death row for an unacceptable length of time.[49]

The problem of pre-trial delay can be addressed by invoking the principle in *Guerra v. Baptiste*,[50] which recognises that the circumstances of some cases

---

[40] See *Briggs v. Baptiste* [2000] 2 A.C. 40 in the Privy Council.
[41] See *Briggs v. Baptiste* [2000] 2 A.C. 40 at p. 54.
[42] See *Thomas v. Baptiste* [2000] 2 A.C. 1.
[43] See *Runyowa v. The Queen* [1967] 1 A.C. 26.
[44] See also *Bradshaw v. Attorney General of Barbados* [1995] 1 W.L.R. 936 where it was held that detention in prison prior to execution was ancillary to the punishment and not separate treatment. Furthermore, in any event, overlong detention would be equally unlawful.
[45] See *Pawala v. State of Maharashira* [1985] 2 S.C.R. 8.
[46] [1994] 2 A.C. 1.
[47] [1998] A.C. 673.
[48] [1994] 2 A.C. 1.
[49] But see the dissenting judgement of Lord Steyn.
[50] [1996] A.C. 397.

might justify a departure from the norm. Where fundamental constitutional rights are in issue, such as those under the Jamaican Constitution, Section 17(1), the possibility of taking into account serious pre-trial delay cannot be excluded.[51,52]

Conditions in which condemned prisoners are kept awaiting execution. 7–14
There is no connection between the death sentence and the manner in which the prisoner is detained. They are not matters connected to the imposition of the death sentence.

The courts have concluded that a "global approach"[53] had to be adopted in considering whether a condemned prisoner's treatment had been such as to render their execution inhuman punishment taking into account all matters which would make the totality of their punishment more than the ordinary death penalty, but that since the delay between the applicant's convictions and in the case of *Higgs*, the reading of the death warrants to them, was less than a 5 year period which would have presumptively made their executions unconstitutional, and there was no nexus between the pre-trial delay or the prison conditions in which the applicants were held and their sentences of death, in all the circumstances their execution would not constitute inhuman treatment or punishment.

Individual breaches of Article 3 will not be sufficient to render the execution inhuman or degrading. Although the prison conditions in which the condemned prisoner is being held may be completely unacceptable in a civilised society, the fact that the applicants have suffered inhuman treatment in prison will entitle them to a remedy to deal with that specific abuse.[54] For instance, in the Zimbabwean case of *Conjwayo v. Minister of Justice, Legal and Parliamentary Affairs*,[55] the prison conditions in which a condemned prisoner was held were considered to be in violation of the Constitution prohibiting inhuman or degrading treatment. As a result of this, the prison authorities were ordered to allow longer periods of exercise, but this did not necessarily mean that the death sentence would be commuted.[56]

Conditions of cells on Death Row. A slightly different approach was taken in 7–15
the Court of Appeal as to whether or not the conditions in which the applicants are kept in prison awaiting execution amounted to a breach of Article 3. Such matters were considered in *Thomas v. Baptiste*[57] to be a value judgement in which it was necessary to take account of local conditions both in and outside prison. The Privy Council of Trinidad and Tobago indicated that they would be slow to depart from the "careful assessment of the Court of Appeal" when they

---

[51] However, in the circumstances of *Fisher v. Minister of Public Safety and Immigration (No. 1)*, the circumstances were not so exceptional as to warrant the application of the principle in *Guerra v. Baptiste*.

[52] In *Higgs v. Minister of National Security* [2000] 2 A.C. 228, Lord Steyn in his powerful dissenting judgement observed that the genesis of Section 17(1) of the Constitution is a verbatim image of the European Convention for the Protection of Human Rights and Fundamental Freedoms, Article 3 and that what is held about the interpretation of Section 17(1) of the Constitution of the Bahamas is therefore of importance for the Human Rights law of the United Kingdom (see p. 252).

[53] See *Higgs v. Minister of National Security* [2000] 2 A.C. 228.

[54] See *Thomas v. Baptiste* [2000] 2 A.C. 1 at p. 28A.

[55] See 1992 (2) SA 56. The court rejected an explanation as to the deprivation based upon prison staffing problems.

[56] But see the minority reasons of the Board in *Thomas v. Baptiste* [2000] 2 A.C. 1.

[57] [2000] 2 A.C. 1 at 27.

concluded that the conditions did not amount to "cruel and unusual treatment".[58]

The Privy Council would not hold in *Thomas v. Baptiste*[59] that any breach of a condemned person's constitutional rights makes it unlawful to carry out a sentence of death. But whether the condemned individual is treated in such a way prior to sentence of death being carried out, that the sentence in itself becomes a violation of Article 3, seems to be a matter of degree. The court in *Thomas v. Baptiste*[60] stated that:

> "The fact that the conditions in which the condemned man has been kept prior to execution infringe his constitutional rights does not make a lawful sentence unconstitutional . . . it would be otherwise if the condemned man were kept in solitary confinement or shackled or flogged or tortured. One would then say 'enough is enough'. A state which imposes such punishments forfeits its right to carry out the death sentence in addition".

Taking into account this "global approach", it is very clear from the authorities that pre-trial delay per se will not constitute a violation of Article 3. Previous decisions may properly have some influence on how the court may interpret whether a violation has occurred but will not be a binding precedent.[61]

Whilst the courts do not condone lengthy pre-trial delays or uncivilised prison conditions and indeed have described them as "unacceptable",[62] the authorities conclude that they differ sharply from the case of delay in execution because whereas a prisoner cannot be expected to put an end to his uncertainty by demanding his own execution, both pre-trial delay and prison conditions are the subject of other legal remedies.

The potential remedies were considered in *Fisher (No. 1)*.[63] When a prisoner has been held in custody for an excessive period of time, pre-trial, they can apply to have the prosecution dismissed as an abuse of process. Furthermore, the prisoner may apply for an order from the court that unless he be tried speedily he should be released on bail. Likewise, in the case of prison conditions, the prisoner may apply for injunctive relief.[64]

Whilst the court will look at all matters in the round that would make the totality of the punishment something more than "the straight forward death penalty",[65] the guideline principle is that the matters to be taken into account must have an aggravation of the punishment of death. In other words there must be a nexus between matters complained of and the sentence of death.

---

[58] in breach of the Constitution of Trinidad and Tobago which came into force on 1 August 1976 which prohibited "cruel and unusual treatment or punishment". In *Thomas v. Baptiste* (citation above) the applicants were detained in cramped and foul-smelling cells and deprived of exercise or access to the open air for long periods of time. When they were allowed to exercise in the fresh air they were handcuffed. The Privy Council accepted that the conditions in which they were kept were in breach of the Prison Rules and thus unlawful. But they emphasised again that it did not follow that they amounted to "cruel and unusual treatment".

[59] [2000] 2 A.C. 1.

[60] At page 28.

[61] *Per* Lord Cooke of Thorndon at p. 260E—p. 261A.

[62] See *Higgs v. Minister of National Security* at p. 248.

[63] See [1998] A.C. 73 at 680–681 *per* Lord Goff of Chieveley.

[64] See *Coljwayo v. Minister of Justice, Legal and Parliamentary Affairs* (see above citation) which has been described as a striking example of the grant of such relief to prisoners under sentence of death (*Higgs v. Minister of National Security* at p. 48, *per* Lord Hoffmann).

[65] See *Thomas v. Baptiste* [2000] 2 A.C. 1.

The courts have not concluded that pre-trial delay or conditions under which prisoners are kept cannot constitute an unlawful aggravation of the death sentence merely because they are also inflicted upon prisoners but have observed that the establishment of the necessary link is more difficult when the conditions in the prison are a generalised consequences of overcrowding and lack of resources.[66]

On the facts of *Higgs v. Minister of National Security*,[67] the pre-trial delay was held to have no connection with the fact that a sentence of death was eventually imposed and furthermore that the conditions under which the applicants were held had no connection (save for them being held in individual cells) with the fact that they were under sentence of death. Indeed, the Privy Council commented that even if the conditions suffered by the applicants had been confined to those on death row, they would not have been inclined to consider them inhuman or degrading and *a fortiori*, did not make a subsequent execution inhuman or degrading. It is also a question of fact and degree.[68]

Execution *per se*. The overwhelming European case law suggests that execution in itself does not breach Article 3.[69]   **7–16**

The proposed manner of execution. It has been argued that the type of   **7–17** execution could also evoke Article 3 arguments. The applicant in *Abdullah Ocalan*, the PKK Political Leader whom the Turks asserted to try[70] was described by Sir Sydney Kentridge Q.C., one of the four counsel representing Ocalan, as:

> "This is one of the most significant and high profile cases ever to come before the European Court of Human Rights . . . it is a case in which a man's life is at stake . . . the first case in which the passing and proposed implementation of the death penalty within a signatory State has resulted in litigation before the European Court of Human Rights".

The applicant argued that hanging would involve a separate violation of his Article 3 Convention rights. Reliance was placed on the medical opinion of Dr Harold Hillman who stated that hanging is a "painful and humiliating procedure"

---

[66] See *Higgs v. Minister of National Security* [2000] 2 A.C. 228 at p. 251.

[67] [2000] 2 A.C. 228.

[68] Lord Hoffmann observed at p. 51 the well known principle that the Privy Council is not a second court of appeal. Its function is to lay down general principles and to correct substantial miscarriages of justice. The court at p. 251 considered that it would create uncertainty and to be detrimental to the administration of justice if the Board were in each case to form its own view on whether local conditions in the prison fell on one side or the other of the imprecise line dividing treatment which is inhuman from that which is not.

[69] Albert Pierrepoint in his autobiography stated that in all his experience as an executioner in Britain from 1931 to 1956, he was of the view that capital punishment had no deterrent effect: "I operated, on behalf of the State, what I am convinced was the most humane and the most dignified method of meeting out death to a delinquent—however justified or unjustified the allotment of death—and on behalf of humanity I trained other nations to adopt the British system of execution. It is a fact which is no source of pride to me at all—it is simple history—but I have carried out the execution of more judicial sentences of death (outside the field of politics) than any executioner in any British record or archive. That fact is the measure of my experience. The fruit of my experience has this bitter aftertaste: that I do not now believe that any one of the hundreds of executions I carried out has in any way acted as a deterrent against future murder. Capital punishment, in my view, achieved nothing except revenge".

[70] Application No. 46221/99.

because, *inter alia*, "the person hanged is masked, his wrists and ankles are bound to restrain him, he cannot react to pain, distress and feeling of asphyxia by the usual psychological responses of crying out or moving violently and he often sweats, drools, micturates and defecates".[71]

Further, in *Aksoy v. Turkey*,[72] the European Court of Human Rights held that hanging an individual by his or her arms constitutes torture and violates Article 3 of the Convention.[73]

7–18   **The grant of mercy.** The exercise of mercy is not a sentencing function. As was stated in *Reyes v. The Queen*[74]:

"Both in language and literature, mercy and justice are contrasted".

The administration of justice involves the determination of what punishment a transgressor deserves, and the fixing of the appropriate sentence for the crime. But the grant of mercy involves the determination that a transgressor need not suffer the punishment he deserves, that the appropriate sentence may for some reason be remitted. The former is a judicial activity and the latter is executive responsibility. Determination of guilt and also determination of the appropriate measure of punishment is a judicial exercise and not an executive function.[75]

7–19   **Prison rules.** Even if the prison conditions in which the applicants are kept contravene Prison Rules and are therefore unlawful and furthermore amount to a breach of Article 3, that will not make a lawful death sentence passed upon an applicant unconstitutional.

2. MANDATORY LIFE IMPRISONMENT

7–20   **Not incompatible with Article 3.** A mandatory term of life imprisonment for murder[76] is incompatible with Article 3. The question of whether a mandatory

---

[71] See Dr Hillman's affidavit in *Maheia & v. Attorney General of Belize* 1999.

[72] (1997) 23 E.H.R.R. 553.

[73] The vast majority of executions which take place each year are carried out by only four countries, China, the Democratic Republic of the Congo, the United States of America and Iran. See also *Aksoy v. Turkey* (2002) 34 E.H.R.R. 57.

[74] [2002] UKPC 11.

[75] See *Hinds v. The Queen* [1977] A.C. 195 at 226D and *R. v. Mollison (No. 2)* May 29, 2000 and *Nicholas v. The Queen* (1998) 193 C.L.R. 173.

[76] See *Reyes v. The Queen* [2002] UKPC 11 which held that the mandatory provision of the Criminal Code of Belize requiring sentence of death to be passed on conviction of murder by shooting, categorised as a class A murder, subjected the convicted person to inhuman or degrading punishment or other treatment incompatible with his constitutional rights, and so that provision was void. Any provision by shooting was, the Board held, to be treated as falling within class B so that if special extenuating circumstances existed a sentence of life imprisonment instead of death could be imposed. The court directed itself that it had to consider the substance of the fundamental right at issue and ensure contemporary protection of that right in the light of evolving standards of decency that marked the progress of a maturing society (see *Trop v. Dulles* (1958) 356 U.S. 86). The Privy Council held that the requirement of humanity had been read as incorporating the precept that consideration of the offender's culpability and of any potentially mitigating circumstances should be regarded as a *sine qua non* of the humane imposition of capital punishment. In many respects the court limited itself to the circumstances of its particular case and they stressed that for the purposes of the appeal the Board did not need to consider the constitutionality of any mandatory penalty other than death, nor such penalty imposed for any murder other than by shooting. They observed that so long as the death penalty was retained, there might well be murders by shooting, which justified the ultimate penalty, but for others the death penalty would be excessive and disproportionate. Interestingly, counsel for

term for other offences is similarly incompatible. In reality, a mandatory life sentence is indeterminate, rarely will there be imprisonment for life. In practice, when the penal element of the sentence has been served, the Secretary of State could release the prisoner on licence. The Court had emphasised that an indeterminate sentence upon a child which allows for the child's continued detention or their recall to detention following release where necessary to protect the public will not be in breach of Article 3.[77]

If the prisoner is then recalled, he will have the opportunity to have his recall considered by the Parole Board.[78] The mandatory life sentence is part penal and part preventative, for which there is no justification in circumstances where the offender is not expected to be a danger if released after he has served the penal element of his sentence.[79]

In *T & V*,[80] a case which deals with the treatment of children and juveniles,[81] the European Court observed that it did not consider "that the punitive element inherent in the tariff approach itself gives rise to a breach of Article 3". Overall, the court's conclusions are expressed in terms which indicate that there is no objection under Article 3 to a mandatory indeterminate sentence for murder. The court in *Lichniak*,[82] in concluding that Article 3 was not violated we are reassured that there was sufficient "individualised consideration of the offender's case within the context of the sentence".

Prisoners aged between 18 and 21 years. The imposition of a mandatory   **7–21** sentence of life imprisonment in respect of the offence of murder committed by young adults between the ages of 18 and 21 does not disclose treatment and punishment prohibited by Article 3 of the Convention.[83]

The Commission have also held that there is no incompatibility with the Convention in the imposition of a life sentence as a security or retributive measure in a particular case or in a decision to keep a recidivist or habitual offender at the disposal of the Government.[84]

While in cases concerning detention during Her Majesty's pleasure, the court commented that a sentence pursuant to which young persons forfeited their liberty for the rest of their lives might raise issues under Article 3 of the Convention,[85] the Commission considers that these remarks apply to sentences of

---

the appellant argued that not everyone convicted of murder or murder classified as capital, deserved to die. He went on to develop his submission that the mandatory imposition of sentence of death on the appellant violated his right not to be subjected to inhuman or degrading punishment or other treatment. This case opens the door to other strongly arguable submissions that the mandatory capital sentence *per se* violates Article 3.

However, in *Morrisey v. R* 9 B.H.R.C. 179, the Canadian Supreme Court affirmed that the deterrent aims of the mandatory sentence were justified in cases of extremely serious crime and did not constitute cruel and unusual punishment on the facts of that case which were essentially that the appellant was convicted of criminal negligence following an incident in which a shotgun that he was holding when intoxicated accidentally discharged, killing his companion, for which he received a 4 year mandatory sentence of imprisonment.

[77] See *T v. U.K.* and *V v. U.K.*, para. 98 above.
[78] See Crime (Sentences) Act 1997, Section 29.
[79] See Crime (Sentences) Act 1997, Section 31.
[80] See 30 E.H.R.R. 121.
[81] See Chapter 8: Children and Juveniles.
[82] [2001] EWHC Admin 294.
[83] See *Bromfield v. United Kingdom* (Application no. 32003/96) July 1, 1998.
[84] See *Weeks v. United Kingdom* (1987) 10 E.H.R.R. 293.
[85] See *Hussain v. United Kingdom* (1996) 22 E.H.R.R. 1.

life imprisonment imposed on children under the age of 18 to whom special considerations apply.[86]

7–22   **Discretionary life sentences.** In *Wynne v. United Kingdom*,[87] the court said:

> "The very nature of the discretionary life sentence which, unlike the mandatory sentence, was imposed not because of the inherent gravity of the offence but because of the presence of factors which were susceptible to change which the passage of time, namely mental instability and dangerousness. A clear distinction was drawn between the discretionary life sentence which was considered to have a protective purpose and a mandatory life sentence which was viewed as essentially punitive in nature".[87a]

Many discretionary life sentence prisoners have committed offences more serious than those serving mandatory life sentences and yet they are entitled to judicial review by the Parole Board of their continuing detention.[88]

7–23   **Crime (Sentences) Act 1997 Section 2(5) and Section 2(6).** The practice when imposing a discretionary life sentence is to fix what would have been the appropriate determinate sentence had an indeterminate sentence not been necessary, and then to specify a proportion of the sentence being between one half and two thirds.[89] In the case of adult offenders, this should be the starting point and, in many cases, would be the appropriate period, but the Judge has a discretion to fix a period up to two thirds of the appropriate determinate sentence.[90]

Section 2 of the 1997 Act, insofar as it is pertinent, reads in the following terms:

> "(1) This section applies where:
>
>> (a) A person is convicted of a serious offence committed after the commencement of this section; and
>> (b) At the time when that offence was committed, he was 18 or over and had been convicted in any part of the United Kingdom of another serious offence;
>
> (2) The court shall impose a life sentence, that is to say . . .
>
>> (a) Where the person is 21 or over, a sentence of imprisonment for life;
>> (b) Where he is under 21, a sentence of custody for life under Section 8(2) of the Criminal Justice Act 1982 (the 1982 Act), unless the court is of the opinion that there are exceptional circumstances relating to either of the offences or to the offender which justify its not doing so.
>
> (3) Where the court does not impose a life sentence, it shall state in open court that it is of that opinion and what the exceptional circumstances are.

---

[86] See Chapter 8 on Children and Juveniles.
[87] (1994) 19 E.H.R.R. 333 at 346, para. 33.
[87a] See para. 7–030.
[88] See also *Singh v. United Kingdom*, para. 61 and *Hussain v. United Kingdom*, para. 53 as to life sentences and genuine protection for the public.
[89] although in the case of young offenders sentenced to an indeterminate period of detention, the general rule should be to fix the period at one half—see *R. v. Secretary of State for the Home Department ex p. Furber* [1998] 1 All E.R. 23, DC.
[90] See Practice Direction (Crime: Life Sentences) [1993] 1 W.L.R. 223 as repealed and replaced by the Crime (Sentences) Act 1997 Section 28 which has in turn been repealed in part and replaced by the Powers of Criminal Courts (Sentencing) Act 2000 Section 82A: *R. v. M* (Discretionary Life Sentence); *R. v. L* [1999] 1 W.L.R. 485 CA.

(4) An offence, the sentence for which is imposed under sub-section (2) above, shall not be regarded as an offence the sentence for which is fixed by law.

(5) An offence committed in England and Wales is a serious offence for the purposes of this section if it is any of the following, namely . . .

    (a) An attempt to commit murder, a conspiracy to commit murder or an incitement to murder;

    (b) An offence under section 4 of the Offences Against the Person Act 1861 (soliciting murder);

    (c) Manslaughter;

    (d) An offence under section 18 of the Offences Against the Person Act 1861 (wounding or causing grievous bodily harm with intent);

    (e) Rape or an attempt to commit rape;

    (f) An offence under section 5 of the Sexual Offences Act 1956 (intercourse with a girl under 13);

    (g) An offence under section 16 (possession of a firearm with intent to injure); section 17 (use of a firearm to resist arrest) or section 18 (carrying a firearm with criminal intent) of the Firearms Act 1968;

    (h) Robbery where, at some time during the commission of the offence, the offender had in his possession a firearm or imitation firearm within the meaning of that Act".

The following features of section 2 will be noted. Firstly, it refers to two offences having been committed by the offender. Secondly, it is only the second offence (the trigger offence) which has to have been committed after the commencement of the section. The earlier offence may have been committed at any time. Thirdly, when the second offence is committed, the offender is required to be over 18 but there is no age requirement in relation to the first offence. Fourthly, the proviso of "exceptional circumstances" applies to both offences. The "exceptional circumstances" can relate either to the offences or to the offender but what constitutes exceptional circumstances is not otherwise defined by the section. Finally, all offences identified as serious offences are offences for which life imprisonment could be imposed quite apart from section 2.

"Exceptional" was defined in *R. v. Kelly (Edward)*,[91] by Lord Bingham:

> "as an ordinary, familiar English adjective, and not as a term of art. It describes a circumstance which is such as to form an exception, which is such as to form an exception, which is out of the ordinary course, or unusual, or special, or uncommon, to be exceptional, a circumstance need not be unique, or unprecedented, or very rare; but it cannot be one that is regularly, or routinely, or normally encountered".

In *R. v. Buckland*,[92] Lord Bingham further described the rationale of Section 2 in the following terms:

> "The section is founded on an assumption that those who have been convicted of two qualifying serious offences present such a serious and continuing danger to the safety of the public that they should be liable to indefinite incarceration and, if released, should be liable indefinitely to recall to prison. In any case where, on all the evidence, it appears that such a danger does or may exist, it is hard to see how the court can consider itself justified in not imposing the statutory penalty, even if exceptional circumstances are found to exist. But if exceptional circumstances are found, and their evidence

---

[91] [2000] Q.B. 198 at 208.
[92] [2000] 1 W.L.R. 1262 at 1268.

suggests that an offender does not present a serious and continuing danger to the safety of the public, the court may be justified in imposing a lesser penalty".

In *R. v. Offen*,[93] considered the expression "exceptional circumstances", and held that those words must be so construed as not to contravene the prohibition on inhuman and degrading treatment, or arbitrary and disproportionate punishment.[94] It has been construed that in enacting the 1997 Act, the Government's intention was that the public should receive proper protection from persistent violent or sex offenders, and the court gave effect to that intention by indicating that in every case Judge must assess the risk tot he public and use the words "exceptional circumstances" to ensure that no offender is sentenced to life imprisonment who does not constitute a significant risk to the public.

7-24   **Post-tariff detentions.** When prisoners reach the preventative stage of their sentence, as opposed to the punishment (tariff) stage of a discretionary life sentence, it is arguable that the State will be obliged to provide treatment to help reduce their dangerousness. One of the criticisms of the present penal system is that no treatment is given to detainees during the preventative stage of their sentence so that they may be released into the community without any risk to society. In the future, where no such programmes are offered to detainees, a violation of Article 3 may be arguable.

7-25   **The Home Secretary's power to increase tariffs.** In *R. v. Secretary of State for the Home Department ex p. Pierson*,[95] the House of Lords equated the Secretary of State's tariff with a sentence.

The European Court is of the view that the tariff or, in other words, the minimum period to be served by a prisoner to satisfy the requirements of retribution and deterrence, comprising the punishment element of the mandatory life sentence, when fixed by the Home Secretary is a sentencing exercise and that after the expiry of the tariff, continued detention depends on elements of dangerousness and risk associated with the objectives of the original sentence of murder. In *Stafford v. United Kingdom*,[96] the European Court considered the application of the Crime (Sentences) Act 1997, Sections 28 to 34, in accordance with which the Secretary of State decides the length of the tariff.[97]

Murder carries a mandatory sentence of life imprisonment under the Murder (Abolition of Death Penalty) Act 1965.[98]

---

[93] [2001] 1 W.L.R. 253.

[94] Therefore, not violating Articles 3 and 5 of the Convention.

[95] [1997] 3 W.L.R. 492; [1997] 3 All E.R. 577.

[96] (2002) E.H.R.R. 32.

[97] The procedure from Crown Court conviction is that the view of the Trial Judge is made known to the prisoner after his trial as is the opinion of the Lord Chief Justice. The prisoner is afforded the opportunity to make representations to the Secretary of State who then proceeds to fix the tariff and is entitled to depart from the judicial view (see *R. v. Secretary of State for the Home Department ex p. Doody* [1994] 1 A.C. 531 and the Policy Statement to Parliament by Michael Howard, the then Home Secretary, July 27, 1993 Hansard (House of Commons Debates) Columns 861–864)

[98] A person convicted of other serious offences (*e.g.* manslaughter or rape) may also be sentenced to life imprisonment at the discretion of the Trial Judge in certain other cases where the offence is grave and where there are exceptional circumstances which demonstrate that the offender is a danger to the public and it is not possible to say when that danger will subside. When an offender is under 18 years of age, when the offence of murder is committed, he or she is sentenced to detention during Her Majesty's pleasure (see the Children and Young Persons Act 1933, Section 53(1) and Chapter ??).

The tariff. The tariff policy was first publicly announced in Parliament by Mr   **7–26**
Leon Brittan on November 30, 1983.[99] The tariff approach involves breaking
down the life sentence into component parts, namely retribution, deterrence and
protection of the public. The tariff represents the minimum period which the
prisoner will have to serve to satisfy the requirements of retribution and deterrence.

The Home Secretary will not refer the case to the Parole Board until 3 years
before the expiry of the tariff period, and will not exercise his discretion to
release on licence until after the tariff period has been completed.[1]

The tariff of a discretionary life prisoner is fixed in open court by the Trial
Judge after conviction pursuant to section 34 of the 1991 Act. After the tariff has
expired, the prisoner may require the Secretary of State to refer his case to the
Parole Board which has the power to order his release if it is satisfied that it is
no longer necessary to detain him for the protection of the public.[2]

Procedure. Following the case of *R. v. Secretary of State for the Home*   **7–27**
Department ex p. Handscomb,[3] the procedure followed in all life sentence cases
in England and Wales, is that the trial judge writes to the Home Secretary,
through the Lord Chief Justice, immediately after the trial, to inform the Home
Secretary of the conviction and to give his views on the necessary period of
detention to meet the requirements of retribution and deterrence. The Lord Chief
Justice adds his own view. Taking these views into account, a junior Minister, on
behalf of the Home Secretary, decides upon the period of imprisonment necessary to meet the requirements of retribution and deterrence. This period of
imprisonment is referred to as the "tariff". The tariff is fixed strictly in accordance with the following judicial recommendation from *Handscomb*.[4]

> "In determining how long such a person should be detained for punitive purposes, the
> Secretary of State should fix the date of the first review . . . strictly in accordance with
> a period of detention (that is to say, the notional determinate sentence less one third in
> remission) recommended by the Judiciary as necessary, to meet the requirements of
> retribution and deterrence".

If and when the Parole Board recommend release, the trial judge and the
Lord Chief Justice are again consulted before the papers are referred to the
Minister.

Criticisms of the tariff system are not new. Lord Lane, the Lord Chief Justice,
stated:

> "It is unsatisfactory, to say the least, that the length of a prisoner's stay in prison should
> be determined or partially determined behind the scenes by someone who has not heard

---

[99] See *Hansard* (House of Commons Debates) Columns 505–507.
[1] See *R. v. Secretary of State for the Home Department ex p. V & T* [1998] A.C. 407 at 492G to
493A.
[2] As at December 3, 2001, there were 3,171 male and 114 female mandatory life prisoners, 220 men
and 11 women serving a sentence of detention under Her Majesty's pleasure and 1,424 male and 25
female discretionary life prisoners.
[3] (1987) 86 Cr.App.R. 59.
[4] At p. 60.

any representations by or on behalf of the prisoner on grounds which the prisoner does not know".[5]

7–28   **Fixing the tariff is equivalent to a judge's sentencing power.** During the case of *Ex p. T & V*, the House of Lords considered the nature of the tariff fixing exercise and confirmed that it was a sentencing power which was being utilised by the Home Secretary.

In guiding the Home Secretary as to how that power should be used, the House of Lords emphasised that the Minister should exercise "dispassionate fairness". Lord Steyn stated:

> "Writing on behalf of the Home Secretary, the Home Office explained that 'the Home Secretary must ensure that, at all times, he acts with the same dispassionate fairness as a sentencing judge'.
>
>   The comparison between the position of the Home Secretary, when he fixes a tariff representing the punitive element of the sentence, and the position of the sentencing judge, is correct. In fixing a tariff the Home Secretary is carrying out, contrary to the constitutional principle of the separation of powers between the executive and the judiciary, a classic judicial function. Parliament entrusted the underlying statutory power, which entailed a discretion to adopt a policy and fix a tariff, to the Home Secretary. But the power to fix a tariff is nevertheless equivalent to a judge's sentencing power".

Lord Hope added:

> "If the Secretary of State wishes to fix a tariff for the case—in order to replace the views of the judiciary with a view of his own about the length of the minimum period—he must be careful to abide by the same rules . . . ".

7–29   **Whole life tariffs can be appropriate.** A whole life tariff may be appropriate in certain exceptional cases "where the crime or crimes are sufficiently heinous".[6] The court held that in the case of Myra Hindley the decision of the Secretary of State to apply a whole life tariff was found in the circumstances to be lawful.

It seems that Hindley's case was distinguished in that the Home Secretary was held to be entitled to revise his view of the tariff which had been based on incomplete knowledge of her role in the three murders upon which she had faced trial and in ignorance of her involvement in two other murders, matters which came to light later.[7]

The Report of the Select Committee on Murder and Life Imprisonment[8] accepted that the full life sentence should remain available both for "particularly outrageous murders and for those where there would be a degree of uncertainty about the risk, by reason in particular of his mental condition, of releasing a

---

[5] See Report of the Select Committee on Murder and Life Imprisonment, Vol. 1, HL Paper 78–I. In the Report, the House of Lords recommended that the life sentence for murder should become discretionary and that the range of penalties for murder should be the same as for that of any other serious crime (para. 175). They further recommended (at para. 177) that in every case the judge should specify in Open Court the period of years which he considers necessary to satisfy the requirements of retribution and deterrence.

[6] See *R. v. Home Secretary ex p. Hindley* [2001] 1 A.C., where a provisional tariff of 30 years had been replaced by a whole life tariff.

[7] There are 22 mandatory life prisoners with whole life tariffs as at December 31, 2001.

[8] See citation above.

prisoner at the end of a determinate sentence".[9] Indeed, the Committee go on to say that they:

> "recognise that the courts have, in recent years, been faced with crimes of the most extreme gravity. They believe that the form of life imprisonment which they recommend would provide a degree of protection which the public rightly demand, and would provide a sufficiently severe sentence to deal with the most outrageous crimes. After the introduction of a discretionary sentence for murder, the Committee appreciate that the average length of time served under a life sentence would be considerably longer than it is now. The Committee expect that their proposals will lead to very lengthy penal sanctions being set in the most grave cases. In some cases, this may result in imprisonment for the rest of the prisoner's life".[10]

No distinction between life sentences. The court in *Stafford v. United King-*   **7–30**
dom,[11] considered that it must now be regarded as established in domestic law that there is no distinction between mandatory life prisoners, discretionary life prisoners and juvenile murderers as regards the nature of tariff fixing. It is a sentencing exercise. The mandatory life sentence does not impose imprisonment for life as a punishment. The tariff, which reflects the individual circumstances of the offence and the offender, represents the element of punishment.

The European Court went on to conclude that the findings in *Wynne*,[12] that the mandatory life sentence constituted punishment for life can no longer be regarded as reflecting the real position in the domestic criminal justice system of the mandatory life prisoner. The court were reinforced as to their view by the fact that a whole life tariff may, in exceptional cases, be imposed where justified by the gravity of the particular offence.[13] Therefore, once the punishment element of a sentence as reflected in the tariff has been satisfied, the grounds for continued detention, as in discretionary life and juvenile murder cases, must be considerations of risk and dangerousness.

The present situation. Although prior to *Stafford v. United Kingdom*[14] it had   **7–31**
been held that there was no violation of Article 3 as a result of the policy changes announced in 1983,[15] the decision in *Stafford* whilst finding violations of Article 5 also opens the door to strongly arguable submissions that Article 3 has also, in those circumstances, been violated.[16]

---

[9] See para. 176.
[10] See para. 178.
[11] (2002) 35 E.H.R.R. 32.
[12] (1995) 19 E.H.R.R. 333.
[13] The European Court referred again to *T & V v. United Kingdom* reiterating that an adult mandatory life sentence constituted punishment for life (*T v. United Kingdom* at para. 109 and *V v. United Kingdom* at para. 110). But the European Court got round this difficulty by observing that in doing so, the courts had merely sought to draw attention to the difference between such a life sentence and a sentence to detention during Her Majesty's pleasure, which was the category of sentence under review in the cases concerned. The court in *Stafford* observed that their colleagues in *V & T* had sought to distinguish previous case law rather than to confirm an analysis deriving from that case law.
[14] (2002) 35 E.H.R.R. 32.
[15] See *Hogben v. United Kingdom* 46 D.R. 231.
[16] There are indications that the Home Secretary is not going to take this lying down, he stated in a press release dated May 28, 2002 that he was considering domestic legislation to enshrine the principle of life sentences meaning life. He stated "If this judgement were to be used to support a legal process to achieve (encouragement for those who would like to remove the Home Secretary's powers to set tariffs for adult murderers), I would seek to use domestic legislation to enshrine the power of Parliament to provide adequate punishment for the guilty, including life meaning life".

3. AUTOMATIC LIFE SENTENCES

7–32   **Article 3 not violated.** Article 3[17] of the European Convention on Human Rights is not contravened when an automatic life sentence is imposed upon a defendant. The court will reach the same conclusion even if the defendant is mentally ill within the definition of the Mental Health Act 1983.

7–33   **Mentally ill defendants.** Notwithstanding the stigma of a life sentence and the fact that the courts have in such cases previously encouraged the use of hospital and restriction orders under the Mental Health Act 1983, it has always been open to Parliament to say, as it did in 1997, that in defined cases there was an assumption that the offender presented such a serious and continuing danger to the safety of the public that a hospital order with a restriction order would afford inadequate protection, and there must therefore be a sentence of life imprisonment.

The European Court of Human Rights has never ruled that it is inconsistent with Article 3 to sentence someone who is mentally ill to a term of imprisonment. But the position may be different if the medical services available in prison are inadequate.

7–34   **Assumption rebuttable.** The assumption that the offender presents such a serious and continuing danger to the safety of the public that a hospital order with a restriction order would afford inadequate protection and that there must therefore be a sentence of life imprisonment, is rebuttable.

7–35   **Prisoner may not receive appropriate medical treatment.** Nevertheless, if it can be established that the offender sentenced to life imprisonment would not receive appropriate medical treatment, it is very arguable indeed that the statutory assumption can be said to have infringed his Convention rights under Article 3.

In *R. v. Drew*,[18] the appellant who was suffering from a mental illness within the meaning of the 1983 Act, received a life sentence by virtue of the provisions under the Criminal Courts (Sentencing) Act 2000, s.109.[19] In that case, the Court of Appeal held that there had been no breach of Article 3 and specifically pointed out that there was no evidence to show that the appellant would be deprived of appropriate medical treatment in prison. *Drew* involved a defendant who was subject to a hospital order[20] under the Mental Health Act 1983, s.37, and a restriction order under section 41 of the same Act. He fell within Section 2 of the Crime (Sentences) Act 1997,[21] for receipt of an automatic life sentence as a result of two qualifying offences. He would receive that sentence unless "exceptional circumstances" arose. The court at first instance, following *R. v. Newman*,[22] declined to find mental illness as an exceptional circumstance for the purposes of section 109.

---

[17] And Article 5.
[18] See *The Times*, January 14, 2002: [2001] EWCA Crim. 2861.
[19] Formerly s.2 of the Crime (Sentences) Act 1997 involving discretionary life sentences.
[20] Hospital and Limitation Directions are at present available only in respect of an offender suffering from psychopathic disorders whose condition is likely to be alleviated by treatment or in whose case treatment will prevent deterioration.
[21] Now s.109 of the Powers of the Criminal Courts (Sentencing) Act 2000.
[22] [2000] 2 Cr.App.R. (S) 227.

It was submitted that to impose a sentence of imprisonment in circumstances where but for the existence of an earlier offence, the court would make a hospital order must be punishment, and therefore must for the purposes of Article 3 be regarded as inhuman and degrading treatment, to label someone who was mentally ill as a culpable and deliberate wrongdoer deserving punishment, even if he received appropriate care and treatment from the moment the sentence was imposed. During the course of argument before the Court of Appeal, no evidence was presented that the appellant had been subjected to inhuman or degrading treatment. For instance, there was no allegation that the appellant had been subjected to physical or mental suffering. In fact, he was in the same institution that he would have been if a hospital order had been made under the Mental Health Act 1983.

In the absence of this evidence, the court had no alternative but to find that there had been no violation of Article 3. A query remains as to what the court would have made of section 109 of the 2000 Act had there been evidence of physical or mental suffering.

4. REMAND

Detention on remand not of itself in breach of Article 3. In *Kudla v.* **7–36** *Poland*,[23] the European Court of Human Rights held that although the applicant had spent more than 2 years in detention on remand during which he twice attempted suicide, detention on remand was not of itself inhuman or degrading treatment but that the State had to ensure that the conditions of detention showed respect for human dignity.[24] The facts of that case seem to disclose that the applicant had regularly sought and obtained medical assistance and that there was insufficient evidence to indicate that his suicide attempts were in any way due to the failures on the part of the authorities.[25]

5. CUSTODIAL SENTENCES GENERALLY

Violation of Article 3 unlikely. Although the Commission and the court have **7–37** indicated that the severity of a criminal sentence could, in principle, constitute inhuman or degrading treatment, in the context of a custodial sentence imposed upon an adult defendant, such a finding is unlikely in practice.[26] The Commission have held that "only in exceptional circumstances could the length of a sentence be relevant under Article 3".[27] The fact that a penalty is more severe than the

---

[23] See 10 B.H.R.C. 269.
[24] See Chapter 4.
[25] Furthermore, Article 3 will not be violated when a prisoner is punished for the commission of a disciplinary offence and loses remission. See *McFeeley v. United Kingdom* (1981) 3 E.H.R.R. 161 at para. 47 and Chapter 4.
[26] See *Treholt v. Norway* (1991) 71 D.R. 168 at 191; *X v. Germany* (1976) 6 D.R. 127.
[27] See *C v. Germany* (1986) 46 D.R. 179.

penalty which would be imposed for the same offence elsewhere in Europe is not sufficient.[28]

Although there is no Article of the Convention which provides an express right to challenge the length of the criminal sentence,[29] an unduly harsh sentence may be incompatible with a defendant's Convention rights if it is so severe in its effects as to violate Article 3.[30]

---

[28] See *C v. Germany* (1986) 46 D.R. 170.
[29] See *X v. United Kingdom* (1974) 1 D.R. 54 which was an application in respect of a 4 year sentence imposed for arson.
[30] or, it is imposed for an offence committed in the normal exercise of the rights protected by Articles 8 to 11 and gives rise to a disproportionate interference with the right concerned.

Chapter 8

CHILDREN AND YOUNG PEOPLE

Bullet points. 8–01

- Not in breach of Article 3 to put child on trial in adult court—see *T and V v. United Kingdom*;

- Juveniles should only be deprived of their liberty as a last resort and for the shortest possible period of time—see Convention on the Rights of the Child, Article 37(b);

- Particular importance is attached to the role of health care services for juveniles in custody—see 9th General Report of the CPT;

1. LEGAL PROCEEDINGS

Generally. All the case law on this subject relates to children and young 8–02 people in criminal courts and it seems that a clear distinction has to be made between their participation in the criminal justice system and the civil courts whereby their very age they are unlikely to participate as parties although in all court hearings the protection of children and young people as vulnerable witnesses will be paramount upon the courts' priorities.

Juveniles tried in the Crown Court. It is not inhuman or degrading treatment 8–03 in breach of Article 3 to put a child on trial in an adult court, or for that court to have a degree of publicity but in the case of juveniles, the right to a fair trial, Article 6, requires a specially adapted procedure which promotes the welfare of the child defendant, adequately respects the child's right to privacy and enables the child to understand and participate fully in the proceedings. In the cases of *T & V v. United Kingdom*,[1] in its ruling on the merits the Commission found a violation of Article 6 but no violation of Article 3. The applicants, T and V were convicted of murder committed when they were aged 10.

The trial took place when the applicants were 11. T and V brought an action in the European Court of Human Rights, arguing that their fundamental rights as enshrined in the European Convention, Article 3, Article 5 and Article 6, had been breached by the way that the trial had been conducted and by their general treatment.

In argument before the Commission, it was asserted that the applicants may have had the intellectual capacity to understand various elements of the trial process but that in the case of V he lacked the emotional strength to follow the trial or to take decisions in his own best interests. As with more recent cases,[2] the applicants did not give evidence.

---

[1] (2000) 30 E.H.R.R. 121.
[2] Damilola Taylor.

The European Court agreed that Article 6 had been breached by the way that the trial had been conducted. Although the Crown Court in which the case had been heard had been modified to take into account the age of the applicants, the degree of formality and ritual was held to have been oppressive to the applicants. The layout of the court had been such that the applicants had been in full view of the media and public. Considering the intense intention the case had attracted, it was impossible to conclude that the applicants could have consorted with their lawyers free of any inhibition.

The Commission stated that:

"Where a child is faced with a criminal charge and the domestic system requires a fact finding procedure, with a view to establishing guilt, it is essential that his age, level of maturity and intellectual and emotional capacities be taken into account in the procedures followed ... the public trial process in an adult court with attendant publicity must be regarded in the case of an 11 year old child as a severely intimidating procedure.

The way in which the trial placed the applicant in a raised dock, as the focus of intense public attention over a period of 3 weeks, must have seriously impinged on his ability to participate in the proceedings in any meaningful manner ... where the alleged offender is a child, the procedures adopted must be conducive to an active participation, as opposed to passive presence. Otherwise, trial risks presenting the appearance of an exercise in the vindication of public outrage".

Nevertheless, despite all this, the court were not of the view that the applicants had been subjected to degrading treatment, contrary to Article 3 by virtue of their age.[3] The selection of 10 for the age of criminal responsibility was not significantly lower than the age of responsibility elsewhere in Europe.[4]

8–04   **Public trials.** In *T & V v. United Kingdom*,[5] the European Court considered the public trials of juveniles and were of the view that a public trial could cause suffering which surpassed the minimum threshold but emphasised that in the absence of any intention to humiliate it did not consider that the effect of the proceedings in the cases of *T & V* would have gone beyond that which would have inevitably been engendered by any attempt to deal with the applicants in the criminal arena following the commission of the offences concerned.[6] The fact that the effect of the proceedings inevitably engenders humiliation is a significant obstacle to a successful application under Article 3 against a procedure which in all other aspects is legitimate.

8–05   **Good practice.** As a result of the court's findings in *T & V v. United Kingdom*,[7] the domestic courts have rationalised how juveniles are to be treated.[8]

---

[3] See para. 8–06 as to the court's observations on sentencing juveniles.

[4] Although England and Wales are unusual in having a low age of responsibility, there was not a sufficiently clear standard amongst the European States or indeed relevant international standards for the court to conclude that the age of 10 was in itself objectionable. The court were clearly taking the stance that it would not treat something as unacceptable where it reflects a significant majority view. See the position of the Isle of Man in respect to birching: *Tyrer v. United Kingdom* (1979–80) 2 E.H.R.R. 1.

[5] (2000) 30 E.H.R.R. 121.

[6] See also *Abdulazi, Cabales and Balkandali v. United Kingdom* (1985) 7 E.H.R.R. 741: the courts also recognised the difficulty of separating the distress caused by the trial and that resulting from guilt.

[7] (2000) 30 E.H.R.R. 121.

[8] See Practice Direction 2000 CAR 483.

Interestingly, the Youth Justice and Criminal Evidence Act 1999 seeks to establish special measures to assist vulnerable witnesses to give evidence. Whilst these provisions only seem to relate to witnesses rather than defendants, they do provide a useful yardstick as to what may be considered by the European Court to be good practice. It is certainly difficult to understand why these quite proper provisions made available to witnesses should not also be applied to juvenile defendants who themselves may be witnesses in their own trial.

Although the existing law makes provision for a variety of special measures, some at common law (for instance, screens) and some by statute (live link; video recording of evidence-in-chief), the 1999 Act consolidates and adds to this panoply. The special measure can be employed to assist witnesses "other than the accused"[9] who are "eligible".

The eligibility requirements are:

1. that they are under 17[10];

2. that they have a mental disorder or otherwise have a significant impairment of intelligence and social functioning which the court considers likely to affect the quality of their evidence[11];

3. that they have a physical disorder or disability which the court considers likely to affect the quality of their evidence[12]; or

4. that the court is satisfied that the quality of their evidence is likely to be diminished by reason of fear or distress on their part connected with testifying in the proceedings.[13]

Section 17 reads:

"Section 17(1):   For the purposes of this chapter, a witness in criminal proceedings (other than the accused) is eligible for assistance by virtue of this sub-section if the court is satisfied that the quality of evidence given by the witness is likely to be diminished by reason of fear or distress on the part of the witness in connection with testifying in the proceedings.

Section 17(2)   In determining whether a witness falls with sub-section (1) the court must take into account, in particular—

(a) the nature and alleged circumstances of the offence to which the proceedings relate;
(b) the age of the witness;
(c) such of the following matters as appear to the court to be relevant, namely—

(i) the social and cultural background and ethnic origins of the witness,
(ii) the domestic and employment circumstances of the witness, and
(iii) any religious beliefs of political opinions of the witness

---

[9] See Section 17.
[10] See Section 16(1)(a).
[11] See Section 16(2)(a).
[12] See Section 16(2)(b).
[13] See Section 17.

(d) any behaviour towards the witness on the part of—

    (i) the accused,

    (ii) members of the family or associates of the accused; or

    (iii) any other person who is likely to be an accused or a witness in the proceedings".

The special measures provided for by the 1999 Act to witnesses, but not the accused, are:

1. screens[14];

2. live link[15];

3. clearing the court[16];

4. removal of wigs and gowns[17];

5. video recorded evidence-in-chief[18];

6. video recorded cross-examination (where evidence-in-chief is so recorded)[19];

7. examination through intermediary[20];

8. affording witnesses aids to communication[21]

A child witness who is not in need of special protection nevertheless has to be dealt with on the assumption that their evidence will benefit from certain special measures. For instance, if a video recording has been made with a view to its admission as evidence-in-chief, the normal rule would be that the recording will be admitted, and any evidence given by the witness which is not so recorded will be by live link.

It is arguable that there is no valid reason why some or all of these provisions should not be made available to the defendant, the absence of which could well assist in an argument to substantiate violation of Article 3. Section 19(6) of the 1999 Act may be of some assistance here:

"Section 19(6):   Nothing in this chapter is to be regarded as affecting any power of a court to make an order or give leave of any description (in the exercise of its inherent jurisdiction or otherwise)—

    (a) in relation to a witness who is not an eligible witness . . ".

There seems absolutely no good reason why these provisions should not therefore apply to the juvenile defendant, the absence of which could undermine any subsequent hearing.

---

[14] See s.23.
[15] See s.24.
[16] See s.25, in sexual cases and cases involving possible intimidation.
[17] See s.26.
[18] See s.27.
[19] See s.28.
[20] See s.29 relating to young or incapacitated witnesses only.
[21] See s.30 relating to young or incapacitated witnesses.

2. Sentencing

Detention of minors is being recognised as a major source of concern. **8–06**
Such concern arising whether as a result of abuse of children by adults entrusted
with their care or on account of inappropriate use of incarceration in the face of
lack of alternatives to custody.[22] In its 9th Report, the Committee for the
Prevention of Torture and Inhuman and Degrading Treatment or Punishment
turned its attention to the detention of juveniles (considered for their purposes as
persons under the age of 18).[23]

In its 1999 Report, the Committee welcomed this approach and emphasised
that juveniles in detention lacked effective voices on account of immaturity and
likely dysfunctional family background: they are, the Report stated: "inherently
more vulnerable than adults" and thus "particular vigilance is required to ensure
that their physical and mental well-being is adequately protected".[24] A cardinal
principle is that "juveniles should only be deprived of their liberty as a last resort
and for the shortest possible period of time".[25]

The Committee have stressed that effective safeguards for minors replicate
many of the principles applicable to adult detainees, but the immaturity and
vulnerability of young people may require additional measure to be put in place.
The Committee have further found that deliberate ill-treatment of juveniles in
places of detention detainees is "comparatively rare",[26] although it has uncov-
ered acceptance of a practice of the "occasional 'Pedagogic slap' to juveniles
who misbehaved", a practice which the Committee considered "entirely unacceptable". It stated that it wished to see all forms of physical chastisement both
formerly prohibited and avoided in practice with misbehaviour addressed only in
accordance with prescribed disciplinary procedures since absolute prohibition is
the only practical way of preventing ill-treatment.[27]

By extension, the Committee were further of the view that the carrying of
batons by custodial staff who have direct contact with juveniles "fails to foster
positive relations: if staff consider it indispensable to carry such, batons should
be hidden from view".[28] The Committee recommend that in terms of detention
policies, juveniles should be accommodated separately from adults.[29]

It is further recommended that appropriate "custodial ethos" and "fostering a
degree of normality in a place of detention" are enhanced by the presence of both
male and female staff as well as implementing the principle that detainees,
regardless of age, should only be searched by staff of the same gender (with any

---

[22] See the European Convention for the Prevention of Torture or Inhuman or Degrading Treatment or
Punishment: Activities in 1999, Report of Jim Murdoch (2000) 25 E.L.Rev. Human Rights Survey.
[23] See *R. v. Stratford Youth Court ex p. S.* [1998] 1 W.L.R. 1758.
[24] See 9th General Report at para. 20, see above.
[25] See Convention on the Rights of the Child, Article 37(b) and Rules 13 and 19 of the Beijing Rules,
otherwise known as the UN Standard Minimum Rules for the Administration of Juvenile Justice
which was adopted in 1985.
[26] See 1999 Report above.
[27] See 9th General Report above, para. 24.
[28] See 9th General Report above, para. 27.
[29] The Committee does however accept "there may be exceptional situations (eg. parents and children
being held as immigration detainees) in which it is plainly in the best interests of juveniles not to be
separated from particular adults": see 9th General Report above, para. 25, and Chapter 5:
Immigration.

search involving undressing being conducted out of the sight of custodial staff of the opposite gender).[30]

Other principles enunciated replicate standards applying to places of detention in general but also include supplementary expectations on account of the perceived vulnerability of young people. It is suggested that juveniles should be held in detention centres specifically designed for persons of their age and which can offer a multi-disciplinary regime offered by a range of professionals (including teachers and psychologists) and tailored to meeting the individual needs of juveniles "within a secure educative and socio-therapeutic environment" employing "special efforts to reduce the risks of long terms social maladjustment".[31]

Staff should be carefully selected on the basis of personal maturity and ability to work with, guiding and motivating, and safeguard the welfare of young people. Specific training, appropriate support and supervision, the Report suggests, is crucial. The management of juvenile detention centres requires "advanced leadership skills" and the ability to respond to the competing demands of detainees and staff.[32]

The 1999 Report goes on to suggest that material conditions should provide "positive and personalised conditions of detention" of an adequate size, well-lit and ventilated, properly furnished, well-decorated and offering "appropriate visual stimulae". In the absence of compelling considerations of security, detainees should be permitted to retain personal items. For female detainees, failure to prepare sanitary and washing facilities and hygiene items (such as sanitary towels) can amount to degrading treatment, the Report suggests.[33]

Regime activities should involve "a full programme of education, sport, vocational training, recreation and other purposeful activities" including in particular physical education with female detainees enjoying equal access to such rather than being provided with stereotypical activities such as sewing or handicrafts.

Rule 26.4 of the Beijing Rules is cited by the Report which provides that female juveniles deprived of their liberty "by no means receive less care, protection, assistance, treatment and training than young male offenders".

Where a regime operates a scheme allowing additional privileges "in exchange for displaying approved behaviour", the Committee suggest that careful consideration should be given to "the content of the base-level regime being offered to juveniles subject to such schemes, and to whether the manner in which they may progress, and regress within a given scheme includes adequate safeguards against arbitrary decision making by staff".[34]

8–07   **Solitary confinement.** Any resort to the placement of a juvenile in conditions resembling solitary confinement can only be justified if for the shortest possible period of time and accompanied by appropriate human contact, access to reading material, and at least one hour of outdoor exercise every day, according to the 1999 Report. These expectations applying to any place of detention but is supplemented by standards reflecting the vulnerability and immaturity of juvenile

---

[30] See 9th General Report above, paras 25–26.
[31] See 9th General Report above, para. 28.
[32] See 9th General Report above, para. 33.
[33] See 9th General Report above, paras 29–30.
[34] See 9th General Report above, paras 31–32.

detainees. Contact with the outside world should never be restricted or denied as a disciplinary measure.

Disciplinary and complaint procedures. As with the imposition of any **8–08** disciplinary measure, formal safeguards which include the right to be heard and to appeal to a higher authority should be made available to the juvenile or young person. Furthermore, proper recording of any sanction imposed is considered to be central to the prevention of ill-treatment.

Similarly, the European Committee for the Prevention of Torture and Inhuman or Degrading Treatment or Punishment[35] were of the view that an effective complaints and inspection procedure, including the right of lodging a complaint both within and outside the detention centres' administrative system, coupled with confidential access to an appropriate authority were vital.[36] The Committee placed particular importance to the existence of a scheme of regular visits to all juvenile establishments to inspect accommodation and facilities by an independent body such as a visiting committee or a judge which can receive and take action on complaints.[37]

Medical care. Of course, the standard expectations apply,[38] including a proper **8–09** interview and physical examination by a medical doctor (or by a fully qualified nurse reporting to a doctor), as soon as possible after admission and on the day of admission with a view to identifying any potential health problems such as drug addiction or suicidal tendencies to enable appropriate preventative action.[39]

This is particularly important when juveniles or young people have already been categorised as vulnerable and with the increasing number of young people attempting, and at times succeeding, in taking their own lives a particular duty is imposed upon those in authority at detention centres to ensure their safety. The Committee also suggest that other guarantees such as confidential access to a

---

[35] The standards laid down by the European Committee for the Prevention of Torture can influence the interpretation of Article 3 in the European Court. Applicants have used the reports to challenge State practices under Article 3 and in particular to assist them to establish whether factual circumstances constitute torture, inhuman or degrading treatment. In *Salman v. Turkey* (2000) 34 E.H.R.R. 17 at para. 113, it was observed "the bruising and swelling on the left foot combined with the grazes on the left ankle were consistent with the application of falaka, which [the CPT] reported was one of the forms of ill-treatment in common use, *inter alia*, in [the particular detention centre]". See also *Dougoz v. Greece* (2002) 34 E.H.R.R. 61 at paras 46–49 where the use of a CPT report to corroborate an applicant's allegations of degrading treatment on account of serious overcrowding and appalling sanitary conditions was used to establish a violation. In *S. M and T v. Austria* (1993) 74, 179, the CPT's views that immigration detainees were being held in acceptable conditions was cited by the Commission in determining that there had been no Article 3 violation. In the case of *Aerts v. Belgium* (2000) 29 E.H.R.R. 50, the Commission acknowledged that the Committee's criticisms of a mental health establishment helped give weight to its conclusion that the conditions in which the applicant had been held had constituted degrading treatment, contrary to Article 3, but the court on the other hand concluded that there was insufficient evidence that the applicant's mental health had deteriorated, nor was it satisfied that the conditions of detention had any serious effects on the applicant's mental health so as to bring them within the scope of Article 3. In that case the issue was one of proof, but importantly, the court had shown itself willing to rely upon the Committee's report both in establishing the factual basis of holding conditions and also the seriousness of their shortcomings in assessing whether there had been a violation of Article 3 (1998-V, 1939, paras 61–67).
[36] See the 1999 Report above.
[37] See 9th General Report above, paras 34–36.
[38] See Chapter 4: Prisoners.
[39] See 1999 Report at p. 225.

doctor at any time and appropriate access to a range of specialist medical care is also an important provision. If there is to be any difference or nuance in contrast with the general expectations it will be one of emphasis rather than of substance.

For instance, particular importance will be attached to the role of health care services in constituting an integrated system of care which will involve the co-ordination between doctors, nurses, psychologists and other health carers to work in tandem with other relevant professionals such as social workers and teachers. The Committee identified that juveniles had two particular needs, that of nutrition and the provision of health education. They observed that monitoring the quality of food is particularly important for juveniles since the consequences of inadequate nutrition may become evident more rapidly and be more serious than for prisoners who have reached full physical maturity. The Committee went on to stress that of equal importance is the need to respond to the tendency of juvenile detainees to engage in risk taking behaviour such as drugs and alcohol abuse and sexual activities and thus necessitating the provision of relevant health education, including the provision of information about the risks of drug abuse and about transmittable diseases.[40]

The Committee of Ministers of the Council of Europe observed in 1987[41] that "The penal system of minors should continue to be characterised by its objective of education and social integration".

It is apparent from the guidance being given by the Committee and from established case law that it will be an accumulation of abuses in this area which will increase the likelihood of a finding under Article 3. The observations of the Committee should not be taken lightly. They give an important indication as to what matters the European Court will take into account when considering violations in respect to juveniles and young people. Various other international conventions enforce the attitude that will be taken to juveniles and young persons in detention. For instance, the International Covenant on Civil and Political Rights 1996, Article 10, states:

"Article 10(1):	All persons deprived of their liberty shall be treated with humanity and with respect for the inherent dignity of the human person.[42]
Article 10(2):	(b) Accused juvenile persons shall be separated from adults and brought as speedily as possible for adjudication.
Article 10(3):	The penitentiary system shall comprise a treatment of prisoners, the essential aim of which shall be their reformation and social rehabilitation. Juvenile offenders shall be segregated from adults and be accorded treatment appropriate to their age and legal status"

The United Nations Convention on the Rights of the Child 1989, Article 37 gave further guidance to how this vulnerable category of persons shall be treated:

---

[40] See 9th General Report above, paras 37–41.
[41] See Recommendation No. R(87)20—"Social Reactions to Juvenile Delinquency" adopted at the 410th meeting of Ministers Deputies on September 17, 1987.
[42] The United Nations Human Rights Committee found a violation of Article 10 in Communication No. 410/1990, *Parkanyi v. Hungary* (1992) 13 H.R.L.J. 345.

"Article 37(c)   Every child deprived of liberty shall be treated with humanity and respect for the inherent dignity of the human person, and in a manner which takes into account the needs of persons of his or her age. In particular, every child deprived of liberty shall be separated from adults unless it is considered in the child's best interest not to do so and shall have the right to maintain contact with his or her family through correspondence and visits, save in exceptional circumstances".

3. LEGAL PROCEEDINGS

The codification of children's rights. In 1989 the United Nations Convention   **8–10** on the Rights of the Child codified certain guarantees which parties to the Convention must put in place. These included:

"Article 40(2)(b)(i)   To be presumed innocent until proven guilty according to the law;

Article 40(2)(b)(ii)   To be informed promptly and directly of the charges against him or her and, if appropriate, through his or her parents or legal guardians, and to have legal or other appropriate assistance in the preparation and presentation of his or her defence;

Article 40(2)(b)(iii)   To have the matter determined without delay by a competent, independent and impartial authority or judicial body in a fair hearing according to law, in the presence of legal or other appropriate assistance and, unless it is considered not to be in the best interest of the child, in particular, taking into account his or her age or situation, his or her parents or legal guardians;

Article 40(2)(b)(iv)   Not to be compelled to give testimony or to confess guilt; to examine or have examined adverse witnesses and to obtain the participation and examination of witnesses on his or her behalf under conditions of equality;

Article 40(2)(b)(v)   If considered to have infringed the penal law, to have this decision and any measures imposed in consequence thereof reviewed by a higher, competent, independent and impartial authority or judicial body according to law;

Article 40(2)(b)(vi)   To have the free assistance of an interpreter if the child cannot understand or speak the language used;

Article 40(2)(b)(vii)   To have his or her privacy fully respected at all stages of the proceedings;

Article 40(3)   States Parties shall seek to promote the establishment of laws, procedures, authorities and institutions specifically applicable to children alleged as, accused of, or recognised as having infringed the penal law, and, in particular:

(a) the establishment of a minimum age below which children shall be presumed not to have the capacity not to infringe the penal law;

(b) whenever appropriate and desirable, measures for dealing with such children without resorting to judicial proceedings, providing that human rights and legal safeguards are fully respected".

It is clear that the European jurisprudence establishes that children accused of criminal offences should be treated differently from adults.

The UN guidelines for the Prevention of Juvenile Delinquency, also known as the "Riyadh Guidelines" were adopted in 1990. This document recognised that:

> "The prevention of juvenile delinquency is an essential part of crime prevention in society".[43]

The guidelines emphasised that any country's policy in dealing with juvenile delinquency should think twice before introducing these individuals into the criminal justice system. They stated that the authorities should "avoid criminalising and penalising a child for behaviour that does not cause serious damage to the development of the child or harm to others".[44]

The United Nations Standard Minimum Rules for the Administration of Juvenile Justice, otherwise known as the "Beijing Rules" which came into force in 1985 also emphasised that the criminalisation of juveniles should only be taken in certain circumstances which will relate to the offender and to the offence.

At Rule 5.1 the Beijing Rules stipulated that "any reaction to juvenile offenders shall always be in proportion to the circumstances of both the offenders and to the offence" and that discretion should be exercised at all stages of proceedings and at different levels of juvenile justice administration "including investigation, prosecution, adjudication and the follow-up of disposals".[45]

4. JUVENILES TRIED IN THE CROWN COURT

8–11   **The age of the juvenile.** The Children and Young Persons Act 1933, Section 50 sets the age of criminal responsibility at 10 years of age.[46] Although the United Nations Standard Minimum Rules for the Administration of Juvenile Justice (the Beijing Rules)[47] laid down at Rule 4.1 that the beginning of the age of criminal responsibility should not be fixed at too low an age level, bearing in mind the facts of emotional, mental and intellectual maturity. The modern approach is to consider whether a child can live up to the moral and psychological components of criminal responsibility, that is whether a child, by virtue of their individual discernment and understanding, can be held responsible for essentially antisocial behaviour. In *T. v. United Kingdom* and *V. v. United Kingdom*,[48] the European Court of Human Rights held that the trial of child applicants aged 11 did not, in itself, violate Article 3. In assessing the United Kingdom's age for criminal responsibility, the court observed that the selection of 10 was not significantly lower than the age of responsibility elsewhere in Europe.[49]

---

[43] See para. 1.1.
[44] See also UN Rules for the Protection of Juveniles Deprive of their Liberty A/RES/45/113 which laid down that "the juvenile justice system should up hold the rights and safety and promote the physical and mental well-being of juveniles" at Rule 1.
[45] See Rule 6.1.
[46] as amended by the Children and Young Persons Act 1963, Section 16(1).
[47] GA Resn 40/33, Annexe GAOR, 40th Sessions, Supp. 53, p. 207, UN Doc A/40/53 (1985).
[48] (2000) 30 E.H.R.R. 121.
[49] See para. 74 above.

Reporting restrictions. The powers conferred by the Children and Young   **8–12**
Persons Act 1933, s.49(4A) as inserted by the Crime (Sentences) Act 1997, to
dispense with reporting restrictions in criminal proceedings concerning a juvenile
is to be exercised with great care, caution and circumspection.[50]

Statutory provisions relating to the welfare of juveniles involved in legal
proceedings and to the imposition of and dispensing with reporting restrictions in
such cases are to be read against the background of international law and practice
which emphasises the need to protect the welfare and privacy of juveniles
involved in such cases.[51]

Terms of a Section 39 Order should be clear. A judge should make it clear   **8–13**
what the terms of an order restricting reporting applied under the Children and
Young Persons Act 1933 s.39(1) are. A bare order is considered too vague to
constitute a sufficient basis for a subsequent prosecution for breach as a result of
publication. In *Briffett v. Director of Public Prosecutions*,[52] the court ordered that
"under section 39 of the Children and Young Persons Act 1933, reporting
restrictions apply in respect of the applicant herein . . . ". This was considered too
vague and too general to constitute a sufficient basis for prosecution under
s.39(2).[53]

Punitive sentences. Imposing a sentence with a punitive element upon a child   **8–14**
does not amount to inhuman or degrading treatment. Nevertheless, in *T. v. United
Kingdom* and *V. v. United Kingdom*,[54] the court held that Article 6, the right to a
fair trial before an impartial tribunal, was breached when the Home Secretary, as
part of the executive, had fixed the tariff.[55]

Imprisonment. Although there will be no breach of Article 3 if a child is   **8–15**
imprisoned,[56] it is suggested that imprisonment should only be used as a last
resort.

The United Nations Rules for the Protection of Juveniles Deprived of their
Liberty[57] asserts that juveniles should only be deprived of their liberty in
accordance with the principles and procedures set out in their Rules and in the
United Nations Standard Minimum Rules for the Administration of Juvenile
Justice (the Beijing Rules).

Rule 2 of the Rules for the Protection of Juveniles Deprived of their Liberty
reads:

"Rule 2: Deprivation of the liberty of a juvenile should be a disposition of last resort
and for the minimum necessary period and should be limited to exceptional
cases. The length of the sanction should be determined by the judicial
authority, without precluding the possibility of his or her early release.

---

[50] See *McKerry v. Teesdale and Wear Valley Justices* [2001] E.M.L.R. 5.
[51] See *T. v. United Kingdom* and *V. v. United Kingdom* (2000) E.H.R.R. 121.
[52] [2001] EWHC Admin 841.
[53] See also *R. v. Central Criminal Court ex p. Crook* [1995] 1 W.L.R. 139 at 146.
[54] (2000) 30 E.H.R.R. 121.
[55] See *Stafford v. United Kingdom* (2002) 152 N.L.J. 880.
[56] See also *Papon v. France* (2001) Crim.L.R. 917 and *Sawoniuk v. United Kingdom* (2001)
Crim.L.R. 918 which deals with the admissibility of cases challenging imprisonment of elderly
persons and whether Article 3 is applicable.
[57] GA Resn 45/113, Annexe, GAOR, 45th Session, Supp 49A, p. 205, UN Doc A/45/49 (1990).

Rule 3:   The rules are intended to establish minimum standards accepted by the United Nations for the protection of juveniles deprived of their liberty in all forms, consistent with human rights and fundamental freedoms, and with a view to counteracting the detrimental effects of all types of detention and to fostering integration in society.

Rule 4:   The rules should be applied impartially, without discrimination of any kind as to race, colour, sex, age, language, religion, nationality, political or other opinion, cultural beliefs or practices, property, birth or family status, ethnic or social origin, and disability. The religious and cultural beliefs, practices and moral concepts of the juvenile should be respected.

Rule 7:   Where appropriate, States should incorporate the Rules into their legislation or amend it accordingly and provide effective remedies for their breach, including compensation when injuries are inflicted on juveniles. States should also monitor the application of the Rules".[58]

Life imprisonment without the possibility of release will probably breach Article 3. Guidance can be obtained from the United Nations Convention on the Rights of the Child 1989, Article 37 which directs that States Parties ensure that:

"(a) No child shall be subjected to torture or other cruel, inhuman or degrading treatment or punishment. Neither capital punishment nor life imprisonment without possibility of release shall be imposed for offences committed by persons below 18 years of age;

(b) No child shall be deprived of his or her liberty unlawfully or arbitrarily. The arrest, detention or imprisonment of a child shall be in conformity with the law and shall be used only as a measure of last resort and for the shortest appropriate period of time;".

In *Weekes v. United Kingdom*,[59] the court held that to sentence a 17 year old to life imprisonment as punishment for an offence of robbery would potentially violate Article 3.

8–16   **The Crime and Disorder Act 1998, Section 98.** This section relates to the custody of 15 to 16 year old boys and girls on remand. Although the matter fell within the scope of Articles 8 and 14, the general principles expressed by Lord Justice Brooke are instructive as to the contrasting treatment of young males and females in custody, when he states that there were "too few juvenile female remandees to allow a network of female specialist juvenile youth offender institutes to be developed", thus finding against a breach of Article 8. Clearly, any discrimination which does arise under section 98 will equally fail to activate Article 3.

8–17   **Non-custodial disposals.** International jurisprudence advocates various disposals. The United Nations Convention on the Rights of the Child 1989[60] at Article 40 Rule 4 lists suggestions:

---

[58] For the purposes of these Rules, a juvenile is every person under the age of 18. (See Rule 11).

[59] (1988) 10 E.H.R.R. 293 at para. 47.

[60] The Convention has been a vital tool in protecting the rights of children and youngsters under the age of 18 in the War Crimes Tribunals of Rwanda and elsewhere who have been accused of genocide and murder. The Convention clauses that protect children in conflict with the law have been cited by UNICEF and the International Committee of the Red Cross to protect child prisoners held in overcrowded adult prisons. See UNICEF, The Progress of Nations (1996).

"such as care, guidance and supervision orders; counselling; probation; foster care; education and vocational training programmes and other alternatives to institutional care shall be available to ensure that children are dealt with in a manner appropriate to their well-being and proportionate both to their circumstances and the offence".

A similar attitude was taken by the United Nations Standard Minimum Rules for the Administration of Juvenile Justice at Rule 18.1 which emphasised the importance of avoiding institutionalisation and added suggestions such as community service orders, financial penalties, compensation and restitution, intermediate treatment and other treatment orders, orders to participate on group counselling and similar activities, orders concerning living communities and a catch-all provision, "other relevant orders". Again, the Rules emphasised that institutionalisation of juveniles should be last resort and for the shortest necessary period.[61]

5. CORPORAL PUNISHMENT

Bullet points. The following propositions can be established with reference to **8–18** key cases—see *R. v. H (Assault of Child: Reasonable Chastisement)* [2001] EWCA Crim 1024; *Costello-Roberts v. United Kingdom* (1993) 19 E.H.R.R. 112; *Tyrer v. United Kingdom* (1979) 2 E.H.R.R. 1; *Campbell and Cousans v. United Kingdom* (1982) 4 E.H.R.R. 293:

- Must attain required level of severity;

- An assessment of severity depends upon nature and context of ill-treatment;

- Its duration;

- Its physical and mental effects upon the victim;

- The victim's age;

- The victim's sex;

- The victim's state of health;

- The reasons for administering chastisement;

- The State is responsible for punishment inflicted by schools and in that context an extra criteria to consider on severity is whether the infliction of punishment was in public or private and therefore degrading;

- The State is responsible for the acts of private individuals (parents);

- The threat of corporal punishment can be sufficient to violate Article 3;

- The object of the balancing exercise in the context of a criminal trial is to balance the rights of the victim under Article 3 and the defendant's right to a fair trial under Article 6 and their rights under Article 7 not to be punished for an act which does not constitute a criminal offence.

---

[61] See Rule 19.1.

8–19 **Generally.** Although this chapter deals with the corporal punishment of children and juveniles, the basic principles apply to the application of corporal punishment[62] to any human being, although such sentences are now very rare if not completely obsolete.[62a]

The post-war drafting committees applying themselves to human rights declarations had struggled with issues relating to corporal punishment. The United Kingdom had particular problems which should be understood as they go some way to explaining the reticence to completely stop the practice of beating children as a form of parental or scholastic punishment. In 1946 as countries were beginning to actively embrace the codification of human rights, the British Navy were still flogging their servicemen with the cat-of-nine-tails and birching was a possible judicial punishment in Britain. Professor A.W. Brian Simpson observes: "As for British schools, both public and private, they were veritable temples of flagellation".[63] In the British Colonies corporal punishment was common although citizens of the colonies were spared the cat-of-nine-tails and received lashes from a cane instead.[64] A recognition of these attitudes is essential when we consider subsequent domestic responses to whether corporal punishment, particularly relating to children and juveniles, is acceptable and the European approach in harmonising the attitude towards beating.

The International Covenant on Civil and Political Rights 1966 stated the position on corporal punishment very clearly. In Article 7 it stated:

"No one shall be subjected to torture or cruel, inhuman or degrading treatment . . .

5. The prohibition in Article 7 relates not only to acts that cause physical pain but also to acts that cause mental suffering to the victim. In the Committee's view, moreover, the prohibition must extend to corporal punishment, including excessive chastisement ordered as punishment for a crime or as an educative or disciplinary measure. It is appropriate to emphasise in this regard that Article 7 protects, in particular, children, pupils and patients in teaching, and medical institutions".

8–20 **The old law.** The long-standing common law position relating to corporal punishment which applied prior to the coming into force of the Human Rights Act 1998 was expressed by Cockburn C.J. in *R. v. Hopley*[65]:

"By the law of England, a parent or a schoolmaster (who for this purpose represents the parent and has the parental authority delegated to him), may for the purpose of correcting what is evil in the child inflict moderate and reasonable corporal punishment, always, however, with this condition, that it is moderate and reasonable.

If it be administered for the gratification of passion or of rage, or if it be immoderate and excessive in its nature or degree, or if it be protracted beyond the child's powers of endurance, or with an instrument unfitted for the purpose and calculated to produce

---

[62] Corporal punishment in prisons was abolished by the Criminal Justice Act 1967, s.65.

[62a] But see *Pinder v. The Queen, The Times,* October 4, 2002 (PC) which held that a sentence of flogging from a Court in the Bahamas was an inhuman and degrading punishment, although not infringing the Constitution of the Bahamas (*per* Lord Millett: Lord Nicholls and Lord Hope dissenting).

[63] *Human Rights and the End of Empire*; published by Oxford University Press (2001).

[64] In the British Annual Corporal Punishment Returns (1950–1958) CO859/1344 we note that in Hong Kong in 1954 corporal punishment had been used on 141 adults and 54 young offenders. In Kenya it could be used for no fewer for 21 different offences. In the Bahamas, lazy prisoners could be punished by the application of beating.

[65] (1860) 2 F and F 202 at 206.

danger to life or limb, in all such cases the punishment is excessive, the violence is unlawful, and if evil consequences to life or limb ensue, then the person inflicting it is answerable to the law, and if death ensues it will be manslaughter".

In that case the jury returned a verdict of guilty in relation to the defendant who had caused the death of a 14 year old boy, by inflicting punishment, with a thick stick, for some $2\frac{1}{2}$ hours.

Reassuringly, attitudes have now changed and the treatment of corporal punishment under the Convention is one of the best examples of how European jurisprudence has adapted and evolved within the society which it purports to serve. The European Court of Human Rights endorses this as a principal merit of Article 3 and Article 8 applications and so litigation under these Articles should and must constantly push at the boundaries.

Consultation Papers were published both in England and in Scotland, seeking views as to the way in which the law should be amended. In the English Consultation Paper, at its introduction,[66] it states:

"The law recognises that there may be occasions when moderate and reasonable physical punishment of a child by a parent, may be appropriate".

It later goes on to state[67]:

"The Government fully accepts the need for change. The harmful and degrading treatment of children can never be justified. We have made it quite clear, however, that we do not consider that the right way forward is to make unlawful all smacking and other forms of physical rebuke and this Paper explicitly rules out this possibility".

This assertion reflects the jurisprudence in Europe.

A balancing exercise. Whether the application of corporal punishment **8–21** amounts to a violation of Article 3 will depend upon various criteria which will include considerations of severity and reasonableness.

Reasonable chastisement. Reasonable chastisement of children by parents or **8–22** others *in loco parentis* is lawful at common law.[68] It has always been a good defence in the law of the United Kingdom that the alleged battery was merely the correcting of a child by its parents or those *in locus parentis*, provided that the correction was moderate in the way it was applied, what instrument was used and the quantity of stokes.[69]

This Victorian approach has now been modified and clarified although the defence is still available to a parent accused of assaulting his child so as to occasion actual bodily harm as was confirmed in *R. v. H (Assault of Child: Reasonable Chastisement)*[70] although the courts have accepted that more detailed directions should be given to a jury as to the factors relevant to the reasonableness of the chastisement.[71] In considering how the courts approach what is

---

[66] At para. 1.3.
[67] At para. 1.5.
[68] See *Halliwell v. Counsell* (1878) 38 L.T. 126; *Cleary v. Booth* [1893] 1 Q.B. 465; *R. v. H (Assault of Child: Reasonable Chastisement)* [2001] EWCA Crim 1024; and [2002] 1 Cr.App.R. 7. See also the Children and Young Persons Act 1933, s.1(7).
[69] *R. v. Hopley* (1860) 2 F.F. 202.
[70] [2001] EWCA Crim 1024.
[71] *A v. United Kingdom* (1998) 27 E.H.R.R. 611.

reasonable chastisement an appreciation of the facts of some of the cases is of assistance. In *A v. United Kingdom*,[72] the child was aged 9 and referred to a paediatrician whose examination revealed a number of bruises which indicated that the child had been beaten with a garden cane, used on more than one occasion with considerable force. The child's stepfather was subsequently charged with assault occasioning actual bodily harm and the case proceeded to trial at which the stepfather raised the defence available under English law that the child's beating represented reasonable chastisement.

Although the stepfather was acquitted by a majority verdict, the child applied to the European Court contending that his treatment constituted a violation of Article 3. The European Court of Justice unanimously held that it did fall within the scope of Article 3 and that the ill-treatment had attained that level of severity which indicated a violation.

Certain important factors assisted the court to come to this conclusion; they considered the nature and context of the ill-treatment, its duration, its physical and mental effects, and, in some cases, the victim's age, sex and state of health. The court were also of the view that the reasons given by a defendant for his conduct is also a factor to be taken into consideration.[73]

In *R. v. H*,[74] it was alleged that a father had assaulted his son, causing him actual bodily harm. The father's defence was that the use of a leather belt for disobedience was punishment he was entitled to use in exercise of his rights as a parent. This was considered by the Court of Appeal as a case worthy of the reasonable chastisement directions. Notwithstanding that an alleged offence may have occurred before the implementation of the Human Rights Act 1998, it is appropriate for a judge to direct the jury in accordance with the current state of the common law as it has been developed in the light of decisions of the European Court of Human Rights.

The object of these directions to the jury is to achieve a balance between maintaining the rights of the child under Article 3, the parents' rights to a fair trial under Article 6 and the parents' rights under Article 7 not to be punished for an act which does not constitute a criminal offence.

8-23   **Schools.** The relationship of teacher and pupil formerly carried with it the right of reasonable chastisement.[75]

The Education Act 1996 Section 548 abolished corporal punishment for the majority of pupils, including, but not limited to, pupils at (a) schools maintained by a local education authority, (b) special schools not so maintained, (c) grant maintained schools, and (d) independent schools maintained or assisted by a Minister of the Crown (including a school of which a government department is the proprietor) or assisted by a local education authority and falling within a prescribed class.[76]

---

[72] (1998) 27 E.H.R.R. 611.

[73] In *R. v. Derrivier* 53 Cr.App.R. 637 CA it was argued that immigrant parents must conform to English standards in the correction of their children, although some regard may be had initially to their different background as, for example, in the case of a first offender who either did not understand what the standards in this country were or was having difficulty adjusting himself.

[74] [2001] EWCA Crim 1024.

[75] *Cleary v. Booth* [1893] 1 Q.B. 465; *Mansell v. Griffin* [1908] 1 K.B. 160; and *R. v. Newpoart (Salop) JJ ex p. Wright* [1929] 2 K.B. 416 at 427, 428.

[76] See also the Education (Abolition of Corporal Punishment) (Independent Schools) Regulations 1987 (SI 1987 No. 1183) and the Education (Abolition of Corporal Punishment) (Independent Schools) (Prescribed Categories of Persons) Regulations 1989 (SI 1989 No. 1825).

Section 458(2) provides that in respect of a pupil at any school, the giving of corporal punishment by or on the authority of a member of the staff cannot be justified if the punishment was inhuman or degrading. Section 549(3) elaborates on when such punishment is to be regarded as inhuman or degrading.

This statute was in response to the judgement of the European Court in *Costello-Roberts v. United Kingdom*,[77] This in case, the punishment was administered in a private school upon a 7 year old child. In holding that there was no violation of Article 3, the European Court applied itself to where the punishment was administered, the quantity of strokes, the instrument used and the consequence to the victim. On this criteria and on the facts of the case, it was held that there was no violation of Article 3 because the punishment was administered in private, three strokes were administered, the instrument was a rubber-soled slipper on the buttocks through shorts, and that there was no evidence of any severe or long term effect upon the applicant. In short, the minimum level of severity had not been attained, although it did express concern, short of the severity threshold being breached, that the three day delay before administration of the punishment and the automatic nature of the punishment caused the court some concern.

Compare *Tyrer v. United Kingdom*[78] where a 15 year old child was sentenced by a criminal court to 3 strokes of the birch. He received this punishment three weeks after sentence by police officers in a police station, two officers restraining the young person and the third applying the birch to his bare buttocks. The European Court were of the view that this punishment and treatment was degrading (although no so severe as to amount to torture or inhuman punishment).

Perhaps we can distinguish *Tyrer* from *Costello-Roberts* on the basis of the instrument used to apply the beating, a birch rather than a slipper, the blows upon bare buttocks rather than those which are covered, and that in *Costello-Roberts* the punishment was administered in private rather than in a police station involving the attentions of two police officers holding the young person and another applying the strokes. As such, the treatment could have humiliated the applicant in his own eyes and was therefore degrading according to the definitions within Article 3.

European jurisprudence in the field of child-related law has consistently emphasised that though there may be special considerations which apply to children and young people, as a basic principle and starting point, they should always be afforded the same protections as that of an adult. This approach is particularly clear in *Tyrer* where it can be seen that if the victim had been an adult there would have been a clear violation of Article 3, the punishment involving infliction of violence by one human being upon another in an institutionalised situation which would normally in general criminal disciplines constitute an assault.[79]

The use of reasonable force to prevent offences. The Education Act 1996, **8–24** s.548(6), provides that a person does not commit an offence by reason of any conduct relating to a pupil which would, apart from s.548, be justified on the

---

[77] (1993) 19 E.H.R.R. 112.
[78] (1979) 2 E.H.R.R. 1.
[79] See also *Warwick v. U.K.* (1986) 60 D.R. 5 where the Commission found punishment degrading because it was inflicted by a man on a 16 year old girl, it caused physical injury (bruising on the girl's hand which was visible 8 days later) and that psychological injury could not be ruled out.

ground that it is done in pursuance of a right exerciseable by a member of staff by virtue of their position as such.

The Education Act 1996, s.550A, provides that a member of staff of a school may use, in relation to any pupil at the school, such force as is reasonable in the circumstances for the purpose of preventing the pupil committing an offence, causing personal injury to, or damage to the property of, any person or engaging in any behaviour prejudicial to the maintenance of good order and discipline at the school or among its pupils.

8–25   **Threat of corporal punishment.** The threat of corporal punishment which crosses the threshold of what is reasonable and therefore breaches Article 3 may in itself violate that Article[80] although the mere fact that it was a possible sanction does not cause sufficient concern and apprehension in a child as to violate Article 3.[81] Although the system of corporal punishment can cause a certain degree of apprehension in those who may be subjected to it, the court in *Campbell and Cousans*[82] shared the Commission's view that the situation in which the applicants found themselves, that is under threat of corporal punishment, did not amount to torture or inhuman treatment within the meaning of Article 3.[83] Nevertheless, the court considered *Tyrer*[84] and were of the view that the facts of that case did indicate certain criteria concerning the notion of degrading punishment.[85]

A particular measure is not excluded from the category of degrading within the meaning of Article 3 simply because the measure has been in use for a long time but even meets with general approval.[86]

8–26   **State responsibility.** The State cannot absolve its responsibility by delegating punishment decisions to schools or private individuals.[87] As for private individuals, and in practice this will mean parental application of corporal punishment, the State still has a duty to provide adequate protection for children and if the Government fails to do so it will constitute a breach of Article 3.

Article 1 of the Convention read with Article 3 demands that Contracting States adopt measures to ensure the protection of those within their jurisdiction and prevent them from suffering torture or inhuman or degrading treatment or punishment, with children and the vulnerable deserving particular protection in the form of effective deterrents.[88] Furthermore, the State has a positive obligation to protect vulnerable individuals from serious breaches of their personal integrity.[89]

---

[80] The Domestic Court is presently considering an imaginative application on behalf of a mother who refuses to send her child to a school where corporal punishment is practised, not under Article 3 complaints but under Article 9, freedom of thought, conscience and religion in that she cannot send her child to a church school because it practices corporal punishment. A decision is awaited.
[81] See *Campbell and Cousans v. U.K.* (1982) 4 E.H.R.R. 293.
[82] *Campbell and Cousans v. U.K.* (1982) 4 E.H.R.R. 293.
[83] There was no evidence in that case that the juveniles underwent suffering of a level inherent within the notions of torture or inhuman treatment as they have been interpreted and applied in *Ireland v. U.K.* (1978) 2 E.H.R.R. 25 at pp. 66–67 and 68, paras 167 and 174.
[84] (1979–80) 2 E.H.R.R. 1.
[85] See p. 15, para. 30.
[86] See *Campbell and Cousans v. U.K.* (1982) 4 E.H.R.R. 293: see also *Tyrer* (1979–80) 2 E.H.R.R. 1. p. 15, para. 31.
[87] As to schools, see *Costello-Roberts v. U.K.* (1995) 19 E.H.R.R. 112 at paras 26–28.
[88] See *A v. U.K.* (1999) 27 E.H.R.R. 611.
[89] See *X & Y v. Netherlands* (1985) 8 E.H.R.R. 235.

Because of the "reasonable and moderate punishment defence" which was open to the stepfather in the case of *A v. United Kingdom*,[90] the courts are of the view that the State should be held responsible for failing to secure the child's rights under Article 3 by reason of the failure of its domestic legal system to protect children within its jurisdiction from degrading treatment or punishment by parents or those in *loco parentis*.

Furthermore, the Commission in *A v. United Kingdom*,[91] observed that the direct responsibility of the State could not attach for acts of the applicant's stepfather or the jury's acquittal. However, they were of the view that State responsibility could be engaged through the obligation imposed by Article 1 of the Convention.[92]

This Article imposes a positive obligation on the State to "ensure a legal system which provides adequate protection for children's physical and emotional integrity".[93] According to the Commission the effective protection of vulnerable individuals such as children against treatment of the kind referred to under Article 3, required the deterrent effect of the criminal law.

In its opinion, the protection afforded to children was significantly reduced by the defence open to parents (and those in *loco parentis*) that the acts in question were lawful, as involving the reasonable and moderate physical punishment of the child as well as the fact that it was for the prosecution to negative the defence and not on the defendant to substitute the punishment applied. This led to a Commission finding that the domestic law "failed to provide the applicant with adequate and effective protection against corporal punishment which was in the circumstances of the case degrading within the meaning of Article 3 of the Convention and that the applicant was a victim of treatment or punishment contrary to Article 3 of the Convention for which the United Kingdom must be held responsible".

The Commission went on to explain that "this finding does not mean that Article 3 is to be interpreted as imposing an obligation on States to protect, through their criminal law, against any form of physical rebuke, however mild, by a parent of a child".[94]

The European Court and the Commission are at pains to outline the limitations of their findings and leave open the issue as to what is a permissible level of physical rebuke. Cases involving "child smacking" will clearly in the future force the Commission and the courts to further rationalise its approach as to what is a permissible level of physical rebuke.

---

[90] (1999) 27 E.H.R.R. 611.

[91] (1999) 27 E.H.R.R. 611.

[92] The Commission relied on Article 3 of the Convention only in the context of the failure of the legal system to provide practical and effective protection of the guarantees contained within it. This was itself founded upon the Article 1 duty to secure the rights contained within the Convention. The limited context in which State responsibility is engaged, according to the Report, is interesting. The Report laid down that the State was so responsible *not* because to the special vulnerability of the children *per se*, a matter that would clearly have significant implications for other forms of private ill-treatment, for instance domestic violence, but from such vulnerability coupled with the apparently reduced protection granted to children by the legal system (the legal defence of reasonable chastisement open to parents). This is why the Commission Report stated that "The obligation on the State under Article 1 of the Convention cannot be interpreted as requiring the State to guarantee its legal system that inhuman and degrading treatment is never inflicted by one individual on another or that, if it is, the perpetrator will be subject to criminal sanctions" (Commission Report, para. 48).

[93] See *Costello-Roberts* (1995) 19 E.H.R.R. 112. Commission Report para. 37.

[94] See Commission Report para. 55.

In a concurring opinion, Commissioner Loucaides cited increased acceptance of the UN Convention on the Rights of the Child, in particular Article 19 which outlines that all Member States should take appropriate measures to "protect the child from all forms of physical or mental violence, injury or abuse", and added that "It is high time to reconsider the existing approach regarding corporal punishment of children as established by the jurisprudence and to adopt the view that such punishment, regardless of the degree of its severity, is by its very nature inhuman and degrading treatment". Although this does not state the present situation in the law, it does indicate the extent to which this area of authority will continue to develop. The Commission Report also referred to the examination by the UN Committee on the Rights of the Child of the United Kingdom's initial report in 1995 where the "reasonable chastisement" issue was criticised.

8–27   **Parental control.** Parents are given a wide measure of discretion in the upbringing of their children. This was recognised by the European Court in *Nielsen v. Denmark*[95] where it was observed that family life in Contracting States encompasses a broad range of parental rights and responsibilities in regard to care and custody of minor children. That case also went on to recognise that the care and upbringing of children normally and necessarily requires that the parents or an only parent imposes or authorises the imposition of various restrictions upon the child. Therefore, children in a school or other educational or recreational institutions must abide by certain rules which limit their freedoms. Likewise, a child may have to be hospitalised for medical treatment.

It was observed in *Nielsen* that:

"The exercise of parental rights constitutes a fundamental element of family life".[96]

8–28   **Local Authorities.** Local authorities have a duty to protect children from abuse and neglect. The State has a positive obligation to protect children from ill-treatment of which it had ought to have had knowledge and this includes potential ill-treatment of children in local authorities. These principles were enshrined in the United Nations General Assembly Declaration on the Rights of the Child 1959 where at Principle 2 it was stated:

"The child shall enjoy special protection, and shall be given opportunities and facilities, by law and by other means, to enable him to develop physically, mentally, morally, spiritually and socially in a healthy and normal manner and in conditions of freedom and dignity. In the enactment of laws for this purpose, the best interests of the child shall be the paramount consideration".

A further statement of principle appears in the United Nations Convention on the Rights of the Child 1989 at Article 3:

"1. In all actions concerning children, whether undertaken by public or private social welfare institutions, courts of law, administrative authorities or legislative bodies, the best interests of the child shall be a primary consideration.

2. States Parties undertake to ensure the child such protection and care as is necessary for his or her well-being, taking into account the rights and duties of his or her parents, legal guardians, or other individuals legally responsible for him or

---

[95] (2001) 33 E.H.R.R. 9.
[96] At pp. 191–192, para. 61: see also *Family T v. Austria* 64 D.R. 176 at 180, para. 1.

her, and, to this end, shall take all appropriate legislative and administrative measures.

3. States Parties shall ensure that the institution, services and facilities responsible for the care or protection of children shall conform with the standards established by competent authorities, particularly in the areas of safety, health, in the manner and suitability of their staff, as well as competent supervision".

It is clear that the guiding principle reflected both in the 1959 Declaration and the 1989 Convention is that of "best interests of the child".

The same criteria which applies to establishing whether the State is responsible for a private individual administering ill-treatment applies to the acts of those with responsibility for looking after the welfare of children and young people in local government, for instance, Social Services.

In *Z v. United Kingdom*,[97] the European Court of Human Rights overturned a decision of the House of Lords and held that local authorities should be held liable in respect of the exercise of their statutory duties in safeguarding the welfare of children. The European Court of Human Rights acknowledged that while the role of Social Services was acknowledged to be a difficult one, the State has a positive obligation to protect children from ill-treatment which it had, ought to have had knowledge.[98]

In *Z v. United Kingdom*, the applicant and his three siblings had been subjected to severe long-term neglect and abuse and argued that the authorities had breached Article 3, *inter alia*, because the behaviour of the parents who were abusing the siblings had been reported to the Social Services on several occasions, yet they had only acted five years after the first complaint, when the children were placed in emergency care at the insistence of their mother. It was not contested in that case that the abuse suffered reached a level of severity prohibited by Article 3 and that the State was responsible for the failure of Social Services to protect these children who were being abused by members of their family.

In *KL v. United Kingdom*,[99] the European Commission on Human Rights accepted that an allegation that a local authority had failed to protect children from abuse and neglect when within a family structure meant that the State had probably failed to protect its most vulnerable citizens from inhuman or degrading punishment.

Secure accommodation orders. A decision by a local authority to restrict the **8–29** liberty of a child is "serious and draconian".[1] Indeed, where the criteria which justifies the making of a secure accommodation order ceases to exist, there is no justification for a local authority to continue to detain a child whom it had agreed was to be moved into non-secure accommodation.[2]

In *Re K (A Child) (Secure Accommodation Order: Right to Liberty)*,[3] the Court of Appeal referred with approval to the observations in *Koniarska v. United Kingdom*,[4] where it was stated that:

---

[97] (2002) 34 E.H.R.R. 3.
[98] See also *Osman v. United Kingdom* [1999] 1 F.L.R. 193.
[99] [2000] 2 F.C.R. 274.
[1] See *Re M (Secure Accommodation Order)* [1995] 1 F.L.R. 418 at 423.
[2] See *LM v. Essex County Council* [1999] 1 F.L.R. 988.
[3] [2001] Fam. 377.
[4] Application No. 33670/96, unreported, October 12, 2000.

"The court notes that the aim of the orders under Section 25 of the Children Act 1989 is to provide 'secure' accommodation, . . . the applicant likens the security regime to that of a medium to high security prison for adult offenders, and this is not contested by the Government".

As such, the court in *K* were satisfied that a secure accommodation order is a deprivation of liberty.[5]

The applicant's submissions under Articles 3 and 8 in the view of the Court of Appeal "crumbled at the first touch". The *prima facie* incarceration of a child within secure accommodation in accordance with Section 25 seems to go nowhere near breaching the minimum severity threshold.

---

[5] Within the meaning of Article 5.

CHAPTER 9

PHYSICAL INTEGRITY

1. Protection Beyond Article 3

Article 8. Conduct not reaching the severity threshold for Article 3 may,   **9–01**
nonetheless, breach Article 8 which protects physical and moral integrity as part
of an individual's fear of privacy. For instance, in *Am v. Italy*,[1] strict conditions
of detention imposed on an account of the applicant's links with the Mafia were
inadmissible under Article 3 but admissible under Article 8.

Article 8, the right to respect for private and family life, reads:

"(1) Everyone has the right to respect for his private and family life, his home and his
correspondence;

(2) There shall be no interference by a public authority with the exercise of this right
except such as is in accordance with the law and is necessary in a democratic
society in the interests of national security, public safety or the economic well
being of the country, for the prevention of disorder or crime, for the protection of
health or morals, or for the protection of the rights and freedoms of others".

Private life. Article 8(1) establishes the right to respect for private life. The   **9–02**
European Court of Human Rights has not formulated an exhaustive definition of
private life, however, one can assume that it means physical integrity and that the
concept goes further than the mere right to privacy.

Private life includes a person's physical and psychological integrity: see *Botta
v. Italy*.[2] Article 8 is intended to ensure the development, without outside
interference, of the personality of each individual in his relations with other
human beings.[3] The European Commission has made it clear that an individual's
right to inter-relate socially with others is also a part of the right to develop and
fulfil one's own personality.[4]

Not limitless. Article 8 does not give an individual limitless rights of liberty   **9–03**
and cannot be invoked to substantiate a person's freedom to do whatever they
want to do.

Article 8 is dynamic. The flexible and developing nature of Article 8 is seen   **9–04**
throughout European jurisprudence, as this aspect of law adapts to the time. In
Smith v. United Kingdom[5] in a case concerning the right of gypsies to protection
from eviction, the European Court of Human Rights observed that:

---

[1] June 8, 1999.
[2] (1998) 26 E.H.R.R. 241 at para. 32.
[3] See *Botta v. Italy* (1998) 26 E.H.R.R. 241.
[4] See *McFeeley v. United Kingdom* (1980) 3 E.H.R.R. 161 at para. 82, a case which considered the
conditions under which the prisoners in the notorious Maze Prison were held.
[5] (2001) 33 E.H.R.R. 30.

"There may be said to be an emerging international consensus throughout Contracting States of the Council of Europe recognising the special needs of minorities and an obligation to protect their security, identity and lifestyle . . . not only for the purpose of safeguarding the interests of the minorities themselves, but to preserve a cultural diversity of value to the whole community".[6]

9–05   **The margin of appreciation.** Even if it is established before the court that private life is a relevant factor, the State is afforded a wider margin of appreciation by the European Court in determining how any such right should be respected. In *Abdulaziz, Cabales and Balkandali v. United Kingdom*,[7] the court stated that:

"The 'notion of respect' is not clear cut: having regard to the diversity of the practices followed and the situations obtaining in the Contracting States, the notion's requirements will vary considerably from case to case. Accordingly, this is an area in which the Contracting Parties enjoy a wide margin of appreciation in determining the steps to be taken to ensure compliance with the Convention with due regard to the needs and resources of the community and of individuals".

The Human Rights Act 1998 recognises the domestic courts as public authorities[8] and the European Court affords the courts and the discretion in applying the margin of appreciation and expects the domestic courts and tribunals to closely scrutinise cases before they reach the European phase of litigation.

9–06   **Rights can be restricted.** It is apparent from a reading of sub-section 2 of Article 8 that the rights under this Article can be restricted. This is in stark contrast with the absolute rights afforded under Article 3.

9–07   **No right of self-determination.** There has been no case which has established a right of self-determination under Article 8,[9] although the European Convention on Human Rights has recognised the notion of personal autonomy as an important principle underlying the interpretation of its guarantees.

The ability to conduct one's life in a manner of one's own choosing may also include the opportunity to pursue activities perceived to be physically or morally harmful or dangerous for the individual concerned. Any imposition of compulsory or criminal sanctions on private life in this respect will require justification in terms of Article 8(2). Furthermore, the prevention of exercising choice will interfere with the right to respect for private life.

9–08   **Direct effect.**[10] In a case considering the legitimacy of fox hunting in Scotland,[11] the Court of Sessions applied themselves to the status of victims under Convention law and concluded that the European Court would not admit a claim by an "association some of whose members could claim to be victims in the

---

[6] See also *Marckx v. Belgium* (1979–80) 2 E.H.R.R. 330 which dealt with the distinction between legitimate and illegitimate children which may have been relevant to society in the 1950s but was incompatible with a reading of Article 8 in the late 1970s, thus highlighting again the observation that Article 8 is "a living instrument": see *Tyrer v. U.K.* (1979–80) 2 E.H.R.R. 1.

[7] (1985) 7 E.H.R.R. 471.

[8] See Appendix 1: The Human Rights Act and International Perspective.

[9] *Diane Pretty v. U.K.* (2002) 35 E.H.R.R. 1.

[10] See also Chapter 5: Immigration, 5–15 Group Persecution.

[11] See *Adams v. Lord Advocate, The Times*, August 8, 2002.

sense of being directly affected by the legislation".[12] Victims must, in some way, be directly affected by the acts of which they complain.

Adams v. Lord Advocate was, in part, a case brought under Article 8 by those who challenged the validity of the Protection of Wild Mammals (Scotland) Act 2002. The court concluded that Article 8 was not engaged because mounted fox hunting with dogs was not an activity of private life as explained in European jurisprudence.[13]

Association with Article 3. Where the minimum severity threshold has not   **9–09**
been reached so as to activate Article 3, a consideration of Article 8 will be appropriate as the threshold for a breach of this Article is lower than under Article 3.[14] Often claims are brought under Article 3 and Article 8. For instance, in *Y v. U.K.*,[15] a private schoolboy was caned across his clothed buttocks by his headmaster. This punishment left four weals. The schoolboy claimed that the punishment constituted degrading treatment contrary to Article 3 and an unjustified interference with his family life contrary to Article 8.

The Commission of the European Communities of Human Rights found that Article 3 had been violated and that no separate issue arose under Article 8.[16] In *Costello-Roberts v. U.K.*,[17] which again involved the corporal punishment of a pupil in a private school, the court was asked to consider applications of Article 3 and Article 8.

Association with Article 2. Article 8 was also argued under a substantive   **9–10**
claim of violation under Article 2[18] in the case of *Osman v. U.K.*[19] where it was argued that the failure of the police to bring to an end a campaign of harassment, vandalism and victimisation, which one of the applicant's teachers waged against their property constituted a breach of Article 8. The applicants further argued that the failure to prevent the wounding of a second applicant also breached Article 8.

Effectively, use was being made of Article 8 to establish a duty upon the police force to take preventative action, either to end the intimidation or to prevent physical assault. The European Court did not criticise this use of the Article which in short was being used to assert a duty upon the police to take reasonable steps to protect privacy, the home and family.

---

[12] See Lord Nimmo-Smith who referred to *Klass v. Germany* (1978) 2 E.H.R.R. 214: *Young, James and Webster v. U.K.* (1981) 3 E.H.R.R. 20; *Krone-Verlag Gmbh v. Austria* March 7, 2000, *Norris v. Ireland* (1989) 13 E.H.R.R. 186; *Purcell v. Ireland* (1991) 70 D.R. 262.
[13] See *Pretty v. U.K.* (2002) 35 E.H.R.R. 1; *Chassagnou v. France* (1999) 29 E.H.R.R. 615; *Laskey, Jaggard and Brown v. U.K.* (1997) 27 E.H.R.R. 39; *Niemietz v. Germany* (1992) 16 E.H.R.R. 97; *X v. Iceland* (1976) 5 D.R. 86; *Bruggemann and Scheuten v. Federal Republic of Germany* (1983) 3 E.H.R.R. 244; *Friedl v. Austria* (1995) 21 E.H.R.R. 83; *Botta v. Italy* (1998) 26 E.H.R.R. 241.
[14] See *Raninen v. Finland* (1998) 26 E.H.R.R. 563.
[15] (1994) 17 E.H.R.R. 238.
[16] Under the Convention System the establishment and verification of facts are primarily a matter for the Commission, the court is not bound by the Commission's findings, nor by the findings of domestic courts, and is free to make its own appreciation of the facts in the light of all the material before it: see *Ireland v. U.K.* (1979–80) 2 E.H.R.R. 25 and *Ribisch v. Austria* (1996) 21 E.H.R.R. 573.
[17] (1995) 19 E.H.R.R. 112.
[18] The right to life.
[19] (1998) 29 E.H.R.R. 245.

2. THE APPLICATION OF ARTICLE 8

9–11   **Generally.** A comprehensive analysis of the range of Article 8 which would of necessity include a consideration of the law of privacy is beyond the scope of this book.[20] But insofar as Article 8 has been used in tandem with an Article 3 application, certain illustrative examples are appropriate. In the paragraphs which follow, I have attempted to extract key principles that will be relevant when one considers Article 8 within the vast range of disciplines in which it operates.

9–12   **Corporal punishment.** See *Costello-Roberts v. United Kingdom*.[21]

9–13   **Physical abuse.** see *X & Y v. Netherlands*[22] which concerned a sexual assault on a 16 year old woman who was mentally deficient.

Sexual assault of the mental handicapped and vulnerable: *X & Y v. Netherlands*[23] imposed a positive obligation on the State to protect mentally handicapped children from sexual assault by enabling their parents to file criminal complaints in respect of assaults upon them.

Domestic violence: see *Airey v. United Kingdom*.[24] There is an argument that Article 3 may also be invoked.

9–14   **Child abuse.** see *A v. United Kingdom*[25]

9–15   **Seeking personal records.** The need to come to terms with emotional and psychological impact of abuse. The case of *MG v. United Kingdom*[26] was an admissibility decision of the European Court of Human Rights which is presently considering the issue where the applicant seeks access to records as he believes that he was abused and needs access to the documentation to help him come to terms with the emotional and psychological impact of the abuse and to understand his own behaviour.

Furthermore, *Odievre v. France* was declared admissible on October 16, 2001 and is currently awaiting a full hearing on the merits. This case concerns the inability of the applicant to obtain disclosure of adoption records. He argues breaches under Articles 8 and 14. What is clear is that disclosure of information relating to the individual identity of the applicant will be in breach of Article 8.

In *The Queen (on the application of Gunn-Russo) v. Nugent Care Society and the Secretary of State for the Department of Health*[27] the court sought to distinguish *Gaskin v. United Kingdom*[28] when Scott Baker J. observed:

"The present case is clearly distinguishable from *Gaskin* where the material sought was about the applicant.

---

[20] But see Appendix 2.
[21] (1995) 19 E.H.R.R. 112.
[22] (1986) 8 E.H.R.R. 235.
[23] (1986) 8 E.H.R.R. 235.
[24] (1979) 2 E.H.R.R. 305.
[25] (1998) 2 F.L.R. 959.
[26] [2002] 3 F.C.R. 289.
[27] [2001] EWHC Admin 566.
[28] (1989) 12 E.H.R.R. 36.

Here the information was provided by a third party and is about a third party. [In *Gaskin*] since the information compiled and maintained by the local authority related to the applicant's basic identity, and indeed provided the only coherent records of his childhood formative years, the court found the refusal to allow him access to the file to be an interference with his right to respect for his family life falling to be justified under Article 8(2)".

Taking preventative measures. An obligation on the police to take pre-   **9–16** ventative measures: see *Osman v. United Kingdom*.[29]

Excessive noise. see *Powell and Rayner v. United Kingdom*,[30] which con-   **9–17** cerned those who lived near Heathrow Airport and complained of excessive aircraft noise.

The obtaining of samples. The obtaining of samples for DNA testing by the   **9–18** police: see *Saunders v. United Kingdom*.[31]

The destruction of fingerprints or samples obtained in connection with investigations. Although the taking of samples may constitute an interference with personal integrity, retention of samples may not. In *The Queen (on the application of S) v. Chief Constable of South Yorkshire and Secretary of State for the Home Department*: and *The Queen (on the application of Marper) v. Chief Constable of South Yorkshire and Secretary of State for the Home Department* in the Administrative Court on March 22, 2002, considered section 64 of the Police and Criminal Evidence Act 1984 which states that fingerprints or samples obtained in connection with the investigation of an offence were to be destroyed as soon as practicable after conclusion of proceedings in which a suspect was cleared.

Section 82 of the Criminal Justice and Police Act 2001 (which came into force on May 11, 2001), retrospectively amends this provision and appears to permit the retention of fingerprints and DNA samples notwithstanding that the person was cleared of the offence.

In *S* a 12 year old boy with no previous convictions was arrested for attempted robbery and fingerprints and DNA samples were taken in January 2001. In June 2001, he was acquitted.

His solicitors wrote to the Chief Constable and asked for destruction of the fingerprints and photographs in his presence contending that retention would breach Article 8. They criticised the Chief Constable's blanket policy under the new law instead of exercising discretion in each case as to whether retention was justified.

In *Marper* an adult of good behaviour was charged with harassing his partner. His fingerprints and DNA were taken in March 2001. The matter between the two individuals was reconciled and the CPS dropped the case in June 2001. His solicitors also wrote to the Chief Constable requesting destruction and subsequently that he exercise his discretion against retaining them. The Chief Constable advised of his general policy of retention.

It was challenged by judicial review that the new provisions breach Articles 8 and 14 and alternatively, the Chief Constable has effected his discretion in exercising a blanket policy of retention. The court were of the view that the

---

[29] (2000) 29 E.H.R.R. 245.
[30] (1990) 12 E.H.R.R. 355.
[31] (1997) 23 E.H.R.R. 313.

taking of samples may constitute an interference with personal integrity but the retention of samples is different. In *McVeigh, O'Neill and Evans v. United Kingdom*, the Commission distinguished between the taking of fingerprints and photographs and records and their retention. A person can only be identified by fingerprint or DNA either by an expert or the use of sophisticated equipment, in both cases it is essential to have some sample from the activity with which to compare the retained data.

Concerning Article 8(2), the court stated that anyone suspected of an offence knew or could find out that the Chief Constable had the power to retain samples irrespective of the outcome of proceedings subject to there being any specific reason to ask him to destroy them. Furthermore, he remained subject to judicial review and therefore the applicant failed to convince the court that the procedure was "not in accordance with law". Furthermore, the court observed that limitation of retention for the purpose of crime detection and prosecution corresponds with a pressing social need. On the issue of "not necessary in a democratic society", the opening question is proportionality.

The court were of the view that the samples served to eliminate most people and only focus on someone implicated. Therefore, the need and interference are proportionate. Indeed, the court observed that section 64 of the Police and Criminal Evidence Act only requires that samples *may* be retained.

9–19   **Secret surveillance.** See *Klass v. Germany*[32]; *Leander v. Sweden*.[33] Although the prevention of crime and protection of the rights of others are legitimate grounds to negate Article 8, the questions the courts will ask themselves are is it lawful and procedurally correct to operation secret surveillance rather than whether it is legitimate.[34]

In *R. v. Loveridge*,[35] it was established that secret filming by the police of a defendant in a cell area of a Magistrates' Court was unlawful and a breach of their right to privacy which, since it was not in accordance with law, could not be justified. This was considered to be a breach of Article 8.[36]

---

[32] (1979) 2 E.H.R.R. 214.

[33] (1987) 9 E.H.R.R. 433.

[34] The regulation of investigatory Powers Act 2000 ensures that the relevant investigatory powers are used in accordance with basic human rights principles. The Act works in conjunction with existing legislation in particular the Intelligence Services Act 1994, the Police Act 1997 and the Human Rights Act 1998. It was the case of *R. v. Khan (Sultan), The Times*, May 13, 2000 in the European Court of Human Rights which instigated the inception of the 2000 Act. The court held that there was no British legislation regulating the use of covert listening devices (only Home Office Guidelines) and there was, therefore, a breach of Article 8 paragraph 2. As such, Article 8 can credit itself with forcing the introduction of a very significant piece of legislation into the United Kingdom's Domestic Statute Book. Interestingly, s.28(3) of the 200 Act repeats to a significant extent Article 8(2). Section 28(3) reads "an authorisation is necessary on grounds falling within this sub-section if it is necessary (a) in the interests of national security; (b) for the purpose of preventing or detecting crime or of preventing disorder; (c) in the interests of the economic well being of the United Kingdom; (d) in the interests of public safety; (e) for a purpose of protecting public health; (f) for the purpose of assessing or collecting any tax, duty, levy or other imposition, contribution or charge payable to a Government department; or (g) for any purpose (not falling within paragraphs (a) to (f)) which is specified for the purposes of this sub-section by an order made by the Secretary of State". This formula is repeated throughout the Act for various aspects of surveillance.

[35] [2001] EWCA Crim 1034.

[36] However, a judge had been entitled to admit the film in evidence at the defendant's trial, as it has not interfered with the fairness of the trial.

Covert surveillance which carried out in an applicant's home is capable of amounting to a breach of Article 8. In *P.G. and J.H. v. United Kingdom*,[37] the United Kingdom Government accepted that the use of covert listening devices in the applicant's flat was not "in accordance with the law" as at the time (1995) no statutory regulation of the use of such devices existed. This case also concerned two applicants who successfully claimed that the use of covert listening devices within a police station violated Article 8.

A similar conclusion was reached in *Armstrong v. United Kingdom*[38] where the police placed covert listening devices in the home of the applicant's co-defendant. The police sought authority for covert surveillance involving the operation and recording of conversations in the home of the applicant's co-defendant from a Chief Superintendent rather than a Chief Constable. As such the operation violated Article 8. This emphasises the need for getting the proper authority. Failure to do so will be fatal to the integrity of the evidence. But see now, the regime introduced by Regulation of Investigatory Powers Act 2000.

In the same case, the European Court of Human Rights were of the opinion that no violation of Article 8 had arisen as a result of the police obtaining British Telecom itemised billing information relating to the telephone in the flat under surveillance, which was later used in court to corroborate the times and dates recorded by the covert listening device. During the course of the case it had not been disputed that the obtaining by the police of information relating to the numbers called on the applicant's telephone amounted to an interference with the applicant's Article 8 rights.

Nevertheless, with reference to Article 8(2), the court decided that as the information was obtained and used by the police in the course of a criminal investigation and trial, interference was both in accordance with the law and necessary in a democratic society.

The third aspect of this case concerned covert listening devices in the cells of the police station in which the applicants were held, so placed, for the purpose of obtaining speech samples to compare with the tapes from the flat. Written authorisation was obtained both to place the devices in the cells and attach listening devices to the officers who were present when the applicants were formally charged. Speech samples were then recorded without the applicant's knowledge or permission. The court were unanimous of the opinion that a violation of Article 8 had arisen by the use of listening devices in this way. Despite the fact that the applicants' voices were recorded for the purpose of obtaining speech samples, this did not prevent the covert recording constituting an interference with the applicants' Article 8 rights.

Interception of emails for preservation purposes. There is no breach of **9–20** Article 8, or of the Regulation of Investigatory Powers Act 2000 if emails are intercepted in the course of transmission and were the subject of an application for production for special procedure material[39] in order to preserve them, pending the hearing of that application.

In *R. [NTL Group Limited] v. Ipswich Crown Court*,[40] a telecommunication company intercepted emails following an order made by the Crown Court for

---

[37] Application No. 44787/89.
[38] *The Times*, August 6, 2002.
[39] Pursuant to the Police and Criminal Evidence Act 1984, s.9 and Sch. 1.
[40] *The Times*, August 6, 2002.

preservation. Provided that they were not transferred to another address in a way that they would become subsequently available if the court later considered that disclosure was inappropriate, the Queen's Bench Divisional Court held[41] that the court had power to take the necessary action to preserve emails.

9–21 **Regulation of Investigatory Powers Act 2000.** Since 1995 the Regulation of Investigatory Powers Act 2000 has been passed which contains provisions concerning covert surveillance in police stations, but in 1995 there was no such statutory system and therefore the interference was not considered to be in accordance with the law. The 2000 Act was a direct result of challenges and potential challenges under Article 8 for breaches of private life and this is a classic example of how Convention law can cause domestic legislation to be enacted. It is clearly important when considering cases which pre-date the 2000 Act to discount the present legislative regime.

9–22 **Random monitoring of telephone calls made by mental health patients.** Random monitoring of telephone calls of mental patients classified as having dangerous, violent or criminal propensities requiring treatment in special hospitals was not considered unlawful and did not interfere with their right to privacy under Article 8.[42]

9–23 **Unborn children.** Unborn children: the father of an unborn child has a right to raise issues on the child's behalf under Article 8 (and Article 2, the right to life). This right does not apply to an ordinary member of the public: see *X v. Austria*.[43]

9–24 **Abortion.** Abortion does not breach the Article 8 rights of a father. See *Paton v. United Kingdom*.[44] Furthermore, the father has no right to be consulted about an abortion.[45] Legislation restricting abortion does not breach the Article 8 right to establish relationships with others, including sexual relations. In *Bruggemann and Scheuten v. Germany*,[46] it was argued that legislation restricting abortion forced the applicants to either cease sexual intercourse or use contraception. The European Court were of the view that this did not breach the Article 8 right.

9–25 **Discrimination.** Racial discrimination can breach Article 8.

9–26 **Arrest and deprivation of liberty.** This concerns the ability to establish and maintain contact with the outside world. The significant rules relating to prisoners' correspondence are contained in prison Rules 37 and 37A[47] and in Standing Order 5, all of which came into being as a result of *Silver v. United Kingdom*.[48] This case established that stopping a letter to a solicitor on the grounds that the complaints it contained had not previously been raised in the internal complaints

---

[41] See Lord Woolf, Lord Chief Justice.
[42] See *R. v. Ashworth Special Health Authority ex p. N* Administrative Court, May 11, 2001.
[43] (1976) 7 D.R. 87: *Knudsen v. Norway* (1985) 42 D.R. 247.
[44] (1980) 19 D.R. 244.
[45] See *Paton v. U.K.* (1981) 3 E.H.R.R. 408.
[46] (1977) 10 D.R. 100.
[47] See also Prison Rules 1964, Rules 33 and 34.
[48] (1983) 5 E.H.R.R. 347: for the Commission's decision see (1980) 3 E.H.R.R. 475.

mechanism violated Article 8 and was not necessary in a democratic society to satisfy any of the legitimate aims set out in Article 8(2).

The case also has significant influence upon the protection of non-legal correspondence. The Rules and Standing Orders deal with correspondence with legal advisors,[49] where the prisoner has become a party to legal proceedings and at the other side of the divide when he has not.

Prisoners' correspondence. Article 8 does not completely prohibit control over prisoners' correspondence. The measures taken by the State must be proportionate. The European Court have recognised the importance that written correspondence plays in the life of a detainee. If the detainee does not receive visits, the written correspondence will be his only contact with the outside world, and interference is taken very seriously indeed. **9–27**

Nevertheless, the applicant should ensure that they have exhausted all available domestic remedies. In *Faulkner v. United Kingdom*,[50] the applicant prisoner complained that his letters had been opened by the authorities. The Under-Secretary of State apologised for the opening of one of the letters which he said had taken place in the context of "random opening of mail" in response to the discovery that a solicitor had improperly enclosed money in a letter whilst stating it was legal correspondence. The European Court of Human Rights considered that in the circumstances of that case, the applicant could not longer be considered a victim under Article 34 of the Convention.[51] The court were of the view that the applicant could have challenged a number of the alleged interferences with his legal correspondence by way of judicial review and had therefore failed to exhaust his domestic remedies. The prison authorities have a relatively wide discretion.

In *R. (on the application of Nilson) v. Governor of Whitemoor Prison*,[52] the claimant in this case was a serving prisoner. He had for a number of years been working on an autobiography. In 1996, his solicitor took a manuscript out of prison without the knowledge of the defendant. In March 2000, he sent it back to the claimant. The defendant refused to give the manuscript to the claimant without being able to examine the contents to ensure that they did not breach Prison Service Standing Order 5(b), para. 34(9). The defendant believed the manuscript was restricted by this order at para. 34(9) which reads:

"General correspondence should not contain (9) material intended for publication if it is (a) in return for payment, or (c) if it is about the inmate's own crime except where it makes serious representations on crime . . . or the process of justice".

The claimant applied for judicial review, in particular that the refusal to convey the manuscript was a violation of Article 8 and (10). The application was dismissed. The court held that para. 34(9) clearly referred to incoming mail. The

---

[49] See Standing Order 5A 34, and are defined as the inmate's counsel, solicitor or a clerk acting on behalf of the solicitor.
[50] (2002) 35 E.H.R.R. 27.
[51] Article 34 concerns individual applications and reads "The court may receive applications from any person, non-Governmental organisation or group of individuals claiming to be the victim of a violation by one of the High Contracting Parties of the rights set forth in the Convention or the Protocols thereto. The High Contracting Parties undertake not to hinder in any way the effective exercise of this right".
[52] Administrative Court on March 19, 2002.

defendant was entitled to check the script to see if it breached the order or not. They did not regard the facts of this case to breach either Articles.

A prisoner's rights of association

- The refusal to transfer a prisoner from one country in which he has been sentenced to his country of origin under the European Convention on the Transfer of Sentenced Prisoners does not infringe Article 8.[53]

- A condition that medication be taken does not violate Article 8 as a result of the application of Article 8(2) with reference to the protection of the applicant's health.[54]

9–28   **Artificial insemination.** A prisoner has no such right to artificial insemination. In *R. v. Secretary of State for the Home Department ex p. Mellor*,[55] the detainee argued, amongst other things, that he had a right to access to facilities for artificial insemination. In dismissing this argument, the court did observe that in exceptional circumstances it may be necessary to relax the imposition of detention in order to avoid a disproportionate interference with a human right:

> "The interference with fundamental human rights which is permitted by Article 8(2) involves an exercise in proportionality. Exceptional circumstances may require the normal consequences of imprisonment to yield, because the effect of its interference with a particular human right is disproportionate" (see paras 43–5).

9–29   **The Crime and Disorder Act 1998, Section 98 regarding custody of boys to girls.** In *S. R. v. Nottingham Magistrates' Court*, unreported, November 19, 2001, S. R. sought a declaration that section 98 of the Act was incompatible with the European Convention on Human Rights because it unlawfully discriminated against 15 and 16 year old boys, in contrast to girls of the same age, when they are remanded in custody pending trial. Lord Justice Brooke accepted that the matter fell within the scope of Articles 8 and 14 and that the alleged discrimination was on the basis of sex. However, he held that the interference was in order to pursue a legitimate aim, and was proportionate to that aim:

> "The dilemma that faced policy makers was that there were too few juvenile female remandees to allow a network of female specialist juvenile youth offender institutes to be developed which would meet the objective of providing secure accommodation for female juveniles close to their homes ... this is the legitimate objective which is asserted as the justification of the discriminatory policy: to detain all juvenile defendants on secure remand in appropriate accommodation within reasonable visiting distance of their homes.
>
> Because STC was not yet available and there are no specialist female youth offender institutes, the alternative would have been to accommodate these girls in female adult prisons ... on the main issue we have to decide, we do not consider that Section 98 of the 1998 Act is incompatible with SR's Convention rights ... in a democratic society, if our elected representatives believe that it is desirable or expedient to detain more children, and younger children, in secure accommodation than was previously thought desirable or expedient, that is a choice they are entitled to make. We do not accept the argument that Parliament should have held back in making these legislative changes

---

[53] See *Hacisuleymanoglu v. Italy*, Application No. 23241/94 79-B D.R. 121.
[54] See *L v. Sweden* (1986) 8 E.H.R.R. 269.
[55] [2001] EWCA Civ 472.

simply because this would entail boys being placed on secure remand in specialist youth offender institutes and girls being placed in LASU when otherwise it might have been possible to accommodate them in LASU's.

It must not be forgotten that no child of this age may lawfully be placed on secure remand unless a court is satisfied that the public would be at risk of serious harm if he/she was not so placed . . . ".

Separation of mother prisoner from her baby. In *R (P) v. Secretary of State*   **9–30**
for the Home Department[56] in the Court of Appeal, there was a challenge to the policy of separation of mother prisoners and baby, once the child reached the age of 18 months.

The policy was challenged under the Children Act 1989, Sections 1 and 17 and Article 8. The Court of Appeal quashed the rigid policy of the Prison Service that children aged 18 months should cease to stay with their mothers in prison. It considered that the Prison Service was entitled to have a policy like the one under challenge. However, it was not entitled to operate it in a rigid fashion, insisting that all children must leave the unit at the age of 18 months, however catastrophic the separation might be in the case of a particular child, however unsatisfactory the alternative placement available for the child, and however attractive the alternative solution of combining day care outside prison (see para. 100).

The court reached its conclusion for two reasons. The first was that the policy's own declared aim was to promote the welfare of the child. The second was because, on the proper construction of Article 8, there might be very rare exceptions where the interests of the mother and child coincide and outweigh any other considerations arising from the fact of the mother's imprisonment and the implications of any relaxation in the policy on the individual prison and the Prison Service generally.

The court drew certain conclusions from earlier Strasbourg authorities:

- The right to respect for family life is not a right which a prisoner necessarily loses by reason of his or her incarceration;

- On the other hand, when a court considers whether the State's reason for interfering with that right are relevant and sufficient it is entitled to take into account:
  — the reasonable requirements of prison organisation and security; and
  — the desirability of maintaining a uniform regime in prison which avoids any appearance of arbitrariness or discrimination;

- Whatever the justification for a general rule, the European Court of Human Rights' jurisprudence requires the court to consider the application of that rule to the particular case, and to determine whether in that case the interference is proportionate to the particular legitimate aim being pursued;

- The more serious the intervention in any given case (and interventions cannot come very much more serious than the act of separating a mother from a very young child), the more compelling must be the justification (see para. 78).

---

[56] *The Times*, August 1, 2001.

The court went on to consider the effect of Article 8 on the sentencing process and stated:

> "If the passing of a custodial sentence involves the separation of a mother from her very young child (or indeed from any of her children) the sentencing court is bound by section 6(1) to carry out the balancing exercise identified by Hale L.J. in the case of *Re W and B (Children)* at para. 54, especially at sub-paragraph (iii) (for which see para. 65 above) before deciding that the seriousness of the offence justifies the separation of mother and child. If the court does not have sufficient information about the likely consequences of the compulsory separation, it must, in compliance with its obligations under section 6(1) as for more.
>
> It will not longer be permissible, if it ever was, for a court to choose a custodial sentence merely because the mother's want of means and her commitments to her children appear to make a fine or community sentence inappropriate, if the seriousness of the offence does not itself warrant a custodial sentence. In such circumstances, it must ensure that the relevant statutory authorities and/or voluntary organisations provide a viable, properly packaged solution designed to ensure that the mother can be punished adequately for her offence without the necessity of taking her into custody away from her children" (see para. 80).

9–31   **Immigration.**[57] Admissions: see *Abdulaziz, Cabales and Balkandali.*[58] Article 8 may be evoked to admit family members of those already in the jurisdiction if it can be shown that there are real obstacles to establishing family life elsewhere or otherwise there are special reasons why the individuals should not be expected to do so. In *Balkandali v. United Kingdom,*[59] the applicants were lawfully and permanently settled in the United Kingdom and complained that their husbands were refused permission to join them in this country. The court found a breach of Article 8 on the basis of sexual discrimination.[60] Furthermore, Article 8 can be invoked to prevent the removal of an applicant to another country, if that interference is not proportionate to the aim that the State wishes to pursue.[61]

Expulsion. As to whether there is an Article 8 violation, similar considerations will be given to the effect of such expulsion upon family life and the chances of establishing family life elsewhere. Of course, close attention will be paid to the provisions in Article 8(2) which will particularly apply if the applicant has been convicted or suspected of criminal offences.

A failure to renew a residents permit which results in an applicant being separated from his wife is capable of violating Article 8. In *Boultif v. Switzerland,*[62] the applicant was an Algerian national who entered Switzerland on a tourist visa and shortly thereafter married a Swiss citizen.

He was later convicted of the unlawful possession of weapons and of robbery and damage to property by attacking a man. The applicant was sentenced to 2 years' imprisonment. Under Swiss domestic law, the criminal conviction of a foreigner serves as a ground for expulsion. Immediately following the date the applicant began his prison sentence, the authorities refused to renew his residents permit. In due course the applicant was ordered to leave Switzerland by January

---

[57] See *East African Asian v. United Kingdom* (1981) 3 E.H.R.R. 76; *X & Y v. Germany* (1977) 9 D.R. 219; *Lukka v. United Kingdom* (1987) 9 E.H.R.R. 552.
[58] (1986) 7 E.H.R.R. 471.
[59] (1985) 7 E.H.R.R. 471.
[60] See also Chapter 5: Immigration.
[61] *Boutlif v. Switzerland* (2001) 33 E.H.R.R. 50.
[62] (2001) 33 E.H.R.R. 50.

15, 2000. The applicant did so but alleged that the failure to renew the residents permit meant that he was separated from his wife in breach of Article 8. The European Court agreed with him unanimously. Although the court were of the view that the interference with the applicant's Article 8 rights was "in accordance with the law" and was within the Article 8(2) criteria of preventing disorder or crime the judgement went on to indicate that the interference was not proportionate to the aim pursued. The separation from his wife had subjected him to a serious handicap in establishing family life, as at the time he was probably in Italy whilst his wife was in Switzerland. This separation and breach of Article 8 was considered to be disproportionate to the danger that the applicant posed to the public.[63]

The balancing exercise. There must be a balance between respect for family   **9–32**
life and the prevention of crime and disorder.

In *Samaroo v. Secretary of State for the Home Department*,[64] the applicant was convicted of serious drugs offences, and given deportation orders on the basis that it would be conducive to the public good and have a deterrent effect. The applicant challenged this under Article 8(1) on the basis of the interference of his family life established in the United Kingdom. The court stated that a fair balance needs to be struck between the applicant's right to respect for family life and the prevention of crime and disorder (Article 8(2)). National courts must also take the fair balance test into account, they must decide whether the Secretary of State for the Home Department struck the balance fairly. The court will allow the Secretary of State for the Home Department "a discretionary area of judgement". The following factors should be considered: The balance also needs to be struck between a right to family life and the need to conduct an effective investigation. The case of *Pannullo and Forte v. France*,[65] concerned the death of the daughter of two Italian nationals in a French hospital in June 1996. Amid controversy, her body was taken by the French authorities to allow them to conduct an investigation into her death. An autopsy took place in July 1996, but the child's body was not returned to the parents until a judge ordered it on February 14, 1997.

The parents complained that this 7 month delay in returning the body breached their Article 8 right to respect for family life. The European Court of Human Rights found that the French authorities had not struck the right balance between the applicant's family life and the need to conduct an effective investigation into their daughter's death. There had, therefore, been a breach of Article 8.

Checklist.   **9–33**

- Is the right absolute, or does it allow a balance to be struck? If the latter, the court is likely to defer to the opinion of the decision maker;

---

[63] See also *Sen v. Netherlands* (Application No. 31465/96) December 21, 2001. The Netherlands refused an application by a Turkish family living together in the Netherlands for a residents permit for their daughter who had remained in Turkey with her aunt for the past six years. The applicants claimed that this decision violated their right to respect of family life, and the Human Rights Court agreed. It was held that, in rejecting the application on the basis that the daughter was no longer part of her parents' family unit, the Netherlands had failed to strike a fair balance between the applicants' interests and their own controlling immigration.
[64] [2001] EWCA Civ 1139.
[65] October 30, 2001.

- The extent to which the issues requires consideration of the social, economic or political factors. In such cases, the court will defer, as the court is not expert in the policy making and is not democratically elected;

- The extent to which the court has special expertise (*i.e.* in criminal matters);

- If the rights claimed are of "especial importance", a high degree of constitutional protection will be appropriate.

Dyson L.J. stated that:

> "The right to respect for family life is not regarded as a right which requires a high degree of constitutional protection. It is true that the issues are not as technical as economic issues often are. But the court does not have expertise in judging how effective a deterrent is a policy of deporting foreign nationals who have been convicted of serious drug trafficking offences once they have served their sentences".

In *R. v. Home Secretary ex p. R*,[66] R was a failed asylum seeker from Colombia. He was convicted of grievous bodily harm, possession of drugs and a serious driving offence. R attempted to challenge removal by way of judicial review. He argued a breach of his Article 8 rights on the basis that he had contact with his separated wife and three children. The court accepted that if the claimant were to be removed and his wife allowed to stay there would be a serious risk of a breach of the claimant's Article 8 rights. It was considered disproportionate to remove R because of his criminal convictions. Nevertheless, the application was dismissed because the Secretary of State then gave an undertaking not to remove the applicant until his wife's application had been determined.

9–34   **Unmarried fathers.** In *R. v. Home Secretary ex p. Montana*,[67] the court considered the provision in the British Nationality Act 1981, s.50(9), which recognises the relationship between a woman and her child, whether the child be legitimate or illegitimate. However, the father of a child who is not married to the mother does not count as a father under the Act. Hence, an illegitimate child born abroad to a British citizen father and non-British citizen mother is not a British citizen. Under section 3 of the British Nationality Act the Secretary of State has power to register any child as a British citizen. It was argued in this case that the refusal to grant citizenship was in breach of Articles 8 and 14 of the Convention. The court held that the relationship between a father and his child amounted to family life within Article 8, but the refusal itself was not an interference with Article 8. The refusal has not affected the appellant's relationship and regular contact with his son.

The differential treatment of children of British fathers and those of British mothers was a direct result of the terms of the British Nationality Act 1981. Those who *acquired* British citizenship under section 2(1) were not in an analogous position to those who could be granted it under section 3(1). There was no Article 14 violation.

9–35   **Blood tests on children.** Although the law does not permit blood tests to be performed on adults against their wishes,[68] the position of children is different.

---

[66] Administrative Court, *The Times*, November 29, 2000.
[67] Court of Appeal, *The Times*, December 5, 2000.
[68] See Blood Tests on Adults.

In their case, the court is occupying the position of a parent and must act as the judicial reasonable parent. The parent is not guilty of assault if he or she physically interferes with the child by way of reasonable restraint or chastisement or for therapeutic reasons.[69] The court observed that so far as health was concerned it has never been suggested that the taking of a minute drop of blood from the human body is likely to be attended with danger, even in the case of haemophiliacs when proper precautions are taken.[70] In deciding whether a blood test is to be carried out upon a child, the test is whether or not it is in the interests of the child and that no other interests are relevant. This assimilates the issue of paternity to the issue which arises in custody cases where there is a dispute usually between parents of children as to where the child is to spend their life until old enough to make their own choice. The court is in loco parantis, and has to make the choice and in doing so the interests of the child are paramount.

Blood tests on adults. The case of *S. v. McC*,[71] concerns the taking of blood   **9–36** for testing in paternity issues. The court emphasised that so far as adults were concerned the law did not permit such an operation to be performed against their wishes and referred to the American decision of *Bednarik v. Bednarik*[72] where the court observed:

"To subject a person against his will to a blood test is an assault and battery, and clearly an invasion of his personal privacy".

The Court of Appeal in the United Kingdom reached a similar conclusion in *W. v. W.*[73]

Consent orders. The case of *Glaser v. United Kingdom*, Application No.   **9–37** 32346/96, September 19, 2000, considered the issue of the enforcement of consent orders and found in the particular circumstances of that case that there was no violation of Article 8.

Security vetting. The holding of information about private individuals which   **9–38** is released to possible employers is an increasing phenomena in modern society and may, subject to Article 8(2), raise issues under the substantive part of Article 8.[74]

Adoption. A decision is awaited in the case of *Frette v. France*[75] concerning   **9–39** the applicant's complaints under Articles 8 and 14 of the Convention that the courts have refused him leave to adopt a child based upon unfavourable prejudice about his sexual orientation.

Removal of Children. The case of *Covelli and Morselli v. Italy* is presently   **9–40** before the court[76] concerning the applicant's allegations that Articles 8, 6(1) and 13 of the Convention have been breached as a result of the removal of their five

---

[69] See *S. v. McC*, at p. 57.
[70] But see whether there are religious or ethical objections to such a course.
[71] [1972] A.C. 24.
[72] (1940) 16 A 2d 80 at p. 90.
[73] [1964] P. 67.
[74] See *Leander v. Sweden* (1987) 9 E.H.R.R. 433.
[75] October 2, 2001.
[76] January 24, 2002.

children from their home and placement them in different homes without contact with each other.

9–41   **Transsexuals.** In *Goodwin v. United Kingdom*,[77] the European Court of Human Rights held in an application under Article 8 that there was clear and uncontested evidence of a continuing international trend in favour of not only increased social accepted of transsexuals but also of the legal recognition of the new sexual identity of post-operative transsexuals. As such, under Article 8 where the notion of personal autonomy is an important principle underlying the interpretation of its guarantees, protection will be given "to the personal sphere of each individual, including the right to establish details of their identity as individual human beings . . . in the 21st century, the rights of transsexuals to personal development and to physical and moral security in the full sense enjoyed by others in society could no longer be regarded as a matter of controversy".

9–42   **Privacy.**[78] In *A. v. United Kingdom*,[79] Lord Justice Brooke observed:

"The Commission appears to be saying that since the authorities in this country have been content to leave it to the judges to develop the law in this sensitive field, it is the judges who must develop the law so that it gives appropriate recognition to Article 8(1) rights".[80]

3. ENVIRONMENTAL PROTECTION

9–43   **Generally.** The European Court have in a series of cases held that certain activities which affect the environment will constitute a violation of Article 8. A reading of Article 8(1) indicates how potential violations sit neatly within the protection offered for one's home, private and family life.

9–44   **Level of interference.** The level of interference complained of will have to be severe.

In *Lopez Ostra v. Spain*,[81] the court observed that:

"Naturally, severe environmental pollution may affect an individual's well being and prevent them from enjoying their homes in such a way as to affect their private and family life adversely, without, however, seriously endangering their health".[82]

The facts of *Lopez Ostra* are instructive. The applicant lived 12 metres away from a waste treatment plant which had no licence and due to a malfunction released noxious fumes causing health problems and nuisance to many local residents. The Town Council relocated the local inhabitants but allowed the waste

---

[77] Times Law Reports, July 12, 2002.
[78] See Appendix 1: "Privacy, Breach of Confidence and the Interception of Communications".
[79] (1998) 27 E.H.R.R. 61.
[80] For consideration as to whether the Article 8 right is enshrined in privacy or the law of confidence, see Appendix 1: "Privacy, Breach of Confidence and the Interception of Communications".
[81] (1995) 20 E.H.R.R. 277.
[82] See para. 51 above.

treatment plant to continue certain activities. When the applicant returned with her family to her home, she continued to suffer health problems.

Following her exhaustion of all domestic remedies, she applied to the Commission alleging that the inactivity of her local authority resulted in the violation of her rights as articulated under Article 8. She further alleged breaches of Article 3. The Commission upheld her first complaint but rejected the Article 3 allegations.[83] She was more successful under Article 8, as the court observed that the local authorities had failed to take steps to protect the applicant's Article 8 rights and had also resisted judicial decisions which would have had that effect. The offer to re-house the applicant's family was not considered by the court to constitute complete redress for the nuisance and inconvenience which they had suffered.

It is clear that the level of interference must be of a certain degree of severity before Article 8 will be evoked by the courts and as such mirrors to some extent the minimum level of severity approach taken by the European Court to be necessary to activate potential breaches of Article 3.

In *Vetterlein v. Hampshire County Council*,[84] Mr Justice Sullivan referred to *Lopez Ostra* when he observed that the facts of that case "were extreme", highlighting again the level of severity that will be required to establish a breach of Article 8 in environmental issues.

Direct effect on home, family or private life. The quality of life of the applicant must be directly affected so as to engage Article 8. In *Vetterlein v. Hampshire County Council*,[85] the defendant had argued that the Council, in granting planning permission for the construction of an energy recovery facility and waste transfer station, breached their Article 8 rights and that there was a direct link between the pollution complained of and the claimant's quality of life.

Significantly, the Council argued that there had been no breach of World Health Organisation Guidelines as to nitrogen dioxide emissions in the defendants' homes. This was accepted by all parties. The judge considered this significant and concluded that there was no reasonably convincing evidence that the applicant's quality of life would be so directly affected by the plant as to engage Article 8. The court laid emphasis upon the fact that Article 8 is concerned with an individual's right to enjoy life in his own home.[86] In emphasising the personal impact that activities potentially in breach of Article 8 must have upon an applicant, the judge remarked:

> "The claimants' is not more than a generalised concern as to the effects of the incinerator in terms of increased nitrogen dioxide emissions. Such generalised environmental concerns do not engage Article 8 which is concerned with an individual's right to enjoy life in his own home".

There is nevertheless a degree of latitude to this interpretation where the court accepted that it was appropriate in the circumstances of each particular case to

9–45

---

[83] The court also rejected her allegations under Article 3 observing that the conditions in which she had lived was certainly very difficult but they did not amount to degrading treatment within the meaning of Article 3.

[84] [2001] EWHC Admin 560.

[85] [2001] EWHC Admin 560.

[86] See para. 61.

look beyond domestic accommodation and to include other community or social activities such as taking children to school.

9–46   **Risk of future violations.** It is only in exceptional circumstances that the risk of future violation will activate Article 8. In *Asselbourg v. Luxembourg*,[87] the court observed that the level of proof required to establish this risk is high and that the applicant must produce "reasonable and convincing evidence of the probability of the occurrence of a violation concerning him or her personally: mere suspicions or conjectures are not enough".

9–47   **The balance between the individual and the community as a whole.** The court will have regard to the competing interests of the individual and the community and strive to strike a fair balance between these competing interests.[88] The plant in *Lopez Ostra* had initially been built to solve the town's serious pollution problems but had resulted in severe environmental pollution which the Town Council resisted taking action upon. As such, on the facts of that case, the court concluded that the State had not succeeded in striking a fair balance between the town's economic well being and the applicant's effective enjoyment of her right to respect for her home and family life.[89]

9–48   **The State's duty to take reasonable and appropriate measures to secure the applicant's rights under Article 8.** The State has a positive duty to secure an applicant's rights under this Article or justify the interference of that right with reference to the criteria laid down in Article 8(2).

Whether such justification can be achieved will particularly rely on the factors under consideration of the balance to be struck between individuals and the community as a whole and these issues are effectively inextricably linked.

9–49   **Local and national interests.** Earlier case law seems to establish that it was upon the State to protect the national interest in respect of environment encroachment,[90] but this approach seems to have been altered by the judgement in *Hatton v. United Kingdom*[91] which concerned noise pollution from aeroplanes flying out of Heathrow Airport.

The court stated:

"States are required to minimise, as far as possible, the interference with the (Article 8) rights by trying to find alternative solutions and by generally seeking to achieve their aims in the least onerous way as regards human rights. In order to do that, a proper and complete investigation and study with the aim of finding the best possible solution which will in reality strike the right balance should precede the relevant project".[92]

9–50   **Relationship with Article 14.** Article 14 is not a free-standing right. It finds its provenance in connection with the enjoyment with other rights. In *R. v. Manchester City Council*,[93] the relationship between Article 8 and Article 14 was expressed in the judgement of Mr Justice Mundy. This case concerned the

---

[87] Appeal No. 2912/95 dated June 29, 1999.
[88] See *Lopez Ostra v. Spain* (1995) 20 E.H.R.R. 277.
[89] See para. 58.
[90] See *Powell and Rayner v. United Kingdom* (1990) 12 E.H.R.R. 355.
[91] Application No. 36022/97.
[92] See para. 98.
[93] Unreported, September 28, 2001 in the Administrative Court.

legality of a local authority's policy under which it paid those of its short-term foster-carers who were friends or relatives of the child at a different and very significantly lower rate than it paid other such foster-carers. The Children Act provides that it is the duty of the authority to safeguard and promote the child's welfare and to provide accommodation and maintain the child in other respects (see sections 22 and 23).

In considering the relationship between Article 8 and Article 14, the court observed:

> "The steps required to be taken by Manchester under ... the Act ... in relation to looked after children are a classic circumstance in which the Article 8 positive obligation comes into play ... the non-discrimination obligation under Article 14 relates to rights, such as those arising under Article 8, which are themselves guaranteed by the Convention. Article 14 extends both to direct discrimination, that is discrimination which is directed at the status of the victim, and to indirect discrimination, that which has a disproportionate effect on a particular group" (Mr Justice Mundy).

A little earlier in the judgment, the court acknowledge the growing concerns over environmental protection when they comment that in "the particularly sensitive field of environmental protection", the State can no longer simply refer to economic well being of the country outweighing the rights of others.[94]

The court was particularly critical of the U.K. Government for its failure to carry out an independent assessment of the economic interest in night flights and for its limited research into the nature of sleep disturbance and prevention.[95]

Provision of housing. Of itself, Article 8 does not require the provision of **9–51** family housing. In *J. R. (on the application of) v. London Borough of Enfield* in the High Court, Queen's Bench Division (Administrative Court),[96] a claimant was seriously ill. This Ghanaen woman had a two year old child. Both the mother and child had overstayed their leave to remain in the United Kingdom and were destitute. The question which fell for the court to consider was whether the general duty of every local authority under section 17 of the Children Act 1989 to promote the welfare of children required assistance to every mother and child to provide housing. The court held that section 17 did not require such assistance.

It considered that after the decision of *R (A) v. Lambeth London Borough Council*,[97] it was clear that a local authority no longer had to provide accommodation for a child under section 17. In the present case, it would not sit well with the rationale of the Lambeth case to conclude that the authority could nonetheless provide financial support for accommodation for the family. Although *obiter*, His Lordship also noted that Section 17 was compatible with Article 8. Article 8 by itself did not require provision of accommodation for the family.

Gypsies. Article 8 can be used to protect the travelling community. *Porter v.* **9–52** *South Bucks District Council*[98] in the Court of Appeal, was a case which

---

[94] See para. 97.
[95] The court found that the limited scope of judicial review as the appropriate remedy also meant that Article 13 had been violated. Each applicant received £4,000 representing non-pecuniary damages.
[96] March 4, 2002.
[97] (2001) L.G.R. 513.
[98] October 12, 2001.

concerned the granting of injunctions against travellers, which were held to be in breach of Article 8.[99]

9–53   **The right to receive information from public authorities about risks to the environment.** Applicants are entitled to essential information that would enable them to assess the risks that they or their families might face.[1]

9–54   **Failure to carry out work.** A failure of a defendant to carry out work which would bring an end to the activity which produces the environmental hazard will be capable of breaching Article 8.[2]

9–55   **Police Searches.** The power to enter and search premises is derived from the Police and Criminal Evidence Act 1984, Section 8 which compels a police officer to apply to a justice of the peace for a search warrant if the police officer has reasonable grounds for believing:

(a)   "That a serious arrestable offence has been committed; and

(b)   that there is material on premises specified in the application which is likely to be of substantial value (whether by itself or together with other material) to the investigation of the offence; and

(c)   that the material is likely to be relevant evidence; and

(d)   that it does not consist of or include items subject to legal privilege, excluding material or special procedure material; and

(e)   that any of the conditions specified in (3) below, applies, he may issue a warrant authorising a constable to enter and search the premises".

Section 8(3) lays down four conditions:

"(a)   That it is not practicable to communicate with any person entitled to grant entry to the premises;

(b)   That it is practicable to communicate with a person entitled to grant entry to the premises but it is not practicable to communicate with any person entitled to grant access to the evidence;

(c)   That entry to the premises will not be granted unless a warrant is produced;

(d)   That the purpose of a search may be frustrated or seriously prejudiced unless a constable arriving at the premises can secure immediate entry to them".

Any breach of these provisions will raise a *prima facie* case under Article 8.

●   Search of a car—see *X v. Belgium*[3]

●   Temporary confiscation of personal papers: see *X v. Germany*[4]

---

[99] See also *Clarke v. Secretary of State for the Environment, Transport and the Regions*, October 9, 2001 concerning planning permission to station a caravan on his land by a Romany man for his own residential use.

[1] See *Guerra v. Italy* (1998) E.H.R.R. 357.

[2] See *Marcic v. Thames Water Utilities Limited*, May 14, 2001, which was subsequently endorsed in the Court of Appeal. See [2002] EWCA Civ 64, at para. 111.

[3] 45 Collection of Decisions 20.

[4] (1976) 3 D.R. 104.

- Taking personal details and/or photographs of suspects: see *Murrey v. United Kingdom*.[5] This case concerned the photographing of a suspect without their consent in a police station which was held to be legitimate in accordance with the application of Article 8(2). But when photographs are taken at a public demonstration rather than in the confines of a police station Article 8 may be infringed.[6]

- Personal searches: In *Home Office v. Wainwright*, the Court of Appeal considered whether a right to privacy existed in common law so as to found a course of action in respect of personal searches which occurred before the Human Rights Act 1998 came into force.[7]

Extradition searches. In extradition cases, there is no police power under   **9–56**
statute or common law either to enter or search a suspect's dwelling house
without a court search warrant. In *Commissioner of Police for the Metropolis:
Secretary of State for the Home Department, ex p. Rottman*,[8] the Divisional Court
ordered delivery up of possessions seized during this illegal search and declared
that the search was unlawful in breach of Article 8.

Checklist.   **9–57**

- Article 8 is a qualified right;

- Below severity threshold;

- The question has to be asked as to whether the State has failed to respect the right;

- Is the failure justified under Article 8(2)?

---

[5] (1995) 19 E.H.R.R. 193 at para. 86.
[6] See *Friedl v. Austria* (1996) 21 E.H.R.R. 83.
[7] [2001] EWCA 2081, *The Times*, January 4, 2002 and Appendix 1: "Privacy, Breach of Confidence and the Interception of Communications".
[8] Queen's Bench Division, July 24, 2001.

CHAPTER 10

EFFECTIVE REMEDY

1. ARTICLE 13

The text. Article 13 establishes the right to an effective remedy before a national body and is often argued in tandem with Article 3 violations. Article 13 reads:

    "Everyone whose rights and freedoms as set forth in this Convention are violated shall have an effective remedy before a national authority notwithstanding that the violation has been committed by persons acting in an official capacity".

The duty. It is the duty of the domestic authority to secure and protect Convention rights.

The nature of the remedy. An effective remedy may entail the payment of compensation where appropriate although this is not exhaustive and, for example, a thorough and effective investigation capable of leading to the identification and punishment of those responsible for violations and including effective access for the complainant to the investigatory procedure may be required.

In *Aydin v. Turkey*,[1] the applicant was entirely reliant on the Public Prosecutor to assemble the evidence necessary for corroborating her complaint under Article 3, a complaint which by its nature should have alerted the Public Prosecutor to the need to conduct promptly a thorough and effective investigation.

The Public Prosecutor's enquiry was ineffective in that, *inter alia*, he accepted too readily the security forces' denial that the applicant had been detained and was content to conduct that part of his investigation by correspondence, accordingly, there had been a violation of Article 3 in the view of the European Court.[2] In *Aksoy v. Turkey*,[3] the Public Prosecutor decided that there were no grounds to institute criminal proceedings against those who had inflicted torture upon the applicant. The European Court found that the Public Prosecutor had ignored clear evidence of torture which was tantamount to undermining the effectiveness of any other remedies that may have been open to the applicant. Compensation was awarded for what the court considered extremely serious violations.

In the Greek cases,[4] The United Kingdom argued that domestic remedies had not been exhausted as required by the Convention.[5] This requirement has been used to control the number of individual petitions, but it was agreed in the Greek case that it could also apply to interstate application.[6]

10–01

10–02

10–03

---

[1] (1998) 25 E.H.R.R. 251.
[2] See also *Aksoy v. Turkey* (2002) 34 E.H.R.R. 57. *Tekin v. Turkey* (2001) 31 E.H.R.R. 4.
[3] (2002) 34 E.H.R.R. 251.
[4] See above.
[5] Rule 41(2) of the Commission's Rules of Procedure required, in furtherance of Article 26, that a party "shall provide evidence to show that all domestic remedies have been exhausted".
[6] This was somewhat surprising as the Greek Government was not acting in any way as agent of the supposed victims, who it seems were not consulted over the conduct of the proceedings.

The application also argued that the local remedies were not of any use and states:

> "Either the victims did not know the names of their tormentors, or else an administrative enquiry conducted in their absence concluded that the accused officials were innocent".[7]

The Greek application went on to say:

> "Even in those cases where it is possible to identify them, a civil suit was not likely to furnish the victims with the moral reparation that would be represented by the punishment of the guilty men".[8]

Therefore, there was no effective remedy as is required by Article 13.[9]

10–04   **The State's first duty to protect human rights.** In *Mills v. HM Advocate*,[10] a case concerning the delayed appeal hearing of a defendant, the court considered the approach to what would be an effective remedy. Lord Hope commented:

> "The approach was first to identify the remedy which would ordinarily be thought to be appropriate in domestic law for a breach of the kind which had taken place, and then to consider whether the remedy which had thus been identified would achieve just satisfaction for the breach as indicated by the jurisprudence of the European Court.
>
> It was important to start with the position in domestic law because as was emphasised in Eckle v. Federal Republic in Germany 5 E.H.R.R. I, 24, para. 66, the Convention left to each Contracting State, in the first place, the task of securing the enjoyment of the rights and freedoms which it enshrined".

10–05   **Article 3.** In matters relating to torture, inhuman or degrading treatment and/or punishment, the irreversible nature of the harm that might occur if the risk of ill-treatment materialises and the importance the court attaches to Article 3 has led the European Court to state that the notion of an effective remedy under Article 13 in the context of Article 3 requires independent scrutiny of the claim that there exists substantial grounds for fearing a real risk of treatment contrary to Article 3.[11] The court in *Chahal v. United Kingdom*[12] stated:

> "The requirement of a remedy which is 'as effective as it can be' is not appropriate in respect of a complaint that a person's deportation will expose him or her to a real risk of treatment in breach of Article 3, where the issues concerning national security are immaterial".[13]

In short, wherever it is established the there is a serious risk of torture, inhuman or degrading treatment, any decision refuting asylum will be struck down as unreasonable.

---

[7] See para. 12.

[8] See para. 15.

[9] because at this time it was impossible to sue the Crown in Cyprus, there being no local equivalent to the Crown Proceedings Act 1947.

[10] [2002] UKPC D2.

[11] See *Chahal v. United Kingdom* (1997) 23 E.H.R.R. 413.

[12] (1997) 23 E.H.R.R. 413.

[13] The Government in *Chahal* argued that judicial review as a remedy was effective as it could be, given the necessity of relying on secret sources of information.

Accountability of public officials. Central to both Articles 3 and 13 is the　**10–06**
accountability of public officials. This requires a right of access to court whereby
the applicant can hold the responsible officials to account in adversarial proceedings and obtain an enforceable order for compensation if the claim is substantiated. The wording of Article 13 also prohibits the creation of immunities for
public officials and any such immunity must be regarded as contrary to the object
and purpose of the Convention. Sometimes, a remedy required by Article 13 need
not always be judicial in character.[14]

Responsibility for investigating allegations. In addition to payment of com-　**10–07**
pensation where appropriate, Article 13 requires a thorough and effective investigation capable of leading to the identification and punishment of those
responsible for inflicting the ill-treatment, including effective access for the
complainant to the investigation procedure.[15]

These cases however concern alleged killings or infliction of treatment contrary to Article 3 involving potential criminal responsibility on the part of
security force officials. Where alleged failure by the authorities to protect persons
from the acts of others is concerned, Article 13 may not always require that the
authorities undertake the responsibility for investigating the allegations. There
should however be available to the victim or the victim's family a mechanism for
establishing any liability of State officials or bodies for acts or omissions
involving the breach of their rights under the Convention. Furthermore, in the
case of breaches of Articles 2 and 3 of the Convention, which rank as the most
fundamental provisions of the Convention, compensation for the non-pecuniary
damage flowing from the breach should in principle be available as part of the
range of redress.[16]

The remedy required by Article 13 must be effective. Article 13's remedy　**10–08**
has to be effective in practice as well as in law.[17]

Police complaints. The system of investigation of complaints against the　**10–09**
police does not meet the required standards of independence needed to constitute
sufficient protection against the abuse of authority. The European Court are of the
view that it does not provide an effective remedy in accordance with Article
3.

In *P.G. and J.H. v. United Kingdom*,[18] the applicant had been the victim of
various examples of covert surveillance, in his home, in the police cell in which
he was detained and by means of listening devices on the person of police
officers dealing with him. It was held that the domestic courts had been incapable
of providing a remedy in 1995 because it was not open to them to deal with the
substance of the Convention complaint that the interference with the applicant's
Article 8 rights was not in accordance with the law or to grant appropriate relief
in connection with the applicant.[19]

---

[14] See *Z v. United Kingdom* [2001] 2 F.L.R. at 638.
[15] See *Kaya v. Turkey* (1999) 28 E.H.R.R. 1.
[16] See *Z v. United Kingdom* [2001] 2 F.L.R. 638 at para. 109.
[17] See *Aydin v. Turkey* (1998) 25 E.H.R.R. 251 and *Kaya v. Turkey* (1999) 28 E.H.R.R. 1.
[18] Application No. 44787/98.
[19] In terms of damages, the court awarded each applicant £1,00 for non-pecuniary damages in respect
of injury to their feelings in addition to costs and expenses.

10–10 **Inquests.** An inquest does not provide an effective remedy sufficient to satisfy Article 13. The issue most often arises during death in custody cases.

10–11 **The International Criminal Tribunal.** The European Court are presently considering whether defendants who have been submitted to the International Criminal Tribunal have any effective remedy in relation to their arrest, detention or criminal proceedings conducted against them in the International Criminal Tribunal. These issues are presently before the court[20] at the instigation of Slobodan Milosevic, the Former President of the Federal Republic of Yugoslavia who filed his application invoking Articles 5, 6, 10, 13 and 14 against the Netherlands. The decision is awaited.

10–12 **Exhausting domestic remedies.** In *William Ballantyne v. United Kingdom*[21] the Government submitted that the applicant had failed to exhaust domestic remedies in respect of his complaints since, *inter alia*, he had not instituted proceedings for damages or for judicial review against the Secretary of State. The Government submitted that even if the applicant can be said to have exhausted all available remedies, his complaints are time barred since he failed to introduce them within the 6 month time limit of the final decision, ie, that replies made to his petitions to the Secretary of State.

But the Commission commented on the exhaustion of domestic remedies and recalled that Article 26 of the Convention only requires the exhaustion of such remedies which related to the breaches of the Convention alleged and, at the same time, can provide effective and sufficient redress. An applicant does not need to exercise remedies which, although theoretically of a nature to constitute a remedy, do not in reality offer any chance of redressing the alleged breach. It was furthermore observed that the burden of proving the existence of the available and sufficient domestic remedies lay upon the State (see *Deweer*[22]). In any event, the application was held to be time barred and rejected under Article 27(3) of the Convention.

Moreover, the Commission were of the view that in this instance the applicant had failed to exhaust his domestic remedies as he had not instituted any proceeding claiming damages in respect of the injury to his hand or alleged medical negligence.

On October 12, 1957, the Commission published its decision, inviting the United Kingdom to answer questions concerning their domestic remedies in Cyprus. These questions probed about the existence of civil remedies against the Crown, the nature of civil remedies against individuals, and the regulations requiring consent for criminal proceedings against officials.

The Commission accepted the Greek argument that:

"Whereas, in accordance with the generally recognised principles of international law, the exhaustion of a domestic remedy is nevertheless not required if the applicant party can prove that in the particular circumstances such remedy will probably prove ineffectual or inadequate . . . ".

The Commission took the view that the British Government had a duty, if it relied on failure to exhaust domestic remedies "to demonstrate the existence of

---

[20] On December 20, 2001.
[21] Commission Admissibility Decision, Application No. 1462/88.
[22] February 27, 1980, Series A, No. 35, p. 15, para. 26.

such remedies". The Commission held that it had failed to do so in regard to suits against the Crown. The Commission stated that:

> "Whereas . . . the United Kingdom Government has shown . . . it is possible to address a demand for compensation by petition addressed either to the Governor of Cyprus, or to the Queen; whereas, however, such a remedy, being a matter of grace, is not among those which must be exhausted by virtue of Article 26 . . . ".[23]

The Commission recognised nevertheless that civil actions could be brought against individuals and ruled that such civil remedies had to be exhausted before the Commission could be seized of the matter. As to the argument concerning criminal proceedings, the Commission did not treat the failure to attempt to bring such proceedings as vital, or they did note that the Attorney General had in fact consented to such proceedings.

Therefore, as far as the Greek cases are concerned, as a result of this ruling, the cases which were admissible were cases in which the identity of the alleged perpetrator of the ill-treatment was not established because the individuals concerned approached the competent authorities in Cyprus for the names of the authors of the alleged acts, but were refused the information requested or those authorities were requested to open an investigation or enquiry into the alleged acts, but considered that there was no reason to prosecute, or, where no such approach or request was made, but the Greek Government established that the British authorities displayed no readiness to indicate the names of the perpetrators of the alleged tortures or ill-treatment, even though an express request for such information was addressed to them. As a matter of deduction, the inadmissible cases were those where the victims knew the identity of the alleged perpetrator and should have brought actions under the civil law.[24]

In *D.P. and J.C. v. U.K.*[24a] the European Court of Human Rights held that Article 13 had been violated where two applicants who had been sexually abused as children by their step-father did not have available to them, appropriate means of obtaining a determination of their allegations that the local authority had failed to protect them from serious ill-treatment. The Court also considered Article 3, but held no violation because Social Services records did not indicate that there had been any suspicion of sexual abuse. Furthermore, no contemporaneous complaint had been made. Given that there was no evidence that the local authority should have been aware of the sexual abuse, the authority could not be regarded as having failed in any positive obligation to the applicants.

---

[23] See the Report of the Commission.

[24] It seems that there was considerable satisfaction in London with the reduction in the number of cases from 49 to 29. Initial but ultimately futile consideration was given to Article 26 which as well as providing that domestic remedies must be exhausted before the Commission could entertain a complaint also imposed a time limit whereby the Commission may only deal with the matter within a period of six months from the date on which the final decision was taken. The United Kingdom postulated that it was possible to argue that if time ran from the date of the incident, then 11 of the 29 cases were out of time. (Cases 2, 3, 5, 6, 7, 8, 10, 11, 12, 13, 14) Arguments within Government were against taking the point. The Solicitor General, Sir Harry Hylton-Foster, dismissed the idea in his letter of December 10, 1957 (CO936/496) when he said: "Frankly, the further argument . . . presented as attractively as possible . . . appears to me to be disreputable. I should certainly feel most embarrassed if required to present it on behalf of HMG. I cannot believe it has any chance of success".

[24a] Times Law Reports, October 23, 2002.

10–13   **Pending civil proceedings.** In *McShane v. United Kingdom*,[25] the court observed that the applicant had lodged civil proceeding which were pending and that it had found no elements which would prevent those proceedings providing the necessary redress in respect of any alleged excessive use of force by the police.

---

[25] (2002) 35 E.H.R.R. 23.

THE HUMAN RIGHTS ACT—AN INTERNATIONAL PERSPECTIVE

A PAPER BY JOHN COOPER, BARRISTER OF THE ENGLISH AND AUSTRALIAN BAR

A Historical Background

In March 1946 the Reconstruction Department of the Foreign Office produced a draft **A.1–01** paper on Human Rights. It was in most part a rambling text. The author had faced the fundamental problem of the lack of cohesion from any previous papers. It considered human rights under a number of categories: national rights, civil rights, religious rights, political rights, the status of women, economic and social rights, scientific rights, and miscellaneous rights. Insofar as the paper discussed the state of British law, it considered equality before the law, freedom from wrongful interference, the right to a fair trial, freedom from arbitrary arrest, respect for private property and non-discrimination on the grounds of race, language or sex, and concluded, somewhat confidently that "our own body of law provides ample safeguards against abuses of all of the above rights".

The paper implied the same self-satisfaction with religious rights and then moved to political rights and observed: "In a western democracy the basis of our political rights are the principles (a) of respect for the human personality; (b) that individuals make up society; and (c) that the consent of the governed is necessary".

From this flowed the rights to free and secret elections, freedom of assembly, freedom of association, and freedom of speech, press and communication. It was rather smugly concluded that the British record over freedom of information was "exemplary" and that all the rights were fully protected. The paper did, however, appear to accept that the state of affairs in the colonies might be more uncertain.

The Colonial Office agreed that the protection of rights did not depend upon formal legal statutes.

They suggested that rights could be as well protected in countries which did not have a bill of rights as in those that did.

In 1946, it was very obvious that as the world emerged from world conflict there was **A.1–02** very little legal coherence upon what actually constituted human rights. As Professor A. W. Brian Simpson puts it in his colossal work, "Human Rights and the End of Empire". There was no clear consensus on what a human right was—a national right perhaps? Or perhaps not. "There was consensus that some rights were fundamental, but no agreement as to what the list should be, or how it should be structured . . . there was uncertainty on the relationship between human rights and democratic forms of government . . . it was thought that the protection of rights depended not on the legal forms in which they were expressed, but in the state of opinion, and the practical mechanisms whereby alleged violations could be remedied".

The General Assembly adopted the Universal Declaration of Human Rights[1] on December 10, 1948[2] and was heralded as "a common standard of achievement for all peoples and all nations, to the end that every individual and every organ of society, keeping this declaration constantly in mind, shall strive for teaching and education to promote respect for these rights and freedoms and by progressive measures, national and international, to secure their universal and effective recognition and observance both among the peoples of Member States themselves and among the peoples of territories under their jurisdiction".[3]

A.1–03   The Declaration provides that the rights and freedoms set forth in its text should be enjoyed by all without distinction of any kind, such as race, colour, sex, language, religion, political or other opinion, national or social origin, property, birth or other status.

As a matter of history, the Declaration was part of a wider reordering of world order, designed to create, as Michael Ignatieff[4] called it "fire walls against barbarism", but it did more than that, it laid down the blue print, the basic principles upon which the recent revolution of human rights has grown.

"Human Rights and fundamental freedoms are the birthright of all human beings"[5] but in practice both individuals and groups remain the victims of human rights violations, abuses sustained for example by refugees, prisoners and detainees in custody, highlight the problems confronting the international enormity.

Today, most modern states have satisfied the international human rights conventions and some states have incorporated their rights and remedies into the structure of their legal systems. The European Court of Human Rights which was established in 1953 affords citizens of European States the capacity to appeal against injustices in civil and state procedure to the European Court. The pressure upon states around the world to embrace the principles of Human Rights increases by the day.

A.1–04   In Europe, states such as Britain now accept that decisions taken by their courts or administrative bodies can be affected by principles laid down in the European Convention for the Protection of Human Rights and Fundamental Freedoms and new nations seeking entry into the European Union must align their domestic law to the compatible with the strictures laid down in the European Convention.

In the developing world, ratifying international human rights covenants has become a condition precedent for entry into the family of nations. As Ignatieff puts it, "while genuflection towards human rights is the homage that vice pays to virtue, the fact that oppressive regimes feel so obliged means that vice can now be shamed and even controlled in ways that were unavailable before 1945".[6]

Back in 1950, only one British dependency, the Kingdom of Tonga, possessed a constitution which came anywhere near to the Declaration and to this day, remains in force. Modelled on the declarations of rights in the Hawaiian constitutions of 1864 and 1852, it dates back from 1875 and was drafted by a Wesleyan Missionary to Reverend Shirley Baker, known to the Tongans as Tcemangoi, or "he who surmounts all difficulties".

A.1–05   The King of Tonga, Tupow I, who gave Baker his title was an astute judge of the problems in introducing a human rights code into domestic law, conception and delivery

---

[1] G. A. Ross, 217 A (III), GAOR, 3rd Session, Part I Resolutions p. 71.
[2] International Human Rights Day is celebrated annually on December 10.
[3] The text of the Universal Declaration.
[4] Human Rights as Politics and Idolatry.
[5] Vienna Declaration, 1995, para. 1.
[6] See n. 4.

is not without trauma, but in a world which sets its norms of moral decency and international acceptability against the provision of human rights in emerging states, that trauma is not an option and it must be endured.

Fundamental Rights and Freedoms

The then Home Secretary, Jack Straw, observed that the Parliamentary Bill, bringing **A.1–06** into effect the incorporation of the European Convention on Human Rights into the law of the United Kingdom will "strengthen representative and democratic government. It does so by enabling citizens to challenge more easily actions of the state if they fail to match the standards set by the European Convention".[7]

The rights protected by the subsequent Human Rights Act 1998, made law in the United Kingdom are referred to as "Convention Rights". Resonant echoes of those somewhat arrogant authors of 1946 can be heard as to the rights that will, to varying degrees, be protected—

- The right to life—Article 2
- Prohibition on torture, inhuman or degrading treatment—Article 3
- Prohibition on slavery and forced labour—Article 4
- A right to liberty and security—Article 5
- A right to a fair trial—Article 6
- No punishment without law—Article 7
- A right to respect for private and family life—Article 8
- Freedom of thought, conscience and religion—Article 9
- Freedom of expression—Article 10
- Freedom of assembly and association—Article 11
- A right to marry—Article 12
- Prohibition on discrimination—Article 14

Further protocols provide:

- Protection for property—Protocol 1, Article 1
- A right to education—Protocol 1, Article 2
- A right to free election—Protocol 1, Article 3
- Abolition of the death penalty—Prohibition 6, Article 1

These are all basic requirements of any hybrid of a Human Rights Legislative document.

Incorporation into Domestic Law

Incorporation of the Convention into the law of the United Kingdom laid down four **A.1–07** main principles which were referred to by the Lord Chancellor as "the British model".

---

[7] 306 HC 769 (February 16, 1998).

Firstly, legislation, enacted into domestic law should be construed compatibly with the Convention as far as possible.

Secondly, the Sovereignty of Parliament should not be disturbed. Where the courts cannot reconcile legislation with Convention rights, Parliament should be able to do so—and more quickly, if thought appropriate, than by enacting primary legislation.

Thirdly, public authorities [now widely defined by case law] should comply with Convention rights or face the prospect of a legal challenge.

Fourthly, remedies should be available for a breach of Convention rights by a public authority.

A.1–08   Put another way, the drafting of the British bill is designed to give the courts as much space as possible to protect human rights, short of a power to set aside or ignore Acts of Parliament.

During Parliamentary debate, the British Government became somewhat confused as to precisely whether they intended to "incorporate" the Convention into domestic law or, as the Lord Chancellor put it, give "further effect in the United Kingdom to Convention rights".[8]

This confusion only goes to highlight the necessity to grasp the nettle of incorporation, nothing short will do.

The Lord Chancellor's reticence may well have stemmed from the immediate post-war era of complacency when analysing domestic compliance with human rights norms. In the modern era, no nation state should start from the premise that their protection of basic human rights is already compliant with international norms, such a position avoids the necessity of incorporation and full, unequivocal submission to the human rights code. This was finally accepted in the United Kingdom, when the Home Secretary announced "Having decided that we should incorporate the Convention, the most fundamental question that we faced was how to do that in a manner that strengthened and did not undermine the sovereignty of Parliament".[9]

A.1–09   For any democratic state, courting incorporation of any model of human rights principles into their domestic legislation, the Sovereignty of Parliament is a vital consideration. In the British model, the Government proposed that there should be a "dialogue" between the executive legislative and the courts about the operation and development of incorporation, "this dialogue is the only way in which we can ensure the legislation is a living development that assists our citizens".[10]

Of course, it would be alarmingly short sighted to restrict the influence of human rights developments and precedents to those "made in Europe".

That is why the British model makes it clear that whilst its domestic courts must take into account Convention jurisprudence they are not bound by it. This leaves the way open for jurisprudence under other international human rights treaties, or from other jurisdictions with comparable human rights legislation to be prayed in aid where appropriate.

Some would argue that the United Kingdom has therefore gone further than simply incorporating the European Convention into its law, it has, in its open door approach to international jurisprudence, gone much further and created a new Bill of Rights.

A.1–10   The European models of incorporation have adhered to the Lord Chancellor's observations that "we have not provided for the Convention rights to be directly justifiable in actions between private individuals. We have sought to protect the rights of individuals against the abuse of power by the state, broadly defined, rather than to protect them against each other".

Section 6 of the Human Rights Act 1998, tells us that "public authorities" may not act in contravention of Convention rights but whether the Act enables an individual citizen to

---

[8] 585 HL 421 (January 29, 1998).
[9] 306 HC 771 (February 16, 1998).
[10] 314 HC 1141 (June 24, 1998).

enforce Convention rights in proceedings against another individual, in what is known as a "horizontal" action remains an area of vibrant debate.

In some circumstances public authorities come under a duty to protect private individuals from breaches of the Convention by other private individuals, for instance, where a father beat his child in the privacy of his own home in violation of Article 3—"The Court considers that the obligation on the High Contracting Parties under Article 1 of the Convention to secure for everyone within their jurisdiction the rights and freedoms defined in the Convention, taken together with Article 3, requires States to take measures designed to ensure that individuals within their jurisdiction are not subjected to torture or inhuman or degrading treatment or punishment, including such ill-treatment administered by private individuals".[11]

Any country considering incorporation of any Human Rights Code should take the **A.1–11** advantage of freeing itself from the straight jacket imposed by some European models and ensuring that not only should the State and its emanations be compelled to respect human rights, but so should individuals *per se*.

The traditional conception of human rights limits them to the relationship between the individual and their government. They are seen as operating only in this sphere, and serving to limit collective or governmental power, to protect the individual against any potential abuse. This is why such rights are typically enshrined in national constitutions.

According to this traditional approach, human rights are limited to the relationship between the individual and their government and to speak of one private individual violating another's rights is wrong. If, for example, a private individual tortures another, the perpetrator is not necessarily an agent of the state,[12] although he may be a criminal. But the modern world requires a more flexible approach.

Considering the growing controversy of media invasions of privacy as cases of genocide and war crimes across international boundaries—there is a strong argument that a mature human rights code must be activated by the nature of violations and the consequent suffering of the victims rather than whether the perpetrators were a state or "public authority".

Much case law has developed in the sphere of asylum claims as to whether it is the state **A.1–12** or rebel forces which offer potential persecution if a refugee is returned to the receiving country. The effect upon the refugee will be the same regardless of whether the state flies the flag of its country when it inflicts the torture or if the abusive behaviour perpetrates from a rebel standard.

The Court of Human Rights has indicated that it considers that so-called "horizontal" violations can occur. In a case concerning corporal punishment in private schools,[13] the European Court held that although the defendant before the court was a state, the primary harm was caused by the actions of non-state persons or bodies. In each such case, the Court has found the State guilty of a violation because it failed to provide protection for one individual from another. For example, although it was a private group that intimidated a group of pro-life doctors in Austria to the point where they could not speak freely, the Austrian government was guilty of a violation of that right because of its failure to protect the doctor's freedom of speech.[14]

We can conclude that the court accepts the conceptual possibility that the actions of private individuals may violate rights. Furthermore, if a domestic court fails to deal with an individual's complaint, then the court may have violated their human rights.

---

[11] *A v. United Kingdom* (1998) 27 E.H.R.R. 611 at para. 22.
[12] But see note 11 above.
[13] *Young, James and Webster v. United Kingdom* (1981) 4 E.H.R.R. 38. See also *X & Y v. Netherlands* (1985) 8 E.H.R.R. 235 and Platform "Arzte fur das Leben", June 21, 1988, No. 139.
[14] Platform Arzte above.

A.1–13 This latter proposition is sound because Courts of Law are, according to Section 6(3) of the Human Rights Act 1998, part of the state. It is clear that a criminal court which convicts a defendant in breach of a Convention right does so unlawfully and therefore itself commits a violation.

It is unclear whether civil courts are similarly constrained within the confines of "the British model". For instance, will a civil court act unlawfully if it decides a case between private parties in a fashion which is irreconcilable with the Convention? It has been argued[15] that since a major element of the court's role as "public authorities" is to settle disputes between individuals, the British Acts horizontality arises as a matter of necessary implication.

American jurisprudence comes to our assistance on this latter point. *Shelley v. Kramer*,[16] a case which goes back to the 1940's, categorised all common law rules, irrespective of the identities of the parties contesting them, as part of the apparatus of government. Although *Shelley v. Kramer* only operates as a negative restraint on a court action by forcing it to withhold previously available remedies and not as a positive requirement to create new remedies, it does create a useful and compelling canvas upon which to fashion a code of human rights available to all humans regardless of whether they are part of the apparatus of state.

The Nepalese Model

A.1–14 It is not without a sense of excitement, flooded with trepidation, that a mature country considers afresh its obligations to a code of human rights and fundamental freedoms. Treaty-making in Nepal is, traditionally and constitutionally, an exclusive prerogative of the executive and as such, the Constitution contains no reference on this aspect. International conventions do not apply automatically in the national administration. If any obligation accepted under such instruments needs to be implemented, it is regulated through executive orders or by framing rules under the existing statute, or, if necessary, by enacting fresh legislation to this effect. The courts may accept an international treaty made with other governments as facts, but not as law.

The Constitution seeks to guarantee certain rights such as the right to equal protection of the law; rights against discrimination; rights to life and personal liberty; rights to some specific freedoms; protection against arbitrary arrest; unlawful persecution or unlawful punishment. Furthermore, the Constitution purports to lay down that any person or citizen whose rights have been infringed has a right to constitutional remedies, under which he can move the Supreme Court to have his rights protected and goes on to guarantee a number of basic human rights, including freedom of expression and freedom of religion.[17]

A.1–15 The promotion of human rights should never be at the expense of dismembering and disintegrating usable democracies, but many would argue that the best guarantee of state stability must be democracy, human rights and remedies for breaches within those states.*

---

[15] Wade HRW (2000) "Horizons of horizontality" L.Q.R. 217–224: Hunt, M. (1998) "The Horizontal Effect of the Human Act Rights" P. L. 423–443.

[16] (1948) 343 US 1.

[17] I am indebted to Dhruba Bar Singh Thapa's paper "The Legal System of Nepal"—Modern Legal Systems Cyclopedia.

* Delivered at the "Human Rights and the Rule of Law" Conference in Nepal, June 21, 2002.

PRIVATE GRIEF: PRIVACY, BREACH OF CONFIDENCE AND INTERCEPTION OF COMMUNICATIONS

A PAPER BY JOHN COOPER

The existence of a law of privacy has taken on almost biblical proportions over the last **A.1–16** year or so. Distinguished lawyers throughout the length and breadth of the country are being asked if they have seen, or are aware of, a law of privacy and in the face of accusations that they have flirted with a categoric right to protect personal liberty, they thrice deny their association

"Privacy—me? I've never met the fellow".

But there is no doubt that a right of privacy is being established in various key areas:

(a) Protecting children;

(b) "Kiss and tell" stories. In the keen balance which must be struck between the rights to a private life and freedom of expression, it is conceivable that revelations of fact will stop at the bedroom door. The publicity-seeking partner will be able to say that they had a relationship but not divulge the secrets of the bedroom;

(c) Illnesses. The media can talk about the facts of an illness but not about particular medical records.

The final approach to a law of privacy began last year when the domestic courts began to close in on the restrictive attitudes taken in *Kaye v. Robertson*[1] when in 1991 the Court of Appeal stated that there was no right to privacy and accordingly there was no right of action for breach of a person's privacy.

In recognising that in modern times the ability to invade a person's private life and to **A.1–17** violate that right has never been more potent. The domestic courts have finally decided to develop the common law to meet the demands of citizens in the 21st Century.
As Lord Justice Sedley said in *Douglas v. Hello!*[2]:

"We have reached a point at which it can be said with confidence that the law recognises and will appropriately protect a right of personal privacy".

But was that commendable statement a false dawn?
The facts of *Douglas v. Hello!* are familiar: photographic rights were sold to OK! Magazine of the marriage between Michael Douglas and Catherine Zeta-Jones which was of its nature a significant celebrity event. Hello! gate-crashed the event and took photographs of the nuptial celebrations. To begin with, their courses of action were somewhat optimistic, there were in malicious falsehood, interference with contractual relations, breach of confidence and infringement of copyright.

---

[1] [1991] F.S.R. 62 at 66.
[2] *Douglas, Zeta-Jones, Northern Shell PLC v. Hello! Limited* [2001] 2 W.L.R. 992.

A.1–18   It was breach of confidence which troubled the court and once again a ripple of excitement spread amongst the legal fraternity when the Court of Appeal acknowledged that the complainant's argument was more in terms of privacy than breach of confidence.[3]

In fact, Lord Justice Keene's concession was born of pragmatism. The identity of the photographer was uncertain. If it had been a guest or employee of the company working at the reception, an action in breach of confidence would have been maintained without any difficulty whatsoever; against the guest because the invitation to the wedding informed them that no photographs were to be taken and against the contractor's employees in that they also had knowledge of the extensive security arrangements. The defendants were aware of this aspect of the case and argued that Hello! had also had notice of the arrangements, so desperate it seems they were to avoid submitting to a new privacy regime.

This fear of the spectre of a new law of privacy is endemic amongst the media, although they need have no cause for concern given the way the domestic courts have developed the approach to this issue over the last few months.

The Court of Appeal in *Douglas v. Hello!*, possibly making a rod for its own back, acknowledged that the photographs could have been the work of an intruder with no relationship of trust or confidence.

Thus began a consideration of domestic common law, the Human Rights Act 1998 and Article 8 of the European Convention on Human Rights, the right to respect for family life.

The full text of Article 8 reads:

"Article 8—the right to respect the private and family life:

(1) Everyone has the right to respect for his private and family life, his home and his correspondence;
(2) There shall be no interference by a public authority with the exercise of this right except such as is in accordance with the law and is necessary in a democratic society in the interest of national security, public safety or the economic well being of the country, of the prevention of disorder or crime, for the protection of health or morals, or for the protection of the rights and freedoms of others".

A.1–19   Lord Justice Sedley recognised the increasing social need to allow people "some private space". But the question which resonates through this case and indeed subsequent cases is, does this recognition of a social need find its protection in a refined law relating to breach of confidence or a new law of privacy? Some say that the title is unimportant, what is vital is the protection of the right.

The right itself was first expressed in *Hellewell v. Chief Constable of Derbyshire.*[4] Mr Justice Laws stated:

"I entertain no doubt that disclosure of a photograph may, in some circumstances, be actionable as a breach of confidence. If someone with a telephoto lens were to take from a distance and with no authority a picture of another engaged in some private act, his subsequent disclosure of the photograph would, in my judgement, as surely amount to a breach of confidence as if he had found or stolen a letter or diary in which the act was recounted and proceeded to publish it. In such a case, the law would protect what might reasonably be called a right of privacy, although the name accorded to the course of action would be breach of confidence".

A.1–20   Just as the European Convention has been referred to as "a living instrument",[5] the same accolade can be given to domestic common law. The courts recognise that social

---

[3] See Lord Justice Keene at para. 164.
[4] [2001] 2 W.L.R. 804 at 807H.
[5] See *Tyrer v. United Kingdom* (1978) 2 E.H.R.R. 1.

attitudes change, attitudes to illegitimacy in 1970 have been accepted by the courts to have changed in the present day. Other examples of the law developing and growing within its community can be seen in its attitude towards corporal punishment and homosexuality.

The court in *Douglas v. Hello!* did make an attempt to distinguish a law relating to breach of confidence to a right of privacy, but this analysis does not rule out a developed breach of confidence law providing adequate protection.

Lord Justice Sedley said:

> "What a concept of privacy does, however, is accord a recognition to the fact that the law has to protect not only those people whose trust has been abused, but those who simply find themselves subject to an unwanted intrusion into their personal lives. The law no longer needs to construct an artificial relationship of confidentiality between intruder and victim: it can recognise privacy itself as a legal principle drawn from the fundamental value of personal autonomy".[6]

Indeed, in an apparent attempt to shore-up breach of confidence jurisprudence so that **A.1–21** it was robust enough to face modern times, Lord Justice Keene observed[7] that there exists persuasive dicta to the effect that a pre-existing confidential relationship between the parties is not required for a breach of confidence action. For instance, the nature of the subject matter or the circumstances of the breach and the defendant's activities may be sufficient in some instances to give rise to liability for a breach of confidence. This is considerably extending the historic ambit of this area of law.

The case of *Attorney General v. Guardian Newspapers (No. 2)*,[8] developed principles so as to establish whether an issue of confidentiality had been made out. The court articulated three points:

1. Confidentiality could not arise in respect of information which was generally accessible;

2. Confidentiality could not apply to useless or trivial information;

3. The public interest in confidentiality could be outweighed by some other counter-vailing public interest which favours disclosure requiring a balancing exercise between confidence and disclosure.

This third aspect was rejected in *Venables and Thompson v. Newsgroup Newspapers* **A.1–22** *and Associated Newspapers Limited*[9] in the light of Section 12[10] of the Human Rights Act 1998 and Article 10[11] which gives an enhanced protection to freedom of expression and the rights of the press to publish.[12]

THE REGULATION OF INVESTIGATORY POWERS ACT 2000

An analogous example of how Article 8 and the positive requirement upon States to **A.1–23** implement strictures of that right has caused domestic law to develop can be seen in the area of interception of communications and the planting of covert surveillance devices.

In *Halford v. United Kingdom*,[13] the European Court observed:

---

[6] At para. 126.
[7] At para. 166.
[8] [1990] 1 A.C. 109.
[9] [2001] 2 W.L.R. 1038.
[10] Freedom of Expression.
[11] Freedom of Expression.
[12] See para. 10.
[13] (1997) 24 E.H.R.R. 523.

" . . . telephone calls made from business premises as well as from the home may be covered by the notions of 'private life' and 'correspondence' within the meaning of Article 8(1)".[14]

If the interception of communications is to be justified under Article 8, certain minimum standards must be complied with:

1. A definition of the categories of people liable to have their telephones tapped;

2. The nature of the offences which may give rise to authorisation for telephone tapping;

3. A limit on the duration of telephone tapping;

4. A procedure for drawing up summaries of intercepted communications;

5. Precautions designed to ensure that the intercepted material remains intact for inspection by the trial judge and the defence; and

6. The circumstances in which intercepted communications should be erased, in particular, where an accused person is acquitted or the charges are dropped.

The 2000 Act enshrines the principles articulated in Article 8.

A.1–24   Part I of the Act is in two chapters. Chapter 1 deals with the interception of communications, an example of this would be tapping a telephone or opening a person's mail. Chapter 2 deals with the acquisition of communications data, an example of this is obtaining the details of a telephone subscriber or an itemised bill. Both activities infringe Article 8. The Act lays down a regime as to the obtaining of authorisation for surveillance, the likely effect of proceeding without such authorisation is that the policing activity will lack a legal basis and not be in accordance with Article 8 rights.

The criteria for authorisation is startlingly similar to the Article 8(2) criteria, in that an authorisation is necessary if it is:

(a) in the interests of national security;

(b) for the purpose of preventing or detecting crime or of preventing disorder;

(c) in the interests of the economic well being of the United Kingdom;

(d) in the interests of public safety;

(e) for the purpose of protecting public health;

(f) for the purpose of assessing or collecting any tax, duty, levy or other imposition, contribution or charge payable to a Government department; or

(g) for any purpose (not falling within paragraphs (a) to (f)) which is specified for the purposes of this sub-section by an order made by the Secretary of State.

These are pretty wide ranging.[15]

ARTICLE 8

A.1–26   The United Kingdom has an obligation to take action to protect Convention rights, and here, Article 8 rights. It has a duty to act positively.

---

[14] See para. 46.
[15] See s.28(3) for directed surveillance: s.29(3) for covert human intelligence.

But here lies another problem. Article 8 appears to be concerned only with interference with privacy by the State and not by private individuals or organisations (see the use of the words "public authority" in the Article).

Much academic debate has centred around whether the Human Rights Act 1998 has a so-called "horizontal" effect, making it possible to be enforced against individuals. Even before the present round of cases in this area, the European Court of Human Rights has made its position clear on whether such horizontal violations can occur—and it thinks that they can. Consider, for example, the 1988 case of *Plattform "Arzte fur das Leben"*[16] which concerned a private group that intimidated pro life doctors in Austria to the point where they could not speak freely. The European Court held that the Austrian Government was guilty of a violation of the right of free speech because of its failure to protect the doctors' freedom of speech.

There could of course be two readings of decisions of this nature. The first being that **A.1–27** the court accepts the conceptual possibility that actions of private parties may compromise a violation of rights and thus open the way to a horizontal interpretation of the Act, or a narrower interpretation that the individuals did not themselves violate the rights, but the Government did in failing to prevent or punish their actions.

This, too, will give effect to a horizontal interpretation of the Act. This is also in harmony in respect of the positive obligations of the State to remedy domestic law, for instance, regarding corporal punishment of children.[17]

In *Venables and Thompson*,[18] Dame Elizabeth Butler-Sloss held that the court was obliged as a public authority to apply Article 10 to the case before her but was at pains to point out that the Convention did not create a free-standing course of action between private individuals and that the court simply had a duty "to act compatibly with Convention rights in adjudicating upon existing common law courses of action, and that includes a positive as well as a negative obligation".[19]

One of the problems with an unencumbered horizontal approach is that of quality **A.1–28** control. There is a big difference between an uncontrolled paparazzo hounding a celebrity without just cause and a child suing her parents for invading her privacy. It would be for the court, in its discretion, to control a petty and litigious society from taking the law into areas where it has no place.

The law of confidence was further stretched to breaking point in *Venables and Thompson*, the case which we will recall concerned two children accused of murdering James Bulger who brought actions seeking a continuation of injunctions preventing the publication of information about them. Having regard to the three principles expressed in the *Guardian Newspapers (No. 2)*[20] case, the court acknowledged the law of breach of confidence as a living and organic instrument but applied the unseen and unacknowledged law of privacy. Her Ladyship observed:

"In my judgment, the court does have jurisdiction, in exceptional cases, to extend the protection of confidentiality of information, even to impose restrictions on the Press, where not to do so would be likely to lead to serious physical injury or to death, of the person seeking that confidentiality and there is no other way to protect the applicants other than by seeking relief from the court".

The courts continued to be reluctant to acknowledge a free-standing law of privacy and **A.1–29** seem more comfortable in bolstering or attempting to bolster the law of confidence.

---

[16] June 21, 1988, No. 139.
[17] See *A v. United Kingdom* (1998) 27 E.H.R.R. 61 at para. 21.
[18] (2000) 30 E.H.R.R. 121.
[19] See para. 4.
[20] (2000) 30 E.H.R.R. 121.

In a reversal of the old adage used of children, the law of privacy continues to be heard but not seen.

In *A v. B and C*,[21] the case concerning the footballer, Gary Flitcroft, the court dealt with a footballer attempting to restrain publication of his details on breach of confidence principles. Mr Justice Jack confirmed that the law of confidentiality should protect "facts concerning sexual relations within marriage . . . and in the context of modern sexual relations, it should be no different to relationships outside marriage".

But a distinction was made for celebrities.

A.1–30   The Court of Appeal laid down 15 guidelines in a breach of confidence context, which was enforced by the strictures of Article 8 and Article 10.

Lord Woolf C.J. side-steps the flirtatious advances of the law of privacy like a haughty Mr Darcy. He states:

"It is most unlikely that any purport will be served by a judge seeking to decide whether there exists a new course of action in tort which protects privacy.

In the great majority of situations, in no all situations, where the protection of privacy is justified, relating to events after the Human Rights Act came into force, an action for breach of confidence now will, where this is appropriate, provide the necessary protection. This means that at first instance it can be readily accepted that it is not necessary to tackle the vexed question of whether there is a separate course of action based upon a new tort involving the infringement of privacy".[22]

A.1–31   This echoes the approach of Lord Justice Keene who felt that a distinction between the law of confidence and a right to privacy was merely a matter of labels.[23]

The courts were emphasising the balancing exercise which needs to be conducted between a right to privacy and freedom of expression.

It seems to be established that a person's right to respect for his or her private life may be affected by the public interest in knowing about certain traits of his or her personality. In a recent speech, the Attorney General Lord Goldsmith, commented that freedom of speech was "the lifeblood of democracy . . . a break on the abuse of power".[24] He went on to say that "the media makes a positive contribution to justice by dissemination to the public the operation of the justice system".

A.1–32   The press mantra appears at Article 10 of the Convention. It reads:

"(1) Everyone has the right to freedom of expression. This right shall include freedom to hold opinions and to receive and impart information and ideas without interference by public authority and regardless of frontiers . . .

(2) The exercise of these freedoms, since it carries with it duties and responsibilities, may be subject to such formalities, conditions, restrictions or penalties as are prescribed by law and are necessary in a democratic society . . . for the protection of the reputation or rights of others . . . ".

A.1–33   John Underwood, the former ITN Home Affairs Correspondent, Director of Communications for the Labour Party and Managing Director of a leading PR company, said:

"Freedom of the press is like any other free gift—great to have but often badly treated by those who have acquired it all too easily".

---

[21] [2002] EWCA Civ 337.
[22] See para. 11(vi).
[23] At para. 166 of the Report (*Douglas v. Hello!*).
[24] Shandwicks. Media Lecture, February 2002.

It is perhaps with this sentiment in mind that the 12th guideline was drafted and I make no apology for reciting this guideline in its entirety as it presents the bedrock of the present state of law:

"Where an individual is a public figure, he is entitled to have his privacy respected in the appropriate circumstances. A public figure is entitled to a private life.

The individual, however, should recognise that because of his public position he must expect and accept that his actions will be more closely scrutinised by the media. Even trivial facts relating to a public figure can be of great interest to readers and other observers of the media. Conduct which in the case of a private individual would not be the appropriate subject of comment can be the proper subject of comment in the case of a public figure.

The public figure may hold a position where higher standards of conduct can be rightly expected by the public. The public figure may be a role model whose conduct could well be emulated by others. He may set the fashion. The higher the profile of the individual concerned the more likely that this will be the position. Whether you have courted publicity or not, you may be a legitimate subject of public attention.

If you have courted public attention then you have less ground to object to the intrusion which follows. In many of these cases it would be overstating the position to say that there is a public interest in the information being published.

It would be more accurate to say that the public had an understandable and so a legitimate interest in being told the information. If this is the situation then it can be appropriate taken into account by a court when deciding on which side of the line a case falls. The courts must not ignore the fact that if newspapers do not publish information which the public are interested in, there will be fewer newspapers published which will not be in the public interest".[25]

From footballers to models, in a brace of cases involving the supermodel Naomi **A.1–34** Campbell. In *Campbell v. Frisbee*,[26] the court considered the duty of confidentiality owed by someone who was engaged under a contract to Miss Campbell. Again, the court evoked the balancing exercise:

"Whether the public interest is such as it overrides an obligation of confidence depends upon the facts of the particular case".

The court observed that various matters should be taken into consideration:

1. Consider the status of the public figure;

2. Consider the respect in which the photograph was false;

3. Consider the nature of the correction and the means taken to effect the correction;

Two other matters should be taken into account:

1. The nature of the confidentiality owed. The relationship between the parties owing and owed to the duty of confidentiality is vital;

2. Where a close confidential relationship exists, the contractually assumed duty of confidentiality, though not sacrosanct, must be given full and serious regard and not be lightly overridden.[27]

---

[25] See Lord Woolf at para. 11(xii).
[26] [2002] EWCA Civ 1374.
[27] See para. 32.

In the second of Miss Campbell's cases, the court considered the publication of details and photographs of the model leaving a meeting of Narcotics Anonymous. She was granted damages for breach of confidence (and breach of the Data Protection Act 1998). But still, a law of privacy, was not acknowledged, but the court recognised that even celebrities are "entitled to some space or privacy".

A.1–35 Mr Justice Morland in *Campbell v. MGN Limited* stated that to succeed in a claim for breach of confidence the claimant had to establish three matters:

1. That the details given by the publication complained of had the necessary quality of confidence about them;

2. That those details must be imparted in circumstances importing an obligation of confidence;

3. And that the publication of those details must be to the claimant's detriment.

This highlights the fact that there is now no need for a relationship of confidence between the giver and receiver of information, a claim can now succeed where the receiver of the information "either knows or ought to know" that the giver can reasonably expect his privacy to be protected.

The details of those medical records were a step too far.

But why are the courts so reluctant to embrace a law of privacy. Perhaps the key to this can be seen in the observations of Lord Justice Buxton in *Home Office v. Wainwright*[28]:

"I have no doubt that in being invited to recognise the existence of a tort of breach of privacy, we are indeed being invited to make the law, and not merely to apply it.

Diffidence in the face of such an invitation is not, in my view, an abdication of our responsibility, but rather a recognition that, in areas involving extremely contested and strongly conflicting social interests, the Judges are extremely ill-equipped to undertake the detailed investigations necessary before the proper shape of the law can be decided".

A.1–36 The judiciary are helpfully and imaginatively giving, as Mr Justice Morland put it in *Campbell v. MGN*, "a new strength and breadth" to the law of confidence. But the reality is that a law of privacy exists in all but name, the challenge for tomorrow, if not today, is to recognise its existence.*

---

[28] [1993] Q.B. 727; decided before *A v. B and C*: at para. 112.
* Delivered at the Law Society, Chancery Lane London, September 2002.

LIST OF AUTHORITIES REFERRED TO IN PAPER

Kaye v. Robertson [1991] F.S.R. 62 **A.1–37**

Douglas, Zeta-Jones and Northern Shell plc v. Hello! Limited [2001] 2 W.L.R. 992

Hellewell v. Chief Constable of Derbyshire [1995] 1 W.L.R. 804

Tyrer v. United Kingdom (1978) 2 E.H.R.R. 1

Attorney General v. Guardian Newspapers (No. 2) 1 A.C. 109

Venables and Thompson v. Newsgroup Newspapers and Associates Newspapers Limited [2001] 2 W.L.R. 1038

Plattform "Artze fur das Leben" (1991) 13 E.H.R.R. 204

A v. United Kingdom (1998) 27 E.H.R.R. 61

A v. B and C [2002] EWCA Civ 337

Campbell v. Frisbee EWHC 328 (Ch)

Campbell v. MGN Limited

Home Office v. Wainwright [1993] Q.B. 727

Halford v. United Kingdom (1997) 24 E.H.R.R. 523

Has there been a failure to properly investigate allegations in breach of Article 3

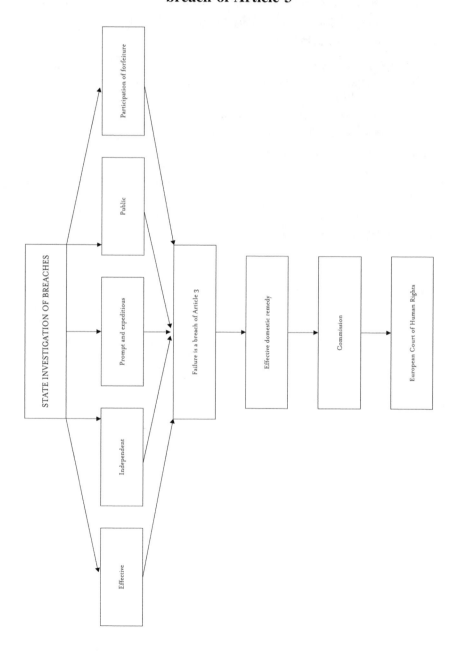

Are the conditions in which a detainee is held in breach of Article 3?

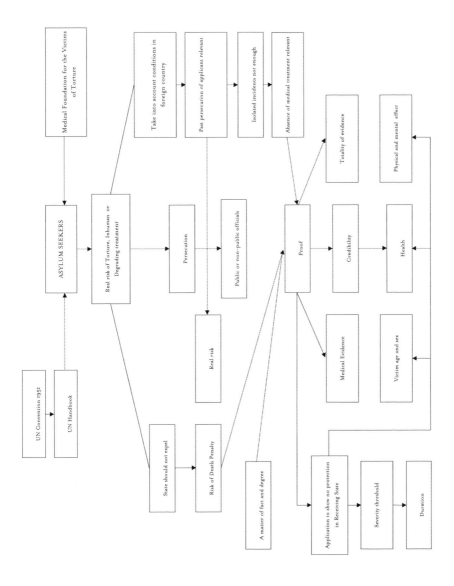

Have the state failed to take appropriate steps to protect in breach of Article 3?

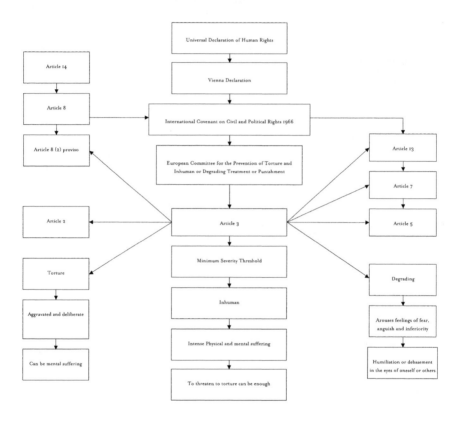

Is the deprivation of a right to reside in a state in breach of Article 3?

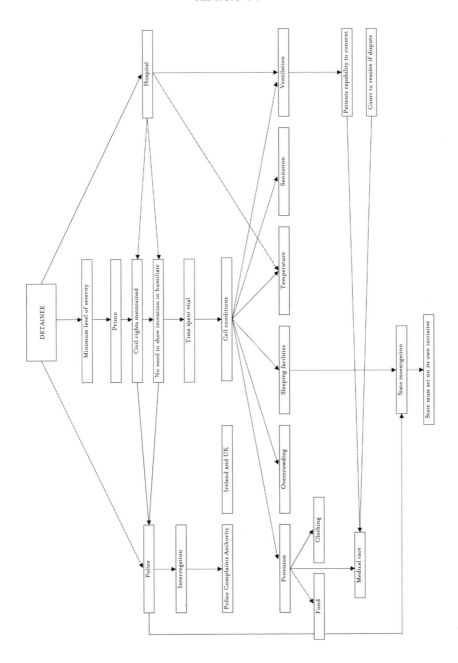

How to prove a breach and its relationship with other convention rights.

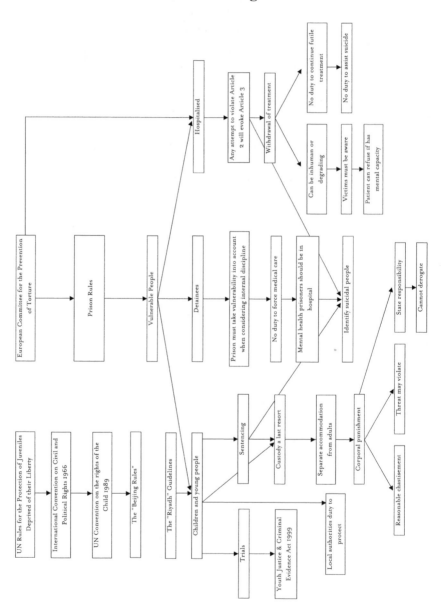

Human Rights Act 1998

Chapter 42

Arrangement of Sections

Introduction

Section   A.2–01

Legislation

Public Authorities

Remedial Action

Other Rights and Proceedings

Human Rights Act 1998

1998 CHAPTER 42

A.2–02   An Act to give further effect to rights and freedoms guaranteed under the European Convention on Human Rights; to make provision with respect to holders of certain judicial offices who become judges of the European Court of Human Rights; and for connected purposes. [9th November 1998]

BE IT ENACTED by the Queen's most Excellent Majesty, by and with the advice and consent of the Lords Spiritual and Temporal, and Commons, in this present Parliament assembled, and by the authority of the same, as follows:

INTRODUCTION

The Convention rights

1.—(1) In this Act "the Convention rights" means the rights and fundamental free- **A.2–03** doms set out in—

(a) Articles 2 to 12 and 14 of the Convention,

(b) Articles 1 to 3 of the First Protocol, and

(c) Articles 1 and 2 of the Sixth Protocol,

as read with Articles 16 to 18 of the Convention.

(2) Those Articles are to have effect for the purposes of this Act subject to any designated derogation or reservation (as to which see sections 14 and 15).

(3) The Articles are set out in Schedule 1.

(4) The Secretary of State may by order make such amendments to this Act as he considers appropriate to reflect the effect, in relation to the United Kingdom, of a protocol.

(5) In subsection (4) "protocol" means a protocol to the Convention—

(a) which the United Kingdom has ratified; or

(b) which the United Kingdom has signed with a view to ratification.

(6) No amendment may be made by an order under subsection (4) so as to come into force before the protocol concerned is in force in relation to the United Kingdom.

Interpretation of Convention rights

2.—(1) A court or tribunal determining a question which has arisen in connection with **A.2–04** a Convention right must take into account any—

(a) judgment, decision, declaration or advisory opinion of the European Court of Human Rights,

(b) opinion of the Commission given in a report adopted under Article 31 of the Convention,

(c) decision of the Commission in connection with Article 26 or 27(2) of the Convention, or

(d) decision of the Committee of Ministers taken under Article 46 of the Convention,

whenever made or given, so far as, in the opinion of the court or tribunal, it is relevant to the proceedings in which that question has arisen.

(2) Evidence of any judgment, decision, declaration or opinion of which account may have to be taken under this section is to be given in proceedings before any court or tribunal in such manner as may be provided by rules.

(3) In this section "rules" means rules of court or, in the case of proceedings before a tribunal, rules made for the purposes of this section—

(a) by the Lord Chancellor or the Secretary of State, in relation to any proceedings outside Scotland;

(b) by the Secretary of State, in relation to proceedings in Scotland; or

(c) by a Northern Ireland department, in relation to proceedings before a tribunal in Northern Ireland—

    (i) which deals with transferred matters; and
    (ii) for which no rules made under paragraph (a) are in force.

LEGISLATION

Intepretation of legislation

A.2–05   3.—(1) So far as it is possible to do so, primary legislation and subordinate legislation must be read and given effect in a way which is compatible with the Convention rights.

(2) This section—

(a) applies to primary legislation and subordinate legislation whenever enacted;

(b) does not affect the validity, continuing operation or enforcement of any incompatible primary legislation; and

(c) does not affect the validity, continuing operation or enforcement of any incompatible subordinate legislation if (disregarding any possibility of revocation) primary legislation prevents removal of the incompatibility.

Declaration of incompatibility

A.2–06   4.—(1) Subsection (2) applies in any proceedings in which a court determines whether a provision of primary legislation is compatible with a Convention right.

(2) If the court is satisfied that the provision is incompatible with a Convention right, it may make a declaration of that incompatibility.

(3) Subsection (4) applies in any proceedings in which a court determines whether a provision of subordinate legislation, made in the exercise of a power conferred by primary legislation, is compatible with a Convention right.

(4) If the court is satisfied—

(a) that the provision is incompatible with a Convention right, and

(b) that (disregarding any possibility of revocation) the primary legislation concerned prevents removal of the incompatibility,

it may make a declaration of that incompatibility.

(5) In this section "court" means—

(a) the House of Lords;

(b) he Judicial Committee of the Privy Council;

(c) the Courts-Martial Appeal Court;

(d) in Scotland, the High Court of Justiciary sitting otherwise than as a trial court or the Court of Session;

(e) in England and Wales or Northern Ireland, the High Court or the Court of Appeal.

(6) A declaration under this section ("a declaration of incompatibility")—

(a) does not affect the validity, continuing operation or enforcement of the provision in respect of which it is given; and

(b) is not binding on the parties to the proceedings in which it is made.

Right of Crown to intervene

5.—(1) Where a court is considering whether to make a declaration of incompatibility, **A.2–07** the Crown is entitled to notice in accordance with rules of court.

(2) In any case to which subsection (1) applies—

(a) a Minister of the Crown (or a person nominated by him),

(b) a member of the Scottish Executive,

(c) a Northern Ireland Minister,

(d) a Northern Ireland department,

is entitled, on giving notice in accordance with rules of court, to be joined as a party to the proceedings.

(3) Notice under subsection (2) may be given at any time during the proceedings.

(4) A person who has been made a party to criminal proceedings (other than in Scotland) as the result of a notice under subsection (2) may, with leave, appeal to the House of Lords against any declaration of incompatibility made in the proceedings.

(5) In subsection (4)—

"criminal proceedings" includes all proceedings before the Courts-Martial Appeal Court; and

"leave" means leave granted by the court making the declaration of incompatibility or by the House of Lords.

PUBLIC AUTHORITIES

Acts of public authorities

6.—(1) It is unlawful for a public authority to act in a way which is incompatible with **A.2–08** a Convention right.

(2) Subsection (1) does not apply to an act if—

(a) as the result of one or more provisions of primary legislation, the authority could not have acted differently; or

(b) in the case of one or more provisions of, or made under, primary legislation which cannot be read or given effect in a way which is compatible with the Convention rights, the authority was acting so as to give effect to or enforce those provisions.

(3) In this section "public authority" includes—

(a) a court or tribunal, and

(b) any person certain of whose functions are functions of a public nature,

but does not include either House of Parliament or a person exercising functions in connection with proceedings in Parliament.

(4) In subsection (3) "Parliament" does not include the House of Lords in its judicial capacity.

(5) In relation to a particular act, a person is not a public authority by virtue only of subsection (3)(b) if the nature of the act is private.

(6) "An act" includes a failure to act but does not include a failure to—

(a) introduce in, or lay before, Parliament a proposal for legislation; or

(b) make any primary legislation or remedial order.

Proceedings

A.2–09   7.—(1) A person who claims that a public authority has acted (or proposes to act) in a way which is made unlawful by section 6(1) may—

(a) bring proceedings against the authority under this Act in the appropriate court or tribunal, or

(b) rely on the Convention right or rights concerned in any legal proceedings,

but only if he is (or would be) a victim of the unlawful act.

(2) In subsection (1)(a) "appropriate court or tribunal" means such court or tribunal as may be determined in accordance with rules; and proceedings against an authority include a counterclaim or similar proceeding.

(3) If the proceedings are brought on an application for judicial review, the applicant is to be taken to have a sufficient interest in relation to the unlawful act only if he is, or would be, a victim of that act.

(4) If the proceedings are made by way of a petition for judicial review in Scotland, the applicant shall be taken to have title and interest to sue in relation to the unlawful act only if he is, or would be, a victim of that act.

(5) Proceedings under subsection (1)(a) must be brought before the end of—

(a) the period of one year beginning with the date on which the act complained of took place; or

(b) such longer period as the court or tribunal considers equitable having regard to all the circumstances,

but that is subject to any rule imposing a stricter time limit in relation to the procedure in question.

(6) In subsection (1)(b) "legal proceedings" includes—

(a) proceedings brought by or at the instigation of a public authority; and

(b) an appeal against the decision of a court or tribunal.

(7) For the purposes of this section, a person is a victim of an unlawful act only if he would be a victim for the purposes of Article 34 of the Convention if proceedings were brought in the European Court of Human Rights in respect of that act.

(8) Nothing in this Act creates a criminal offence.

(9) In this section "rules" means—

(a) in relation to proceedings before a court or tribunal outside Scotland, rules made by the Lord Chancellor or the Secretary of State for the purposes of this section or rules of court,

(b) in relation to proceedings before a court or tribunal in Scotland, rules made by the Secretary of State for those purposes,

(c) in relation to proceedings before a tribunal in Northern Ireland—

    (i) which deals with transferred matters; and
    (ii) for which no rules made under paragraph (a) are in force,

rules made by a Northern Ireland department for those purposes,

and includes provision made by order under section 1 of the Courts and Legal Services Act 1990.

(10) In making rules, regard must be had to section 9.

(11) The Minister who has power to make rules in relation to a particular tribunal may, to the extent he considers it necessary to ensure that the tribunal can provide an appropriate remedy in relation to an act (or proposed act) of a public authority which is (or would be) unlawful as a result of section 6(1), by order add to—

(a) the relief or remedies which the tribunal may grant; or

(b) the grounds on which it may grant any of them.

(12) An order made under subsection (11) may contain such incidental, supplemental, consequential or transitional provision as the Minister making it considers appropriate.

(13) "The Minister" includes the Northern Ireland department concerned.

Judicial remedies

8.—(1) In relation to any act (or proposed act) of a public authority which the court   **A.2–10** finds is (or would be) unlawful, it may grant such relief or remedy, or make such order, within its powers as it considers just and appropriate.

(2) But damages may be awarded only by a court which has power to award damages, or to order the payment of compensation, in civil proceedings.

(3) No award of damages is to be made unless, taking account of all the circumstances of the case, including—

(a) any other relief or remedy granted, or order made, in relation to the act in question (by that or any other court), and

(b) the consequences of any decision (of that or any other court) in respect of that act,

the court is satisfied that the award is necessary to afford just satisfaction to the person in whose favour it is made.

(4) In determining—

(a) whether to award damages; or

(b) the amount of an award,

the court must take into account the principles applied by the European Court of Human Rights in relation to the award of compensation under Article 41 of the Convention.

(5) A public authority against which damages are awarded is to be treated—

(a) in Scotland, for the purposes of section 3 of the Law Reform (Miscellaneous Provisions) (Scotland) Act 1940 as if the award were made in an action of damages in which the authority has been found liable in respect of loss or damage to the person to whom the award is made;

(b) for the purposes of the Civil Liability (Contribution) Act 1978 as liable in respect of damage suffered by the person to whom the award is made.

(6) In this section—

"court" includes a tribunal;

"damages" means damages for an unlawful act of a public authority; and

"unlawful" means unlawful under section 6(1).

Judicial acts

A.2–11   9.—(1) Proceedings under section 7(1)(a) in respect of a judicial act may be brought only—

(a) by exercising a right of appeal;

(b) on an application (in Scotland a petition) for judicial review; or

(c) in such other forum as may be prescribed by rules.

(2) That does not affect any rule of law which prevents a court from being the subject of judicial review.

(3) In proceedings under this Act in respect of a judicial act done in good faith, damages may not be awarded otherwise than to compensate a person to the extent required by Article 5(5) of the Convention.

(4) An award of damages permitted by subsection (3) is to be made against the Crown; but no award may be made unless the appropriate person, if not a party to the proceedings, is joined.

(5) In this section—

"appropriate person" means the Minister responsible for the court concerned, or a person or government department nominated by him;

"court" includes a tribunal;

"judge" includes a member of a tribunal, a justice of the peace and a clerk or other officer entitled to exercise the jurisdiction of a court;

"judicial act" means a judicial act of a court and includes an act done on the instructions, or on behalf, of a judge; and

"rules" has the same meaning as in section 7(9).

REMEDIAL ACTION

Power to take remedial action

A.2–12   10.—(1) This section applies if—

(a) a provision of legislation has been declared under section 4 to be incompatible with a Convention right and, if an appeal lies—

    (i) all persons who may appeal have stated in writing that they do not intend to do so;

    (ii) the time for bringing an appeal has expired and no appeal has been brought within that time; or

    (iii) an appeal brought within that time has been determined or abandoned; or

(b) it appears to a Minister of the Crown or Her Majesty in Council that, having regard to a finding of the European Court of Human Rights made after the coming into force of this section in proceedings against the United Kingdom, a provision of legislation is incompatible with an obligation of the United Kingdom arising from the Convention.

(2) If a Minister of the Crown considers that there are compelling reasons for proceeding under this section, he may by order make such amendments to the legislation as he considers necessary to remove the incompatibility.

(3) If, in the case of subordinate legislation, a Minister of the Crown considers—

(a) that it is necessary to amend the primary legislation under which the subordinate legislation in question was made, in order to enable the incompatibility to be removed, and

(b) that there are compelling reasons for proceeding under this section,

he may by order make such amendments to the primary legislation as he considers necessary.

(4) This section also applies where the provision in question is in subordinate legislation and has been quashed, or declared invalid, by reason of incompatibility with a Convention right and the Minister proposes to proceed under paragraph 2(b) of Schedule 2.

(5) If the legislation is an Order in Council, the power conferred by subsection (2) or (3) is exercisable by Her Majesty in Council.

(6) In this section "legislation" does not include a Measure of the Church Assembly or of the General Synod of the Church of England.

(7) Schedule 2 makes further provision about remedial orders.

OTHER RIGHTS AND PROCEEDINGS

Safeguard for existing human rights

11. A person's reliance on a Convention right does not restrict—   **A.2–13**

(a) any other right or freedom conferred on him by or under any law having effect in any part of the United Kingdom; or

(b) his right to make any claim or bring any proceedings which he could make or bring apart from sections 7 to 9.

Freedom of expression

12.—(1) This section applies if a court is considering whether to grant any relief which, **A.2–14** if granted, might affect the exercise of the Convention right to freedom of expression.

(2) If the person against whom the application for relief is made ("the respondent") is neither present nor represented, no such relief is to be granted unless the court is satisfied—

(a) that the applicant has taken all practicable steps to notify the respondent; or

(b) that there are compelling reasons why the respondent should not be notified.

(3) No such relief is to be granted so as to restrain publication before trial unless the court is satisfied that the applicant is likely to establish that publication should not be allowed.

(4) The court must have particular regard to the importance of the Convention right to freedom of expression and, where the proceedings relate to material which the respondent claims, or which appears to the court, to be journalistic, literary or artistic material (or to conduct connected with such material), to—

(a) the extent to which—

    (i) the material has, or is about to, become available to the public; or
    (ii) it is, or would be, in the public interest for the material to be published;

(b) any relevant privacy code.

(5) In this section—

"court" includes a tribunal; and

"relief" includes any remedy or order (other than in criminal proceedings).

Freedom of thought, conscience and religion

A.2–15   13.—(1) If a court's determination of any question arising under this Act might affect the exercise by a religious organisation (itself or its members collectively) of the Convention right to freedom of thought, conscience and religion, it must have particular regard to the importance of that right.

(2) In this section "court" includes a tribunal.

DEROGATIONS AND RESERVATIONS

Derogations

A.2–16   14.—(1) In this Act "designated derogation" means—

(a) the United Kingdom's derogation from Article 5(3) of the Convention; and

(b) any derogation by the United Kingdom from an Article of the Convention, or of any protocol to the Convention, which is designated for the purposes of this Act in an order made by the Secretary of State.

(2) The derogation referred to in subsection (1)(a) is set out in Part I of Schedule 3.

(3) If a designated derogation is amended or replaced it ceases to be a designated derogation.

(4) But subsection (3) does not prevent the Secretary of State from exercising his power under subsection (1)(b) to make a fresh designation order in respect of the Article concerned.

(5) The Secretary of State must by order make such amendments to Schedule 3 as he considers appropriate to reflect—

(a) any designation order; or

(b) the effect of subsection (3).

(6) A designation order may be made in anticipation of the making by the United Kingdom of a proposed derogation.

Reservations

15.—(1) In this Act "designated reservation" means—   **A.2–17**

(a) the United Kingdom's reservation to Article 2 of the First Protocol to the Convention; and

(b) any other reservation by the United Kingdom to an Article of the Convention, or of any protocol to the Convention, which is designated for the purposes of this Act in an order made by the Secretary of State.

(2) The text of the reservation referred to in subsection (1)(a) is set out in Part II of Schedule 3.

(3) If a designated reservation is withdrawn wholly or in part it ceases to be a designated reservation.

(4) But subsection (3) does not prevent the Secretary of State from exercising his power under subsection (1)(b) to make a fresh designation order in respect of the Article concerned.

(5) The Secretary of State must by order make such amendments to this Act as he considers appropriate to reflect—

(a) any designation order; or

(b) the effect of subsection (3).

Period for which designated derogations have effect

16.—(1) If it has not already been withdrawn by the United Kingdom, a designated   **A.2–18** derogation ceases to have effect for the purposes of this Act—

(a) in the case of the derogation referred to in section 14(1)(a), at the end of the period of five years beginning with the date on which section 1(2) came into force;

(b) in the case of any other derogation, at the end of the period of five years beginning with the date on which the order designating it was made.

(2) At any time before the period—

(a) fixed by subsection (1)(a) or (b), or

(b) extended by an order under this subsection,

comes to an end, the Secretary of State may by order extend it by a further period of five years.

(3) An order under section 14(1)(b) ceases to have effect at the end of the period for consideration, unless a resolution has been passed by each House approving the order.

(4) Subsection (3) does not affect—

(a) anything done in reliance on the order; or

(b) the power to make a fresh order under section 14(1)(b).

(5) In subsection (3) "period for consideration" means the period of forty days beginning with the day on which the order was made.

(6) In calculating the period for consideration, no account is to be taken of any time during which—

(a) Parliament is dissolved or prorogued; or

(b) both Houses are adjourned for more than four days.

(7) If a designated derogation is withdrawn by the United Kingdom, the Secretary of State must by order make such amendments to this Act as he considers are required to reflect that withdrawal.

Periodic review of designated reservations

A.2–19   17.—(1) The appropriate Minister must review the designated reservation referred to in section 15(1)(a)—

(a) before the end of the period of five years beginning with the date on which section 1(2) came into force; and

(b) if that designation is still in force, before the end of the period of five years beginning with the date on which the last report relating to it was laid under subsection (3).

(2) The appropriate Minister must review each of the other designated reservations (if any)—

(a) before the end of the period of five years beginning with the date on which the order designating the reservation first came into force; and

(b) if the designation is still in force, before the end of the period of five years beginning with the date on which the last report relating to it was laid under subsection (3).

(3) The Minister conducting a review under this section must prepare a report on the result of the review and lay a copy of it before each House of Parliament.

JUDGES OF THE EUROPEAN COURT OF HUMAN RIGHTS

Appointment to European Court of Human Rights

A.2–20   18.—(1) In this section "judicial office" means the office of—

(a) the Lord Justice of Appeal, Justice of the High Court or Circuit judge, in England and Wales;

(b) a judge of the Court of Session or sheriff, in Scotland;

(c) the Lord Justice of Appeal, judge of the High Court or county court judge, in Northern Ireland.

(2) The holder of a judicial office may become a judge of the European Court of Human Rights ("the Court") without being required to relinquish his office.

(3) But he is not required to perform the duties of his judicial office while he is a judge of the Court.

(4) In respect of any period during which he is a judge of the Court—

(a) a Lord Justice of Appeal or Justice of the High Court is not to count as a judge of the relevant court for the purposes of section 2(1) or 4(1) of the Supreme Court Act

1981 (maximum number of judges) nor as a judge of the Supreme Court for the purposes of section 12(1) to (6) of that Act (salaries etc.);

(b) a judge of the Court of Session is not to count as a judge of that court for the purposes of section 1(1) of the Court of Session Act 1988 (maximum number of judges) or of section 9(1)(c) of the Administration of Justice Act 1973 ("the 1973 Act") (salaries etc.);

(c) a Lord Justice of Appeal or judge of the High Court in Northern Ireland is not to count as a judge of the relevant court for the purposes of section 2(1) or 3(1) of the Judicature (Northern Ireland) Act 1978 (maximum number of judges) nor as a judge of the Supreme Court of Northern Ireland for the purposes of section 9(1)(d) of the 1973 Act (salaries etc.);

(d) a Circuit judge is not to count as such for the purposes of section 18 of the Courts Act 1971 (salaries etc.);

(e) a sheriff is not to count as such for the purposes of section 14 of the Sheriff Courts (Scotland) Act 1907 (salaries etc.);

(f) a county court judge of Northern Ireland is not to count as such for the purposes of section 106 of the County Courts Act (Northern Ireland) 1959 (salaries etc.).

(5) If a sheriff principal is appointed a judge of the Court, section 11(1) of the Sheriff Courts (Scotland) Act 1971 (temporary appointment of sheriff principal) applies, while he holds that appointment, as if his office is vacant.

(6) Schedule 4 makes provision about judicial pensions in relation to the holder of a judicial office who serves as a judge of the Court.

(7) The Lord Chancellor or the Secretary of State may by order make such transitional provision (including, in particular, provision for a temporary increase in the maximum number of judges) as he considers appropriate in relation to any holder of a judicial office who has completed his service as a judge of the Court.

PARLIAMENTARY PROCEDURE

Statements of compatibility

19.—(1) A Minister of the Crown in charge of a Bill in either House of Parliament   **A.2–21**
must, before Second Reading of the Bill—

(a) make a statement to the effect that in his view the provisions of the Bill are compatible with the Convention rights ("a statement of compatibility"); or

(b) make a statement to the effect that although he is unable to make a statement of compatibility the government nevertheless wishes the House to proceed with the Bill.

(2) The statement must be in writing and be published in such manner as the Minister making it considers appropriate.

SUPPLEMENTAL

Orders etc. under this Act

20.—(1) Any power of a Minister of the Crown to make an order under this Act is   **A.2–22**
exercisable by statutory instrument.

(2) The power of the Lord Chancellor or the Secretary of State to make rules (other than rules of court) under section 2(3) or 7(9) is exercisable by statutory instrument.

(3) Any statutory instrument made under section 14, 15 or 16(7) must be laid before Parliament.

(4) No order may be made by the Lord Chancellor or the Secretary of State under section 1(4), 7(11) or 16(2) unless a draft of the order has been laid before, and approved by, each House of Parliament.

(5) Any statutory instrument made under section 18(7) or Schedule 4, or to which subsection (2) applies, shall be subject to annulment in pursuance of a resolution of either House of Parliament.

(6) The power of a Northern Ireland department to make—

(a) rules under section 2(3)(c) or 7(9)(c), or

(b) an order under section 7(11),

is exercisable by statutory rule for the purposes of the Statutory Rules (Northern Ireland) Order 1979.

(7) Any rules made under section 2(3)(c) or 7(9)(c) shall be subject to negative resolution; and section 41(6) of the Interpretation Act (Northern Ireland) 1954 (meaning of "subject to negative resolution") shall apply as if the power to make the rules were conferred by an Act of the Northern Ireland Assembly.

(8) No order may be made by a Northern Ireland department under section 7(11) unless a draft of the order has been laid before, and approved by, the Northern Ireland Assembly.

INTERPRETATION, ETC.

A.2–23   21.—(1) In this Act—

"amend" includes repeal and apply (with or without modifications);

"the appropriate Minister" means the Minister of the Crown having charge of the appropriate authorised government department (within the meaning of the Crown Proceedings Act 1947);

"the Commission" means the European Commission of Human Rights;

"the Convention" means the Convention for the Protection of Human Rights and Fundamental Freedoms, agreed by the Council of Europe at Rome on 4th November 1950 as it has effect for the time being in relation to the United Kingdom;

"declaration of incompatibility" means a declaration under section 4;

"Minister of the Crown" has the same meaning as in the Ministers of the Crown Act 1975;

"Northern Ireland Minister" includes the First Minister and the deputy First Minister in Northern Ireland;

"primary legislation" means any—

(a) public general Act;

(b) local and personal Act;

(c) private Act;

(d) Measure of the Church Assembly;

(e) Measure of the General Synod of the Church of England;

(f) Order in Council—

    (i) made in exercise of Her Majesty's Royal Prerogative;

    (ii) made under section 38(1)(a) of the Northern Ireland Constitution Act 1973 or the corresponding provision of the Northern Ireland Act 1998; or

    (iii) amending an Act of a kind mentioned in paragraph (a), (b) or (c);

and includes an order or other instrument made under primary legislation (otherwise than by the National Assembly for Wales, a member of the Scottish Executive, a Northern Ireland Minister or a Northern Ireland department) to the extent to which it operates to bring one or more provisions of that legislation into force or amends any primary legislation;

"the First Protocol" means the protocol to the Convention agreed at Paris on 20th March 1952;

"the Sixth Protocol" means the protocol to the Convention agreed at Strasbourg on 28th April 1983;

"the Eleventh Protocol" means the protocol to the Convention (restructuring the control machinery established by the Convention) agreed at Strasbourg on 11th May 1994;

"remedial order" means an order under section 10;

"subordinate legislation" means any—

(a) Order in Council other than one—

    (i) made in exercise of Her Majesty's Royal Prerogative;

    (ii) made under section 38(1)(a) of the Northern Ireland Constitution Act 1973 or the corresponding provision of the Northern Ireland Act 1998; or

    (iii) amending an Act of a kind mentioned in the definition of primary legislation;

(b) Act of the Scottish Parliament;

(c) Act of the Parliament of Northern Ireland;

(d) Measure of the Assembly established under section 1 of the Northern Ireland Assembly Act 1973;

(e) Act of the Northern Ireland Assembly;

(f) order, rules, regulations, scheme, warrant, byelaw or other instrument made under primary legislation (except to the extent to which it operates to bring one or more provisions of that legislation into force or amends any primary legislation);

(g) order, rules, regulations, scheme, warrant, byelaw or other instrument made under legislation mentioned in paragraph (b), (c), (d) or (e) or made under an Order in Council applying only to Northern Ireland;

(h) order, rules, regulations, scheme, warrant, byelaw or other instrument made by a member of the Scottish Executive, a Northern Ireland Minister or a Northern Ireland department in exercise of prerogative or other executive functions of Her Majesty which are exercisable by such a person on behalf of Her Majesty;

"transferred matters" has the same meaning as in the Northern Ireland Act 1998; and

"tribunal" means any tribunal in which legal proceedings may be brought.

(2) The references in paragraphs (b) and (c) of section 2(1) to Articles are to Articles of the Convention as they had effect immediately before the coming into force of the Eleventh Protocol.

(3) The reference in paragraph (d) of section 2(1) to Article 46 includes a reference to Articles 32 and 54 of the Convention as they had effect immediately before the coming into force of the Eleventh Protocol.

(4) The references in section 2(1) to a report or decision of the Commission or a decision of the Committee of Ministers include references to a report or decision made as provided by paragraphs 3, 4 and 6 of Article 5 of the Eleventh Protocol (transitional provisions).

(5) Any liability under the Army Act 1955, the Air Force Act 1955 or the Naval Discipline Act 1957 to suffer death for an offence is replaced by a liability to imprisonment for life or any less punishment authorised by those Acts; and those Acts shall accordingly have effect with the necessary modifications.

Short title, commencement, application and extent

A.2–24   22.—(1) This Act may be cited as the Human Rights Act 1998.

(2) Sections 18, 20 and 21(5) and this section come into force on the passing of this Act.

(3) The other provisions of this Act come into force on such day as the Secretary of State may by order appoint; and different days may be appointed for different purposes.

(4) Paragraph (b) of subsection (1) of section 7 applies to proceedings brought by or at the instigation of a public authority whenever the act in question took place; but otherwise that subsection does not apply to an act taking place before the coming into force of that section.

(5) This Act binds the Crown.

(6) This Act extends to Northern Ireland.

(7) Section 21(5), so far as it relates to any provision contained in the Army Act 1955, the Air Force Act 1955 or the Naval Discipline Act 1957, extends to any place to which that provision extends.

SCHEDULES

Schedule 1

The Articles

PART I

THE CONVENTION

Rights and freedoms

Article 2

Right to life

1. Everyone's right to life shall be protected by law. No one shall be deprived of his life   **A.2–25** intentionally save in the execution of a sentence of a court following his conviction of a crime for which this penalty is provided by law.

2. Deprivation of life shall not be regarded as inflicted in contravention of this Article when it results from the use of force which is no more than absolutely necessary:

(a) in defence of any person from unlawful violence;

(b) in order to effect a lawful arrest or to prevent the escape of a person lawfully detained;

(c) in action lawfully taken for the purpose of quelling a riot or insurrection.

Article 3

Prohibition of torture

No one shall be subjected to torture or to inhuman or degrading treatment or punish-   **A.2–26** ment.

Article 4

Prohibition of slavery and forced labour

1. No one shall be held in slavery or servitude.   **A.2–27**

2. No one shall be required to perform forced or compulsory labour.

3. For the purpose of this Article the term "forced or compulsory labour" shall not include:

(a) any work required to be done in the ordinary course of detention imposed according to the provisions of Article 5 of this Convention or during conditional release from such detention;

(b) any service of a military character or, in case of conscientious objectors in countries where they are recognised, service exacted instead of compulsory military service;

(c) any service exacted in case of an emergency or calamity threatening the life or well-being of the community;

(d) any work or service which forms part of normal civic obligations.

Article 5

Right to liberty and security

A.2–28   1. Everyone has the right to liberty and security of person. No one shall be deprived of his liberty save in the following cases and in accordance with a procedure prescribed by law:

(a) the lawful detention of a person after conviction by a competent court;

(b) the lawful arrest or detention of a person for non-compliance with the lawful order of a court or in order to secure the fulfilment of any obligation prescribed by law;

(c) the lawful arrest or detention of a person effected for the purpose of bringing him before the competent legal authority on reasonable suspicion of having committed an offence or when it is reasonably considered necessary to prevent his committing an offence or fleeing after having done so;

(d) the detention of a minor by lawful order for the purpose of educational supervision or his lawful detention for the purpose of bringing him before the competent legal authority;

(e) the lawful detention of persons for the prevention of the spreading of infectious diseases, of persons of unsound mind, alcoholics or drug addicts or vagrants;

(f) the lawful arrest or detention of a person to prevent his effecting an unauthorised entry into the country or of a person against whom action is being taken with a view to deportation or extradition.

2. Everyone who is arrested shall be informed promptly, in a language which he understands, of the reasons for his arrest and of any charge against him.

3. Everyone arrested or detained in accordance with the provisions of paragraph 1(c) of this Article shall be brought promptly before a judge or other officer authorised by law to exercise judicial power and shall be entitled to trial within a reasonable time or to release pending trial. Release may be conditioned by guarantees to appear for trial.

4. Everyone who is deprived of his liberty by arrest or detention shall be entitled to take proceedings by which the lawfulness of his detention shall be decided speedily by a court and his release ordered if the detention is not lawful.

5. Everyone who has been the victim of arrest or detention in contravention of the provisions of this Article shall have an enforceable right to compensation.

Article 6

Right to a fair trial

A.2–29   1. In the determination of his civil rights and obligations or of any criminal charge against him, everyone is entitled to a fair and public hearing within a reasonable time by an independent and impartial tribunal established by law. Judgment shall be pronounced publicly but the press and public may be excluded from all or part of the trial in the interest of morals, public order or national security in a democratic society, where the interests of juveniles or the protection of the private life of the parties so require, or to the extent strictly necessary in the opinion of the court in special circumstances where publicity would prejudice the interests of justice.

2. Everyone charged with a criminal offence shall be presumed innocent until proved guilty according to law.

3. Everyone charged with a criminal offence has the following minimum rights:

(a) to be informed promptly, in a language which he understands and in detail, of the nature and cause of the accusation against him;

(b) to have adequate time and facilities for the preparation of his defence;

(c) to defend himself in person or through legal assistance of his own choosing or, if he has not sufficient means to pay for legal assistance, to be given it free when the interests of justice so require;

(d) to examine or have examined witnesses against him and to obtain the attendance and examination of witnesses on his behalf under the same conditions as witnesses against him;

(e) to have the free assistance of an interpreter if he cannot understand or speak the language used in court.

Article 7

No punishment without law

1. No one shall be held guilty of any criminal offence on account of any act or omission **A.2–30** which did not constitute a criminal offence under national or international law at the time when it was committed. Nor shall a heavier penalty be imposed than the one that was applicable at the time the criminal offence was committed.

2. This Article shall not prejudice the trial and punishment of any person for any act or omission which, at the time when it was committed, was criminal according to the general principles of law recognised by civilised nations.

Article 8

Right to respect for private and family life

1. Everyone has the right to respect for his private and family life, his home and his **A.2–31** correspondence.

2. There shall be no interference by a public authority with the exercise of this right except such as is in accordance with the law and is necessary in a democratic society in the interests of national security, public safety or the economic well-being of the country, for the prevention of disorder or crime, for the protection of health or morals, or for the protection of the rights and freedoms of others.

Article 9

Freedom of thought, conscience and religion

1. Everyone has the right to freedom of thought, conscience and religion; this right **A.2–32** includes freedom to change his religion or belief and freedom, either alone or in community with others and in public or private, to manifest his religion or belief, in worship, teaching, practice and observance.

2. Freedom to manifest one's religion or beliefs shall be subject only to such limitations as are prescribed by law and are necessary in a democratic society in the interests of public safety, for the protection of public order, health or morals, or for the protection of the rights and freedoms of others.

Article 10

Freedom of expression

1. Everyone has the right to freedom of expression. This right shall include freedom to **A.2–33** hold opinions and to receive and impart information and ideas without interference by

public authority and regardless of frontiers. This Article shall not prevent States from requiring the licensing of broadcasting, television or cinema enterprises.

2. The exercise of these freedoms, since it carries with it duties and responsibilities, may be subject to such formalities, conditions, restrictions or penalties as are prescribed by law and are necessary in a democratic society, in the interests of national security, territorial integrity or public safety, for the prevention of disorder or crime, for the protection of health or morals, for the protection of the reputation or rights of others, for preventing the disclosure of information received in confidence, or for maintaining the authority and impartiality of the judiciary.

Article 11

Freedom of assembly and association

A.2–34   1. Everyone has the right to freedom of peaceful assembly and to freedom of association with others, including the right to form and to join trade unions for the protection of his interests.

2. No restrictions shall be placed on the exercise of these rights other than such as are prescribed by law and are necessary in a democratic society in the interests of national security or public safety, for the prevention of disorder or crime, for the protection of health or morals or for the protection of the rights and freedoms of others. This Article shall not prevent the imposition of lawful restrictions on the exercise of these rights by members of the armed forces, of the police or of the administration of the State.

Article 12

Right to marry

A.2–35   Men and women of marriageable age have the right to marry and to found a family, according to the national laws governing the exercise of this right.

Article 14

Prohibition of discrimination

A.2–36   The enjoyment of the rights and freedoms set forth in this Convention shall be secured without discrimination on any ground such as sex, race, colour, language, religion, political or other opinion, national or social origin, association with a national minority, property, birth or other status.

Article 16

Restrictions on political activity of aliens

A.2–37   Nothing in Articles 10, 11 and 14 shall be regarded as preventing the High Contracting Parties from imposing restrictions on the political activity of aliens.

Article 17

Prohibition of abuse of rights

A.2–38   Nothing in this Convention may be interpreted as implying for any State, group or person any right to engage in any activity or perform any act aimed at the destruction of any of the rights and freedoms set forth herein or at their limitation to a greater extent than is provided for in the Convention.

Article 18

Limitation on use of restrictions on rights

A.2–39   The restrictions permitted under this Convention to the said rights and freedoms shall not be applied for any purpose other than those for which they have been prescribed.

Part II

The First Protocol

Article 1

Protection of property

Every natural or legal person is entitled to the peaceful enjoyment of his possessions.   **A.2–40**
No one shall be deprived of his possessions except in the public interest and subject to the
conditions provided for by law and by the general principles of international law.

The preceding provisions shall not, however, in any way impair the right of a State to
enforce such laws as it deems necessary to control the use of property in accordance
with the general interest or to secure the payment of taxes or other contributions or
penalties.

Article 2

Right to education

No person shall be denied the right to education. In the exercise of any functions which   **A.2–41**
it assumes in relation to education and to teaching, the State shall respect the right of
parents to ensure such education and teaching in conformity with their own religious and
philosophical convictions.

Article 3

Right to free elections

The High Contracting Parties undertake to hold free elections at reasonable intervals by   **A.2–42**
secret ballot, under conditions which will ensure the free expression of the opinion of the
people in the choice of the legislature.

Part III

The Sixth Protocol

Article 1

Abolition of the death penalty

The death penalty shall be abolished. No one shall be condemned to such penalty or   **A.2–43**
executed.

Article 2

Death penalty in time of war

A State may make provision in its law for the death penalty in respect of acts committed   **A.2–44**
in time of war or of imminent threat of war: such penalty shall be applied only in the
instances laid down in the law and in accordance with its provisions. The State shall
communicate to the Secretary General of the Council of Europe the relevant provisions of
that law.

Schedule 2

Remedial Orders

ORDERS

A.2–45   1.—(1) A remedial order may—

(a) contain such incidental, supplemental, consequential or transitional provision as the person making it considers appropriate;

(b) be made so as to have effect from a date earlier than that on which it is made;

(c) make provision for the delegation of specific functions;

(d) make different provision for different cases.

(2) The power conferred by sub-paragraph (1)(a) includes—

(a) power to amend primary legislation (including primary legislation other than that which contains the incompatible provision); and

(b) power to amend or revoke subordinate legislation (including subordinate legislation other than that which contains the incompatible provision).

(3) A remedial order may be made so as to have the same extent as the legislation which it affects.

(4) No person is to be guilty of an offence solely as a result of the retrospective effect of a remedial order.

Procedure

A.2–46   2. No remedial order may be made unless—

(a) a draft of the order has been approved by a resolution of each House of Parliament made after the end of the period of 60 days beginning with the day on which the draft was laid; or

(b) it is declared in the order that it appears to the person making it that, because of the urgency of the matter, it is necessary to make the order without a draft being so approved.

Orders laid in draft

A.2–47   3.—(1) No draft may be laid under paragraph 2(a) unless—

(a) the person proposing to make the order has laid before Parliament a document which contains a draft of the proposed order and the required information; and

(b) the period of 60 days, beginning with the day on which the document required by this sub-paragraph was laid, has ended.

(2) If representations have been made during that period, the draft laid under paragraph 2(a) must be accompanied by a statement containing—

    (a) a summary of the representations; and

    (b) if, as a result of the representations, the proposed order has been changed, details of the changes.

Urgent cases

4.—(1) If a remedial order ("the original order") is made without being approved in draft, the person making it must lay it before Parliament, accompanied by the required information, after it is made.   **A.2–48**

(2) If representations have been made during the period of 60 days beginning with the day on which the original order was made, the person making it must (after the end of that period) lay before Parliament a statement containing—

    (a) a summary of the representations; and

    (b) if, as a result of the representations, he considers it appropriate to make changes to the original order, details of the changes.

(3) If sub-paragraph (2)(b) applies, the person making the statement must—

    (a) make a further remedial order replacing the original order; and

    (b) lay the replacement order before Parliament.

(4) If, at the end of the period of 120 days beginning with the day on which the original order was made, a resolution has not been passed by each House approving the original or replacement order, the order ceases to have effect (but without that affecting anything previously done under either order or the power to make a fresh remedial order).

Definitions

5. In this Schedule—   **A.2–49**

    "representations" means representations about a remedial order (or proposed remedial order) made to the person making (or proposing to make) it and includes any relevant Parliamentary report or resolution; and

    "required information" means—

        (a) an explanation of the incompatibility which the order (or proposed order) seeks to remove, including particulars of the relevant declaration, finding or order; and

        (b) a statement of the reasons for proceeding under section 10 and for making an order in those terms.

Calculating periods

6. In calculating any period for the purposes of this Schedule, no account is to be taken of any time during which—   **A.2–50**

    (a) Parliament is dissolved or prorogued; or

    (b) both Houses are adjourned for more than four days.

Schedule 3

Derogation and Reservation

PART I

DEROGATION

The 1998 notification

A.2–51   The United Kingdom Permanent Representative to the Council of Europe presents his compliments to the Secretary General of the Council, and has the honour to convey the following information in order to ensure compliance with the obligations of Her Majesty's Government in the United Kingdom under Article 15(3) of the Convention for the Protection of Human Rights and Fundamental Freedoms signed at Rome on 4 November 1950.

There have been in the United Kingdom in recent years campaigns of organised terrorism connected with the affairs of Northern Ireland which have manifested themselves in activities which have included repeated murder, attempted murder, maiming, intimidation and violent civil disturbance and in bombing and fire raising which have resulted in death, injury and widespread destruction of property. As a result, a public emergency within the meaning of Article 15(1) of the Convention exists in the United Kingdom.

The Government found it necessary in 1974 to introduce and since then, in cases concerning persons reasonably suspected of involvement in terrorism connected with the affairs of Northern Ireland, or of certain offences under the legislation, who have been detained for 48 hours, to exercise powers enabling further detention without charge, for periods of up to five days, on the authority of the Secretary of State. These powers are at present to be found in Section 12 of the Prevention of Terrorism (Temporary Provisions) Act 1984, Article 9 of the Prevention of Terrorism (Supplemental Temporary Provisions) Order and Article 10 of the Prevention of Terrorism (Supplemental Temporary Provisions) (Northern Ireland) Order 1984.

Section 12 of the Prevention of Terrorism (Temporary Provisions) Act 1984 provides for a person whom a constable has arrested on reasonable grounds of suspecting him to be guilty of an offence under Section 1, 9 or 10 of the Act, or to be or to have been involved in terrorism connected with the affairs of Northern Ireland, to be detained in right of the arrest for up to 48 hours and thereafter, where the Secretary of State extends the detention period, for up to a further five days. Section 12 substantially re-enacted Section 12 of the Prevention of Terrorism (Temporary Provisions) Act 1976 which, in turn, substantially re-enacted Section 7 of the Prevention of Terrorism (Temporary Provisions) Act 1974.

Article 10 of the Prevention of Terrorism (Supplemental Temporary Provisions) (Northern Ireland) Order and Article 9 of the Prevention of Terrorism (Supplemental Temporary Provisions) Order were both made under Sections 13 and 14 of and Schedule 3 to the 1984 Act and substantially re-enacted powers of detention in Orders made under the 1974 and 1976 Acts. A person who is being examined under Article 4 of either Order on his arrival in, or on seeking to leave, Northern Ireland or Great Britain for the purpose of determining whether he is or has been involved in terrorism connected with the affairs of Northern Ireland, or whether there are grounds for suspecting that he has committed an offence under Section 9 of the 1984 Act, may be detained under Article 9 or 10, as appropriate, pending the conclusion of his examination. The period of this examination may exceed 12 hours if an examining officer has reasonable grounds for suspecting him to be or to have been involved in acts of terrorism connected with the affairs of Northern Ireland.

Where such a person is detained under the said Article 9 or 10 he may be detained for up to 48 hours on the authority of an examining officer and thereafter, where the Secretary of State extends the detention period, for up to a further five days.

In its judgment of 29 November 1988 in the Case of *Brogan and Others*, the European Court of Human Rights held that there had been a violation of Article 5(3) in respect of each of the applicants, all of whom had been detained under Section 12 of the 1984 Act. The Court held that even the shortest of the four periods of detention concerned, namely four days and six hours, fell outside the constraints as to time permitted by the first part of Article 5(3). In addition, the Court held that there had been a violation of Article 5(5) in the case of each applicant.

Following this judgment, the Secretary of State for the Home Department informed Parliament on 6 December 1988 that, against the background of the terrorist campaign, and the over-riding need to bring terrorists to justice, the Government did not believe that the maximum period of detention should be reduced. He informed Parliament that the Government were examining the matter with a view to responding to the judgment. On 22 December 1988, the Secretary of State further informed Parliament that it remained the Government's wish, if it could be achieved, to find a judicial process under which extended detention might be reviewed and where appropriate authorised by a judge or other judicial officer. But a further period of reflection and consultation was necessary before the Government could bring forward a firm and final view.

Since the judgment of 29 November 1988 as well as previously, the Government have found it necessary to continue to exercise, in relation to terrorism connected with the affairs of Northern Ireland, the powers described above enabling further detention without charge for periods of up to 5 days, on the authority of the Secretary of State, to the extent strictly required by the exigencies of the situation to enable necessary enquiries and investigations properly to be completed in order to decide whether criminal proceedings should be instituted. To the extent that the exercise of these powers may be inconsistent with the obligations imposed by the Convention the Government has availed itself of the right of derogation conferred by Article 15(1) of the Convention and will continue to do so until further notice.

Dated 23 December 1988.

The 1989 notification

The United Kingdom Permanent Representative to the Council of Europe presents his **A.2–52** compliments to the Secretary General of the Council, and has the honour to convey the following information.

In his communication to the Secretary General of 23 December 1988, reference was made to the introduction and exercise of certain powers under section 12 of the Prevention of Terrorism (Temporary Provisions) Act 1984, Article 9 of the Prevention of Terrorism (Supplemental Temporary Provisions) Order 1984 and Article 10 of the Prevention of Terrorism (Supplemental Temporary Provisions) (Northern Ireland) Order 1984.

These provisions have been replaced by section 14 of and paragraph 6 of Schedule 5 to the Prevention of Terrorism (Temporary Provisions) Act 1989, which make comparable provision. They came into force on 22 March 1989. A copy of these provisions is enclosed.

The United Kingdom Permanent Representative avails himself of this opportunity to renew to the Secretary General the assurance of his highest consideration.

23 March 1989.

PART II

RESERVATION

A.2–53   At the time of signing the present (First) Protocol, I declare that, in view of certain provisions of the Education Acts in the United Kingdom, the principle affirmed in the second sentence of Article 2 is accepted by the United Kingdom only so far as it is compatible with the provision of efficient instruction and training, and the avoidance of unreasonable public expenditure.

Dated 20 March 1952. Made by the United Kingdom Permanent Representative to the Council of Europe.

Schedule 4

Judicial Pensions

DUTY TO MAKE ORDERS ABOUT PENSIONS

A.2–54   1.—(1) The appropriate Minister must by order make provision with respect to pensions payable to or in respect of any holder of a judicial office who serves as an ECHR judge.

(2) A pensions order must include such provision as the Minister making it considers is necessary to secure that—

  (a) an ECHR judge who was, immediately before his appointment as an ECHR judge, a member of a judicial pension scheme is entitled to remain as a member of that scheme;

  (b) the terms on which he remains a member of the scheme are those which would have been applicable had he not been appointed as an ECHR judge; and

  (c) entitlement to benefits payable in accordance with the scheme continues to be determined as if, while serving as an ECHR judge, his salary was that which would (but for section 18(4) have been payable to him in respect of his continuing service as the holder of his judicial office.

Contributions

A.2–55   2. A pensions order may, in particular, make provision—

  (a) for any contributions which are payable by a person who remains a member of a scheme as a result of the order, and which would otherwise be payable by deduction from his salary, to be made otherwise than by deduction from his salary as an ECHR judge; and

  (b) for such contributions to be collected in such manner as may be determined by the administrators of the scheme.

Amendments of other enactments

A.2–56   3. A pensions order may amend any provision of, or made under, a pensions Act in such manner and to such extent as the Minister making the order considers necessary or expedient to ensure the proper administration of any scheme to which it relates.

[266]

Definitions

4. In this Schedule—   **A.2–57**

"appropriate Minister" means—

(a) in relation to any judicial office whose jurisdiction is exercisable exclusively in relation to Scotland, the Secretary of State; and

(b) otherwise, the Lord Chancellor;

"ECHR judge" means the holder of a judicial office who is serving as a judge of the Court;

"judicial pension scheme" means a scheme established by and in accordance with a pensions Act;

"pensions Act" means—

(a) the Country Courts Act (Northern Ireland) 1959;

(b) the Sheriffs' Pensions (Scotland) Act 1961;

(c) the Judicial Pensions Act 1981; or

(d) the Judicial Pensions and Retirement Act 1993; and

"pensions order" means an order made under paragraph 1.

CONVENTION FOR THE PROTECTION OF HUMAN RIGHTS AND FUNDAMENTAL FREEDOMS AS AMENDED BY PROTOCOL NO. 11

Rome, 4.XI.1950

The text of the Convention had been amended according to the provisions of Protocol No. 3 (ETS No. 45), which entered into force on 21 September 1970, of Protocol No. 5 (ETS No. 55), which entered into force on 20 December 1971 and of Protocol No. 8 (ETS No. 118), which entered into force on 1 January 1990, and comprised also the text of Protocol No. 2 (ETS No. 44) which, in accordance with Article 5, paragraph 3 thereof, had been an integral part of the Convention since its entry into force on 21 September 1970. All provisions which had been amended or added by these Protocols are replaced by Protocol No. 11 (ETS No. 155), as from the date of its entry into force on 1 November 1998. As from that date, Protocol No. 9 (ETS No. 140), which entered into force on 1 October 1994, is repealed and Protocol No. 10 (ETS No. 146) has lost its purpose.   **A.3–01**

The governments signatory hereto, being members of the Council of Europe,

Considering the Universal Declaration of Human Rights proclaimed by the General Assembly of the United Nations on 10th December 1948;

Considering that this Declaration aims at securing the universal and effective recognition and observance of the Rights therein declared;

Considering that the aim of the Council of Europe is the achievement of greater unity between its members and that one of the methods by which that aim is to be pursued is the maintenance and further realisation of human rights and fundamental freedoms;

Reaffirming their profound belief in those fundamental freedoms which are the foundation of justice and peace in the world and are best maintained on the one hand by an effective political democracy and on the other by a common understanding and observance of the human rights upon which they depend;

Being resolved, as the governments of European countries which are like-minded and have a common heritage of political traditions, ideals, freedom and the rule of law, to take the first steps for the collective enforcement of certain of the rights stated in the Universal Declaration,

Have agreed as follows:

ARTICLE 1—OBLIGATION TO RESPECT HUMAN RIGHTS[1]

The High Contracting Parties shall secure to everyone within their jurisdiction the rights and freedoms defined in Section I of this Convention.   **A.3–02**

Section I—Rights and freedoms[1]

Article 2—Right to Life

A.3–03
1. Everyone's right to life shall be protected by law. No one shall be deprived of his life intentionally save in the execution of a sentence of a court following his conviction of a crime for which this penalty is provided by law.
2. Deprivation of life shall not be regarded as inflicted in contravention of this article when it results from the use of force which is no more than absolutely necessary:

   a. in defence of any person from unlawful violence;

   b. in order to effect a lawful arrest or to prevent the escape of a person lawfully detained;

   c. in action lawfully taken for the purpose of quelling a riot or insurrection.

Article 3—Prohibition of Torture

A.3–04 No one shall be subjected to torture or to inhuman or degrading treatment or punishment.

Article 4—Prohibition of Slavery and Forced Labour

A.3–05
1. No one shall be held in slavery or servitude.
2. No one shall be required to perform forced or compulsory labour.
3. For the purpose of this article the term "forced or compulsory labour" shall not include:

   a. any work required to be done in the ordinary course of detention imposed according to the provisions of Article 5 of this Convention or during conditional release from such detention;

   b. any service of a military character or, in case of conscientious objectors in countries where they are recognised, service exacted instead of compulsory military service;

   c. any service exacted in case of an emergency or calamity threatening the life or well-being of the community;

   d. any work or service which forms part of normal civic obligations.

Article 5—Right to Liberty and Security

A.3–06
1. Everyone has the right to liberty and security of person. No one shall be deprived of his liberty save in the following cases and in accordance with a procedure prescribed by law:

   a. the lawful detention of a person after conviction by a competent court;

   b. the lawful arrest or detention of a person for non-compliance with the lawful order of a court or in order to secure the fulfilment of any obligation prescribed by law;

---

[1] Heading added according to the provisions of Protocol No. 11 (ETS No. 155).

   c. the lawful arrest or detention of a person effected for the purpose of bringing him before the competent legal authority on reasonable suspicion of having committed an offence or when it is reasonably considered necessary to prevent his committing an offence or fleeing after having done so;

   d. the detention of a minor by lawful order for the purpose of educational supervision or his lawful detention for the purpose of bringing him before the competent legal authority;

   e. the lawful detention of persons for the prevention of the spreading of infectious diseases, of persons of unsound mind, alcoholics or drug addicts or vagrants;

   f. the lawful arrest or detention of a person to prevent his effecting an unauthorised entry into the country or of a person against whom action is being taken with a view to deportation or extradition.

2. Everyone who is arrested shall be informed promptly, in a language which he understands, of the reasons for his arrest and of any charge against him.

3. Everyone arrested or detained in accordance with the provisions of paragraph 1.c of this article shall be brought promptly before a judge or other officer authorised by law to exercise judicial power and shall be entitled to trial within a reasonable time or to release pending trial. Release may be conditioned by guarantees to appear for trial.

4. Everyone who is deprived of his liberty by arrest or detention shall be entitled to take proceedings by which the lawfulness of his detention shall be decided speedily by a court and his release ordered if the detention is not lawful.

5. Everyone who has been the victim of arrest or detention in contravention of the provisions of this article shall have an enforceable right to compensation.

ARTICLE 6—RIGHT TO A FAIR TRIAL

1. In the determination of his civil rights and obligations or of any criminal charge **A.3–07** against him, everyone is entitled to a fair and public hearing within a reasonable time by an independent and impartial tribunal established by law. Judgment shall be pronounced publicly but the press and public may be excluded from all or part of the trial in the interests of morals, public order or national security in a democratic society, where the interests of juveniles or the protection of the private life of the parties so require, or to the extent strictly necessary in the opinion of the court in special circumstances where publicity would prejudice the interests of justice.

2. Everyone charged with a criminal offence shall be presumed innocent until proved guilty according to law.

3. Everyone charged with a criminal offence has the following minimum rights:

   a. to be informed promptly, in a language which he understands and in detail, of the nature and cause of the accusation against him;

   b. to have adequate time and facilities for the preparation of his defence;

   c. to defend himself in person or through legal assistance of his own choosing or, if he has not sufficient means to pay for legal assistance, to be given it free when the interests of justice so require;

   d. to examine or have examined witnesses against him and to obtain the attendance and examination of witnesses on his behalf under the same conditions as witnesses against him;

   e. to have the free assistance of an interpreter if he cannot understand or speak the language used in court.

ARTICLE 7—NO PUNISHMENT WITHOUT LAW

1. No one shall be held guilty of any criminal offence on account of any act or omission **A.3–08** which did not constitute a criminal offence under national or international law at the

time when it was committed. Nor shall a heavier penalty be imposed than the one that was applicable at the time the criminal offence was committed.

2. This article shall not prejudice the trial and punishment of any person for any act or omission which, at the time when it was committed, was criminal according to the general principles of law recognised by civilised nations.

A<small>RTICLE</small> 8—R<small>IGHT TO</small> R<small>ESPECT FOR</small> P<small>RIVATE AND</small> F<small>AMILY</small> L<small>IFE</small>

A.3–09   1. Everyone has the right to respect for his private and family life, his home and his correspondence.

2. There shall be no interference by a public authority with the exercise of this right except such as is in accordance with the law and is necessary in a democratic society in the interests of national security, public safety or the economic well-being of the country, for the prevention of disorder or crime, for the protection of health or morals, or for the protection of the rights and freedoms of others.

A<small>RTICLE</small> 9—F<small>REEDOM OF</small> T<small>HOUGHT</small>, C<small>ONSCIENCE AND</small> R<small>ELIGION</small>

A.3–10   1. Everyone has the right to freedom of thought, conscience and religion; this right includes freedom to change his religion or belief and freedom, either alone or in community with others and in public or private, to manifest his religion or belief, in worship, teaching, practice and observance.

2. Freedom to manifest one's religion or beliefs shall be subject only to such limitations as are prescribed by law and are necessary in a democratic society in the interests of public safety, for the protection of public order, health or morals, or for the protection of the rights and freedoms of others.

A<small>RTICLE</small> 10—F<small>REEDOM OF</small> E<small>XPRESSION</small>

A.3–11   1. Everyone has the right to freedom of expression. This right shall include freedom to hold opinions and to receive and impart information and ideas without interference by public authority and regardless of frontiers. This article shall not prevent States from requiring the licensing of broadcasting, television or cinema enterprises.

2. The exercise of these freedoms, since it carries with it duties and responsibilities, may be subject to such formalities, conditions, restrictions or penalties as are prescribed by law and are necessary in a democratic society, in the interests of national security, territorial integrity or public safety, for the prevention of disorder or crime, for the protection of health or morals, for the protection of the reputation or rights of others, for preventing the disclosure of information received in confidence, or for maintaining the authority and impartiality of the judiciary.

A<small>RTICLE</small> 11—F<small>REEDOM OF</small> A<small>SSEMBLY AND</small> A<small>SSOCIATION</small>

A.3–12   1. Everyone has the right to freedom of peaceful assembly and to freedom of association with others, including the right to form and to join trade unions for the protection of his interests.

2. No restrictions shall be placed on the exercise of these rights other than such as are prescribed by law and are necessary in a democratic society in the interests of national security or public safety, for the prevention of disorder or crime, for the protection of

health or morals or for the protection of the rights and freedoms of others. This article shall not prevent the imposition of lawful restrictions on the exercise of these rights by members of the armed forces, of the police or of the administration of the State.

ARTICLE 12—RIGHT TO MARRY

Men and women of marriageable age have the right to marry and to found a family, according to the national laws governing the exercise of this right.   **A.3–13**

ARTICLE 13—RIGHT TO AN EFFECTIVE REMEDY

Everyone whose rights and freedoms as set forth in this Convention are violated shall have an effective remedy before a national authority notwithstanding that the violation has been committed by persons acting in an official capacity.   **A.3–14**

ARTICLE 14—PROHIBITION OF DISCRIMINATION

The enjoyment of the rights and freedoms set forth in this Convention shall be secured without discrimination on any ground such as sex, race, colour, language, religion, political or other opinion, national or social origin, association with a national minority, property, birth or other status.   **A.3–15**

ARTICLE 15—DEROGATION IN TIME OF EMERGENCY

1. In time of war or other public emergency threatening the life of the nation any High Contracting Party may take measures derogating from its obligations under this Convention to the extent strictly required by the exigencies of the situation, provided that such measures are not inconsistent with its other obligations under international law.   **A.3–16**
2. No derogation from Article 2, except in respect of deaths resulting from lawful acts of war, or from Articles 3, 4 (paragraph 1) and 7 shall be made under this provision.
3. Any High Contracting Party availing itself of this right of derogation shall keep the Secretary General of the Council of Europe fully informed of the measures which it has taken and the reasons therefor. It shall also inform the Secretary General of the Council of Europe when such measures have ceased to operate and the provisions of the Convention are again being fully executed.

ARTICLE 16—RESTRICTIONS ON POLITICAL ACTIVITY OF ALIENS

Nothing in Articles 10, 11 and 14 shall be regarded as preventing the High Contracting Parties from imposing restrictions on the political activity of aliens.   **A.3–17**

ARTICLE 17—PROHIBITION OF ABUSE OF RIGHTS

Nothing in this Convention may be interpreted as implying for any State, group or person any right to engage in any activity or perform any act aimed at the destruction of any of   **A.3–18** the rights and freedoms set forth herein or at their limitation to a greater extent than is provided for in the Convention.

ARTICLE 18—LIMITATION ON USE OF RESTRICTIONS ON RIGHTS

A.3–19 The restrictions permitted under this Convention to the said rights and freedoms shall not be applied for any purpose other than those for which they have been prescribed.

Section II—European Court of Human Rights[2]

ARTICLE 19—ESTABLISHMENT OF THE COURT

A.3–20 To ensure the observance of the engagements undertaken by the High Contracting Parties in the Convention and the Protocols thereto, there shall be set up a European Court of Human Rights, hereinafter referred to as "the Court". It shall function on a permanent basis.

ARTICLE 20—NUMBER OF JUDGES

A.3–21 The Court shall consist of a number of judges equal to that of the High Contracting Parties.

ARTICLE 21—CRITERIA FOR OFFICE

A.3–22
1. The judges shall be of high moral character and must either possess the qualifications required for appointment to high judicial office or be jurisconsults of recognised competence.
2. The judges shall sit on the Court in their individual capacity.
3. During their term of office the judges shall not engage in any activity which is incompatible with their independence, impartiality or with the demands of a full-time office; all questions arising from the application of this paragraph shall be decided by the Court.

ARTICLE 22—ELECTION OF JUDGES

A.3–23
1. The judges shall be elected by the Parliamentary Assembly with respect to each High Contracting Party by a majority of votes cast from a list of three candidates nominated by the High Contracting Party.
2. The same procedure shall be followed to complete the Court in the event of the accession of new High Contracting Parties and in filling casual vacancies.

---

[2] New Section II according to the provisions of Protocol No. 11 (ETS No. 155).

Article 23—Terms of Office

1. The judges shall be elected for a period of six years. They may be re-elected.   **A.3–24**
   However, the terms of office of one-half of the judges elected at the first election shall
   expire at the end of three years.
2. The judges whose terms of office are to expire at the end of the initial period of three
   years shall be chosen by lot by the Secretary General of the Council of Europe
   immediately after their election.
3. In order to ensure that, as far as possible, the terms of office of one-half of the judges
   are renewed every three years, the Parliamentary Assembly may decide, before
   proceeding to any subsequent election, that the term or terms of office of one or more
   judges to be elected shall be for a period other than six years but not more than nine
   and not less than three years.
4. In cases where more than one term of office is involved and where the Parliamentary
   Assembly applies the preceding paragraph, the allocation of the terms of office shall
   be effected by a drawing of lots by the Secretary General of the Council of Europe
   immediately after the election.
5. A judge elected to replace a judge whose term of office has not expired shall hold
   office for the remainder of his predecessor's term.
6. The terms of office of judges shall expire when they reach the age of 70.
7. The judges shall hold office until replaced. They shall, however, continue to deal with
   such cases as they already have under consideration.

Article 24—Dismissal

No judge may be dismissed from his office unless the other judges decide by a majority   **A.3–25**
of two-thirds that he has ceased to fulfil the required conditions.

Article 25—Registry and Legal Secretaries

The Court shall have a registry, the functions and organisation of which shall be laid down   **A.3–26**
in the rules of the Court. The Court shall be assisted by legal secretaries.

Article 26—Plenary Court

The plenary Court shall: **A.3–27**
   a. elect its President and one or two Vice-Presidents for a period of three years; they
      may be re-elected;
   b. set up Chambers, constituted for a fixed period of time;
   c. elect the Presidents of the Chambers of the Court; they may be re-elected;
   d. adopt the rules of the Court, and
   e. elect the Registrar and one or more Deputy Registrars.

Article 27—Committees, Chambers and Grand Chamber

1. To consider cases brought before it, the Court shall sit in committees of three judges,   **A.3–28**
   in Chambers of seven judges and in a Grand Chamber of seventeen judges. The
   Court's Chambers shall set up committees for a fixed period of time.

2. There shall sit as an *ex officio* member of the Chamber and the Grand Chamber the judge elected in respect of the State Party concerned or, if there is none or if he is unable to sit, a person of its choice who shall sit in the capacity of judge.
3. The Grand Chamber shall also include the President of the Court, the Vice-Presidents, the Presidents of the Chambers and other judges chosen in accordance with the rules of the Court. When a case is referred to the Grand Chamber under Article 43, no judge from the Chamber which rendered the judgment shall sit in the Grand Chamber, with the exception of the President of the Chamber and the judge who sat in respect of the State Party concerned.

ARTICLE 28—DECLARATIONS OF INADMISSIBILITY BY COMMITTEES

A.3–29 A committee may, by a unanimous vote, declare inadmissible or strike out of its list of cases an application submitted under Article 34 where such a decision can be taken without further examination. The decision shall be final.

ARTICLE 29—DECISIONS BY CHAMBERS ON ADMISSIBILITY AND MERITS

A.3–30 1. If no decision is taken under Article 28, a Chamber shall decide on the admissibility and merits of individual applications submitted under Article 34.
2. A Chamber shall decide on the admissibility and merits of inter-State applications submitted under Article 33.
3. The decision on admissibility shall be taken separately unless the Court, in exceptional cases, decides otherwise.

ARTICLE 30—RELINQUISHMENT OF JURISDICTION TO THE GRAND CHAMBER

A.3–31 Where a case pending before a Chamber raises a serious question affecting the interpretation of the Convention or the protocols thereto, or where the resolution of a question before the Chamber might have a result inconsistent with a judgment previously delivered by the Court, the Chamber may, at any time before it has rendered its judgment, relinquish jurisdiction in favour of the Grand Chamber, unless one of the parties to the case objects.

ARTICLE 31—POWERS OF THE GRAND CHAMBER

A.3–32 The Grand Chamber shall:
a. determine applications submitted either under Article 33 or Article 34 when a Chamber has relinquished jurisdiction under Article 30 or when the case has been referred to it under Article 43; and
b. consider requests for advisory opinions submitted under Article 47.

ARTICLE 32—JURISDICTION OF THE COURT

A.3–33 1. The jurisdiction of the Court shall extend to all matters concerning the interpretation and application of the Convention and the protocols thereto which are referred to it as provided in Articles 33, 34 and 47.

2. In the event of dispute as to whether the Court has jurisdiction, the Court shall decide.

ARTICLE 33—INTER-STATE CASES

Any High Contracting Party may refer to the Court any alleged breach of the provisions of the Convention and the protocols thereto by another High Contracting Party.   **A.3–34**

ARTICLE 34—INDIVIDUAL APPLICATIONS

The Court may receive applications from any person, non-governmental organisation or group of individuals claiming to be the victim of a violation by one of the High Contracting Parties of the rights set forth in the Convention or the protocols thereto. The High Contracting Parties undertake not to hinder in any way the effective exercise of this right.   **A.3–35**

ARTICLE 35—ADMISSIBILITY CRITERIA

1. The Court may only deal with the matter after all domestic remedies have been exhausted, according to the generally recognised rules of international law, and within a period of six months from the date on which the final decision was taken.   **A.3–36**
2. The Court shall not deal with any application submitted under Article 34 that:

   a. is anonymous; or
   b. is substantially the same as a matter that has already been examined by the Court or has already been submitted to another procedure of international investigation or settlement and contains no relevant new information.

3. The Court shall declare inadmissible any individual application submitted under Article 34 which it considers incompatible with the provisions of the Convention or the protocols thereto, manifestly ill-founded, or an abuse of the right of application.
4. The Court shall reject any application which it considers inadmissible under this Article. It may do so at any stage of the proceedings.

ARTICLE 36—THIRD PARTY INTERVENTION

1. In all cases before a Chamber or the Grand Chamber, a High Contracting Party one of whose nationals is an applicant shall have the right to submit written comments and to take part in hearings.   **A.3–37**
2. The President of the Court may, in the interest of the proper administration of justice, invite any High Contracting Party which is not a party to the proceedings or any person concerned who is not the applicant to submit written comments or take part in hearings.

ARTICLE 37—STRIKING OUT APPLICATIONS

1. The Court may at any stage of the proceedings decide to strike an application out of its list of cases where the circumstances lead to the conclusion that: **A.3–38**

    a. the applicant does not intend to pursue his application; or
    b. the matter has been resolved; or
    c. for any other reason established by the Court, it is no longer justified to continue the examination of the application.

However, the Court shall continue the examination of the application if respect for human rights as defined in the Convention and the protocols thereto so requires.

2. The Court may decide to restore an application to its list of cases if it considers that the circumstances justify such a course.

ARTICLE 38—EXAMINATION OF THE CASE AND FRIENDLY SETTLEMENT PROCEEDINGS

A.3–39   1. If the Court declares the application admissible, it shall:

    a. pursue the examination of the case, together with the representatives of the parties, and if need be, undertake an investigation, for the effective conduct of which the States concerned shall furnish all necessary facilities;
    b. place itself at the disposal of the parties concerned with a view to securing a friendly settlement of the matter on the basis of respect for human rights as defined in the Convention and the protocols thereto.

2. Proceedings conducted under paragraph 1.b shall be confidential.

ARTICLE 39—FINDING OF A FRIENDLY SETTLEMENT

A.3–40   If a friendly settlement is effected, the Court shall strike the case out of its list by means of a decision which shall be confined to a brief statement of the facts and of the solution reached.

ARTICLE 40—PUBLIC HEARINGS AND ACCESS TO DOCUMENTS

A.3–41   1. Hearings shall be in public unless the Court in exceptional circumstances decides otherwise.
2. Documents deposited with the Registrar shall be accessible to the public unless the President of the Court decides otherwise.

ARTICLE 41—JUST SATISFACTION

A.3–42   If the Court finds that there has been a violation of the Convention or the protocols thereto, and if the internal law of the High Contracting Party concerned allows only partial reparation to be made, the Court shall, if necessary, afford just satisfaction to the injured party.

ARTICLE 42—JUDGMENTS OF CHAMBERS

Judgments of Chambers shall become final in accordance with the provisions of Article 44, paragraph 2.

ARTICLE 43—REFERRAL TO THE GRAND CHAMBER

1. Within a period of three months from the date of the judgment of the Chamber, any **A.3–43** party to the case may, in exceptional cases, request that the case be referred to the Grand Chamber.
2. A panel of five judges of the Grand Chamber shall accept the request if the case raises a serious question affecting the interpretation or application of the Convention or the protocols thereto, or a serious issue of general importance.
3. If the panel accepts the request, the Grand Chamber shall decide the case by means of a judgment.

ARTICLE 44—FINAL JUDGMENTS

1. The judgment of the Grand Chamber shall be final. **A.3–44**
2. The judgment of a Chamber shall become final:

   a. when the parties declare that they will not request that the case be referred to the Grand Chamber; or
   b. three months after the date of the judgment, if reference of the case to the Grand Chamber has not been requested; or
   c. when the panel of the Grand Chamber rejects the request to refer under Article 43.

3. The final judgment shall be published.

ARTICLE 45—REASONS FOR JUDGMENTS AND DECISIONS

1. Reasons shall be given for judgments as well as for decisions declaring applications **A.3–45** admissible or inadmissible.
2. If a judgment does not represent, in whole or in part, the unanimous opinion of the judges, any judge shall be entitled to deliver a separate opinion.

ARTICLE 46—BINDING FORCE AND EXECUTION OF JUDGMENTS

1. The High Contracting Parties undertake to abide by the final judgment of the Court **A.3–46** in any case to which they are parties.
2. The final judgment of the Court shall be transmitted to the Committee of Ministers, which shall supervise its execution.

ARTICLE 47—ADVISORY OPINIONS

1. The Court may, at the request of the Committee of Ministers, give advisory opinions **A.3–47** on legal questions concerning the interpretation of the Convention and the protocols thereto.
2. Such opinions shall not deal with any question relating to the content or scope of the rights or freedoms defined in Section I of the Convention and the protocols thereto, or with any other question which the Court or the Committee of Ministers might have to consider in consequence of any such proceedings as could be instituted in accordance with the Convention.

3. Decisions of the Committee of Ministers to request an advisory opinion of the Court shall require a majority vote of the representatives entitled to sit on the Committee.

Article 48—Advisory Jurisdiction of the Court

A.3–48 The Court shall decide whether a request for an advisory opinion submitted by the Committee of Ministers is within its competence as defined in Article 47.

Article 49—Reasons for Advisory Opinions

A.3–49
1. Reasons shall be given for advisory opinions of the Court.
2. If the advisory opinion does not represent, in whole or in part, the unanimous opinion of the judges, any judge shall be entitled to deliver a separate opinion.
3. Advisory opinions of the Court shall be communicated to the Committee of Ministers.

Article 50—Expenditure on the Court

A.3–50 The expenditure on the Court shall be borne by the Council of Europe.

Article 51—Privileges and Immunities of Judges

A.3–51 The judges shall be entitled, during the exercise of their functions, to the privileges and immunities provided for in Article 40 of the Statute of the Council of Europe and in the agreements made thereunder.

Section III—Miscellaneous provisions[3]

Article 52—Inquiries by the Secretary General

A.3–52 On receipt of a request from the Secretary General of the Council of Europe any High Contracting Party shall furnish an explanation of the manner in which its internal law ensures the effective implementation of any of the provisions of the Convention.

Article 53—Safeguard for Existing Human Rights

A.3–53 Nothing in this Convention shall be construed as limiting or derogating from any of the human rights and fundamental freedoms which may be ensured under the laws of any High Contracting Party or under any other agreement to which it is a Party.

---

[3] The articles of this Section are renumbered according to the provisions of Protocol No. 11 (ETS No. 155).

ARTICLE 54—POWERS OF THE COMMITTEE OF MINISTERS

Nothing in this Convention shall prejudice the powers conferred on the Committee of **A.3–54**
Ministers by the Statute of the Council of Europe.

ARTICLE 55—EXCLUSION OF OTHER MEANS OF DISPUTE SETTLEMENT

The High Contracting Parties agree that, except by special agreement, they will not avail **A.3–55**
themselves of treaties, conventions or declarations in force between them for the purpose
of submitting, by way of petition, a dispute arising out of the interpretation or application
of this Convention to a means of settlement other than those provided for in this Convention.

ARTICLE 56—TERRITORIAL APPLICATION

1. [4]Any State may at the time of its ratification or at any time thereafter declare by
   notification addressed to the Secretary General of the Council of Europe that the
   present Convention shall, subject to paragraph 4 of this Article, extend to all or any
   of the territories for whose international relations it is responsible.
2. The Convention shall extend to the territory or territories named in the notification as
   from the thirtieth day after the receipt of this notification by the Secretary General of
   the Council of Europe.
3. The provisions of this Convention shall be applied in such territories with due regard,
   however, to local requirements.
4. [4]Any State which has made a declaration in accordance with paragraph 1 of this
   article may at any time thereafter declare on behalf of one or more of the territories
   to which the declaration relates that it accepts the competence of the Court to receive
   applications from individuals, non-governmental organisations or groups of individuals as provided by Article 34 of the Convention.

ARTICLE 57—RESERVATIONS

1. Any State may, when signing this Convention or when depositing its instrument of **A.3–56**
   ratification, make a reservation in respect of any particular provision of the Convention to the extent that any law then in force in its territory is not in conformity with
   the provision. Reservations of a general character shall not be permitted under this
   article.
2. Any reservation made under this article shall contain a brief statement of the law
   concerned.

ARTICLE 58—DENUNCIATION

1. A High Contracting Party may denounce the present Convention only after the expiry **A.3–57**
   of five years from the date on which it became a party to it and after six months'

---

[4] Text amended according to the provisions of Protocol No. 11 (ETS No. 155).

notice contained in a notification addressed to the Secretary General of the Council of Europe, who shall inform the other High Contracting Parties.

2. Such a denunciation shall not have the effect of releasing the High Contracting Party concerned from its obligations under this Convention in respect of any act which, being capable of constituting a violation of such obligations, may have been performed by it before the date at which the denunciation became effective.

3. Any High Contracting Party which shall cease to be a member of the Council of Europe shall cease to be a Party to this Convention under the same conditions.

4. The Convention may be denounced in accordance with the provisions of the preceding paragraphs in respect of any territory to which it has been declared to extend under the terms of Article 56.

ARTICLE 59—SIGNATURE AND RATIFICATION

A.3–58   1. This Convention shall be open to the signature of the members of the Council of Europe. It shall be ratified. Ratifications shall be deposited with the Secretary General of the Council of Europe.

2. The present Convention shall come into force after the deposit of ten instruments of ratification.

3. As regards any signatory ratifying subsequently, the Convention shall come into force at the date of the deposit of its instrument of ratification.

4. The Secretary General of the Council of Europe shall notify all the members of the Council of Europe of the entry into force of the Convention, the names of the High Contracting Parties who have ratified it, and the deposit of all instruments of ratification which may be effected subsequently.

Done at Rome this 4th day of November 1950, in English and French, both texts being equally authentic, in a single copy which shall remain deposited in the archives of the Council of Europe. The Secretary General shall transmit certified copies to each of the signatories.

CONVENTION RELATING TO THE STATUS OF REFUGEES

Adopted on 28 July 1951 by the United Nations Conference of Plenipotentiaries on the Status of Refugees and Stateless Persons convened under General Assembly resolution 429 (V) of 14 December 1950

ENTRY INTO FORCE 22 APRIL 1954, IN ACCORDANCE WITH ARTICLE 43

Preamble

The High Contracting Parties,   **A.4–01**

Considering that the Charter of the United Nations and the Universal Declaration of Human Rights approved on 10 December 1948 by the General Assembly have affirmed the principle that human beings shall enjoy fundamental rights and freedoms without discrimination,

Considering that the United Nations has, on various occasions, manifested its profound concern for refugees and endeavoured to assure refugees the widest possible exercise of these fundamental rights and freedoms,

Considering that it is desirable to revise and consolidate previous international agreements relating to the status of refugees and to extend the scope of and the protection accorded by such instruments by means of a new agreement,

Considering that the grant of asylum may place unduly heavy burdens on certain countries, and that a satisfactory solution of a problem of which the United Nations has recognized the international- scope and nature cannot therefore be achieved without international co-operation,

Expressing the wish that all States, recognizing the social and humanitarian nature of the problem of refugees, will do everything within their power to prevent this problem from becoming a cause of tension between States,

Noting that the United Nations High Commissioner for Refugees is charged with the task of supervising international conventions providing for the protection of refugees, and recognizing that the effective co-ordination of measures taken to deal with this problem will depend upon the co-operation of States with the High Commissioner,

Have agreed as follows:

CHAPTER I

GENERAL PROVISIONS

Article 1. Definition of the term "refugee"

A. For the purposes of the present Convention, the term "refugee" shall apply to any   **A.4–02**
person who:

(1) Has been considered a refugee under the Arrangements of 12 May 1926 and 30 June 1928 or under the Conventions of 28 October 1933 and 10 February 1938, the Protocol of 14 September 1939 or the Constitution of the International Refugee Organization;

Decisions of non-eligibility taken by the International Refugee Organization during the period of its activities shall not prevent the status of refugee being accorded to persons who fulfil the conditions of paragraph 2 of this section;

(2) As a result of events occurring before 1 January 1951 and owing to well-founded fear of being persecuted for reasons of race, religion, nationality, membership of a particular social group or political opinion, is outside the country of his nationality and is unable, or owing to such fear, is unwilling to avail himself of the protection of that country; or who, not having a nationality and being outside the country of his former habitual residence as a result of such events, is unable or, owing to such fear, is unwilling to return to it.

In the case of a person who has more than one nationality, the term "the country of his nationality" shall mean each of the countries of which he is a national, and a person shall not be deemed to be lacking the protection of the country of his nationality if, without any valid reason based on well-founded fear, he has not availed himself of the protection of one of the countries of which he is a national.

B. (1) For the purposes of this Convention, the words "events occurring before 1 January 1951" in article 1, section A, shall be understood to mean either (a) "events occurring in Europe before 1 January 1951"; or (b) "events occurring in Europe or elsewhere before 1 January 1951"; and each Contracting State shall make a declaration at the time of signature, ratification or accession, specifying which of these meanings it applies for the purpose of its obligations under this Convention.

(2) Any Contracting State which has adopted alternative (a) may at any time extend its obligations by adopting alternative (b) by means of a notification addressed to the Secretary-General of the United Nations.

A.4–03 C. This Convention shall cease to apply to any person falling under the terms of section A if:

(1) He has voluntarily re-availed himself of the protection of the country of his nationality; or

(2) Having lost his nationality, he has voluntarily reacquired it; or

(3) He has acquired a new nationality, and enjoys the protection of the country of his new nationality; or

(4) He has voluntarily re-established himself in the country which he left or outside which he remained owing to fear of persecution; or

(5) He can no longer, because the circumstances in connection with which he has been recognized as a refugee have ceased to exist, continue to refuse to avail himself of the protection of the country of his nationality;

Provided that this paragraph shall not apply to a refugee falling under section A (I) of this article who is able to invoke compelling reasons arising out of previous persecution for refusing to avail himself of the protection of the country of nationality;

(6) Being a person who has no nationality he is, because the circumstances in connection with which he has been recognized as a refugee have ceased to exist, able to return to the country of his former habitual residence;

Provided that this paragraph shall not apply to a refugee falling under section A (I) of this article who is able to invoke compelling reasons arising out of previous persecution for refusing to return to the country of his former habitual residence.

D. This Convention shall not apply to persons who are at present receiving from organs or agencies of the United Nations other than the United Nations High Commissioner for Refugees protection or assistance.

When such protection or assistance has ceased for any reason, without the position of such persons being definitively settled in accordance with the relevant resolutions adopted by the General Assembly of the United Nations, these persons shall *ipso facto* be entitled to the benefits of this Convention.

E. This Convention shall not apply to a person who is recognized by the competent authorities of the country in which he has taken residence as having the rights and obligations which are attached to the possession of the nationality of that country.

F. The provisions of this Convention shall not apply to any person with respect to whom there are serious reasons for considering that.

    (a) He has committed a crime against peace, a war crime, or a crime against humanity, as defined in the international instruments drawn up to make provision in respect of such crimes;

    (b) He has committed a serious non-political crime outside the country of refuge prior to his admission to that country as a refugee;

    (c) He has been guilty of acts contrary to the purposes and principles of the United Nations.

Article 2. General obligations

Every refugee has duties to the country in which he finds himself, which require in particular that he conform to its laws and regulations as well as to measures taken for the maintenance of public order.   **A.4–04**

Article 3. Non-discrimination

The Contracting States shall apply the provisions of this Convention to refugees without discrimination as to race, religion or country of origin.   **A.4–05**

Article 4. Religion

The Contracting States shall accord to refugees within their territories treatment at least as favourable as that accorded to their nationals with respect to freedom to practise their religion and freedom as regards the religious education of their children.   **A.4–06**

Article 5. Rights granted apart from this Convention

Nothing in this Convention shall be deemed to impair any rights and benefits granted by a Contracting State to refugees apart from this Convention.   **A.4–07**

Article 6. The term "in the same circumstances"

For the purposes of this Convention, the term "in the same circumstances" implies that any requirements (including requirements as to length and conditions of sojourn or residence) which the particular individual would have to fulfil for the enjoyment of the   **A.4–08** right in question, if he were not a refugee, must be fulfilled by him, with the exception of requirements which by their nature a refugee is incapable of fulfilling.

Article 7. Exemption from reciprocity

A.4–09 1. Except where this Convention contains more favourable provisions, a Contracting State shall accord to refugees the same treatment as is accorded to aliens generally.

2. After a period of three years' residence, all refugees shall enjoy exemption from legislative reciprocity in the territory of the Contracting States.

3. Each Contracting State shall continue to accord to refugees the rights and benefits to which they were already entitled, in the absence of reciprocity, at the date of entry into force of this Convention for that State.

4. The Contracting States shall consider favourably the possibility of according to refugees, in the absence of reciprocity, rights and benefits beyond those to which they are entitled according to paragraphs 2 and 3, and to extending exemption from reciprocity to refugees who do not fulfil the conditions provided for in paragraphs 2 and 3.

5. The provisions of paragraphs 2 and 3 apply both to the rights and benefits referred to in Articles 13, 18, 19, 21 and 22 of this Convention and to rights and benefits for which this Convention does not provide.

Article 8. Exemption from exceptional measures

A.4–10 With regard to exceptional measures which may be taken against the person, property or interests of nationals of a foreign State, the Contracting States shall not apply such measures to a refugee who is formally a national of the said State solely on account of such nationality. Contracting States which, under their legislation, are prevented from applying the general principle expressed in this article, shall, in appropriate cases, grant exemptions in favour of such refugees.

Article 9. Provisional measures

A.4–11 Nothing in this Convention shall prevent a Contracting State, in time of war or other grave and exceptional circumstances, from taking provisionally measures which it considers to be essential to the national security in the case of a particular person, pending a determination by the Contracting State that that person is in fact a refugee and that the continuance of such measures is necessary in his case in the interests of national security.

Article 10. Continuity of residence

A.4–12 1. Where a refugee has been forcibly displaced during the Second World War and removed to the territory of a Contracting State, and is resident there, the period of such enforced sojourn shall be considered to have been lawful residence within that territory.

2. Where a refugee has been forcibly displaced during the Second World War from the territory of a Contracting State and has, prior to the date of entry into force of this Convention, returned there for the purpose of taking up residence, the period of residence before and after such enforced displacement shall be regarded as one uninterrupted period for any purposes for which uninterrupted residence is required.

Article 11. Refugee seamen

A.4–13 In the case of refugees regularly serving as crew members on board a ship flying the flag of a Contracting State, that State shall give sympathetic consideration to their establishment on its territory and the issue of travel documents to them or their temporary admission to its territory particularly with a view to facilitating their establishment in another country.

CHAPTER II

JURIDICAL STATUS

Article 12. Personal status

1. The personal status of a refugee shall be governed by the law of the country of his domicile or, if he has no domicile, by the law of the country of his residence.   **A.4–14**

2. Rights previously acquired by a refugee and dependent on personal status, more particularly rights attaching to marriage, shall be respected by a Contracting State, subject to compliance, if this be necessary, with the formalities required by the law of that State, provided that the right in question is one which would have been recognized by the law of that State had he not become a refugee.

Article 13. Movable and immovable property

The Contracting States shall accord to a refugee treatment as favourable as possible and, in any event, not less favourable than that accorded to aliens generally in the same circumstances, as regards the acquisition of movable and immovable property and other rights pertaining thereto, and to leases and other contracts relating to movable and immovable property.   **A.4–15**

Article 14. Artistic rights and industrial property

In respect of the protection of industrial property, such as inventions, designs or models, trade marks, trade names, and of rights in literary, artistic and scientific works, a refugee shall be accorded in the country in which he has his habitual residence the same protection as is accorded to nationals of that country. In the territory of any other Contracting States, he shall be accorded the same protection as is accorded in that territory to nationals of the country in which he has his habitual residence.   **A.4–16**

Article 15. Right of association

As regards non-political and non-profit-making associations and trade unions the Contracting States shall accord to refugees lawfully staying in their territory the most favourable treatment accorded to nationals of a foreign country, in the same circumstances.   **A.4–17**

Article 16. Access to courts

1. A refugee shall have free access to the courts of law on the territory of all Contracting States.   **A.4–18**

2. A refugee shall enjoy in the Contracting State in which he has his habitual residence the same treatment as a national in matters pertaining to access to the courts, including legal assistance and exemption from *cautio judicatum solvi.*

3. A refugee shall be accorded in the matters referred to in paragraph 2 in countries other than that in which he has his habitual residence the treatment granted to a national of the country of his habitual residence.

[287]

CHAPTER III

GAINFUL EMPLOYMENT

Article 17. Wage-earning employment

A.4–19 1. The Contracting States shall accord to refugees lawfully staying in their territory the most favourable treatment accorded to nationals of a foreign country in the same circumstances, as regards the right to engage in wage-earning employment.

2. In any case, restrictive measures imposed on aliens or the employment of aliens for the protection of the national labour market shall not be applied to a refugee who was already exempt from them at the date of entry into force of this Convention for the Contracting State concerned, or who fulfils one of the following conditions:

(a) He has completed three years' residence in the country;

(b) He has a spouse possessing the nationality of the country of residence. A refugee may not invoke the benefit of this provision if he has abandoned his spouse;

(c) He has one or more children possessing the nationality of the country of residence.

3. The Contracting States shall give sympathetic consideration to assimilating the rights of all refugees with regard to wage-earning employment to those of nationals, and in particular of those refugees who have entered their territory pursuant to programmes of labour recruitment or under immigration schemes.

Article 18. Self-employment

A.4–20 The Contracting States shall accord to a refugee lawfully in their territory treatment as favourable as possible and, in any event, not less favourable than that accorded to aliens generally in the same circumstances, as regards the right to engage on his own account in agriculture, industry, handicrafts and commerce and to establish commercial and industrial companies.

Article 19. Liberal professions

A.4–21 1. Each Contracting State shall accord to refugees lawfully staying in their territory who hold diplomas recognized by the competent authorities of that State, and who are desirous of practising a liberal profession, treatment as favourable as possible and, in any event, not less favourable than that accorded to aliens generally in the same circumstances.

2. The Contracting States shall use their best endeavours consistently with their laws and constitutions to secure the settlement of such refugees in the territories, other than the metropolitan territory, for whose international relations they are responsible.

CHAPTER IV

WELFARE

Article 20. Rationing

A.4–22 Where a rationing system exists, which applies to the population at large and regulates the general distribution of products in short supply, refugees shall be accorded the same treatment as nationals.

Article 21. Housing

As regards housing, the Contracting States, in so far as the matter is regulated by laws or   **A.4–23**
regulations or is subject to the control of public authorities, shall accord to refugees
lawfully staying in their territory treatment as favourable as possible and, in any event, not
less favourable than that accorded to aliens generally in the same circumstances.

Article 22. Public education

1. The Contracting States shall accord to refugees the same treatment as is accorded to   **A.4–24**
nationals with respect to elementary education.

2. The Contracting States shall accord to refugees treatment as favourable as possible,
and, in any event, not less favourable than that accorded to aliens generally in the same
circumstances, with respect to education other than elementary education and, in particular, as regards access to studies, the recognition of foreign school certificates, diplomas
and degrees, the remission of fees and charges and the award of scholarships.

Article 23. Public relief

The Contracting States shall accord to refugees lawfully staying in their territory the same   **A.4–25**
treatment with respect to public relief and assistance as is accorded to their nationals.

Article 24. Labour legislation and social security

1. The Contracting States shall accord to refugees lawfully staying in their territory the   **A.4–26**
same treatment as is accorded to nationals in respect of the following matters;

   (a) In so far as such matters are governed by laws or regulations or are subject to the
control of administrative authorities: remuneration, including family allowances
where these form part of remuneration, hours of work, overtime arrangements,
holidays with pay, restrictions on home work, minimum age of employment,
apprenticeship and training, women's work and the work of young persons, and the
enjoyment of the benefits of collective bargaining;

   (b) Social security (legal provisions in respect of employment injury, occupational
diseases, maternity, sickness, disability, old age, death, unemployment, family
responsibilities and any other contingency which, according to national laws or
regulations, is covered by a social security scheme), subject to the following
limitations:

      (i) There may be appropriate arrangements for the maintenance of acquired rights
and rights in course of acquisition;

      (ii) National laws or regulations of the country of residence may prescribe special
arrangements concerning benefits or portions of benefits which are payable
wholly out of public funds, and concerning allowances paid to persons who do
not fulfil the contribution conditions prescribed for the award of a normal
pension.

2. The right to compensation for the death of a refugee resulting from employment injury
or from occupational disease shall not be affected by the fact that the residence of the
beneficiary is outside the territory of the Contracting State.

3. The Contracting States shall extend to refugees the benefits of agreements concluded
between them, or which may be concluded between them in the future, concerning the
maintenance of acquired rights and rights in the process of acquisition in regard to social
security, subject only to the conditions which apply to nationals of the States signatory to
the agreements in question.

4. The Contracting States will give sympathetic consideration to extending to refugees so far as possible the benefits of similar agreements which may at any time be in force between such Contracting States and non-contracting States.

CHAPTER V

ADMINISTRATIVE MEASURES

Article 25. Administrative assistance

A.4–27 1. When the exercise of a right by a refugee would normally require the assistance of authorities of a foreign country to whom he cannot have recourse, the Contracting States in whose territory he is residing shall arrange that such assistance be afforded to him by their own authorities or by an international authority.

2. The authority or authorities mentioned in paragraph I shall deliver or cause to be delivered under their supervision to refugees such documents or certifications as would normally be delivered to aliens by or through their national authorities.

3. Documents or certifications so delivered shall stand in the stead of the official instruments delivered to aliens by or through their national authorities, and shall be given credence in the absence of proof to the contrary.

4. Subject to such exceptional treatment as may be granted to indigent persons, fees may be charged for the services mentioned herein, but such fees shall be moderate and commensurate with those charged to nationals for similar services.

5. The provisions of this article shall be without prejudice to articles 27 and 28.

Article 26. Freedom of movement

A.4–28 Each Contracting State shall accord to refugees lawfully in its territory the right to choose their place of residence and to move freely within its territory subject to any regulations applicable to aliens generally in the same circumstances.

Article 27. Identity papers

A.4–29 The Contracting States shall issue identity papers to any refugee in their territory who does not possess a valid travel document.

Article 28. Travel documents

A.4–30 1. The Contracting States shall issue to refugees lawfully staying in their territory travel documents for the purpose of travel outside their territory, unless compelling reasons of national security or public order otherwise require, and the provisions of the Schedule to this Convention shall apply with respect to such documents. The Contracting States may issue such a travel document to any other refugee in their territory; they shall in particular give sympathetic consideration to the issue of such a travel document to refugees in their territory who are unable to obtain a travel document from the country of their lawful residence.

2. Travel documents issued to refugees under previous international agreements by Parties thereto shall be recognized and treated by the Contracting States in the same way as if they had been issued pursuant to this article.

[290]

Article 29. Fiscal charges

1. The Contracting States shall not impose upon refugees duties, charges or taxes, of any description whatsoever, other or higher than those which are or may be levied on their nationals in similar situations.

2. Nothing in the above paragraph shall prevent the application to refugees of the laws and regulations concerning charges in respect of the issue to aliens of administrative documents including identity papers.

Article 30. Transfer of assets

1. A Contracting State shall, in conformity with its laws and regulations, permit refugees to transfer assets which they have brought into its territory, to another country where they have been admitted for the purposes of resettlement.

2. A Contracting State shall give sympathetic consideration to the application of refugees for permission to transfer assets wherever they may be and which are necessary for their resettlement in another country to which they have been admitted.

Article 31. Refugees unlawfully in the country of refuge

1. The Contracting States shall not impose penalties, on account of their illegal entry or presence, on refugees who, coming directly from a territory where their life or freedom was threatened in the sense of Article 1, enter or are present in their territory without authorization, provided they present themselves without delay to the authorities and show good cause for their illegal entry or presence.

2. The Contracting States shall not apply to the movements of such refugees restrictions other than those which are necessary and such restrictions shall only be applied until their status in the country is regularized or they obtain admission into another country. The Contracting States shall allow such refugees a reasonable period and all the necessary facilities to obtain admission into another country.

Article 32. Expulsion

1. The Contracting States shall not expel a refugee lawfully in their territory save on grounds of national security or public order.

2. The expulsion of such a refugee shall be only in pursuance of a decision reached in accordance with due process of law. Except where compelling reasons of national security otherwise require, the refugee shall be allowed to submit evidence to clear himself, and to appeal to and be represented for the purpose before competent authority or a person or persons specially designated by the competent authority.

3. The Contracting States shall allow such a refugee a reasonable period within which to seek legal admission into another country. The Contracting States reserve the right to apply during that period such internal measures as they may deem necessary.

Article 33. Prohibition of expulsion or return ("refoulement")

1. No Contracting State shall expel or return ("refouler") a refugee in any manner whatsoever to the frontiers of territories where his life or freedom would be threatened on account of his race, religion, nationality, membership of a particular social group or political opinion.

2. The benefit of the present provision may not, however, be claimed by a refugee whom there are reasonable grounds for regarding as a danger to the security of the country in which he is, or who, having been convicted by a final judgment of a particularly serious crime, constitutes a danger to the community of that country.

Article 34. Naturalization

A.4–36 The Contracting States shall as far as possible facilitate the assimilation and naturalization of refugees. They shall in particular make every effort to expedite naturalization proceedings and to reduce as far as possible the charges and costs of such proceedings.

CHAPTER VI

EXECUTORY AND TRANSITORY PROVISIONS

Article 35. Co-operation of the national authorities with the United Nations

A.4–37 1. The Contracting States undertake to co-operate with the Office of the United Nations High Commissioner for Refugees, or any other agency of the United Nations which may succeed it, in the exercise of its functions, and shall in particular facilitate its duty of supervising the application of the provisions of this Convention.

2. In order to enable the Office of the High Commissioner or any other agency of the United Nations which may succeed it, to make reports to the competent organs of the United Nations, the Contracting States undertake to provide them in the appropriate form with information and statistical data requested concerning:

(a) The condition of refugees,

(b) The implementation of this Convention, and

(c) Laws, regulations and decrees which are, or may hereafter be, in force relating to refugees.

Article 36. Information on national legislation

A.4–38 The Contracting States shall communicate to the Secretary-General of the United Nations the laws and regulations which they may adopt to ensure the application of this Convention.

Article 37. Relation to previous conventions

A.4–39 Without prejudice to Article 28, paragraph 2, of this Convention, this Convention replaces, as between Parties to it, the Arrangements of 5 July 1922, 31 May 1924, 12 May 1926, 30 June 1928 and 30 July 1935, the Conventions of 28 October 1933 and 10 February 1938, the Protocol of 14 September 1939 and the Agreement of 15 October 1946.

CHAPTER VII

FINAL CLAUSES

Article 38. Settlement of disputes

A.4–40 Any dispute between Parties to this Convention relating to its interpretation or application, which cannot be settled by other means, shall be referred to the International Court of Justice at the request of any one of the parties to the dispute.

Article 39. Signature, ratification and accession

A.4–41 1. This Convention shall be opened for signature at Geneva on 28 July 1951 and shall thereafter be deposited with the Secretary-General of the United Nations. It shall be open for signature at the European Office of the United Nations from 28 July to 31 August 1951 and shall be re-opened for signature at the Headquarters of the United Nations from 17 September 1951 to 31 December 1952.

2. This Convention shall be open for signature on behalf of all States Members of the United Nations, and also on behalf of any other State invited to attend the Conference of Plenipotentiaries on the Status of Refugees and Stateless Persons or to which an invitation to sign will have been addressed by the General Assembly. It shall be ratified and the instruments of ratification shall be deposited with the Secretary-General of the United Nations.

3. This Convention shall be open from 28 July 1951 for accession by the States referred to in paragraph 2 of this article. Accession shall be effected by the deposit of an instrument of accession with the Secretary-General of the United Nations.

Article 40. Territorial application clause

1. Any State may, at the time of signature, ratification or accession, declare that this **A.4–42** Convention shall extend to all or any of the territories for the international relations of which it is responsible. Such a declaration shall take effect when the Convention enters into force for the State concerned.

2. At any time thereafter any such extension shall be made by notification addressed to the Secretary-General of the United Nations and shall take effect as from the ninetieth day after the day of receipt by the Secretary-General of the United Nations of this notification, or as from the date of entry into force of the Convention for the State concerned, whichever is the later.

3. With respect to those territories to which this Convention is not extended at the time of signature, ratification or accession, each State concerned shall consider the possibility of taking the necessary steps in order to extend the application of this Convention to such territories, subject, where necessary for constitutional reasons, to the consent of the Governments of such territories.

Article 41. Federal clause

In the case of a Federal or non-unitary State, the following provisions shall apply: **A.4–43**

(a) With respect to those articles of this Convention that come within the legislative jurisdiction of the federal legislative authority, the obligations of the Federal Government shall to this extent be the same as those of parties which not Federal States;

(b) With respect to those articles of this Convention that come within the legislative jurisdiction of constituent States, provinces or cantons which are not, under the constitutional system of the Federation, bound to take legislative action, the Federal Government shall bring such articles with a favourable recommendation to the notice of the appropriate authorities of States, provinces or cantons at the earliest possible moment;

(c) A Federal State Party to this Convention shall, at the request of any other Contracting State transmitted through the Secretary-General of the United Nations, supply a statement of the law and practice of the Federation and its constituent units in regard to any particular provision of the Convention showing the extent to which effect has been given to that provision by legislative or other action.

Article 42. Reservations

1. At the time of signature, ratification or accession, any State may make reservations to **A.4–44** articles of the Convention other than to Articles 1, 3, 4, 16(1), 33, 36–46 inclusive.

2. Any State making a reservation in accordance with paragraph I of this article may at any time withdraw the reservation by a communication to that effect addressed to the Secretary-General of the United Nations.

Article 43. Entry into force

A.4–45 1. This Convention shall come into force on the ninetieth day following the day of deposit of the sixth instrument of ratification or accession.

2. For each State ratifying or acceding to the Convention after the deposit of the sixth instrument of ratification or accession, the Convention shall enter into force on the ninetieth day following the date of deposit by such State of its instrument of ratification or accession.

Article 44. Denunciation

A.4–46 1. Any Contracting State may denounce this Convention at any time by a notification addressed to the Secretary-General of the United Nations.

2. Such denunciation shall take effect for the Contracting State concerned one year from the date upon which it is received by the Secretary-General of the United Nations.

3. Any State which has made a declaration or notification under Article 40 may, at any time thereafter, by a notification to the Secretary-General of the United Nations, declare that the Convention shall cease to extend to such territory one year after the date of receipt of the notification by the Secretary-General. Article 45.—Revision

1. Any Contracting State may request revision of this Convention at any time by a notification addressed to the Secretary-General of the United Nations.

2. The General Assembly of the United Nations shall recommend the steps, if any, to be taken in respect of such request.

Article 46. Notifications by the Secretary-General of the United Nations

A.4–47 The Secretary-General of the United Nations shall inform all Members of the United Nations and non-member States referred to in Article 39;

(a) Of declarations and notifications in accordance with section B of Article 1;

(b) Of signatures, ratifications and accessions in accordance with Article 39;

(c) Of declarations and notifications in accordance with Article 40;

(d) Of reservations and withdrawals in accordance with Article 42;

(e) Of the date on which this Convention will come into force in accordance with Article 43;

(f) Of denunciations and notifications in accordance with Article 44;

(g) Of requests for revision in accordance with Article 45.

IN FAITH WHEREOF the undersigned, duly authorized, have signed this Convention on behalf of their respective Governments.

DONE at Geneva, this twenty-eighth day of July, one thousand nine hundred and fifty-one, in a single copy, of which the English and French texts are equally authentic and which shall remain deposited in the archives of the United Nations, and certified true copies of which shall be delivered to all Members of the United Nations and to the non-member States referred to in Article 39.

CONVENTION AGAINST TORTURE AND OTHER CRUEL, INHUMAN OR DEGRADING TREATMENT OR PUNISHMENT

Adopted and opened for signature, ratification and accession by General Assembly resolution 39/46 of 10 December 1984

ENTRY INTO FORCE 26 JUNE 1987, IN ACCORDANCE WITH ARTICLE 27(1)

The States Parties to this Convention

Considering that, in accordance with the principles proclaimed in the Charter of the United Nations, recognition of the equal and inalienable rights of all members of the human family is the foundation of freedom, justice and peace in the world.   A.5–01

Recognizing that those rights derive from the inherent dignity of the human person,

Considering the obligation of States under the Charter, in particular Article 55, to promote universal respect for, and observance of, human rights and fundamental freedoms,

Having regard to Article 5 of the Universal Declaration of Human Rights and Article 7 of the International Covenant on Civil and Political Rights, both of which provide that no one shall be subjected to torture or to cruel, inhuman or degrading treatment or punishment,

Having regard also to the Declaration on the Protection of All Persons from Being Subjected to Torture and Other Cruel, Inhuman or Degrading Treatment or Punishment, adopted by the General Assembly on 9 December 1975,

Desiring to make more effective the struggle against torture and other cruel, inhuman or degrading treatment or punishment throughout the world,

Have agreed as follows:

PART I

Article 1

1. For the purposes of this Convention, the term "torture" means any act by which severe pain or suffering, whether physical or mental, is intentionally inflicted on a person for such purposes as obtaining from him or a third person information or a confession, punishing him for an act he or a third person has committed or is suspected of having committed, or intimidating or coercing him or a third person, or for any reason based on discrimination of any kind, when such pain or suffering is inflicted by or at the instigation of or with the consent or acquiescence of a public official or other person acting in an official   A.5–02

capacity. It does not include pain or suffering arising only from, inherent in or incidental to lawful sanctions.

2. This article is without prejudice to any international instrument or national legislation which does or may contain provisions of wider application.

Article 2

A.5–03   1. Each State Party shall take effective legislative, administrative, judicial or other measures to prevent acts of torture in any territory under its jurisdiction.

2. No exceptional circumstances whatsoever, whether a state of war or a threat of war, internal political in stability or any other public emergency, may be invoked as a justification of torture.

3. An order from a superior officer or a public authority may not be invoked as a justification of torture.

Article 3 General comment on its implementation

A.5–04   1. No State Party shall expel, return ("refouler") or extradite a person to another State where there are substantial grounds for believing that he would be in danger of being subjected to torture.

2. For the purpose of determining whether there are such grounds, the competent authorities shall take into account all relevant considerations including, where applicable, the existence in the State concerned of a consistent pattern of gross, flagrant or mass violations of human rights.

Article 4

A.5–05   1. Each State Party shall ensure that all acts of torture are offences under its criminal law. The same shall apply to an attempt to commit torture and to an act by any person which constitutes complicity or participation in torture.

2. Each State Party shall make these offences punishable by appropriate penalties which take into account their grave nature.

Article 5

A.5–06   1. Each State Party shall take such measures as may be necessary to establish its jurisdiction over the offences referred to in article 4 in the following cases:

(a) When the offences are committed in any territory under its jurisdiction or on board a ship or aircraft registered in that State;

(b) When the alleged offender is a national of that State;

(c) When the victim is a national of that State if that State considers it appropriate.

2. Each State Party shall likewise take such measures as may be necessary to establish its jurisdiction over such offences in cases where the alleged offender is present in any territory under its jurisdiction and it does not extradite him pursuant to article 8 to any of the States mentioned in paragraph I of this article.

3. This Convention does not exclude any criminal jurisdiction exercised in accordance with internal law.

Article 6

A.5–07   1. Upon being satisfied, after an examination of information available to it, that the circumstances so warrant, any State Party in whose territory a person alleged to have committed any offence referred to in Article 4 is present shall take him into custody or take other legal measures to ensure his presence. The custody and other legal measures shall be as provided in the law of that State but may be continued only for such time as is necessary to enable any criminal or extradition proceedings to be instituted.

2. Such State shall immediately make a preliminary inquiry into the facts.

3. Any person in custody pursuant to paragraph I of this article shall be assisted in communicating immediately with the nearest appropriate representative of the State of which he is a national, or, if he is a stateless person, with the representative of the State where he usually resides.

4. When a State, pursuant to this article, has taken a person into custody, it shall immediately notify the States referred to in Article 5, paragraph 1, of the fact that such person is in custody and of the circumstances which warrant his detention. The State which makes the preliminary inquiry contemplated in paragraph 2 of this article shall promptly report its findings to the said States and shall indicate whether it intends to exercise jurisdiction.

Article 7

1. The State Party in the territory under whose jurisdiction a person alleged to have   **A.5–08**
committed any offence referred to in Article 4 is found shall in the cases contemplated in article 5, if it does not extradite him, submit the case to its competent authorities for the purpose of prosecution.

2. These authorities shall take their decision in the same manner as in the case of any ordinary offence of a serious nature under the law of that State. In the cases referred to in Article 5, paragraph 2, the standards of evidence required for prosecution and conviction shall in no way be less stringent than those which apply in the cases referred to in article 5, paragraph 1.

3. Any person regarding whom proceedings are brought in connection with any of the offences referred to in Article 4 shall be guaranteed fair treatment at all stages of the proceedings.

Article 8

1. The offences referred to in Article 4 shall be deemed to be included as extraditable   **A.5–09**
offences in any extradition treaty existing between States Parties. States Parties undertake to include such offences as extraditable offences in every extradition treaty to be concluded between them.

2. If a State Party which makes extradition conditional on the existence of a treaty receives a request for extradition from another State Party with which it has no extradition treaty, it may consider this Convention as the legal basis for extradition in respect of such offences. Extradition shall be subject to the other conditions provided by the law of the requested State.

3. States Parties which do not make extradition conditional on the existence of a treaty shall recognize such offences as extraditable offences between themselves subject to the conditions provided by the law of the requested State.

4. Such offences shall be treated, for the purpose of extradition between States Parties, as if they had been committed not only in the place in which they occurred but also in the territories of the States required to establish their jurisdiction in accordance with Article 5, paragraph 1.

Article 9

1. States Parties shall afford one another the greatest measure of assistance in connection   **A.5–10**
with criminal proceedings brought in respect of any of the offences referred to in Article 4, including the supply of all evidence at their disposal necessary for the proceedings.

2. States Parties shall carry out their obligations under paragraph I of this article in conformity with any treaties on mutual judicial assistance that may exist between them.

Article 10

A.5–11 1. Each State Party shall ensure that education and information regarding the prohibition against torture are fully included in the training of law enforcement personnel, civil or military, medical personnel, public officials and other persons who may be involved in the custody, interrogation or treatment of any individual subjected to any form of arrest, detention or imprisonment.

2. Each State Party shall include this prohibition in the rules or instructions issued in regard to the duties and functions of any such person.

Article 11

A.5–12 Each State Party shall keep under systematic review interrogation rules, instructions, methods and practices as well as arrangements for the custody and treatment of persons subjected to any form of arrest, detention or imprisonment in any territory under its jurisdiction, with a view to preventing any cases of torture.

Article 12

A.5–13 Each State Party shall ensure that its competent authorities proceed to a prompt and impartial investigation, wherever there is reasonable ground to believe that an act of torture has been committed in any territory under its jurisdiction.

Article 13

A.5–14 Each State Party shall ensure that any individual who alleges he has been subjected to torture in any territory under its jurisdiction has the right to complain to, and to have his case promptly and impartially examined by, its competent authorities. Steps shall be taken to ensure that the complainant and witnesses are protected against all ill-treatment or intimidation as a consequence of his complaint or any evidence given.

Article 14

A.5–15 1. Each State Party shall ensure in its legal system that the victim of an act of torture obtains redress and has an enforceable right to fair and adequate compensation, including the means for as full rehabilitation as possible. In the event of the death of the victim as a result of an act of torture, his dependants shall be entitled to compensation.

2. Nothing in this article shall affect any right of the victim or other persons to compensation which may exist under national law.

Article 15

A.5–16 Each State Party shall ensure that any statement which is established to have been made as a result of torture shall not be invoked as evidence in any proceedings, except against a person accused of torture as evidence that the statement was made.

Article 16

A.5–17 1. Each State Party shall undertake to prevent in any territory under its jurisdiction other acts of cruel, inhuman or degrading treatment or punishment which do not amount to torture as defined in Article I, when such acts are committed by or at the instigation of or with the consent or acquiescence of a public official or other person acting in an official capacity. In particular, the obligations contained in Articles 10, 11, 12 and 13 shall apply with the substitution for references to torture of references to other forms of cruel, inhuman or degrading treatment or punishment.

2. The provisions of this Convention are without prejudice to the provisions of any other international instrument or national law which prohibits cruel, inhuman or degrading treatment or punishment or which relates to extradition or expulsion.

PART II

Article 17

1. There shall be established a Committee against Torture (hereinafter referred to as the **A.5–18** Committee) which shall carry out the functions hereinafter provided. The Committee shall consist of ten experts of high moral standing and recognized competence in the field of human rights, who shall serve in their personal capacity. The experts shall be elected by the States Parties, consideration being given to equitable geographical distribution and to the usefulness of the participation of some persons having legal experience.

2. The members of the Committee shall be elected by secret ballot from a list of persons nominated by States Parties. Each State Party may nominate one person from among its own nationals. States Parties shall bear in mind the usefulness of nominating persons who are also members of the Human Rights Committee established under the International Covenant on Civil and Political Rights and who are willing to serve on the Committee against Torture.

3. Elections of the members of the Committee shall be held at biennial meetings of States Parties convened by the Secretary-General of the United Nations. At those meetings, for which two thirds of the States Parties shall constitute a quorum, the persons elected to the Committee shall be those who obtain the largest number of votes and an absolute majority of the votes of the representatives of States Parties present and voting.

4. The initial election shall be held no later than six months after the date of the entry into force of this Convention. At least four months before the date of each election, the Secretary-General of the United Nations shall address a letter to the States Parties inviting them to submit their nominations within three months. The Secretary-General shall prepare a list in alphabetical order of all persons thus nominated, indicating the States Parties which have nominated them, and shall submit it to the States Parties.

5. The members of the Committee shall be elected for a term of four years. They shall be eligible for re-election if renominated. However, the term of five of the members elected at the first election shall expire at the end of two years; immediately after the first election the names of these five members shall be chosen by lot by the chairman of the meeting referred to in paragraph 3 of this article.

6. If a member of the Committee dies or resigns or for any other cause can no longer perform his Committee duties, the State Party which nominated him shall appoint another expert from among its nationals to serve for the remainder of his term, subject to the approval of the majority of the States Parties. The approval shall be considered given unless half or more of the States Parties respond negatively within six weeks after having been informed by the Secretary-General of the United Nations of the proposed appointment.

7. States Parties shall be responsible for the expenses of the members of the Committee while they are in performance of Committee duties. (amendment (see General Assembly resolution 47/111 of 16 December 1992; *status of ratification*)

Article 18

1. The Committee shall elect its officers for a term of two years. They may be **A.5–19** re-elected.

2. The Committee shall establish its own rules of procedure, but these rules shall provide, *inter alia*, that:

(a) Six members shall constitute a quorum;

(b) Decisions of the Committee shall be made by a majority vote of the members present.

3. The Secretary-General of the United Nations shall provide the necessary staff and facilities for the effective performance of the functions of the Committee under this Convention.

4. The Secretary-General of the United Nations shall convene the initial meeting of the Committee. After its initial meeting, the Committee shall meet at such times as shall be provided in its rules of procedure.

5. The States Parties shall be responsible for expenses incurred in connection with the holding of meetings of the States Parties and of the Committee, including reimbursement to the United Nations for any expenses, such as the cost of staff and facilities, incurred by the United Nations pursuant to paragraph 3 of this article. (amendment (see General Assembly resolution 47/111 of 16 December 1992); *status of ratification*)

Article 19

A.5–20 1. The States Parties shall submit to the Committee, through the Secretary-General of the United Nations, reports on the measures they have taken to give effect to their undertakings under this Convention, within one year after the entry into force of the Convention for the State Party concerned. Thereafter the States Parties shall submit supplementary reports every four years on any new measures taken and such other reports as the Committee may request.

2. The Secretary-General of the United Nations shall transmit the reports to all States Parties.

3. Each report shall be considered by the Committee which may make such general comments on the report as it may consider appropriate and shall forward these to the State Party concerned. That State Party may respond with any observations it chooses to the Committee.

4. The Committee may, at its discretion, decide to include any comments made by it in accordance with paragraph 3 of this article, together with the observations thereon received from the State Party concerned, in its annual report made in accordance with Article 24. If so requested by the State Party concerned, the Committee may also include a copy of the report submitted under paragraph I of this article.

Article 20

A.5–21 1. If the Committee receives reliable information which appears to it to contain well-founded indications that torture is being systematically practised in the territory of a State Party, the Committee shall invite that State Party to co-operate in the examination of the information and to this end to submit observations with regard to the information concerned.

2. Taking into account any observations which may have been submitted by the State Party concerned, as well as any other relevant information available to it, the Committee may, if it decides that this is warranted, designate one or more of its members to make a confidential inquiry and to report to the Committee urgently.

3. If an inquiry is made in accordance with paragraph 2 of this article, the Committee shall seek the co-operation of the State Party concerned. In agreement with that State Party, such an inquiry may include a visit to its territory.

4. After examining the findings of its member or members submitted in accordance with paragraph 2 of this article, the Commission shall transmit these findings to the State Party concerned together with any comments or suggestions which seem appropriate in view of the situation.

5. All the proceedings of the Committee referred to in paragraphs 1 to 4 of this article shall be confidential, and at all stages of the proceedings the co-operation of the State Party shall be sought. After such proceedings have been completed with regard to an inquiry made in accordance with paragraph 2, the Committee may, after consultations with the State Party concerned, decide to include a summary account of the results of the proceedings in its annual report made in accordance with Article 24.

Article 21

1. A State Party to this Convention may at any time declare under this article that it **A.5–22** recognizes the competence of the Committee to receive and consider communications to the effect that a State Party claims that another State Party is not fulfilling its obligations under this Convention. Such communications may be received and considered according to the procedures laid down in this article only if submitted by a State Party which has made a declaration recognizing in regard to itself the competence of the Committee. No communication shall be dealt with by the Committee under this article if it concerns a State Party which has not made such a declaration. Communications received under this article shall be dealt with in accordance with the following procedure;

(a) If a State Party considers that another State Party is not giving effect to the provisions of this Convention, it may, by written communication, bring the matter to the attention of that State Party. Within three months after the receipt of the communication the receiving State shall afford the State which sent the communication an explanation or any other statement in writing clarifying the which should include, to the extent possible and pertinent, reference to domestic procedures and remedies taken, pending or available in the matter;

(b) If the matter is not adjusted to the satisfaction of both States Parties concerned within six months after the receipt by the receiving State of the initial communication, either State shall have the right to refer the matter to the Committee, by notice given to the Committee and to the other State;

(c) The Committee shall deal with a matter referred to it under this article only after it has ascertained that all domestic remedies have been invoked and exhausted in the matter, in conformity with the generally recognized principles of international law. This shall not be the rule where the application of the remedies is unreasonably prolonged or is unlikely to bring effective relief to the person who is the victim of the violation of this Convention;

(d) The Committee shall hold closed meetings when examining communications under this article;

(e) Subject to the provisions of subparagraph (c), the Committee shall make available its good offices to the States Parties concerned with a view to a friendly solution of the matter on the basis of respect for the obligations provided for in this Convention. For this purpose, the Committee may, when appropriate, set up an ad hoc conciliation commission;

(f) In any matter referred to it under this article, the Committee may call upon the States Parties concerned, referred to in subparagraph (b), to supply any relevant information;

(g) The States Parties concerned, referred to in subparagraph (b), shall have the right to be represented when the matter is being considered by the Committee and to make submissions orally and/or in writing;

(h) The Committee shall, within twelve months after the date of receipt of notice under subparagraph (b), submit a report:

(i) If a solution within the terms of subparagraph (e) is reached, the Committee shall confine its report to a brief statement of the facts and of the solution reached;

(ii) If a solution within the terms of subparagraph (e) is not reached, the Committee shall confine its report to a brief statement of the facts; the written submissions and record of the oral submissions made by the States Parties concerned shall be attached to the report.

In every matter, the report shall be communicated to the States Parties concerned.

2. The provisions of this article shall come into force when five States Parties to this Convention have made declarations under paragraph 1 of this article. Such declarations shall be deposited by the States Parties with the Secretary-General of the United Nations, who shall transmit copies thereof to the other States Parties. A declaration may be withdrawn at any time by notification to the Secretary-General. Such a withdrawal shall not prejudice the consideration of any matter which is the subject of a communication already transmitted under this article; no further communication by any State Party shall be received under this article after the notification of withdrawal of the declaration has been received by the Secretary-General, unless the State Party concerned has made a new declaration.

Article 22

A.5–23 1. A State Party to this Convention may at any time declare under this article that it recognizes the competence of the Committee to receive and consider communications from or on behalf of individuals subject to its jurisdiction who claim to be victims of a violation by a State Party of the provisions of the Convention. No communication shall be received by the Committee if it concerns a State Party which has not made such a declaration.

2. The Committee shall consider inadmissible any communication under this article which is anonymous or which it considers to be an abuse of the right of submission of such communications or to be incompatible with the provisions of this Convention.

3. Subject to the provisions of paragraph 2, the Committee shall bring any communications submitted to it under this article to the attention of the State Party to this Convention which has made a declaration under paragraph I and is alleged to be violating any provisions of the Convention. Within six months, the receiving State shall submit to the Committee written explanations or statements clarifying the matter and the remedy, if any, that may have been taken by that State.

4. The Committee shall consider communications received under this article in the light of all information made available to it by or on behalf of the individual and by the State Party concerned.

5. The Committee shall not consider any communications from an individual under this article unless it has ascertained that:

(a) The same matter has not been, and is not being, examined under another procedure of international investigation or settlement;

(b) The individual has exhausted all available domestic remedies; this shall not be the rule where the application of the remedies is unreasonably prolonged or is unlikely to bring effective relief to the person who is the victim of the violation of this Convention.

6. The Committee shall hold closed meetings when examining communications under this article.

7. The Committee shall forward its views to the State Party concerned and to the individual.

8. The provisions of this article shall come into force when five States Parties to this Convention have made declarations under paragraph 1 of this article. Such declarations

shall be deposited by the States Parties with the Secretary-General of the United Nations, who shall transmit copies thereof to the other States Parties. A declaration may be withdrawn at any time by notification to the Secretary-General. Such a withdrawal shall not prejudice the consideration of any matter which is the subject of a communication already transmitted under this article; no further communication by or on behalf of an individual shall be received under this article after the notification of withdrawal of the declaration has been received by the Secretary-General, unless the State Party has made a new declaration.

Article 23

The members of the Committee and of the ad hoc conciliation commissions which may   **A.5–24** be appointed under Article 21, paragraph I (e), shall be entitled to the facilities, privileges and immunities of experts on mission for the United Nations as laid down in the relevant sections of the Convention on the Privileges and Immunities of the United Nations.

Article 24

The Committee shall submit an annual report on its activities under this Convention to the   **A.5–25** States Parties and to the General Assembly of the United Nations.

Part III

Article 25

1. This Convention is open for signature by all States.   **A.5–26**

2. This Convention is subject to ratification. Instruments of ratification shall be deposited with the Secretary-General of the United Nations.

Article 26

This Convention is open to accession by all States. Accession shall be effected by the   **A.5–27** deposit of an instrument of accession with the Secretary-General of the United Nations.

Article 27

1. This Convention shall enter into force on the thirtieth day after the date of the deposit   **A.5–28** with the Secretary-General of the United Nations of the twentieth instrument of ratification or accession.

2. For each State ratifying this Convention or acceding to it after the deposit of the twentieth instrument of ratification or accession, the Convention shall enter into force on the thirtieth day after the date of the deposit of its own instrument of ratification or accession.

Article 28

1. Each State may, at the time of signature or ratification of this Convention or accession   **A.5–29** thereto, declare that it does not recognize the competence of the Committee provided for in Article 20.

2. Any State Party having made a reservation in accordance with paragraph I of this article may, at any time, withdraw this reservation by notification to the Secretary-General of the United Nations.

Article 29

1. Any State Party to this Convention may propose an amendment and file it with the   **A.5–30** Secretary-General of the United Nations. The Secretary-General shall thereupon communicate the proposed amendment to the States Parties with a request that they notify him

whether they favour a conference of States Parties for the purpose of considering and voting upon the proposal. In the event that within four months from the date of such communication at least one third of the States Parties favours such a conference, the Secretary-General shall convene the conference under the auspices of the United Nations. Any amendment adopted by a majority of the States Parties present and voting at the conference shall be submitted by the Secretary-General to all the States Parties for acceptance.

2. An amendment adopted in accordance with paragraph I of this article shall enter into force when two thirds of the States Parties to this Convention have notified the Secretary-General of the United Nations that they have accepted it in accordance with their respective constitutional processes.

3. When amendments enter into force, they shall be binding on those States Parties which have accepted them, other States Parties still being bound by the provisions of this Convention and any earlier amendments which they have accepted.

Article 30

A.5–31   1. Any dispute between two or more States Parties concerning the interpretation or application of this Convention which cannot be settled through negotiation shall, at the request of one of them, be submitted to arbitration. If within six months from the date of the request for arbitration the Parties are unable to agree on the organization of the arbitration, any one of those Parties may refer the dispute to the International Court of Justice by request in conformity with the Statute of the Court.

2. Each State may, at the time of signature or ratification of this Convention or accession thereto, declare that it does not consider itself bound by paragraph I of this article. The other States Parties shall not be bound by paragraph I of this article with respect to any State Party having made such a reservation.

3. Any State Party having made a reservation in accordance with paragraph 2 of this article may at any time withdraw this reservation by notification to the Secretary-General of the United Nations.

Article 31

A.5–32   1. A State Party may denounce this Convention by written notification to the Secretary-General of the United Nations. Denunciation becomes effective one year after the date of receipt of the notification by the Secretary-General.

2. Such a denunciation shall not have the effect of releasing the State Party from its obligations under this Convention in regard to any act or omission which occurs prior to the date at which the denunciation becomes effective, nor shall denunciation prejudice in any way the continued consideration of any matter which is already under consideration by the Committee prior to the date at which the denunciation becomes effective.

3. Following the date at which the denunciation of a State Party becomes effective, the Committee shall not commence consideration of any new matter regarding that State.

Article 32

A.5–33   The Secretary-General of the United Nations shall inform all States Members of the United Nations and all States which have signed this Convention or acceded to it of the following:

(a) Signatures, ratifications and accessions under Articles 25 and 26;

(b) The date of entry into force of this Convention under Article 27 and the date of the entry into force of any amendments under Article 29;

(c) Denunciations under Article 31.

Article 33

1. This Convention, of which the Arabic, Chinese, English, French, Russian and Spanish **A.5–34** texts are equally authentic, shall be deposited with the Secretary-General of the United Nations.

2. The Secretary-General of the United Nations shall transmit certified copies of this Convention to all States.

UNIVERSAL DECLARATION OF HUMAN RIGHTS

Preamble

Whereas recognition of the inherent dignity and of the equal and inalienable rights of all **A.6–01** members of the human family is the foundation of freedom, justice and peace in the world,

Whereas disregard and contempt for human rights have resulted in barbarous acts which have outraged the conscience of mankind, and the advent of a world in which human beings shall enjoy freedom of speech and belief and freedom from fear and want has been proclaimed as the highest aspiration of the common people,

Whereas it is essential, if man is not to be compelled to have recourse, as a last resort, to rebellion against tyranny and oppression, that human rights should be protected by the rule of law,

Whereas it is essential to promote the development of friendly relations between nations,

Whereas the peoples of the United Nations have in the Charter reaffirmed their faith in fundamental human rights, in the dignity and worth of the human person and in the equal rights of men and women and have determined to promote social progress and better standards of life in larger freedom,

Whereas Member States have pledged themselves to achieve, in cooperation with the **A.6–02** United Nations, the promotion of universal respect for and observance of human rights and fundamental freedoms,

Whereas a common understanding of these rights and freedoms is of the greatest importance for the full realization of this pledge,

Now, therefore,

The General Assembly,

Proclaims this Universal Declaration of Human Rights as a common standard of achievement for all peoples and all nations, to the end that every individual and every organ of society, keeping this Declaration constantly in mind, shall strive by teaching and education to promote respect for these rights and freedoms and by progressive measures, national and international, to secure their universal and effective recognition and observance, both among the peoples of Member States themselves and among the peoples of territories under their jurisdiction.

Article 1

All human beings are born free and equal in dignity and rights. They are endowed with **A.6–03** reason and conscience and should act towards one another in a spirit of brotherhood.

Article 2

A.6–04 Everyone is entitled to all the rights and freedoms set forth in this Declaration, without distinction of any kind, such as race, colour, sex, language, religion, political or other opinion, national or social origin, property, birth or other status.

Furthermore, no distinction shall be made on the basis of the political, jurisdictional or international status of the country or territory to which a person belongs, whether it be independent, trust, non-self-governing or under any other limitation of sovereignty.

Article 3

A.6–05 Everyone has the right to life, liberty and security of person.

Article 4

A.6–06 No one shall be held in slavery or servitude; slavery and the slave trade shall be prohibited in all their forms.

Article 5

A.6–07 No one shall be subjected to torture or to cruel, inhuman or degrading treatment or punishment.

Article 6

A.6–08 Everyone has the right to recognition everywhere as a person before the law.

Article 7

A.6–09 All are equal before the law and are entitled without any discrimination to equal protection of the law. All are entitled to equal protection against any discrimination in violation of this Declaration and against any incitement to such discrimination.

Article 8

A.6–10 Everyone has the right to an effective remedy by the competent national tribunals for acts violating the fundamental rights granted him by the constitution or by law.

Article 9

A.6–11 No one shall be subjected to arbitrary arrest, detention or exile.

Article 10

A.6–12 Everyone is entitled in full equality to a fair and public hearing by an independent and impartial tribunal, in the determination of his rights and obligations and of any criminal charge against him.

Article 11

A.6–13 1. Everyone charged with a penal offence has the right to be presumed innocent until proved guilty according to law in a public trial at which he has had all the guarantees necessary for his defence.

2. No one shall be held guilty of any penal offence on account of any act or omission which did not constitute a penal offence, under national or international law, at the time when it was committed. Nor shall a heavier penalty be imposed than the one that was applicable at the time the penal offence was committed.

Article 12

A.6–14 No one shall be subjected to arbitrary interference with his privacy, family, home or correspondence, nor to attacks upon his honour and reputation. Everyone has the right to the protection of the law against such interference or attacks.

Article 13

1. Everyone has the right to freedom of movement and residence within the borders of   **A.6–15**
each State.

2. Everyone has the right to leave any country, including his own, and to return to his
country.

Article 14

1. Everyone has the right to seek and to enjoy in other countries asylum from persecu-   **A.6–16**
tion.

2. This right may not be invoked in the case of prosecutions genuinely arising from non-
political crimes or from acts contrary to the purposes and principles of the United
Nations.

Article 15

1. Everyone has the right to a nationality.   **A.6–17**

2. No one shall be arbitrarily deprived of his nationality nor denied the right to change his
nationality.

Article 16

1. Men and women of full age, without any limitation due to race, nationality or religion,   **A.6–18**
have the right to marry and to found a family. They are entitled to equal rights as to
marriage, during marriage and at its dissolution.

2. Marriage shall be entered into only with the free and full consent of the intending
spouses.

3. The family is the natural and fundamental group unit of society and is entitled to
protection by society and the State.

Article 17

1. Everyone has the right to own property alone as well as in association with others.   **A.6–19**

2. No one shall be arbitrarily deprived of his property.

Article 18

Everyone has the right to freedom of thought, conscience and religion; this right includes   **A.6–20**
freedom to change his religion or belief, and freedom, either alone or in community with
others and in public or private, to manifest his religion or belief in teaching, practice,
worship and observance.

Article 19

Everyone has the right to freedom of opinion and expression; this right includes freedom   **A.6–21**
to hold opinions without interference and to seek, receive and impart information and
ideas through any media and regardless of frontiers.

Article 20

1. Everyone has the right to freedom of peaceful assembly and association.   **A.6–22**

2. No one may be compelled to belong to an association.

Article 21

1. Everyone has the right to take part in the government of his country, directly or through   **A.6–23**
freely chosen representatives.

2. Everyone has the right to equal access to public service in his country.

3. The will of the people shall be the basis of the authority of government; this will shall be expressed in periodic and genuine elections which shall be by universal and equal suffrage and shall be held by secret vote or by equivalent free voting procedures.

Article 22

A.6–24 Everyone, as a member of society, has the right to social security and is entitled to realization, through national effort and international co-operation and in accordance with the organization and resources of each State, of the economic, social and cultural rights indispensable for his dignity and the free development of his personality.

Article 23

A.6–25 1. Everyone has the right to work, to free choice of employment, to just and favourable conditions of work and to protection against unemployment.

2. Everyone, without any discrimination, has the right to equal pay for equal work.

3. Everyone who works has the right to just and favourable remuneration ensuring for himself and his family an existence worthy of human dignity, and supplemented, if necessary, by other means of social protection.

4. Everyone has the right to form and to join trade unions for the protection of his interests.

Article 24

A.6–26 Everyone has the right to rest and leisure, including reasonable limitation of working hours and periodic holidays with pay.

Article 25

A.6–27 1. Everyone has the right to a standard of living adequate for the health and well-being of himself and of his family, including food, clothing, housing and medical care and necessary social services, and the right to security in the event of unemployment, sickness, disability, widowhood, old age or other lack of livelihood in circumstances beyond his control.

2. Motherhood and childhood are entitled to special care and assistance. All children, whether born in or out of wedlock, shall enjoy the same social protection.

Article 26

A.6–28 1. Everyone has the right to education. Education shall be free, at least in the elementary and fundamental stages. Elementary education shall be compulsory. Technical and professional education shall be made generally available and higher education shall be equally accessible to all on the basis of merit.

2. Education shall be directed to the full development of the human personality and to the strengthening of respect for human rights and fundamental freedoms. It shall promote understanding, tolerance and friendship among all nations, racial or religious groups, and shall further the activities of the United Nations for the maintenance of peace.

3. Parents have a prior right to choose the kind of education that shall be given to their children.

Article 27

A.6–29 1. Everyone has the right freely to participate in the cultural life of the community, to enjoy the arts and to share in scientific advancement and its benefits.

2. Everyone has the right to the protection of the moral and material interests resulting from any scientific, literary or artistic production of which he is the author.

Article 28

Everyone is entitled to a social and international order in which the rights and freedoms **A.6–30** set forth in this Declaration can be fully realized.

Article 29

1. Everyone has duties to the community in which alone the free and full development of **A.6–31** his personality is possible.

2. In the exercise of his rights and freedoms, everyone shall be subject only to such limitations as are determined by law solely for the purpose of securing due recognition and respect for the rights and freedoms of others and of meeting the just requirements of morality, public order and the general welfare in a democratic society.

3. These rights and freedoms may in no case be exercised contrary to the purposes and principles of the United Nations.

Article 30

Nothing in this Declaration may be interpreted as implying for any State, group or person **A.6–32** any right to engage in any activity or to perform any act aimed at the destruction of any of the rights and freedoms set forth herein.

INTERNATIONAL COVENANT ON CIVIL AND POLITICAL RIGHTS

Adopted and opened for signature, ratification and accession by General Assembly resolution 2200A (XXI) of 16 December 1966

Entry into Force 23 March 1976, in Accordance with Article 49

Preamble

The States Parties to the present Covenant,　　　　　　　　　　　　　　　　**A.7–01**

Considering that, in accordance with the principles proclaimed in the Charter of the United Nations, recognition of the inherent dignity and of the equal and inalienable rights of all members of the human family is the foundation of freedom, justice and peace in the world,

Recognizing that these rights derive from the inherent dignity of the human person,

Recognizing that, in accordance with the Universal Declaration of Human Rights, the ideal of free human beings enjoying civil and political freedom and freedom from fear and want can only be achieved if conditions are created whereby everyone may enjoy his civil and political rights, as well as his economic, social and cultural rights,

Considering the obligation of States under the Charter of the United Nations to promote universal respect for, and observance of, human rights and freedoms,

Realizing that the individual, having duties to other individuals and to the community to which he belongs, is under a responsibility to strive for the promotion and observance of the rights recognized in the present Covenant,

Agree upon the following articles:

Part I

Article 1

1. All peoples have the right of self-determination. By virtue of that right they freely　**A.7–02** determine their political status and freely pursue their economic, social and cultural development.

2. All peoples may, for their own ends, freely dispose of their natural wealth and resources without prejudice to any obligations arising out of international economic co-operation, based upon the principle of mutual benefit, and international law. In no case may a people be deprived of its own means of subsistence.

3. The States Parties to the present Covenant, including those having responsibility for the administration of Non-Self-Governing and Trust Territories, shall promote the realization of the right of self-determination, and shall respect that right, in conformity with the provisions of the Charter of the United Nations.

PART II

Article 2

A.7–03 1. Each State Party to the present Covenant undertakes to respect and to ensure to all individuals within its territory and subject to its jurisdiction the rights recognized in the present Covenant, without distinction of any kind, such as race, colour, sex, language, religion, political or other opinion, national or social origin, property, birth or other status.

2. Where not already provided for by existing legislative or other measures, each State Party to the present Covenant undertakes to take the necessary steps, in accordance with its constitutional processes and with the provisions of the present Covenant, to adopt such laws or other measures as may be necessary to give effect to the rights recognized in the present Covenant.

3. Each State Party to the present Covenant undertakes:

(a) To ensure that any person whose rights or freedoms as herein recognized are violated shall have an effective remedy, notwithstanding that the violation has been committed by persons acting in an official capacity;

(b) To ensure that any person claiming such a remedy shall have his right thereto determined by competent judicial, administrative or legislative authorities, or by any other competent authority provided for by the legal system of the State, and to develop the possibilities of judicial remedy;

(c) To ensure that the competent authorities shall enforce such remedies when granted.

Article 3

A.7–04 The States Parties to the present Covenant undertake to ensure the equal right of men and women to the enjoyment of all civil and political rights set forth in the present Covenant.

Article 4

A.7–05 1. In time of public emergency which threatens the life of the nation and the existence of which is officially proclaimed, the States Parties to the present Covenant may take measures derogating from their obligations under the present Covenant to the extent strictly required by the exigencies of the situation, provided that such measures are not inconsistent with their other obligations under international law and do not involve discrimination solely on the ground of race, colour, sex, language, religion or social origin.

2. No derogation from Articles 6, 7, 8 (paragraphs 1 and 2), 11, 15, 16 and 18 may be made under this provision.

3. Any State Party to the present Covenant availing itself of the right of derogation shall immediately inform the other States Parties to the present Covenant, through the intermediary of the Secretary-General of the United Nations, of the provisions from which it has derogated and of the reasons by which it was actuated. A further communication shall be

made, through the same intermediary, on the date on which it terminates such derogation.

Article 5

1. Nothing in the present Covenant may be interpreted as implying for any State, group **A.7–06** or person any right to engage in any activity or perform any act aimed at the destruction of any of the rights and freedoms recognized herein or at their limitation to a greater extent than is provided for in the present Covenant.

2. There shall be no restriction upon or derogation from any of the fundamental human rights recognized or existing in any State Party to the present Covenant pursuant to law, conventions, regulations or custom on the pretext that the present Covenant does not recognize such rights or that it recognizes them to a lesser extent.

PART III

Article 6

1. Every human being has the inherent right to life. This right shall be protected by law. **A.7–07** No one shall be arbitrarily deprived of his life.

2. In countries which have not abolished the death penalty, sentence of death may be imposed only for the most serious crimes in accordance with the law in force at the time of the commission of the crime and not contrary to the provisions of the present Covenant and to the Convention on the Prevention and Punishment of the Crime of Genocide. This penalty can only be carried out pursuant to a final judgement rendered by a competent court.

3. When deprivation of life constitutes the crime of genocide, it is understood that nothing in this article shall authorize any State Party to the present Covenant to derogate in any way from any obligation assumed under the provisions of the Convention on the Prevention and Punishment of the Crime of Genocide.

4. Anyone sentenced to death shall have the right to seek pardon or commutation of the sentence. Amnesty, pardon or commutation of the sentence of death may be granted in all cases.

5. Sentence of death shall not be imposed for crimes committed by persons below eighteen years of age and shall not be carried out on pregnant women.

6. Nothing in this article shall be invoked to delay or to prevent the abolition of capital punishment by any State Party to the present Covenant.

Article 7

No one shall be subjected to torture or to cruel, inhuman or degrading treatment or **A.7–08** punishment. In particular, no one shall be subjected without his free consent to medical or scientific experimentation.

Article 8

1. No one shall be held in slavery; slavery and the slave-trade in all their forms shall be **A.7–09** prohibited.

2. No one shall be held in servitude.

3. (a) No one shall be required to perform forced or compulsory labour;

   (b) Paragraph 3 (a) shall not be held to preclude, in countries where imprisonment with hard labour may be imposed as a punishment for a crime, the performance of hard labour in pursuance of a sentence to such punishment by a competent court;

(c) For the purpose of this paragraph the term "forced or compulsory labour" shall not include:

    (i) Any work or service, not referred to in subparagraph (b), normally required of a person who is under detention in consequence of a lawful order of a court, or of a person during conditional release from such detention;

    (ii) Any service of a military character and, in countries where conscientious objection is recognized, any national service required by law of conscientious objectors;

    (iii) Any service exacted in cases of emergency or calamity threatening the life or well-being of the community;

    (iv) Any work or service which forms part of normal civil obligations.

Article 9

A.7–10 1. Everyone has the right to liberty and security of person. No one shall be subjected to arbitrary arrest or detention. No one shall be deprived of his liberty except on such grounds and in accordance with such procedure as are established by law.

2. Anyone who is arrested shall be informed, at the time of arrest, of the reasons for his arrest and shall be promptly informed of any charges against him.

3. Anyone arrested or detained on a criminal charge shall be brought promptly before a judge or other officer authorized by law to exercise judicial power and shall be entitled to trial within a reasonable time or to release. It shall not be the general rule that persons awaiting trial shall be detained in custody, but release may be subject to guarantees to appear for trial, at any other stage of the judicial proceedings, and, should occasion arise, for execution of the judgment.

4. Anyone who is deprived of his liberty by arrest or detention shall be entitled to take proceedings before a court, in order that court may decide without delay on the lawfulness of his detention and order his release if the detention is not lawful.

5. Anyone who has been the victim of unlawful arrest or detention shall have an enforceable right to compensation.

Article 10

A.7–11 1. All persons deprived of their liberty shall be treated with humanity and with respect for the inherent dignity of the human person.

2. (a) Accused persons shall, save in exceptional circumstances, be segregated from convicted persons and shall be subject to separate treatment appropriate to their status as unconvicted persons;

    (b) Accused juvenile persons shall be separated from adults and brought as speedily as possible for adjudication. 3. The penitentiary system shall comprise treatment of prisoners the essential aim of which shall be their reformation and social rehabilitation. Juvenile offenders shall be segregated from adults and be accorded treatment appropriate to their age and legal status.

Article 11

A.7–12 No one shall be imprisoned merely on the ground of inability to fulfil a contractual obligation.

Article 12

A.7–13 1. Everyone lawfully within the territory of a State shall, within that territory, have the right to liberty of movement and freedom to choose his residence.

2. Everyone shall be free to leave any country, including his own.

3. The above-mentioned rights shall not be subject to any restrictions except those which are provided by law, are necessary to protect national security, public order (ordre public), public health or morals or the rights and freedoms of others, and are consistent with the other rights recognized in the present Covenant.

4. No one shall be arbitrarily deprived of the right to enter his own country.

Article 13

An alien lawfully in the territory of a State Party to the present Covenant may be expelled   **A.7–14**
therefrom only in pursuance of a decision reached in accordance with law and shall, except where compelling reasons of national security otherwise require, be allowed to submit the reasons against his expulsion and to have his case reviewed by, and be represented for the purpose before, the competent authority or a person or persons especially designated by the competent authority.

Article 14

1. All persons shall be equal before the courts and tribunals. In the determination of any   **A.7–15**
criminal charge against him, or of his rights and obligations in a suit at law, everyone shall be entitled to a fair and public hearing by a competent, independent and impartial tribunal established by law. The press and the public may be excluded from all or part of a trial for reasons of morals, public order (*ordre public*) or national security in a democratic society, or when the interest of the private lives of the parties so requires, or to the extent strictly necessary in the opinion of the court in special circumstances where publicity would prejudice the interests of justice; but any judgment rendered in a criminal case or in a suit at law shall be made public except where the interest of juvenile persons otherwise requires or the proceedings concern matrimonial disputes or the guardianship of children.

2. Everyone charged with a criminal offence shall have the right to be presumed innocent until proved guilty according to law.

3. In the determination of any criminal charge against him, everyone shall be entitled to the following minimum guarantees, in full equality:

   (a) To be informed promptly and in detail in a language which he understands of the nature and cause of the charge against him;

   (b) To have adequate time and facilities for the preparation of his defence and to communicate with counsel of his own choosing;

   (c) To be tried without undue delay;

   (d) To be tried in his presence, and to defend himself in person or through legal assistance of his own choosing; to be informed, if he does not have legal assistance, of this right; and to have legal assistance assigned to him, in any case where the interests of justice so require, and without payment by him in any such case if he does not have sufficient means to pay for it;

   (e) To examine, or have examined, the witnesses against him and to obtain the attendance and examination of witnesses on his behalf under the same conditions as witnesses against him;

   (f) To have the free assistance of an interpreter if he cannot understand or speak the language used in court;

   (g) Not to be compelled to testify against himself or to confess guilt.

4. In the case of juvenile persons, the procedure shall be such as will take account of their age and the desirability of promoting their rehabilitation.

5. Everyone convicted of a crime shall have the right to his conviction and sentence being reviewed by a higher tribunal according to law.

6. When a person has by a final decision been convicted of a criminal offence and when subsequently his conviction has been reversed or he has been pardoned on the ground that a new or newly discovered fact shows conclusively that there has been a miscarriage of justice, the person who has suffered punishment as a of such conviction shall be compensated according to law, unless it is proved that the non-disclosure of the unknown fact in time is wholly or partly attributable to him.

7. No one shall be liable to be tried or punished again for an offence for which he has already been finally convicted or acquitted in accordance with the law and penal procedure of each country.

Article 15

A.7–16 1. No one shall be held guilty of any criminal offence on account of any act or omission which did not constitute a criminal offence, under national or international law, at the time when it was committed. Nor shall a heavier penalty be imposed than the one that was applicable at the time when the criminal offence was committed. If, subsequent to the commission of the offence, provision is made by law for the imposition of the lighter penalty, the offender shall benefit thereby.

2. Nothing in this article shall prejudice the trial and punishment of any person for any act or omission which, at the time when it was committed, was criminal according to the general principles of law recognized by the community of nations.

Article 16

A.7–17 Everyone shall have the right to recognition everywhere as a person before the law.

Article 17

A.7–18 1. No one shall be subjected to arbitrary or unlawful interference with his privacy, family, home or correspondence, nor to unlawful attacks on his honour and reputation.

2. Everyone has the right to the protection of the law against such interference or attacks.

Article 18

A.7–19 1. Everyone shall have the right to freedom of thought, conscience and religion. This right shall include freedom to have or to adopt a religion or belief of his choice, and freedom, either individually or in community with others and in public or private, to manifest his religion or belief in worship, observance, practice and teaching.

2. No one shall be subject to coercion which would impair his freedom to have or to adopt a religion or belief of his choice.

3. Freedom to manifest one's religion or beliefs may be subject only to such limitations as are prescribed by law and are necessary to protect public safety, order, health, or morals or the fundamental rights and freedoms of others.

4. The States Parties to the present Covenant undertake to have respect for the liberty of parents and, when applicable, legal guardians to ensure the religious and moral education of their children in conformity with their own convictions.

Article 19

A.7–20 1. Everyone shall have the right to hold opinions without interference.

2. Everyone shall have the right to freedom of expression; this right shall include freedom to seek, receive and impart information and ideas of all kinds, regardless of frontiers, either orally, in writing or in print, in the form of art, or through any other media of his choice.

3. The exercise of the rights provided for in paragraph 2 of this article carries with it special duties and responsibilities. It may therefore be subject to certain restrictions, but these shall only be such as are provided by law and are necessary:

(a) For respect of the rights or reputations of others;

(b) For the protection of national security or of public order (ordre public), or of public health or morals.

Article 20

1. Any propaganda for war shall be prohibited by law.   **A.7–21**

2. Any advocacy of national, racial or religious hatred that constitutes incitement to discrimination, hostility or violence shall be prohibited by law.

Article 21

The right of peaceful assembly shall be recognized. No restrictions may be placed on the   **A.7–22** exercise of this right other than those imposed in conformity with the law and which are necessary in a democratic society in the interests of national security or public safety, public order (*ordre public*), the protection of public health or morals or the protection of the rights and freedoms of others.

Article 22

1. Everyone shall have the right to freedom of association with others, including the right   **A.7–23** to form and join trade unions for the protection of his interests.

2. No restrictions may be placed on the exercise of this right other than those which are prescribed by law and which are necessary in a democratic society in the interests of national security or public safety, public order (*ordre public*), the protection of public health or morals or the protection of the rights and freedoms of others. This article shall not prevent the imposition of lawful restrictions on members of the armed forces and of the police in their exercise of this right.

3. Nothing in this article shall authorize States Parties to the International Labour Organisation Convention of 1948 concerning Freedom of Association and Protection of the Right to Organize to take legislative measures which would prejudice, or to apply the law in such a manner as to prejudice, the guarantees provided for in that Convention.

Article 23

1. The family is the natural and fundamental group unit of society and is entitled to   **A.7–24** protection by society and the State.

2. The right of men and women of marriageable age to marry and to found a family shall be recognized.

3. No marriage shall be entered into without the free and full consent of the intending spouses.

4. States Parties to the present Covenant shall take appropriate steps to ensure equality of rights and responsibilities of spouses as to marriage, during marriage and at its dissolution. In the case of dissolution, provision shall be made for the necessary protection of any children.

Article 24

1. Every child shall have, without any discrimination as to race, colour, sex, language,   **A.7–25** religion, national or social origin, property or birth, the right to such measures of protection as are required by his status as a minor, on the part of his family, society and the State.

2. Every child shall be registered immediately after birth and shall have a name.

3. Every child has the right to acquire a nationality.

Article 25

A.7–26   Every citizen shall have the right and the opportunity, without any of the distinctions mentioned in article 2 and without unreasonable restrictions:

> (a) To take part in the conduct of public affairs, directly or through freely chosen representatives;
>
> (b) To vote and to be elected at genuine periodic elections which shall be by universal and equal suffrage and shall be held by secret ballot, guaranteeing the free expression of the will of the electors;
>
> (c) To have access, on general terms of equality, to public service in his country.

Article 26

A.7–27   All persons are equal before the law and are entitled without any discrimination the equal protection of the law. In this respect, the law shall prohibit any discrimination and guarantee to all persons equal and effective protection against discrimination on any ground such as race, colour, sex, language, religion, political or other opinion, national or social origin, property, birth or other status.

Article 27

A.7–28   In those States in which ethnic, religious or linguistic minorities exist, persons belonging to such minorities shall not be denied the right, in community with the other members of their group, to enjoy their own culture, to profess and practise their own religion, or to use their own language.

PART IV

Article 28

A.7–29   1. There shall be established a Human Rights Committee (hereafter referred to in the present Covenant as the Committee). It shall consist of eighteen members and shall carry out the functions hereinafter provided.

2. The Committee shall be composed of nationals of the States Parties to the present Covenant who shall be persons of high moral character and recognized competence in the field of human rights, consideration being given to the usefulness of the participation of some persons having legal experience.

3. The members of the Committee shall be elected and shall serve in their personal capacity.

Article 29

A.7–30   1. The members of the Committee shall be elected by secret ballot from a list of persons possessing the qualifications prescribed in Article 28 and nominated for the purpose by the States Parties to the present Covenant.

2. Each State Party to the present Covenant may nominate not more than two persons. These persons shall be nationals of the nominating State.

3. A person shall be eligible for renomination.

Article 30

1. The initial election shall be held no later than six months after the date of the entry into   **A.7–31**
force of the present Covenant.

2. At least four months before the date of each election to the Committee, other than an election to fill a vacancy declared in accordance with Article 34, the Secretary-General of the United Nations shall address a written invitation to the States Parties to the present Covenant to submit their nominations for membership of the Committee within three months.

3. The Secretary-General of the United Nations shall prepare a list in alphabetical order of all the persons thus nominated, with an indication of the States Parties which have nominated them, and shall submit it to the States Parties to the present Covenant no later than one month before the date of each election.

4. Elections of the members of the Committee shall be held at a meeting of the States Parties to the present Covenant convened by the Secretary General of the United Nations at the Headquarters of the United Nations. At that meeting, for which two thirds of the States Parties to the present Covenant shall constitute a quorum, the persons elected to the Committee shall be those nominees who obtain the largest number of votes and an absolute majority of the votes of the representatives of States Parties present and voting.

Article 31

1. The Committee may not include more than one national of the same State.   **A.7–32**

2. In the election of the Committee, consideration shall be given to equitable geographical distribution of membership and to the representation of the different forms of civilization and of the principal legal systems.

Article 32

1. The members of the Committee shall be elected for a term of four years. They shall be   **A.7–33**
eligible for re-election if renominated. However, the terms of nine of the members elected at the first election shall expire at the end of two years; immediately after the first election, the names of these nine members shall be chosen by lot by the Chairman of the meeting referred to in Article 30, paragraph 4.

2. Elections at the expiry of office shall be held in accordance with the preceding articles of this part of the present Covenant.

Article 33

1. If, in the unanimous opinion of the other members, a member of the Committee has   **A.7–34**
ceased to carry out his functions for any cause other than absence of a temporary character, the Chairman of the Committee shall notify the Secretary-General of the United Nations, who shall then declare the seat of that member to be vacant.

2. In the event of the death or the resignation of a member of the Committee, the Chairman shall immediately notify the Secretary-General of the United Nations, who shall declare the seat vacant from the date of death or the date on which the resignation takes effect.

Article 34

1. When a vacancy is declared in accordance with article 33 and if the term of office of   **A.7–35**
the member to be replaced does not expire within six months of the declaration of the vacancy, the Secretary-General of the United Nations shall notify each of the States Parties to the present Covenant, which may within two months submit nominations in accordance with Article 29 for the purpose of filling the vacancy.

2. The Secretary-General of the United Nations shall prepare a list in alphabetical order of the persons thus nominated and shall submit it to the States Parties to the present Covenant. The election to fill the vacancy shall then take place in accordance with the relevant provisions of this part of the present Covenant.

3. A member of the Committee elected to fill a vacancy declared in accordance with Article 33 shall hold office for the remainder of the term of the member who vacated the seat on the Committee under the provisions of that article.

Article 35

A.7–36 The members of the Committee shall, with the approval of the General Assembly of the United Nations, receive emoluments from United Nations resources on such terms and conditions as the General Assembly may decide, having regard to the importance of the Committee's responsibilities.

Article 36

A.7–37 The Secretary-General of the United Nations shall provide the necessary staff and facilities for the effective performance of the functions of the Committee under the present Covenant.

Article 37

A.7–38 1. The Secretary-General of the United Nations shall convene the initial meeting of the Committee at the Headquarters of the United Nations.

2. After its initial meeting, the Committee shall meet at such times as shall be provided in its rules of procedure.

3. The Committee shall normally meet at the Headquarters of the United Nations or at the United Nations Office at Geneva.

Article 38

A.7–39 Every member of the Committee shall, before taking up his duties, make a solemn declaration in open committee that he will perform his functions impartially and conscientiously.

Article 39

A.7–40 1. The Committee shall elect its officers for a term of two years. They may be re-elected.

2. The Committee shall establish its own rules of procedure, but these rules shall provide, *inter alia*, that:

(a) Twelve members shall constitute a quorum;

(b) Decisions of the Committee shall be made by a majority vote of the members present.

Article 40

A.7–41 1. The States Parties to the present Covenant undertake to submit reports on the measures they have adopted which give effect to the rights recognized herein and on the progress made in the enjoyment of those rights:

(a) Within one year of the entry into force of the present Covenant for the States Parties concerned;

(b) Thereafter whenever the Committee so requests.

2. All reports shall be submitted to the Secretary-General of the United Nations, who shall transmit them to the Committee for consideration. Reports shall indicate the factors and difficulties, if any, affecting the implementation of the present Covenant.

3. The Secretary-General of the United Nations may, after consultation with the Committee, transmit to the specialized agencies concerned copies of such parts of the reports as may fall within their field of competence.

4. The Committee shall study the reports submitted by the States Parties to the present Covenant. It shall transmit its reports, and such general comments as it may consider appropriate, to the States Parties. The Committee may also transmit to the Economic and Social Council these comments along with the copies of the reports it has received from States Parties to the present Covenant.

5. The States Parties to the present Covenant may submit to the Committee observations on any comments that may be made in accordance with paragraph 4 of this article.

Article 41

1. A State Party to the present Covenant may at any time declare under this article that **A.7–42** it recognizes the competence of the Committee to receive and consider communications to the effect that a State Party claims that another State Party is not fulfilling its obligations under the present Covenant. Communications under this article may be received and considered only if submitted by a State Party which has made a declaration recognizing in regard to itself the competence of the Committee. No communication shall be received by the Committee if it concerns a State Party which has not made such a declaration. Communications received under this article shall be dealt with in accordance with the following procedure:

(a) If a State Party to the present Covenant considers that another State Party is not giving effect to the provisions of the present Covenant, it may, by written communication, bring the matter to the attention of that State Party. Within three months after the receipt of the communication the receiving State shall afford the State which sent the communication an explanation, or any other statement in writing clarifying the matter which should include, to the extent possible and pertinent, reference to domestic procedures and remedies taken, pending, or available in the matter;

(b) If the matter is not adjusted to the satisfaction of both States Parties concerned within six months after the receipt by the receiving State of the initial communication, either State shall have the right to refer the matter to the Committee, by notice given to the Committee and to the other State;

(c) The Committee shall deal with a matter referred to it only after it has ascertained that all available domestic remedies have been invoked and exhausted in the matter, in conformity with the generally recognized principles of international law. This shall not be the rule where the application of the remedies is unreasonably prolonged;

(d) The Committee shall hold closed meetings when examining communications under this article;

(e) Subject to the provisions of subparagraph (c), the Committee shall make available its good offices to the States Parties concerned with a view to a friendly solution of the matter on the basis of respect for human rights and fundamental freedoms as recognized in the present Covenant;

(f) In any matter referred to it, the Committee may call upon the States Parties concerned, referred to in subparagraph (b), to supply any relevant information;

(g) The States Parties concerned, referred to in subparagraph (b), shall have the right to be represented when the matter is being considered in the Committee and to make submissions orally and/or in writing;

(h) The Committee shall, within twelve months after the date of receipt of notice under subparagraph (b), submit a report:

(i) If a solution within the terms of subparagraph (e) is reached, the Committee shall confine its report to a brief statement of the facts and of the solution reached;

(ii) If a solution within the terms of subparagraph (e) is not reached, the Committee shall confine its report to a brief statement of the facts; the written submissions and record of the oral submissions made by the States Parties concerned shall be attached to the report. In every matter, the report shall be communicated to the States Parties concerned.

2. The provisions of this article shall come into force when ten States Parties to the present Covenant have made declarations under paragraph I of this article. Such declarations shall be deposited by the States Parties with the Secretary-General of the United Nations, who shall transmit copies thereof to the other States Parties. A declaration may be withdrawn at any time by notification to the Secretary-General. Such a withdrawal shall not prejudice the consideration of any matter which is the subject of a communication already transmitted under this article; no further communication by any State Party shall be received after the notification of withdrawal of the declaration has been received by the Secretary-General, unless the State Party concerned has made a new declaration.

Article 42

A.7–43 1. (a) If a matter referred to the Committee in accordance with article 41 is not resolved to the satisfaction of the States Parties concerned, the Committee may, with the prior consent of the States Parties concerned, appoint an ad hoc Conciliation Commission (hereinafter referred to as the Commission). The good offices of the Commission shall be made available to the States Parties concerned with a view to an amicable solution of the matter on the basis of respect for the present Covenant;

(b) The Commission shall consist of five persons acceptable to the States Parties concerned. If the States Parties concerned fail to reach agreement within three months on all or part of the composition of the Commission, the members of the Commission concerning whom no agreement has been reached shall be elected by secret ballot by a two-thirds majority vote of the Committee from among its members.

2. The members of the Commission shall serve in their personal capacity. They shall not be nationals of the States Parties concerned, or of a State not Party to the present Covenant, or of a State Party which has not made a declaration under Article 41.

3. The Commission shall elect its own Chairman and adopt its own rules of procedure.

4. The meetings of the Commission shall normally be held at the Headquarters of the United Nations or at the United Nations Office at Geneva. However, they may be held at such other convenient places as the Commission may determine in consultation with the Secretary-General of the United Nations and the States Parties concerned.

5. The secretariat provided in accordance with article 36 shall also service the commissions appointed under this article.

6. The information received and collated by the Committee shall be made available to the Commission and the Commission may call upon the States concerned to supply any other relevant information.

7. When the Commission has fully considered the matter, but in any event not later than twelve months after having been seized of the matter, it shall submit to the Chairman of the Committee a report for communication to the States Parties concerned:

(a) If the Commission is unable to complete its consideration of the matter within twelve months, it shall confine its report to a brief statement of the status of its consideration of the matter;

(b) If an amicable solution to the matter on tie basis of respect for human rights as recognized in the present Covenant is reached, the Commission shall confine its report to a brief statement of the facts and of the solution reached;

(c) If a solution within the terms of subparagraph (b) is not reached, the Commission's report shall embody its findings on all questions of fact relevant to the issues between the States Parties concerned, and its views on the possibilities of an amicable solution of the matter. This report shall also contain the written submissions and a record of the oral submissions made by the States Parties concerned;

(d) If the Commission's report is submitted under subparagraph (c), the States Parties concerned shall, within three months of the receipt of the report, notify the Chairman of the Committee whether or not they accept the contents of the report of the Commission.

8. The provisions of this article are without prejudice to the responsibilities of the Committee under Article 41.

9. The States Parties concerned shall share equally all the expenses of the members of the Commission in accordance with estimates to be provided by the Secretary-General of the United Nations.

10. The Secretary-General of the United Nations shall be empowered to pay the expenses of the members of the Commission, if necessary, before reimbursement by the States Parties concerned, in accordance with paragraph 9 of this article.

Article 43

The members of the Committee, and of the ad hoc conciliation commissions which may be appointed under Article 42, shall be entitled to the facilities, privileges and immunities of experts on mission for the United Nations as laid down in the relevant sections of the Convention on the Privileges and Immunities of the United Nations.   **A.7–44**

Article 44

The provisions for the implementation of the present Covenant shall apply without prejudice to the procedures prescribed in the field of human rights by or under the constituent instruments and the conventions of the United Nations and of the specialized agencies and shall not prevent the States Parties to the present Covenant from having recourse to other procedures for settling a dispute in accordance with general or special international agreements in force between them.   **A.7–45**

Article 45

The Committee shall submit to the General Assembly of the United Nations, through the Economic and Social Council, an annual report on its activities.   **A.7–46**

PART V

Article 46

Nothing in the present Covenant shall be interpreted as impairing the provisions of the Charter of the United Nations and of the constitutions of the specialized agencies which   **A.7–47** define the respective responsibilities of the various organs of the United Nations and of the specialized agencies in regard to the matters dealt with in the present Covenant.

Article 47

A.7–48   Nothing in the present Covenant shall be interpreted as impairing the inherent right of all peoples to enjoy and utilize fully and freely their natural wealth and resources.

PART VI

Article 48

A.7–49   1. The present Covenant is open for signature by any State Member of the United Nations or member of any of its specialized agencies, by any State Party to the Statute of the International Court of Justice, and by any other State which has been invited by the General Assembly of the United Nations to become a Party to the present Covenant.

2. The present Covenant is subject to ratification. Instruments of ratification shall be deposited with the Secretary-General of the United Nations.

3. The present Covenant shall be open to accession by any State referred to in paragraph 1 of this article.

4. Accession shall be effected by the deposit of an instrument of accession with the Secretary-General of the United Nations.

5. The Secretary-General of the United Nations shall inform all States which have signed this Covenant or acceded to it of the deposit of each Instrument of ratification or accession.

Article 49

A.7–50   1. The present Covenant shall enter into force three months after the date of the deposit with the Secretary-General of the United Nations of the thirty-fifth instrument of ratification or instrument of accession.

2. For each State ratifying the present Covenant or acceding to it after the deposit of the thirty-fifth instrument of ratification or instrument of accession, the present Covenant shall enter into force three months after the date of the deposit of its own instrument of ratification or instrument of accession.

Article 50

A.7–51   The provisions of the present Covenant shall extend to all parts of federal States without any limitations or exceptions.

Article 51

A.7–52   1. Any State Party to the present Covenant may propose an amendment and file it with the Secretary-General of the United Nations. The Secretary-General of the United Nations shall thereupon communicate any proposed amendments to the States Parties to the present Covenant with a request that they notify him whether they favour a conference of States Parties for the purpose of considering and voting upon the proposals. In the event that at least one third of the States Parties favours such a conference, the Secretary-General shall convene the conference under the auspices of the United Nations. Any amendment adopted by a majority of the States Parties present and voting at the conference shall be submitted to the General Assembly of the United Nations for approval.

2. Amendments shall come into force when they have been approved by the General Assembly of the United Nations and accepted by a two-thirds majority of the States

Parties to the present Covenant in accordance with their respective constitutional processes. 3. When amendments come into force, they shall be binding on those States Parties which have accepted them, other States Parties still being bound by the provisions of the present Covenant and any earlier amendment which they have accepted.

Article 52

Irrespective of the notifications made under Article 48, paragraph 5, the Secretary-General   **A.7–53**
of the United Nations shall inform all States referred to in paragraph I of the same article of the following particulars:

    (a) Signatures, ratifications and accessions under Article 48;

    (b) The date of the entry into force of the present Covenant under Article 49 and the date of the entry into force of any amendments under Article 51.

Article 53

1. The present Covenant, of which the Chinese, English, French, Russian and Spanish   **A.7–54**
texts are equally authentic, shall be deposited in the archives of the United Nations.

2. The Secretary-General of the United Nations shall transmit certified copies of the present Covenant to all States referred to in Article 48.

CODE OF PRACTICE FOR THE DETENTION, TREATMENT AND QUESTIONING OF PERSONS BY POLICE OFFICERS

C:1 General

C:1.1 All persons in custody must be dealt with expeditiously, and released as soon as the need for detention has ceased to apply. **A.8–01**

C:1.1A A custody officer is required to perform the functions specified in this code as soon as is practicable. A custody officer shall not be in breach of this code in the event of delay provided that the delay is justifiable and that every reasonable step is taken to prevent unnecessary delay. The custody record shall indicate where a delay has occurred and the reason why. [See *Note 1H*].

C:1.2 This code of practice must be readily available at all police stations for consultation by police officers, detained persons and members of the public.

C:1.3 The notes for guidance included are not provisions of this code, but are guidance to police officers and others about its application and interpretation. Provisions in the annexes to this code are provisions of this code.

C:1.4 If an officer has any suspicion, or is told in good faith, that a person of any age may be mentally disordered or mentally handicapped, or mentally incapable of understanding the significance of questions put to him or his replies, then that person shall be treated as a mentally disordered or mentally handicapped person for the purposes of this code. [See *Note 1G.*]

C:1.5 If anyone appears to be under the age of 17 then he shall be treated as a juvenile for the purposes of this code in the absence of clear evidence to show that he is older.

C:[1.5A If anyone appears to be under the age of 18 then he shall be exempt from drug testing under section 17 of this code in the absence of clear evidence to show that he is older.]

C:1.6 If a person appears to be blind or seriously visually handicapped, deaf, unable to read, unable to speak or has difficulty orally because of a speech impediment, he shall be treated as such for the purpose of this code in the absence of clear evidence to the contrary.

C:1.7 In this code "the appropriate adult" means:

(a) in the case of a juvenile:

    (i) his parent or guardian (or, if he is in care, the care authority or voluntary organisation. The term "in care" is used in this code to cover all cases in which a juvenile is "looked after" by a local authority under the terms of the *Children Act* 1989);

    (ii) a social worker;

    (iii) failing either of the above, another responsible adult aged 18 or over who is not a police officer or employed by the police.

(b) in the case of a person who is mentally disordered or mentally handicapped:

    (i) a relative, guardian or other person responsible for his care and custody;

    (ii) someone who has experience of dealing with mentally disordered or mentally handicapped people but who is not a police officer or employed by the police (such as an approved social worker as defined by the *Mental Health Act* 1983 or a specialist social worker); or

    (iii) failing either of the above, some other responsible adult aged 18 or over who is not a police officer or employed by the police.

[See *Note 1E.*]

C:1.8 Whenever this code requires a person to be given certain information he does not have to be given it if he is incapable at the time of understanding what is said to him or is violent or likely to become violent or is in urgent need of medical attention, but he must be given it as soon as practicable.

C:1.9 Any reference to a custody officer in this code includes an officer who is performing the functions of a custody officer.

C:1.10 Subject to paragraph 1.12, this code applies to people who are in custody at police stations in England and Wales whether or not they have been arrested for an offence and to those who have been removed to a police station as a place of safety under sections 135 and 136 of the *Mental Health Act* 1983. Section 15 (reviews and extensions of detention) however applies solely to people in police detention, for example those who have been brought to a police station under arrest for an offence or have been arrested at a police station for an offence after attending there voluntarily.

C:1.11 People in police custody include anyone taken to a police station after being arrested under section 14 of the *Prevention of Terrorism (Temporary Provisions) Act* 1989 or under paragraph 6 of Schedule 5 to that *Act* by an examining officer who is a constable.

C:1.12 This code does not apply to the following groups of people in custody:

(i) people who have been arrested by officers from a police force in Scotland exercising their powers of detention under section 137(2) of the *Criminal Justice and Public Order Act* 1994 (Cross Border powers of arrest etc.);

(ii) people arrested under section 3(5) of the *Asylum and Immigration Appeals Act* 1993 for the purpose of having their fingerprints taken;

(iii) people who have been served a notice advising them of their detention under powers contained in the *Immigration Act* 1971;

(iv) convicted or remanded prisoners held in police cells on behalf of the Prison Service under the *Imprisonment (Temporary Provisions) Act* 1980;

but the provisions on conditions of detention and treatment in sections 8 and 9 of this code must be considered as the minimum standards of treatment for such detainees.

NOTES FOR GUIDANCE

C:1A *Although certain sections of this code (e.g. section 9—treatment of detained* **A.8–02** *persons) apply specifically to people in custody at police stations, those there voluntarily to assist with an investigation should be treated with no less consideration (e.g. offered refreshments at appropriate times) and enjoy an absolute right to obtain legal advice or communicate with anyone outside the police station.*

C:1B *This code does not affect the principle that all citizens have a duty to help police officers to prevent crime and discover offenders. This is a civic rather than a legal duty; but when a police officer is trying to discover whether, or by whom, an offence has been committed he is entitled to question any person from whom he thinks useful information can be obtained, subject to the restrictions imposed by this code. A person's declaration that he is unwilling to reply does not alter this entitlement.*

C:1C *A person, including a parent or guardian, should not be an appropriate adult if he is suspected of involvement in the offence in question, is the victim, is a witness, is involved in the investigation or has received admissions prior to attending to act as the appropriate adult. If the parent of a juvenile is estranged from the juvenile, he should not be asked to act as the appropriate adult if the juvenile expressly and specifically objects to his presence.*

C:1D *If a juvenile admits an offence to or in the presence of a social worker other than during the time that the social worker is acting as the appropriate adult for that juvenile, another social worker should be the appropriate adult in the interest of fairness.*

C:1E *In the case of people who are mentally disordered or mentally handicapped, it may in certain circumstances be more satisfactory for all concerned if the appropriate adult is someone who has experience or training in their care rather than a relative lacking such qualifications. But if the person himself prefers a relative to a better qualified stranger or objects to a particular person as the appropriate adult, his wishes should if practicable be respected.*

C:1EE *A person should always be given an opportunity, when an appropriate adult is called to the police station, to consult privately with a solicitor in the absence of the appropriate adult if they wish to do so.*

C:1F *A solicitor or lay visitor who is present at the police station in that capacity may not act as the appropriate adult.*

C:1G *The generic term "mental disorder" is used throughout this code. "Mental disorder" is defined in section 1(2) of the* Mental Health Act 1983 *as "mental illness, arrested or incomplete development of mind, psychopathic disorder and any other dis-order or disability of mind". It should be noted that "mental disorder" is different from "mental handicap" although the two are dealt with similarly throughout this code. Where the custody officer has any doubt as to the mental state or capacity of a person detained an appropriate adult should be called.*

C:1H *Paragraph 1.1A is intended to cover the kinds of delays which may occur in the processing of detained persons because, for example, a large number of suspects are brought into the police station simultaneously to be placed in custody, or interview rooms are all being used, or where there are difficulties in contacting an appropriate adult, solicitor or interpreter.*

C:1I *It is important that the custody officer reminds the appropriate adult and the detained person of the right to legal advice and records any reasons for waiving it in accordance with section 6 of this code.*

C:2 Custody records

A.8–03   C:2.1 A separate custody record must be opened as soon as practicable for each person who is brought to a police station under arrest or is arrested at the police station having attended there voluntarily. All information which has to be recorded under this code must be recorded as soon as practicable in the custody record unless otherwise specified. Any audio or video recording made in the custody area is not part of the custody record.

C:2.2 In the case of any action requiring the authority of an officer of a specified rank, his name and rank must be noted in the custody record. The recording of names does not apply to officers dealing with people detained under the *Prevention of Terrorism (Tempo-rary Provisions) Act* 1989. Instead the record shall state the warrant or other identification number and duty station of such officers.

C:2.3 The custody officer is responsible for the accuracy and completeness of the custody record and for ensuring that the record or a copy of the record accompanies a detained person if he is transferred to another police station. The record shall show the time of and reason for transfer and the time a person is released from detention.

C:2.4 A solicitor or appropriate adult must be permitted to consult the custody record of a person detained as soon as practicable after their arrival at the police station. When a person leaves police detention or is taken before a court, he or his legal representative or his appropriate adult shall be supplied on request with a copy of the custody record as soon as practicable. This entitlement lasts for 12 months after his release.

C:2.5 The person who has been detained, the appropriate adult, or the legal representa-tive shall be permitted to inspect the original custody record after the person has left police detention provided they give reasonable notice of their request. A note of any such inspection shall be made in the custody record.

C:2.6 All entries in custody records must be timed and signed by the maker. In the case of a record entered on a computer this shall be timed and contain the operator's identifica-tion. Warrant or other identification numbers shall be used rather than names in the case of detention under the *Prevention of Terrorism (Temporary Provisions) Act* 1989.

C:2.7 The fact and time of any refusal by a person to sign a custody record when asked to do so in accordance with the provisions of this code must itself be recorded.

C:3 Initial action

(a) DETAINED PERSONS: NORMAL PROCEDURE

A.8–04   C:3.1 When a person is brought to a police station under arrest or is arrested at the police station having attended there voluntarily, the custody officer must tell him clearly of the following rights and of the fact that they are continuing rights which may be exercised at any stage during the period in custody:

(i) the right to have someone informed of his arrest in accordance with section 5 below;

(ii) the right to consult privately with a solicitor and the fact that independent legal advice is available free of charge; and

(iii) the right to consult these codes of practice.

[See *Note 3E.*]

C:3.2 In addition the custody officer must give the person a written notice setting out the above three rights, the right to a copy of the custody record in accordance with paragraph 2.4 above and the caution in the terms prescribed in section 10 below. The notice must also explain the arrangements for obtaining legal advice. The custody officer must also give the person an additional written notice briefly setting out his entitlements while in custody. [See *Notes 3A and 3B.*] The custody officer shall ask the person to sign the custody record to acknowledge receipt of these notices and any refusal to sign must be recorded on the custody record.

C:3.3 A citizen of an independent Commonwealth country or a national of a foreign country (including the Republic of Ireland) must be informed as soon as practicable of his rights of communication with his High Commission, Embassy or Consulate. [See *Section 7.*]

C:3.4 The custody officer shall note on the custody record any comment the person may make in relation to the arresting officer's account but shall not invite comment. If the custody officer authorises a person's detention he must inform him of the grounds as soon as practicable and in any case before that person is then questioned about any offence. The custody officer shall note any comment the person may make in respect of the decision to detain him but, again, shall not invite comment. The custody officer shall not put specific questions to the person regarding his involvement in any offence, nor in respect of any comments he may make in response to the arresting officer's account or the decision to place him in detention. Such an exchange is likely to constitute an interview as defined by paragraph 11.1A and would require the associated safeguards included in section 11. [See also paragraph 11.13 in respect of unsolicited comments.]

C:3.5 The custody officer shall ask the detained person whether at this time he would like legal advice (see paragraph 6.5). The person shall be asked to sign the custody record to confirm his decision. The custody officer is responsible for ensuring that in confirming any decision the person signs in the correct place.

C:3.5A If video cameras are installed in the custody area, notices which indicate that cameras are in use shall be prominently displayed. Any request by a detained person or other person to have video cameras switched off shall be refused.

(b) DETAINED PERSONS: SPECIAL GROUPS

C:3.6 If the person appears to be deaf or there is doubt about his hearing or speaking **A.8–05** ability or ability to understand English, and the custody officer cannot establish effective communication, the custody officer must as soon as practicable call an interpreter and ask him to provide the information required above. [See Section 13.]

C:3.7 If the person is a juvenile, the custody officer must, if it is practicable, ascertain the identity of a person responsible for his welfare. That person may be his parent or guardian (or, if he is in care, the care authority or voluntary organisation) or any other person who has, for the time being, assumed responsibility for his welfare. That person must be informed as soon as practicable that the juvenile has been arrested, why he has been arrested and where he is detained. This right is in addition to the juvenile's right in section 5 of the code not to be held incommunicado. [See *Note 3C.*]

C:3.8 In the case of a juvenile who is known to be subject to a supervision order, reasonable steps must also be taken to notify the person supervising him.

C:3.9 If the person is a juvenile, is mentally handicapped or appears to be suffering from a mental disorder, then the custody officer must, as soon as practicable, inform the appropriate adult (who in the case of a juvenile may or may not be a person responsible for his welfare, in accordance with paragraph 3.7 above) of the grounds for his detention and his whereabouts and ask the adult to come to the police station to see the person.

C:3.10 It is imperative that a mentally disordered or mentally handicapped person who has been detained under section 136 of the *Mental Health Act* 1983 shall be assessed as soon as possible. If that assessment is to take place at the police station, an approved social worker and a registered medical practitioner shall be called to the police station as soon as possible in order to interview and examine the person. Once the person has been interviewed and examined and suitable arrangements have been made for his treatment or care, he can no longer be detained under section 136. The person should not be released until he has been seen by both the approved social worker and the registered medical practitioner.

C:3.11 If the appropriate adult is already at the police station, then the provisions of paragraphs 3.1 to 3.5 above must be complied with in his presence. If the appropriate adult is not at the police station when the provisions of paragraphs 3.1 to 3.5 above are complied with, then these provisions must be complied with again in the presence of the appropriate adult once that person arrives.

C:3.12 The person shall be advised by the custody officer that the appropriate adult (where applicable) is there to assist and advise him and that he can consult privately with the appropriate adult at any time.

C:3.13 If, having been informed of the right to legal advice under paragraph 3.11 above, either the appropriate adult or the person detained wishes legal advice to be taken, then the provisions of section 6 of this code apply. [See *Note 3G*.]

C:3.14 If the person is blind or seriously visually handicapped or is unable to read, the custody officer shall ensure that his solicitor, relative, the appropriate adult or some other person likely to take an interest in him (and not involved in the investigation) is available to help in checking any documentation. Where this code requires written consent or signification then the person who is assisting may be asked to sign instead if the detained person so wishes. [See *Note 3F*.]

(c) PERSONS ATTENDING A POLICE STATION VOLUNTARILY

A.8–06 C:3.15 Any person attending a police station voluntarily for the purpose of assisting with an investigation may leave at will unless placed under arrest. If it is decided that he should not be allowed to leave then he must be informed at once that he is under arrest and brought before the custody officer, who is responsible for ensuring that he is notified of his rights in the same way as other detained persons. If he is not placed under arrest but is cautioned in accordance with section 10 below, the officer who gives the caution must at the same time inform him that he is not under arrest, that he is not obliged to remain at the police station but if he remains at the police station he may obtain free and independent legal advice if he wishes. The officer shall point out that the right to legal advice includes the right to speak with a solicitor on the telephone and ask him if he wishes to do so.

C:3.16 If a person who is attending the police station voluntarily (in accordance with paragraph 3.15) asks about his entitlement to legal advice, he shall be given a copy of the notice explaining the arrangements for obtaining legal advice. [See paragraph 3.2.]

(d) DOCUMENTATION

C:3.17 The grounds for a person's detention shall be recorded, in his presence if **A.8–07** practicable.

C:3.18 Action taken under paragraphs 3.6 to 3.14 shall be recorded.

NOTES FOR GUIDANCE

C:3A *The notice of entitlements is intended to provide detained persons with brief* **A.8–08** *details of their entitlement over and above the statutory rights which are set out in the notice of rights. The notice of entitlements should list the entitlements contained in this code, including visits and contact with outside parties (including special provisions for Commonwealth citizens and foreign nationals), reasonable standards of physical comfort, adequate food and drink, access to toilets and washing facilities, clothing, medical attention, and exercise where practicable. It should also mention the provisions relating to the conduct of interviews, the circumstances in which an appropriate adult should be available to assist the detained person and his statutory rights to make representation whenever the period of his detention is reviewed.*

C:3B *In addition to the notices in English, translations should be available in Welsh, the main ethnic minority languages and the principal European languages whenever they are likely to be helpful.*

C:3C *If the juvenile is in the care of a local authority or voluntary organisation but is living with his parents or other adults responsible for his welfare then, although there is no legal obligation on the police to inform them, they as well as the authority or organisation should normally be contacted unless suspected of involvement in the offence concerned. Even if a juvenile in care is not living with his parents, consideration should be given to informing them as well.*

C:3D *Most local authority Social Services Departments can supply a list of interpreters who have the necessary skills and experience to interpret for deaf people at police interviews. The local Community Relations Council may be able to provide similar information in cases where the person concerned does not understand English. [See section 13.]*

C:3E *The right to consult the codes of practice under paragraph 3.1 above does not entitle the person concerned to delay unreasonably any necessary investigative or administrative action while he does so. Procedures requiring the provision of breath, blood or urine specimens under the terms of the* Road Traffic Act *1988 need not be delayed.*

C:3F *Blind or seriously visually handicapped people may be unwilling to sign police documents. The alternative of their representative signing on their behalf seeks to protect the interests of both police and detained people.*

C:3G *The purpose of paragraph 3.13 is to protect the rights of a juvenile, mentally disordered or mentally handicapped person who may not understand the significance of what is being said to him. If such a person wishes to exercise the right to legal advice the appropriate action should be taken straightaway and not delayed until the appropriate adult arrives.*

C:4 Detained person's property

(a) ACTION

C:4.1 The custody officer is responsible for: **A.8–09**

(a) ascertaining:

    (i) what property a detained person has with him when he comes to the police station (whether on arrest, re-detention on answering to bail, commitment to prison custody on the order or sentence of a court, lodgement at the police station with a view to his production in court from such custody, arrival at a police station on transfer from detention at another police station or from hospital or on detention under section 135 or 136 of the *Mental Health Act* 1983);

    (ii) what property he might have acquired for an unlawful or harmful purpose while in custody;

  (b) the safekeeping of any property which is taken from him and which remains at the police station.

To these ends the custody officer may search him or authorise his being searched to the extent that he considers necessary (provided that a search of intimate parts of the body or involving the removal of more than outer clothing may be made only in accordance with Annex A to this code). A search may be only carried out by an officer of the same sex as the person searched. [See *Note 4A*.]

    C:4.2 A detained person may retain clothing and personal effects at his own risk unless the custody officer considers that he may use them to cause harm to himself or others, interfere with evidence, damage property or effect an escape or they are needed as evidence. In this event the custody officer may withhold such articles as he considers necessary. If he does so he must tell the person why.

    C:4.3 Personal effects are those items which a person may lawfully need or use or refer to while in detention but do not include cash and other items of value.

(b) DOCUMENTATION

A.8–10   C:4.4 The custody officer is responsible for recording all property brought to the police station which a detained person had with him, or had taken from him on arrest. The detained person shall be allowed to check and sign the record of property as correct. Any refusal to sign shall be recorded.

    C:4.5 If a detained person is not allowed to keep any article of clothing or personal effects the reason must be recorded.

NOTES FOR GUIDANCE

A.8–11   C:4A *Section 54(1) of* PACE *and paragraph 4.1 require a detained person to be searched where it is clear that the custody officer will have continuing duties in relation to that person or where that person's behaviour or offence makes an inventory appropriate. They do not require* every *detained person to be searched. Where, for example, it is clear that a person will only be detained for a short period and is not to be placed in a cell, the custody officer may decide not to search him. In such a case the custody record will be endorsed "not searched", paragraph 4.4 will not apply, and the person will be invited to sign the entry. Where the person detained refuses to sign, the custody officer will be obliged to ascertain what property he has on him in accordance with paragraph 4.1.*

    C:4B *Paragraph 4.4 does not require the custody officer to record on the custody record property in the possession of the person on arrest, if by virtue of its nature, quantity or size, it is not practicable to remove it to the police station.*

    C:4C *Paragraph 4.4 above is not to be taken as requiring that items of clothing worn by the person be recorded unless withheld by the custody officer in accordance with paragraph 4.2.*

C:5 Right not to be held incommunicado

(a) ACTION

C:5.1 Any person arrested and held in custody at a police station or other premises may   **A.8–12**
on request have one person known to him or who is likely to take an interest in his welfare
informed at public expense of his whereabouts as soon as practicable. If the person cannot
be contacted the person who has made the request may choose up to two alternatives. If
they too cannot be contacted the person in charge of detention or of the investigation has
discretion to allow further attempts until the information has been conveyed. [See *Notes
5C and 5D.*]

C:5.2 The exercise of the above right in respect of each of the persons nominated may
be delayed only in accordance with *Annex B* to this code.

C:5.3 The above right may be exercised on each occasion that a person is taken to
another police station.

C:5.4 The person may receive visits at the custody officer's discretion. [See *Note
5B.*]

C:5.5 Where an enquiry as to the whereabouts of the person is made by a friend,
relative or person with an interest in his welfare, this information shall be given, if he
agrees and if Annex B does not apply. [See *Note 5D.*]

C:5.6 Subject to the following condition, the person shall be supplied with writing
materials on request and allowed to speak on the telephone for a reasonable time to one
person [See *Notes 5A and 5E*]. Where an officer of the rank of Inspector or above
considers that the sending of a letter or the making of a telephone call may result in:

(a) any of the consequences set out in the first and second paragraphs of *Annex B* and
the person is detained in connection with an arrestable or a serious arrestable
offence, for which purpose, any reference to a serious arrestable offence in *Annex
B* includes an arrestable offence; or

(b) either of the consequences set out in paragraph 8 of *Annex B* and the person is
detained under the *Prevention of Terrorism (Temporary Provisions) Act* 1989;

that officer can deny or delay the exercise of either or both these privileges. However,
nothing in this section permits the restriction or denial of the rights set out in paragraphs
5.1 and 6.1.

C:5.7 Before any letter or message is sent, or telephone call made, the person shall be
informed that what he says in any letter, call or message (other than in the case of a
communication to a solicitor) may be read or listened to as appropriate and may be given
in evidence. A telephone call may be terminated if it is being abused. The costs can be at
public expense at the discretion of the custody officer.

(b) DOCUMENTATION

C:5.8 A record must be kept of: **A.8–13**

(a) any request made under this section and the action taken on it;

(b) any letters, messages or telephone calls made or received or visits received; and

(c) any refusal on the part of the person to have information about himself or his
whereabouts given to an outside enquirer. The person must be asked to countersign
the record accordingly and any refusal to sign shall be recorded.

NOTES FOR GUIDANCE

A.8–14   C:5A *An interpreter may make a telephone call or write a letter on a person's behalf.*

C:5B *In the exercise of his discretion the custody officer should allow visits where possible in the light of the availability of sufficient manpower to supervise a visit and any possible hindrance to the investigation.*

C:5C *If the person does not know of anyone to contact for advice or support or cannot contact a friend or relative, the custody officer should bear in mind any local voluntary bodies or other organisations who might be able to offer help in such cases. But if it is specifically legal advice that is wanted, then paragraph 6.1 below will apply.*

C:5D *In some circumstances it may not be appropriate to use the telephone to disclose information under paragraphs 5.1 and 5.5 above.*

C:5E *The telephone call at paragraph 5.6 is an addition to any communication under paragraphs 5.1 and 6.1.*

C:6 Right to legal advice

(a) ACTION

A.8–15   C:6.1 Subject to the provisos in Annex B all people in police detention must be informed that they may at any time consult and communicate privately, whether in person, in writing or by telephone with a solicitor, and that independent legal advice is available free of charge from the duty solicitor. [See paragraph 3.1 and *Note 6B* and *Note 6J*.]

C:6.2 [Not Used.]

C:6.3 A poster advertising the right to have legal advice must be prominently displayed in the charging area of every police station. [See *Note 6H*.]

C:6.4 No police officer shall at any time do or say anything with the intention of dissuading a person in detention from obtaining legal advice.

C:6.5 The exercise of the right of access to legal advice may be delayed only in accordance with Annex B to this code. Whenever legal advice is requested (and unless Annex B applies) the custody officer must act without delay to secure the provision of such advice to the person concerned. If, on being informed or reminded of the right to legal advice, the person declines to speak to a solicitor in person, the officer shall point out that the right to legal advice includes the right to speak with a solicitor on the telephone and ask him if he wishes to do so. If the person continues to waive his right to legal advice the officer shall ask him the reasons for doing so, and any reasons shall be recorded on the custody record or the interview record as appropriate. Reminders of the right to legal advice must be given in accordance with paragraphs 3.5, 11.2, 15.3, 16.4 and 16.5 of this code and paragraphs 2.15(ii) and 5.2 of Code D. Once it is clear that a person neither wishes to speak to a solicitor in person nor by telephone he should cease to be asked his reasons. [See *Note 6K*.]

C:6.6 A person who wants legal advice may not be interviewed or continue to be interviewed until he has received it unless:

(a) Annex B applies; or

(b) an officer of the rank of superintendent or above has reasonable grounds for believing that:

(i) delay will involve an immediate risk of harm to persons or serious loss of, or damage to, property; or

(ii) where a solicitor, including a duty solicitor, has been contacted and has agreed to attend, awaiting his arrival would cause unreasonable delay to the process of investigation; or

(c) the solicitor nominated by the person, or selected by him from a list:

(i) cannot be contacted; or

(ii) has previously indicated that he does not wish to be contacted; or

(iii) having been contacted, has declined to attend;

and the person has been advised of the Duty Solicitor Scheme but has declined to ask for the duty solicitor, or the duty solicitor is unavailable. (In these circumstances the interview may be started or continued without further delay provided that an officer of the rank of Inspector or above has given agreement for the interview to proceed in those circumstances—see *Note 6B*.)

(d) the person who wanted legal advice changes his mind. In these circumstances the interview may be started or continued without further delay provided that the person has given his agreement in writing or on tape to being interviewed without receiving legal advice and that an officer of the rank of Inspector or above, having inquired into the person's reasons for his change of mind, has given authority for the interview to proceed. Confirmation of the person's agreement, his change of mind, his reasons where given and the name of the authorising officer shall be recorded in the taped or written interview record at the beginning or recommencement of interview. [See *Note 61*.]

C:6.7 Where 6.6(b)(i) applies, once sufficient information to avert the risk has been obtained, questioning must cease until the person has received legal advice unless 6.6(a), (b)(ii), (c) or (d) apply.

C:6.8 Where a person has been permitted to consult a solicitor and the solicitor is available (*i.e.* present at the station or on his way to the station or easily contactable by telephone) at the time the interview begins or is in progress, the solicitor must be allowed to be present while he is interviewed.

C:6.9 The solicitor may only be required to leave the interview if his conduct is such that the investigating officer is unable properly to put questions to the suspect. [See *Notes 6D* and *6E*.]

C:6.10 If the investigating officer considers that a solicitor is acting in such a way, he will stop the interview and consult an officer not below the rank of superintendent, if one is readily available, and otherwise an officer not below the rank of inspector who is not connected with the investigation. After speaking to the solicitor, the officer who has been consulted will decide whether or not the interview should continue in the presence of that solicitor. If he decides that it should not, the suspect will be given the opportunity to consult another solicitor before the interview continues and that solicitor will be given an opportunity to be present at the interview.

C:6.11 The removal of a solicitor from an interview is a serious step and, if it occurs, the officer of superintendent rank or above who took the decision will consider whether the incident should be reported to the Law Society. If the decision to remove the solicitor has been taken by an officer below the rank of superintendent, the facts must be reported to an officer of superintendent rank or above who will similarly consider whether a report to the Law Society would be appropriate. Where the solicitor concerned is a duty solicitor, the report should be both to the Law Society and to the Legal Aid Board.

C:6.12 In Codes of Practice issued under the *Police and Criminal Evidence Act* 1984, "solicitor" means a solicitor who holds a current practising certificate, a trainee solicitor, a duty solicitor representative or an accredited representative included on the register of representatives maintained by the Legal Aid Board. If a solicitor wishes to send a non-accredited or probationary representative to provide advice on his behalf, then that person shall be admitted to the police station for this purpose unless an officer of the rank of inspector or above considers that such a visit will hinder the investigation of crime and directs otherwise. (Hindering the investigation of a crime does not include giving proper legal advice to a detained person in accordance with *Note 6D.*) Once admitted to the police station, the provisions of paragraphs 6.6 to 6.10 apply.

C:6.13 In exercising his discretion under paragraph 6.12, the officer should take into account in particular whether the identity and status of the non-accredited or probationary representative have been satisfactory [*sic*] established; whether he is of suitable character to provide legal advice (a person with a criminal record is unlikely to be suitable unless the conviction was for a minor offence and is not of recent date); and any other matters in any written letter of authorisation provided by the solicitor on whose behalf the person is attending the police station. [See *Note 6F.*]

C:6.14 If the inspector refuses access to a non-accredited or probationary representative or a decision is taken that such a person should not be permitted to remain at an interview, he must forthwith notify a solicitor on whose behalf the non-accredited or probationary representative was to have acted or was acting, and give him an opportunity to make alternative arrangements. The detained person must also be informed and the custody record noted.

C:6.15 If a solicitor arrives at the station to see a particular person, that person must (unless Annex B applies) be informed of the solicitor's arrival whether or not he is being interviewed and asked whether he would like to see him. This applies even if the person concerned has already declined legal advice or having requested it, subsequently agreed to be interviewed without having received advice. The solicitor's attendance and the detained person's decision must be noted in the custody record.

(b) DOCUMENTATION

C:6.16 Any request for legal advice and the action taken on it shall be recorded.

C:6.17 If a person has asked for legal advice and an interview is begun in the absence of a solicitor or his representative (or the solicitor or his representative has been required to leave an interview), a record shall be made in the interview record.

NOTES FOR GUIDANCE

C:6A *In considering whether paragraph 6.6(b) applies, the officer should where practicable ask the solicitor for an estimate of the time that he is likely to take in coming to the station, and relate this information to the time for which detention is permitted, the time of day (i.e. whether the period of rest required by paragraph 12.2 is imminent) and the requirements of other investigations in progress. If the solicitor says that he is on his way to the station or that he will set off immediately, it will not normally be appropriate to begin an interview before he arrives. If it appears that it will be necessary to begin an interview before the solicitor's arrival he should be given an indication of how long the police would be able to wait before paragraph 6.6(b) applies so that he has an opportunity to make arrangements for legal advice to be provided by someone else.*

C:6B *A person who asks for legal advice should be given an opportunity to consult a specific solicitor or another solicitor from that solicitor's firm or the duty solicitor. If advice is not available by these means, or he does not wish to consult the duty solicitor, the person should be given an opportunity to choose a solicitor from a list of those willing to provide legal advice. If this solicitor is unavailable, he may choose up to two alternatives. If these attempts to secure legal advice are unsuccessful, the custody officer has discretion to allow further attempts until a solicitor has been contacted and agrees to provide legal advice. Apart from carrying out his duties under Note 6B, a police officer must not advise the suspect about any particular firm of solicitors.*

C:6C *[Not used.]*

C:6D *A detained person has a right to free legal advice and to be represented by a solicitor. The solicitor's only role in the police station is to protect and advance the legal rights of his client. On occasions this may require the solicitor to give advice which has the effect of his client avoiding giving evidence which strengthens a prosecution case. The solicitor may intervene in order to seek clarification or to challenge an improper question to his client or the manner in which it is put, or to advise his client not to reply to particular questions, or if he wishes to give his client further legal advice. Paragraph 6.9 will only apply if the solicitor's approach or conduct prevents or unreasonably obstructs proper questions being put to the suspect or his response being recorded. Examples of unacceptable conduct include answering questions on a suspect's behalf or providing written replies for him to quote.*

C:6E *In a case where an officer takes the decision to exclude a solicitor, he must be in a position to satisfy the court that the decision was properly made. In order to do this he may need to witness what is happening himself.*

C:6F *If an officer of at least the rank of inspector considers that a particular solicitor or firm of solicitors is persistently sending non-accredited or probationary representatives who are unsuited to provide legal advice, he should inform an officer of at least the rank of superintendent, who may wish to take the matter up with the Law Society.*

C:6G *Subject to the constraints of* Annex B, *solicitor may advise more than one client in an investigation if he wishes. Any question of a conflict of interest is for the solicitor under his professional code of conduct. If, however, waiting for a solicitor to give advice to one client may lead to unreasonable delay to the interview with another, the provisions of paragraph 6.6(b) may apply.*

C:6H *In addition to a poster in English advertising the right to legal advice, a poster or posters containing translations into Welsh, the main ethnic minority languages and the principal European languages should be displayed wherever they are likely to be helpful and it is practicable to do so.*

C:6I *Paragraph 6.6(d) requires the authorisation of an officer of the rank of Inspector or above, to the continuation of an interview, where a person who wanted legal advice changes his mind. It is permissible for such authorisation to be given over the telephone, if the authorising officer is able to satisfy himself as to the reason for the person's change of mind and is satisfied that it is proper to continue the interview in those circumstances.*

C:6J *Where a person chooses to speak to a solicitor on the telephone, he should be allowed to do so in private unless this is impractical because of the design and layout of the custody area or the location of telephones.*

C:6K *A person is not obliged to give reasons for declining legal advice and should not be pressed if he does not wish to do so.*

C:7 Citizens of Independent Commonwealth countries or foreign nationals

(a) ACTION

C:7.1 Any citizen of an independent Commonwealth country or a national of a foreign country (including the Republic of Ireland) may communicate at any time with his High Commission, Embassy or Consulate. He must be informed of this right as soon as practicable. He must also be informed as soon as practicable of his right, upon request to have his High Commission, Embassy or Consulate told of his whereabouts and the grounds for his detention. Such a request should be acted upon as soon as practicable.

C:7.2 If a person is detained who is a citizen of an independent Commonwealth or foreign country with which a bilateral consular convention or agreement is in force requiring notification of arrest, the appropriate High Commission, Embassy or Consulate shall be informed as soon as practicable, subject to paragraph 7.4 below. The countries to which this applies as at 1 January 1995 are listed in Annex F.

C:7.3 Consular officers may visit one of their nationals who is in police detention to talk to him and, if required, to arrange for legal advice. Such visits shall take place out of the hearing of a police officer.

C:7.4 Notwithstanding the provisions of consular conventions, where the person is a political refugee (whether for reasons of race, nationality, political opinion or religion) or is seeking political asylum, a consular officer shall not be informed of the arrest of one of his nationals or given access or information about him except at the person's express request.

(b) DOCUMENTATION

A.8–18　　C:7.5 A record shall be made when a person is informed of his rights under this section and of any communications with a High Commission, Embassy or Consulate.

NOTE FOR GUIDANCE

A.8–19　　C:7A *The exercise of the rights in this section may not be interfered with even though* <u>Annex B</u> *applies.*

C:8 Conditions of Detention

(a) ACTION

A.8–20　　C:8.1 So far as is practicable, not more than one person shall be detained in each cell.

C:8.2 Cells in use must be adequately heated, cleaned and ventilated. They must be adequately lit, subject to such dimming as is compatible with safety and security to allow people detained overnight to sleep. No additional restraints shall be used within a locked cell unless absolutely necessary, and then only suitable handcuffs. In the case of a mentally handicapped or mentally disordered person, particular care must be taken when deciding whether to use handcuffs. [See Annex E paragraph 13.]

C:8.3 Blankets, mattresses, pillows and other bedding supplied shall be of a reasonable standard and in a clean and sanitary condition. [See *Note 8B.*]

C:8.4 Access to toilet and washing facilities must be provided.

C:8.5 If it is necessary to remove a person's clothes for the purposes of investigation, for hygiene or health reasons or for cleaning, replacement clothing of a reasonable standard of comfort and cleanliness shall be provided. A person may not be interviewed unless adequate clothing has been offered to him.

C:8.6 At least two light meals and one main meal shall be offered in any period of 24 hours. [See *Note 8C.*] Drinks should be provided at meal times and upon reasonable request between meal times. Whenever necessary, advice shall be sought from the police surgeon on medical and dietary matters. As far as practicable, meals provided shall offer a varied diet and meet any special dietary needs or religious beliefs that the person may have; he may also have meals supplied by his family or friends at his or their own expense. [See *Note 8B.*]

C:8.7 Brief outdoor exercise shall be offered daily if practicable.

C:8.8 A juvenile shall not be placed in a police cell unless no other secure accommodation is available and the custody officer considers that it is not practicable to supervise him if he is not placed in a cell or the custody officer considers that a cell provides more comfortable accommodation than other secure accommodation in the police station. He may not be placed in a cell with a detained adult.

C:8.9 Reasonable force may be used if necessary for the following purposes;

> (i) to secure compliance with reasonable instructions, including instructions given in pursuance of the provisions of a code of practice; or
> (ii) to prevent escape, injury, damage to property or the destruction of evidence.

C:8.10 People detained shall be visited every hour, and those who are drunk, at least every half hour. A person who is drunk shall be roused and spoken to on each visit. [See *Note 8A.*] Should the custody officer feel in any way concerned about the person's condition, for example because he fails to respond adequately when roused, then the officer shall arrange for medical treatment in accordance with paragraph 9.2 of this code.

(b) DOCUMENTATION

C:8.11 A record must be kept of replacement clothing and meals offered. **A.8–21**

C:8.12 If a juvenile is placed in a cell, the reason must be recorded.

NOTES FOR GUIDANCE

C:8A *Whenever possible juveniles and other people at risk should be visited more* **A.8–22** *frequently.*

C:8B *The provisions in paragraphs 8.3 and 8.6 respectively regarding bedding and a varied diet are of particular importance in the case of a person detained under the* Prevention of Terrorism (Temporary Provisions) Act *1989, immigration detainees and others who are likely to be detained for an extended period.*

C:8C *Meals should so far as practicable be offered at recognised meal times.*

C:9 Treatment of Detained Persons
(a) GENERAL

C:9.1 If a complaint is made by or on behalf of a detained person about his treatment **A.8–23** since his arrest, or it comes to the notice of any officer that he may have been treated improperly, a report must be made as soon as practicable to an officer of the rank of inspector or above who is not connected with the investigation. If the matter concerns a possible assault or the possibility of the unnecessary or unreasonable use of force then the police surgeon must also be called as soon as practicable.

(b) MEDICAL TREATMENT

C:9.2 The custody officer must immediately call the police surgeon (or, in urgent **A.8–24** cases,—for example, where a person does not show signs of sensibility or awareness,—must send the person to hospital or call the nearest available medical practitioner) if a person brought to a police station or already detained there:

(a) appears to be suffering from physical illness or a mental disorder; or

(b) is injured; or

(c) [Not used]

(d) fails to respond normally to questions or conversation (other than through drunkenness alone); or

(e) otherwise appears to need medical attention.

This applies even if the person makes no request for medical attention and whether or not he has already had medical treatment elsewhere (unless brought to the police station direct from hospital). It is not intended that the contents of this paragraph should delay the transfer of a person to a place of safety under section 136 of the *Mental Health Act* 1983 where that is applicable. Where an assessment under that Act is to take place at the police station, the custody officer has discretion not to call the police surgeon so long as he believes that the assessment by a registered medical practitioner can be undertaken without undue delay. [See *Note 9A*.]

C:9.3 If it appears to the custody officer, or he is told, that a person brought to the police station under arrest may be suffering from an infectious disease of any significance he must take steps to isolate the person and his property until he has obtained medical directions as to where the person should be taken, whether fumigation should take place and what precautions should be taken by officers who have been or will be in contact with him.

C:9.4 If a detained person requests a medical examination the police surgeon must be called as soon as practicable. He may in addition be examined by a medical practitioner of his own choice at his own expense.

C:9.5 If a person is required to take or apply any medication in compliance with medical directions, but prescribed before the person's detention, the custody officer should consult the police surgeon prior to the use of the medication. The custody officer is responsible for the safekeeping of any medication and for ensuring that the person is given the opportunity to take or apply medication which the police surgeon has approved. However no police officer may administer medicines which are also controlled drugs subject to the *Misuse of Drugs Act* 1971 for this purpose. A person may administer a controlled drug to himself only under the personal supervision of the police surgeon. The requirement for personal supervision will have been satisfied if the custody officer consults the police surgeon (this may be done by telephone) and both the police surgeon and the custody officer are satisfied that, in all the circumstances, self administration of the controlled drug will not expose the detained person, police officers or anyone to the risk of harm or injury. If so satisfied, the police surgeon may authorise the custody officer to permit the detained person to administer the controlled drug. If the custody officer is in any doubt, the police surgeon should be asked to attend. Such consultation should be noted in the custody record.

C:9.6 If a detained person has in his possession or claims to need medication relating to a heart condition, diabetes, epilepsy or a condition of comparable potential seriousness then, even though paragraph 9.2 may not apply, the advice of the police surgeon must be obtained.

(c) DOCUMENTATION

A.8–25 C:9.7 A record must be made of any arrangements made for an examination by a police surgeon under paragraph 9.1 above and of any complaint reported under that paragraph together with any relevant remarks by the custody officer.

C:9.8 A record must be kept of any request for a medical examination under paragraph 9.4, of the arrangements for any examinations made, and of any medical directions to the police.

C:9.9 Subject to the requirements of section 4 above the custody record shall include not only a record of all medication that a detained person has in his possession on arrival at the police station but also a note of any such medication he claims he needs but does not have with him.

NOTES FOR GUIDANCE

C:9A *The need to call a police surgeon need not apply to minor ailments or injuries* **A.8–26** *which do not need attention. However, all such ailments or injuries must be recorded in the custody record and any doubt must be resolved in favour of calling the police surgeon.*

C:9B *It is important to remember that a person who appears to be drunk or behaving abnormally may be suffering from illness or the effects of drugs or may have sustained injury (particularly head injury) which is not apparent, and that someone needing or addicted to certain drugs may experience harmful effects within a short time of being deprived of their supply. Police should therefore always call the police surgeon when in any doubt, and act with all due speed.*

C:9C *If a medical practitioner does not record his clinical findings in the custody record, the record must show where they are recorded.*

C:10 Cautions

(a) WHEN A CAUTION MUST BE GIVEN

C:10.1 A person whom there are grounds to suspect of an offence must be cautioned **A.8–27** before any questions about it (or further questions if it is his answers to previous questions which provide the grounds for suspicion) are put to him regarding his involvement or suspected involvement in that offence if his answers or his silence (*i.e.* failure or refusal to answer a question or to answer satisfactorily) may be given in evidence to a court in a prosecution. He therefore need not be cautioned if questions are put for other purposes, for example, solely to establish his identity or his ownership of any vehicle or to obtain information in accordance with any relevant statutory requirement (see paragraph 10.5C) or in furtherance of the proper and effective conduct of a search, (for example to determine the need to search in the exercise of powers of stop and search or to seek co-operation while carrying out a search) or to seek verification of a written record in accordance with paragraph 11.13.

C:10.2 Whenever a person who is not under arrest is initially cautioned or is reminded that he is under caution (see paragraph 10.5) he must at the same time be told that he is not under arrest and is not obliged to remain with the officer (see paragraph 3.15).

C:10.3 A person must be cautioned upon arrest for an offence unless:

(a) it is impracticable to do so by reason of his condition or behaviour at the time; or

(b) he has already been cautioned immediately prior to arrest in accordance with paragraph 10.1 above.

(b) ACTION: GENERAL

A.8–28 C:10.4 The caution shall be in the following terms:

"You do not have to say anything. But it may harm your defence if you do not mention when questioned something which you later rely on in court. Anything you do say may be given in evidence."

Minor deviations do not constitute a breach of this requirement provided that the sense of the caution is preserved. [See *Note 10C*.]

C:10.5 When there is a break in questioning under caution the interviewing officer must ensure that the person being questioned is aware that he remains under caution. If there is any doubt the caution shall be given again in full when the interview resumes. [See *Note 10A*.]

SPECIAL WARNINGS UNDER SECTIONS 36 AND 37 OF THE CRIMINAL JUSTICE AND PUBLIC ORDER ACT 1994

A.8–29 C:10.5A When a suspect who is interviewed after arrest fails or refuses to answer certain questions, or to answer them satisfactorily, after due warning, a court or jury may draw such inferences as appear proper under sections 36 and 37 of the *Criminal Justice and Public Order Act* 1994. This applies when:

(a) a suspect is arrested by a constable and there is found on his person, or in or on his clothing or footwear, or otherwise in his possession, or in the place where he was arrested, any objects, marks or substances, or marks on such objects, and the person fails or refuses to account for the objects, marks or substances found; or

(b) an arrested person was found by a constable at a place at or about the time the offence for which he was arrested, is alleged to have been committed, and the person fails or refuses to account for his presence at that place.

C:10.5B For an inference to be drawn from a suspect's failure or refusal to answer a question about one of these matters or to answer it satisfactorily, the interviewing officer must first tell him in ordinary language:

(a) what offence he is investigating;

(b) what fact he is asking the suspect to account for;

(c) that he believes this fact may be due to the suspect's taking part in the commission of the offence in question;

(d) that a court may draw a proper inference if he fails or refuses to account for the fact about which he is being questioned;

(e) that a record is being made of the interview and that it may be given in evidence if he is brought to trial.

C:10.5C Where, despite the fact that a person has been cautioned, failure to co-operate may have an effect on his immediate treatment, he should be informed of any relevant consequences and that they are not affected by the caution. Examples are when his refusal to provide his name and address when charged may render him liable to detention, or when his refusal to provide particulars and information in accordance with a statutory requirement, for example, under the *Road Traffic Act* 1988, may amount to an offence or may make him liable to arrest.

(c) JUVENILES, THE MENTALLY DISORDERED AND THE MENTALLY HANDICAPPED

C:10.6 If a juvenile or a person who is mentally disordered or mentally handicapped is cautioned in the absence of the appropriate adult, the caution must be repeated in the adult's presence.

A.8–30

(d) DOCUMENTATION

C:10.7 A record shall be made when a caution is given under this section, either in the officer's pocket book or in the interview record as appropriate.

A.8–31

NOTES FOR GUIDANCE

C:10A *In considering whether or not to caution again after a break, the officer should bear in mind that he may have to satisfy a court that the person understood that he was still under caution when the interview resumed.*

A.8–32

C:10B *[Not used]*

C:10C *If it appears that a person does not understand what the caution means, the officer who has given it should go on to explain it in his own words.*

C:10D *[Not used]*

C:11 Interviews: general

(a) ACTION

C:11.1A An interview is the questioning of a person regarding his involvement or suspected involvement in a criminal offence or offences which, by virtue of paragraph 10.1 of Code C, is required to be carried out under caution. Procedures undertaken under section 7 of the *Road Traffic Act* 1988 do not constitute interviewing for the purpose of this code.

A.8–33

C:11.1 Following a decision to arrest a suspect he must not be interviewed about the relevant offence except at a police station or other authorised place of detention unless the consequent delay would be likely:

(a) to lead to interference with or harm to evidence connected with an offence or interference with or physical harm to other people; or

(b) to lead to the alerting of other people suspected of having committed an offence but not yet arrested for it; or

(c) to hinder the recovery of property obtained in consequence of the commission of an offence.

Interviewing in any of these circumstances shall cease once the relevant risk has been averted or the necessary questions have been put in order to attempt to avert that risk.

C:11.2 Immediately prior to the commencement or re-commencement of any interview at a police station or other authorised place of detention, the interviewing officer shall remind the suspect of his entitlement to free legal advice and that the interview can be delayed for him to obtain legal advice (unless the exceptions in paragraph 6.6 or Annex C apply). It is the responsibility of the interviewing officer to ensure that all such reminders are noted in the record of interview.

C:11.2A At the beginning of an interview carried out in a police station, the interviewing officer, after cautioning the suspect, shall put to him any significant statement or silence which occurred before his arrival at the police station, and shall ask him whether he confirms or denies that earlier statement or silence and whether he wishes to add anything. A "significant" statement or silence is one which appears capable of being used in evidence against the suspect, in particular a direct admission of guilt, or failure or refusal to answer a question or to answer it satisfactorily, which might give rise to an inference under Part III of the *Criminal Justice and Public Order Act* 1994.

C:11.3 No police officer may try to obtain answers to questions or to elicit a statement by the use of oppression. Except as provided for in paragraph 10.5C, no police officer shall indicate, except in answer to a direct question, what action will be taken on the part of the police if the person being interviewed answers questions, makes a statement or refuses to do either. If the person asks the officer directly what action will be taken in the event of his answering questions, making a statement or refusing to do either, then the officer may inform the person what action the police propose to take in that event provided that action is itself proper and warranted.

C:11.4 As soon as a police officer who is making enquiries of any person about an offence believes that a prosecution should be brought against him and that there is sufficient evidence for it to succeed, he shall ask the person if he has anything further to say. If the person indicates that he has nothing more to say the officer shall without delay cease to question him about that offence. This should not, however, be taken to prevent officers in revenue cases or acting under the confiscation provisions of the *Criminal Justice Act* 1988 or the *Drug Trafficking Offences Act* 1986 from inviting suspects to complete a formal question and answer record after the interview is concluded.

(b) INTERVIEW RECORDS

A.8–34   (a) An accurate record must be made of each interview with a person suspected of an offence, whether or not the interview takes place at a police station.

(b) The record must state the place of the interview, the time it begins and ends, the time the record is made (if different), any breaks in the interview and the names of all those present; and must be made on the forms provided for this purpose or in the officer's pocket book or in accordance with the code of practice for the tape-recording of police interviews with suspects (Code E).

(c) The record must be made during the course of the interview, unless in the investigating officer's view this would not be practicable or would interfere with conduct of the interview, and must constitute either a verbatim record of what has been said or failing this, an account of the interview which adequately and accurately summarises it.

C:11.6 The requirement to record the names of all those present at any interview does not apply to police officers interviewing people detained under the *Prevention of Terrorism (Temporary Provisions) Act* 1989. Instead the record shall state the warrant or other identification number and duty station of such officers.

C:11.7 If an interview record is not made during the course of the interview it must be made as soon as practicable after its completion.

C:11.8 Written interview records must be timed and signed by the maker.

C:11.9 If an interview record is not completed in the course of the interview the reason must be recorded in the officer's pocket book.

C:11.10 Unless it is impracticable the person interviewed shall be given the opportunity to read the interview record and to sign it as correct or to indicate the respects in which he considers it inaccurate. If the interview is tape-recorded the arrangements set out in Code E apply. If the person concerned cannot read or refuses to read the record or to sign it, the senior police officer present shall read it to him and ask him whether he would like to sign it as correct (or make his mark) or to indicate the respects in which he considers it inaccurate. The police officer shall then certify on the interview record itself what has occurred. [See *Note 11D.*]

C:11.11 If the appropriate adult or the person's solicitor is present during the interview, he shall also be given an opportunity to read and sign the interview record (or any written statement taken down by a police officer).

C:11.12 Any refusal by a person to sign an interview record when asked to do so in accordance with the provisions of the code must itself be recorded.

C:11.13 A written record shall also be made of any comments made by a suspected person, including unsolicited comments, which are outside the context of an interview but which might be relevant to the offence. Any such record must be timed and signed by the maker. Where practicable the person shall be given the opportunity to read that record and to sign it as correct or to indicate the respects in which he considers it inaccurate. Any refusal to sign shall be recorded. [See *Note 11D.*]

(c) JUVENILES, MENTALLY DISORDERED PEOPLE AND MENTALLY HANDICAPPED PEOPLE

C:11.14 A juvenile or a person who is mentally disordered or mentally handicapped, whether suspected or not, must not be interviewed or asked to provide or sign a written statement in the absence of the appropriate adult unless paragraph 11.1 or Annex C applies. **A.8–35**

C:11.15 Juveniles may only be interviewed at their places of education in exceptional circumstances and then only where the principal or his nominee agrees. Every effort should be made to notify both the parent(s) or other persons responsible for the juvenile's welfare and the appropriate adult (if this is a different person) that the police want to interview the juvenile and reasonable time should be allowed to enable the appropriate adult to be present at the interview. Where awaiting the appropriate adult would cause unreasonable delay and unless the interviewee is suspected of an offence against the educational establishment, the principal or his nominee can act as the appropriate adult for the purposes of the interview.

C:11.16 Where the appropriate adult is present at an interview, he shall be informed that he is not expected to act simply as an observer; and also that the purposes of his presence are, first, to advise the person being questioned and to observe whether or not the interview is being conducted properly and fairly, and secondly, to facilitate communication with the person being interviewed.

NOTES FOR GUIDANCE

C:11A *[Not used]* **A.8–36**

C:11B *It is important to bear in mind that, although juveniles or people who are mentally disordered or mentally handicapped are often capable of providing reliable evidence, they may, without knowing or wishing to do so, be particularly prone in certain circumstances to provide information which is unreliable, misleading or self-incriminating. Special care should therefore always be exercised in questioning such a person, and the appropriate adult should be involved, if there is any doubt about a person's age, mental state or capacity. Because of the risk of unreliable evidence it is also important to obtain corroboration of any facts admitted whenever possible.*

C:11C *It is preferable that a juvenile is not arrested at his place of education unless this is unavoidable. Where a juvenile is arrested at his place of education, the principal or his nominee must be informed.*

C:11D *When a suspect agrees to read records of interviews and of other comments and to sign them as correct, he should be asked to endorse the record with words such as "I agree that this is a correct record of what was said" and add his signature. Where the suspect does not agree with the record, the officer should record the details of any disagreement and then ask the suspect to read these details and then sign them to the effect that they accurately reflect his disagreement. Any refusal to sign when asked to do so shall be recorded.*

C:12 Interviews in police stations

(a) ACTION

C:12.1 If a police officer wishes to interview, or conduct enquiries which require the presence of a detained person, the custody officer is responsible for deciding whether to deliver him into his custody.

C:12.2 In any period of 24 hours a detained person must be allowed a continuous period of at least 8 hours for rest, free from questioning, travel or any interruption by police officers in connection with the investigation concerned. This period should normally be at night. The period of rest may not be interrupted or delayed, except at the request of the person, his appropriate adult or his legal representative, unless there are reasonable grounds for believing that it would:

   (i) involve a risk of harm to people or serious loss of, or damage to, property; or
   (ii) delay unnecessarily the person's release from custody; or
   (iii) otherwise prejudice the outcome of the investigation.

If a person is arrested at a police station after going there voluntarily, the period of 24 hours runs from the time of his arrest and not the time of arrival at the police station. Any action which is required to be taken in accordance with section 8 of this code, or in accordance with medical advice or at the request of the detained person, his appropriate adult or his legal representative, does not constitute an interruption to the rest period such that a fresh period must be allowed.

C:12.3 A detained person may not be supplied with intoxicating liquor except on medical directions. No person, who is unfit through drink or drugs to the extent that he is unable to appreciate the significance of questions put to him and his answers, may be questioned about an alleged offence in that condition except in accordance with Annex C. [See *Note 12B.*]

C:12.4 As far as practicable interviews shall take place in interview rooms which must be adequately heated, lit and ventilated.

C:12.5 People being questioned or making statements shall not be required to stand.

C:12.6 Before the commencement of an interview each interviewing officer shall identify himself and any other officers present by name and rank to the person being interviewed, except in the case of people detained under the *Prevention of Terrorism (Temporary Provisions) Act* 1989 when each officer shall identify himself by his warrant or other identification number and rank rather than his name.

C:12.7 Breaks from interviewing shall be made at recognised meal times. Short breaks for refreshment shall also be provided at intervals of approximately two hours, subject to the interviewing officer's discretion to delay a break if there are reasonable grounds for believing that it would:

   (i) involve a risk of harm to people or serious loss of, or damage to property;

(ii) delay unnecessarily the person's release from custody; or

(iii) otherwise prejudice the outcome of the investigation.

[See *Note 12C.*]

C:12.8 If in the course of the interview a complaint is made by the person being questioned or on his behalf concerning the provisions of this code then the interviewing officer shall:

(i) record it in the interview record; and

(ii) inform the custody officer, who is then responsible for dealing with it in accordance with section 9 of this code.

(b) DOCUMENTATION

C:12.9 A record must be made of the time at which a detained person is not in the   **A.8–38**
custody of the custody officer, and why; and of the reason for any refusal to deliver him out of that custody.

C:12.10 A record must be made of any intoxicating liquor supplied to a detained person, in accordance with paragraph 12.3 above.

C:12.11 Any decision to delay a break in an interview must be recorded, with grounds, in the interview record.

C:12.12 All written statements made at police stations under caution shall be written on the forms provided for the purpose.

C:12.13 All written statements made under caution shall be taken in accordance with Annex D to this code.

NOTES FOR GUIDANCE

C:12A *If the interview has been contemporaneously recorded and the record signed by*   **A.8–39**
the person interviewed in accordance with paragraph 11.10 above, or has been tape recorded, it is normally unnecessary to ask for a written statement. Statements under caution should normally be taken in these circumstances only at the person's express wish. An officer may, however, ask him whether or not he wants to make such a statement.

C:12B *The police surgeon can give advice about whether or not a person is fit to be interviewed in accordance with paragraph 12.3 above.*

C:12C *Meal breaks should normally last at least 45 minutes and shorter breaks after two hours should last at least 15 minutes. If the interviewing officer delays a break in accordance with paragraph 12.7 of this code and prolongs the interview, a longer break should then be provided. If there is a short interview, and a subsequent short interview is contemplated, the length of the break may be reduced if there are reasonable grounds to believe that this is necessary to avoid any of the consequences in paragraph 12.7(i) to (iii).*

C:13 Interpreters

(a) GENERAL

C:13.1 Information on obtaining the services of a suitably qualified interpreter for the   **A.8–40**
deaf or for people who do not understand English is given in *Note for Guidance 3D.*

(b) FOREIGN LANGUAGES

A.8–41   C:13.2 Except in accordance with paragraph 11.1 or unless Annex C applies, a person must not be interviewed in the absence of a person capable of acting as interpreter if:

(a) he has difficulty in understanding English;

(b) the interviewing officer cannot speak the person's own language; and

(c) the person wishes an interpreter to be present.

C:13.3 The interviewing officer shall ensure that the interpreter makes a note of the interview at the time in the language of the person being interviewed for use in the event of his being called to give evidence, and certifies its accuracy. He shall allow sufficient time for the interpreter to make a note of each question and answer after each has been put or given and interpreted. The person shall be given an opportunity to read it or have it read to him and sign it as correct or to indicate the respects in which he considers it inaccurate. If the interview is tape-recorded the arrangements set out in Code E apply.

C:13.4 In the case of a person making a statement in a language other than English:

(a) the interpreter shall take down the statement in the language in which it is made;

(b) the person making the statement shall be invited to sign it; and

(c) an official English translation shall be made in due course.

(c) DEAF PEOPLE AND PEOPLE WITH A SPEECH HANDICAP

A.8–42   C:13.5 If a person appears to be deaf or there is doubt about his hearing or speaking ability, he must not be interviewed in the absence of an interpreter unless he agrees in writing to be interviewed without one or paragraph 11.1 or Annex C applies.

C:13.6 An interpreter shall also be called if a juvenile is interviewed and the parent or guardian present as the appropriate adult appears to be deaf or there is doubt about his hearing or speaking ability, unless he agrees in writing that the interview should proceed without one or paragraph 11.1 or Annex C applies.

C:13.7 The interviewing officer shall ensure that the interpreter is given an opportunity to read the record of the interview and to certify its accuracy in the event of his being called to give evidence.

(d) ADDITIONAL RULES FOR DETAINED PERSONS

A.8–43   C:13.8 All reasonable attempts should be made to make clear to the detained person that interpreters will be provided at public expense.

C:13.9 Where paragraph 6.1 applies and the person concerned cannot communicate with the solicitor, whether because of language, hearing or speech difficulties, an interpreter must be called. The interpreter may not be a police officer when interpretation is needed for the purposes of obtaining legal advice. In all other cases a police officer may only interpret if he first obtains the detained person's (or the appropriate adult's) agreement in writing or if the interview is tape-recorded in accordance with Code E.

C:13.10 When a person is charged with an offence who appears to be deaf or there is doubt about his hearing or speaking ability or ability to understand English, and the custody officer cannot establish effective communication, arrangements must be made for an interpreter to explain as soon as practicable the offence concerned and any other information given by the custody officer.

(e) DOCUMENTATION

C:13.11 Action taken to call an interpreter under this section and any agreement to be interviewed in the absence of an interpreter must be recorded.   **A.8–44**

NOTES FOR GUIDANCE

C:13A *If the interpreter is needed as a prosecution witness at the person's trial, a   **A.8–45** second interpreter must act as the court interpreter.*

C:14 Questioning: special restrictions

C:14.1 If a person has been arrested by one police force on behalf of another and the   **A.8–46** lawful period of detention in respect of that offence has not yet commenced in accordance with section 41 of the *Police and Criminal Evidence Act* 1984 no questions may be put to him about the offence while he is in transit between the forces except in order to clarify any voluntary statement made by him.

C:14.2 If a person is in police detention at a hospital he may not be questioned without the agreement of a responsible doctor. [See *Note 14A.*]

NOTE FOR GUIDANCE

C:14A *If questioning takes place at a hospital under paragraph 14.2 (or on the way to   **A.8–47** or from a hospital) the period concerned counts towards the total period of detention permitted.*

C:15 Reviews and extensions of detention

(a) ACTION

C:15.1 The review officer is responsible under section 40 of the *Police and Criminal   **A.8–48** Evidence Act* 1984, (or, in terrorist cases, under Schedule 3 to the *Prevention of Terrorism (Temporary Provisions) Act* 1989) for determining whether or not a person's detention continues to be necessary. In reaching a decision he shall provide an opportunity to the detained person himself to make representations (unless he is unfit to do so because of his condition or behaviour) or to his solicitor or to the appropriate adult if available at the time. Other people having an interest in the person's welfare may make representations at the review officer's discretion.

C:15.2 The same people may make representations to the officer determining whether further detention should be authorised under section 42 of the Act or under Schedule 3 to the 1989 Act. [See *Note 15A.*]

C:15.2A After hearing any representations, the review officer or officer determining whether further detention should be authorised shall note any comment the person may make if the decision is to keep him in detention. The officer shall not put specific questions to the suspect regarding his involvement in any offence, nor in respect of any comments he may make in response to the decisions to keep him in detention. Such an exchange is likely to constitute an interview as defined by paragraph 11.1A and would require the associated safeguards included in section 11. [See also paragraph 11.13.]

(b) DOCUMENTATION

A.8–49 C:15.3 Before conducting a review the review officer must ensure that the detained person is reminded of his entitlement to free legal advice (see paragraph 6.5). It is the responsibility of the review officer to ensure that all such reminders are noted in the custody record.

C:15.4 The grounds for and extent of any delay in conducting a review shall be recorded.

C:15.5 Any written representations shall be retained.

C:15.6 A record shall be made as soon as practicable of the outcome of each review and application for a warrant of further detention or its extension.

NOTES FOR GUIDANCE

A.8–50 C:15A *If the detained person is likely to be asleep at the latest time when a review of detention or an authorisation of continued detention may take place, the appropriate officer should bring it forward so that the detained person may make representations without being woken up.*

C:15B *An application for a warrant of further detention or its extension should be made between 10 a.m. and 9 p.m., and if possible during normal court hours. It will not be practicable to arrange for a court to sit specially outside the hours of 10 a.m. to 9 p.m. If it appears possible that a special sitting may be needed (either at a weekend, Bank/ Public Holiday or on a weekday outside normal court hours but between 10 a.m. and 9 p.m.) then the clerk to the justices should be given notice and informed of this possibility, while the court is sitting if possible.*

C:15C *If in the circumstances the only practicable way of conducting a review is over the telephone then this is permissible, provided that the requirements of section 40 of the* Police and Criminal Evidence Act *1984 or of Schedule 3 to the* Prevention of Terrorism (Temporary Provisions) Act *1989 are observed. However, a review to decide whether to authorise a person's continued detention under section 42 of the* 1984 Act *must be done in person rather than over the telephone.*

C:16 Charging of detained persons

(a) ACTION

A.8–51 C:16.1 When an officer considers that there is sufficient evidence to prosecute a detained person, and that there is sufficient evidence for a prosecution to succeed, and that the person has said all that he wishes to say about the offence, he shall without delay (and subject to the following qualification) bring him before the custody officer who shall then be responsible for considering whether or not he should be charged. When a person is detained in respect of more than one offence it is permissible to delay bringing him before the custody officer until the above conditions are satisfied in respect of all the offences (but see paragraph 11.4). Any resulting action shall be taken in the presence of the appropriate adult if the person is a juvenile or mentally disordered or mentally handicapped.

C:16.2 When a detained person is charged with or informed that he may be prosecuted for an offence he shall be cautioned in the following terms:

"You do not have to say anything. But it may harm your defence if you do not mention now something which you later rely on in court. Anything you do say may be given in evidence."

C:16.3 At the time a person is charged he shall be given a written notice showing particulars of the offence with which he is charged and including the name of the officer in the case (in terrorist cases, the officer's warrant or other identification number instead), his police station and the reference number for the case. So far as possible the particulars of the charge shall be stated in simple terms, but they shall also show the precise offence in law with which he is charged. The notice shall begin with the following words:

"You are charged with the offence(s) shown below. You do not have to say anything. But it may harm your defence if you do not mention now something which you later rely on in court. Anything you do say may be given in evidence."

If the person is a juvenile or is mentally disordered or mentally handicapped the notice shall be given to the appropriate adult.

C:16.4 If at any time after a person has been charged with or informed that he may be prosecuted for an offence, a police officer wishes to bring to the notice of that person any written statement made by another person or the content of an interview with another person, he shall hand to that person a true copy of any such written statement or bring to his attention the content of the interview record, but shall say or do nothing to invite any reply or comment save to warn him that he does not have to say anything but that anything he does say may be given in evidence and to remind him of his right to legal advice in accordance with paragraph 6.5 above. If the person cannot read then the officer may read it to him. If the person is a juvenile or mentally disordered or mentally handicapped the copy shall also be given to, or the interview record brought to the attention of, the appropriate adult.

C:16.5 Questions relating to an offence may not be put to a person after he has been charged with that offence, or informed that he may be prosecuted for it, unless they are necessary for the purpose of preventing or minimising harm or loss to some other person or to the public or for clearing up an ambiguity in a previous answer or statement, or where it is in the interests of justice that the person should have put to him and have an opportunity to comment on information concerning the offence which has come to light since he was charged or informed that he might be prosecuted. Before any such questions are put to him, he shall be warned that he does not have to say anything but that anything he does say may be given in evidence and reminded of his right to legal advice in accordance with paragraph 6.5 above. [See *Note 16A*.]

C:16.6 Where a juvenile is charged with an offence and the custody officer authorises his continued detention he must try to make arrangements for the juvenile to be taken into care of a local authority to be detained pending appearance in court unless he certifies that it is impracticable to do so, or, in the case of a juvenile of at least 12 years of age, no secure accommodation is available and there is a risk to the public of serious harm from that juvenile, in accordance with section 38(6) of the *Police and Criminal Evidence Act* 1984, as amended by section 59 of the *Criminal Justice Act* 1991 and section 24 of the *Criminal Justice and Public Order Act* 1994. [See *Note 16B*.]

(b) DOCUMENTATION

C:16.7 A record shall be made of anything a detained person says when charged.   **A.8–52**

C:16.8 Any questions put after charge and answers given relating to the offence shall be contemporaneously recorded in full on the forms provided and the record signed by that person or, if he refuses, by the interviewing officer and any third parties present. If the questions are tape-recorded the arrangements set out in Code E apply.

C:16.9 If it is not practicable to make arrangements for the transfer of a juvenile into local authority care in accordance with paragraph 16.6 above the custody officer must record the reasons and make out a certificate to be produced before the court together with the juvenile.

NOTES FOR GUIDANCE

A.8–53   C:16A *The service of the Notice of Intended Prosecution under sections 1 and 2 of the* Road Traffic Offenders Act *1988 does not amount to informing a person that he may be prosecuted for an offence and so does not preclude further questioning in relation to that offence.*

C:16B *Except as provided for in 16.6 above, neither a juvenile's behaviour nor the nature of the offence with which he is charged provides grounds for the custody officer to decide that it is impracticable to seek to arrange for his transfer to the care of the local authority. Similarly, the lack of secure local authority accommodation shall not make it impracticable for the custody officer to transfer him. The availability of secure accommodation is only a factor in relation to a juvenile aged 12 or over when the local authority accommodation would not be adequate to protect the public from serious harm from the juvenile. The obligation to transfer a juvenile to local authority accommodation applies as much to a juvenile charged during the daytime as it does to a juvenile to be held overnight, subject to a requirement to bring the juvenile before a court under section 46 of the* Police and Criminal Evidence Act *1984.*

C:17 Testing persons for the presence of specified Class A drugs

(a) ACTION

A.8–54   C:17.1 A sample of urine or a non-intimate sample may be taken from a person in police detention for the purpose of ascertaining whether he has any specified Class A drugs in his body if:

(a) that person has been charged with a trigger offence, or

(b) he has been charged with any offence and a police officer of inspector rank or above, who has reasonable grounds for suspecting that the misuse by that person of any specified Class A drug caused or contributed to the offence, has authorised the sample to be taken.

C:17.2 The person from whom the sample is taken must have attained the age of 18.

C:17.3 A police officer must have requested the person concerned to give the sample.

C:17.4 Before requesting a sample from the person concerned, an officer must:

(a) inform him that the purpose of taking the sample is for drug testing under the *Police and Criminal Evidence Act* 1984. This is to ascertain whether he has a specified Class A drug present in his body;

(b) warn him that if, when requested, he fails without good cause to provide a sample he may be liable to prosecution;

(c) where the taking of the sample has been authorised by an inspector or above under paragraph 17.1(b) of this code, inform him that the authorisation has been given and the grounds for giving it;

(d) remind him of the following rights, which may be exercised at any stage during the period in custody:

(i) the right to have someone informed of his arrest [see section 5];

(ii) the right to consult privately with a solicitor and the fact that independent legal advice is available free of charge [see section 6]; and

(iii) the right to consult these codes of practice [see note 3E].

C:17.5 Authorisation by an officer of the rank of inspector or above may be given orally or in writing, but if it is given orally it must be confirmed in writing as soon as practicable.

C:17.6 Custody officers may authorise continued detention for up to six hours from the time of charge to enable a sample to be taken.

(b) DOCUMENTATION

C:17.7 If a sample is taken following authorisation by an officer of the rank of **A.8–55** inspector or above, the authorisation and the grounds for suspicion must be recorded in the custody record.

C:17.8 The giving of a warning on the consequences of failure to provide a specimen must be recorded in the custody record.

C:17.9 The time of charge and the time at which the sample was given must be recorded in the custody record.

(c) GENERAL

C:17.10 A sample may only be taken by a prescribed person. **A.8–56**

C:17.11 Force may not be used to take any sample for the purpose of drug testing.

C:17.12 The terms "Class A drug" and "misuse" have the same meaning as in the *Misuse of Drugs Act* 1971. "Specified" (in relation to a Class A drug) and "trigger offence" have the same meanings as in Part III of the *Criminal Justice and Court Services Act* 2000.

C:17.13 Any sample taken:

(a) may not be used for any purpose other than to ascertain whether the person concerned has a specified Class A drug present in his body; and

(b) must be retained until court proceedings have been concluded.

NOTES FOR GUIDANCE

C:17A *When warning a person who is asked to provide a urine or non-intimate sample* **A.8–57** *in accordance with paragraph 17.1, the following form of words may be used:*

"You do not have to provide a sample, but I must warn you that if you fail or refuse without good cause to do so, you will commit an offence for which you may be imprisoned, or fined, or both."

C:17B *A sample has to be sufficient and suitable. A sufficient sample is sufficient in quantity and quality to enable drug testing analysis to take place. A suitable sample is one, which by its nature, is suitable for a particular form of drug analysis.*

C:17C *A prescribed person in paragraph 17.10 is one who is prescribed in regulations made by the Secretary of State under section 63B(6) of the* Police and Criminal Evidence Act *1984.*

C:17D *The retention of the sample in paragraph 17.13 allows for the sample to be sent to the Forensic Science Service laboratory for confirmatory testing and analysis if the detainee disputes the test. But such samples, and the information derived from them, may not be subsequently used in the investigation of any offence or in evidence against the persons from whom they were taken.*

C:17E *The trigger offences are: from the* Theft Act *1968—theft, robbery, burglary, aggravated burglary, taking a motor vehicle (or other conveyance) without authority, aggravated vehicle-taking, obtaining property by deception, going equipped for stealing etc.; and from the* Misuse of Drugs Act *1971 (but only if committed in respect of a specified Class A drug)—producing and supplying a controlled drug, possessing a controlled drug, possessing a controlled drug with intent to supply.*]

As to the limited application of paragraph 17, see *ante*, A-38 in this supplement.

Annex A

Intimate and strip searches [See paragraph 4.1]

A INTIMATE SEARCH

A.8–58   C:1. An "intimate search" is a search which consists of the physical examination of a person's body orifices other than the mouth.

(a) ACTION

A.8–59   C:2. Body orifices other than the mouth may be searched only if an officer of the rank of superintendent or above has reasonable grounds for believing:

(a) that an article which could cause physical injury to the detained person or others at the police station has been concealed; or

(b) that the person has concealed a Class A drug which he intended to supply to another or to export; and

(c) that in either case an intimate search is the only practicable means of removing it.

The reasons why an intimate search is considered necessary shall be explained to the person before the search takes place.

C:3. An intimate search may only be carried out by a registered medical practitioner or registered nurse, unless an officer of at least the rank of superintendent considers that this is not practicable and the search is to take place under sub-paragraph 2(a) above.

C:4. An intimate search under sub-paragraph 2(a) above may take place only at a hospital, surgery, other medical premises or police station. A search under sub-paragraph 2(b) may take place only at a hospital, surgery or other medical premises.

C:5. An intimate search at a police station of a juvenile or a mentally disordered or mentally handicapped person may take place only in the presence of an appropriate adult of the same sex (unless the person specifically requests the presence of a particular adult of the opposite sex who is readily available). In the case of a juvenile the search may take place in the absence of the appropriate adult only if the juvenile signifies in the presence of the appropriate adult that he prefers the search to be done in his absence and the appropriate adult agrees. A record shall be made of the juvenile's decision and signed by the appropriate adult.

C:6. Where an intimate search under sub-paragraph 2(a) above is carried out by a police officer, the officer must be of the same sex as the person searched. Subject to paragraph 5 above, no person of the opposite sex who is not a medical practitioner or nurse shall be present, nor shall anyone whose presence is unnecessary but a minimum of two people, other than the person searched, must be present during the search. The search shall be conducted with proper regard to the sensitivity and vulnerability of the person in these circumstances.

(b) DOCUMENTATION

C:7. In the case of an intimate search the custody officer shall as soon as practicable record which parts of the person's body were searched, who carried out the search, who was present, the reasons for the search and its result. **A.8–60**

C:8. If an intimate search is carried out by a police officer, the reason why it was impracticable for a suitably qualified person to conduct it must be recorded.

B STRIP SEARCH

C:9. A strip search is a search involving the removal of more than outer clothing. **A.8–61**

(a) ACTION

C:10. A strip search may take place only if it is considered necessary to remove an article which a person would not be allowed to keep, and the officer reasonably considers that the person might have concealed such an article. Strip searches shall not be routinely carried out where there is no reason to consider that articles have been concealed. **A.8–62**

THE CONDUCT OF STRIP SEARCHES

C:11. The following procedures shall be observed when strip searches are conducted: **A.8–63**

(a) a police officer carrying out a strip search must be of the same sex as the person searched;

(b) the search shall take place in an area where the person being searched cannot be seen by anyone who does not need to be present, nor by a member of the opposite sex (except an appropriate adult who has been specifically requested by the person being searched);

(c) except in cases of urgency, where there is a risk of serious harm to the person detained or to others, whenever a strip search involves exposure of intimate parts of the body, there must be at least two people present other than the person searched, and if the search is of a juvenile or a mentally disordered or mentally handicapped person, one of the people must be the appropriate adult. Except in urgent cases as above, a search of a juvenile may take place in the absence of the appropriate adult only if the juvenile signifies in the presence of the appropriate adult that he prefers the search to be done in his absence and the appropriate adult agrees. A record shall be made of the juvenile's decision and signed by the appropriate adult. The presence of more than two people, other than an appropriate adult, shall be permitted only in the most exceptional circumstances;

(d) the search shall be conducted with proper regard to the sensitivity and vulnerability of the person in these circumstances and every reasonable effort shall be made to secure the person's co-operation and minimise embarrassment. People who are searched should not normally be required to have all their clothes removed at the same time, for example, a man shall be allowed to put on his shirt before removing his trousers, and a woman shall be allowed to put on her blouse and upper garments before further clothing is removed;

(e) where necessary to assist the search, the person may be required to hold his or her arms in the air or to stand with his or her legs apart and to bend forward so that a visual examination may be made of the genital and anal areas provided that no physical contact is made with any body orifice;

(f) if, during a search, articles are found, the person shall be asked to hand them over. If articles are found within any body orifice other than the mouth, and the person refuses to hand them over, their removal would constitute an intimate search, which must be carried out in accordance with the provisions of Part A of this Annex;

(g) a strip search shall be conducted as quickly as possible, and the person searched allowed to dress as soon as the procedure is complete.

(b) DOCUMENTATION

A.8–64 C:12. A record shall be made on the custody record of a strip search including the reason it was considered necessary to undertake it, those present and any result.

Annex B

Delay in notifying arrest or allowing access to legal advice

A. Persons detained under the Police and Criminal Evidence Act 1984

(a) ACTION

A.8–65 C:1. The rights set out in sections 5 or 6 of the code or both may be delayed if the person is in police detention in connection with a serious arrestable offence, has not yet been charged with an offence and an officer of the rank of superintendent or above has reasonable grounds for believing that the exercise of either right:

(i) will lead to interference with or harm to evidence connected with a serious arrestable offence or interference with or physical injury to other people; or

(ii) will lead to the alerting of other people suspected of having committed such an offence but not yet arrested for it; or

(iii) will hinder the recovery of property obtained as a result of such an offence.

[See *Note B3.*]

C:2. These rights may also be delayed where the serious arrestable offence is either:

(i) a drug trafficking offence and the officer has reasonable grounds for believing that the detained person has benefited from drug trafficking, and that the recovery of the value of that person's proceeds of drug trafficking will be hindered by the exercise of either right or;

(ii) an offence to which Part VI of the *Criminal Justice Act* 1988 (covering confiscation orders) applies and the officer has reasonable grounds for believing that the detained person has benefited from the offence, and that the recovery of the value of the property obtained by that person from or in connection with the offence, or if [*sic*] the pecuniary advantage derived by him from or in connection with it, will be hindered by the exercise of either right.

C:3. Access to a solicitor may not be delayed on the grounds that he might advise the person not to answer any questions or that the solicitor was initially asked to attend the police station by someone else, provided that the person himself then wishes to see the solicitor. In the latter case the detained person must be told that the solicitor has come to the police station at another person's request, and must be asked to sign the custody record to signify whether or not he wishes to see the solicitor.

C:4. These rights may be delayed only for as long as is necessary and, subject to paragraph 9 below, in no case beyond 36 hours after the relevant time as defined in section 41 of the *Police and Criminal Evidence Act* 1984. If the above grounds cease to apply within this time, the person must as soon as practicable be asked if he wishes to exercise either right, the custody record must be noted accordingly, and action must be taken in accordance with the relevant section of the code.

C:5. A detained person must be permitted to consult a solicitor for a reasonable time before any court hearing.

(b) DOCUMENTATION

C:6. The grounds for action under this Annex shall be recorded and the person informed of them as soon as practicable.   **A.8–66**

C:7. Any reply given by a person under paragraphs 4 or 9 must be recorded and the person asked to endorse the record in relation to whether he wishes to receive legal advice at this point.

B. Persons detained under the Prevention of Terrorism (Temporary Provisions) Act 1989

(a) ACTION

C:8. The rights set out in sections 5 or 6 of this code or both may be delayed if paragraph 1 above applies or if an officer of the rank of superintendent or above has reasonable grounds for believing that the exercise of either right: **A.8–67**

(a) will lead to interference with the gathering of information about the commission, preparation or instigation of acts of terrorism; or

(b) by alerting any person, will make it more difficult to prevent an act of terrorism or to secure the apprehension, prosecution or conviction of any person in connection with the commission, preparation or instigation of an act of terrorism.

C:9. These rights may be delayed only for as long as is necessary and in no case beyond 48 hours from the time of arrest. If the above grounds cease to apply within this time, the person must as soon as practicable be asked if he wishes to exercise either right, the custody record must be noted accordingly, and action must be taken in accordance with the relevant section of this code.

C:10. Paragraphs 3 and 5 above apply.

(b) DOCUMENTATION

C:11. Paragraphs 6 and 7 above apply.

NOTES FOR GUIDANCE

A.8–68   C:B1 *Even if Annex B applies in the case of a juvenile, or a person who is mentally disordered or mentally handicapped, action to inform the appropriate adult (and the person responsible for a juvenile's welfare, if that is a different person) must nevertheless be taken in accordance with paragraph 3.7 and 3.9 of this code.*

C:B2 *In the case of Commonwealth citizens and foreign nationals see Note 7A.*

C:B3 *Police detention is defined in section 118(2) of the* Police and Criminal Evidence Act *1984.*

C:B4 *The effect of paragraph 1 above is that the officer may authorise delaying access to a specific solicitor only if he has reasonable grounds to believe that specific solicitor will, inadvertently or otherwise, pass on a message from the detained person or act in some other way which will lead to any of the three results in paragraph 1 coming about. In these circumstances the officer should offer the detained person access to a solicitor (who is not the specific solicitor referred to above) on the Duty Solicitor Scheme.*

C:B5 *The fact that the grounds for delaying notification of arrest under paragraph 1 above may be satisfied does not automatically mean that the grounds for delaying access to legal advice will also be satisfied.*

Annex C

Vulnerable suspects: urgent interviews at police stations

A.8–69   C:1. When an interview is to take place in a police station or other authorised place of detention if, and only if, an officer of the rank of superintendent or above considers that delay will lead to the consequences set out in paragraph 11.1(a) to (c) of this Code:

(a) a person heavily under the influence of drink or drugs may be interviewed in that state; or

(b) a juvenile or a person who is mentally disordered or mentally handicapped may be interviewed in the absence of the appropriate adult; or

(c) a person who has difficulty in understanding English or who has a hearing disability may be interviewed in the absence of an interpreter.

C:2. Questioning in these circumstances may not continue once sufficient information to avert the immediate risk has been obtained.

C:3. A record shall be made of the grounds for any decision to interview a person under paragraph 1 above.

NOTE FOR GUIDANCE

A.8–70   C:C1 *The special groups referred to in this Annex are all particularly vulnerable. The provisions of the Annex, which override safeguards designed to protect them and to minimise the risk of interviews producing unreliable evidence, should be applied only in exceptional cases of need.*

Annex D

Written statements under caution (See paragraph 12.13)

(a) WRITTEN BY A PERSON UNDER CAUTION

C:1. A person shall always be invited to write down himself what he wants to say. A.8–71

C:2. Where the person wishes to write it himself, he shall be asked to write out and sign, before writing what he wants to say, the following:

"I make this statement of my own free will. I understand that I do not have to say anything but that it may harm my defence if I do not mention when questioned something which I later rely on in court. This statement may be given in evidence."

C:3. Any person writing his own statement shall be allowed to do so without any prompting except that a police officer may indicate to him which matters are material or question any ambiguity in the statement.

(b) WRITTEN BY A POLICE OFFICER

C:4. If a person says that he would like someone to write it for him, a police officer A.8–72 shall write the statement, but, before starting, he must ask him to sign, or make his mark, to the following:

"I, . . . , wish to make a statement. I want someone to write down what I say. I understand that I do not have to say anything but that it may harm my defence if I do not mention when questioned something which I later rely on in court. This statement may be given in evidence."

C:5. Where a police officer writes the statement, he must take down the exact words spoken by the person making it and he must not edit or paraphrase it. Any questions that are necessary (*e.g.* to make it more intelligible) and the answers given must be recorded contemporaneously on the statement form.

C:6. When the writing of a statement by a police officer is finished the person making it shall be asked to read it and to make any corrections, alterations or additions he wishes. When he has finished reading it he shall be asked to write and sign or make his mark on the following certificate at the end of the statement:

"I have read the above statement, and I have been able to correct, alter or add anything I wish. This statement is true. I have made it of my own free will."

C:7. If the person making the statement cannot read, or refuses to read it, or to write the above mentioned certificate at the end of it or to sign it, the senior police officer present shall read it to him and ask him whether he would like to correct, alter or add anything and to put his signature or make his mark at the end. The police officer shall then certify on the statement itself what has occurred.

Annex E

Summary of provisions relating to mentally disordered and mentally handicapped people

C:1. If an officer has any suspicion, or is told in good faith, that a person of any age A.8–73 may be mentally disordered or mentally handicapped, or mentally incapable of understanding the significance of questions put to him or his replies, then that person shall be treated as mentally disordered or mentally handicapped for the purposes of this code. [See paragraph 1.4.]

C:2. In the case of a person who is mentally disordered or mentally handicapped, "the appropriate adult" means:

(a) a relative, guardian or some other person responsible for his care or custody;

(b) someone who has experience of dealing with mentally disordered or mentally handicapped people but is not a police officer or employed by the police; or

(c) failing, either of the above, some other responsible adult aged 18 or over who is not a police officer or employed by the police.

[See paragraph 1.7(b).]

C:3. If the custody officer authorises the detention of a person who is mentally handicapped or appears to be suffering from a mental disorder he must as soon as practicable inform the appropriate adult of the grounds for the person's detention and his whereabouts, and ask the adult to come to the police station to see the person. If the appropriate adult is already at the police station when information is given as required in paragraphs 3.1 to 3.5 the information must be given to the detained person in the appropriate adult's presence. If the appropriate adult is not at the police station when the provisions of 3.1 to 3.5 are complied with then these provisions must be complied with again in the presence of the appropriate adult once that person arrives. [See paragraphs 3.9 and 3.11.]

C:4. If the appropriate adult, having been informed of the right to legal advice, considers that legal advice should be taken, the provisions of section 6 of the code apply as if the mentally disordered or mentally handicapped person had requested access to legal advice. [See paragraph 3.13 and *Note E2*.]

C:5. If a person brought to a police station appears to be suffering from mental disorder or is incoherent other than through drunkenness alone, or if a detained person subsequently appears to be mentally disordered, the custody officer must immediately call the police surgeon or, in urgent cases, send the person to hospital or call the nearest available medical practitioner. It is not intended that these provisions should delay the transfer of a person to a place of safety under section 136 of the *Mental Health Act* 1983 where that is applicable. Where an assessment under that Act is to take place at the police station, the custody officer has discretion not to call the police surgeon so long as he believes that the assessment by a registered medical practitioner can be undertaken without undue delay. [See paragraph 9.2.]

C:6. It is imperative that a mentally disordered or mentally handicapped person who has been detained under section 136 of the *Mental Health Act* 1983 should be assessed as soon as possible. If that assessment is to take place at the police station, an approved social worker and a registered medical practitioner shall be called to the police station as soon as possible in order to interview and examine the person. Once the person has been interviewed and examined and suitable arrangements have been made for his treatment or care, he can no longer be detained under section 136. The person should not be released until he has been seen by both the approved social worker and the registered medical practitioner. [See paragraph 3.10.]

C:7. If a mentally disordered or mentally handicapped person is cautioned in the absence of the appropriate adult, the caution must be repeated in the appropriate adult's presence. [See paragraph 10.6.]

C:8. A mentally disordered or mentally handicapped person must not be interviewed or asked to provide or sign a written statement in the absence of the appropriate adult unless the provisions of paragraph 11.1 or Annex C of this code apply. Questioning in these circumstances may not continue in the absence of the appropriate adult once sufficient information to avert the risk has been obtained. A record shall be made of the grounds for any decision to begin an interview in these circumstances. [See paragraphs 11.1 and 11.14 and Annex C.]

C:9. Where the appropriate adult is present at an interview, he shall be informed that he is not expected to act simply as an observer; and also that the purposes of his presence are, first, to advise the person being interviewed and to observe whether or not the interview is being conducted properly and fairly, and, secondly, to facilitate communication with the person being interviewed. [See paragraph 11.16.]

C:10. If the detention of a mentally disordered or mentally handicapped person is reviewed by a review officer or a superintendent, the appropriate adult must, if available at the time, be given opportunity to make representations to the officer about the need for continuing detention. [See paragraphs 15.1 and 15.2.]

C:11. If the custody officer charges a mentally disordered or mentally handicapped person with an offence or takes such other action as is appropriate when there is sufficient evidence for a prosecution this must be done in the presence of the appropriate adult. The written notice embodying any charge must be given to the appropriate adult. [See paragraphs 16.1 to 16.3.]

C:12. An intimate or strip search of a mentally disordered or mentally handicapped person may take place only in the presence of the appropriate adult of the same sex, unless the person specifically requests the presence of a particular adult of the opposite sex. A strip search may take place in the absence of an appropriate adult only in cases of urgency where there is a risk of serious harm to the person detained or to others. [See *Annex A*, paragraphs 5 and 11(c).]

C:13. Particular care must be taken when deciding whether to use handcuffs to restrain a mentally disordered or mentally handicapped person in a locked cell. [See paragraph 8.2.]

NOTES FOR GUIDANCE

C:E1 *In the case of mentally disordered or mentally handicapped people, it may in* **A.8–74** *certain circumstances be more satisfactory for all concerned if the appropriate adult is someone who has experience or training in their care rather than a relative lacking such qualifications. But if the person himself prefers a relative to a better qualified stranger or objects to a particular person as the appropriate adult, his wishes should if practicable be respected. [See Note 1E.]*

C:E2 *The purpose of the provision at paragraph 3.13 is to protect the rights of a mentally disordered or mentally handicapped person who does not understand the significance of what is being said to him. If the person wishes to exercise the right to legal advice, the appropriate action should be taken and not delayed until the appropriate adult arrives. [See Note 3G.] A mentally disordered or mentally handicapped person should always be given an opportunity, when an appropriate adult is called to the police station, to consult privately with a solicitor in the absence of the appropriate adult if he wishes to do so. [See Note 1EE.]*

C:E3 *It is important to bear in mind that although mentally disordered or mentally handicapped are [sic] people often capable of providing reliable evidence, they may, without knowing or wishing to do so, be particularly prone in certain circumstances to provide information which is unreliable, misleading or self-incriminating. Special care should therefore always be exercised in questioning such a person, and the appropriate adult involved, if there is any doubt about a person's mental state or capacity. Because of the risk of unreliable evidence, it is important to obtain corroboration of any facts admitted whenever possible. [See Note 11B.]*

C:E4 *Because of the risks referred to in Note E3, which the presence of the appropriate adult is intended to minimise, officers of superintendent rank or above should exercise their discretion to authorise the commencement of an interview in the adult's absence only in exceptional cases, where it is necessary to avert an immediate risk of serious harm. [See paragraph 11.1 and Annex C and Note C1.]*

Annex F

Countries with which bilateral consular conventions or agreements requiring notification of the arrest and detention of their nationals are in force as at 1 January 1995

A.8–75

Armenia	Kyrgyzstan
Austria	Macedonia
Azerbaijan	Mexico
Belarus	Moldova
Belgium	Mongolia
Bosnia-Hercegovina	Norway
Bulgaria	Poland
China*	Romania
Croatia	Russia
Cuba	Slovak Republic
Czech Republic	Slovenia
Denmark	Spain
Egypt	Sweden
France	Tajikistan
Georgia	Turkmenistan
German Federal Republic	Ukraine
Greece	USA
Hungary	Uzbekistan
Kazakhstan	Yugoslavia

*Police are required to inform Chinese officials of arrest/detention in the Manchester consular district only. This comprises Derbyshire, Durham, Greater Manchester, Lancashire, Merseyside, North, South and West Yorkshire, and Tyne and Wear.

DECLARATION ON THE PROTECTION OF ALL PERSONS FROM BEING SUBJECTED TO TORTURE AND OTHER CRUEL, INHUMAN OR DEGRADING TREATMENT OR PUNISHMENT

Adopted by General Assembly resolution 3452 (XXX) of 9 December 1975

Article 1

1. For the purpose of this Declaration, torture means any act by which severe pain or suffering, whether physical or mental, is intentionally inflicted by or at the instigation of a public official on a person for such purposes as obtaining from him or a third person information or confession, punishing him for an act he has committed or is suspected of having committed, or intimidating him or other persons. It does not include pain or suffering arising only from, inherent in or incidental to, lawful sanctions to the extent consistent with the Standard Minimum Rules for the Treatment of Prisoners.

A.9–01

2. Torture constitutes an aggravated and deliberate form of cruel, inhuman or degrading treatment or punishment.

Article 2

Any act of torture or other cruel, inhuman or degrading treatment or punishment is an offence to human dignity and shall be condemned as a denial of the purposes of the Charter of the United Nations and as a violation of the human rights and fundamental freedoms proclaimed in the Universal Declaration of Human Rights.

A.9–02

Article 3

No State may permit or tolerate torture or other cruel, inhuman or degrading treatment or punishment. Exceptional circumstances such as a state of war or a threat of war, internal political instability or any other public emergency may not be invoked as a justification of torture or other cruel, inhuman or degrading treatment or punishment.

A.9–03

Article 4

Each State shall, in accordance with the provisions of this Declaration, take effective measures to prevent torture and other cruel, inhuman or degrading treatment or punishment from being practised within its jurisdiction.

A.9–04

Article 5

The training of law enforcement personnel and of other public officials who may be responsible for persons deprived of their liberty shall ensure that full account is taken of the prohibition against torture and other cruel, inhuman or degrading treatment or punishment. This prohibition shall also, where appropriate, be included in such general rules or

A.9–05

instructions as are issued in regard to the duties and functions of anyone who may be involved in the custody or treatment of such persons.

Article 6

A.9–06 Each State shall keep under systematic review interrogation methods and practices as well as arrangements for the custody and treatment of persons deprived of their liberty in its territory, with a view to preventing any cases of torture or other cruel, inhuman or degrading treatment or punishment.

Article 7

A.9–07 Each State shall ensure that all acts of torture as defined in article 1 are offences under its criminal law. The same shall apply in regard to acts which constitute participation in, complicity in, incitement to or an attempt to commit torture.

Article 8

A.9–08 Any person who alleges that he has been subjected to torture or other cruel, inhuman or degrading treatment or punishment by or at the instigation of a public official shall have the right to complain to, and to have his case impartially examined by, the competent authorities of the State concerned.

Article 9

A.9–09 Wherever there is reasonable ground to believe that an act of torture as defined in article 1 has been committed, the competent authorities of the State concerned shall promptly proceed to an impartial investigation even if there has been no formal complaint.

If an investigation under Article 8 or Article 9 establishes that an act of torture as defined in Article 1 appears to have been committed, criminal proceedings shall be instituted against the alleged offender or offenders in accordance with national law. If an allegation of other forms of cruel, inhuman or degrading treatment or punishment is considered to be well founded, the alleged offender or offenders shall be subject to criminal, disciplinary or other appropriate proceedings.

Article 11

A.9–10 Where it is proved that an act of torture or other cruel, inhuman or degrading treatment or punishment has been committed by or at the instigation of a public official, the victim shall be afforded redress and compensation in accordance with national law.

Article 12

A.9–11 Any statement which is established to have been made as a result of torture or other cruel, inhuman or degrading treatment or punishment may not be invoked as evidence against the person concerned or against any other person in any proceedings.

THE MENTAL HEALTH ACT 1983

PART IV

CONSENT TO TREATMENT

s.56 Patients to whom Part IV applies.

(1) This Part of this Act applies to any patient liable to be detained under this Act **A.10–01** except—

   (a) a patient who is liable to be detained by virtue of an emergency application and in respect of whom the second medical recommendation referred to in section 4(4)(a) above has not been given and received;

   (b) a patient who is liable to be detained by virtue of section 5(2) or (4) or 35 above or section 125 or 126 below or by virtue of a direction under section 37(4) above; and

   (c) a patient who has been conditionally discharged under section 42(2) above or section 73 or 74 below and has not been recalled to hospital.

(2) Section 57 and, so far as relevant to that section, sections 59, 60 and 62 below, apply also to any patient who is not liable to be detained under this Act.

Notes:
Act excluded by Mental Health (Scotland) Act 1984 (c.36), ss.17(2), 79(1) Act modified by Repatriation of Prisoners Act 1984 (c.47), s.3, Sch. para. 5(1)(a)

s.57 Treatment requiring consent and a second opinion.

(1) This section applies to the following forms of medical treatment for mental dis- **A.10–02** order—

   (a) any surgical operation for destroying brain tissue or for destroying the functioning of brain tissue; and

   (b) such other forms of treatment as may be specified for the purposes of this section by regulations made by the Secretary of State.

(2) Subject to section 62 below, a patient shall not be given any form of treatment to which this section applies unless he has consented to it and—

(a) a registered medical practitioner appointed for the purposes of this Part of this Act by the Secretary of State (not being the responsible medical officer) and two other persons appointed for the purposes of this paragraph by the Secretary of State (not being registered medical practitioners) have certified in writing that the patient is capable of understanding the nature, purpose and likely effects of the treatment in question and has consented to it; and

(b) the registered medical practitioner referred to in paragraph (a) above has certified in writing that, having regard to the likelihood of the treatment alleviating or preventing a deterioration of the patient's condition, the treatment should be given.

(3) Before giving a certificate under subsection (2)(b) above the registered medical practitioner concerned shall consult two other persons who have been professionally concerned with the patient's medical treatment, and of those persons one shall be a nurse and the other shall be neither a nurse nor a registered medical practitioner.

(4) Before making any regulations for the purpose of this section the Secretary of State shall consult such bodies as appear to him to be concerned.

Notes:

Act excluded by Mental Health (Scotland) Act 1984 (c.36), ss.17(2), 79(1) Act modified by Repatriation of Prisoners Act 1984 (c.47), s.3, Sch. para. 5(1)(a)

s.58 Treatment requiring consent or a second opinion.

A.10–03   (1) This section applies to the following forms of medical treatment for mental disorder—

(a) such forms of treatment as may be specified for the purposes of this section by regulations made by the Secretary of State;

(b) the administration of medicine to a patient by any means (not being a form of treatment specified under paragraph (a) above or section 57 above) at any time during a period for which he is liable to be detained as a patient to whom this Part of this Act applies if three months or more have elapsed since the first occasion in that period when medicine was administered to him by any means for his mental disorder.

(2) The Secretary of State may by order vary the length of the period mentioned in subsection (1)(b) above.

(3) Subject to section 62 below, a patient shall not be given any form of treatment to which this section applies unless—

(a) he has consented to that treatment and either the responsible medical officer or a registered medical practitioner appointed for the purposes of this Part of this Act by the Secretary of State has certified in writing that the patient is capable of understanding its nature, purpose and likely effects and has consented to it; or

(b) a registered medical practitioner appointed as aforesaid (not being the responsible medical officer) has certified in writing that the patient is not capable of understanding the nature, purpose and likely effects of that treatment or has not consented to it but that, having regard to the likelihood of its alleviating or preventing a deterioration of his condition, the treatment should be given.

(4) Before giving a certificate under subsection (3)(b) above the registered medical practitioner concerned shall consult two other persons who have been professionally

concerned with the patient's medical treatment, and of those persons one shall be a nurse and the other shall be neither a nurse nor a registered medical practitioner.

(5) Before making any regulations for the purposes of this section the Secretary of State shall consult such bodies as appear to him to be concerned.

Notes:

Act excluded by Mental Health (Scotland) Act 1984 (c.36), ss.17(2), 79(1) Act modified by Repatriation of Prisoners Act 1984 (c.47), s.3, Sch. para. 5(1)(a)

s.59 Plans of treatment.

Any consent or certificate under section 57 or 58 above may relate to a plan of treatment   **A.10–04** under which the patient is to be given (whether within a specified period or otherwise) one or more of the forms of treatment to which that section applies.

Notes:

Act excluded by Mental Health (Scotland) Act 1984, (c.36), ss.17(2), 79(1) Act modified by Repatriation of Prisoners Act 1984 (c.47), s.3, Sch. para. 5(1)(a).

s.60 Withdrawal of consent.

(1) Where the consent of a patient to any treatment has been given for the purposes of   **A.10–05** section 57 or 58 above, the patient may, subject to section 62 below, at any time before the completion of the treatment withdraw his consent, and those sections shall then apply as if the remainder of the treatment were a separate form of treatment.

(2) Without prejudice to the application of subsection (1) above to any treatment given under the plan of treatment to which a patient has consented, a patient who has consented to such a plan may, subject to section 62 below, at any time withdraw his consent to further treatment, or to further treatment of any description, under the plan.

Notes:

Act excluded by Mental Health (Scotland) Act 1984 (c.36), ss.17(2), 79(1) Act modified by Repatriation of Prisoners Act 1984 (c.47), s.3, Sch. para. 5(1)(a)

s.61 Review of treatment.

(1) Where a patient is given treatment in accordance with section 57(2) or 58(3)(b)   **A.10–06** above a report on the treatment and the patient's condition shall be given by the responsible medical officer to the Secretary of State—

(a) on the next occasion on which the responsible medical officer furnishes a report under section 20(3) or 21B(2) above renewing the authority for the detention of the patient; and

(b) at any other time if so required by the Secretary of State.

(2) In relation to a patient who is subject to a restriction order, limitation direction or restriction direction subsection (1) above shall have effect as if paragraph (a) required the report to be made—

(a) in the case of treatment in the period of six months beginning with the date of the order or direction, at the end of that period;

(b) in the case of treatment at any subsequent time, on the next occasion on which the responsible medical officer makes a report in respect of the patient under [section 41 (6), 45B(3) or 49(3)] [FN1] above.

(3) The Secretary of State may at any time give notice to the responsible medical officer directing that, subject to section 62 below, a certificate given in respect of a patient

under section 57(2) or 58(3)(b) above shall not apply to treatment given to him after a date specified in the notice and sections 57 and 58 above shall then apply to any such treatment as if that certificate had not been given.

[FN1] words inserted by Crime (Sentences) Act (1997 c.43), Sch. 4 Para. 12(7)(b)

s.62 Urgent treatment.

A.10–07   (1) Sections 57 and 58 above shall not apply to any treatment—

(a) which is immediately necessary to save the patient's life; or

(b) which (not being irreversible) is immediately necessary to prevent a serious deterioration of his condition; or

(c) which (not being irreversible or hazardous) is immediately necessary to alleviate serious suffering by the patient; or

(d) which (not being irreversible or hazardous) is immediately necessary and represents the minimum interference necessary to prevent the patient from behaving violently or being a danger to himself or to others.

(2) Sections 60 and 61(3) above shall not preclude the continuation of any treatment or of treatment under any plan pending compliance with section 57 or 58 above if the responsible medical officer considers that the discontinuance of the treatment or of treatment under the plan would cause serious suffering to the patient.

(3) For the purposes of this section treatment is irreversible if it has unfavorable irreversible physical or psychological consequences and hazardous if it entails significant physical hazard.

Notes:

Act excluded by Mental Health (Scotland) Act 1984 (c.36), ss.17(2), 79(1) Act modified by Repatriation of Prisoners Act 1984 (c.47), s.3, Sch. para. 5(1)(a)

s.63 Treatment not requiring consent.

A.10–08   The consent of a patient shall not be required for any medical treatment given to him for the mental disorder from which he is suffering, not being treatment falling within section 57 or 58 above, if the treatment is given by or under the direction of the responsible medical officer.

Notes:

Act excluded by Mental Health (Scotland) Act 1984 (c.36), ss.17(2), 79(1) Act modified by Repatriation of Prisoners Act 1984 (c.47), s.3, Sch. para. 5(1)(a)

s.64 Supplementary provisions for Part IV.

A.10–09   (1) In this Part of this Act "the responsible medical officer" means the registered medical practitioner in charge of the treatment of the patient in question and "hospital" includes a [registered establishment] [FN1]. [. . .] [FN2].

(2) Any certificate for the purposes of this Part of this Act shall be in such form as may be prescribed by regulations made by the Secretary of State.

[FN1] words substituted by Care Standards Act (2000 c.14), Sch. 4 Para. 9(2).
[FN2] words substituted by Care Standards Act (2000 c.14), Sch. 4 Para. 9(2).

CONVENTION ON THE RIGHTS OF THE CHILD

Adopted and opened for signature, ratification and accession by General Assembly resolution 44/25 of 20 November 1989

ENTRY INTO FORCE 2 SEPTEMBER 1990, IN ACCORDANCE WITH ARTICLE 49

Preamble

The States Parties to the present Convention,   A.11–01

Considering that, in accordance with the principles proclaimed in the Charter of the United Nations, recognition of the inherent dignity and of the equal and inalienable rights of all members of the human family is the foundation of freedom, justice and peace in the world,

Bearing in mind that the peoples of the United Nations have, in the Charter, reaffirmed their faith in fundamental human rights and in the dignity and worth of the human person, and have determined to promote social progress and better standards of life in larger freedom,

Recognizing that the United Nations has, in the Universal Declaration of Human Rights and in the International Covenants on Human Rights, proclaimed and agreed that everyone is entitled to all the rights and freedoms set forth therein, without distinction of any kind, such as race, colour, sex, language, religion, political or other opinion, national or social origin, property, birth or other status,

Recalling that, in the Universal Declaration of Human Rights, the United Nations has proclaimed that childhood is entitled to special care and assistance,

Convinced that the family, as the fundamental group of society and the natural environment for the growth and well-being of all its members and particularly children, should be afforded the necessary protection and assistance so that it can fully assume its responsibilities within the community,

Recognizing that the child, for the full and harmonious development of his or her personality, should grow up in a family environment, in an atmosphere of happiness, love and understanding,

Considering that the child should be fully prepared to live an individual life in society, and brought up in the spirit of the ideals proclaimed in the Charter of the United Nations, and in particular in the spirit of peace, dignity, tolerance, freedom, equality and solidarity,

Bearing in mind that the need to extend particular care to the child has been stated in the Geneva Declaration of the Rights of the Child of 1924 and in the Declaration of the Rights of the Child adopted by the General Assembly on 20 November 1959 and recognized in the Universal Declaration of Human Rights, in the International Covenant on Civil and Political Rights (in particular in articles 23 and 24), in the International Covenant on Economic, Social and Cultural Rights (in particular in article 10) and in the statutes and relevant instruments of specialized agencies and international organizations concerned with the welfare of children,

Bearing in mind that, as indicated in the Declaration of the Rights of the Child, "the child, by reason of his physical and mental immaturity, needs special safeguards and care, including appropriate legal protection, before as well as after birth",

Recalling the provisions of the Declaration on Social and Legal Principles relating to the Protection and Welfare of Children, with Special Reference to Foster Placement and Adoption Nationally and Internationally; the United Nations Standard Minimum Rules for the Administration of Juvenile Justice (The Beijing Rules); and the Declaration on the Protection of Women and Children in Emergency and Armed Conflict,

Recognizing that, in all countries in the world, there are children living in exceptionally difficult conditions, and that such children need special consideration,

Taking due account of the importance of the traditions and cultural values of each people for the protection and harmonious development of the child,

Recognizing the importance of international co-operation for improving the living conditions of children in every country, in particular in the developing countries,

Have agreed as follows:

PART I

Article 1

A.11–02   For the purposes of the present Convention, a child means every human being below the age of eighteen years unless under the law applicable to the child, majority is attained earlier.

Article 2

A.11–03   1. States Parties shall respect and ensure the rights set forth in the present Convention to each child within their jurisdiction without discrimination of any kind, irrespective of the child's or his or her parent's or legal guardian's race, colour, sex, language, religion, political or other opinion, national, ethnic or social origin, property, disability, birth or other status.

2. States Parties shall take all appropriate measures to ensure that the child is protected against all forms of discrimination or punishment on the basis of the status, activities, expressed opinions, or beliefs of the child's parents, legal guardians, or family members.

Article 3

A.11–04   1. In all actions concerning children, whether undertaken by public or private social welfare institutions, courts of law, administrative authorities or legislative bodies, the best interests of the child shall be a primary consideration.

2. States Parties undertake to ensure the child such protection and care as is necessary for his or her well-being, taking into account the rights and duties of his or her parents, legal guardians, or other individuals legally responsible for him or her, and, to this end, shall take all appropriate legislative and administrative measures.

3. States Parties shall ensure that the institutions, services and facilities responsible for the care or protection of children shall conform with the standards established by competent

authorities, particularly in the areas of safety, health, in the number and suitability of their staff, as well as competent supervision.

Article 4

States Parties shall undertake all appropriate legislative, administrative, and other meas-   **A.11–05**
ures for the implementation of the rights recognized in the present Convention. With regard to economic, social and cultural rights, States Parties shall undertake such measures to the maximum extent of their available resources and, where needed, within the framework of international co-operation.

Article 5

States Parties shall respect the responsibilities, rights and duties of parents or, where   **A.11–06**
applicable, the members of the extended family or community as provided for by local custom, legal guardians or other persons legally responsible for the child, to provide, in a manner consistent with the evolving capacities of the child, appropriate direction and guidance in the exercise by the child of the rights recognized in the present Convention.

Article 6

1. States Parties recognize that every child has the inherent right to life.   **A.11–07**

2. States Parties shall ensure to the maximum extent possible the survival and development of the child.

Article 7

1. The child shall be registered immediately after birth and shall have the right from birth   **A.11–08**
to a name, the right to acquire a nationality and, as far as possible, the right to know and be cared for by his or her parents.

2. States Parties shall ensure the implementation of these rights in accordance with their national law and their obligations under the relevant international instruments in this field, in particular where the child would otherwise be stateless.

Article 8

1. States Parties undertake to respect the right of the child to preserve his or her identity,   **A.11–09**
including nationality, name and family relations as recognized by law without unlawful interference.

2. Where a child is illegally deprived of some or all of the elements of his or her identity, States Parties shall provide appropriate assistance and protection, with a view to re-establishing speedily his or her identity.

Article 9

1. States Parties shall ensure that a child shall not be separated from his or her parents   **A.11–10**
against their will, except when competent authorities subject to judicial review determine, in accordance with applicable law and procedures, that such separation is necessary for the best interests of the child. Such determination may be necessary in a particular case such as one involving abuse or neglect of the child by the parents, or one where the parents are living separately and a decision must be made as to the child's place of residence.

2. In any proceedings pursuant to paragraph 1 of the present article, all interested parties shall be given an opportunity to participate in the proceedings and make their views known.

3. States Parties shall respect the right of the child who is separated from one or both parents to maintain personal relations and direct contact with both parents on a regular basis, except if it is contrary to the child's best interests.

4. Where such separation results from any action initiated by a State Party, such as the detention, imprisonment, exile, deportation or death (including death arising from any cause while the person is in the custody of the State) of one or both parents or of the child, that State Party shall, upon request, provide the parents, the child or, if appropriate, another member of the family with the essential information concerning the whereabouts of the absent member(s) of the family unless the provision of the information would be detrimental to the well-being of the child. States Parties shall further ensure that the submission of such a request shall of itself entail no adverse consequences for the person(s) concerned.

Article 10

A.11–11 1. In accordance with the obligation of States Parties under Article 9, paragraph 1, applications by a child or his or her parents to enter or leave a State Party for the purpose of family reunification shall be dealt with by States Parties in a positive, humane and expeditious manner. States Parties shall further ensure that the submission of such a request shall entail no adverse consequences for the applicants and for the members of their family.

2. A child whose parents reside in different States shall have the right to maintain on a regular basis, save in exceptional circumstances personal relations and direct contacts with both parents. Towards that end and in accordance with the obligation of States Parties under Article 9, paragraph 1, States Parties shall respect the right of the child and his or her parents to leave any country, including their own, and to enter their own country. The right to leave any country shall be subject only to such restrictions as are prescribed by law and which are necessary to protect the national security, public order (ordre public), public health or morals or the rights and freedoms of others and are consistent with the other rights recognized in the present Convention.

Article 11

A.11–12 1. States Parties shall take measures to combat the illicit transfer and non-return of children abroad.

2. To this end, States Parties shall promote the conclusion of bilateral or multilateral agreements or accession to existing agreements.

Article 12

A.11–13 1. States Parties shall assure to the child who is capable of forming his or her own views the right to express those views freely in all matters affecting the child, the views of the child being given due weight in accordance with the age and maturity of the child.

2. For this purpose, the child shall in particular be provided the opportunity to be heard in any judicial and administrative proceedings affecting the child, either directly, or through a representative or an appropriate body, in a manner consistent with the procedural rules of national law.

Article 13

A.11–14 1. The child shall have the right to freedom of expression; this right shall include freedom to seek, receive and impart information and ideas of all kinds, regardless of frontiers, either orally, in writing or in print, in the form of art, or through any other media of the child's choice.

2. The exercise of this right may be subject to certain restrictions, but these shall only be such as are provided by law and are necessary:

(a) For respect of the rights or reputations of others; or

(b) For the protection of national security or of public order (ordre public), or of public health or morals.

Article 14

1. States Parties shall respect the right of the child to freedom of thought, conscience and   **A.11–15**
religion.

2. States Parties shall respect the rights and duties of the parents and, when applicable, legal guardians, to provide direction to the child in the exercise of his or her right in a manner consistent with the evolving capacities of the child.

3. Freedom to manifest one's religion or beliefs may be subject only to such limitations as are prescribed by law and are necessary to protect public safety, order, health or morals, or the fundamental rights and freedoms of others.

Article 15

1. States Parties recognize the rights of the child to freedom of association and to freedom   **A.11–16**
of peaceful assembly.

2. No restrictions may be placed on the exercise of these rights other than those imposed in conformity with the law and which are necessary in a democratic society in the interests of national security or public safety, public order (ordre public), the protection of public health or morals or the protection of the rights and freedoms of others.

Article 16

1. No child shall be subjected to arbitrary or unlawful interference with his or her privacy,   **A.11–17**
family, home or correspondence, nor to unlawful attacks on his or her honour and reputation.

2. The child has the right to the protection of the law against such interference or attacks.

Article 17

States Parties recognize the important function performed by the mass media and shall   **A.11–18**
ensure that the child has access to information and material from a diversity of national and international sources, especially those aimed at the promotion of his or her social, spiritual and moral well-being and physical and mental health. To this end, States Parties shall:

   (a) Encourage the mass media to disseminate information and material of social and cultural benefit to the child and in accordance with the spirit of article 29;

   (b) Encourage international co-operation in the production, exchange and dissemination of such information and material from a diversity of cultural, national and international sources;

   (c) Encourage the production and dissemination of children's books;

   (d) Encourage the mass media to have particular regard to the linguistic needs of the child who belongs to a minority group or who is indigenous;

   (e) Encourage the development of appropriate guidelines for the protection of the child from information and material injurious to his or her well-being, bearing in mind the provisions of Articles 13 and 18.

Article 18

1. States Parties shall use their best efforts to ensure recognition of the principle that both   **A.11–19**
parents have common responsibilities for the upbringing and development of the child. Parents or, as the case may be, legal guardians, have the primary responsibility for the upbringing and development of the child. The best interests of the child will be their basic concern.

2. For the purpose of guaranteeing and promoting the rights set forth in the present Convention, States Parties shall render appropriate assistance to parents and legal guardians in the performance of their child-rearing responsibilities and shall ensure the development of institutions, facilities and services for the care of children.

3. States Parties shall take all appropriate measures to ensure that children of working parents have the right to benefit from child-care services and facilities for which they are eligible.

Article 19

A.11–20 1. States Parties shall take all appropriate legislative, administrative, social and educational measures to protect the child from all forms of physical or mental violence, injury or abuse, neglect or negligent treatment, maltreatment or exploitation, including sexual abuse, while in the care of parent(s), legal guardian(s) or any other person who has the care of the child.

2. Such protective measures should, as appropriate, include effective procedures for the establishment of social programmes to provide necessary support for the child and for those who have the care of the child, as well as for other forms of prevention and for identification, reporting, referral, investigation, treatment and follow-up of instances of child maltreatment described heretofore, and, as appropriate, for judicial involvement.

Article 20

A.11–21 1. A child temporarily or permanently deprived of his or her family environment, or in whose own best interests cannot be allowed to remain in that environment, shall be entitled to special protection and assistance provided by the State.

2. States Parties shall in accordance with their national laws ensure alternative care for such a child.

3. Such care could include, inter alia, foster placement, kafalah of Islamic law, adoption or if necessary placement in suitable institutions for the care of children. When considering solutions, due regard shall be paid to the desirability of continuity in a child's upbringing and to the child's ethnic, religious, cultural and linguistic background.

Article 21

A.11–22 States Parties that recognize and/or permit the system of adoption shall ensure that the best interests of the child shall be the paramount consideration and they shall:

(a) Ensure that the adoption of a child is authorized only by competent authorities who determine, in accordance with applicable law and procedures and on the basis of all pertinent and reliable information, that the adoption is permissible in view of the child's status concerning parents, relatives and legal guardians and that, if required, the persons concerned have given their informed consent to the adoption on the basis of such counselling as may be necessary;

(b) Recognize that inter-country adoption may be considered as an alternative means of child's care, if the child cannot be placed in a foster or an adoptive family or cannot in any suitable manner be cared for in the child's country of origin; (c) Ensure that the child concerned by inter-country adoption enjoys safeguards and standards equivalent to those existing in the case of national adoption;

(d) Take all appropriate measures to ensure that, in inter-country adoption, the placement does not result in improper financial gain for those involved in it;

(e) Promote, where appropriate, the objectives of the present article by concluding bilateral or multilateral arrangements or agreements, and endeavour, within this framework, to ensure that the placement of the child in another country is carried out by competent authorities or organs.

Article 22

1. States Parties shall take appropriate measures to ensure that a child who is seeking   **A.11–23**
refugee status or who is considered a refugee in accordance with applicable international
or domestic law and procedures shall, whether unaccompanied or accompanied by his or
her parents or by any other person, receive appropriate protection and humanitarian
assistance in the enjoyment of applicable rights set forth in the present Convention and in
other international human rights or humanitarian instruments to which the said States are
Parties.

2. For this purpose, States Parties shall provide, as they consider appropriate,
co-operation in any efforts by the United Nations and other competent intergovernmental
organizations or non-governmental organizations co-operating with the United Nations to
protect and assist such a child and to trace the parents or other members of the family of
any refugee child in order to obtain information necessary for reunification with his or her
family. In cases where no parents or other members of the family can be found, the child
shall be accorded the same protection as any other child permanently or temporarily
deprived of his or her family environment for any reason, as set forth in the present
Convention.

Article 23

1. States Parties recognize that a mentally or physically disabled child should enjoy a full   **A.11–24**
and decent life, in conditions which ensure dignity, promote self-reliance and facilitate the
child's active participation in the community.

2. States Parties recognize the right of the disabled child to special care and shall
encourage and ensure the extension, subject to available resources, to the eligible child
and those responsible for his or her care, of assistance for which application is made and
which is appropriate to the child's condition and to the circumstances of the parents or
others caring for the child. 3. Recognizing the special needs of a disabled child, assistance
extended in accordance with paragraph 2 of the present article shall be provided free of
charge, whenever possible, taking into account the financial resources of the parents or
others caring for the child, and shall be designed to ensure that the disabled child has
effective access to and receives education, training, health care services, rehabilitation
services, preparation for employment and recreation opportunities in a manner conducive
to the child's achieving the fullest possible social integration and individual development,
including his or her cultural and spiritual development.

4. States Parties shall promote, in the spirit of international cooperation, the exchange of
appropriate information in the field of preventive health care and of medical, psychological and functional treatment of disabled children, including dissemination of and
access to information concerning methods of rehabilitation, education and vocational
services, with the aim of enabling States Parties to improve their capabilities and skills and
to widen their experience in these areas. In this regard, particular account shall be taken
of the needs of developing countries.

Article 24

1. States Parties recognize the right of the child to the enjoyment of the highest attainable   **A.11–25**
standard of health and to facilities for the treatment of illness and rehabilitation of health.
States Parties shall strive to ensure that no child is deprived of his or her right of access
to such health care services.

2. States Parties shall pursue full implementation of this right and, in particular, shall take
appropriate measures:

  (a) To diminish infant and child mortality;

  (b) To ensure the provision of necessary medical assistance and health care to all
       children with emphasis on the development of primary health care;

(c) To combat disease and malnutrition, including within the framework of primary health care, through, inter alia, the application of readily available technology and through the provision of adequate nutritious foods and clean drinking-water, taking into consideration the dangers and risks of environmental pollution;

(d) To ensure appropriate pre-natal and post-natal health care for mothers;

(e) To ensure that all segments of society, in particular parents and children, are informed, have access to education and are supported in the use of basic knowledge of child health and nutrition, the advantages of breastfeeding, hygiene and environmental sanitation and the prevention of accidents;

(f) To develop preventive health care, guidance for parents and family planning education and services.

3. States Parties shall take all effective and appropriate measures with a view to abolishing traditional practices prejudicial to the health of children.

4. States Parties undertake to promote and encourage international co-operation with a view to achieving progressively the full realization of the right recognized in the present article. In this regard, particular account shall be taken of the needs of developing countries.

Article 25

A.11–26 States Parties recognize the right of a child who has been placed by the competent authorities for the purposes of care, protection or treatment of his or her physical or mental health, to a periodic review of the treatment provided to the child and all other circumstances relevant to his or her placement.

Article 26

A.11–27 1. States Parties shall recognize for every child the right to benefit from social security, including social insurance, and shall take the necessary measures to achieve the full realization of this right in accordance with their national law.

2. The benefits should, where appropriate, be granted, taking into account the resources and the circumstances of the child and persons having responsibility for the maintenance of the child, as well as any other consideration relevant to an application for benefits made by or on behalf of the child.

Article 27

A.11–28 1. States Parties recognize the right of every child to a standard of living adequate for the child's physical, mental, spiritual, moral and social development.

2. The parent(s) or others responsible for the child have the primary responsibility to secure, within their abilities and financial capacities, the conditions of living necessary for the child's development.

3. States Parties, in accordance with national conditions and within their means, shall take appropriate measures to assist parents and others responsible for the child to implement this right and shall in case of need provide material assistance and support programmes, particularly with regard to nutrition, clothing and housing.

4. States Parties shall take all appropriate measures to secure the recovery of maintenance for the child from the parents or other persons having financial responsibility for the child, both within the State Party and from abroad. In particular, where the person having financial responsibility for the child lives in a State different from that of the child, States Parties shall promote the accession to international agreements or the conclusion of such agreements, as well as the making of other appropriate arrangements.

Article 28

1. States Parties recognize the right of the child to education, and with a view to achieving   **A.11–29**
this right progressively and on the basis of equal opportunity, they shall, in particular:

    (a) Make primary education compulsory and available free to all;

    (b) Encourage the development of different forms of secondary education, including
general and vocational education, make them available and accessible to every
child, and take appropriate measures such as the introduction of free education and
offering financial assistance in case of need;

    (c) Make higher education accessible to all on the basis of capacity by every appro-
priate means;

    (d) Make educational and vocational information and guidance available and acces-
sible to all children;

    (e) Take measures to encourage regular attendance at schools and the reduction of
drop-out rates.

2. States Parties shall take all appropriate measures to ensure that school discipline is
administered in a manner consistent with the child's human dignity and in conformity with
the present Convention.

3. States Parties shall promote and encourage international cooperation in matters relating
to education, in particular with a view to contributing to the elimination of ignorance and
illiteracy throughout the world and facilitating access to scientific and technical knowledge and modern teaching methods. In this regard, particular account shall be taken of the
needs of developing countries.

Article 29

1. States Parties agree that the education of the child shall be directed to: **A.11–30**

    (a) The development of the child's personality, talents and mental and physical
abilities to their fullest potential;

    (b) The development of respect for human rights and fundamental freedoms, and for
the principles enshrined in the Charter of the United Nations;

    (c) The development of respect for the child's parents, his or her own cultural identity,
language and values, for the national values of the country in which the child is
living, the country from which he or she may originate, and for civilizations
different from his or her own;

    (d) The preparation of the child for responsible life in a free society, in the spirit of
understanding, peace, tolerance, equality of sexes, and friendship among all peoples, ethnic, national and religious groups and persons of indigenous origin;

    (e) The development of respect for the natural environment.

2. No part of the present article or article 28 shall be construed so as to interfere with the
liberty of individuals and bodies to establish and direct educational institutions, subject
always to the observance of the principle set forth in paragraph 1 of the present article and
to the requirements that the education given in such institutions shall conform to such
minimum standards as may be laid down by the State.

Article 30

In those States in which ethnic, religious or linguistic minorities or persons of indigenous   **A.11–31**
origin exist, a child belonging to such a minority or who is indigenous shall not be denied

the right, in community with other members of his or her group, to enjoy his or her own culture, to profess and practise his or her own religion, or to use his or her own language.

Article 31

A.11–32   1. States Parties recognize the right of the child to rest and leisure, to engage in play and recreational activities appropriate to the age of the child and to participate freely in cultural life and the arts.

2. States Parties shall respect and promote the right of the child to participate fully in cultural and artistic life and shall encourage the provision of appropriate and equal opportunities for cultural, artistic, recreational and leisure activity.

Article 32

A.11–33   1. States Parties recognize the right of the child to be protected from economic exploitation and from performing any work that is likely to be hazardous or to interfere with the child's education, or to be harmful to the child's health or physical, mental, spiritual, moral or social development.

2. States Parties shall take legislative, administrative, social and educational measures to ensure the implementation of the present article. To this end, and having regard to the relevant provisions of other international instruments, States Parties shall in particular:

(a) Provide for a minimum age or minimum ages for admission to employment;

(b) Provide for appropriate regulation of the hours and conditions of employment;

(c) Provide for appropriate penalties or other sanctions to ensure the effective enforcement of the present article.

Article 33

A.11–34   States Parties shall take all appropriate measures, including legislative, administrative, social and educational measures, to protect children from the illicit use of narcotic drugs and psychotropic substances as defined in the relevant international treaties, and to prevent the use of children in the illicit production and trafficking of such substances.

Article 34

A.11–35   States Parties undertake to protect the child from all forms of sexual exploitation and sexual abuse. For these purposes, States Parties shall in particular take all appropriate national, bilateral and multilateral measures to prevent:

(a) The inducement or coercion of a child to engage in any unlawful sexual activity;

(b) The exploitative use of children in prostitution or other unlawful sexual practices;

(c) The exploitative use of children in pornographic performances and materials.

Article 35

A.11–36   States Parties shall take all appropriate national, bilateral and multilateral measures to prevent the abduction of, the sale of or traffic in children for any purpose or in any form.

Article 36

A.11–37   States Parties shall protect the child against all other forms of exploitation prejudicial to any aspects of the child's welfare.

Article 37

States Parties shall ensure that: **A.11–38**

(a) No child shall be subjected to torture or other cruel, inhuman or degrading treatment or punishment. Neither capital punishment nor life imprisonment without possibility of release shall be imposed for offences committed by persons below eighteen years of age;

(b) No child shall be deprived of his or her liberty unlawfully or arbitrarily. The arrest, detention or imprisonment of a child shall be in conformity with the law and shall be used only as a measure of last resort and for the shortest appropriate period of time;

(c) Every child deprived of liberty shall be treated with humanity and respect for the inherent dignity of the human person, and in a manner which takes into account the needs of persons of his or her age. In particular, every child deprived of liberty shall be separated from adults unless it is considered in the child's best interest not to do so and shall have the right to maintain contact with his or her family through correspondence and visits, save in exceptional circumstances;

(d) Every child deprived of his or her liberty shall have the right to prompt access to legal and other appropriate assistance, as well as the right to challenge the legality of the deprivation of his or her liberty before a court or other competent, independent and impartial authority, and to a prompt decision on any such action.

Article 38

1. States Parties undertake to respect and to ensure respect for rules of international   **A.11–39**
humanitarian law applicable to them in armed conflicts which are relevant to the child.

2. States Parties shall take all feasible measures to ensure that persons who have not attained the age of fifteen years do not take a direct part in hostilities.

3. States Parties shall refrain from recruiting any person who has not attained the age of fifteen years into their armed forces. In recruiting among those persons who have attained the age of fifteen years but who have not attained the age of eighteen years, States Parties shall endeavour to give priority to those who are oldest.

4. In accordance with their obligations under international humanitarian law to protect the civilian population in armed conflicts, States Parties shall take all feasible measures to ensure protection and care of children who are affected by an armed conflict.

Article 39

States Parties shall take all appropriate measures to promote physical and psychological   **A.11–40**
recovery and social reintegration of a child victim of: any form of neglect, exploitation, or abuse; torture or any other form of cruel, inhuman or degrading treatment or punishment; or armed conflicts. Such recovery and reintegration shall take place in an environment which fosters the health, self-respect and dignity of the child.

Article 40

1. States Parties recognize the right of every child alleged as, accused of, or recognized   **A.11–41**
as having infringed the penal law to be treated in a manner consistent with the promotion of the child's sense of dignity and worth, which reinforces the child's respect for the human rights and fundamental freedoms of others and which takes into account the child's age and the desirability of promoting the child's reintegration and the child's assuming a constructive role in society.

2. To this end, and having regard to the relevant provisions of international instruments, States Parties shall, in particular, ensure that:

(a) No child shall be alleged as, be accused of, or recognized as having infringed the penal law by reason of acts or omissions that were not prohibited by national or international law at the time they were committed;

(b) Every child alleged as or accused of having infringed the penal law has at least the following guarantees:

(i) To be presumed innocent until proven guilty according to law;

(ii) To be informed promptly and directly of the charges against him or her, and, if appropriate, through his or her parents or legal guardians, and to have legal or other appropriate assistance in the preparation and presentation of his or her defence;

(iii) To have the matter determined without delay by a competent, independent and impartial authority or judicial body in a fair hearing according to law, in the presence of legal or other appropriate assistance and, unless it is considered not to be in the best interest of the child, in particular, taking into account his or her age or situation, his or her parents or legal guardians;

(iv) Not to be compelled to give testimony or to confess guilt; to examine or have examined adverse witnesses and to obtain the participation and examination of witnesses on his or her behalf under conditions of equality;

(v) If considered to have infringed the penal law, to have this decision and any measures imposed in consequence thereof reviewed by a higher competent, independent and impartial authority or judicial body according to law;

(vi) To have the free assistance of an interpreter if the child cannot understand or speak the language used;

(vii) To have his or her privacy fully respected at all stages of the proceedings. 3. States Parties shall seek to promote the establishment of laws, procedures, authorities and institutions specifically applicable to children alleged as, accused of, or recognized as having infringed the penal law, and, in particular:

(a) The establishment of a minimum age below which children shall be presumed not to have the capacity to infringe the penal law;

(b) Whenever appropriate and desirable, measures for dealing with such children without resorting to judicial proceedings, providing that human rights and legal safeguards are fully respected.

4. A variety of dispositions, such as care, guidance and supervision orders; counselling; probation; foster care; education and vocational training programmes and other alternatives to institutional care shall be available to ensure that children are dealt with in a manner appropriate to their well-being and proportionate both to their circumstances and the offence.

Article 41

A.11–42 Nothing in the present Convention shall affect any provisions which are more conducive to the realization of the rights of the child and which may be contained in:

(a) The law of a State party; or

(b) International law in force for that State.

PART II

Article 42

A.11–43 States Parties undertake to make the principles and provisions of the Convention widely known, by appropriate and active means, to adults and children alike.

Article 43

1. For the purpose of examining the progress made by States Parties in achieving the **A.11–44** realization of the obligations undertaken in the present Convention, there shall be established a *Committee on the Rights of the Child*, which shall carry out the functions hereinafter provided.

2. The Committee shall consist of ten experts of high moral standing and recognized competence in the field covered by this Convention. The members of the Committee shall be elected by States Parties from among their nationals and shall serve in their personal capacity, consideration being given to equitable geographical distribution, as well as to the principal legal systems.

3. The members of the Committee shall be elected by secret ballot from a list of persons nominated by States Parties. Each State Party may nominate one person from among its own nationals.

4. The initial election to the Committee shall be held no later than six months after the date of the entry into force of the present Convention and thereafter every second year. At least four months before the date of each election, the Secretary-General of the United Nations shall address a letter to States Parties inviting them to submit their nominations within two months. The Secretary-General shall subsequently prepare a list in alphabetical order of all persons thus nominated, indicating States Parties which have nominated them, and shall submit it to the States Parties to the present Convention.

5. The elections shall be held at meetings of States Parties convened by the Secretary-General at United Nations Headquarters. At those meetings, for which two thirds of States Parties shall constitute a quorum, the persons elected to the Committee shall be those who obtain the largest number of votes and an absolute majority of the votes of the representatives of States Parties present and voting.

6. The members of the Committee shall be elected for a term of four years. They shall be eligible for re-election if renominated. The term of five of the members elected at the first election shall expire at the end of two years; immediately after the first election, the names of these five members shall be chosen by lot by the Chairman of the meeting.

7. If a member of the Committee dies or resigns or declares that for any other cause he or she can no longer perform the duties of the Committee, the State Party which nominated the member shall appoint another expert from among its nationals to serve for the remainder of the term, subject to the approval of the Committee.

8. The Committee shall establish its own rules of procedure.

9. The Committee shall elect its officers for a period of two years.

10. The meetings of the Committee shall normally be held at United Nations Headquarters or at any other convenient place as determined by the Committee. The Committee shall normally meet annually. The duration of the meetings of the Committee shall be determined, and reviewed, if necessary, by a meeting of the States Parties to the present Convention, subject to the approval of the General Assembly.

11. The Secretary-General of the United Nations shall provide the necessary staff and facilities for the effective performance of the functions of the Committee under the present Convention.

12. With the approval of the General Assembly, the members of the Committee established under the present Convention shall receive emoluments from United Nations resources on such terms and conditions as the Assembly may decide.

Article 44

1. States Parties undertake to submit to the Committee, through the Secretary-General of **A.11–45** the United Nations, reports on the measures they have adopted which give effect to the rights recognized herein and on the progress made on the enjoyment of those rights:

(a) Within two years of the entry into force of the Convention for the State Party concerned;

(b) Thereafter every five years.

2. Reports made under the present article shall indicate factors and difficulties, if any, affecting the degree of fulfilment of the obligations under the present Convention. Reports shall also contain sufficient information to provide the Committee with a comprehensive understanding of the implementation of the Convention in the country concerned.

3. A State Party which has submitted a comprehensive initial report to the Committee need not, in its subsequent reports submitted in accordance with paragraph 1(b) of the present article, repeat basic information previously provided.

4. The Committee may request from States Parties further information relevant to the implementation of the Convention.

5. The Committee shall submit to the General Assembly, through the Economic and Social Council, every two years, reports on its activities.

6. States Parties shall make their reports widely available to the public in their own countries.

Article 45

A.11–46 In order to foster the effective implementation of the Convention and to encourage international co-operation in the field covered by the Convention:

(a) The specialized agencies, the United Nations Children's Fund, and other United Nations organs shall be entitled to be represented at the consideration of the implementation of such provisions of the present Convention as fall within the scope of their mandate. The Committee may invite the specialized agencies, the United Nations Children's Fund and other competent bodies as it may consider appropriate to provide expert advice on the implementation of the Convention in areas falling within the scope of their respective mandates. The Committee may invite the specialized agencies, the United Nations Children's Fund, and other United Nations organs to submit reports on the implementation of the Convention in areas falling within the scope of their activities;

(b) The Committee shall transmit, as it may consider appropriate, to the specialized agencies, the United Nations Children's Fund and other competent bodies, any reports from States Parties that contain a request, or indicate a need, for technical advice or assistance, along with the Committee's observations and suggestions, if any, on these requests or indications;

(c) The Committee may recommend to the General Assembly to request the Secretary-General to undertake on its behalf studies on specific issues relating to the rights of the child;

(d) The Committee may make suggestions and general recommendations based on information received pursuant to articles 44 and 45 of the present Convention. Such suggestions and general recommendations shall be transmitted to any State Party concerned and reported to the General Assembly, together with comments, if any, from States Parties.

PART III

Article 46

A.11–47 The present Convention shall be open for signature by all States.

Article 47

The present Convention is subject to ratification. Instruments of ratification shall be deposited with the Secretary-General of the United Nations.

A.11–48

Article 48

The present Convention shall remain open for accession by any State. The instruments of accession shall be deposited with the Secretary-General of the United Nations.

A.11–49

Article 49

1. The present Convention shall enter into force on the thirtieth day following the date of deposit with the Secretary-General of the United Nations of the twentieth instrument of ratification or accession.

A.11–50

2. For each State ratifying or acceding to the Convention after the deposit of the twentieth instrument of ratification or accession, the Convention shall enter into force on the thirtieth day after the deposit by such State of its instrument of ratification or accession.

Article 50

1. Any State Party may propose an amendment and file it with the Secretary-General of the United Nations. The Secretary-General shall thereupon communicate the proposed amendment to States Parties, with a request that they indicate whether they favour a conference of States Parties for the purpose of considering and voting upon the proposals. In the event that, within four months from the date of such communication, at least one third of the States Parties favour such a conference, the Secretary-General shall convene the conference under the auspices of the United Nations. Any amendment adopted by a majority of States Parties present and voting at the conference shall be submitted to the General Assembly for approval.

A.11–51

2. An amendment adopted in accordance with paragraph 1 of the present article shall enter into force when it has been approved by the General Assembly of the United Nations and accepted by a two-thirds majority of States Parties.

3. When an amendment enters into force, it shall be binding on those States Parties which have accepted it, other States Parties still being bound by the provisions of the present Convention and any earlier amendments which they have accepted.

Article 51

1. The Secretary-General of the United Nations shall receive and circulate to all States the text of reservations made by States at the time of ratification or accession.

A.11–52

2. A reservation incompatible with the object and purpose of the present Convention shall not be permitted.

3. Reservations may be withdrawn at any time by notification to that effect addressed to the Secretary-General of the United Nations, who shall then inform all States. Such notification shall take effect on the date on which it is received by the Secretary-General.

Article 52

A State Party may denounce the present Convention by written notification to the Secretary-General of the United Nations. Denunciation becomes effective one year after the date of receipt of the notification by the Secretary-General.

A.11–53

Article 53

The Secretary-General of the United Nations is designated as the depositary of the present Convention.

A.11–54

Article 54

A.11–55　The original of the present Convention, of which the Arabic, Chinese, English, French, Russian and Spanish texts are equally authentic, shall be deposited with the Secretary-General of the United Nations.

IN WITNESS THEREOF the undersigned plenipotentiaries, being duly authorized thereto by their respective governments, have signed the present Convention.

INDEX

[389]

[401]